# COSMOLOGY REBORN

# COSMOLOGY REBORN

## STAR WISDOM, VOLUME 1
### 2019

EDITOR
JOEL PARK

CONSULTING EDITORS
Robert Powell & Claudia McLaren Lainson

EDITORIAL BOARD
Brian Gray • Lacquanna Paul • Robert Schiappacasse

Lindisfarne Books

LINDISFARNE BOOKS
an imprint of Steinerbooks/Anthroposophic Press, Inc.
610 Main Street, Suite 1
Gr. Barrington, MA, 01230
www.steinerbooks.org

*Cosmology Reborn: Star Wisdom,* vol. 1 (former volumes published as *Journal for Star Wisdom*) © 2018 by Joel Park and Robert Powell. All contributions are used by permission of the authors. All rights reserved. No part of this publication may be reproduced, stored in a retrieval system, or transmitted in any form or by any means, electronic, mechanical, photocopying, recording, or otherwise without the prior written permission of the publisher.

With grateful acknowledgment to Peter Treadgold (1943–2005), who wrote the Astrofire program (available from the Sophia Foundation), with which the ephemeris pages in *Star Wisdom* are computed each year.

Disclaimer: The views expressed in the articles published in *Star Wisdom* are the sole responsibility of the authors of these articles and do not necessarily reflect those of the editorial board of *Star Wisdom*.

DESIGN: JENS JENSEN

ISBN: 978-1-58420-934-8 (Paperback)
ISBN: 978-1-58420-935-5 (eBook)

Printed in the United States of America

# CONTENTS

Preface
    *by Robert Powell* . . . . . . . . . . . 9

The Seven Ideals of the Rose of the World
    *by Robert Powell* . . . . . . . . . . . 14

Editorial Foreword
    *by Joel Park* . . . . . . . . . . . 15

Working with *Star Wisdom* . . . . . . . . . . . 17

Cosmogony, Freedom, Altruism in the Light of Astrogeography
    *by Joel Park* . . . . . . . . . . . 18

The Year 2019 and the Opening to the Angelic Realm: The New Star Wisdom
    *by Robert Powell* . . . . . . . . . . . 24

Communion of Love with Holiness: Saturn–Pluto Conjunctions
    *by Claudia McLaren Lainson* . . . . . . . . . . . 42

First Steps toward a Grail Timeline
    *by Joel Park* . . . . . . . . . . . 64

Healing Miracles: The Destiny Task of Our Time
    *by Estelle Isaacson* . . . . . . . . . . . 82

American Cosmogony: Retrospects and Prospects
    *by Kevin Dann* . . . . . . . . . . . 84

Uranus in Aries: Disturbing Cosmic Parallels
    *by Julie Humphreys* . . . . . . . . . . . 90

The Rising of the Dharma Sun: A Hermetic Perspective
    *by Claudia McLaren Lainson* . . . . . . . . . . . 103

Classics in Astrosophy, Part II: The Lunar Calendar, Concluded
    *by Robert Powell* . . . . . . . . . . . 110

Working with the *Star Wisdom* Calender
    *by Robert Powell* . . . . . . . . . . . 120

Symbols Used in Charts / Time . . . . . . . . . . . 122

Commentaries and Ephemerides, January – December 2019
    *by Claudia McLaren Lainson*
    including Monthly Stargazing Preview & Astronomical Sky Watch
    *by Julie Humphreys* . . . . . . . . . . . 125

Glossary . . . . . . . . . . . 244

Bibliography and References . . . . . . . . . . . 251

About the Contributors . . . . . . . . . . . 254

# ASTROSOPHY

The Sophia Foundation was founded and exists to help usher in the new Age of Sophia and the corresponding Sophianic culture, the Rose of the World, prophesied by Daniel Andreev and other spiritual teachers. Part of the work of the Sophia Foundation is the cultivation of a new star wisdom, *Astro-Sophia* (Astrosophy), now arising in our time in response to the descent of Sophia, who is the bearer of Divine Wisdom, just as Christ (the Logos, or the Lamb) is the bearer of Divine Love. Like the star wisdom of antiquity, astrosophy is sidereal, which means "of the stars." Astrosophy, inspired by Divine Sophia, descending from stellar heights, directs our consciousness toward the glory and majesty of the starry heavens, to encompass the entire celestial sphere of our cosmos and, beyond this, to the galactic realm—the realm that Daniel Andreev referred to as "the heights of our universe"—from which Sophia is descending on her path of approach into our cosmos. Sophia draws our attention not only to the star mysteries of the heights, but also to the cosmic mysteries connected with Christ's deeds of redemption wrought two thousand years ago. To penetrate these mysteries is the purpose of the annual volumes of *Star Wisdom*.

For information about Astrosophy/Choreocosmos/Cosmic Dance workshops
Contact the Sophia Foundation:
4500 19th Street, #369, Boulder, CO 80304
Phone: (303) 242-5388; sophia@sophiafoundation.org;
www.sophiafoundation.org

# PREFACE
## Robert Powell, PhD

This is the first volume of the annual *Star Wisdom* (formerly *Journal for Star Wisdom*), intended to help all people interested in the new star wisdom of astrosophy and in the cosmic dimension of Christianity, which began with the star of the magi. The calendar comprises an ephemeris page for each month of the year, computed with the help of Peter Treadgold's *Astrofire* computer program, with a monthly commentary by Claudia McLaren Lainson. The monthly commentary relates the geocentric and heliocentric planetary movements to events in the life of Jesus Christ.

Jesus Christ united the levels of the earthly personality (geocentric = Earth-centered) and the higher self (heliocentric = Sun-centered) in so far as he was the most highly evolved earthly personality (Jesus) embodying the higher self (Christ) of all existence, the Divine "I AM." To see the life of Jesus Christ in relation to the world of stars opens the door to a profound experience of the cosmos, giving rise to a new star wisdom (astrosophy) that is the Spiritual Science of Cosmic Christianity.

*Star Wisdom* is scientific, resting upon a solid mathematical-astronomical foundation and also upon a secure chronology of the life of Jesus Christ, and at the same time it is spiritual, aspiring to the higher dimension of existence that is expressed outwardly in the world of stars. The scientific and the spiritual come together in the sidereal zodiac that originated with the Babylonians and was used by the three magi who beheld the star of Bethlehem and came to pay homage to Jesus a few months after his birth. In continuity of spirit with the origins of Cosmic Christianity with the three magi, the sidereal zodiac is the frame of reference used for the computation of the geocentric and heliocentric planetary movements that are commented upon in the light of the life of Jesus Christ in *Star Wisdom*.

Thus, all zodiacal longitudes indicated in the text and presented in the following calendar are in terms of the sidereal zodiac, which has to be distinguished from the tropical zodiac in widespread use in contemporary astrology in the West. The tropical zodiac was introduced into astrology in the middle of the second century AD by the Greek astronomer Claudius Ptolemy. Prior to this the sidereal zodiac was in use. Such was the influence of Ptolemy upon the Western astrological tradition that the tropical zodiac became substituted for the sidereal zodiac used by the Babylonians, Egyptians, and early Greek astrologers. Yet the astrological tradition in India was not influenced by Ptolemy, and so the sidereal zodiac is still used to this day by Hindu astrologers.

The sidereal zodiac originated with the Babylonians in the sixth to fifth centuries BC and was defined by them in relation to certain bright stars. For example, Aldebaran ("the Bull's Eye") is located in the middle of the sidereal sign/constellation of the Bull at 15° Taurus, and Antares ("the Scorpion's heart") is in the middle of the sidereal sign/constellation of the Scorpion at 15° Scorpio. The sidereal signs, each 30° long, coincide closely with the twelve astronomical zodiacal constellations of the same name, whereas the signs of the tropical zodiac, since they are defined in relation to the vernal point, now have little or no relationship to the corresponding zodiacal constellations. This is because the vernal point, the zodiacal location of the Sun on March 20/21, shifts slowly backward through the sidereal zodiac at a rate of 1° in seventy-two years ("the precession of the equinoxes"). When Ptolemy introduced the tropical zodiac into astrology, there was an almost exact coincidence between the tropical and the sidereal zodiac, as the vernal point, which is defined to be 0° Aries in the tropical zodiac, was at 1° Aries in the sidereal zodiac in the middle of the second century AD. Thus, there was only 1° difference between the two zodiacs. So, it made hardly any difference to Ptolemy or his contemporaries to use the tropical zodiac instead of the sidereal zodiac. But now—the vernal point, on account of precession, having shifted back from 1° Aries to 5° Pisces—there is a 25° difference and so there is virtually no correspondence between the two. Without going into further detail concerning the complex issue of the zodiac, as shown in the *Hermetic Astrology* trilogy, the sidereal zodiac is the zodiac used by the three magi, who were the last representatives of the true star wisdom of antiquity. For this reason the sidereal zodiac is used throughout *Star Wisdom*.

Readers interested in exploring the scientific (astronomical and chronological) foundations of Cosmic Christianity are referred to the works listed below under "Literature." The *Chronicle of the Living Christ: Foundations of Cosmic Christianity,* listed on the next page, is an indispensable source of reference (abbreviated *Chron.*) for *Star Wisdom,* as, too, are the four Gospels (Matthew = Mt.; Mark = Mk.; Luke = Lk.; John = Jn.). The chronology of the life of Jesus Christ rests upon Robert Powell's research based on the description of Christ's daily life by Anne Catherine Emmerich in her three-volume work *The Visions of Anne Catherine Emmerich* (abbreviated *ACE*). Further details concerning *Star Wisdom* and how to work with it on a daily basis may be found in the general introduction to the *Christian Star Calendar.* The general introduction explains all the features of *Star Wisdom*. The new edition, published in 2003, includes sections on the megastars (stars of great luminosity) and on the 36 decans (10° subdivisions of the twelve signs of the zodiac) in relation to their planetary rulers and to the extra-zodiacal constellations, those constellations above or below the circle of the twelve constellations/signs of the zodiac. Further material on the decans, including examples of historical personalities born in the various decans, and also a wealth of other material on the signs of the sidereal zodiac, is to be found in *Cosmic Dances of the Zodiac,* listed below. Also foundational is *History of the Zodiac,* published by Sophia Academic Press, listed below under "Works by Robert Powell."

## Literature

*(See also "References" section)*

*General Introduction to the Christian Star Calendar: A Key to Understanding,* 2nd ed. Palo Alto, CA: Sophia Foundation, 2003.

Bento, William, Robert Schiappacasse, and David Tresemer, *Signs in the Heavens: A Message for our Time*. Boulder: StarHouse, 2000.

Emmerich, Anne Catherine, *The Visions of Anne Catherine Emmerich* (new edition, with material by Robert Powell). Kettering, OH: Angelico Press, 2015.

Paul, Lacquanna, and Robert Powell, *Cosmic Dances of the Planets*. San Rafael, CA: Sophia Foundation Press, 2007.

———, *Cosmic Dances of the Zodiac*. San Rafael, CA: Sophia Foundation Press, 2007.

Smith, Edward, *The Burning Bush: An Anthroposophical Commentary on the Bible*. Gr. Barrington, MA: SteinerBooks, 1997.

Steiner, Rudolf, *Astronomy and Astrology: Finding a Relationship to the Cosmos*. London: Rudolf Steiner Press, 2009.

Sucher, Willi, *Cosmic Christianity and the Changing Countenance of Cosmology*. Gr. Barrington, MA: SteinerBooks, 1993. *Isis Sophia* and other works by Willi Sucher are available from the Astrosophy Research Center, PO Box 13, Meadow Vista, CA 95722.

Tidball, Charles S., and Robert Powell, *Jesus, Lazarus, and the Messiah: Unveiling Three Christian Mysteries*. Gr. Barrington, MA: SteinerBooks, 2005. This book offers a penetrating study of the Christ mysteries against the background of *Chronicle of the Living Christ* and contains two chapters by Robert Powell on the Apostle John and John the Evangelist (Lazarus).

Tresemer, David (with Robert Schiappacasse), *Star Wisdom & Rudolf Steiner: A Life Seen Through the Oracle of the Solar Cross*. Gr. Barrington, MA: SteinerBooks, 2007.

## Astrosophical Works by Robert Powell, PhD

**Starcrafts (formerly Astro Communication Services, or ACS):**
*History of the Houses* (1997)
*History of the Planets* (1989)
*The Zodiac: A Historical Survey* (1984)
www.acspublications.com
www.astrocom.com
Business Address:
Starcrafts Publishing
334 Calef Hwy.
Epping, NH 03042
Phone: 603-734-4300
Fax: 603-734-4311
Contact maria@starcraftseast.com

### SteinerBooks:

Orders: (703) 661-1594; www.steinerbooks.org
PO Box 960, Herndon, VA 20172

*The Astrological Revolution: Unveiling the Science of the Stars as a Science of Reincarnation and Karma*, coauthor Kevin Dann (Gr. Barrington, MA: SteinerBooks, 2010). After reestablishing the sidereal zodiac as a basis for astrology that penetrates the mystery of the stars' relationship to human destiny, the reader is invited to discover the astrological significance of the totality of the vast sphere of stars surrounding the Earth. This book points to the astrological significance of the entire celestial sphere, including all the stars and constellations beyond the twelve zodiacal signs. This discovery is revealed by the study of megastars, illustrating how they show up in an extraordinary way in Christ's healing miracles by aligning with the Sun at the time of those events. This book offers a spiritual, yet scientific, path toward a new relationship to the stars.

*Christian Hermetic Astrology: The Star of the Magi and the Life of Christ* (Hudson, NY: Anthroposophic Press, 1998). Twenty-five discourses set in the "Temple of the Sun," where Hermes and his pupils gather to meditate on the Birth, the Miracles, and the Passion of Jesus Christ. The discourses offer a series of meditative contemplations on the deeds of Christ in relation to the mysteries of the cosmos. They are an expression of the age-old hermetic mystery wisdom of the ancient Egyptian sage, Hermes Trismegistus. This book offers a meditative approach to the cosmic correspondences between major events in the life of Christ and the heavenly configurations at that time 2,000 years ago.

*Chronicle of the Living Christ: Foundations of Cosmic Christianity* (Hudson, NY: Anthroposophic Press, 1996). An account of the life of Christ, day by day, throughout most of the 3½ years of his ministry, including the horoscopes of conception, birth, and death of Jesus, Mary, and John the Baptist, together with a wealth of material relating to a new star wisdom focused on the life of Christ. This work provides the chronological basis for *Christian Hermetic Astrology* and *Star Wisdom*.

*Elijah Come Again: A Prophet for our Time: A Scientific Approach to Reincarnation* (Gr. Barrington, MA: SteinerBooks, 2009). By way of horoscope comparisons from conception–birth–death in one incarnation to conception–birth–death in the next, this work establishes scientifically two basic astrosophical research findings. These are: the importance 1) of the sidereal zodiac and 2) of the heliocentric positions of the planets. Also, for the first time, the identity of the "saintly nun" is revealed, of whom Rudolf Steiner spoke in a conversation with Marie von Sivers about tracing Novalis's karmic background. The focus throughout the book is on the Elijah individuality in his various incarnations, and is based solidly on Rudolf Steiner's indications. It also can be read as a karmic biography by anyone who chooses to omit the astrosophical material.

*Journal for Star Wisdom* (Gr. Barrington, MA: Lindisfarne Books, 2010–2018), edited by Robert Powell and others engaged in astrosophic research. A guide to the correspondences of Christ in the stellar and etheric world. Includes articles of interest, a complete geocentric and heliocentric sidereal ephemeris, and an aspectarian. Published yearly in November for the coming years. According to Rudolf Steiner, every step taken by Christ during his ministry between the baptism in the Jordan and the resurrection was in harmony with, and an expression of, the cosmos. The journal is concerned with these heavenly correspondences during the life of Christ. It is intended to help provide a foundation for Cosmic Christianity, the cosmic dimension of Christianity. It is this dimension that has been missing from Christianity in its 2,000-year history. A starting point is to contemplate the movements of the Sun, Moon, and planets against the background of the zodiacal constellations (sidereal signs) today in relation to corresponding stellar events during the life of Christ. This opens the possibility of attuning to the life of Christ in the etheric cosmos in a living way.

## Sophia Foundation Press and Sophia Academic Press Publications

Books available from Amazon.com
JamesWetmore@mac.com
www.logosophia.com

*History of the Zodiac* (San Rafael, CA: Sophia Academic Press, 2007). Book version of Robert Powell's PhD thesis on the *History of the Zodiac*. This penetrating study of the *History of the Zodiac* restores the sidereal zodiac to its rightful place as the original zodiac, tracing it back to fifth-century-BC Babylonians. Available in paperback and hard cover.

*Hermetic Astrology: Volume 1, Astrology and Reincarnation* (San Rafael, CA: Sophia Foundation Press, 2007). This book seeks to give the ancient science of the stars a scientific basis. This new foundation for astrology based on research into reincarnation and karma (destiny) is the primary focus. It includes numerous reincarnation examples, the study of which reveals the existence of certain astrological "laws" of reincarnation, on the basis of which it is evident that the ancient sidereal zodiac is the authentic astrological zodiac, and that the heliocentric movements of the planets are of great significance. Foundational for the new star wisdom of astrosophy.

*Hermetic Astrology: Volume 2, Astrological Biography* (San Rafael, CA: Sophia Foundation Press, 2007). Concerned with karmic relationships and the unfolding of destiny in seven-year periods through one's life. The seven-year rhythm underlies the human being's astrological biography, which can be studied in relation to the movements of the Sun, Moon, and planets around the sidereal zodiac between conception and birth. The "rule of Hermes" is used to determine the moment of conception.

*Sign of the Son of Man in the Heavens: Sophia and the New Star Wisdom* (San Rafael, CA: Sophia Foundation Press, 2008). Revised and expanded with new material, this edition deals with a new wisdom of stars in the light of Divine Sophia. It is intended as a help in our time, when we are called on to be extremely wakeful during the period leading up to the end of the Mayan calendar in 2012.

*Cosmic Dances of the Zodiac* (San Rafael, CA: Sophia Foundation Press, 2007), coauthor Lacquanna Paul. Study material describing the twelve signs of the zodiac and their forms and gestures in cosmic dance, with diagrams, including a wealth of information on the twelve signs and the 36 decans (the subdivision of the signs into decans, or 10° sectors, corresponding to constellations above and below the zodiac).

*Cosmic Dances of the Planets* (San Rafael, CA: Sophia Foundation Press, 2007), coauthor Lacquanna Paul. Study material describing the seven classical planets and their forms and gestures in cosmic dance, with diagrams, including much information on the planets.

## American Federation of Astrologers (AFA) Publications (currently not in print)

www.astrologers.com

*The Sidereal Zodiac*, coauthor Peter Treadgold (Tempe, AZ: AFA, 1985). A *History of the Zodiac* (sidereal, tropical, Hindu, astronomical) and a formal definition of the sidereal zodiac with the star Aldebaran ("the Bull's Eye") at 15° Taurus. This is an abbreviated version of *History of the Zodiac*.

## Rudolf Steiner College Press Publications

9200 Fair Oaks Blvd., Fair Oaks, CA 95628

*The Christ Mystery: Reflections on the Second Coming* (Fair Oaks, CA: Rudolf Steiner College Press, 1999). The fruit of many years of reflecting on the Second Coming and its cosmological aspects. Looks at the approaching trial of humanity and the challenges of living in apocalyptic times, against the background of "great signs in the heavens."

## The Sophia Foundation

4500 19th Street, #369, Boulder, CO 80304; distributes many of the books listed here and other works by Robert Powell.
Tel: (303) 242-5388
sophia@sophiafoundation.org
www.sophiafoundation.org

Computer program for charts and ephemerides, with grateful acknowledgment to Peter Treadgold, who wrote the computer program

## Preface

*Astrofire* (with research module, star catalog of over 4,000 stars, and database of birth and death charts of historical personalities), capable of printing geocentric and heliocentric/hermetic sidereal charts and ephemerides throughout history. The hermetic charts, based on the astronomical system of the Danish astronomer Tycho Brahe, are called "Tychonic" charts in the program. This program can:

- compute birth charts in a large variety of systems (tropical, sidereal, geocentric, heliocentric, hermetic);
- calculate conception charts using the hermetic rule, in turn applying it for correction of the birth time;
- produce charts for the period between conception and birth;
- print out an "astrological biography" for the whole of lifework with the geocentric, heliocentric (and even lemniscatory) planetary system;
- work with the sidereal zodiac according to the definition of your choice (Babylonian sidereal, Indian sidereal, unequal-division astronomical, etc.);
- work with planetary aspects with orbs of your choice.

The program includes eight house systems and a variety of chart formats. The program also includes an ephemeris program with a search facility. The geocentric/heliocentric sidereal ephemeris pages in the annual volumes of *Star Wisdom* are produced by the software program *Astrofire,* which is compatible with Microsoft Windows.

Those interested in obtaining the *Astrofire* program should contact:

**The Sophia Foundation**
4500 19th Street, #369
Boulder, CO 80304
Tel: (303) 242-5388
sophia@sophiafoundation.org
www.sophiafoundation.org

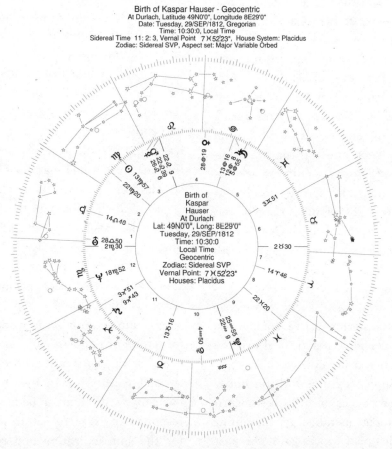

*A horoscope generated by the* Astrofire *program*

# THE SEVEN IDEALS OF THE ROSE OF THE WORLD
## *Robert Powell, PhD*

*In gratitude to Daniel Andreev (1906–1959), the Russian prophet of the Rose of the World as the coming world culture, inspired by Sophia—a culture based on Love and Wisdom.*

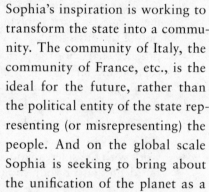

The Rose of the World is arising through the approach of Divine Sophia toward the Earth. Her approach is calling forth the following basic qualities or attributes of the new world culture that She is creating and inspiring:

1. First and foremost: interreligion. For Sophia all true religious and spiritual traditions are different layers of spiritual reality, which She seeks to weave together as petals of the Rose of the World. Sophia is not founding a new world religion as She approaches, descending from cosmic heights, and draws ever closer to our solar system. On Her path of descent, approaching our planet to incarnate into the Earth's aura during the Age of Aquarius, She is bestowing insight concerning each religion and spiritual tradition, thus awaking interreligiosity, signifying a heartfelt interest in religious and spiritual traditions other than one's own. This signifies the blossoming and unfolding of the petals of the Rose of the World, creating brother-/sisterhood between all peoples.

2. Sophia's approach toward our planet is bringing about an awaking of social conscience on a global scale, inspiring active compassion combined with unflagging practical efforts on behalf of social justice around the world.

3. Through Sophia a framework for understanding the higher dimension of historical processes is coming about: metahistory, illumining the meaning of historical processes of the past, present, and future in relation to humankind's spiritual evolution. This entails glimpses into the mystical consciousness of humanity such as may be found in the Book of Revelation.

4. On the national sociopolitical level, Sophia's inspiration is working to transform the state into a community. The community of Italy, the community of France, etc., is the ideal for the future, rather than the political entity of the state representing (or misrepresenting) the people. And on the global scale Sophia is seeking to bring about the unification of the planet as a world community through bringing the different country communities into a harmonious relationship with one another on a religious, cultural, and economic level.

5. This world community, the Rose of the World, inspired by Sophia, will seek to establish the economic wellbeing of every man, woman, and child on the planet, to ensure that everyone has a roof over their heads and sufficient food to live on. Here it is a matter of ensuring a decent standard of living for all peoples of the Earth.

6. A high priority of the Rose of the World will be the ennobling of education. New methods of education are being inspired by Sophia to help bring out everyone's creative talents. To ennoble education so that each person's creativity can unfold is the goal here.

7. Finally, Sophia is working for the transformation of the planet into a garden and, moreover, for the spiritualization of Nature. Humanity and Nature are to live in cooperation and harmony, with human beings taking up their responsibility toward Nature, which is to work for the spiritualization and redemption of the kingdoms of Nature.

# EDITORIAL FOREWORD

## Joel Park

As of the writing of this foreword (Aug. 2, 2018), it is now fifty-three years since Willi Sucher began to publish his *Monthly Star Journal*. This *Journal* was in publication from 1965 to 1974, at which point, the *Journal* went through a transformation, which showed itself in several ways: 1) the title was changed to *Mercury Star Journal*; 2) it became a quarterly rather than a monthly publication; and 3) the editor changed from Willi Sucher to Robert Powell. Willi Sucher, in 1974, was seventy-two years of age; Robert Powell was twenty-seven. Although Robert was quite young and the two had only known each other for a short time, Willi Sucher had the confidence to "pass the baton," as it were, to Robert.

The *Mercury Star Journal* continued its publication until 1980. The final issue changed the format to an annual rather than a quarterly publication; unfortunately, owing to a variety of circumstances, the *Journal* ceased publication at that time. It was resurrected eleven years later in 1991 the first issue of the *Christian Star Calendar* appeared. Whereas prior to this point, the purpose of the *Monthly Star Journal* and *Mercury Star Journal* had always been focused on Astrosophy, the new star wisdom emerging from an anthroposophical, spiritual scientific exploration of astronomy and astrology, a new and higher octave of this purpose began to come about in the pages of the *Christian Star Calendar*. Due to Robert Powell's penetrating investigation of the visions of Anne Catherine Emmerich, a precise chronology of the life of Christ could be established. Based on this, the stellar configurations during the life of Christ could be known. These stellar configurations "imprinted" the starry heavens with the deeds and words of Christ; every time these configurations come about again above us, these deeds and words are remembered by the Cosmos and the Earth. The *Christian Star Calendar* began the practice of looking at the ephemerides of the coming year as an expression of memories from the life of Christ. A new Star Wisdom was truly born.

The *Christian Star Calendar* was published until 2009; in 2010, another change in title occurred. The editorial board realized that the publication was more of a journal than a calendar, and hence the *Journal for Star Wisdom* was born. The daily commentaries on the annual configurations were taken up by Claudia McLaren Lainson; through her efforts the commentaries became more richly realized each year. As the years went on, *Journal for Star Wisdom* increasingly became the responsibility of Robert Powell and Claudia McLaren Lainson.

I met Robert Powell on April 16, 2015, when he visited Peterborough, New Hampshire, for a retreat with Estelle Isaacson. Within the next four months, I and a few others began to assist Robert in his lifelong task of finding astrosophical "rules" of karma and reincarnation. We developed a strong rapport over the course of the following year and a half as I entered this research more and more deeply.

In February 2016, I began to publish articles anonymously on my website, TreeHouse (www.treehouse.live). By the end of 2016, Claudia McLaren Lainson had read some of my work on the website and reached out to me for contributions to *Journal for Star Wisdom* 2018. Work on the *Journal* was a natural fit; I ended up contributing one original article and aiding in some of the editorial work. By the end of this process, Robert proposed that I take up the position of editor, to which I agreed in June 2017.

Now we have come to 2019; both Robert and Claudia find themselves in a position similar to that of Willi Sucher in 1974. Both have a need, even an obligation, to pull back from a variety of activities they pioneered over the years and "pass the baton." I find myself in a position similar to that of Robert Powell at the age of twenty-seven; I have the honor of being able to take on the role of editor for a publication that has thus far existed for fifty-three years under four different titles. With another change of editorship, a new title has also come about. Rather than a journal or calendar, one can view this publication as the first in a series, the name of which is simply *Star Wisdom*. Each annual volume of *Star Wisdom* will have its own unique title that encapsulates the general theme of the articles within it. This year, to commemorate a lecture by Rudolf Steiner called "Cosmogony, Freedom, Altruism" (Oct. 10, 1919), we have chosen the title *Cosmology Reborn*.

The emphasis, as indicated, of both the *Christian Star Calendar* and *Journal for Star Wisdom* has been the experience of Christ's ether body (which bears his entire biography) through the stellar configurations, recalling his life events and hence his etheric body. As those of us schooled in Anthroposophy know very well, since 1933 Christ has been making his presence known to humanity in the *etheric* realm, by contrast to his manifestation on the physical plane approximately 2,000 years ago. Experiencing the movements of the stars as expressions of the etheric Christ is a potent method for coming into closer relationship with Christ at this time. Keeping in mind that the birth and death horoscope of individuals expresses their karma (i.e., their destiny), the development of this relationship also potentially heightens our understanding of Christ at this time in history as the Lord of Karma.

The reader is encouraged to practice stargazing as much as possible; this grounds our understanding and experience of the etheric Christ in a direct experience of the natural world. In this way, a bridge is formed from Nature to Spirit and back again. Conveniently, because *Star Wisdom* is written from a sidereal perspective, there will be no difference between the astrological position of the planets listed in the ephemeris and commentary in relation to their actual (astronomical) position in the starry heavens. For example, right now, a calendar of tropical astrology would place the Sun in Leo, opposite Aquarius. But if I were to go outside tonight as the Sun sets, I would see that it is opposite Capricorn, meaning it is in the sign of Cancer. This confusion does not exist in sidereal astrology, since the astronomical and astrological positions of the planets are identical.

As *Star Wisdom* moves into the future, it is my wish to continue these aspects that have been a feature of this publication for twenty-seven years, while simultaneously broadening its offerings to readers. Willi Sucher was greatly inspired by Rudolf Steiner's lecture "Cosmogony, Freedom, Altruism" commemorated in this volume. He began to see clearly that the accomplishment of the mission of the West (Anglo-America) in creating an authentic spiritual Cosmology depended on the establishment of Astrosophy. However, whereas Christian Astrosophy must be the core of a living cosmology, it is not the only topic that could be considered "cosmological." It is my intention to feature over the years articles from an increasingly wider spectrum of disciplines that mutually complement the perspectives presented in each volume of *Star Wisdom*. This is the deeper reason for the change of title; authentic Christian Astrosophy has been established. Therefore, the foundation has been laid and the door opened to the discovery and establishment of authentic Christian Cosmology.

I extend the deepest gratitude to those who have made this publication possible. Certainly to all of the contributors, who have so much of my respect, as I have been reading some of your work for years. To Gene Gollogly and Jens Jensen of SteinerBooks; thank you not only for your work but also for the excellent feedback and suggestions as we move forward into a new incarnation of this publication. And particularly to Robert Powell and Claudia McLaren Lainson, for your unwavering guidance and confidence in me as I move into this new role. I would also like to extend my thanks and warm greetings to our readers, who are ultimately the reason for the existence of *Star Wisdom*.

# WORKING WITH
## *STAR WISDOM*

The listing of major planetary events each month is intended as a stimulus toward attunement with the Universal Christ, the Logos, whose being encompasses the entire galaxy. The deeds of the historical Christ wrought two thousand years ago are of eternal significance—inscribed into the cosmos—and they resonate with the movements of the heavenly bodies, especially when certain alignments or planetary configurations occur bearing a resemblance with those prevailing at the time of events in the life of Jesus Christ. With the rare astronomical event of the transit of Venus across the face of the Sun that took place June 8, 2004, at exactly the zodiacal degree (23° Taurus), where the Sun stood at Christ's Ascension, a new impulse was given from divine-spiritual realms for the further unfolding of star wisdom, *Astro-Sophia*.

The calendar (see table of contents) comprises ephemeris pages for the twelve months of the year with accompanying monthly commentaries on the astronomical events listed on the ephemeris pages. Indications regarding the similarity of contemporary planetary configurations with those at events in the life of Christ are given in the lower part of the monthly commentaries, and the upper part gives a commentary on the notable astronomical occurrences each month. Unless otherwise stated, all astronomical indications regarding visibility mean "visible to the naked eye." See the note concerning time on the page preceding the monthly commentaries.

With this calendar, astronomy and astrology, which were a unity in the ancient star wisdom of the Egyptians and Babylonians, are reunited and provide a foundation for astrosophy, the all-encompassing star wisdom, *Astro-Sophia*, an expression of Sophia and referred to in the Revelation of John as the "Bride of the Lamb."

# COSMOGONY, FREEDOM, ALTRUISM IN THE LIGHT OF ASTROGEOGRAPHY

## Joel Park

Last year, the editorial board of the *Journal for Star Wisdom* wished to commemorate a special address by Rudolf Steiner on October 9, 1918, "What Does the Angel Do in Our Astral Body?"[1] The reasons for this were twofold: on the one hand, the year 2018 saw the end of three 33⅓-year cycles, totaling 100 years since the lecture was first given; on the other hand, the year 2018 was a year that portended a greater awaking for a part of humanity to the work of the Angels, in that it was the end of the thirty-nine Cosmic Days of Temptation in the Wilderness, and the beginning of the fortieth day in the Wilderness, when Jesus Christ was ministered unto by Angels after having successfully passed through the three temptations on the thirty-seventh, thirty-eighth, and thirty-ninth days.[2]

In his lecture, Rudolf Steiner emphasized three gifts that could be bestowed on humanity by becoming conscious of the activity of the Angels in the astral body. Three images are being placed in the subconscious of the human being: the first is an impulse to freedom, through the recognition of the eternal and unique individuality residing in each human being. The second is an impulse to brotherhood and sisterhood, to the point of being unable to feel happiness if another is suffering. The third is to cultivate the ability to cross the abyss into the spiritual world through the transformation of thinking into spiritual perception, and to come to a living awareness of the spiritual reality underlying the manifold expression of Nature.

When the editors of *Star Wisdom* were searching for a theme for this year's edition, we began to look at what could be commemorated a hundred years from 1919. Very quickly we encountered a lecture from October 10, 1919 (almost exactly one year after the lecture "What Does the Angel Do in Our Astral Body?") titled "Cosmogony, Freedom, Altruism."[3] From one perspective, it seemed to us that a hundred years after the social impulse that gave birth to the idea of the "threefold social order" it would be important to give some recognition to this revolutionary social movement, and to the possibility of its resurrection in our time. Refreshingly, however, rather than the straightforward approach of Freedom in the cultural sphere, Equality in the rights sphere, and Fraternity in the economic sphere, the ideas presented in the lecture of October 10, 1919, offer an image of the social organism that is from a slightly different angle.

Throughout this lecture, Steiner emphasizes the different tasks that different portions of the world are drawn to due to their fundamental temperament. Rather than a threefolding of the social organism itself, it is a threefolding of global culture that arises. Steiner characterizes the Central nations of the world (he speaks specifically of Europe) as being concerned primarily with the idea of freedom, of elaborating philosophically a true understanding of Freedom. We might see Steiner's own work, *The Philosophy of Freedom*,[4] as the highest accomplishment of this mission of the center. He sees this impulse to freedom coming to expression especially in the philosophical and artistic spheres.

On the other hand, Steiner characterizes the temperament of Eastern nations (specifically Asia) as that of altruism, a fundamental urge toward selflessness and fellow feeling, expressing itself in the religious and economic spheres. He goes on to characterize the temperament of the Western nations (specifically Anglo-America) as seeking

---

1 That lecture is in Steiner, *Death as Metamorphosis of Life*.
2 See Powell, "The Apocalypse Code and the Year 2018," *Journal for Star Wisdom* 2018, pp. 24–41.
3 See Steiner, *Understanding Society*.
4 See Steiner, *Intuitive Thinking as a Spiritual Path: A Philosophy of Freedom*.

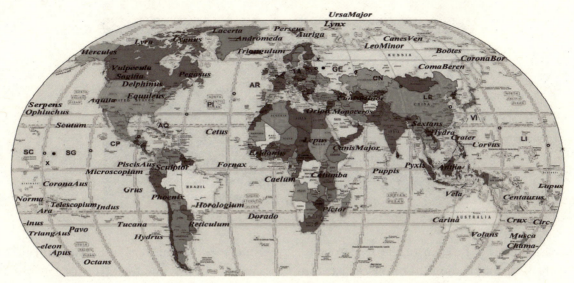

Map 1: Astrogeographia map of 82 constellations (AD 2000)

a true, living cosmology. He states that Western individuals do not just seek to be citizens of a state, nation, or even the world, but citizens of the entire cosmos. They wish to see the spiritual thread connecting them to all of Nature. This perspective of the West offered by Steiner led us quite naturally to the title and overlighting theme of this year's issue, *Cosmology Reborn*.

One reason this lecture is remarkable is the way the content is a metamorphosis of what was given one year prior, when Rudolf Steiner was describing the activity of the angels in the astral body. The first image given by the angels is that of a free meeting from "I" to "I"; we can see this image as being taken up particularly by the peoples of the Center. The second image, relating to a strong feeling of empathy with other human beings who are suffering belongs especially to the Eastern peoples. The third image, that of crossing the abyss into the spiritual world through the transformation of thinking, dwells as inspiration primarily within the Western peoples.

If we wish to have further clarity of these three different regions of Earth, we need look no further than Astrogeography. As described in great detail in Robert Powell and David Bowden's *Astrogeographia*, there is a relationship between each star in the heavens and every point on Earth. When we look at these three regions through the lens of Astrogeography, we can draw some remarkable conclusions.

When we look at an Astrogeographical map of the globe (Map 1),[5] we can see that by the "Central region" of the Earth, Steiner means specifically the realm of the globe under the rulership of Taurus—more specifically, under the rulership of Taurus, Gemini, and Cancer. This portion of the globe extends from 1°12' east at its western limit to 91°12' east at its eastern limit. More or less, this is the portion of the globe that is to the east of London and to the west of Mongolia. It contains three of the seven Earth Chakras, or centers of spiritual receptivity. Mt. Kailash in the Himalayas (the Mars Chakra), Jerusalem in Israel (the Sun Chakra), and the Externsteine in Northern Germany (the Jupiter Chakra; see Map 2).

Significantly, we can see that the trajectory of the development of the successive cultural epochs since the end of the Atlantean Age up to the present day is contained within this geographical portion of the globe: India, Persia, Egypt–Chaldea–Babylonia, Greece–Rome, Europe, and even the western half of Russia are in this broad strip. We can infer from this that the entire mission and meaning of the post-Atlantean time (thus far) has been the achievement of true human freedom.[6] In

---

5 Powell and Bowden, *Astrogeographia: Correspondences between the Stars and Earthly Locations*, pp. 185, 196.

6 For an adequate description of the different epochs and ages of Earth evolution, see Steiner, *Cosmic Memory* and *An Outline of Esoteric Science* (ch. 4).

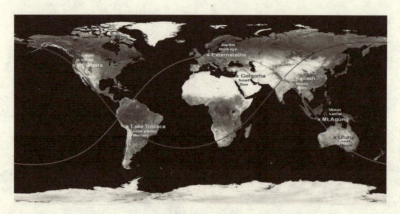

*Map 2: Mercator's map of Earth*

particular, this is a freedom of the kind sought for by the German philosophers of the eighteenth, nineteenth, and twentieth centuries: to find inner freedom. One of the great German Idealist philosophers, Hegel, argued that one is not free by doing whatever one chooses, for if one is unconscious of the motivations for one's actions, one is not free.[1] It is not until we are able to discover what underlies the different motivations for our actions that we can achieve true freedom. Therefore, it is above all a living *philosophy of freedom* that is sought for in this part of the world, and at this time in history.

Inseparable from this is the search for the eternal core of the human being, which lives beyond and above the lower drives of the psyche. It is only this eternal core that can investigate motivations for action, and it is only those originating from this eternal core that can truly be called motivations that originate in a state of freedom rather than in a state of coercion or conditioning (biological or environmental). We can see in the cultures in the vicinity of the three Earth Chakras of this region (in the Himalayas, Jerusalem, and Northern Germany) a call to inner liberation through the awaking of the eternal within the human being, for here we have the regions of Buddha, Christ, and the modern union of the two streams in Anthroposophy, which could be described as a "Christian Buddhism" or "Buddhist Christianity."[2]

Note, too, that this region is under the rulership of Taurus, whose influence streams into the larynx and eustachian tubes. It is the *head* that seeks redemption here. This is the region of the globe that falls under the aegis of the Church of Peter, the head of the Church. It has been primarily in correspondence with the development of Catholicism that a philosophy of freedom (Aquinas and Scholasticism) has been able to develop. It may seem ironic to some, but is true none-the-less, that Roman Catholicism has brought about a culture primed to achieve Liberty in the Spiritual/Cultural/Artistic sphere.

Moving to the Eastern portion of the globe, we see that it is under the rulership of Leo, in addition to Virgo and Libra. This extends from 91°12' east at its western boundary to 178°48' west in its eastern boundary. This is the entire region of the globe east of India and west of Alaska. This region contains two of the Earth Chakras—the Moon Chakra at Uluru in Australia, and the Venus Chakra at Mount Agung in Bali.

Whereas the Central portion of the globe virtually extends over the geographical extent of our post-Atlantean cultural centers, this Eastern region is related to Ancient Lemuria, which was centered on the area taken up currently by the Indian Ocean. How can we understand the relationship of this region and time period to the second image offered to the astral body by the Angels, that of an inability to feel happiness if another suffers? The fundamental state of the human being at this time period was naturally one of complete fraternity. The human being at this time lacked a completely

---

[1] See Hegel, *Philosophy of Right*, particularly section 3, "The Ethical Life."

[2] See especially Steiner, *Esoteric Christianity and the Mission of Christian Rosenkreuz*, for a full elaboration of Anthroposophy as a harmonizing of the impulses of Buddha and Christ.

formed and incarnated "I." Humanity existed not as a collection of distinct individuals but as one being, a united family. The divide between "self" and "other" was not yet distinct.

When we look at the cultures of this region today, there is an echo of this fundamental Lemurian quality. We see this, for example, in the ancestor worship of many Asian cultures. The "self" in such a cultural perspective does not exist primarily as an independent being, but as one shaped by the family, tribe, nation as a member of a greater whole. We see a caricatured and empty form of this in the doctrine of Communism, in which the individual is not of primary significance but the State. Furthermore, indigenous tribal cultures in some of these regions still have a natural understanding of the oneness of the tribe, or the reliance of the individual on the rest of the people in the tribe.

Each of these phenomena—ancestor worship, Communism, and tribal identity—gives a foretaste of what will be achieved in the Russian cultural epoch to come. The mission of our current cultural epoch—centered on Indo-Europe—is the achievement of Freedom. The mission of Russia, on the other hand, is a reborn Fraternity. This fraternity, however, is built on a foundation of individual freedom; rather than a natural, instinctual gravitation toward altruism, or the enforcement of altruism via the state, as in Communism, the hallmark of this time will be an altruism that flows from the completely developed "I."

This is a region ruled by Leo, related to the heart. The warmth of compassion flowing from the heart is the striving brought about by the fundamental temperament of the East. Whereas the head forces of Taurus work via the Church of Peter to facilitate Freedom in the spiritual–cultural–artistic sphere, we see here the activity of the Church of John. The Church of John, as embodied in the Eastern Orthodox faiths, facilitates authentic altruism, an authentic religious life that will flow into the economic sphere. An author of the twentieth century who supplied a foretaste of this phenomenon was E. F. Schumacher. In his book *Small Is Beautiful*, he describes what he calls "Buddhist economics." According to Schumacher, economics presupposes a moral underpinning; if this is not supplied through some form of religious life, the void is filled by amoral, materialistic philosophy (usually unconsciously). The Buddhist economics he describes is precisely the economics to be brought about by the East; but they require the foundation built by the freedom of the Central regions. In fact, Steiner emphasizes that no one region can accomplish its mission without what is supplied by the other two regions; in other words, Europe cannot implement cultural freedom effectively without the altruism developed by the East and the cosmogony developed by the West.

And what of the West? This is the region under the rulership of Aquarius—actually, Aquarius, Pisces, and Aries. This region extends from 88°48' west at its western border through 1°12' east at its eastern border. More or less, this covers the region of the globe east of the Mississippi River and west of London. There is one Earth Chakra in this region—the Mercury Chakra at Lake Titicaca in South America.

Note that Rudolf Steiner attributed the mission of developing a living cosmogony to Anglo-America. Through Astrogeography, we see clearly why he spoke of Anglo-America and not just about America. This region begins in the British Isles and ends part way through the North American continent. It contains all of South America within its realm. Whereas our current age exists in the region of Freedom in the Center, and ancient Lemuria covered the region of Altruism in the East, here we have exactly the region where ancient Atlantis existed—the Atlantic Ocean and most of the land masses bordering it.

The Celtic peoples of the British Isles represent a cultural memory of the final peoples that populated Ancient Atlantis, prior to the migration that led across Europe to the Gobi Desert, where the seeds for the next cultures could develop undisturbed. Across the ocean, the indigenous peoples of North and South America represent a cultural memory of Atlantis in its prime. We can see a deeply embedded cosmogony in both the Celtic and Native American cultures, both in their mythologies and in their fundamental approach to Nature.

There is no separation between Spirit and Nature for these cultures; rather, it is a *pan-en-theism,* or God-in-Nature. Furthermore, there is no separation between Nature and Humanity; rather, human beings form a vital link in the chain of all creation. Every deed performed was weighed and measured in relation to Nature and her wellbeing. A crime against Nature was a crime against both God and Self. When we read Steiner's descriptions of ancient Atlantis, the keynote is humanity's ability to influence Nature through the power of the Word. Humanity was not divorced from or at the whim of a mechanical universe; rather, there was a magical breathing back and forth between human deeds and forces of the natural world.

How can we understand the living cosmogony Steiner discusses in this lecture when put in this particular context? It is not merely a theoretical musing on the cosmic origin of the world and the human being. No, it is much more; it is to discover how human beings can be true "citizens of the cosmos." We see this urge to find our place as citizens by finding our place in the cosmos in the Declaration of Independence: "We hold these truths to be self-evident, that all men are created equal, that they are endowed by their Creator with certain unalienable Rights, that among these are Life, Liberty and the Pursuit of Happiness."

It is only when humanity understands the beginning, middle, and end of the cosmic drama that it can know its place in Nature. When we human beings understand our common divine origin in the Garden of Eden, our common divine goal in the New Jerusalem and our collective turning point within Christ, then we no longer see ourselves as mindless products and victims of mechanical forces. We can begin to see ourselves as co-creators with the Divine, co-creators in training. Our relationship to Nature must begin to reverse; rather than taking from Nature to preserve our survival, we must learn to give of ourselves to lift Nature to a higher octave.

The emphasis in the realm of Aquarius is on the limbs, as Aquarius forms both the shins and the forearms. Whereas the Church of Peter develops Freedom in the head, and the Church of John develops Altruism in the heart, there is a third church that encourages Cosmogony in the limbs, or human activity. We see the beginnings of this in Anthroposophical initiatives in agriculture, medicine, and therapy. All of these realms have a deep relationship to Astrosophy, to coming to a true understanding of the deeds of the starry heavens (particularly at the time of Christ). In fact, none of these realms can truly accomplish its task without some degree of star wisdom. The work of this publication is to further develop and encourage the existence of a living cosmogony in the West.

The church associated with this impulse is the third church, the Church of Paul. The Pauline Church has come to limited exoteric expression in the third orthodoxy after Roman Catholicism and Eastern Orthodoxy—the Anglican–Episcopalian Church. In reality, the true being of this church exists as Celtic Christianity, the Church of the Holy Grail. The ultimate goal of this church is not just to elevate Nature, but to redeem of the sub-Natural, the subearthly spheres. It is a Church of Grail knighthood, confronting the "dragons" of fallen nature in service to the Grail maiden of unfallen Nature. These Knights find the inspiration for their work by coming into a deeper relationship with the starry script and the angelic hierarchies who authored it. It will not be until the far future, until the seventh post-Atlantean cultural epoch centered in America, that this work will be completely possible. It is from this perspective that we can understand the third image offered to the astral body by the Angels: that of *crossing the abyss* to gain a living grasp of the spiritual behind nature.

To summarize briefly[1]:

---

1 One might find a contradiction between the characterization of the three Churches given here vs. what is found for example in appendix 2 of Robert Powell's *Hermetic Astrology,* vol. 1, in which he makes the correspondence of the Church of Peter with Willing and the Church of Paul with Thinking. To resolve this dilemma, one needs to regard the development of the Church as analogous to the development of the human being. The young child (from 0 to 7) has an exceptionally large head vs. a full-grown adult, and yet it expresses itself primarily through the will via the limbs. On the other hand, the teenage child (from 14 to 21) has disproportionately long limbs, yet expresses itself

| Peter | John | Paul |
|-------|------|------|
| head | heart | limbs |
| Taurus | Leo | Aquarius |

But what of Scorpio? Is there a fourth region of the globe, and if so what is its mission? When we look at the region of the globe onto which the constellations Scorpio, Sagittarius, and Capricorn project, we find a region bounded on the western side at 178°48' west, and at its eastern side at 88°48' west. This is the region lying to the east of far eastern Russia and to the west of South America—more or less the Pacific ocean, the western portion of Canada and the U.S., and all of Mexico. The sole Earth Chakra within this region is the Saturn Chakra at Mount Shasta, California. Notice that the path of the Earth Chakras from Root to Crown leads through four great Ages: Lemuria (Moon and Venus), Atlantis (Mercury), the current Age (Sun, Mars, Jupiter) and the future Age (Saturn).

Within this region of the globe the future age will come about, or what will arise from the ashes of the War of All Against All, thousands of years from now. The existence of this future age will rely on each of the other three portions of the globe and the accomplishing to a degree their respective missions. This depends, as we have already pointed out, on each portion of the globe coming to the aid of the others with what they lack. A fourth stage can come out of this harmony: Synthesis. The New Jerusalem, where Freedom, Equality, and Brotherhood exist in a perfect harmony, can arise in this region. This is the environment in which religion, art, and science can reunite and find their original wholeness.

While Taurus relates to the head, Leo to the heart, and Aquarius to the limbs, Scorpio is related to the human procreative organs. This implies the transformation of human reproduction into a process centered in the larynx through the magical transformation of speech, which will come about in this region through the synthesis of the three earthly missions. We might call the church leading this realm of fruition the Church of the Lamb and his Bride, which is by and large an etheric congregation, its earthly fulfillment yet to come.

It may be many years before this fulfillment can come about. The trend we see is the impulse to Fraternity streaming east out of Europe into Russia (ultimately coming to fruition in the next cultural epoch, that of the spirit self), whereas the impulse to cosmogony streams west out of Europe into Anglo-America (ultimately coming to fruition in the final cultural epoch of our age, that of spirit life). These two impulses become increasingly estranged from each other, with a growing tension and inability to reconcile. But at the very boundary of the future region of Scorpio, at 178° west longitude, we see far East Russia reaching out to touch Alaska, the far West—a geographical sign of the peace that will someday come, once tensions have been stretched beyond their limit.

It is no small matter that from early on in Willi Sucher's career, Rudolf Steiner's lecture of 1919 became the guiding star in his astrosophical and therapeutic striving. It is the conscious intention of this publication to continue to be inspired in this way and to cultivate the development of the mission of the West—to become co-creators of the New Earth through a living cosmogony. We do so through a conscious unification of our Astrosophy with what is offered to us from the East and the Center—or example, Sophiology and Anthroposophy, respectively (although one might look just as readily to Buddhism and Catholicism, among the many possibilities). Through this, it is our hope that one day "good may become what from our hearts we would found, and from our heads direct with single purpose."

---

primarily through thinking in the head. We might say that the Church of Peter works from above to below to enact a philosophy (head-centered) of freedom (will-activating), while the Church of Paul works from periphery to center to enact a participatory (limb-focused) cosmogony (thought-enlivening): the so-called Cosmic Drama.

# THE YEAR 2019 AND THE OPENING TO THE ANGELIC REALM—THE NEW STAR WISDOM

## *Robert Powell, PhD*

In my article "The Apocalypse Code and the Year 2018," published in *Journal for Star Wisdom* 2018, I indicated that the future for humanity according to the Apocalypse Code signifies a continuing unfolding and enactment of Christ's life—in relation to the whole of humankind—over the next 36,000 years. As stated in the article, the astronomical basis of the Apocalypse Code is that one day in the life of Christ corresponds to 29½ years in the life of humanity. Clearly, in the unfolding of the Book of Revelation, the underlying dating of which is specified by the Apocalypse Code, there are many wondrous miracles ahead, once humanity makes it through the *three temptations of humankind in the wilderness*, which have been precisely dated according to the Apocalypse Code. For now it can be said that, against the background of the Apocalypse Code, humanity has had to face—in the course of the twentieth century and continuing up to the present time in the twenty-first century—*the three temptations of humankind in the wilderness*. More precisely, as discussed in the article, the three temptations unfolded in this time frame:

### Dating of the Three Temptations of Humanity

(1) 1929 to 1958 (dates according to the Apocalypse Code) was a period when humanity faced in particular *the temptation of the will-to-power*, which at that time came most vividly to manifestation through Hitler in relation to the German people (but not only through him; consider also Stalin, for example, who at the same time as Hitler presented the same temptation to the Russian people). This temptation could be expressed in these (or similar) words: "I shall give you the kingdom (German: *Reich*), if you bow down and worship me." This could be called the Dictator/Guru temptation. There are, of course, plenty of examples of "good dictators" and "good gurus," who have not fallen prey to the temptation of the will-to-power.

(2) 1958 to 1988 (dates according to the Apocalypse Code): This was a time when humanity was powerfully faced with the temptation directed to the feeling life of *casting oneself down from the pinnacle of the temple*, which came most strikingly to expression through the drug epidemic—for example, through LSD guru Timothy Leary's injunction, "Turn on, tune in, drop out"—a modern-day version of *casting oneself down from the pinnacle of the temple*. In the human being the higher faculties of conscience and reason are the "pinnacle of the temple" and the temptation is—by way of alcohol, drugs, hedonism, etc.—to temporarily blot out reason and conscience and thereby to plunge into the realm of the subconscious, instinctual forces, allowing them to lead one.

And now, 2019, we have (potentially, at least) made it through the cosmically appointed day of the third temptation of *turning stones into bread*:

(3) 1988 to 2018 (dates according to the Apocalypse Code) was the period of the powerful temptation directed to the human being's thought life through modern technology—such as virtual reality, and so on, substituting the lifeless for the living—that is, in the language of the Gospels, "Turning stones into bread."

Now, in light of the Apocalypse Code, there is—potentially—a precious and wondrous future ahead, beginning in the years 2018/2019, denoting the end of the three temptations of humankind in the wilderness. I say "potentially" for a good reason, which will be discussed below.

To summarize these indications from the previous article: in the year 869, according to the Apocalypse Code, there began the first "day" of the forty "days" of humankind's temptations in the wilderness—each "day" lasting 29½ years. At that time, Saturn was in sidereal Sagittarius.[1] Every time—once every 29½ years, this being the orbital period around the zodiac of this distant planet—Saturn returns to sidereal Sagittarius, we have a further day in the unfolding of these forty days of temptation of humanity. If we take the forty days and reckon 40 x 29½ (to be more precise: 40 x 29.4578) = 1,178 years, and add this onto 869, we find that the *end* of the period of forty days of temptation of humankind is in 2047, almost the middle of this century.

Going back one Saturn revolution from the year 2047, we arrive at *the start of the last day*, the fortieth day, in 2018, with Saturn in Sagittarius, where it was located in the sidereal zodiac at the start of the forty days of temptation of humanity in the wilderness in 869. Now, in the year 2019, Saturn remains in Sagittarius for the whole year, and last year we have already commenced the *fortieth* day of temptation of humanity in the wilderness. And, as stated in the Gospels, on this fortieth day, when Christ had overcome the three temptations, "Angels came and ministered unto him" (Matt. 4:11).

## Christ Jesus: The Representative of Humanity

The potential for human beings at the present time, if one considers Christ Jesus as having passed through the temptations in the wilderness as the *Representative of Humanity* [2] and who therefore is able to show each one of us the way forward, not only meeting and overcoming temptation, but also entering into a new relationship with the

**The Representative of Humanity**, *by Edith Maryon and Rudolf Steiner; wood sculpture, approximately 30 feet high*

angelic realm, as described in my previous article and is now discussed further below. However, this depends upon each individual's *alignment with Christ*, since he leaves us free, and it is only if we consciously choose to align ourselves with him, that he as our *Divine-Human Representative* will guide us into spiritual reality—that is, into connection with the angelic realm.

On the other hand, for many of those human beings who have not consciously aligned themselves with the *Representative of Humanity*, instead of coming into connection with the angelic realm, the forces at work behind the three temptations may be able to take hold of them on various levels (thought, feeling, will) with increasing force. The end result of this will be a polarization

---

1  All references made to the zodiac in this article are to the original zodiac of the Babylonians, Egyptians, Greeks, and Romans—now called the *sidereal zodiac*. See Robert Powell, *History of the Zodiac*.

2  Some readers will know that Rudolf Steiner's great statue of Christ titled *The Representative of Humanity* depicts Christ in the midst of the three temptations. Rudolf Steiner, who worked on this statue from 1914 to 1921, knew full well that soon—he even specified the year 1933 as the beginning—humanity would be subject to unprecedented temptations. The creation of the statue *The Representative of Humanity* was a gift to the world to help human beings through the three temptations that would be soon unleashed, starting in 1929, just four years after Rudolf Steiner's unexpected death in 1925.

of human beings into two groups: those who follow Christ and align themselves with him, and those who become more and more swept along by the Antichrist forces underlying the three temptations.[1] The latter human beings, instead of receiving the impulse to connect with the angelic realm, may instead—consciously or not—become open to demonic influences.[2] It is against this background that what is more and more apparent all around us in our time may be understood—modern-day phenomena related to increasing cultural and moral degeneration, the growing manifestation of corruption at various levels of government, law enforcement, the judicial system, and business, and the direction taken by the media of promoting "fake news," as well as other disturbing contemporary phenomena too numerous to mention.[3]

What will be discussed in the following is how the opening up to humanity of a new relationship with the angelic realm (from 2018 on) signifies the possibility, now, of the development of a new and living star wisdom—one aspect of which is a *true astrology*. The reason for this, as described in my book *Hermetic Astrology, volume 2: Astrological Biography* and elsewhere, is that each human soul descends from heavenly heights through the various planetary spheres upon their descent into incarnation, finally to enter the Moon sphere, which is the realm of the angels, prior to conception, and remaining in that sphere during the entire period between conception and birth. It is in this realm of the Moon sphere where, together with one's guardian angel, the "details" of one's earthly destiny are elaborated upon between conception and birth in relation to the planetary movements against the background of the starry heavens. This is the foundation for true astrology, as touched upon briefly in the following quote from Valentin Tomberg's *Studies of the Old Testament*.

Connecting with the angelic realm and the opening up of true astrology

> As [the Old Testament patriarch] Jacob had conquered the falsehood connected with his birth, the mission to which his birth called him was revealed to him through the realm of the angels—that is, his conscious perception of the angels came to him from the...enter[ing] conscious interaction with the beings of the angelic hierarchy...entering conscious interaction with the beings who know the mysteries of birth. The true horoscope will not be reached by a path of calculation but through a path of interaction with suprasensory beings. What angels have imparted to humankind, that is the "horoscope" in the true sense.[4]

It is against this background that in my fortieth year of life the impulse to write and publish a series of three volumes on the new astrology arose—see below—and these three volumes can be looked upon as a preparation for what is now, since the year 2018, opening up increasingly to human beings who are seriously and devotedly seeking in this direction.

Generally speaking, some guidelines are offered in each issue of *Star Wisdom* concerning the basis of an astrology leading to a new wisdom of the stars (astrosophy). The line of development involved here can be stated quite simply as: astronomy → astrology → astrosophy.

---

1  Indeed, the vast majority of those human beings who do not decide to align themselves with Christ will sooner or later fall prey to one or more of the three temptations, because without the help of Christ, who met and overcame these temptations on our behalf, it is virtually impossible to withstand them.

2  See, for example: https://www.naturalnews.com/2018-06-10-demons-really-are-possessing-people-warns-psychiatrist.html.

3  As a counter-impulse to the possibility, through Christ, of human beings taking an ascending path of evolution and thereby coming into connection with the angelic realm, the Antichrist forces are unleashing more and more possibilities for human beings to take a descending path of evolution, thereby coming into connection with very dark forces. See, for example, my two *Shambhala* articles in the 2017 issue of the JSW. The increasing focus in our time upon the development of artificial intelligence (AI)—and all that is associated therewith—is becoming very obvious as a push to lead human beings along a "nonhuman" path of development into the future as a development from the third temptation.

4  Tomberg, *Christ and Sophia: Anthroposophic Meditations on the Old Testament, New Testament, and Apocalypse*, p. 47.

## Astronomy, Astrology, and Astrosophy

In a general sense, it may be understood that astronomy, astrology, and astrosophy comprise the "body," "soul," and "spirit" of star wisdom as a whole. Considered from this general point of view, the trilogy of these works I wrote (originally published, and then republished, in the years indicated) relate, respectively, to the body, soul, and spirit of a new star wisdom:

1. *Astrology and Reincarnation* (1987, 2006),
2. *Astrological Biography* (1989, 2006), and
3. *The Star of the Magi and the Life of Christ* (1991, 1998).

As shown, these three volumes were originally published approximately one Saturn cycle (29½ years) prior to the opening in 2018, through Christ, of the angelic realm to humanity. They can be considered a preparation for this new time into which we have now entered.[5]

What are the main features of the astronomy ("body") of a new star wisdom as presented in volume 1, *Astrology and Reincarnation*? These may be stated concisely as follows:

1. Conclusive research reveals, the authentic astronomical-astrological zodiac is demonstrated to be the sidereal zodiac of the Babylonians, Egyptians, and ancient Greeks.[6]

2. In addition to the geocentric planetary positions usual in traditional astrology, the heliocentric positions of the planets in the sidereal zodiac, as these come to expression in Tycho Brahe's astronomical system, are shown to be astrologically significant. Tycho Brahe's astronomical system can be viewed as a kind of "resurrection" in scientific form of the ancient Egyptian hermetic astronomical system, which, however, was purely intuitive, having no scientific basis (at that time). On this account, and also for other important reasons, in the aforementioned trilogy of books, the term *hermetic astrology* is used to describe the new approach to star wisdom outlined in these three volumes.

These two scientific findings, discovered by way of the astrological reincarnation research presented in volume 1 of the trilogy, form part of the astronomical foundation upon which hermetic astrology is based, and the latter, in turn, provides a foundation for a new wisdom of the stars. At this stage, therefore, it is helpful once again to briefly consider these two astronomical pillars supporting the new star wisdom outlined in volume 1 of this trilogy of hermetic-astrological works.

## The Zoa ("Holy Living Creatures") form the Zodiac

The Greek word *zodiac* means "animal circle" and refers to the circle of constellations made up of animal figures such as the Ram, Bull, Crab, Lion, and so on—including some human figures (Twins, Virgo, and Water Bearer), as well as a half-human–half-animal figure, the Centaur (Sagittarius). The importance of this particular circle of constellations comprising the zodiac is that these constellations provide the background against which the movements of the planets were observed and recorded.[7] The word *zodiac* derives from the Greek word *zoa*, used in the Bible to designate the holy living creatures beheld in John's vision (Apocalypse, ch. 4–5) as surrounding the Throne of God.[8]

Concerning the zodiac, the initiates of antiquity spiritually beheld the signs of the zodiac embedded in the stellar constellations: the Ram, the Bull, the Twins, and so on.[9] With clairvoyant vision they perceived that the twelve visible stellar

---

5  The first two volumes of the *Hermetic Astrology* trilogy, (1) and (2), were republished in 2006 and are available from Amazon. The third volume [3] was republished by SteinerBooks in 1998 and is available either directly from SteinerBooks or from Amazon.

6  Powell, *History of the Zodiac*.

7  This was the essence of Babylonian astronomy underlying the development of astrology in Babylonia, Egypt (especially Alexandria), Greece and Rome—these being the cultures in which the original zodiac of the Babylonians was utilized, as described in my book *History of the Zodiac* and in *The Astrological Revolution*, coauthored with Kevin Dann.

8  Powell and Dann, *Christ and the Maya Calendar*, appendix 2 ("The Central Sun") identifies the Throne of God with the *Galactic Center*, also known as the *Central Sun*.

9  Paul and Powell, *Cosmic Dances of the Zodiac*.

### The sidereal zodiac
### Dates of the Sun's ingresses into the twelve signs of the zodiac

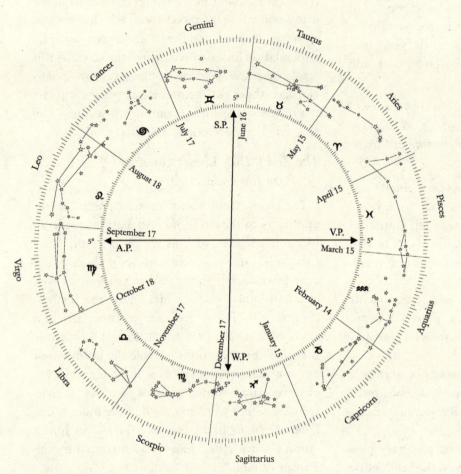

configurations of the zodiac are the outer manifestation ("body") of twelve highly evolved spiritual beings known as the *holy living creatures*. In the Apocalypse of St. John four of these twelve holy living creatures are referred to, one on each side of the Throne of God:

> And round the throne, on each side of the throne, are four living creatures, full of eyes in front and behind: the first living creature like a lion, the second living creature like an ox, the third living creature with the face of a man, and the fourth living creature like a flying eagle. And the four living creatures, each of them with six wings, are full of eyes all round and within, and day and night they never cease to sing: "Holy, holy, holy, is the Lord God Almighty, who was, and is, and is to come!" (Rev. 4:6–8)

Here St. John depicts his clairvoyant vision of the holy living creatures whose "bodies" are visible externally in the zodiacal constellations of the Lion, the Bull (Ox), the Waterman (Man), and the Scorpion (Eagle).[1] St. John refers to only four of the holy living creatures—those manifesting through the four fixed zodiacal signs: Taurus, Leo, Scorpio, and Water-Bearer—but each of these four is flanked on either side by two holy living creatures, so that the full circle of holy living creatures surrounding the throne of God comprises twelve.[2]

In contemplating the inner reality of the sidereal zodiac, we draw near to the throne of God. The inner side of that which is presented to us externally as the twelve sidereal signs (zodiacal constellations) is revealed to clairvoyant vision as the twelve holy living creatures who assisted in the divine creation, and who continue to assist in the guidance of the evolution of the world and in the shaping of the destiny of humankind. In trying to delineate the spheres of influence of the twelve holy living creatures, as hermetic astrology—both ancient and modern—sets out to do, an attempt is made to take account of the spiritual influence of these divine beings upon the Earth and humanity. In this respect,

---

1  For a discussion as to why the Eagle came to be seen as the Scorpion, see my book *Christian Hermetic Astrology: The Star of the Magi and the Life of Christ*.

2  See, for example, Steiner, *The Spiritual Hierarchies and the Physical World*, in which the vision of the twelve holy living creatures around the throne is described.

hermetic astrology aspires to the same sphere of divine reality as that of the age-old star wisdom of antiquity cultivated by Zarathustra in ancient Persia, Hermes in ancient Egypt, Zoroaster (Zaratas) in Babylon, and which radiates through the revelations of the prophet Ezekiel of Ancient Israel and the Christian initiate John the Evangelist in the Book of Revelation.

It was the deed of Zoroaster, who lived in Babylon in the sixth century BC and was known to the priests there as Zaratas, to first arrive at a scientific understanding of the spheres of influence of the twelve holy living creatures comprising the being of the zodiac. On the basis of Zoroaster's indications, the Babylonians defined the twelve sidereal signs, each 30° long, so that the star Aldebaran (the Bull's eye) is located at 15° Taurus and the star Antares (the heart of the Scorpion), which is directly opposite Aldebaran in the zodiac, is placed at 15° Scorpio. It is this zodiac, defined on the basis of the revelation of the great initiate Zoroaster, which is the original astronomical-astrological zodiac of the spiritual tradition to which hermetic astrology belongs.[3]

Now known as the *sidereal zodiac*, this zodiac of the ancient mystery wisdom tradition became reintroduced into Western astrology in the middle of the twentieth century by Cyril Fagan with the publication of his book *Zodiacs Old and New*,[4] and received—in outline—a formal astronomical definition in the work by Robert Powell and Peter Treadgold *The Sidereal Zodiac*.[5] This is the first of the above-mentioned astronomical pillars upon which hermetic astrology rests.

Often the idea is put forward that the sidereal zodiac may well have been valid in antiquity, but that since Christ's sacrifice, known as the *Mystery of Golgotha*, it is the tropical zodiac—defined by Greek astronomers and now used by the majority of Western astrologers—that is the true astrological zodiac. Here it is only necessary to point out that St. John's vision of the holy living creatures from the post-Christian era is more or less in agreement with that of Ezekiel from the Old Testament. The continuity in visionary experience of these two initiates—one from the pre-Christian and one from the post-Christian era—indicates that the twelve holy living creatures did not depart from the zodiacal constellations at the time of the Mystery of Golgotha to take up their abode elsewhere, but that they still continue to work from the realm of the constellations (sidereal signs) of the zodiac, streaming down from there. Moreover, astrological reincarnation research, with the discovery of the second "law" of astrological reincarnation, shows beyond any shadow of doubt that the ancient sidereal zodiac is still to this day the true zodiac underlying astrology.[6]

Moreover, the twentieth-century Christian initiate Rudolf Steiner—in agreement with the initiates of antiquity such as Hermes and Zoroaster—also described clairvoyantly the passage of the Sun through the constellations of the sidereal zodiac. To emphasize that it is the passage of the Sun through the zodiacal constellations which is spiritually significant, Rudolf Steiner published the *Kalender 1912/1913* describing this phenomenon, and wrote in the preface:

> Just as we can describe the simple experience of "I feel the nocturnal darkness giving way to the light" with the words, "the Sun is rising," so the more complicated soul experiences such as "I feel how in spring-time the Earth prepares itself for new growth and for taking in the power of Sun" may find itself expressed

---

3   Powell, *History of the Zodiac*. See also Powell, *Christian Hermetic Astrology: The Star of the Magi and the Life of Christ*.

4   Fagan, *Zodiacs Old and New*; see also his book *Astrological Origins*.

5   Powell and Treadgold, *The Sidereal Zodiac*. In the meantime, this work has been superseded by the publication of my comprehensive PhD thesis, published as *History of the Zodiac*.

6   The second "law" of astrological reincarnation is described in volume 1 of the *Hermetic Astrology* trilogy. It shows empirically that when an individual reincarnates, the planetary configuration at birth echoes the configuration at death in the preceding incarnation *in the sidereal zodiac* (not in the tropical zodiac). The discovery of the second "law" confirmed what Rudolf Steiner had already outlined in a more general way in his lecture of November 28, 1912, in Steiner, *Life between Death and Rebirth*, p. 97.

in the words, "the rising Sun is perceived in the constellation of Pisces."[1]

Here the word *perceived* clearly does not refer to physical perception, as the Sun cannot be observed physically against the background of the stars of the zodiacal constellations (except on the rare occasion of a total solar eclipse). Rather, Rudolf Steiner is referring here to clairvoyant perception of the Sun in the constellation of Pisces. In other words, he described from clairvoyant perception that from the time of the spring equinox, around March 20/21, when spring begins, the Sun can be seen in the constellation of Pisces (and not in Aries, as maintained in modern Western astrology).

## The Hermetic–Tychonic Astronomical System

As referred to previously, another astronomical pillar underlying the foundation of hermetic astrology is the astronomical system of Tycho Brahe, which, as described in *Hermetic Astrology, volume 1: Astrology and Reincarnation*, represents a modern scientific definition of the hermetic astronomical system of the ancient Egyptians. While not denying the validity of the Ptolemaic geocentric astronomical system as the basis for classical geocentric astrology, astrological reincarnation research not only demonstrates conclusively that the sidereal zodiac is the star template for the astrological zodiac but also shows that the heliocentric movements of the planets through the zodiacal signs—that is, through the twelve 30° regions of the sidereal zodiac—are *definitely an astrological reality*.[2]

Moreover, although the Sun-centered Copernican heliocentric system is applicable with regard to physical phenomena (planetary motion, orbits of comets around the Sun, etc.), it is the Tychonic helio-geocentric system that applies to the soul-spiritual side of existence, which is the domain of astrology. For, whereas returning comets (such as Halley's) orbit around the Sun as their focal point, human beings reincarnate upon the Earth, and therefore the Earth is central from an astrological point of view.

As described in the third volume of the trilogy, *Christian Hermetic Astrology: The Star of the Magi and the Life of Christ*, whereas the Copernican heliocentric system applies well on the physical plane of existence, on the astral (soul) plane it is Ptolemy's geocentric system which holds good, and on the devachanic (spiritual) plane the Tychonic system comes into its own.[3] Each plane of existence—physical, astral, devachanic—has its own laws and requires a corresponding astronomical system. From the physical point of view the Tychonic system may seem "stupid," but from the devachanic plane of existence it is a definite validity. That there is a deeper significance to Tycho Brahe's astronomical system is indicated in the following words of Rudolf Steiner:

> The world really knows nothing about Tycho Brahe except that he was "stupid" enough to devise a plan of the cosmos in which the Earth stands still and the Sun together with the planets revolve around it. That is what the world in general knows today. The fact that we have to do here with a significant personality of the sixteenth century, with one who accomplished an infinite amount that even today is still useful to astronomy, that untold depths of wisdom are contained in what he gave—none of this is usually recorded, for the simple reason that in presenting the system in detail, out of his own deep knowledge, Tycho Brahe saw difficulties which Copernicus did not see. If such a thing dare be said—for it does indeed seem paradoxical—even with the Copernican cosmic system the last word has not been uttered. And the conflict between the two systems will still occupy the minds of a later humanity.[4]

As outlined here, there need not to be a conflict between the Copernican and Tychonic systems if it is recognized that they apply to different levels of existence. Similarly, the replacement of the

---

[1] This English translation of the words of Rudolf Steiner from his preface to his *Kalender 1912/1913* can be found in Robert Powell-Peter Treadgold, *The Sidereal Zodiac*, p. 24.

[2] See, for example, the second "law" of astrological reincarnation described in *Hermetic Astrology*, volume 1, appendix 4.

[3] Regarding the Tychonic system, see Powell and Dann, *The Astrological Revolution*, p. 45.

[4] Steiner, *Occult History*, p. 79.

Ptolemaic geocentric system by the heliocentric system of Copernicus meant that by the sixteenth century AD, when in 1543 Copernicus published his system, the transition by human consciousness—effected over centuries from the astral plane to the physical plane—was at its final stage of completion. The Ptolemaic system in its turn had replaced the still earlier hermetic astronomical system of the ancient Egyptians, signifying the transition made in antiquity by human consciousness (again over a long period of time) from the devachanic plane to the astral plane.

By continuing to adhere to the Ptolemaic system right down to the present time, traditional geocentric astrology shows that it is a science applied to the astral plane and not to the physical plane. And by reintroducing the hermetic (Egyptian–Tychonic) system in the twentieth century, modern hermetic astrology is simply taking account of the fact that the deeper spiritual nature of human beings—rooted in the devachanic plane—can only be explored by means of an astronomical system appropriate to that plane.

This deeper spiritual nature comes to expression in the seven lotus flowers (chakras) of the human being. And by way of the correspondences between the seven lotus flowers of the microcosm and the seven planets of the macrocosm, it is possible to arrive at insight into the human being's deeper spiritual talents and faculties. This is achieved by casting a horoscope, within the framework of the Tychonic system, for the moment of birth of the human being, where the resulting horoscope in the trilogy is called the *hermetic chart*. The hermetic chart, relating more to the human being's spiritual nature (belonging essentially to the devachanic plane), complements and supplements the traditional geocentric sidereal chart, cast within the framework of the geocentric astronomical system—that is, the positions of the planets are computed as if the Earth is at the center of our solar system—which offers a picture more of the human being's soul nature (belonging essentially to the astral plane).[5]

Having briefly reviewed some essential points concerning these two aforementioned *astronomical* pillars—the sidereal zodiac and the Tychonic system, discussed especially in volume 1 of the trilogy—let us now turn to one of the main *astrological* pillars upon which hermetic astrology rests. Here we shall make the transition from the "body" of star wisdom (astronomical level) to the "soul" (astrological level) of a new wisdom of the stars. Correspondingly, we shall redirect our attention from the content of volume 1 to that of volume 2 of the *Hermetic Astrology* trilogy. Fundamentally, the central astrological pillar underlying the science of astrological biography outlined in *Hermetic Astrology*, volume 2 can be summarized as follows:

## Astrological Biography

The human being's destiny is mapped out in the cosmic world during the embryonic period, between conception and birth, and unfolds in seven-year periods between birth and death according to the correspondence between each seven-year period of earthly life and each lunar orbit of the sidereal zodiac during the embryonic period.

This key correspondence between the embryonic period and the course of life was discovered by Willi Sucher during the 1930s. Intrinsic to any practical application of this correspondence underlying astrological biography is the use of the hermetic rule (rule of Hermes), which has been handed down from the days when hermetic astrology flourished in Hellenistic Egypt during the first and second centuries BC.[6] The hermetic rule, therefore, is an astrological rule essentially belonging to the central pillar underlying the foundation of hermetic astrology.

Although there is some evidence from the corpus of astrological manuscripts surviving from antiquity that a few astrologers were interested in delving into the cosmic mysteries belonging to the embryonic period, there is no explicit mention of the key correspondence discovered (or re-discovered) by Willi Sucher in the 1930s. There were

---

5  It needs to be borne in mind that this exposition greatly oversimplifies something that is in reality much more complex than what is described here.

6  See Powell, *Hermetic Astrology*, vol. 1, appendix 1 for a description of the hermetic rule in a historical context.

certainly astrologers in antiquity who utilized the hermetic rule for determining the moment of conception,[1] but even if they had known of the previously mentioned key correspondence, the sheer complexity of following the planetary movements throughout the embryonic period would surely have been a sufficiently daunting reason for them not to have undertaken this.

But now, given modern ephemerides and computing facilities, the mapping out of an individual's astrological biography—by following the planetary movements during the embryonic period and applying the key correspondence to transpose to the course of life—has become quite feasible.[2] Willi Sucher, without ever making use of a computer, was adept at applying the hermetic rule and mapping out the astrological biography of a person. He even developed a graphical method for plotting the geocentric and heliocentric movements of the planets throughout the entire embryonic period, a feat which no astrologer in antiquity could ever have attempted without an enormous expenditure of time and a vast number of computations. From his graphs of planetary movements during the embryonic period, Willi Sucher could see at a glance the destiny images, prefigured in the formation of the web of destiny during the embryonic period, relating to events taking place in the course of the individual's life. Sucher was therefore not only the pioneer of astrological biography, he was also an exceptionally accomplished practitioner of this arcane discipline.[3]

In this respect, just as Zoroaster and Tycho Brahe are the names associated with the previously discussed two astronomical pillars underlying a new star wisdom, so the names of Hermes and Willi Sucher are significant in connection with the central astrological pillar under discussion—Hermes having inspired the hermetic rule for the computation of the moment of conception retrogressively from the moment of birth, and Sucher having pioneered the science of astrological biography for exploring the unfolding of destiny in relation to the planetary movements between conception and birth. Just as *Hermetic Astrology,* volume 1 is intended as a source work concerning two of the astronomical pillars underlying a new star wisdom, so *Hermetic Astrology,* volume 2 can be thought of as a practical handbook outlining *astrological biography* as one of the central astrological pillars and its application.[4]

## Christ and the New Star Wisdom

In turning to a brief consideration of the next step: astrology to astrosophy, our attention is directed to the third volume in this trilogy of hermetic, astrological works, *Christian Hermetic Astrology: The Star of the Magi and the Life of Christ.* Here the explicitly Christian nature of a new star wisdom becomes apparent, for the entire work is devoted to the stars during the life of Christ, starting with the *Star of the Magi*.

For some readers of this trilogy, in which in the first two volumes the Christian aspect has also been emphasized throughout, the question has surely arisen: Are not Christianity and astrology essentially incompatible, since any Christian who believes in divine providence is bound to reject the idea that human life is linked to the movements of the planets against the background of the stars? Yet the very fact that the Magi were led to the birth of the Messiah by way of a revelation connected with a specific planetary-stellar configuration, as

---

1 It needs to be borne in mind that the conception horoscope is valid in its own right. The geocentric conception horoscope relates to the etheric body of the human being, and the heliocentric—or rather the hermetic/Tychonic—conception horoscope relates to the human being's physical body: visit the astrogeographia.org website; here with a direct link: http://www.astrogeographia.org/about_us/conception_epoch_chart/index.html.

2 Use of the hermetic rule to compute the horoscope of conception and also the featuring of the astrological biography (as well as many other remarkable features) is made possible through Peter Treadgold's *Astrofire* program, available through the Sophia Foundation—sophiafoundation.org.

3 The features of astrological biography mentioned here are included in Peter Treadgold's *Astrofire*

program, which thus makes this "arcane discipline" referred to above readily accessible to everyone capable of using a computer.

4 *Hermetic Astrology,* volume 2 gives the astrological biography of the composer Richard Wagner as an example.

described in *Christian Hermetic Astrology: The Star of the Magi and the Life of Christ*, shows that Christianity from its very inception had a relationship with the star wisdom of the ancients, of whom the Magi were perhaps the last true representatives. And, more importantly, they were the first followers of Christ.

The whole of *Christian Hermetic Astrology* is written in the same spirit as that which prevailed when the Magi learnt from the world of stars concerning the birth of the Messiah. In the same way in which the Star of the Magi is discussed—connected with the divine birth—so the planetary configurations at the most significant events in the life of Christ are looked at in the same spirit. But, as many readers will undoubtedly ask: to what purpose? Can this help our understanding of the human being's relationship to the world of the stars?

Readers of the predecessor to this publication, the *Journal for Star Wisdom*, know that the monthly commentaries presented by Claudia McLaren Lainson in each issue, are based upon the same findings as that which forms the basis for the astrosophical research presented in *Christian Hermetic Astrology: The Star of the Magi and the Life of Christ*.[5] Taking up the spirit of this book and developing it further, these monthly commentaries represent the central impulse of a new star wisdom (astrosophy) that is coming to birth in our time. The work of Claudia McLaren Lainson can be understood as pioneering the way to a new and spiritual understanding of stellar events taking place in the starry heavens month by month during the cycle of the year. This is something completely new, which offers tremendous help in elevating consciousness to the angelic realm that is now opening up anew to humanity.

---

5 This basis is to be found in Powell, *Chronicle of the Living Christ*, which in turn rests on the content of the 3-volume work, *The Visions of Anne Catherine Emmerich*. As indicated in both of these works, the dating of the life of Christ presented in these works—discovered in the early 1990s by Robert Powell—is demonstrably accurate with well-nigh one-hundred percent certainty. This dating of Christ's life is thus a third scientific pillar upon which the new star wisdom rests.

Here it should be pointed out that Willi Sucher, the leading pioneer of astrosophy in the twentieth century, also placed great importance upon contemplating the geocentric and heliocentric movements of the planets against the background of the stars at the time of Christ. For him (at that time in the twentieth century) this was the heart of astrosophy, through which an immeasurable deepening of the human being's relationship to the star world can take place. How is this to be understood?

Just as the twelve zodiacal constellations, considered in their outer aspect, comprise the "body" of the twelve holy living creatures surrounding the throne of God, so the planets—or rather the spheres traced out by the planets on their orbits—are the abodes of spiritual beings in service of the Creator, whom Christ Jesus called *the Father*. The movements of the planets against the background of the zodiacal constellations, taken in their totality, represent the bringing to realization of the will of the Father through manifold spiritual beings. In this respect the cosmos as a whole can be considered as an expression of the Father. But since the Mystery of Golgotha the words of Christ apply: "No one comes to the Father, but by me" (John 14:6). This means to say, no mortal can find a true relationship with the cosmic world without the mediation of Christ. The step from astrology to astrosophy—astrosophy being concerned with the spiritual side of existence (i.e., with the spiritual beings of the universe)—can be undertaken by way of the Christ, who acts as the Great Guardian to the Threshold to the cosmic world.

In view of the central importance of Christ for a new wisdom of the stars, already in *Hermetic Astrology*, volume 1, especially in appendix 2 ("The second coming"), an attempt was made to indicate a path toward a new understanding of Christ in the twentieth century. It was precisely this, however, which gave rise to misunderstanding and even outright criticism of *Hermetic Astrology*, volume 1, although on the whole the purely astronomical and astrological content of the *Hermetic Astrology* trilogy has been well-received.

## The Second Coming of Christ

The criticism directed against the content of appendix 2 of *Hermetic Astrology,* volume 1 generally overlooked the central idea—or rather ideal—of this appendix, an ideal toward the realization of which the Russian philosopher Vladimir Solovyov (1853–1900) devoted much of his life. The significance of this ideal for a new understanding of Christ in our time should be evident from the following train of thought: there is only one Christ Being, and all true Christians are united in this Being, therefore on a higher level there exists only one Christianity. UNITY IN CHRIST was the ideal which inspired Solovyov,[1] and it is this ideal which inspired the writing of *Hermetic Astrology,* volume 1, appendix 2, which is nothing other than a modern-day exposition of Solovyov's line of thought, taking account of certain developments in humankind's spiritual life since Solovyov's death in 1900.

The main difference between Solovyov's time and our own can be summarized with the words. *the second coming of Christ.* When Solovyov was alive, there existed only traditional Christianity. As he described in poetic form in his work *A Short Narrative about Antichrist* (written during the last few months of his life), traditional Christianity comprises three streams: Roman Catholic, Eastern Orthodox, and Protestant. These in turn, using an analogy with the human being, as we can observe, correspond to the will, feeling, and thinking aspects of Christianity, which may be represented in the form of a triangle.

As described in *Hermetic Astrology,* volume 1, appendix 2, continuing further the analogy with the development of the human being, Rudolf Steiner (1861–1925) came as a messenger of the Self of Christianity, as opposed to the will, feeling, and thinking aspects represented by the three main Christian confessions. The message of Rudolf Steiner—Anthroposophy ("spiritual science")—signified the beginning of the in-streaming of Christ taking place through the second coming, the onset of which commenced in the twentieth century: 1933 is the date indicated for this by Rudolf Steiner. The second coming of Christ signifies the coming to birth of the Self of Christianity, which can be represented by placing a point in the middle of the triangle.

In this analogy with the human being, what is new since the time of Solovyov is the advent or *parousia* ("presence") of the unifying principle, the Self, which alone can truly unite thinking, feeling, and willing. Applying this analogy to Christianity as a whole, there still remains the question as to how the unifying principle (the Self of Christianity, Christ himself) can accomplish the task of unification, and in *Hermetic Astrology,* volume 1, appendix 2, although it was possible to give only the briefest of indications there, mention was made as to how the spiritual teachers of humanity (known as *bodhisattvas* in the East) assist Christ in this work. Also, the descent of Christ from cosmic realms, on his path of return to the onset of his second coming, is another important consideration with regard to Christ's work of re-uniting humanity in brotherhood and sisterhood—as expressed in the words: "Where two or three [meaning "two or more"] are gathered together in my name, there am I in the midst of them" (Matt. 18:20).

However, just as Solovyov met with incomprehension and antagonism when he espoused the ideal of UNITY IN CHRIST, so this immeasurably powerful and inspiring ideal, which is capable in our time of leading to an inner nearness to Christ, may well again evoke misunderstanding and even outright criticism.

Part of the criticism directed against appendix 2 of *Hermetic Astrology,* volume 1, where certain time indications are given relating to the second coming, concerns the application of the correspondence: one year of human life corresponds to one century in the history of Christianity. After the publication of appendix 2 in volume 1 of *Hermetic Astrology,* I came across a reference by Rudolf Steiner to a similar correspondence: one year of human life corresponds to one century in the history of the Sophia Being. (Sophia is the source of inspiration for philosophy and astrosophy, and is described in the vision of St. John as "a woman clothed with the

---

1 In the words of Christ: "By this everyone will know that you are my disciples, if you love one another" (John 13:35).

Sun, with the Moon under her feet, and on her head a crown of twelve stars"—Rev. 12:1).

Rudolf Steiner traced the history of philosophy, which is an expression of Sophia,[2] within the context of the history of philosophy, looking at 700-year periods corresponding to seven-year periods in the development of the human being. He drew this conclusion: "A year for a human being is a century for philosophy [the being of Sophia]. And so we see a being moving through history for whom a century is comparable to a year."[3] If this correspondence holds for Sophia, who is referred to in the book of Revelation as the *Bride of the Lamb*— that is, the *Bride of Christ*—it is not unreasonable to look at 700-year periods of development in the history of Christianity as undertaken in appendix 2 of volume 1 of the *Hermetic Astrology* trilogy.

## A New Science of Reincarnation and Karma

Rudolf Steiner also emphasized the need for the permeation of astrology with the Christ Impulse:

> It became clearer and clearer to me—as the outcome of many years of research—that in our epoch there is really something like a resurrection of the astrology of the third epoch (that of the Egyptian and Babylonian civilizations), but permeated with the Christ Impulse. Today we must search again among the stars in a way different from the old ways, but the stellar script must once again become something that speaks to us.[4]

These words of Rudolf Steiner summarize the overriding essence of hermetic astrology as represented in this trilogy of works. The original hermetic astrology, which was cultivated in and around Alexandria during the first two or three centuries BC and AD, was a continuation of the star wisdom of ancient Egypt stemming from the great initiate Hermes Trismegistus. Modern hermetic astrology is a resurrection of this ancient star wisdom, arising in our time as a result of the permeation of the ancient astrology with the Christ Impulse.

However, it is not only the inclusion of an explicitly Christian orientation which distinguishes modern hermetic astrology from its predecessor in antiquity; it is also the inclusion of reincarnation. As presented in *Hermetic Astrology*, volumes 1 and 2, reincarnation research opens up altogether new dimensions for the science of the stars, but this has only become possible, as Rudolf Steiner pointed out, since the Age of Michael (1879–2233) began in 1879.

> We see here how great the difficulties are when one wishes to approach the wisdom of the stars rightly and righteously. Indeed the true approach to the wisdom of the stars, which we need to penetrate the facts of karma, is only possible in the light of a true insight into Michael's domain. It is only possible at Michael's side. I have shown you a single example today.... It will show you once more, how through the whole reality of modern life there has come forth a certain stream of spiritual life which makes it very difficult to approach with an open mind the science of the stars, and the science, too, of karma. But difficult as it is, it can be done. Despite the attacks that are possible from those quarters that I have described today, we can nevertheless go forward with assurance, and approach the wisdom of the stars and the real shaping of karma.[5]

The call issued by Rudolf Steiner (in the above words, from 1924) for a new science of the stars as a science of karma provided the central motivation for the extensive research and subsequent writing down and publication of *Hermetic Astrology*, volumes 1 and 2, the writing of which I began at Easter 1983. *Hermetic Astrology* thus arose in response to Rudolf Steiner's call issued two Saturn cycles (fifty-nine years) previously. And just as Rudolf Steiner's reincarnation research provided the initial material forming the foundation for modern hermetic astrology— indeed, it would not have been possible without it—so Willi Sucher's example in pioneering a

---

2 The Greek philosopher Pythagoras, who is said to have been the first person to use the word "philosophy," understood this word to mean "love of Sophia"—*Sophia* being the Greek word for wisdom. Thus, according to Pythagoras, Sophia can be conceived of as the *being of philosophy*.
3 Steiner, *Artistic Sensitivity as a Spiritual Approach to Knowing Life and the World*, p. 32.
4 Steiner, *Christ and the Spiritual World and the Search for the Holy Grail*, p. 106.
5 Steiner, *Karmic Relationships*, vol. 4, p. 111.

new star wisdom inspired *Hermetic Astrology* to come into being.

Between Rudolf Steiner (1861–1925) and Willi Sucher (1902–1985), it is important to mention Elisabeth Vreede (1879–1943), who not only was a coworker of Rudolf Steiner, but also was Sucher's mentor in pioneering a new wisdom of the stars (astrosophy). In the introduction to her book concerning the foundations of a modern star wisdom, she wrote: "Knowledge of the universe rises upward through three degrees: from astronomy to astrology, and from astrology to *astrosophy*."[1] Elisabeth Vreede actively encouraged Willi Sucher in the development of a new and Christian wisdom of the stars, and it was she who pointed out to him the importance of the hermetic rule for determining the moment of conception, given the moment of birth. In this way she contributed at an early stage to the resurrection of hermetic astrology in the twentieth century.

In making the transition from astronomy to astrology, in passing from *Hermetic Astrology*, volume 1 to *Hermetic Astrology*, volume 2, we move from study of the "body" to consideration of the "soul" of star wisdom. Whereas volume 1 is essentially concerned with the right astronomical frame of reference for casting horoscopes (the sidereal zodiac, the Tychonic system, the hermetic chart, etc.), volume 2 is devoted primarily to astrological biography, through which the "soul" of star wisdom is revealed in the unfolding of human destiny, as indicated by Rudolf Steiner.

> If we make the attempt with the kind of knowledge I have described, we begin to gaze upon the destiny of a single human being with holy awe. For what is it that works in the destiny of each human being? In very truth it is star wisdom—all-embracing star wisdom![2]

### The Astrological Biography of Richard Wagner

A significant shift in orientation has to be made, in making the transition from the body to the soul of star wisdom, in that the more technical astronomical aspects have to be left aside to "gaze upon the destiny of a single human being with holy awe," as attempted in *Hermetic Astrology*, volume 2 with respect to the destiny of Richard Wagner. As long as one is concerned primarily with casting horoscopes, it is difficult to devote oneself in the right way to the more subtle task of contemplating the unfolding of destiny through human biography. Yet it must be remembered that the horoscope and all computations resulting therefrom provide only the "bare bones," and it is by way of contemplating the biography that "life and soul" are allowed to enter in. The deep and intensive study of biography—the more biographies of historical personalities that are studied the better—is indispensible for a new and "all-embracing star wisdom."

A further shift in orientation is called for to make the transition from astrology to astrosophy. Whereas reincarnation research plays an important role in hermetic astrology, another level of spiritual activity is called for when it comes to contemplation of the cosmic mysteries in the domain of astrosophy—for example, those connected with the life of Christ, as described in *Christian Hermetic Astrology: The Star of the Magi and the Life of Christ*. For example, the knowledge that Richard Wagner was the reincarnation of a nun who was one of the greatest mystics in the history of Christianity, although it helps to illumine Wagner's biography, may divert our attention from the cosmic mystery surrounding Richard Wagner's life work, which was bound up with the Grail mystery. Here this Grail mystery can only be hinted at.[3] Briefly, Wagner's life work culminated with *Parsifal*, in which "the urge to give a musical expression of the Christ Impulse existed. It was anticipated in Richard Wagner and was ultimately responsible for the creation of *Parsifal*."[4]

What was this Christ Impulse to which Wagner sought to give musical expression in *Parsifal*? It had little to do with traditional Christianity, with which Wagner had hardly any relationship.

---

1 Vreede, *Astronomy and Spiritual Science: The Astronomical Letters of Elisabeth Vreede*, p. xviii.
2 Steiner, *Karmic Relationships*, vol. 4, p. 119.
3 For a deeper study see my article "The Grail in Relation to the Stars" in *Shoreline*, vol. 1 (1988).
4 Steiner, *True and False Paths in Spiritual Investigation*, p. 219.

No, it was the beginning of a radiating in of the Christ Impulse in connection with the descent of Christ from cosmic realms through the ranks of the hierarchies, as described in *Hermetic Astrology*, volume 1, appendix 2 ("The second coming"). Exactly at the time that Wagner was composing *Parsifal* (1877–1879), the Russo-Turkish war was taking place, which mirrored on Earth the resistance encountered by Christ on his passage—within the sphere of the Sun—through the ranks of the spiritual beings known as *Dynameis* ("the spirits of movement"). The Russo-Turkish war signified a negative reflection of the descent of Christ through the realm of the Dynameis, whereas the composition of *Parsifal* was a positive reflection of this Christ event. Such knowledge, concerning the spiritual dimensions of cosmic events, belongs to the domain of astrosophy. We are led into this domain through contemplation of the Christ Mystery. This Mystery occupies the central position in astrosophy, and *Christian Hermetic Astrology: The Star of the Magi and the Life of Christ* is intended as a contribution toward this highest level of a new wisdom of the stars.

## A Word of Caution with Regard to Reincarnation Research

There is still a further reason for making this point here. Some readers may have gained the impression from reading *Hermetic Astrology*, volumes 1 and 2 that reincarnation research can be undertaken without too much difficulty. Nothing could be further from the truth. According to Rudolf Steiner, true reincarnation research can be undertaken only through a special spiritual calling. As he indicated in his 1924 lectures titled *Karmic Relationships*, it is a matter of destiny—preparation in a previous incarnation—if one is able to carry out reincarnation research in the present incarnation. In the intervening time since Rudolf Steiner spoke of this in 1924, the possibility of reincarnation research has become opened up on a wider scale—through the grace of Christ, through the onset of his second coming in 1933 (Rudolf Steiner's dating). Certainly, an intensive preparation is required in order not to fall into error when engaged in reincarnation research. Guidelines concerning an appropriate preparation for reincarnation research are outlined in *Hermetic Astrology*, volume 1, chapter 7.[5]

It cannot be emphasized strongly enough that without appropriate preparation it is better to leave reincarnation research alone. This preparation helps to minimize the possibility of making a mistake. Otherwise, the risk of arriving at false conclusions concerning previous incarnations is very great. This is one of the most formidable temptations facing humanity in our time and on into the future. Already in esoteric circles in the twentieth century serious mistakes were made in the domain of reincarnation research, mistakes which wreaked havoc in the lives of numerous people.

One example suffices to illustrate how damaging false reincarnation statements may be: the example of the Indian boy Alcyone (Krishnamurti), who was put forward in the Theosophical Society by Annie Besant and C. W. Leadbeater as the reincarnated Jesus or Jeshu, the new World Teacher. Thousands of people were taken in by this, and it was only through Krishnamurti's honesty that the spiritual movement surrounding him became disbanded in 1929, when he publicly disavowed himself from the false reincarnation statement attached to him. Since most people are not in a position to prove or disprove the authenticity of a reincarnation statement, if a reincarnation statement is attached to a spiritual teacher, either his followers have to believe it uncritically, or else they will retain their critical consciousness and question it, perhaps then even rejecting it.

In the case of Krishnamurti, the false reincarnation statement about him propagated by C. W. Leadbeater and Annie Besant had a hypnotizing effect on large numbers of people who accepted it unquestioningly, and at the same time it created an aura of mystery and spiritual authority surrounding the young Indian. His words, because they were believed to be those of the new World Teacher, acquired formidable power and authority.

---

5  See also Powell and Dann, *The Astrological Revolution*, ch. 3.

In a mood approaching fanatical devotion, thousands of people accepted uncritically everything he said. Fortunately, Krishnamurti was honest enough not to perpetuate the illusion built up around him. Indeed, he shattered this illusion when he proclaimed publicly that he was not the one whom his followers believed him to be.

> The lesson that may be learnt from this example is clear. There is a deep-seated tendency to look to spiritual authority, and this may be misused—as it was by C. W. Leadbeater and Annie Besant with regard to the young Krishnamurti. The ultimate spiritual authority, however, is to be found within ("Christ within"),[1] and may be approached through moral deepening. It is here, within the inner light of conscience, aided by reasoning and common sense, that discrimination has to be learned as an essential step on the spiritual path. Whosoever learns to discriminate is offered a high measure of protection from falling prey to the subtle temptations presented in the domain of the esoteric life—one of these subtle temptations being that of falsely identifying previous incarnations of oneself or others.

Discrimination involves weighing up, subjecting to scrutiny, but without making an overhasty judgment. Both open-mindedness (being open to believe something might be true) and scepticism (to question the truth of an assertion, not accepting it uncritically) are called for, and these two attitudes should balance each other out in a healthy and harmonious way. It is precisely a combination of these two attitudes, which is appropriate with regard to consideration of the results of reincarnation research—for example, in relation to the reincarnation examples presented in volumes 1 and 2 of *Hermetic Astrology*.

## Christ and the Galaxy

Finally, returning now to consider again the level of astrosophy: as referred to above, contemplation of the Christ Mystery in relation to the stars occupies the central position here,[2] as is evident in *Star Wisdom* from perusing the monthly commentaries for the ongoing stellar events.[3] This new astrosophical star wisdom shares with Cosmic Christianity a focus upon the cosmos—a very different realm than that of traditional Christian theology.

As detailed in chapter 5 of *The Astrological Revolution*, it was precisely through empirical research into the cosmic dimension of Christ that one of the most significant breakthroughs came with regard to research into the mysteries of the stars. This breakthrough demonstrates the truly cosmic nature of Christ in relation to the stars in the heavens. In connection with this far-reaching empirical discovery of Christ's connection with the starry realm, the intuition came that the cosmic dimension of Christ's life is of such a magnitude as to expand far beyond the sidereal zodiac to include the *entire celestial sphere of fixed stars*.

This signified a quantum leap with respect to the traditional astrological world view. In this expansion of consciousness the nature of each sidereal sign—that is, each 30° division of the zodiacal belt—is perceived as a constellation or kind of "group effect" of each star belonging to that constellation and that, over and beyond the stars comprising each zodiacal sign/constellation *all the stars* of the constellations above and below the zodiacal constellations also have an effect. In other words, the entire celestial sphere is the real domain not only of astronomy but also of astrology and astrosophy. In other words, each and every star in the heavens is of significance to human beings and life here on the Earth.

It will take some time to assimilate the extraordinary consequences of this discovery. The following is an attempt to communicate the deeper implications of the expansion of consciousness to include the starry heavens in their entirety—this being a step into galactic consciousness. Specifically, it is through an understanding of the cosmic dimension

---

1 In the words of St. Paul, "Not I, but Christ in me" (Gal. 2:20).
2 See Powell and Dann, *The Astrological Revolution*, ch. 5: "Christ and the Starry Heavens."
3 With heartfelt acknowledgment and great appreciation to Claudia McLaren Lainson for her extraordinary contributions each year—for the past ten years—laying the foundations through her monthly commentaries for true star wisdom (*astrosophy*).

of Christ that conclusive proof is offered of the *astrological significance of the entire celestial sphere*, as elaborated upon with regard to several examples in chapter 5 of *The Astrological Revolution*.

In relation to the foregoing statement, these words of Rudolf Steiner need to be carefully considered:

> In Palestine during the time that Jesus of Nazareth walked on Earth as Christ Jesus—during the three years of his life, from his thirtieth to his thirty-third year—the entire being of the Cosmic Christ was acting uninterruptedly upon him, and was working into him. The Christ stood always under the influence of the entire cosmos; he made no step without this working of the cosmic forces into and in him.... It was always in accordance with the collective being of the whole universe with whom the Earth is in harmony, that all which Christ Jesus did took place.[4]

Here we need to remember that in 1911, when Rudolf Steiner gave voice to these words, there was no conception of galaxies beyond our own Milky Way galaxy. In other words, his listeners would have understood "the whole universe" as the entire Milky Way galaxy.

### The Galactic Equator and the Galactic Center

Let us also recall that the term *Milky Way* originally meant the band of stars encircling the starry heavens at an angle of about 60° to the circle of the zodiacal constellations. These two great circles immediately catch the eye when gazing up to the starry heaven on a clear night—the Milky Way band of stars being most visible when the light of the Moon is diminished. In our time, now knowing the spiral structure of the Milky Way galaxy, it is generally known that the Milky Way band of stars comprises a vast conglomeration of stars—the band being about 16° wide—running through the center of the Milky Way galaxy. The central line though the Milky Way band of stars is called the *Galactic Equator*. The Milky Way band of stars extends approximately eight degrees above and eight degrees below the Galactic Equator.

For those who are practiced in stargazing and are familiar with the findings of my research,[5] the most inspiring aspect about beholding the Milky Way band of stars extending approximately eight degrees above and eight degrees below the Galactic Equator, is that through meditative stargazing, in due course of time the possibility arises of coming to the experience that long ago Christ descended from the galactic realm whence he came on his journey of incarnation. As Christ said: "I and the Father are one" (John 10:30). In terms of my research findings concerning Christ's relationship with the fixed stars, Christ was originally born from the Galactic Center, regarding which the Russian mystic Daniel Andreev said, "I remember seeing a glowing mist of stunning majesty, as though the creative heart of our universe had revealed itself to me in visible form for the first time. It was *Astrofire*, the great center of our galaxy."[6]

In Christ's language, the "creative heart of our universe" can be considered as the *heart of the Father* or the *heart of the Creator*. Now, given that there are manifold galaxies, the heart of the Creator manifests mystically at the center of each galaxy, including the Milky Way galaxy.

Taking the center of the Milky Way galaxy as 0° on the Galactic Equator, a new twelvefold division of constellations around the Galactic Equator opens up, having to do with the Divine level of existence, where Christ's words "I and the Father are one" hold good in the sense of this being the realm of the Creator, the realm from which Christ originated.

### The Galactic Circle

In the hitherto unpublished work of David Bowden and myself relating to this realm, we have chosen to call this new twelvefold division of constellations the *Galactic Circle*. It should be noted

---

4 Steiner, *Spiritual Guidance of the Individual and Humanity*, p. 28.

5 Of particular importance here are the research findings summarized in chapter 5 of *The Astrological Revolution*.

6 Andreev, *The Rose of the World*, p. 198.

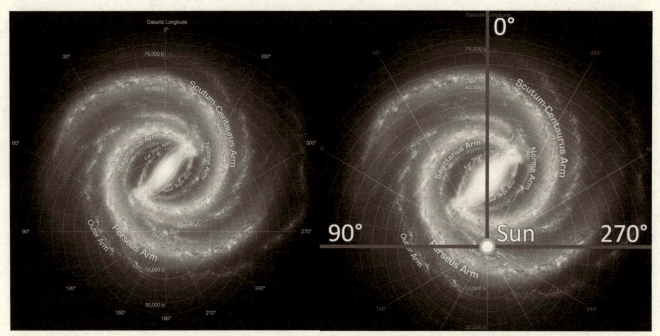

*Diagram of the Sun's location in the Milky Way, where the angles represent longitudes in the galactic coordinate system*

that the Galactic Circle is not galactocentric. In any case, we do not have names for most of the constellations as viewed from the Galactic Center. Rather, the framework of the Galactic Circle is helio-galactocentric, utilizing the *galactic coordinate system* (see images, in particular the second image showing the galactic coordinate system).

The Galactic Circle, like the Zodiacal Circle, comprises twelve constellations. Whereas the zodiacal constellations straddle or are close to the ecliptic, the constellations belonging to the Galactic Circle straddle or are close to the Galactic Equator, the central axis through the Milky Way galaxy as seen from the perspective of our solar system—hence the expression *helio-galactocentric*.

The constellations—such as Canis Major (CMa), Orion (Ori), Auriga (Aur), Cassiopeia (Cas), Cepheus (Cep), Cygnus (Cyg), etc.—comprising the Galactic Circle, are mostly prominent constellations (see figure).

These constellations are not reckoned to be equal-division (30°) constellations in terms of their visible appearance. And, clearly, they do not perfectly straddle the Galactic Equator. However, they are close enough to the Galactic Equator to be included in the list of constellations making up the Galactic Circle. Also they are big enough to occupy many degrees in the designated 30° divisions, without necessarily occupying their respective divisions completely.

In the case of the biggest constellation identified in antiquity, Argo Navis—the ship Argo of Jason and the Argonauts in search of the Golden Fleece—its stars stretch across much of two 30° divisions in the Galactic Circle. However, in the eighteenth/nineteenth centuries Argo Navis was divided into three constellations (Puppis [Pup], Carina [Car], Vela [Vel])—first by the astronomer Nicolas Louis de Lacaille in 1763 and then again by the astronomer Sir John Herschel in 1841. These constellations relate to two of the 30° divisions of the Galactic Circle, designated Pup and Vel in the figure.

It needs to be taken into consideration that there is some overlap between various constellations by virtue of being positioned above each other in terms of the 30° divisions of the Galactic Circle straddling or close to the Galactic Equator—just as in the Zodiacal Circle, Ophiuchus, close to the ecliptic, is above the zodiacal constellation of Scorpio in terms of the 30° division of the ecliptic occupied by Scorpio. However, it is the more prominent

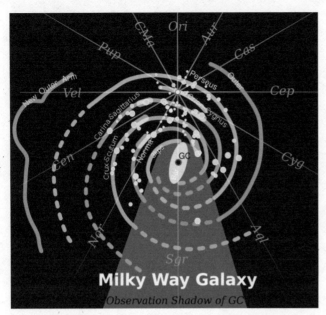

A "God's view" map of the Milky Way as seen from far Galactic North (in Coma Berenices). The star-like lines center in a yellow dot representing the position of Sun. The spokes of that "star" are marked with constellation abbreviations, "Cas" for Cassiopeia, etc. The spiral arms are colored differently to highlight what structure belongs to which arm. (Krisciunas and Yenne, The Pictorial Atlas of the Universe, p. 145)

Scorpio that is named as the zodiacal constellation representing the corresponding 30° division of the Zodiacal Circle. In the same way, the constellations tabulated in the Galactic Circle are generally the more prominent ones within their respective 30° divisions of the Galactic Circle, beginning with the Galactic Center at 0°. Proximity and prominence (and thus also size) are decisive factors in determining which constellation represents its particular 30° division of the Galactic Circle, whereby in some cases the possibility arises that two overlapping constellations might be named.

In *Star Wisdom*, volume 2, the Galactic Circle will be specified more precisely. Also, it will be shown how it is possible, within the definition of the twelve 30° divisions comprising the Galactic Circle, to cast *galactocentric* horoscopes—or rather *heliocentric-galactic* horoscopes. The foregoing is intended as an introduction to this new breakthrough in the domain of astrosophy or star wisdom explored by David Bowden and Robert Powell[1]—a breakthrough now further facilitated by the opening up of consciousness to the angelic realm beginning 2018/2019.

---

[1] Powell and Bowden, *Astrogeographia: Correspondences between the Stars and Earthly Locations*, brings forward the research of these two authors into something indicated by Rudolf Steiner in his *Astronomy Course*, that every place on the Earth corresponds to some star or other in the heavens. More recently they have begun exploring the galactic dimension of existence.

---

> "Whether we acknowledge the work of the angels for our future or deny it does not matter at all. The angels are working on our ideals for the future regardless. Their work is guided by a specific principle, namely, that in the future nobody shall enjoy happiness in peace as long as there are others who are unhappy. That is, a certain impulse of universal fellowship, of community—fellowship understood in the right way, that is—prevails in regard to social conditions in the physical world. This is one of the impulses according to which the angels form pictures in our astral body."
>
> —RUDOLF STEINER, "What Does the Angel Do in Our Astral Body?"

# COMMUNION OF LOVE WITH HOLINESS
## *Saturn–Pluto Conjunctions*
### *Claudia McLaren Lainson*

Pluto is one of three *transcendental* planets. The influence of such planets tends to govern the collective, and through this it affects individuals. It takes Pluto 248 years to complete one revolution around the Sun. To the Greeks, Pluto was the "giver of wealth"; and to the Romans he was the "god of the dead and the underworld."

Hades marks the lower aspect of Pluto. Pluto–Hades is connected with the will-to-power (a negative force rising from the interior of the Earth), which is the result of the union between human will and subhuman will. Indeed, shortly after the discovery of Pluto as a planet (in 1930), scientists experimented with splitting the nucleus of atoms. This was a crucial step toward the development of nuclear power. Soon afterward, Hitler rose to power as a sorrowful example of the terrible forces unleashed when Pluto–Hades drives the will, releasing "trapped life"[1] from the Earth's interior.

That which splits the physical atom, however, will later express division in human souls. Ultimately, it threatens to become the splintering of the human spirit.

In the power struggles among an increasing number of nations throughout the world, nuclear armaments are once again at the forefront. This is a testament to the burgeoning presence of the most sinister agents of evil—for massively destructive weaponry is born of the lords of the underworld, and the insanity of nuclear war can only be born of a malevolent will-to-power.

The word *plutocracy* (from the Greek *ploutos*, wealth, and *kratos*, rule) means "rule of the wealthy," whereby society is controlled by the god of money—i.e., Mammon. Saturn–Pluto cycles are commonly associated with corruption and abuse of power. David Rockefeller, who was born in 1915 under a Saturn–Pluto conjunction, exemplifies rule by the power of money. The exposure of corruption and abuse is also a signature of this aspect, as is exemplified by Edward Snowden, who was born under the Saturn–Pluto conjunction of 1983.

Pluto is a planetary body long known for intensity, depth, and wild passions. From a higher vantage, however, Pluto is Phanes (*the Divine Love of the Father*). From Phanes, vials of blessings are poured out upon humankind. When the heart is closed to Love, on the other hand, the lower aspect (Hades) manifests—for the vials then bestow wrath instead. *Moral will*, living in the collective body of humanity, ultimately determines the outcome.

Saturn is the outermost planet of our classical solar system (i.e., not including the three transcendental planets), and takes 29½ years to make one revolution around the Sun. To the Greeks, Saturn is known as *Cronos*. The Saturn glyph represents a scythe, invoking images of the reaper and harvester. Moreover, it is the cosmic memory-keeper, recording all things into the Great Book of Life. And on the descent through the planetary spheres, the Saturn sphere determines our karma as well as the spiritual resolves we will carry into our new incarnation. Thus karma weaves its continuity from life to life.

Being farthest from the Sun, Saturn has the reputation—in common astrology—for rigidity, death, and malefic influences; it represents restriction and deprivation. Yet, from the vantage of higher worlds, Saturn represents the Holy Virgin, whose restraining mantle guides us to fulfill on Earth the promises made in heaven. As such, she is the

---

1  See Powell, *Hermetic Astrology,* vol. 2, p. 305.

consummate scribe, not only for the cosmos but also for each individual.

Thus, when Saturn and Pluto come into conjunction, we can imagine a heavenly discourse occurring between Divine Love and Holiness. Unfortunately, as the lower aspects of each planetary sphere tend to work against this, it is also imperative that we *collectively* awake to the blessings and warnings such conjunctions herald.

Will we continue to align with Hades-born Mammon? We must break the cycle that has long paralyzed the human soul and spirit, a cycle that has allowed the Plutocracy to seize power geopolitically, militarily, economically, and culturally. Hope lies in the fact that ever more people around the world are peacefully rising, crying out for new systems of just and collaborative governance.

## A Dystopian Scenario: Communion between the Unloving and the Unholy

The world of *1984* (George Orwell's famous novel) has arrived. Public enemy number one, as described in the book, is "the theory and practice of oligarchical collectivism." This can otherwise be described as economic-military rule by a small group of billionaires who have effectively taken control of a country. In the US, their mouthpiece is the whole of corporate-owned mass media. The American military-industrial complex (perhaps now, more accurately, the American military-*technical* complex) is the ultimate plutocracy, out of which billionaires who manufacture privatized weapons continue to build markets. Thus are wars inevitable. When the global superpowers moved away from MAD ("mutually assured destruction"), another means had to be set up to fill the pockets of greed; hence there arose a new covert paradigm, known as Nuclear Primacy, which is aimed at destroying the retaliatory capabilities of *any* adversary. This, nonetheless, is a perilous ruse.

It is therefore not surprising that Orwell's novel (published in 1949)[2] came into reality shortly after the onset of the Saturn–Pluto cycle we are concluding this year, for the Orwellian prophecy of *1984* has indeed come into being. Big Brother and billionaires rule through military might. If we are to disengage from their grip (which began after World War II and has now delivered the human race to the precipice of World War III), we will have to look behind the headlines. Only then can we hope to unmask the conquest-obsessed government under which Americans live.

Indeed, we are breathing a deadly potion brewed by those whom Orwell calls the "thought police"—i.e., the propaganda mongers who have molded mass consciousness. The need for independent "I"-consciousness inspired by a spiritual thought sense has never been more necessary.

## The Cosmogony of America: Wake Up!

Rudolf Steiner gave a series of lectures in October of 1919, published under the title: *Understanding Society through Spiritual-Scientific Knowledge*. He spoke therein of three missions, each of which is linked to a particular global region: altruism (religion) as the mission of the East–Russia; freedom (philosophy) as the mission of the Central Europe; and cosmogony (cosmology) as the mission of Western Anglo-America. The Slavic East gave us Sophiology; the European middle gave us Anthroposophy; and in the West we are to awake to Astrosophy (i.e., wisdom of the stars). Reclaiming the American mission of cosmogony–cosmology (i.e., a sense of spirit connection) is the overlighting theme of this year's edition of *Star Wisdom*.[3]

In times past, we have missed the mark, for we have not comprehended how the stars rightly guide us and how they reveal the hidden background to world events. In his lectures to the priests,[4] Steiner coined the term *apocalyptist*, referring to one who can read the signs of the times as they are occurring. To this end he brought the priests together, hoping to form a council through which revelation could be recognized as it entered into time. We must all become priests in the sense

---

2 Note that Orwell's *1984* was published in June 1949, shortly after the onset of the Saturn–Pluto cycle of 1947. The onset of the Saturn–Pluto cycle 33½ years later, in 1982, would herald the beginning of his dystopian nightmare.

3 See Joel Park's article in this issue of *Star Wisdom*.
4 Steiner, *The Book of Revelation and the Work of the Priest*.

that we, too, can read the signs of our time *in* our time, which is the mission particular to the Anglo-American cosmological West.

The work of Willi Sucher (the pioneer of Astrosophy) and Elisabeth Vreede (appointed by Steiner to head the mathematical–astronomical section at the Goetheanum) served to advance the understanding of star wisdom in accordance with the indications Steiner had given. Robert Powell picked up the threads of these luminaries; moreover, he has continuously unfolded profound new mysteries that we must apply if we are to fulfill the American mission. Indeed, he has proved himself to be among the most significant apocalyptists of the twentieth and twenty-first centuries.

Understanding the astrosophical wisdom underlying the Saturn–Pluto cycles allows us to awake to the nature of the specific themes each cycle presents. The zodiacal constellations in which such conjunctions occur tell us much, preparing us to recognize how both blessings and warnings will be coming into manifestation. Thus can we become conscious witnesses of the battle of good and evil that is not only a fact, but is also a necessity for our time. Merely to know is not enough; the light of one's intellect must become fire if it is to penetrate one's will. And one's will must become as steel, unflinching in its ability to stand firmly before the tasks the fire "entrusts" to it.

## Saturn–Pluto Cycles

The Saturn–Pluto cycle has a long history of geopolitical upheavals. The duration of this period varies from 31 to 38 years, with the average length being 33 years. This is a most significant number to Hermeticists who are aware of the onset of Christ's Second Coming, his *Parousia* ("presence") in the etheric realm, and who are following the wave of Christ's etheric unfolding in history (in 33⅓-year rhythms).

As the current 1982-to-2020 cycle approaches the last year of its duration (2019), we see that the global geopolitical order has entered into a stage of grave uncertainty. This cycle began with the heliocentric conjunction of Saturn and Pluto at 2°36' Libra, occurring just past the star Spica (29° Virgo). High above Spica, located (in terms of its ecliptic longitude) at the transition from Virgo to Libra, is Arcturus in the constellation of Bootes, the Ploughman or Herdsman. The great star Arcturus, the fourth brightest in the heavens and the brightest in the northern celestial hemisphere, is located some 30° north of the ecliptic. In terms of its ecliptic longitude, positioned high above the point of transition from Virgo to Libra at the midpoint of the zodiac, this star stands as a "Watcher" or "Guardian," which is the very meaning of the name *Arcturus*. It stands as a Michaelic figure representing the Lesser Guardian of the Threshold, between worlds. Just as Michael holds the scale of justice, so, too, does Arcturus represent this Michaelic quality of the Lesser Guardian—the sign of Libra, the Scales, being traditionally associated with Michael.

Christ is traditionally associated with the entire zodiac, and, as indicated in Robert Powell's article in this issue of *Star Wisdom*, actually with the entire Milky Way galaxy. However, it is striking that at Christ's incarnation into Jesus at the Baptism in the River Jordan, the Sun had just entered Libra. This reveals something of the great mission of Christ: to balance heaven and Earth. Holding this in consciousness, the fulcrum point of balance between the two pans of the scale can be seen as representative of Christ, the Greater Guardian of the Threshold. Christ's light of certainty streams into the fulcrum point, guiding and shepherding all who seek union with the fiery forces of conscience. To receive such wisdom, we must stand in stalwart uprightness, regardless of how the winds of change may bluster.

The fulcrum point measures the balance among all things. Despite the fact that reality is in continual movement, the fulcrum point is to remain stationary, continuously aligned with the altar of truth. The glyph of Libra is the image of two horizontal parallel lines that ask us to mirror in worlds below what has been ordained in worlds above, ever sounding the word of truth through the raised center of its upper band. The Hermetic axiom thus resounds from this constellation.

We return now to consider the significance of the heliocentric Saturn–Pluto conjunction at 2½° Libra, bearing in mind that the Sun, at the moment of Christ's Baptism in the Jordan, had just entered Libra. Clearly the Sun was then close to the degree of this conjunction. We can thus imagine that this cycle has asked us to choose between the enlightenment of truth (whereby the fulcrum holds steady) and the intoxication of mass consciousness (whereby the fulcrum falters). Moreover, we will continue to reap the consequences of our collective decision as the cycle moves forward toward it completion.

Carl Gustav Jung was well aware of the danger residing in mass consciousness, the hazardous realms of *psychic epidemics*:

> Indeed, it is apparent with an increasingly blinding clarity that what constitutes the greatest danger threatening humankind is not famine or earthquakes or microbes or cancer but man's wellbeing. The cause of this is quite straightforward: there still does not exist any effective protection against psychic epidemics—and these epidemics are infinitely more devastating than the worst catastrophes of Nature! The supreme danger that menaces both the individual and the populace as a whole is *psychic danger*. With regard to this, our understanding proves to be quite powerless, which is explained by the fact that rational arguments act on the conscious—but on the conscious alone—without having the least effect on the unconscious. Consequently, a major danger for humankind emanates from the mass, i.e., the crowd, at whose core the working of the unconscious accumulates—first muzzling, then stifling the pleas for reason on the part of the conscious. Every organization of a crowd constitutes a latent danger, like that of piling up dynamite. Because it produces effects that no one wanted, and which no one is able to hold in check. For this reason, one must ardently hope that psychology—knowledge of psychology and achievements in the domain of psychology—will spread on such a scale that human beings will finally understand the source of the supreme danger hanging over their heads. It is not by arming themselves to the teeth, every country of itself, that nations will be able, in the long run, to preserve themselves from the terrible catastrophes occasioned by modern war. Accumulated arms demand war! On the contrary, would it not be preferable in future to guard against and to avoid the conditions delineated at present—in which the unconscious breaks down the dams of the conscious and dispossesses the latter, making the world run the risk of inestimable devastation?[1]

The constellation of balance calls for all relationships to find equilibrium and to penetrate subconscious realms through the power of conscience. As the early degrees of Libra mark the transition point between the Michaelic guardian and the one he protects, Virgin Sophia, we may awake to the fact that we have allowed ourselves to be led into the muddy waters of mass consciousness. Spurious cunning from anti-Michaelic beings has spun webs of horrendous deceit. Behind the scenes, the one force that stands against evil—purity—has been stalked with the intent to kill. As these psychic epidemics have lured the masses into sinister entanglements that have dispossessed populations of free and independent thought, the grave danger Jung foresaw has indeed fallen upon us.

Many are no longer obedient to the sacred measure of goodness and purity, but have instead been swept away in compromise after compromise. In a sense, we could say human souls have been "dethroned." The Virgin (Virgo), too, was dethroned. The Egyptians and Babylonians depicted her standing upright, whereas Ptolemy depicted her lying down, reaching halfway into the Babylonian constellation of Libra. In such a depiction, the Virgin displaces the Michaelic figure who holds the scales, reducing the image related to this sign to something that is merely mechanical—i.e., scales without the Holder:

> Ptolemy's Virgin, on the other hand, is not upright but reclining. It can be said that Ptolemy thus "dethroned" the Virgin. As the Virgin represents the heavenly wisdom (Sophia), the

---

1 Jung, *L'homme a la decouverte de son ame*, quoted in Anon., *Meditations on the Tarot*, pp. 646–647.

dethroning of the Virgin signifies the loss of the divine wisdom that was accessible through the ancient clairvoyance. Moreover, Ptolemy's Virgin is not only lying down, but has her legs and feet extending halfway into the Babylonian sign of Libra. In this way Ptolemy displaced the figure of the Balance Holder from the heavens, who was seen holding the scales in his right hand, as depicted also in various Egyptian portrayals of the zodiac.[1]

A time has come when all humanity must regain the throne of our free and independent thinking. We are to align with Michael and the Holy Virgin as we battle for the reestablishment of hope and prophecy. This alone allows us to stand against the forces of evil that would rather we succumb to treachery against life itself.

Thus, as the current Saturn–Pluto conjunction comes to its conclusion, we must reenvision the standing Virgin, for her dethroning has, by analogy, resulted in immorality and degeneration. Furthermore, as this conjunction remembers Christ entering into the sheaths of the immaculate Jesus being, we must heighten our awareness of what the Holy Virgin protects. And what is that? Purity! She is the protector of children, sacred procreation, and the elemental kingdoms of earth, water, air, and fire. She serves as the blessed protector of the entirety of our natural environment. Moreover, the Virgin is the mediator for right relationships between men and women.

As with all things in our world, however, the Virgin has her inversion, her opponent, which is the Woman of Babylon—the whore. Within the mantle of the Babylonian woman is hidden all that is impure: sexual perversity, the secrets of black magic, and things consecrated to death. While the Virgin devotes herself to the altar of Christ consciousness, the Babylonian woman devotes herself to the altar of the Antichrist—for the fulcrum point of Libra, whose dome reaches to worlds above, *inverts* when situated in the hands of the Woman of Babylon. Instead of rising to worlds above, it focuses attention on worlds below. Indeed, those who become intoxicated with her covert perversions find immorality pleasing. Have we not seen exactly this kind of moral decline over the past thirty-seven years? Moreover, as this conjunction occurred close to the place of Christ's Baptism, we may ask: What was approaching humanity? Was it the enlightenment of goodness and purity, or was it a possession by the ahrimanic hordes rising from under-worldly depths?

The Saturn–Pluto cycle through which we have been passing since 1982 has called us to join with one or the other of the two women archetypes—for Saturn ever represents the Holy Virgin, regardless of where it may be situated amongst the twelve constellations. The "Me too" movement,[2] which began at the close of 2017, gave hope (along with the dismissals of various sexual predators) for the possibility that evil may yet be unmasked, at least in some of its more sordid quarters. Time will tell how enduring this change will be. Yet, if creation is to evolve into a future in which we would *want* to live, the fulcrum point of balance must regain its upward striving.

At the midpoint between the waxing and waning phases of this cycle, we witnessed the event of 9/11. We stood then with the Lesser Guardian, Michael, measuring and weighing at the threshold between worlds. To which altar did the fulcrum point? Instead of humanity choosing the upward path leading to a new and peaceful world, the fulcrum pointed downward to the path below, for war resulted—and war is a travesty against humankind. Furthermore, at this midpoint in the cycle, the consciousness of Christ was descending through the sixth subearthly layer, the *fire earth* (1992–2004), the source of all evil passions.[3] The antidote to the evil beings that indwell this realm is: *Blessed are the pure in heart, for they shall see God*. To "see God" means to behold him in the sacredness of Nature, creation's magical work of art. However, with the scales flipped to realms below, we instead transgressed through aggression toward the so-called "enemy." We also

---

1 Powell, *The Astrological Revolution*, pp. 13–14.

2 The "Me too" movement is an international movement against sexual harassment and assault, especially in the workplace.

3 See Powell, "The Descent of Christ," in the *Journal for Star Wisdom* 2017.

transgressed against nature by way of the "war machine," heightening the machine assault against the kingdoms of Mother Nature.

After the tragedy of 9/11, the empires of East and West again collided in what would grow into an apocalyptic battle that still rages on endlessly. Democracy and freedom were the collateral damage. Yet we witness much that continues to unfold in the hearts of many across the globe: the longing for harmony, the revealing of dark secrets, and the eradication of perversity. This is despite the fact that the *Whore of Babylon*, in opposition to the Holy Virgin, has ripped harmony to shreds, splintering the psyches of the masses, while her consort has swept the fractured pieces into his kingdom to fabricate a world of his own making. Her consort is known as Ahriman.[4]

The overarching question posed by this thirty-seven-year cycle, from the 1982 Saturn–Pluto conjunction until now, is: *What do we stand for*? Further, this cycle has asked us if we have the will, as custodians of our blessed Earth and all her creatures, to maintain our uprightness in allegiance to the spiritual altar of enchristed truth.

## Fiery Beginnings

On January 3, 1983, one month after the beginning of the current Saturn–Pluto cycle, the Kilauea volcano in Hawaii erupted.[5] In almost constant eruption ever since then, it has been one of the most continuously active volcanoes in human experience. Legend tells us that the Goddess Pele's home is the crater at the summit of Kilauea. Known as the Goddess of fire, lightning, wind, dance, and volcanoes, Pele is also known in mythology as the creator of the Hawaiian Islands. We could say, by analogy, that Kilauea's eruption in January 1983 (just after the start the current Saturn–Pluto cycle in December 1982) announced a period of critical environmental unrest; it was a time of consuming fires, massively destructive hurricanes and tornadoes, apocalyptic floods, and other natural catastrophes.

The survivors of the Bangladesh cyclone of 1991, the survivors of the Indian Ocean earthquake and tsunami in 2004, the survivors of hurricane Katrina in 2005, and the survivors of the Haiti earthquake in 2010 have all witnessed such traumatic environmental events. Moreover, California's fires, Colorado's biblical flood, and the deadly heat waves across Europe have recently made clear that the Goddess Pele had issued a warning, as it were, at the onset of this Saturn–Pluto cycle; she reprimanded all who agitate for perpetuation of the materialistic trends that are launching wars and ever greater assaults on the pristine purity of our Mother Earth. Pele's fire dance, in hindsight, was the enactment of a future already written. She was the prophetess of imminent sorrows that would leave the Great Mother groaning in travail, ceaselessly weeping lava tears into the waiting arms of the sea.

We can also imagine the Kilauea eruption as the bleeding wound of Anfortas, a wound that will not heal until human beings right the scale of justice by addressing certain miscarriages. In "First Steps Toward a Grail Timeline," Joel Park's article in this volume of *Star Wisdom*, he reveals the mirroring in 2018 of the Grail event marking Parsifal's healing of Anfortas. In this time of the unfolding fortieth day in the wilderness,[6] much is at stake and much is possible.

On the level of the soul, however, telluric agitation such as earthquakes and volcanic eruptions become revolutions—and the origin of this unrest is *fear of death*. The transhumanism movement is a manifestation of such fear. Death stands as a "spiritual brother" at the threshold between worlds, revealing to consciousness all the errors to which we have succumbed. Avoidance of this

---

4  Concerning Ahriman, see the Glossary at the end of this issue. And regarding the Whore of Babylon, see Revelation 17:4–18. She represents the entanglement in worldly desires, in opposition to striving toward the heavenly Jerusalem, the holy city of the Lamb and His Bride, Sophia, who is united with the Holy Virgin.

5  This article was written in February of 2018. It is interesting to note that Kilauea erupted again in late March 2018.

6  This refers to the day angels came to minister to Jesus Christ soon after his 39 days of continuous temptation. The historic unfolding of the 40th day began early in 2018 (see, Powell, "The Apocalypse Code and the Year 2018," *Journal for Star Wisdom* 2018).

encounter by a people and/or nation creates pressure in worlds below that will eventually erupt into revolution. The Arab Spring resonated in the West as the Occupy Wall Street movement. Although suppressed, incredible tensions resulted, warning of mounting pressure that may yet rise in violence, from below to above.[1]

When we remember our primal beginnings as citizens of a vast and ineffable cosmos, our attention is turned to the next higher level of thinking, *manas* thinking, which finds its inversion in *blood thinking*—i.e., in union with the brooding blood of Hades, who skulks in the soul's darkest regions. Such thinking inflames telluric cataclysms. In the *Lord's Prayer Course*, Valentin Tomberg calls blood "a moral sap in the world, presenting [both] good and evil in the physical world. Everything else can become the *object* [of the working] of good and evil in the world, but blood alone can be the *bearer* of good or evil." To strengthen the blood, as the bearer of the good, we must turn our attention to what is coming newly into being from spiritual Imaginations. This alone will appease the forces at work behind destructive upheavals—influences that work through the body, soul, and spirit, rendering continual disruption until egoism is conquered. Only then will we begin to see the fruits of harmonious relationships between human and divine will.

Thus do volcanic eruptions and telluric cataclysms warn us of the tragic consequences of disharmony between what is above and what is below (i.e., when human will acts against cosmic unity). The calamitous abuse being set upon our environment through chemically spraying our atmosphere[2] is one clear and *visible* example of work inspired from the inverted scales of Libra. This kind of activity reveals the degree to which we have lost our way. When human beings are subjugated to experiments imposed upon them in secret, they can be certain that they live under the rule of tyranny. All such activity is further proof that our global family now collectively lives under Mammon's delusional ideations, thereby setting a course that can only end in disaster. Yet we must not see ourselves as victims of the madness now before us; instead we must enact deeds that birth hope into the world's future promise. Each and every decision—in thought, deed, and word—contributes to one or the other of the two feminine archetypes: the Whore of Babylon or the Holy Virgin-Sophia. What Pele abhors most is inaction and denial, for such is the fate of those who "bury their heads in the sand" or remain passive in times of grave endangerment such as those of the present time.

## Doubles

[In the future] magic will work on both sides: the white magic of advanced humanity, and the black magic consisting of electricity coming from the ground. At the present time black magic is more advanced, further developed, than white magic. Therefore, a miracle is necessary: the coming of the Etheric Christ. For there is a tendency toward a "false resurrection"; a kind of "doppelganger" will arise that

---

1 The various layers of the Earth "are connected by means of rays that unite the center of the Earth with its surface. Underneath the solid Earth there are a large number of subterranean spaces that communicate to the sixth layer, that of fire. This element, the fire earth, is intimately connected with the human will. It is this element that produced the tremendous eruptions that ended the Lemurian epoch. The forces that then nourished the human will went through a trial that unleashed a fire catastrophe that destroyed the Lemurian continent. In the course of evolution, this sixth layer receded continually toward the center and, as a result, volcanic eruptions became less frequent. However, they are still produced as a result of the human will when it is evil and chaotic, which magnetically affects and disrupts that layer. When the human will is without egoism, it can appease this fire. Materialistic periods are usually accompanied and followed by natural cataclysms, earthquakes, and such. Growth powers of evolution are the only alchemy capable of transforming, gradually, the organism and the soul of the Earth" (Steiner, *An Esoteric Cosmology*, pp 93–93).

2 Despite an enormous amount of disinformation, chemtrails have proved scientifically real. They are *not* fantasies born from the minds of "conspiracy theorists." The truth about chemtrails has been buried under mountains of deceit; see Freeland, *Chemtrails, HAARP, and the Full Spectrum Dominance of Planet Earth*. Chemtrails are caused by airplanes spraying aluminum, barium, strontium, etc. into the atmosphere as nanoparticles.

cannot pass through the gate of death. This is the aim [of black magic].[3]

Our "double" dwells within each of us. This being is the sum of all our impurities and errors. It lives alongside the other aspect of our self that is moral and good. At death, the double excarnates downward, into the subearthly realms of evil, while our enlightened self excarnates upward, into the supra-sensible realms above. At birth, the two different aspects are again reunited. Imagine the joy celebrated in evil realms when the double of someone like Vlad Dracula, Joseph Stalin, Adolf Hitler, or Pol Pot dies or is reborn. These humans travel with doubles that are infinitely more powerful than whatever threads of decency such souls may have preserved and strengthened in higher spheres. Indeed, the consciousness of souls who have terrorized their fellow human beings is greater in the School of Ahriman, below, than it can possibly become in the School of Christ, in worlds above. The School of Ahriman initiates souls into secret brotherhoods who for millennia have viciously stood against Christ.

The collective double of humankind is the garment through which the Antichrist has come into manifestation. Rudolf Steiner foresaw the dangers humanity would encounter when transitioning from the Industrial Age to the Digital Age, knowing full well that technological developments would work against the profound potential the New Age could rightly begin unfolding from the year 1899 onward. When Steiner delivered a momentous lecture in 1918—*The Work of the Angels in the Human Astral Body*—he gave due warning that if humanity allowed the fifth kingdom (technology) free reign, the fifth light that streams from angelic worlds (reflecting the work of the angels in our consciousness) would fall upon a forsaken human race.

The world of wireless technology imitates consciousness, replacing the neural-mirror (whose task is to reflect higher consciousness) with the mirror of Narcissus, who looked into a pool of water and fell in love with himself. Unable to leave the beauty of his own reflection, Narcissus lost his will to live, staring at his reflection until death terminated his self-rapture. Does not the Narcissus myth underlie the "selfie" culture? Dying into egoistic self-love may well be the fate of those who have bound themselves to matter instead of devoting themselves to the work of the angels—and the death they encounter may indeed be the "second death"—the death of their spiritual self.

We are free in the human nervous system. Nerves are empty, hollow spaces, and this emptiness allows the nervous system to reflect the great world thoughts.[4] This is precisely where soul and spirit are able to enter, and to imprint their supra-sensible Imaginations. Not only does the excessive use of technological devices fulfill the plan of adversaries, it also threatens to utterly destroy entire generations whose task would have otherwise been the recognition of a new level of consciousness. Indeed, the digitalization of the intellect *is* the great danger Steiner foresaw, since

---

3 Tomberg, *The Lord's Prayer Course*, p. 218.

4 "The nervous system is the only system that has no direct connection to the spirit–soul. Blood, muscles and so forth always have some direct connection to the spirit–soul; however, the nervous system never has a direct connection. That it has any connection to the spirit–soul is only because it continuously shuts itself off from human functioning [i.e., by not being present within it]; it is not present because it continuously decays. The other elements live, and therefore form direct connections to the spirit–soul. The nervous system is in a continuous *state of dying*. It is always saying to the human being, 'You can develop because I present you with no hindrance, because I make sure that I am not there with my life!' That is what is so peculiar. In psychology and physiology you will find the nervous system presented as the organ from which we receive sensations, thinking and the spirit–soul in general. However, how is it that this organ is the intermediary? It is possible only because the nervous system removes itself from life and thereby presents no hindrance to thinking and sensing; it, in fact, has absolutely no connection to thinking and feeling, and, where it exists, it allows the human being to be empty in relationship to the spirit–soul. Where the nerves exist, the spirit–soul meets only *spaces, or gaps*; where these gaps exist, the spirit–soul can enter. We must be thankful to the nervous system that it is not concerned with the spirit–soul and that it, in fact, does not do any of the things physiologists and psychologists say it does" (Steiner, *Foundations of Human Experience*, p. 130; italics added).

it merely imitates in the world of *maya* that which consciousness would otherwise be called to nurture if it instead opened to higher worlds of wonder.

Although we live in the time of a degenerating physical world, the very fact of such degeneration allows the inner forces of soul–spirit to free themselves.

> Because of this brittleness [decay], however, we must not rely on the physical but instead turn to the spiritual element. Everything physical is growing brittle and already in decline on Earth; we should no longer place our hope in this physical level of things. Instead, we can expect only something of what (to put it trivially) is sprinkling out—the spirit and soul—precisely because the physical realm is in decline.[1]

This "spiritual element" makes forces available to us, and we must freely choose whether to unite with them. Such forces in turn unite us with the ministration of angels. In contrast, the "caricature-kingdom" of virtual and augmented realities contracts human souls into self-love. The antidote to self-love is cosmogony, for when we acknowledge that we are a part of a great and wondrous creation, we are humbled—and we thereby find the will to serve the world.

In the second Arcanum of the Tarot, The High Priestess, the anonymous author of *Meditations on the Tarot* tells us of the two principles of integrated consciousness—the activating principle and the reflecting principle, which together awake conscience. He begins by quoting the Master:

> *Truly, truly, I say to you, unless one is born of Water and the Spirit, he cannot enter the Kingdom of God.* (John 3:5)
>
> "Truly, truly"—the Master refers here twice to "truth" in this mantric (i.e., magical) formula of the reality of consciousness. By these words he states that full consciousness of the truth is the result of "inbreathed" truth and reflected truth. Reintegrated consciousness, which is the Kingdom of God, presupposes two renovations, of a significance comparable to birth, in the two constituent elements of consciousness—active Spirit and reflecting Water. Spirit must become divine Breath in place of arbitrary, personal activity, and Water must become a perfect mirror of the divine Breath instead of being agitated by disturbances of the imagination, passions, and personal desires. Reintegrated consciousness must be born of Water and Spirit, after Water has once again become Virginal and Spirit has once again become divine Breath or the Holy Spirit. Reintegrated consciousness therefore becomes born within the human soul in a way *analogous* to birth or historical incarnation of the WORD.[2]

Now, the double we carry alongside us directs our attention to the personal agitations and materialistic information of the degenerating world that surrounds us. The angel, on the other hand, helps us learn how to reflect spiritual fire (spirit) in the stillness of the empty consciousness (water). As we are currently living in the 29½-years of the fortieth day in the wilderness[3] (the day angels came to minister to Christ), we must turn our mind's eye to what the angels are placing in our astral body (our astro–star body), which is seated in the nerve-sense system within us. *We are to quiet our minds so that we may see what angels are bringing to us as the true light we are to follow.* This fulfills the American mission of awaking to Astrosophy–cosmogony.

### The *Homo Economicus* Double: The True Plutocrat

During the time of the initiate-rulers, people were very aware of the fact that worlds of spirit inwardly filled them. "They had no doubt at all that their essential aspect was not passed down to them by father and mother, but had descended from worlds above to unite and combine with what came from the parents."[4] The people of this time were rooted in spirituality and could therefore be

---

1 Steiner, *Understanding Society through Spiritual-Scientific Knowledge*, p. 84.

2 Anon., *Meditations on the Tarot*, p. 30.

3 See Powell and Dann, *Christ and the Maya Calendar*, for understanding the "Apocalypse Code," which explains the period of temptation in relation to unfolding history and the significance of 2018 as the beginning of the disclosure of the fortieth day.

4 Steiner, *Understanding Society*, p. 77.

led by initiates. Steiner tells us how a real spiritual connection was lost during the time of the forming of Rome. Though people no longer remembered themselves as spiritually descending beings, they nonetheless still felt their intellects were spiritually appointed. "Human beings had a clear awareness that their intelligence, their world of thoughts, was not dependent on their blood or physical corporeality, but that it was instead of spiritual origin."[5] Steiner goes on to tell us how even the belief in the spiritual origins of intelligence was eventually lost. Once intelligence became inseparable from the human body, the rule of priests came to an end and something new emerged. This was *"Homo economicus,"*[6] which views human beings as the essential bearers of thinking by means of their own physical organ, the brain. Thus the way was paved for plutocracy.

Indeed, the inevitable destiny trajectory of humanity has been the fall, in stages, from spiritual awareness of our descent from higher worlds, to regarding the human intellect as the sole manifestation of spirit, and—ultimately—to the purely physical and spiritless intellectualism of modern times. Now we have fallen even further, into sub-earthly realms. How far will this descent go? Being in love with spiritless thoughts enslaves people in a prison of their own making, which is the fate of all who are infected with the will-to-power that is the hallmark of Pluto–Hades. This disease of materialism has caused many to work for the evolution of material progress at the expense of spiritual progress. A spiritual void has thus been created into which the spiritless elite marches onward. Materialism has tragically become the choice of the West. Like the phoenix, however, spirit is nonetheless capable of rising from the ashes of such decay.

As we awake our cosmological understanding of the world, through which economics will achieve the fraternity necessary for social harmony, *Homo economicus* will be defeated. On the other hand, economic thinking may eventually result in revolution if this worldview becomes regenerated through the tired ideas that have created past systems.[7] Steiner tells us that *Homo economicus* types are "those who had lived only a short time in the world of spirit and were entirely pervaded by what only the Earth as such can give."[8] He mentions that many of those who were "selected least fit" are now ruling. The antidote to this is to return to the autonomous life of spirit as the source of economic renewal, i.e., to a healthy cosmogony (connection with the cosmos).

"We have to realize that the time of *Homo economicus* is past, [and] that another type of human being must come: the cosmic human being who knows that, besides physical earthly heredity, there live in him also the forces of the Sun, the Moon, the starry heavens, and the supersensible world."[9] When Steiner spoke of this, he was looking toward the East, which was cultivating Leninism, an economic system born from *Homo economicus*. Leninism imposed an abstract intellectuality upon the more altruistic Russians, but this way of thinking was very foreign to them. Thus the experiment failed and instead led to the horror of Stalin. Steiner made it clear that social impulses could no longer be drawn from economic factors; they could arise only from new ideas born from spiritual worlds. By 1917, of course, it was too late; the Bolshevik Revolution had already erupted by then.

In the West, one must choose between uniting with the declining forces of decay and opening to the cosmic (cosmological) connections that constitute the actual gift of the West. In the Middle, in Europe, one must choose between fatalism and the gift of authentic freedom that is the gift appointed to central Europe. In the East, one must choose between

---

5   Ibid., p. 77.
6   This term, coined by Rudolf Steiner, reveals his sense of humor.
7   "People ask what means can be employed to counteract revolutions. Well, the revolution will come once enough crises have accumulated their impulses of demise and destruction. You can only counteract revolutions by continually employing the strength that works against them. If you do not balance economic life with a continual healing life of spirit, then economic life will gather and compress itself into revolutions" (ibid., p. 86).
8   Ibid., p. 82.
9   Ibid., p. 88.

the fanaticism of egoism and being open to the altruism that is the inherent gift of the East. In Joel Park's insightful article in this volume of *Star Wisdom*, he depicts the three branches of Christianity as spread throughout these same three geographic locations; the Petrine stream is at home in Europe; the Johannine stream is at home in the East; and the Celtic–Grail–Pauline stream seeks to be born in the Anglo-American West. Indeed, awaking to cosmogony will lead naturally to a Grail quest, the searching for our lost sense of spirit.

When the people of the West turn consciously to the stars, to cosmogony–astrosophy, they will unite with angels. They must then embrace the *freedom impulse* of the Middle, of central Europe, so as to unite with archangels. Ultimately, as this cosmic consciousness finds freedom extending to all groups of people, Westerners will become *altruistic seekers* of the great plan of evolution and will thereby unite with the mighty archai. This will result in miracles, for each of us must seek collaboration with the seed impulses that can only be found when the people of the East, West, and Center work together.

## Looking Back into History: One Hundred Years of Saturn–Pluto Cycles following the War in Heaven[1]

> For all things arise from the grave historically in a metamorphosed form after thirty-three years through a force that has to do with what is most holy and most redemptive, which humanity has received through the Mystery of Golgotha.... A seed of thought or of deed takes a whole human generation—33 years—to ripen. When it is ripened, it goes on working in historic evolution for 66 years more. Thus the intensity of an impulse planted by a human being in the stream of history can truly be recognized in its working through three generations, i.e., through a whole century.[2]

The Saturn–Pluto cycle of 1883 to 1914 began a hundred years before the onset of the Saturn–Pluto cycle we are currently concluding (1982–2020). Furthermore, the 1883 cycle began a mere 3½ years *after* Michael's 1879 victory in heaven, when he threw the evil spirits from the heavens, casting them down to Earth. The period from 1879 to 1979 marked the hundred-year integration of the fallen spirits of darkness into terrestrial realms below. This changed the nature of all things upon the Earth; for, after the War in Heaven, evil gained new footholds in human terrestrial life.

The hundred-year interval marks the advance of these beings, in 33⅓-year cycles, into the willing, feeling, and thinking life of human beings. And this period concluded just 3½ years before the onset of the 1982 Saturn–Pluto cycle we are currently completing. The culmination of the hundred years resulted in humanity confronting a full-fledged assault—in thinking, feeling, *and* willing—that brought about an entirely new level of temptation. This fourth temptation asks us this: In whose name do we come, God or Mammon? For we have already been told that we cannot serve two masters; we must choose one.[3]

Reorienting our thinking toward a new astrology, new wisdom of the stars, is made easier if we bear in mind that all things in material life have their origins in cosmic worlds. Not only is there the 33⅓-year rhythm, there is also a mirroring of events:

> Things go in cycles or periods. Anything that happens in the physical world is really a kind of projection, or shadow, of what happens in the spiritual world, except that it would have happened earlier in the spiritual world. Let us assume this line here [he drew an image of a line on the chalkboard] was the line or plane separating the spiritual and the physical worlds. What I have just said could then be characterized as follows: Let us assume an event—for example, the battle between Michael and the dragon—happens first of all in the spiritual

---

[1] The term *War in Heaven* originates in the book of Revelation (12:7–10). It is also a term used by Rudolf Steiner, who dated the onset of the event in 1841 and its conclusion in 1879.

[2] Steiner, Dornach, Dec. 26, 1917 (CW 180).

[3] Matt. 6:24: "No one can serve two masters: Either he will hate the one and love the other, or he will be devoted to the one and despise the other. You cannot serve both God and Mammon."

world. It finally comes to an end when the dragon is cast down from heaven to Earth.

On Earth, then, the cycle is brought to completion after a time interval which approximately equals the time between the beginning of the battle in the spiritual world and the time when the dragon was cast down. We might say that the dawn, the very beginning of this battle between Michael and the dragon, was in 1841. Things were particularly lively in 1845. It is thirty-four years from 1845 to 1879; and if we move on thirty-four years after 1879, we come to the mirroring event: we get 1913, the year preceding 1914. You see, the developments that started in the physical world in 1913 are the *mirror image* of the prime reasons for the spiritual battle.

And now consider 1841, 1879, and 1917. The year 1841 was the crucial year in the nineteenth century. The year 1917 is its mirror image. If one realizes that the exertions of the crowd of ahrimanic spirits in 1841 (when the dragon started to fight Michael in the spiritual world) are mirrored right now in 1917, much of what is happening now will not really come as a surprise. *Events in the physical world cannot really be understood unless one knows that they have been in preparation in the spiritual worlds.*[4]

As the last year of the 1883 Saturn–Pluto cycle was 1914, the time when the Great War and the approaching Bolshevik Revolution (1917) began, we can see the mirroring in worlds below of what Steiner mentions as having already occurred in worlds above. The thoughts seeded by evil into human beings resulted in an incredible abomination from Michael's vantage. Steiner's call to awake from the decadence of all old ideas arose from his knowledge of the fall of the spirits of darkness—which necessitated that human beings find *new* ideas. Yet this would not become our destiny, for the old ideas would lead, soon after, to Word War II:

> What matters today is not what people did in 1914, but that they get themselves out of this situation. The problem we have to face now is how to get out of it again. Unless people realize that old ideas will not get us out of it and that new ideas are needed, the result will be failure. Anyone who thinks we will get out of this with the old ideas is barking up the wrong tree. The effort must be made to gain new ideas, and this is possible only with insight into the spiritual world.[5]

Steiner saw that the catastrophe of 1914 was, in truth, a battle between East and West, and that the middle was simply being ground to dust between the two. Anthroposophy was the hope for building such a bridge between them. Yet, sadly, this was not to be. Not only was the middle conceding, but both East and West were far too invested in the economics of Mammon. This suppressed any hope that might rise from socioeconomic altruism. The intelligence of the fallen spirits far surpasses the wisdom humanity has yet gained. Consequently, we have been living through, and indeed *continue* to live through, a time of "catching up" as we struggle to develop the consciousness that awakes us to angelic worlds.[6] The forces of cosmic good have not, however, gone unnoticed by fallen spirits, for they have always known how to seize—and cunningly invert—the good.

The first of the three Saturn/Pluto cycles within that hundred-year period (1883–1914) occurred just past the Pleiades:[7] the seven sisters of Harmony in the constellation of the Bull. And the Earth did tremble! At this time the Etheric Christ was completing his descent through angelic realms (1799–1899) and was beginning his appearance in the aura of the Earth (from 1899 on). Humankind was unknowingly entering a New Age.

Three months after the beginning of this Taurus cycle, seeds of modern fundamentalism were sown in the Dutch East Indies (now Indonesia), from which a new kind of imperialism would rear its ugly head in both Islamic and Western countries; the new imperialism would seal a wretched fate, one that was doomed to change the world. Just as

---

4 Steiner, *The Fall of the Spirits of Darkness*, pp. 144–145.

5 Ibid., p. 147.

6 See Steiner, "What Does the Angel Do in Our Astral Body?" (in *Death as Metamorphosis of Life*); also *Journal for Star Wisdom* 2018.

7 The Pleiades are 5° Taurus, which is an earth sign.

Kilauea erupted at the onset of our current cycle, so, too, was a volcanic eruption the signature of the onset of this cycle a hundred years earlier. This eruption, however, was not the weeping tears of Pele; rather was it the wrath of Satan exploding from sub-depths, announcing his near appearance onto the global stage as the archenemy the Etheric Christ. The volcano was Krakatoa, whose eruption (in 1883) obliterated two-thirds of the original Krakatoa Island, killing an estimated 36,000 people. This remains the second deadliest volcanic eruption in recent history. Two years later, Nevado del Ruiz would erupt in Columbia, killing 23,000 people. Nineteen years later, in the same cycle, Mount Pelée in Martinique erupted, killing approximately 30,000 people.

Three of the four deadliest volcanic eruptions in history would thus occur during this first Saturn–Pluto cycle subsequent to the fall of the spirits of darkness. Meanwhile, in Europe, Britain was threatened by the rising wealth of Germany; according to Rudolf Steiner (in his lecture cycle *The Karma of Untruthfulness*), this was one of the primary and most hidden causes leading to World War I. Greed thereby sowed seeds that would end in brutal wars. In the final years of this cycle, the volcano Novarupta would dramatically erupt on the Alaskan Peninsula.

The fallen spirits of darkness were indeed exciting the fire earth. And as the hundred-year period unfolded, the activity within evil subearthly layers would quietly seep into the subconscious of individuals, from which it would spread to cultures. By the twenty-first century, it would become a systemic global epidemic—"a psychic disease embedded in the masses" (as Jung put it).

Imperialism did not begin in the nineteenth century, yet prior to this time it is called "old imperialism." The age of "new imperialism" is considered to have begun in the 1870s as a result of the second Industrial Revolution. Colonial power was one aspect of the new imperialism, which was propelled into expansion as a result of the needs that were created by the growth of industry. Social Darwinism then came into being. This arose from Darwin's "survival of the fittest," granting justification for superior people to rule over inferior people to improve their lot. (The "naturally selected" superior people were, of course, those of the Western, white race.) The thought was seeded like a worm into Western culture that the conquest of "inferior" people, often resulting in the destruction of "weaker" races, was simply the way things work. Hitler then rose to power as the Frankenstein monster of Social Darwinism. The growth of new imperialism was brought about by the demand for new markets, military bases, raw materials, national security and pride, expansion of the weapons industry, transportation needs (such as railroads), and the continuing search for new sources for investments. In the ever-zealous religious sphere, a need grew to spread the religion of choice to a broader number of people. Christians went forth to proselytize "inferior" people, and Islamic pilgrims were sent forth to spread the true faith. Pressure built as East and West lived into their own versions of the new imperialism. The following study, pertaining to the Saturn–Pluto cycle of 1883 to 1914, exemplifies this situation.

## Krakatoa

The story of the Krakatoa eruption reveals the inevitable destiny of new imperialism, both the Eastern and the Western varieties. Imperialism (with the rise of imperialistic Plutocracy) is defined as the policy of extending the rule or authority of an empire or nation over foreign countries; it is also defined as the policy of acquiring and holding colonies and dependencies. The term *new imperialism* itself was first recorded in 1878, just as the War in Heaven was concluding. West and East have been in conflict ever since the Crusades. With the birth of modern imperialism, however, a pathological component entered both factions, one that would change the course of history as each side came to view the other as its diabolical enemy. Evil would face evil, while both failed to realize they were actually seeing themselves a mirror.

At the time of the Krakatoa eruption, Java–Indonesia was under the rule of the Dutch, who demanded exorbitant tithes from the Javanese–Indonesian people. By treating them as slave laborers, they were rendered destitute. The people were predominantly Muslim, and although Islam was imperialistic in the Middle East, the Indonesians practiced a more tolerant version of Islam, being tempered by Hinduism, one of its other sanctioned religions. At the time, the mounting threat of Western imperialism was exacting trepidation in the minds of the Islamic imperialists. The seeds sown during this Saturn–Pluto cycle would later bear bitter fruit as the collision between Eastern and Western imperialists would swell and grow into a systemic, worldwide catastrophe.

Javanese Islam was syncretic—that is, influenced by multiple beliefs. Yet the central feature still held to the importance of making one's pilgrimage to Mecca, the *Hajj*. However, owing to the high taxation imposed by the Dutch authority and the fact that permission was needed to take a leave from work, such pilgrimages were very difficult. Those who could travel to Mecca were encouraged by the Islamic hierarchy to stay. The longer they stayed, the more Arabized they became, which ultimately festered into rising hostility toward the rule of Dutch infidels. Rebellion was thus seeded in their hearts—a smoldering flame that would erupt against the oppression of their Christian rulers.

Toward the end of the nineteenth century, the Mullahs in Mecca were already experiencing the ominous threat coming toward them from Western imperialism. They saw pilgrims from the east as useful messengers for spreading Islamic purity to the Javanese upon their return home. Adding flames to these mounting fires was a Javanese-born mystic, Hajji Abdul Karim, who fed the conflagration of the rebellion by setting himself up as a seer and messenger of Allah. Tens of thousands of people came to him daily, hoping for a few words or a laying on of hands. As the number of his disciples grew, a dark cloud of uncertainty gathered above the heads of the Dutch.[1]

Hajji Abdul prophesied that Mahdi, a Christ-like messianic figure known to the Islamic religion, was soon to appear. Hajji predicted that terrible signs would offer proof of Mahdi's coming—volcanic eruption, cattle disease, floods, blood-colored rain, and the deaths of many people. Then came the eruption of Krakatoa. As it happened, disease was killing cattle, a tsunami caused by the eruption killed thousands, volcanic ash caused blood-colored rain, and death was everywhere. This was the proof people needed to believe in their coming messiah. Thus Islamic fundamentalism overcame the more tempered Islam once practiced by these people.

As Krakatoa erupted, a perfect storm of unrest rapidly developed. Smoldering embers of rebellion burst into flames of hatred. Islamic martyrs in white robes assassinated Dutch officials. The Mullahs and their propaganda had whipped the Javanese population into fury, aided and abetted by the mystical prophecy of their messiah. Dutch authority was rapidly losing ground.

Five years after the eruption of Krakatoa, an uprising known as the 1888 Rebellion set off a daylong massacre of the Dutch. When the Dutch cavalry arrived later with modern weaponry, the rebels found that piety alone would not protect them as they had believed while in the fever of Holy War. The rebellion was crushed and talk of Mahdi's coming evaporated. That rebellion is considered an important link in the path to Indonesian independence, which did not culminate until 1949.

The ruin and devastation caused by the Krakatoa eruption was exploited by the Muslim leaders, Mullahs, and scholars who were eager to recruit soldiers to help them face their evil Western enemies. Thus, as people of the Middle East recognized the dire threat coming toward them from Western imperialists, the seeds of a new kind of imperialism were sown. At the same time, people of the West recognized the dire threat coming toward them from Eastern Imperialism. The die was thereby cast.

It would take another fourteen years, in 1897, before the thorn in the side of the East entered a new chapter of hostility. This was the first Zionist Congress, held in Switzerland, and the establishment of the World Zionist Organization, whose goal was to create a Jewish homeland in the region surrounding Jerusalem. Israel would not become a state until May 1948, but the Congress (in the

---

1 See, for example, Winchester, *Krakatoa,* pp. 328ff.

minds of Islamic rulers) was tantamount to rattling sabers.

### *The Years that Followed*

The intense volcanic activity during the first Saturn/Pluto cycle since the end of the War in Heaven marked the beginning of this hundred-year process. From one perspective, we could say that the three deadly eruptions were manifestations of the physical effects consequent to *the fall of the spirits of darkness*. The outbreak of World War I, which also occurred during the first third of this hundred-year period, seemed to mirror, in the human will, *evil* impulses being agitated in the fire earth. In the ensuing middle 33⅓ years, the fallen spirits of darkness would inspire the Bolshevik Revolution, World War II, and the atrocity of the atomic bomb. How could the feeling life of humanity digest such horrors? In the final 33⅓ years, moreover, these same fallen beings would seek a body of consciousness through which to "conceive themselves" into the intellectual planes of existence. By the end of this hundred-year period in 1982, we were entering the age of technology, thus providing the dark spirits exactly what they needed to capture human intelligence.

We now stand on a precipice before a "5G world" (an abbreviation for fifth-generation wireless service). The ubiquitous broadcasting of such extreme high-frequency radiation will inevitably pose new levels of danger, threatening humanity's potential to attain higher capacities of thought (or *manas* thinking). We can ask ourselves: When will the Internet finally be fast enough? Our atmosphere already carries trillions of bits of information, which have created a systemic field around us that also penetrates *through* us. Imagine standing at the side of an eight-lane superhighway on which cars and trucks are hurtling past. By analogy, electromagnetic airwaves have placed us exactly there!

We must *not* enter a network that holds such an overwhelming capacity to influence us surreptitiously. Indeed, in a 5G world the capacity for causing people to be "thoughted" will increase a thousandfold, for the *neural emptiness* into which spirit can make itself manifest would instead be drawn into powerful grids of electromagnetism. Escape is difficult once we enter electromagnetic systems of extreme frequencies. *Is this not the fate of all who enter Klingsor's castle?*

The Saturn–Pluto cycle beginning in 2020 will occur in Sagittarius. Truth will be under an even greater assault. Cyber realities must be controlled lest they increasingly enshroud us. The image of Sagittarius is that of the centaur who *rides* the horse, signifying rule over the lower passions and impulses by those who master their intelligence. The victorious will find truth in discourse with angels. We will be asked to model this stance; as we sublimate the lower, we open ourselves to the higher.

Our nerve–sense system is the only system of our physicality in which we are free to mediate between higher and lower worlds. Rudolf Steiner has this to say:

> In psychology and physiology, you will find the nervous system portrayed as the mediating organ for our sensing, our thinking, and our soul–spiritual life as a whole. But in what way is it able to act as this mediating organ? It is able to do so only by perpetually *excluding* itself from our life, by not creating any obstacles for our thinking and feeling. In other words, *it does not establish any connections with our thinking and feeling.* Where it is located, it leaves the human being empty with regard to the soul–spirit. Where the nerves are located, there are just empty spaces for the soul–spirit. Where there are these empty spaces, the soul–spirit is therefore able to enter.[1]

As a reflecting organ for soul–spirit, the nerves constitute the sacred ground of thought life. They are not to be filled with trillions of bits of cyber data. In a state of *wakeful expectation*, they are instead to remain empty—awaiting the approach of divine soul/spiritual content. Such emptiness prepares us to receive the "thoughts of the gods," as spoken in the third panel of the Foundation Stone Meditation. The sucking force of electromagnetic fields, on the other hand, infiltrates these hollow neural tubes, filling them with the content of "the thoughts of others." Going from 4G to 5G will therefore result in an even more

---

1 Steiner, *The Electronic Doppelgänger: The Mystery of the Double in the Age of the Internet*, p. 129 (italics added).

refined body for the Antichrist to achieve his ultimate aim of proving to the Father that human beings have chosen *him*—over and above the rightful Son.

Today we worship the god of technology, whose tempestuous sermons sound through us—day and night—sowing fear, egoism, and neediness born of endless desire. This stands in abject opposition to the stance we are instead to achieve—reverent emptiness that allows angels to draw near to us. We must extend the effort to preserve our strength of consciousness. We must know that a "web" now exists, and that we should not become the "spider's" flies.

## *Initiates*

Initiates regularly come to Earth to model new capacities that striving individualities will eventually acquire on their paths of spiritual development. In the same manner, *anti*-initiates come to Earth to model capacities that will later constitute the prison in which all non-striving individualities will eventually find themselves encapsulated. Christ incarnated into Jesus at the Baptism to open hearts to divine revelation: the wine of Divine Love. Analogously, the intention of the Antichrist (who is an initiate of the secret brotherhoods) is to seduce human hearts with a *narcotic* wine that renders them uncaring when confronted with the suffering of their brothers and sisters. Furthermore, given that the current Saturn–Pluto cycle began so close to where the Sun was positioned at the Baptism, we bear witness as to which of the two feminine archetypes has prevailed—the Holy Virgin or the woman of Babylon? Sadly, moreover, the collective state of our world gives ample proof that a destructive force has actually triumphed and has taken hold of cultural, political, and economic realms.

Someone had to open the door as an initiate from the School of Ahriman, just as Christ opened the door as an initiate from the School of Devachan. After incarnating into Jesus, Christ gained entrance to the hierarchy of humanity, and his immortal presence will eternally bless all who continue to seek him. Inversely, the ahrimanic initiate continues his Machiavellian work. The difference between the two is unmistakable, for whereas Christ enlightens, the "other" one possesses.

## *The Fifth Kingdom of Grace*

"Enlightenment—or possession?" This is the question we face. Two kingdoms have been forming; one comprises a new ether (the fifth, or *moral*, ether), and the other comprises the technological caricature of the moral ether. The Second Coming of Christ indicates his presence within the radiant kingdom of the moral ether that has formed in the etheric aura of the Earth. There is also the second coming of the ahrimanic initiate, whose presence is found within the *enfolded field* of dead light (electricity) and dead sound (magnetism) that has formed out of the negative energies of the sub-realms of the inner Earth.

The fifth kingdom of grace streams holy light from the presence of the Angel Jesus, calling us to awake into a new age of mercy. We are challenged to discover this new light, understanding that (in the words of Goethe) "when we leap, a net will appear." The fifth kingdom of technology, on the other hand, also has a "net"; but instead of bridging into higher spheres, this net imprisons its captives, luring them into a fearfully dense and coagulated mass.

Just as we live in the time of the Second Coming of Christ, similarly we live in the time of the second coming of the ahrimanic initiate. We must choose which "net" we seek. *The fifth light of the fifth sacrifice, in this time of the fifth cultural epoch of Sardis, is synonymous with the fifth kingdom of grace.* Indeed, we are living in pentagrams of new possibilities.

Ahriman, having found his doorway into time, seeks his immortal "second coming" in the fifth kingdom of technology. Are we not forming an even more ideal body for him in the development of 5G technology?

## *The Inner Character of the Twentieth Century*

Through the miracle of his ascent through the various spheres of the celestial hierarchies (from

Ascension in AD 33 to 966), the etheric Christ was *ascending* through all the heavenly hierarchies. From 966 on, he descended through those same spheres. During these nearly two millennia of his ascension and descension, something new was added in each of the various hierarchies he passed through.[1] In 1899, Christ departed from the sphere of the angels, and he gradually began integrating into the Earth's etheric spheres. Thirty-three years later, his etheric manifestation would be countered by the rising of the prophesied beast. The prophet was Rudolf Steiner; the beast was Hitler.

As the Saturn–Pluto conjunction of 1883 began, the etheric Christ was still moving through angelic spheres (1799–1899), the fallen spirits of darkness beheld his near approach. At the close of this cycle (1914), he was already manifesting in Earth's aura (from 1899 on). By 1933, the first third of his integration was complete; by 1967, the middle third of his integration was complete; and by 1999, the last third of his integration was complete. In each of the three periods of manifestation, he was infusing new possibilities into the human life of willing, feeling, and thinking on Earth. Consequently, we can further imagine the spirits of darkness spuriously influencing human willing, feeling, and thinking, while ceaselessly plotting to destroy any possibility that the appearance of the Etheric Christ could be recognized. As yet, humanity has proven to be no match for their cunning genius.

In 1933, the will-to-power was exemplified with Hitler; in 1967 the plunge from the pinnacle of the temple of consciousness was exemplified in the drug epidemic (connected entirely with the current opioid epidemic); and by 1999, technology was exemplifying the turning of bread to stones; since then, the true glory of our earthly kingdom has been viciously abused and totally eclipsed by virtual and augmented glamor. Moreover, as part of this virtual revolution, the machine assault on nature has rapidly advanced. Mechanistic thinking has driven both of these phenomena. Sadly, today's skies of ubiquitous graffiti chemtrails remain unnoticed by most people.

We can apply the Christ rhythm in any hundred-year cycle, just as we have done with the hundred-year period in which the three previous Saturn/Pluto conjunctions (1883, 1914, and 1947) occurred subsequent to the War in Heaven. This hundred-year period came to its conclusion (in 1979) a mere 3½ years before the onset of the Saturn–Pluto cycle we are concluding this year. As the 1982 cycle began, the evil seeds that were sown over the past hundred years had ripened into maturity.

The 1883 conjunction was in Taurus, an earth sign. A call for reverence toward creation was thereby proclaimed. The middle cycle (1914–1947) was in Gemini, an air sign, which is the medium through which spiritual messages reach us. The detonation of atomic bombs poisoned hundreds of thousands of innocent people, sending out venomous plumes that were the utter inversion of spiritual air. The last cycle (1947–1983) began in Cancer, a water sign. Three years before its conclusion (1980), Mt. St. Helens erupted. The blast was estimated to have had a power 500 times greater than the Hiroshima atomic bomb. Fifty-seven people were killed, and the damage was assessed at three billion dollars. This was also the time when the AIDS virus was first identified. Cancer is the constellation of "home," of "mother," wherein spirit must ensoul matter. The inversion of this is an *encapsulation in matter* that leads to disease in thinking, feeling, and willing. Indeed, from 1947 to 1982, the West was becoming ever more enveloped in the hard shell of materialism.

Having failed to heed the warnings inherent in the previous earth, air, and water conjunctions, we were quite unprepared to meet the new air trial brought by the 1982 conjunction cycle in Libra. How could we possibly have known, without a spiritual awaking, that the virtue of *purity* was at stake, or that the fulcrum would flip? Through the vehicle of technology, the hundred-year period of the integration of the fallen spirits would result in a full-fledged attack against the Anglo-American mission of spirit remembering (cosmology). How could we have predicted this? The fact that Saturn–Pluto conjunction of 2020 will occur in the fire sign of Sagittarius, wherein the towering

---

1   See Powell, *The Christ Mystery*.

guardians of Truth find their abode, may yet give us hope.

What is truth? Only the heart can know in times such as ours—when propaganda, hysteria, and innuendo have become the authors of our news. As the new conjunction draws near, however, we may already find in-streaming forces that serve to sustain us. In the meantime, we have created tragically apocalyptic predicaments that are right out of the book of Revelation, predicaments to which we are now bound. Yet, *never* is all lost. The new cycle beginning in 2020 will invite us to awake as Archers, as human spirits setting a course toward radically different shores. If, however, the physical disruptions that have arisen over the past hundred years manifest instead on a *soul* level, we may still have to face the tragedy of revolution.

Before looking ahead, we will briefly look at the closing years of the current cycle.

## Closing Years of the Current Saturn–Pluto Cycle

The early beginnings of 2018 were announced by volcanic eruptions in Japan and the Philippines, as well as by a 7.9-magnitude earthquake off the coast of Alaska. Analogously, we could say that the first month of a given year reveals the signature of that year, just as the timing of a human being's first breath reveals the signature of that person's biography. In the quaking Earth and trembling mountains—exemplifying rules of chaos and revolution—we witness powers striving to send that which is below into the above, and, inversely, throwing that which is above into the below. Indeed, the sixth subearthly sphere (the fire earth) was reminding us of its power to stir bloody rebellions. This we must avoid.

As noted previously, the consciousness of Christ was descending through the sixth subearthly sphere (the fire earth) from 1992 to 2004. From 2004 to 2016, he was descending through the seventh subearthly sphere: the earth mirror. The crash of 2008 is an example of this, as the mortgage crisis revealed how enmeshed we were in a hall of mirrors when mortgages were endlessly bought and sold—until no one understood where they all had gone or how the "game" was being played. The schemes simply became too complex to comprehend, and so the money simply disappeared into that hall of mirrors.

At the same time, the political war machine also entered into a hall of mirrors: it became increasingly difficult to discern exactly who the enemy was—and this continues to be true. The antidote to this realm is the seventh Beatitude: *Blessed are the peacemakers, for they shall be called the children of God*. Unfortunately, since the US was at war for the duration of these twelve years, we can assume that the peacemakers were in fact *not* in positions of power. Nor can those who operate against this Beatitude be considered children of God; rather do they see through the eyes of Ahriman—wherein evil is seen as good, and good is seen as evil.

From 2016 to 2028, the consciousness of Christ will be further permeating the inner Earth. (It is currently manifesting in the eighth subearthly sphere, the divisive layer.) Those who operate from this sphere have united with Ahriman in the fight against righteousness. The antidote to this sphere is the eighth Beatitude: *Blessed are the persecuted, for theirs is the kingdom of heaven*.

We will most assuredly continue to bear witness to division among individuals, communities, and nations, as well as between natural and virtual kingdoms. The 2016 election and subsequent inauguration of the new US president is ample evidence of how easily we divide into groups and end up hating each other.

## We Need a Map

If we are venturing on a trip to a foreign country, we need a map. By analogy, we can say that the cosmological map depicts the region of the zodiac wherein a certain aspect is occurring; for a cosmological understanding inevitably increases conscious awareness *of* a time *in* its time—i.e., *we know where we are*. Having determined the place, we will more readily understand the blessings and warnings surrounding a given cosmic event. Indeed, had we thus comprehended the Saturn–Pluto conjunction in Libra, we could have awaked to the enshrouding web of deceit that was falling upon us.

Purity is evil's greatest enemy—and it is now up to us to rescue this virtue from the gutters of perversity. If we cannot do this, the future course of our existence will continue to be manipulated by beings that are hostile to life. As creative beings, should we not direct our every effort toward supporting only those endeavors and products that serve truth, as well as a sustainable future?

We will inevitably be exposed to ever more techno-wars, for this has already been "written" by the spider that formed the Web. Drones, bots, and other horrors continue to emerge right out of the most heinous corridors of the dark psyches of those who perpetuate them. Yet we may also remember that evil cannot actually create—it can only imitate. Thus we must devote our attention to what evil would otherwise invert—*the creative path being illumined by cosmic and human light-bearers.*

### Looking Ahead: Sacred Conversations

We must educate ourselves to imagine the forces at work when Pluto and Saturn engage in conversation—i.e., when they come into conjunction every thirty to thirty-eight years. Given that the onset of the new conversation will begin in January of 2020, in Sagittarius, we are wise to recognize the potential these conjunctions tend to foster. Cosmic discourses are ever benevolent; they only become diabolical when inverted by forces lurking in worlds below. Our task, as outlined in previous articles in this publication, is to re-envision the meaning streaming from stellar worlds. This has been especially so since 2018, for then began a 29½-year cycle in which human beings can awake to the fact that angels are standing by, ready to offer healing ministry to our weary souls.

The Holy Virgin (Saturn) bore witness to the entire life of Jesus Christ, taking into her immaculate heart all the pain and sorrow living in the hearts of others. In January 2020, she will conjunct Pluto at 27° Sagittarius, from which yet another sacred conversation will ensue. This can be likened to a New Moon, a time of new beginnings. To prepare ourselves for the new conversation of 2020, it is urgently necessary that we take hold of what the closing year of the current cycle offers.

Let us imagine the angels watching us day and night, as we ask ourselves: Is my current activity such that I am drawing angels near to me? How quickly this measures virtue! There is a thin line between sin and evil. When we engage in activities, thoughts, feelings, and deeds that kill something (life, trust, faith, hope, goodness), we are actively sinning. GMOs, for example, kill the seeds' life. Lies kill trust; demeaning comments kill faith; criticism kills hope; and immorality kills goodness. We cross over into evil, however, when we call sin a good thing. This is the dangerous folly of materialism, for it justifies that which kills. And in so doing, it becomes the *servant* of evil.

Jupiter rules Sagittarius. The 2020 conjunction (January 12) finds Jupiter within a few degrees of its position at the birth of the Virgin Mary. This will be accompanied by a "stellium" of planets (Jupiter, Sun, Saturn, Pluto, and Mercury) that will line up in Sagittarius. Jupiter will stand nearby the conjunction of Sun, Saturn, Pluto, and Mercury as witness to the potential inherent in this new conversation between the Holy Virgin and Divine Love (*Phanes*, the higher aspect of Pluto). The stars indeed decree that this thirty-four-year Saturn–Pluto cycle has everything to do with truth and the restraint of lower impulses.

We can imagine Saturn as the mantle of the Virgin, who embraces us to protect us from wandering off the moral path of the narrow way that has been set before us. Upon her blue outer mantle are inscribed all the stars of the heavens; her inner mantle is red, bestowing the gift of the awaking of our "I." The Virgin remembers not only every moment in the life of Jesus Christ, she also remembers each moment in the history of time. She is the great scribe of the cosmos, the authoress of all that is written into the eternal records of time (the *akashic record*).

As the Virgin converses with Phanes, divine love pours into her. She opens her mantle before him, taking into her immaculate heart what the Father "wills" as humanity's destiny over the course of the duration of this cycle. In thirty-four years, in 2053, she will return to Phanes, where he will then rest in the constellation of Aquarius (19°). Thus does the soon-to-begin conversation hail from Sagittarius to Aquarius, from the throne of truth to the throne of the angel–human. And thus is it foreordained that the golden thread of truth shall lead ever more of us into discourse with our angels.

## Sagittarius

Above the position of the 2020 conjunction (27° Sagittarius), we find the star Sulaphat, which along with Vega is one of the stars in the constellation Lyra (the lyre). Vega is the fifth brightest star (in terms of apparent magnitude) that we can see with the naked eye. The constellation of the Eagle (Aquila) also stretches above the longitude of this conjunction wherein we find the star Altair. Altair, Vega, and Deneb (9° Aquarius) are three stars that form the *Summer Triangle*. And far below, in the southern skies, we find the star Alpha Pavonis, also known as Peacock. This star is found in the constellation Pavo, which is the Latin name for peacock.

Greek mythology tells how the peacock was Hera's sacred bird. The goddess would fly through the air in her chariot pulled by peacocks. The eyes on the peacock's tail are said to be the eyes of the giant Argus, killed by Hermes to free the nymph the giant had captured. After his death, Hera placed the eyes of Argus on the tail of her sacred bird. Indeed, the peacock sees with the eye of spirit when humble, and when inflated, the peacock's eyes merely reflect the self. This offers a fine metaphor for the Sagittarius conversation between Pluto and Saturn, for Jupiter rules Sagittarius and is related to the third-eye of wisdom. We can easily imagine the necessity of strengthening this higher sense organ during the course of the new Saturn–Pluto dialogue.

A sacred covenant governs creation; the world will behave in the way it is beheld. When we behold the good, we increase our capacity to see in spiritual realms; when we behold what is ugly, we decrease this capacity. Those who find pleasure in *subjectively* conversing of evil, feed evil. Those who know the fine art of *objectively* casting the knowing glance, starve evil. A thin sword edge determines the integrity of the latter over and above the former.

The constellation Lyra was sacred to Apollo, and its music was known to soothe anger. How fitting that the upcoming conjunction in Sagittarius has the potential to tame wild passions, thus returning the soul to its intended dignity. Furthermore, legend tells of how the musician of the Argonauts and the son of Apollo, Orpheus, played the lyre. Orpheus played his lyre so beautifully that he charmed even the wild beasts, rocks, and trees. He fell in love with the nymph Eurydice, but soon lost her to death caused from a serpent's bite. Orpheus journeyed into the underworld to find her. Yet he failed and lost her for the second time in the gloomy darkness of worlds below. So heartbroken was Orpheus, that he forswore the company of women. This so enraged the ladies of Thrace that they tore him apart. The God Zeus retrieved the lyre of Orpheus and placed it in the heavens.

We can imagine the cosmic lyre resounding with angelic harmonies. Hermes, the wing-footed messenger of the gods, passed it to Apollo, the consummate Archer (Sagittarian). Apollo is also said to be the father of Ophiuchus, who (among others) holds the secrets of healing and of raising the dead. He bears continuous faithfulness in regard to the necessities of evolution. Are not the healing sounds issuing forth from the heavenly lyre the music of the spheres? Are we not each to receive this symphony of grace and translate it according to the directives of our individual "I"—our hallowed "name?"

The myths surrounding the Lyre and the Peacock tell well the inner secrets of Saturn and Pluto conjunct in the late degrees of Sagittarius. We must open our spirit eye, part through the darkness of deceit and illusion, to take hold of the lyre that tames all instincts and desires rising from the lower realms of human nature. The bite of the serpent that killed Eurydice is the herald of death for all who fail to pierce through evil's tangled web of lies—the soul death of all who continue to immerse themselves in the psychic epidemic of mass deceit.

Having passed through the trials presented by the Woman of Babylon during the entire cycle now concluding, we must prepare to "re-tune" our souls to Apollo's harp—for only then may we participate in the heavenly Manna that will be in-streaming as the new conversation between love and holiness (between Phanes and the Virgin) begins anew. Moreover, we are to humble ourselves to strengthen our spirit sight.

The Nathan Jesus was born when the Sun was in Sagittarius. Was not his heart continuously attuned to the music of the spheres? The shepherds who adored him at his birth knew the secrets of nature, Shambhala mysteries, which whisper into hearts open to love. This Jesus was the very incarnation of love—*thus Christ could incarnate into his sheaths*. Each of us is one spark from the divine flame of Christ's sacred heart. The "I" that radiates above our head is our illumining star. As occurred also with the shepherds of olden times, our star is ever guiding us to discover the manger of holiness that rests in the quietude of our innermost heart. Herein we long for truth, virtue, and self-mastery. And in each heart, we find the Holy Virgin keeping silent vigil.

The Nathan Jesus is now the Angel Jesus, through whom the Grail light streams to Earth. The Blessed Virgin (Saturn) protects the sacred opening between that which is above and that which is below. Through this opening, the Angel Jesus seeks to approach each one of us. And as we find our "song"—the resounding glory of our one true "name"—we, too, will find the Grail light of Jesus.

As noted, the conjunction of 1982 occurred close to the position of the Sun at the Baptism of the Nathan Jesus. The conjunction of 2020 occurs in the constellation of his birth. This reminds us that star stories are not separate events; instead they are consecutive chapters in a continuing drama. Moreover, as the current conjunction occurs with the constellation of Lyra shining above, we recall the Summer Triangle: Altair, Vega, and Deneb. Deneb is the luminous megastar that overlit the miracle of the feeding of the 5,000. It is filled with the promise of the future:

When we gaze at Deneb, we are looking exactly in the direction in which our Sun is moving as it orbits around the galactic center. In this sense, too, Deneb is our guiding star.

Deneb, seen by the Greeks as marking the tail of the Swan, is at the head of the Northern Cross. It is remarkable to consider that the cross is the symbol of Christ, and that—in the sense of "as above, so below"—his central miracles (the feeding of the 5,000 and the walking on the water) were aligned via the Sun with Deneb at the head of the cross, and the miracle he performed shortly before these two (the healing of the paralyzed man at the pool of Bethesda) was aligned via the Sun with Sadr—marking the breast of the Swan, located at the center of the Northern Cross.[1]

The Pluto/Saturn conjunction of 2053 occurs at 19° Aquarius, just past Deneb at 10½° Aquarius. Thus we see that the cosmic drama unfolding in the 2020 conjunction is already pointing us to the 2053 conjunction. For, just as the 2020 conjunction is related to the constellation of Lyra that holds the star Vega, as well as the constellation of the Eagle that holds the star Altair, the 2053 conjunction leads us to the third star in the Summer Triangle, Deneb—the head of the Northern Cross. We are being led to the future through these stars of the Summer Triangle. And during the time when both the 2020 and 2053 conjunctions open their chapters in the continuous telling of the cosmic drama in which we live, they will radiate their blessings.

As the Angel Jesus, the Nathan Jesus, is the being through whom the fifth sacrifice of Christ is now taking place, we can easily imagine how profound is the call—issuing forth from the Pluto-Saturn conjunction in Sagittarius—to align ourselves with cosmic truths. In response to this call, we, too, may follow the stars to the angel-human.

The Sagittarian Centaur asks us to aim our arrows true. For as we part the curtain that has long veiled the secrets of heaven, we too will develop mastery over the rising vapors of disorder that Lucifer and Ahriman spew upward from the underworldly depths of Hades (lower Pluto): "The Greek placed

---

1 Powell and Dann, *The Astrological Revolution*, p. 150.

the Pythia over the steam clouds that rose out of the Earth and, through Lucifer and Ahriman, would bring the passions into disorder."[2]

Jesus Christ heals all that is impure, immoral, and isolated in us. When we breathe in his light, radiating from the Angel Jesus, the heavens open. As apocalyptists of our time, we can then learn how to read the cosmic script. Indeed, we live in a new era, wherein many more Christianized sibyls will appear. The dragon of Earth's sorrow is tamed each time we believe in spirit over matter, light over darkness, and love over hate. For Apollo's harp is naught but the purity of love seeking to reveal its virtue in time:

> But Apollo spread his light over Pythia and defeated the wildness of the passions. And she became a prophet. The Greek felt the Sun-spirit Apollo to be the Christ of the third Christ event. In Apollo's protection in relationship to the passion-ruling temperament of the Pythia, the Greeks saw the effect of the third sacrifice of Christ in which the human passions that were lapsing into disorder were harmonized. For the Greeks, the Sun-spirit Apollo is basically the same as what is represented in the pictures of Michael or St. George, who conquer the dragon.[3]

We have lost so much by bartering with the devil! We cannot barter with God, we can only pray that his will be done on Earth as it is in Heaven. When this prayer streams from human hearts, the world will change. We will rise out of the misery of the serpent's closed circle in celebration of the dawning of a new Sun, the Dharma Sun of the Satya Yuga. Even now its rays are cresting the horizon, and angels rejoice when human souls behold this new day. The rays of this Sun stream from the cosmic Lyre, heralding possibilities as yet unimaginable. And in whose hand does this harp rest? In the hand of Christ, at this time of his Second Coming, who speaks to us through the Angel Jesus:

> The theologians of today know nothing about this any more, but the Christian martyrs of the first period of Christianity still knew that the ancient Greek wise men, even if they did not perhaps use the name of Christ, would have known from their knowledge of the mysteries that Apollo was the great Sun-spirit, who would later live in a human being. If asked who Apollo was, they would have said that *the Sun-Spirit was ensouled in Apollo, as in an archangelic form.*[4]

The cosmic lyre has seven strings, representing the seven tones of our soul's eternal nature. As the seven come into harmony, a *new* tone resounds. This is the sound of the fifth ether, the moral ether. To this we strive, for it signals the beginning of a true Grail Quest—*to achieve the cosmological mission that has been entrusted to us as citizens of Western worlds.*

May we seek to be baptized in starlight, in wondrous flames of hope, as the Virgin and Phanes pour forth vials of love from their communion within the citadel of the Archer. Indeed, the forms of deceit may yet surrender to the discerning nobility of truth.

---

2 Steiner, *Approaching the Mystery of Golgotha*, p. 125.
3 Ibid.
4 Ibid., p. 126 (italics added).

# FIRST STEPS TOWARD A GRAIL TIMELINE
## *Joel Park*

### *Finding an Outer Limit*

When we compare the time of Christ at the beginning of our era 2,000 years ago with the time of the Holy Grail around the eighth to ninth centuries AD, the number of connecting threads creates a complicated tapestry. One of the primary common threads connecting the events of the two time periods is the special realm in which they exist—the realm in which history and myth meet and become one in a very special way. Whereas a myth is a story consisting of symbols meant to represent events in the soul or spiritual worlds, and history is a collection of mundane facts occurring on the physical plane, the events of these two time periods are both "mystical facts," to use Rudolf Steiner's parlance. The events described in the Gospels (in fact, in the Bible as a whole), as well as in the Grail legends (e.g., Wolfram von Eschenbach's *Parzival*), describe actual historical events that were heavily symbolic; we might say that, during these times, spiritual archetypes found expression on the physical plane. Unfortunately, this special unification of history and myth creates the possibility for the details of the historical element to become lost or ambiguous. With the visions of Anne Catherine Emmerich and the subsequent penetration of those visions astronomically by Robert Powell, an accurate historical and chronological picture has been crafted of the time of Jesus Christ.[1] The historical and chronological elucidation of the time of the Grail, however, is still coming into focus.

Efforts to bring this time into focus were put forth particularly by W. J. Stein in 1928, with his attempt to find both the timing and historical personalities of the Grail legend in *The Ninth Century and the Holy Grail*.[2] This massive work contains many significant findings, such as the identification of Trevrizent as Hugo de Tours. Werner Greub brought this research to the next level in his *How the Grail Sites Were Found*, by authentically discovering the geography of the Grail through a special form of clairvoyance.[3] He, too, sought to pinpoint the authentic historical personalities involved in the Grail story, with the key identification of Kyot as William of Orange. Unfortunately, what remained a mystery for both of these men (despite their best efforts), and remains a mystery, is an accurate chronology of events. Both Greub and Stein posited that the advent of Parzival becoming the Grail King took place around the middle of the ninth century (despite Steiner's clear indication that the Parzival events took place at the time of Charlemagne, at the turn of the eighth to the ninth centuries AD).[4]

Werner Greub offers substantial astrological evidence to indicate that Parzival's coronation as Grail King and the healing of Anfortas occurred on Whit Sunday, May 12, 848, during a Great Conjunction of Saturn and Jupiter in Pisces.[5] Despite the evidence supplied by Greub in support of this date, further investigation reveals that it is problematic. As Robert Powell describes on page 133 of *Journal for Star Wisdom* 2016:

> Rudolf Steiner's indication is explored in William Bento's article "Saturn in the Crab and

---

1 Powell, *Chronicle of the Living Christ*.
2 Stein, *The Ninth Century and the Holy Grail* (Forest Row, UK: Temple Lodge, 2009).
3 Greub, *How the Grail Sites Were Found*.
4 We need look no further than the first chapter of *The Ninth Century and the Holy Grail*. In the first few pages, an anecdote is related in which Rudolf Steiner repeats several times that the Parzival story occurred at the turn of the 8th to the 9th centuries AD.
5 For a full description, see Werner Greub, *How the Grail Sites Were Found*, Part One: Willehalm-Kyot, Chapter Six: Willehalm and Arabel. The entire text of this chapter can also be found at http://willehalminstitute.blogspot.com/2007/12/willehalm-and-arabel.html.

the Mysteries of the Holy Grail" in the 2005 issue of the *Christian Star Calendar*, the predecessor of *Journal for Star Wisdom*. In that article, using Rudolf Steiner's indication about the Sun and Saturn being in conjunction in the constellation of Cancer at the time of Parzival's first visit to the Grail castle, William Bento identifies the New Moon in Cancer, with Saturn close by, which took place on July 15 in the year 828, as being the heavenly configuration that Rudolf Steiner was referring to. Six planets were in Cancer on that day of the New Moon in the year 828, and the conjunction of the Sun and Moon was at exactly the same location in the zodiac where Saturn had been at Christ's crucifixion.

According to the account of Wolfram von Eschenbach in *Parzival*, it was not until some five years later (*Parzival* 799, 3) that Parzival returned to the Grail castle and became Grail king. Symbolically, it could be that Parzival became Grail king at Pentecost (Sunday, June 1) in the year 833, some five years after his first visit to the Grail castle. Here, however, is not the place to go into the details of this complex theme of the timing of the Grail events. Perhaps, though, it is important to point out the following: according to Walter Johannes Stein in his book *The Ninth Century: World History in the Light of the Holy Grail*, the historical personage called Trevrizent in the Grail story was the French Count Hugo de Tours, who was also one of Charlemagne's twelve paladins. It is known that Hugo de Tours died on October 20 in the year 837, which provides an upper limit for the dating of the Grail events. Whereas June 1, 833, lies within this limit, and is thus a possible date for when Parzival became Grail king, the date offered by Werner Greub on May 13, 848, falls after the death date of Hugo de Tours ("Trevrizent"). This date is simply too late, historically, to be the date when Parzival became Grail king, if we accept that Trevrizent was Hugo de Tours.

William Bento's solution, however, is equally problematic. Another key player in the Parzival tale, Kyot (aka William of Orange, aka St. Guilhem, aka Willehalm) died sometime between 812 and 814 (Charlemagne, too, died around this time, in 814).[6] This sets the upper limit much earlier than 837. The Grail story must have happened prior to this time; a date as late as 828 is impossible.

## The Zenith of Saturn

Another indication that William Bento is incorrect in choosing July 15, 828, as the date of Parzival's first visit to the Grail Castle (Munsalvaesche) comes from Eschenbach's own indications in the text of *Parzival*. After failing to ask the "Grail question" upon meeting the suffering King Anfortas at the first visit to Munsalvaesche, Parzival wanders for years. Eventually he encounters a hermit in the woods; unknown to either of them for a time, the hermit is Trevrizent, brother of Anfortas and Parzival's uncle. Eschenbach reports that this meeting occurs on Good Friday. Trevrizent informs Parzival that four and a half years and three days earlier, Parzival reunited the estranged couple, Jeschute and Orilus.[7] This occurred the day after his first visit to the Grail Castle. This means his first visit to Munsalvaesche was four and a half years and four days prior to Good Friday. Four and a half years prior to Good Friday never brings us to July 15 (the date proposed by William Bento); rather, it takes us to the period of Michaelmas. Eschenbach's descriptions of "summer snow" on the ground at the first visit make much more sense at Michaelmas than in July.

What inspired William Bento to look toward July, when the text clearly indicates Michaelmas? He based his timing on an indication of Rudolf Steiner that it was a "Cancer time" when Parzival visited Anfortas. In fact, Steiner's exact words

---

6 See https://en.wikipedia.org/wiki/William_of_Gellone, which lists two possible death dates for St. Guilhem: either AD May 28, 812 or May 28, 814. Robert Powell has indicated in the course of our astrosophical karma research that the earlier date is the more likely. According to most sources, Charlemagne died on Jan. 28, 814.

7 See Wolfram von Eschenbach, *Parzival*, ch. 9, p. 235. Jeschute and her husband, Orilus, became estranged after Parzival met Jeschute. Parzival had just left his mother, in fool's garb, and with fool's instructions. He greeted Jeschute with a kiss and stole her jewelry, leading her husband Orilus to believe she had been unfaithful. This is described in full in ch. 3; their reuniting in ch. 5.

are, "Saturn and the Sun stood together in Cancer, approaching culmination."[1] This, however, comes not from Steiner's spiritual insight, but from what appears to be a superficial reading of Eschenbach, as Ellen Schalk points out in her article "Kyot and the Stellar Script of Parsifal." For her, the interpretation of the word "zil" or "zenith" is the heart of the matter:

> According to Kyot-astronomy, every planet has its goal. The term *zil*—the meaning of which is the issue at hand—is referred to in contemporary astrology as "domicile" or "house." Every planet has its home or its "zil" in a certain constellation of the zodiac; the return of the planet to its "zil" describes its entry into this constellation. (Saturn requires approximately thirty years for this; its "zil" is Capricorn.)[2]

From this we see that, even if we are talking about the "domicile" of Saturn, we are also talking of Capricorn, not Cancer. However, Saturn did not enter Capricorn until 812 to 813, too late in terms of our "upper limit." Four and a half years later would take us into 816 to 818, when Kyot was no longer living. Something else must be meant by "zenith" than the domicile of the planet. What exactly is meant by *zenith,* as used by Eschenbach? It is possible that what is meant is the *exaltation* of Saturn. The points of exaltation for each of the planets are realms in the starry heavens in which they are able to exert a particularly strong influence. This is due, on the one hand, to the conjunction of the planet in question with a certain luminous star. In the case of Saturn, this is the star Zubenelgenubi, the brightest star in Libra, marking the southwestern end of the beam of the Balance at 20½° Libra.[3]

This is the fixed point of exaltation for the planet Saturn. However, another interpretation and determination of exaltation comes even closer to our search for "zenith," if we interpret this word to mean "summit." This interpretation sees the point of exaltation as determined by the maximum northerly latitude of the planet in question.[4] We can think of latitude as analogous to the path of the Sun through the course of a year: at the summer solstice, it achieves its "enthronement," its maximum northerly point. At the winter solstice, it is "imprisoned" (i.e., it has reached its southernmost point in the year). At the two equinoxes, it achieves a balance between enthronement and imprisonment. Each of the planets follows an analogous path through summer solstice (maximum northerly latitude), to autumn equinox, to winter solstice (maximum southerly latitude), to spring equinox. However, each planet has its own "year," which varies in length from the Solar year of 365.25 days. One Saturn year, for example, is equal to 29.4571 Solar years; within this time period, it has its own summer, fall, spring, and winter—in this case, it is the Saturn summer we are interested in finding.

---

1 It is important to note Steiner's choice of words in this case. He uses the word *culmination,* which is used almost exclusively in astrology to mean Midheaven. It is very unlikely that he was speaking of Saturn's declination or latitude but simply referring to a time of day when both the Sun and Saturn were more or less directly overhead. In other words, Parzival approached the Grail Castle at midday, when both Saturn and Sun were at their "high noon." It makes sense that Eschenbach would emphasize Saturn's awful effect on Anfortas when we understand it in this way; this indicates that, on a *daily* basis, Saturn would have a negative effect on Anfortas. If we understand the reference to *culmination* as referring solely to maximum northerly latitude, for example, Eschenbach directs our attention to something that occurs only once every 29.5 years. There would have been no repeated exposure to Anfortas of this baleful influence, and it would be pointless for Eschenbach to emphasize it. However, we are still left with one loose thread: *Why does Steiner refer to Cancer?* Perhaps our question should be: *Is there an astrological framework that relates the Sign of Cancer to the Midheaven?* It is my intention to investigate this question in a future article.

2 See https://sophiafoundation.org/wp-content/uploads/2017/04/kyotandthestellarscriptofparsifal.pdf.

3 Powell and Bowden, *Astrogeographia*, p. 34.

4 See Powell, *Hermetic Astrology*, vol I, ch. 1, particularly pp. 23–26. The only difference between Robert Powell's approach and my own is that he uses the heliocentric maximum northerly latitude, whereas I am referring to the geocentric maximum northerly latitude, as the heliocentric perspective was both unknown and incalculable to the peoples of the time of Eschenbach.

*First Steps toward a Grail Timeline*

## Accident of Anfortas Wounding - Geocentric/Heliocentric
At Dornach, Switzerland, Latitude 47N29', Longitude 7E37'
Date: Saturday, APR 5, 805, Julian
Time: 0: 0 pm, Local Time
Sidereal Time 1: 9:59, Vernal Point 21 ♓53'39", House System: Equal
Zodiac: Sidereal SVP, Aspect set: Conjunction/Square/Opposition

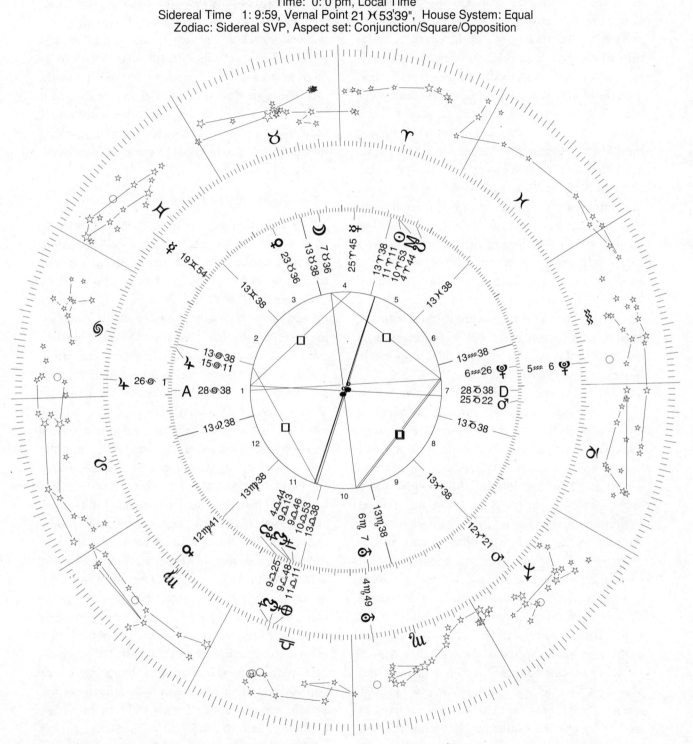

*Chart 1*

- 67 -

From here on out we will refer to the first interpretation of exaltation as the *fixed exaltation* and the second interpretation as the *moving exaltation*. How would we find the moving exaltation of Saturn in the time period of the Grail, from the turn of the eighth to the ninth centuries AD? In this case, we are concerned with the planet Saturn in the time period leading up to AD 812 (our outer limit). For the entire Saturn period (29.4571 years) prior to AD 812, the maximum northerly latitude, the "High Summer" of Saturn occurred in AD April 805, when Saturn was at 2°48' north latitude. Saturn's position in relation to the fixed stars on this date was 9°31' Libra; once again, we find an indication to look for Saturn in Libra! Looking at some of the positions of other planets around this time, particularly on April 5, 805, we find the Sun in Aries, Saturn in Libra, the Moon in Taurus, Mars in Capricorn and Jupiter in Cancer. Five of the seven classical planets were in their signs of fixed exaltation (see chart 1)![1] We will return to this remarkable date later to consider its possible significance to the Parzival saga.

However, as stated, the date of Parzival's first visit to Monsalvaesche was around Michaelmas, not in April. This means we should direct our search to the Michaelmas season in both 804 and 805 to find the day on which Parzival first met Anfortas. These are the two Michaelmas dates during which Saturn was closest to its moving exaltation (maximum northerly latitude) during the turn of the eighth to ninth centuries. Specifically, we will look for dates that are four and a half years plus four days prior to a Good Friday, paying close attention to whether Saturn and Sun stand close to each other (if not conjunct). Four and a half years forward from Michaelmas 805 takes us to the year 810, when Good Friday fell on March 29. When we cast our gaze four and half years and four days back to September 25, 805, we see Saturn at 13°18' Libra—very close to both its fixed as well as its moving exaltation. However, the Sun was 28°5' Virgo, half a sign away (see chart 2). On the other hand, looking one year earlier, Good Friday in 809 was April 6. When we look to October 2, 804, the date four and half years and four days earlier, we see Saturn and Sun within two degrees of each other. Saturn was 3°45' Libra, and the Sun was 5°19' Libra on this date (see chart 3). The latter date, then, seems to be more likely. In fact, for some time this was the date I assumed it to be, until I had investigated other astrological indications given by Eschenbach. Before looking into these other indications, a stronger foundation needs to be laid.

## From Beginning to End

Parzival's first action in Eschenbach's tale is to leave his mother, Herzeloyde (resulting in her untimely death, out of despair at losing her son), to become a knight. She has dressed him as a fool, and given him fool's instructions. This results in his assault on the Lady Jeschute, who is punished undeservedly by her husband, Orilus. They are estranged, according to Eschenbach's narrative, for "a year and more."[2] This implies that Parzival left his mother over a year before his arrival at Monsalvaesche (as stated before, it was the day after his first visit to Monsalvaesche that Orilus and Jeschute were reunited). Soon after this, he comes for the first time upon Sigune with her love the knight Schionatulander, who has just died in her arms. Then, after confronting and killing Ither at King Arthur's Court, Parzival spends two weeks training to be a knight under Gurnemanz. Upon leaving Gurnemanz, he comes to the city of Belrepeire, which is under siege. He fights for the hand of the Lady Condwiramurs, the Queen of Belrepeire, and saves the city. The two are wed at Pentecost. This implies that Parzival left home in the spring, sometime prior to Pentecost. So we know, then, that: Parzival left home in the spring; a year and a half later, at Michaelmas, he fails to ask the question; four and a half years and four days later, on Good Friday, he visits with Trevrizent.

What of the time after this? A close reading of chapters 12 through 16 of *Parzival* gives strong evidence that some sixteen days after Ascension

---

1 The primal or fixed exaltations are: Sun 19° Aries; Moon 3° Taurus; Mercury 15° Virgo; Venus 27° Pisces; Mars 28° Capricorn; Jupiter 15° Cancer; and Saturn 21° Libra.

2 See von Eschenbach, *Parzival*, ch. 3, p. 80.

*First Steps toward a Grail Timeline*

# Historic Event of FIRST GRAIL CASTLE VISIT - Geocentric/Heliocentric

At Dornach, Switzerland, Latitude 47N29', Longitude 7E37'
Date: Thursday, SEP 25, 805, Julian
Time: 2:44 pm, Local Time
Sidereal Time 15:16:30, Vernal Point 21 ♓ 53'15", House System: Equal
Zodiac: Sidereal SVP, Aspect set: Conjunction/Square/Opposition

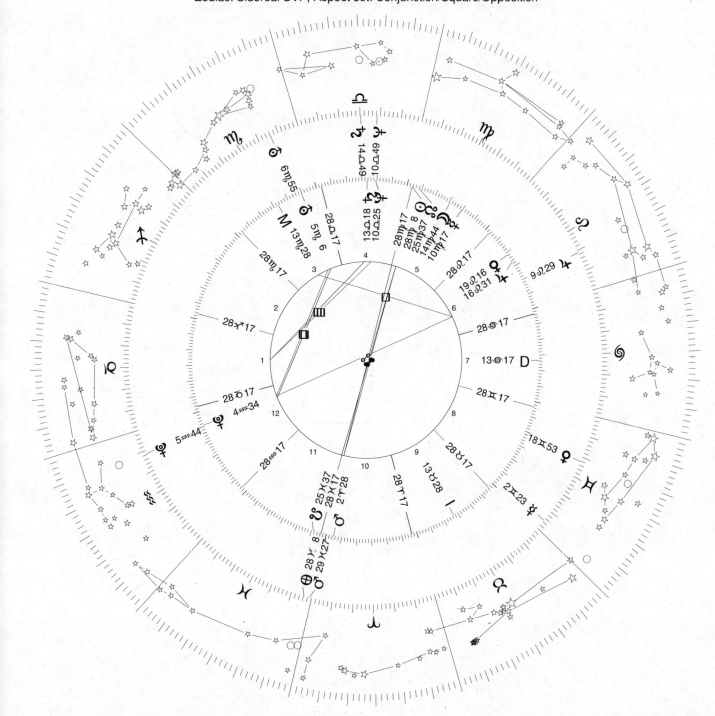

Chart 2

COSMOLOGY REBORN: STAR WISDOM, VOLUME 1

# Historic Event of FIRST GRAIL CASTLE VISIT - Geocentric/Heliocentric
At Dornach, Switzerland, Latitude 47N29', Longitude 7E37'
Date: Wednesday, OCT 2, 804, Julian
Time: 1:44 pm, Local Time
Sidereal Time 14:44:54, Vernal Point 21♓54' 4", House System: Equal
Zodiac: Sidereal SVP, Aspect set: Conjunction/Square/Opposition

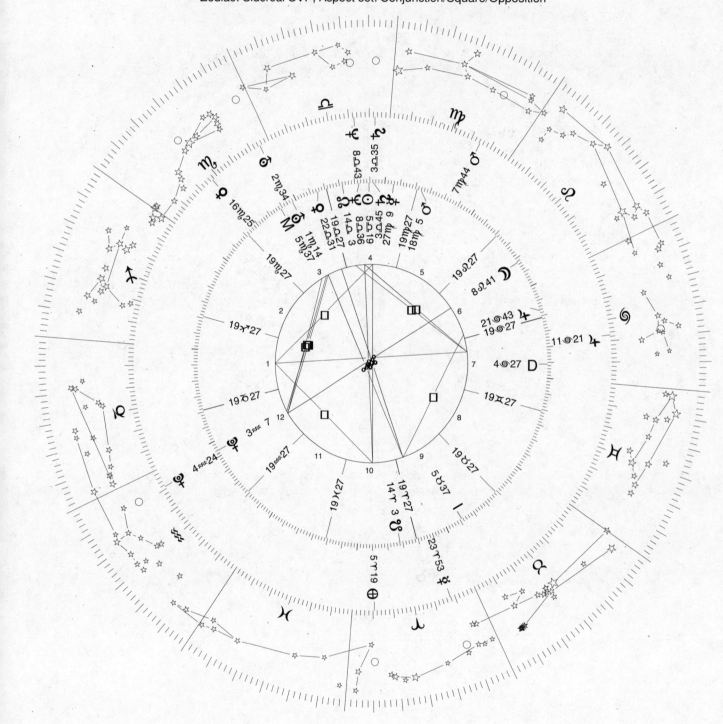

Chart 3

Thursday, Parzival is reunited with his brother Feirefiz, and the following day they journey to Monsalvaesche together. In chapter 12, the knight Gawan confronts King Gramoflanz. Gramoflanz holds a grudge against Gawan, whom he falsely believes has slain his father. He challenges Gawan to a duel to settle the score: "I myself shall appear on the field at Joflanze on the sixteenth day from today to exact payment for this Garland" (page 306). Gawan then sends a messenger to his aunt, the Queen Ginover to summon King Arthur and his troops to his assistance.

When this messenger arrives the next morning to Arthur's encampment, the Queen is kneeling at her psalter in the chapel. She later tells the messenger that it has been four and a half years and six weeks since she last saw Parzival (this was two days after he reunited Jeschute and Orilus, described in chapter 6). If Jeschute and Orilus were reunited four and a half years and *three* days prior to Good Friday, then Ginover last saw Parzival four and a half years and *one* day prior to Good Friday. Yet in the scene in question, she refers to four and a half years and six weeks, or forty-two days. This means forty-one days have elapsed since Good Friday; in other words, it is Ascension Thursday.

The duel of Gramoflanz and Gawan, then, was meant to fall fifteen days after Ascension Thursday (this day is the time period during which the events of chapter 14 of *Parzival* take place). The next day, during the events of chapter 15, Parzival confronts and is eventually reunited with his half-brother Feirefiz. The following day, seventeen days after Ascension Thursday, the two ride to Monsalvaesche together. Seventeen days after Ascension Thursday is Trinity Sunday, eight weeks from Easter Sunday. In 809, this was on June 4; in 810, it was May 26.

Putting all of this together, we see that the bulk of the story of Parzival, from the time Parzival leaves his mother to the time he becomes Grail King, covers just over six years, either from spring 803 through June 4, 809, or from spring 804 through May 26, 810. Is there any way of knowing which six-year period is correct?

## Mars or Jupiter?

> And so was it with Anfortas till the day when Parzival
> And Feirefis his brother, rode swift to Monsalvasch' hall;
> And the time was near when the planet, its course in high heaven run,
> Mars or Jupiter, glowing wrathful, its station had well-nigh won,
> And the spot whence it took its journey—Ah! then was an evil day...[1]

This quote is very mysterious. It occurs in the final chapter of *Parzival*, as Parzival and Feirefiz make their approach to Monsalvaesche. Yet once the secret of this astrological indication is unlocked, it holds the key to the question posed at the end of the previous section, as to when the particular six-year period we are looking for took place. In fact, when we begin to look at the motion of Mars and Jupiter through the same lens by which we have observed Saturn, that is, by taking note of the latitude of these planets, we begin to see the story of Parzival playing itself out in the starry heavens in harmony with the earthly events playing out below.

To reiterate: one way of understanding latitude is by looking to the Sun. The Sun achieves its high point in the heavens at the summer solstice. This is its moving exaltation, versus its fixed exaltation of 19° Aries. It then has its maximum southern point at the winter solstice, and its points of equilibrium at the two equinoxes.

A similar journey takes place for each of the planets as it progresses through its "year." As we noted above, during the Saturn "year" of 29.4571 years leading up to Kyot's death in 812, the Summer Solstice of this "year" took place in April 805. Likewise, Jupiter and Mars each has its own spring, summer, fall, and winter. The above quote refers to the course of Mars or Jupiter in high heaven being run, its station very nearly being won. One gets the impression that the "High Summer" of both planets is over; they are both approaching autumn,

---

1  von Eschenbach, *Parzival* (David Nutt, 1894), p. 166.

returning to their "stations" or balance points of the equinox. It is uncommon for both Mars and Jupiter to be approaching equinox simultaneously. Does this happen to occur in either 809 or 810?

First, consider the journey of Jupiter during the time period in question. This journey, in particular, seems to tell us the story of Parzival. On September 26, 801, Jupiter was at its maximum southerly latitude, its winter solstice, at 1°38'14" south. Its position in relation to the signs of the zodiac was 8° Aries. Here Parzival is yet withdrawn, dwelling in the naive comfort of his home with his mother, Herzeloyde. By March 15, 807, Jupiter has reached its summer solstice: 1°40'40" north, at 20° Virgo. This is analogous to Parzival's complete loss as to his identity, his spirituality, and his destiny, after his failure to ask the question. The time in between, around June 804 when Jupiter was in Gemini, represents the spring equinox of Jupiter. As the growing plant begins to emerge from the earth in complete fresh innocence, so Parzival, around this time, emerged from the loving arms of his mother in complete foolishness.

The closing of this Jupiter year occurred September 6, 812, when Jupiter again reached its maximum southerly latitude of 1°39'42" south, this time at 5° Pisces. The time, then, when Jupiter would have run its course in high heaven and "won its station," coming to its fall equinox, would have been somewhere around June of 810, when Jupiter was in Sagittarius. The Prodigal Son, coming to the other side of his foolishness and ignorance, returns home transformed by his journey. Jupiter's path argues strongly, therefore, that the six-year period lies between "Jupiter spring" 804 and "Jupiter autumn" 810.

What of the path of Mars? Mars has a shorter year than that of Jupiter. Whereas a Jupiter "year" is equal to 11.86 solar years, a Mars year is only 1.88 solar years. Therefore, four Mars years took their course between 803 and 811. We will focus specifically on the time around spring 804, to see if there was a "Mars spring" occurring, and the time around spring 810, to see if there was a "Mars autumn," each occurring simultaneously with the "Jupiter spring" and "Jupiter autumn."

Mars achieved its maximum southerly latitude on July 21, 803, at 6°42'7" south, at 15° Capricorn. By June 29, 804, it had achieved a maximum northerly latitude of 1°10'6" at 17° Cancer. Therefore, around January 804, Mars was approaching its spring equinox. Certainly, then, if we look to March and April 804 as the time when Parzival set out on his quest, we could classify both Jupiter and Mars as experiencing the springtime of their respective years.

Mars achieved maximum northerly latitude again on January 5, 810 at 4°5'33" north, 27° Gemini. By February 18, 811, it reached its maximum southerly latitude of 1°5'55" south at 13° Aquarius. The fall equinox between this summer and winter would have occurred around July 810. Once again, we can see that it would not be inappropriate to describe both Mars and Jupiter as experiencing the autumn of their years on May 26, 810, Trinity Sunday.

If we accept this interpretation of the indicated movement of Jupiter and Mars, the time period 803 to 809 is ruled out, while the time period 804 to 810 seems much more likely to be that of the story of Parzival. We can now attempt a summary.

## Approaching a Timeline

**Spring 804:** Parzival leaves home. His mother, Herzeloyde, dies after his departure. He disturbs the relationship of Jeschute and Orilus, and comes upon his cousin Sigune and her dead love Schionatulander. He kills Ither at King Arthur's Court, and lives for a time under the tutelage of Gurnemanz.

**May 21 804 (Whitsun):** Parzival rescues Belrepeire and Queen Condwiramurs, taking her hand in marriage. They have two sons together (implying he is with her for at least a year).[1]

**April 805:** Here Saturn reaches its moving exaltation, and the Sun, the Moon, Mars, and Jupiter all approach their fixed (or archetypal) exaltations (see chart 1). It is very likely that it was around this time that the Lance wounded Anfortas. Estelle Isaacson indicates in her book *The Grail Bearer*

---
1  See von Eschenbach, *Parzival*, ch. 4, p. 116, for the reference to Whitsun.

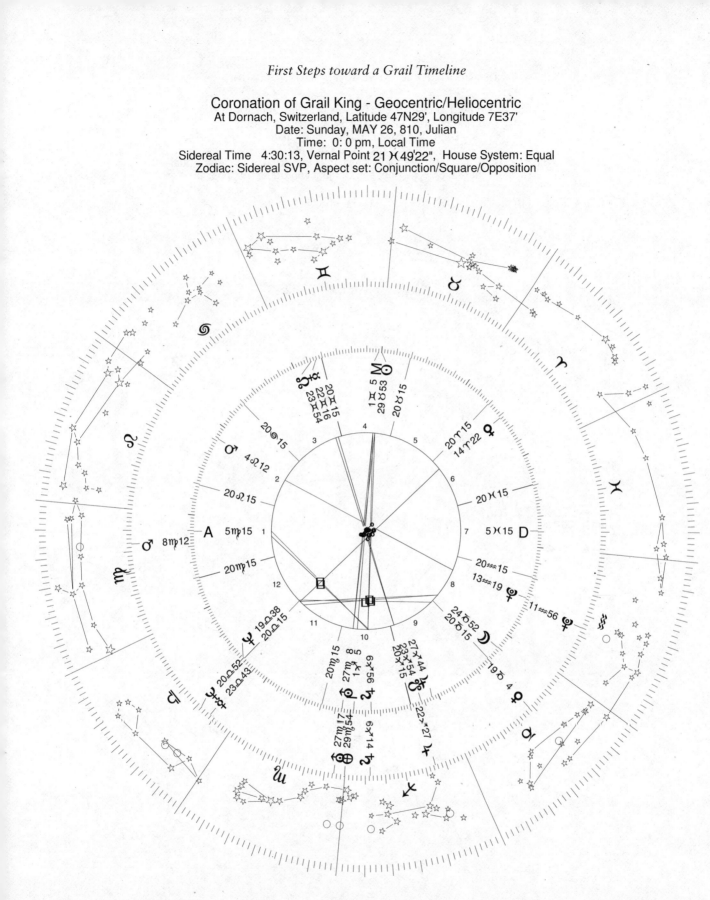

Chart 4

# Cosmology Reborn: Star Wisdom, Volume 1

## Birth of Tycho Brahe (V. ^) - Geocentric/Heliocentric
At Knudstrup, Latitude 55N59', Longitude 13E05'
Date: Tuesday, DEC 14, 1546, Julian
Time: 10:53 am, Local Time
Sidereal Time 17: 1:46, Vernal Point 11♓34'40", House System: Equal
Zodiac: Sidereal SVP, Aspect set: Conjunction/Square/Opposition

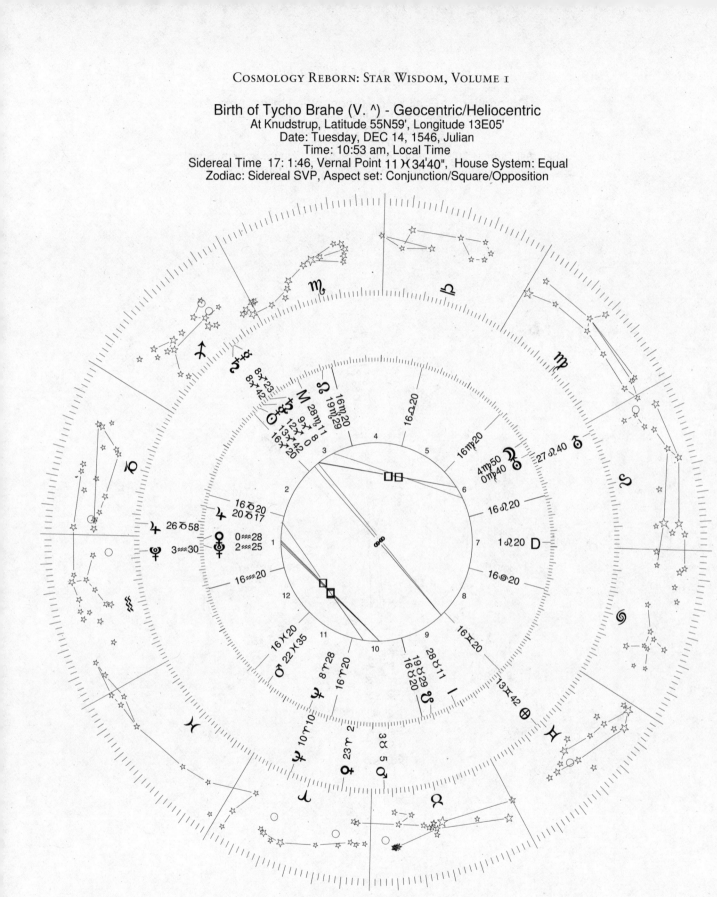

*Chart 5*

that this occurred in the late winter or early spring, shortly before Parzival set out on his quest that would lead him to the Grail King.[1]

**September 25, 805:** Parzival, who has recently left Condwiramurs in search of adventure, stumbles upon Monsalvaesche. He fails to ask the question (see chart 2). The next day, he reunites Jeschute and Orilus. Soon after this, he confronts the Knights of the Round Table, and is made to feel the shame of his actions by Cundrie. He wanders for many years.

**March 29, 810 (Good Friday):** Parzival comes upon the hermit Trevrizent (his uncle) and learns of the true nature of the Grail and of his mission. He stays with him for a time and sets out with a repentant fervor to make good out of his errors.

**May 26, 810 (Festival of the Holy Trinity):** Parzival and Feirefiz ride to Monsalvaesche. Parzival heals Anfortas, becoming the Grail King. Feirefiz weds Repanse de Schoye (see chart 4, page 73).[2]

Through Astrosophy, we may be able to narrow the date of Parzival's departure even further. Herzeloyde reincarnated as Tycho Brahe in the sixteenth century. Schionatulander, who must have died within a few days of Herzeloyde based on Eschenbach's narrative in chapter 3, reincarnated subsequently as Thomas Aquinas and Rudolf Steiner. Hypothetically, comparing the death horoscope of Herzeloyde and birth horoscope of Tycho Brahe on the one hand, and the death horoscope of Schionatulander and birth horoscope of Rudolf Steiner on the other, at least one of Robert Powell's rules of reincarnation ought to be fulfilled. Can we find a date in late winter, early spring 804, that would, for example, fulfill the rule of reincarnation concerning the angular relationship of the Sun and Saturn for both of these individualities?[3]

At Tycho Brahe's birth on December 14, 1546, the Sun stood at 13°42' Sagittarius, while Saturn stood at 9°8' Sagittarius. This is an angular separation of 4°34', which is equivalent to 175°26' (180° - 4°34' = 175°26'; see chart 5). On the day of Rudolf Steiner's birth, February 25, 1861, the Sun stood at 14°33' Aquarius, while Saturn stood at 13°14' Leo. This is an angular separation of 178°41', which is equivalent to 1°19' (180°−178°41' = 1°19'; see chart 6, page 76). Therefore, we should be looking for a time period during which the Sun and Saturn were either close to conjunct (only a few degrees separated) or else close to opposition (only a few degrees shy of 180°). For the year 804, this applies to more or less the entire month of March, during which the Sun was in Pisces and Saturn in Virgo. This would further corroborate the claim that Parzival left Herzeloyde (resulting in her death) in late winter to early spring.

### The Life of Kyot

One of Werner Greub's greatest contributions to Grail research was his identification of the mysterious Kyot as the historical personality St. William (Guilhem) of Gellone. Unfortunately, at the time he made his discovery, less was known about the biography of St. William. Werner Greub was under the impression that he lived between the years 770 to 850, leading to the erroneous identification of the 840s as the time period of the Grail story. In reality, St. William was born around 755 and very likely died on May 28, 812 (it is possible, but astrosophically unlikely, that he died May 28, 814).

There are many remarkable legends associated with the life of St. William. One remarkable piece of his life story involves his decision to retire from

---

1 Isaacson, *The Grail Bearer*, ch. 17, p. 176, and ch. 18, p. 186.

2 It is significant that at the first meeting of Parzival and Anfortas on Sept. 25, 805, the Sun was at 28° Virgo, within a few degrees of its position at the baptism of Christ in the River Jordan, while at the second meeting of Parzival and Anfortas, the Sun was at 29° Taurus, within a few degrees of its position at the first Whitsun. The tale of Parzival retraces, in a metamorphosed way, the path from the start of Christ's ministry on Sept. 23, 29, to its end on May 24, 33.

3 The First Rule of Reincarnation states that the angular relationship (aspect) between the Sun and Saturn at an individual's birth is the same as—or is the complement of—that at death in his or her previous incarnation. This Rule also manifests itself as an alignment of Sun–Sun, Sun–Saturn, or Saturn–Sun, between death in one incarnation and birth in a subsequent incarnation.

# Cosmology Reborn: Star Wisdom, Volume 1

## Birth of Rudolf Steiner (V. ^) - Geocentric/Heliocentric
At Kraljavec/Yugoslavia, Latitude 46N22', Longitude 16E39'
Date: Monday, FEB 25, 1861, Gregorian
Time: 11:26 pm, Local Time
Sidereal Time 9:48:40, Vernal Point 7♓11'52", House System: Equal
Zodiac: Sidereal SVP, Aspect set: Conjunction/Square/Opposition

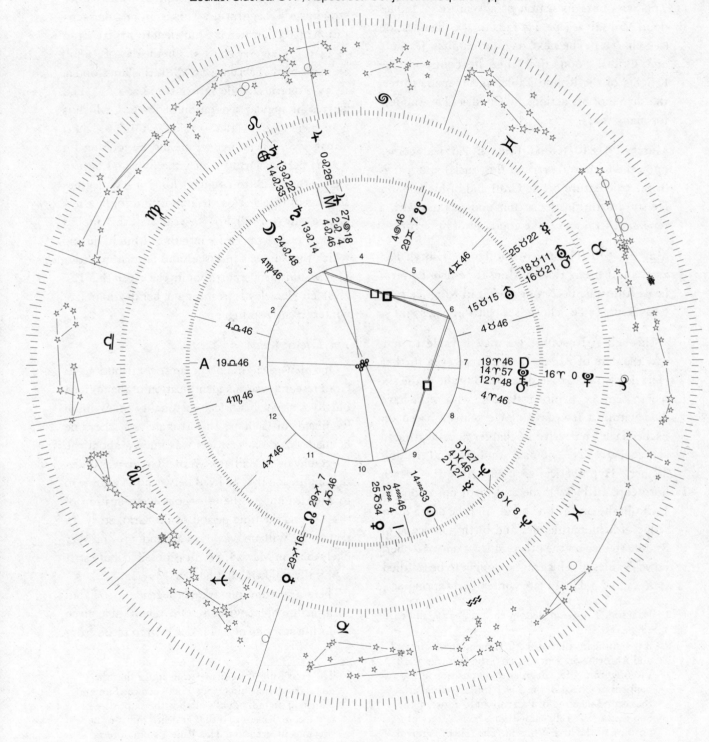

Chart 6

a life of warfare under the service of Charlemagne to establish a monastery, Saint-Guilhem-le-Désert. What is very interesting for our purposes is the time period during which he decided to make this transition. After his last great campaign with Louis the Pious in 801, during which they captured Barcelona from the Moors, William founded the abbey in Gellone in 804. William bestowed upon the abbey a piece of the True Cross of Christ, which he had received from Charlemagne, who in turn had been gifted the piece of the Cross from the Patriarch of Jerusalem. After two years of working on establishing the abbey, William retired there in the year 806, after the death of his wife, Arabel.[1] It was this same Arabel whom he met and married while in captivity in the 790s, and who introduced him to the ancient star wisdom of Flegetanis.[2]

It is no coincidence that the year that Parzival left home (AD 804) was the same year that St. William/Kyot began to establish his monastery, completely changing the course of his career. According to the visions of Estelle Isaacson in *The Grail Bearer*, Parzival spends time training with Kyot at some point between 805 and 810, just around the time that Arabal dies and Kyot retires to the abbey permanently.[3] Just as Kyot is the spiritual guide and inspiration of Eschenbach in the penning of the story of Parzival, one gets the impression that the actions of Kyot behind the scenes, as it were, are intimately related to the course of events in the story of Parzival, guiding them into their true course via star wisdom.

William/Kyot's journey with the Grail Family is a more than thirty-year journey; in fact, one might wonder if it was a span of about 33⅓ years (from about 779 to 812) that Kyot spent weaving in and out of the lives of this mythical family. On what basis do we make such a claim?

According to tradition,[4] Parzival was about fifteen years old, quite young, when he set out on his foolish quest. This would place his birth around 789. According to Eschenbach, he was conceived in May, and so assuming a normal gestation period, his birthday would be in February.[5] One might wonder if he was born February 14, 789, during a conjunction of Saturn and Jupiter in Pisces (see chart 7, page 78). The two planets would have been remembering the Star of the Magi, an aspect of great importance to the karmic threads tying together the various individualities in the story of the Grail.

According to Estelle Isaacson, Parzival's cousin, Sigune, was around nine years old when Parzival was born.[6] This would place her birthdate around 780. Sigune and Parzival were cousins on their mothers' sides; Herzeloyde, Parzival's mother, was the sister of Schoysiane, Sigune's mother. Schoysiane had the esteemed position of Grail Bearer in her youth, until she met the young Kyot and the two fell in love. She was relieved of her duty as Grail Bearer so the two could be wed, and her older sister, Repanse de Schoye, took over the role of Bearer. When Parzival arrives years later to the Grail Castle, it is the same Repanse de Schoye who is the caretaker and Bearer of the Grail.

Shortly after marrying Kyot, Schoysiane became pregnant with Sigune. Tragically, she died giving birth to her. Again, this must have been around 780; hence, we can assume that Kyot's relationship to the Grail Family (in particular Schoysiane) began shortly before this time—possibly in 779.

It was after this time period that Kyot set out on his many campaigns to drive the Saracens out of Christendom. In the 780s, he became the Count of Toulouse; in the 790s, he was under captivity and married Arabel (also known as Giburc). Through Arabel, he came into contact with the mysterious astronomer Flegetanis, who introduced Kyot to the ancient Star Wisdom. When Kyot returned home with Arabel, after twenty years of campaigning for Charlemagne, he had a spiritual experience with the True Cross, and decided to serve penance for all the lives he had taken by setting up a monastery specifically enlisting former knights to find a path of peace in the monastic life. He moved to his

---

1   See https://en.wikipedia.org/wiki/William_of _Gellone.
2   See http://willehalminstitute.blogspot.com/2007/12 /willehalm-and-arabel.html.
3   See Estelle Isaacson, *The Grail Bearer*, part 5.
4   See https://fr.wikipedia.org/wiki/Perceval.

5   See von Eschenbach, *Parzival*, ch. 2, pp. 58–60.
6   See Isaacson, *The Grail Bearer*, ch. 11, pp. 95–97.

COSMOLOGY REBORN: STAR WISDOM, VOLUME 1

## Birth of PARZIVAL - Geocentric/Heliocentric
At Toledo, Spain, Latitude 39N53', Longitude 4W2'
Date: Saturday, FEB 14, 789, Julian
Time: 7:40 pm, Local Time
Sidereal Time 5:33:45, Vernal Point 22 ♓ 7' 6", House System: Equal
Zodiac: Sidereal SVP, Aspect set: Conjunction/Square/Opposition

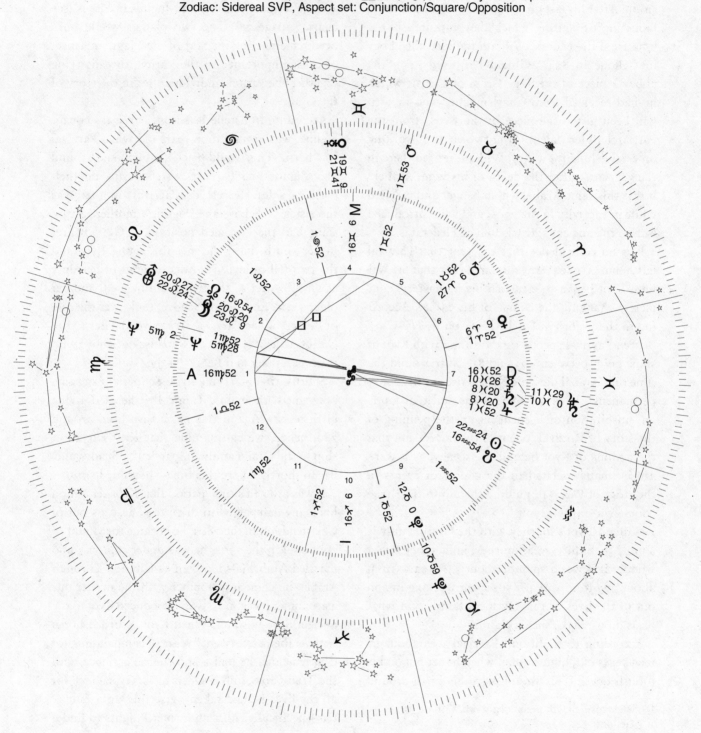

Chart 7

monastery, Saint-Guilhem-le-Désert, permanently after the death of Arabel in 806.[1]

We can now further flesh out the timeline given:

**About 779–780:** Kyot weds Schoysiane, who dies giving birth to Sigune. Repanse de Schoye becomes the Bearer of the Grail.

**789 (possibly Feb. 14):** Herzeloyde gives birth to Parzival. Kyot becomes Count of Toulouse and sets out on various campaigns against the Saracens.

**790s: Kyot** is under captivity. He meets and marries Arabel, who introduces him to the star wisdom of Flegetanis.

**801–806: Kyot** goes on his final campaign against the Saracens. He has a transformative experience with the True Cross and founds Saint-Guilhem-le-Désert. He trains Parzival in the ways of knighthood. He retires to the monastery after the death of Arabel.

Just as Kyot is invisibly telling the story of Parzival through Eschenbach, one begins to get the impression that important events in the Parzival story have been shaped and determined by actions of Kyot behind the scenes. In fact, a good portion of the visions of Estelle Isaacson recorded in *The Grail Bearer* fill in the gaps in the narrative of Eschenbach (the missing years between 804 and 810), and it is indicated when Parzival meets Kyot that he is only just initiating his monastery. On the other hand, Estelle Isaacson's second book of Grail visions fills in the time period prior to Kyot meeting the Grail family.[2]

This timeline is just a beginning, a scratching of the surface. Based on the experience of greater researchers than I, it could in fact be partially or completely incorrect! What it should be is an encouragement to readers to continue to seek for the Truth. The visionary retellings of the original Grail story and the life of Christ should be refashioned accurately before the eyes of the soul, a process of "lunar imagining," leading to "solar thinking" and "zodiacalized willing," per the indications of the anonymous author of *Meditations on the Tarot*.[3]

## The Modern Grail Story

Two questions arise in the aftermath of this research. We might ask in what way (if any) does the chronology of the Grail Story relate to our time? Following up from this, we might wonder what this might indicate spiritually for this moment in human history? In this regard, there are a few key points of orientation. The first is the movement of Saturn in the heavens, specifically the journey from Libra into Sagittarius that Saturn took between the two visits of Parzival to the Grail Castle in 805 and 810. Has this journey recapitulated in recent times? The second point of orientation has to do with the beginning of the Cosmic Temptation in the Wilderness, which began according to Robert Powell's research around October 5, 869, with the Eighth Ecumenical Council.[4] The third point of orientation has to do with the start of the Age of the Consciousness Soul, which takes its course during the 2,160 years from 1414 to 3574. It is very enlightening to take the starting year of this time period, 1414, as a mirror, to see how events happening after 1414 are a reflection of what was happening an equivalent amount of time prior to 1414.

To begin with, however, we will allow our gaze to fall on the entire time period encompassing the life of Charlemagne (742–814), until the time of the Eighth Ecumenical Council in 869, a 127-year period. What was happening, spiritually, in Europe during this time? From Rome in the South came the influence of the Petrine Catholic Church, which would gradually come to dominate the creation of external European culture. In the East, there was gradually developing the Johannine Church, the Byzantine Orthodox Church. Here we find a type of Christianity that is more inward,

---

1 St. Guillaume's will mentions a third wife, Cunegunde, with whom he had several children; see https://fr.wikipedia.org/wiki/Guillaume_de_Gellone.
2 Isaacson, *The Younger Kyot*.
3 See Anon., *Meditations on the Tarot*, 12th Letter-Meditation.
4 The Cosmic Temptation in the Wilderness from 869 to 2047 has been described by Robert Powell and others. See, for example, Powell and Dann, *Christ and the Maya Calendar*, ch. 2.

devotional, and mystical than that which was cultivated in Rome. And from the West, from Britain, there came the influence of Celtic Christianity—the Grail Christianity that could be characterized as Pauline.[1] Considering the karmic background of Charlemagne, who was St. Paul in his previous incarnation, this seems quite appropriate.

Charlemagne lived on the balance point of the development of European culture. With Kyot–St. William as his main paladin, and with an individuality such as Alcuin of York[2] as one of the leading scholars of the Carolingian Court, the first half of his adult life saw a great influence of Pauline Christianity pouring into him, and through him, into the rest of Europe. After he became Emperor at the turn of the 8th to the 9th centuries, and increasingly under the rule of his son Louis the Pious after Charlemagne's death in 814, the sphere of influence on Europe became increasingly Petrine. Werner Greub has characterized John Scotus Eriugena as the last of the Celtic Christian Scholars; with his passing in 877 and the Eighth Ecumenical Council in 869, we might say that the door was shut upon any integration of the three Christian streams of Peter, John, and Paul.[3]

We can see these three streams in relation to the characterization of East, West, and middle by Rudolf Steiner in his lecture "Cosmogony, Freedom, Altruism," October 10, 1919.[4] The East, including Russia, has the task of bringing a true Altruism, a religious feeling of brotherly and sisterly devotion into the world. We can see this in relation to the deeply devotional religion of Johannine Christianity; in our time, this has particularly come to expression in the Russian Sophiologists, such as Vladimir Solovyov. For the middle, for Europe, the mission is the development of a true philosophical understanding of Freedom. We can see this in relationship to the Petrine Christianity that expressed itself at its pinnacle in the philosophy of the Scholastics (reborn, in a modern form, in Rudolf Steiner's *Philosophy of Freedom*), but also in the medieval cultures that built the cathedrals out of a free expression of soul. Finally, the mission of the Anglo-American West is to develop a true cosmogony and cosmology, by crossing the abyss into spiritual perception. It is this element that was laid to rest over the course of the eighth and ninth centuries. The Grail Christianity that came from Britain was Christianity aware of the stars, of the cosmic origin and destiny of Humanity. It is this Pauline Christianity that has yet to properly develop—and until it does, the split between Petrine Catholicism (Europe) and Johannine Orthodoxy (Russia) cannot be healed.

If we take 1414 as a mirror, and look to the year 869, we find that this year is 545 years prior. When we cast our gaze 545 years forward from 1414, we come to the year 1959. We could think of the 55 years between 814 (the death of Charlemagne) and 869 as the gradual death of the Pauline Christianity, and hence the gradual divorce of East from West, and Soul from Spirit, that became set in stone at the 8th Ecumenical Council in 869. Correspondingly, we could look at the fifty-five years between 1959 and 2014 as the gradual *resurrection* of this dead Grail Christianity, and the gradual reopening of the possibility of renewal of the whole Church: East, West, and Middle.

---

1 See "Cosmogony, Freedom, Altruism" in this issue of *Star Wisdom*.

2 Alcuin of York lived from 735 to May 19, 804. During the 780s and '90s, he was a prominent figure in the Carolingian Court. "This early Christianity of the Gospel of John, which in the first Christian centuries had come to Ireland through Spain, had gained a strong foothold there. West and central Europe were at that time Christianised by monks coming from Ireland. Alcuin was the most outstanding representative of this Celtic Christianity at Charlemagne's Court. He was a master of the seven liberal arts and regarded these arts as the pillars for developing a true philosophy of Christianity. He furthered speech training and scientific-practical theology and as such prepared the way for the scholastics" (http://willehalminstitute.blogspot.com/2007/12/willehalm-and-arabel.html).

3 "The last professor of this Celtic line at the Court School was Johannes Scotus Erigena, who was opposed, denounced, and murdered by those on the side of the Petrine Christians. After Erigena died, the Frankish Court became Roman, and the Court School, which under Alcuin could still be compared with the Palace School of Baghdad, lost its fame and glory" (ibid.). John Scotus Eriugena lived 815 to 877.

4 Steiner, *Understanding Society through Spiritual-Scientific Knowledge*.

It is interesting to note that the 1950s saw the beginning of the publication of Willi Sucher's major works, and 1960 was the year that Valentin Tomberg began to pen his *Meditations on the Tarot*. Starting from the 1970s, up until the present day, it became Robert Powell's task to harmonize the complementary expressions of Grail Christianity brought forth by these two authors in the forms of Astrosophy and Christian Hermeticism. The year 2014, as a reflection of the death year of Charlemagne in 814, saw the baptismal descent of Kalki Avatar into his vessel, the Maitreya Bodhisattva, marking the beginning of this individuality's work in the twenty-first century. Robert Powell spent most of his life prying a door that now stands open wide for those who can find it. The true Pauline Christianity can begin to flow into and reunite the Petrine and Johannine.

Finally, what about the path of Saturn during the time of the Grail, from 13° Libra on September 25, 805, to 6° Sagittarius on May 26, 810? This is an approximately fifty-six-month period. When has Saturn traversed this same path in modern times? Saturn journeyed this way over a similar fifty-six-month period, from April 28, 2013, through January 5, 2018. The starting time of April 28, 2013, when Saturn was once again at 13° Libra, fell just over one month before the date of Ahriman's incarnation into his vessel, which according to Robert Powell occurred June 19, 2013.[5] The ending time of January 5, 2018, when Saturn was once again at 6° Sagittarius, fell precisely at the end of the thirty-ninth Cosmic Day of Temptation, the end of humanity's collective Ahrimanic Temptation. The Grail Crisis of our time manifested in the form of the confrontation of humanity with the incarnation of Ahriman! It is very interesting that a modern Orthodox Biblical scholar, David Bentley Hart, has made the case that the essence of the Gospel preached by Paul in his epistles is that of *spiritual warfare*.[6] From the beginning, Paul's mission has been related to Grail Knighthood.

Moreover, 2018 holds a particular place in relation to the year 1414; it is precisely 604 years after 1414. The year 810, when Parzival healed Anfortas and became Grail King, was 604 years prior to 1414. This means that 2018 recapitulated the healing of Anfortas, both in terms of the path of Saturn remembering 810 and in terms of the mirroring of 810 via 1414.

It is only now, since 2018, that the modern Grail story can really begin to unfold. In fact, it is possible that the 56 months *after* January 5, 2018 (inasmuch as they mirror the time period from September 25, 805 through May 26, 810) offer the opportunity for a redemptive force to come into action to counterbalance what occurred between April 28, 2013 and January 5, 2018 (the fifty-six-month period from the ninth century as remembered by the path of Saturn). Those of us who have "eyes to see and ears to hear" can assist the work of the angels in restoring the spiritual wasteland left in the wake of Ahriman's incarnation as we look toward September 2022.

Above and beyond that relatively near future, over the course of the next thirty years in particular we have the opportunity to create a Grail Knighthood guided by a true Cosmosophy—to work toward accomplishing the mission of America and of bringing Europe–Peter and Russia–John back into healthy relationship. Why the next thirty years? On the one hand, the year 779, when Kyot's relationship to the Grail Family began, is reflected via the mirror of 1414 in the year 2049. On the other hand, this last Cosmic Day of Temptation—when we have the opportunity of being ministered unto by Angels, of aligning our thinking, feeling, and willing with that of Angels in a more conscious way than was previously possible for humanity—this last Day carries on until the year 2047. Therefore, the next thirty years is our window for cultivating and manifesting a threefold Christianity of Paul, Peter, and John and for cultivating the threefold global culture of Cosmogony, Freedom, and Altruism.

---

5  Powell and Isaacson, *Gautama Buddha's Successor*, p. 27.

6  See https://aeon.co/ideas/the-gospels-of-paul-dont-say-what-you-think-they-say.

# HEALING MIRACLES
## *The Destiny Task of Our Time*
### Estelle Isaacson

*Editor's Note: Estelle brought forth the following message when Sirius and Pluto were in exact opposition to each other, and Saturn was in Sagittarius (2½°), conjunct its position at the healing of the man born blind. As Pluto is currently in Sagittarius, and Sirius is found across the heavens in Gemini, this teaching will resound throughout the coming year. The "being" speaking to her, and to those there assembled, asked that we practice the art of reading the stellar script to gain wisdom. This reminds us that it is the desire of the starry beings that we receive such wisdom as sustenance for our souls, especially at this tumultuous period in world history.*

We were asked to turn our mind's eye to the star Sirius, and imagine that the light radiating from this star can enlighten and awake our own third eye. For, through this starlight, we may see more clearly the truth that we must behold at this particular time.

It was clearly expressed that we are now being asked to behold the world-evil and name it, as we stand with Sirius, allowing this star's light to flow into us. And, at the same time, we are to keep our gaze on the fact that Pluto stands opposite this mighty star, reminding us of the divine love of the Father.

**Message:** We are to keep our faith certain and pure so that we may maintain an open and loving heart. Yes, we must be able to behold the truth now, when the world is heaving lies everywhere we look.

There are times when evil is hidden and completely cloaked. This can cause us to become passive and complacent. There are other times, however, when through the aid of the starry beings we are able to unveil the mystery of evil—beholding what evil is doing in our world and yet not faint in this beholding. To do this with understanding of what we are witnessing, we need the assistance of spiritual beings, for they support us as we come to understand the mystery of evil.

At the time of the Second Coming there will come to pass seven healing miracles just as there were seven healing miracles performed by Christ during the time of his First Coming.

One of these healing miracles may be especially invoked at this time (when Sirius is ascending and concurrently Saturn is in Sagittarius). At the First Coming, Christ healed the man born blind when the Sun was 2½° Sagittarius. Saturn is drawing very near the exact remembrance of this healing. Thus we may now receive wisdom regarding this miracle and how it will manifest anew during the time of the Second Coming.

The sixth of the seven healing miracles, the healing of the man born blind, will manifest as an opening of the third eye on a vast scale, in which the words written by the Revelator shall come to pass: "*Every eye shall see him.*" Further, in the New Testament it is written that when we see him *we will become like him.* For, when we behold Christ in his Second Coming we shall be in a process of coming closer to him. With purified hearts we behold Him, and our spiritual eye then opens as a seeing organ of the purified heart.

We will begin to use our eyes in the way Christ uses his eyes. We will then begin to truly see, beholding the world as He beholds it. We will have reclaimed our sense of sight from the Fall. All of the senses have fallen, not just sight. Our senses, for the most part, are no longer used in the manner that was originally ordained. We must, through Christ, regain our true sight. We have lost this true sight over time and therefore the gift of sight has become misused.

Christ sees truly, with bright clarity, all that is! He is not afraid to behold the evil in the world. He asks us to look through his eyes. Just as he restored sight to the man born blind 2,000 years ago, now *all* of humanity is in need of true sight if we are to make it through the trials which now face us.

Our sight must become more like His if we are to see the truth. Only in the clear knowing of the truth are we able to then speak the truth, through which we will have real impact on the world situation. The blind man once healed, began to proclaim the miracle to everyone who would listen. His heart was filled with joy and wonder. Consequently, he drew the attention of the authorities who wanted to stop him from proclaiming the miracle of his healing. The ones who know the truth light up like a flame, which shines a great light. They attract both those who are ready to see the truth, as well as those who fear the truth—for they have grown comfortable living in the lie.

The lighthouse can guide ships through storms, and we become lighthouses when the truth streams out from our hearts. Yet, those who hate the truth, and who are disturbed by it, may instead crash against the rocks, being tossed to and fro in storms of confusion.

Most of us do not like to disturb others, nor do we want to make great changes in our lives, therefore we may block ourselves from seeing the truth. The blind man only wanted to say *"Look, the miracle has happened! I see, and it was through the power of the Word that this man Jesus spoke, that I was healed. Go and find him that you also may be healed."*

Likewise, if we are to receive a greater sight that we might know the truth, we must be able to direct all who seek and question to the One who shall appear in red robes of victory. It was he who performed the miracles during the First Coming. Now it is "Christ in us" who shall perform the miracles of the Second Coming. Our will aligned with his will brings about *new* miracles.

If we consecrate our eyes to Christ, our eyes shall be made holy, and we will not abuse them by subjecting them to that which denigrates and destroys. We will offer up our sight to the hierarchies who need to see *through* us the human predicament. As we do this, our capacity for truth, for *spiritual* sight, will increase.

When we consciously behold beauty in other human beings, we are calling forth their star. Our gaze becomes softened and our ability to uphold beauty in the world increases. We can become knights of beauty!

Satan has a plan to destroy true beauty both in human beings and in the world. He intends our sight to become so greatly dimmed, that we would no longer want to see at all. This does not have to come to pass, but it is the evil one's desire that our sight fall even further into his wretched realm, causing us to desire blindness to escape the ugliness.

The antidote to this is to use our sight to take in the beauty all around us. Beauty has her servants. They are angelic beings who love to increase beauty. They do this in joy. True beauty is under attack. True beauty chases away the demons.

When we behold beauty, we aid in its increase and we heal ourselves as well as nature and other human beings—or whatever it is that we behold in beauty.

The man born blind is a special individuality, who will work to bring this miracle to pass during the time of the Second Coming. The miracle wherein every eye will see, and every tongue confess, and every knee will bow in awe of the glory of Christ in his victorious red robes of the Second Coming.

Do not be afraid of the evil one. Cast the knowing glance and name the evil. Then heal your eyes by offering that which you have seen to the spiritual hierarchies. Practice seeing the world through the eyes of Christ, through his soft and loving gaze, which at the same time is ever so piercing.

To be pierced by his gaze is to be transformed. He will transform the world through his piercing gaze. Nothing escapes his compassionate gaze. Nothing!

Beloved disciples of the truth, you are sincere seekers. Your questions are a blessing to the angels. Your questions are strengthening for the angelic realm. Through questions your *spiritual sight* is prepared for a great opening. Your questions shall lead you to the truth. In this you are blessed.

# AMERICAN COSMOGONY
*Retrospects and Prospects*

*Kevin Dann, PhD*

THE YERKES TELESCOPE.
Clear Aperture of Objective, 40 inches.
Photographed by S. W. Burnham at World's Columbian Exposition.

## Prodigies

On August 23, 1893, when astronomer and telescope maker Alvan Graham Clark spoke of 15-inch refracting telescopes having, in the 1840s, been considered "monsters," his audience surely appreciated the irony. Over the heads of the hundred or so astronomers and physicists gathered to hear Clark's "Great Telescopes of the Future" address loomed the Yerkes Telescope, its 40-inch refracting lens (built by Clark's firm) set at the end of a fifty-five-foot-long steel tube which stood upon a thirty-foot-high pedestal. Monstrously large American flags were draped all along the walls of the gargantuan Liberal Arts and Manufactures Building, one of dozens erected seemingly overnight on the grounds of the World's Columbian Exposition, the largest world's fair ever held. The enormous scope of the Exposition delayed the opening until a year after 1892, the 400th anniversary of Christopher Columbus's voyage to the New World. Chicago, like America, was itself a prodigy; a tiny frontier village of two hundred people at its founding in 1833, it had grown to over a million in 1890.

Astronomy's salient presence at the World's Fair was thanks to the Chicago-born scientific prodigy George Ellery Hale. Elected Fellow of the Royal Astronomical Society at age twenty-three for his invention of the spectroheliograph and his study of solar prominences, Hale at age twenty-four had been hired in 1892 as assistant professor at the University of Chicago. The Yerkes Telescope was the first of four times that Hale would build the largest telescope in the world; his last, the Hale Telescope at Palomar Observatory, remains the world's largest refracting telescope. Young Hale had singlehandedly organized the Congress of Astronomy and Astro-physics at the Exposition, having written hundreds of invitation letters to scientists from all over the globe.[1]

The year-and-a-half leading up to the Congress had been a prodigious one for astronomy. January to December 1892, twenty-seven new planetoids were discovered by photographic methods. January 23 to 30, a new star of magnitude 4.5, Nova Aurigae, was discovered. February 11, a record large cluster of sunspots extending over 150,000 miles of longitude reached the Sun's central meridian. August,

---

[1] For a description of the Congress, see *Astronomy and Astro-physics* 12 (1893): 640–645; Alvan Clark's "Great Telescopes of the Future" address is in the same volume, pp. 673–678. A dozen other papers from the Congress appear in the Oct., Nov. and Dec. issues of the journal.

multiple observers, during the opposition of Mars, verified Schiaparelli's *canali*, eventually shown to be optical illusions. Also in August, a new comet was found in Auriga. September 9, Edward Emerson Barnard, 282 years after Galileo's sighting of the "Medicean stars" (moons of Jupiter), sighted the innermost moon of Jupiter. October and November, three new comets were discovered. November 23, a brilliant meteor shower was observed in various parts of America and Canada. During the first six months of 1893, forty more planetoids were identified between Mars and Jupiter, and three comets were discovered.[2]

This great volume of discoveries was a consequence of both the increasing size and power of telescopes and improved photographic methods, and Americans were conspicuous in the number of discoveries made, but they were harbingers of an even more significant development in astronomical science—the shift from astronomy (the "old astronomy") to the "new astronomy"—astrophysics, and with it, the triumph of an evolutionary view of the Cosmos. Even before 1893, the word "cosmogony" over the course of the nineteenth century had come to signify almost exclusively "Mosaic cosmogony," the discarded *Genesis* account of the origin of the Cosmos. In the early twentieth century, "cosmic evolution" would replace "cosmogony" as a popular phrase both among scientists, philosophers, and journalists, reflecting the extension of a Darwinian view to the origin and development of the universe. George Ellery Hale led these developments; a year after the Chicago Congress, he took steps to found the world's first professional journal of astrophysics, and his 1908 *Study of Stellar Evolution* was the first explicitly evolutionary description of stars. Its opening chapter noted the fateful coincidence in 1859 of the publication of *The Origin of Species* and the invention by Kirchoff and Bunsen of the spectroscope—two of the three developments (the third being the investigation of hypnosis and other states of consciousness) Rudolf Steiner noted had long been known in Rosicrucian circles as the necessary preconditions before an esoteric cosmology could be effectively and safely brought before the public.[3]

Both Hale's *Stellar Evolution* and Percival Lowell's *Evolution of Worlds* (1910)—as well as a host of discoveries continuing for the first half of the twentieth century—merely gave evidence for chemical, not *biological*, evolution. At the very same moment (1908–1910), Rudolf Steiner was presenting (in *An Outline of Esoteric Science* (1909) and

---

2   W. F. Denning, "Notes on Astronomical Discoveries in 1892," *The Observatory* 16 (1893): 49–56; George A. Hill, "The Progress of Astronomy in 1893," *Science* 23 (1894): 129–131.

3   Hale, *The Study of Stellar Evolution*, pp. 1–2. Rudolf Steiner in the "Barr Manuscript," written in 1907 for Éduard Schuré, cites the developments in natural science; see Steiner and Steiner-von Sivers, *Correspondence and Documents 1901–1925*, pp. 9–19.

in lectures—a comprehensive and interwoven cosmogony, planetology, cosmology, and anthropology, all essentially *biological* in the sense of elucidating parallel and consonant principles of cosmic origin, growth, and metamorphosis, and in describing cosmic evolution as a consequence of the activity of spiritual beings. What made "American Cosmogony"—unique national scientific and popular understandings in the United States of the origin and development of the cosmos—"prodigious," or "monstrous," was its unabashed materialism, its embrace of an epic narrative of stellar explosions and contractions; a solar system with a history and future totally divorced from the evolution of the human bodily form, consciousness, and spiritual faculties; and of an exclusively physical universe that most astronomers and the general public assumed harbored life—"more advanced" life—on innumerable other planetary bodies.

In 1919, Rudolf Steiner identified the development of a spiritual, planetary, and *true* cosmogony as the destiny task of America.[1] The history of astronomy in America before and after 1919 suggests both hopeful affirmations and troubling contradictions of Rudolf Steiner's statement.

## Frontiers

From its inception, the United States has had a uniquely democratic and relatively egalitarian scientific community, aside from a handful of European-trained college and university professors, astronomy and the other natural sciences were practiced by a wide array of dedicated amateurs. The prestige of making natural scientific contributions was closely tied to republican virtue—to ideals of the independent, free-thinking citizen of the new American republic. In 1846, when Ormsby MacKnight Mitchel founded *The Sidereal Messenger* in Cincinnati, Ohio (America's sixth largest metropolis, with a population of 46,000), it was the first popular astronomical periodical ever attempted in any language. Mitchel's Cincinnati Observatory, which sported the second largest refracting telescope in the world, embodied the democratic ideal; the 800 members who funded its construction were promised access to the instrument, and in its first year of operation the observatory welcomed 4,000 visitors. Whereas European observatories depended on royal patronage and hosted scientific aristocracy, Mitchel's observatory—like a host of other American scientific institutions of the antebellum era—both expected and encouraged patriotic citizen support.

*Discovery* was a hallmark of the development of the American character, and of the ambitions of American astronomy of the nineteenth century. Both America and the solar system presented a succession of frontiers over the course of the nineteenth century, right up to the time of the Columbian Exposition. But 1893 literally brought the end of this era of discovery. The 1890 census had shown that a frontier line, a point beyond which the population density was less than two persons per square mile, no longer existed. A few months before the Congress of Astronomy and Astrophysics, in a presentation to the American Historical Association at the Columbian Exposition, Professor Frederick Jackson Turner argued that the frontier had been the seminal influence shaping American history. Hale's Congress, and the development of the new astronomy, signaled the end of the old astronomy's naked eye discoveries, and a dramatic shift to new quantitative, instrument-driven "frontiers" of discovery. In Chicago, New York, and other large American cities, Gilded Age barons of finance and industry were gaining wide powers that eroded old republican ideals; in astronomical research, a parallel figure appeared—the astronomer and entrepreneur. For men such as Hale, Percival Lowell, and Harvard's Edward Charles Pickering, astronomy needed to be organized on a massive, imperial scale. New systematizations and standardizations were put into place, such as definitions of stellar magnitude and a system of spectroscopic classification.

Alongside this "industrialization" of American astronomy, there proceeded a continued tradition of amateur science, and also a uniquely American stream of "popularization." American writers of each generation produced works to acquaint

---

1 Steiner, "Cosmogony, Freedom, Altruism," Oct. 10, 1919, in *Understanding Society*.

readers (particularly youth) with the wonders of the stars. Perhaps because of the coincidence with expanding industrialization, these popular works were distinctive in their presentation of the heavens as a *sublime* (if now wholly secularized and largely disenchanted) realm. British–American astronomer Richard Proctor's daughter Mary gave popular lectures on star lore at the Columbian Exposition, and then made a nationwide lecture tour the following year. From 1892 to 1894, newspaper writer and editor Garrett Putnam Serviss (who cofounded with Leon Burritt the *Monthly Evening Sky Map* in 1906) wrote a popular astronomy column and chart, syndicated in hundreds of American newspapers. For decades they also manufactured and marketed the *Burritt–Serviss Star Finder*, an inexpensive planisphere, and took an elaborate astronomical lantern slide show on the road. Serviss's "Urania" show was explicitly *evolutionary* (the second season's performance was titled "From Chaos to Man") and characteristically theatrical. *The New York Times* reported, "There never had been such a combination of the magical powers of electricity with the ingenuity of stagecraft."[2] More than a thousand public schoolteachers attended the performance by Serviss at Carnegie Hall, which was underwritten by industrial titan Andrew Carnegie.

### Space Opera and the Sublime

In February 1898, the *New York Journal* began serial publication of G. P. Serviss's *Edison's Conquest of Mars*, arguably America's first science fiction "space opera," complete with alien abductions, spacesuits, interplanetary battles, oxygen pills, asteroid mining, disintegrator rays, and the destruction of New York City by Martians. Heavily illustrated, and later published as a popular book, the serial adventure tale has Thomas Edison, America's premier inventor, vanquish the Martians by way of his technological wizardry. *Edison's Conquest of Mars* presaged the sort of narrative to which America would become addicted, combining exotic imaginary worlds alongside the familiar terrain of advanced technology.[3] The fact that Serviss—perhaps the foremost American astronomical educator (his popular science books include *Other Worlds: Their Nature, Possibilities and Habitability in the Light of the Latest Discoveries*, 1901; *Astronomy with the Naked Eye*, 1908; *Curiosities of the Sky*, 1909; *Astronomy in a Nutshell*, 1912)—was also the author of science fiction is actually characteristic of American expositors of astronomy, as shown by writers and scientific educators such as Arthur C. Clarke, Issac Asimov, and Carl Sagan.[4]

More than any other nation on Earth, beginning in earnest in the 1890s with Percival Lowell's Mars fantasies, America became the leading champion, advocate, and fan of the "plurality of worlds" hypothesis—the belief that other planets, stars, and galaxies are home to intelligent life with whom we might make contact.[5] Whether seen as a continuation of America's "frontier spirit," a quest for the sublime, or a substitute for the belief in a transcendent Supreme Being, America in the twentieth century emerged as the preeminent place of

---

2 *Scientific American*, Apr, 9, 1892: 229; *Brooklyn Daily Eagle* June 17, 1894; *The New York Times* Apr. 9, 1893: 20. At the suggestion of Cornell University President Andrew Dickson White, Carnegie enlisted Serviss to revamp what had originally been the "scientific theater" of German science journalist Max Wilhelm Meyer. When Meyer had brought the production to the United States, it had been a complete failure with American audiences. See Geyer and Paulmann, *The Mechanics of Internationalism*, pp, 311–313.

3 Serviss's tale was most likely inspired by H. G. Wells' *War of the Worlds*, which had been serialized (and pirated) as "Fighters from Mars" in the *NY Journal*, Dec. 1897–Feb. 1898.

4 Ed. Note: It may be of interest to some readers that what might be considered the first science fiction novel was penned by Johannes Kepler in 1608 (published posthumously in 1634), titled *Somnium* (The Dream). See https://en.wikipedia.org/wiki/Somnium_(novel).

5 Decades before Mars, the Moon was widely speculated to harbor life. As Michael J. Crowe shows in his *The Extraterrestrial Life Debate, 1750–1900*, the so-called "Great Moon Hoax" of 1835 was no hoax at all, but a *satire* of English plurality of worlds enthusiast Thomas Dick. That *NY Sun* editor Richard Adams Locke's articles were taken so widely in America to be actual reports of "selenites" (moon dwellers) shows the predisposition Americans had to believe in physical (not spiritual) beings on other planets.

astronomical research and education. At each step of the nation's increasing commitment to space exploration, one finds the most enthusiastic advocates of astrophysical research to cling tenaciously to the belief—despite all evidence to the contrary—that communication with extraterrestrial civilizations is imminent, and largely a matter of improving current technology. The apotheosis of this faith in plurality was reached in the 1970s with Carl Sagan's *Pioneer* plaque (launched in 1972, *Pioneer 10* became the first human-made object to leave the solar system), the "Golden Discs" aboard the *Voyager* spacecraft, and the creation of the SETI (Search for Extraterrestrial Intelligence) program within NASA. Despite Rose Space Center/Hayden Planetarium Director and premier contemporary popularizer Neil DeGrasse Tyson's punchy put-downs of UFO enthusiasts, he clings to the "ET faith" as tenaciously as his predecessor Carl Sagan had done.

There is in today's pervasive popular culture landscape of science fiction a tension between the Romantic Sublime—the sheer awe felt in the face of a vast, supposedly expanding universe—and the Technological Sublime—an awe reserved for powerful machines and instruments of exploration such as deep space telescopes that continue to be sent out toward the stars in the blind faith that they will reward us both with cosmogonic knowledge and possible extraterrestrial contact. Rudolf Steiner, in his 1919 lecture, stated that "Real science must be cosmic—otherwise it is not science. It must be cosmic, must be a cosmogony—otherwise it cannot give inward human impulses which will carry man on through life. The man of modern times cannot live instinctively; he must live consciously. He needs a cosmogony; and he needs a freedom that is real." It is as if America has succumbed to an inversion of this truth; we are caught between the Romantic Sublime's Luciferic tendency to flee the Earth, and the Technological Sublime's impulse to trust our fates to Ahriman, via the promise of technologies that will take us to the outer limits of the Cosmos.

## *Cosmic Expansion, Human Contraction*

Six months after Rudolf Steiner's lecture, astronomers Harlow Shapley and Heber Curtis met at the Smithsonian Institution to publicly debate the size of the Universe. Shapley argued that the spiral nebulae that had been photographed in recent decades were part of the Milky Way, and that our home galaxy encompassed the entire known universe; Curtis countered that Andromeda and other nebulae were separate galaxies. Though later work partially verified aspects of both astronomers' arguments, Curtis's view is now seen as more accurate. Ever since American astronomer Edwin Hubble observed in 1929 that the distances to faraway galaxies were strongly correlated with their redshifts, the idea of an ever-expanding universe gained traction with astronomers as an alternative to the steady-state hypothesis. Given its propensity for evolutionary models and its proclivity for expansion, it is perhaps no surprise that American scientists would embrace first the idea of an expanding universe, and then the "Big Bang" as explanation of its origin. Used originally by detractors like Fred Hoyle to deride the theory, "Big Bang" was a phrase and image perfectly suited to the American psyche, and by 1947, when Russian-born astronomer George Gamow (he moved to the US in 1934) described the Big Bang for a general readership in *One, Two, Three, Infinity*, he assumed it to be widely accepted in both scientific and popular circles. The popularity of Gamow's book underscores the paradoxical American affinity for both the assumed bounded certainty of the quantitative, and the dizzying possibility of a limitless spatial universe.

An expanding universe guaranteed scientific frontiers for astrophysicists to study; it also shrank the seeming significance of the human being within that universe. Journalists routinely spoke of the 1920 Great Debate as "completing the Copernican Revolution," and in 1961, astrophysicist Frank Drake formulated the "Drake equation," a completely abstract, conjectural hypothesis that estimated the existence of between 1,000 and 100 million civilizations in the Milky Way galaxy alone. Though it encouraged the fantasies of SETI enthusiasts and science fiction writers, the Drake equation had no basis in phenomenological observation. Drake's colleague and friend Carl Sagan popularized the term *principle of mediocrity* to describe the human being's contracted cosmic status.[1] Though as unfounded in scientific fact as the Drake equation, Sagan's cherished principle has become an article of faith among both scientists and the lay public. Fed upon *Star Trek*, *Star Wars*, and dozens of other space operas, the typical American teenager today, when asked if there is life on other planets, will answer: "Of course! How can *we* be the only intelligent beings in the universe?"

## Turning Inside Out

On the eve of the hundredth anniversary of his "Cosmogony, Freedom, Altruism" lecture, Neil DeGrasse Tyson's *Astrophysics For People in a Hurry* (2017) sold 50,000 copies its first week after publication, and now has sold over a million copies. The book's opening sentence ("In the beginning, nearly fourteen billion years ago, all the space and all the matter and all the energy of the known universe was contained in a volume less than one-trillionth the size of the period that ends this sentence")—either an unconscious allusion to or a self-conscious assault on the opening of *Genesis*—echoes the rhetorical strategies of earlier American astronomical popularizers. Vast, humbling horizons are thrown up before us, then brought under control with some glib numerical turn-of-phrase. Dr. Tyson receives 200 speaking requests a month, has 7.3 million Twitter followers, and is Stephen Colbert's favorite guest. Tyson's popularity suggests that Americans continue to have a prodigious appetite for knowledge about the Cosmos, but Tyson's bleak, ultramaterialist, solipsistic outlook raises the question as to what possibility exists for "America"—in whatever form such a geographic and metahistorical term might mean in the sixth or seventh post-Atlantean epoch—to realize the destiny identified in 1919 by Rudolf Steiner.

One of the hallmarks of *Star Wisdom* (and its predecessor, the *Journal for Star Wisdom*) is that its authors and editors have sought to turn knowledge into *deeds*, through courses of practical and artistic instruction. Astrosophy as founded by Rudolf Steiner and brought forward by succeeding generations has immense gifts to offer America as it strives for a Christ-centered Cosmogony, but perhaps there are in America's leading cosmological impulses hints as to how astrosophy can help lead America toward its destiny. "Prodigy" can mean exceptionally large and exceptionally sensitive, insightful, or generous; a future spiritual scientific cosmogony forged out of American culture has the potential to be "prodigious" in its cosmopolitan and democratic outlook. The widespread expectation for encountering other sentient beings—the faith in the plurality of worlds—could be transformed into the search for *spiritual*, rather than physical, beings across the threshold. "Popularization," in the sense of bringing a wide public into heartfelt intimacy with potentially intimidating intellectual concepts, can and should be part of this striving. Spiritual science imparts the inspiring truth that all of our organs, our bodily forms, our spiritual and cognitive faculties, are given by the cosmos and its beings. Successively, each of our organs, once macrocosmically "spread out" during Old Saturn, Sun, and Moon conditions, became microcosmically manifested in us, and now we stand at a still point, poised to turn these cosmically given organs inside out, to give back to the stars. Perhaps the prophesied American Cosmogony will form from a parallel turning-inside-out of our collective gaze, away from the far reaches of the galaxy, toward the microcosmic expressions—our heads, hearts, limbs, and literally every other organ of our physical bodies—within us.

---

1  Carl Sagan and William I. Newman, "The Solipsist Approach to Extraterrestrial Intelligence," *Quarterly Journal of the Royal Astronomical Society* 24 (1983): 113–121.

# URANUS IN ARIES
## *Disturbing Cosmic Parallels*
### Julie Humphreys

*"The truth is incontrovertible. Panic may resent it. Ignorance may deride it. Malice may distort it. But there it is."* —WINSTON CHURCHILL

Uranus demands the truth. The great awakeer, Uranus draws us toward new impulses. It fosters the unexpected, events that are "out of the blue." Through its influence, our thoughts are illumined, our hearts long to serve the whole human family, and our deeds lead us consciously to a better future. Conversely, Uranus also has the ability to lure us to engage in thinking that is devoid of spiritual light. It can well serve the egotist and autocrat. To the extent that we are asleep to universal, moral law, Uranus, instead of being a vehicle for divine truth, can electrify our thinking, trapping it inside our skulls. This egotistic ideation can bear earthly fruit for a time, but will inevitably be struck down, reduced to rubble, by the requirements of moral law: through the influence of Uranus, we are forced to face the truth eventually. The rays of cosmic illumination can only reach us once we have sacrificed our personal ideas and position.

It takes an average of eighty-four years for Uranus to make its way around the zodiacal circle. This year, 2019, begins with Uranus at 3°36' Aries, reaching a maximum zodiacal degree of 11°36' Aries in August, when its seasonal retrograde movement commences. (By year's end Uranus will arrive back at 7°40' Aries.) The arc of its movement this year is exactly eight degrees, the midpoint of which, 7°36' Aries, coincidentally marks the position of the Sun at the birth of Adolf Hitler.

As Uranus passes in front of Aries (which takes approximately seven years), there is the potentially explosive combination of the independent and rebellious nature of Uranus that facilitates the influx of new ways of looking at things with the forceful and sometimes unyielding idealism of the Ram. Together the two cry out for something new, something that might be too hot to touch for a while. Narcissism, egoism, and false systems of belief are also distinct possibilities.

When did Uranus last travel past these stars of the Ram? The most recent period falls between April 1934 and April 1936, which will be called Period A. At the start of this period, Uranus was in a tight conjunction with both the Sun and Mars, which lends, when not ennobled toward the higher good, the capacity for unbridled egotism, the inclination to play by one's own rules, the imposition of one's will on others—and even violence. Indeed, one interpretation of the combined influence of Uranus and Mars is *blitzkrieg*, or "lightning war"—the military strategy that relied on momentum and speed to overrun the enemy that would be favored by the Nazis beginning in 1939. During the last three weeks of Period A, we can again find Uranus in conjunction with Mars and the Sun (although not, in this case, a triple conjunction, as the conjunction of Mars with Uranus fell eighteen days before its conjunction with the Sun). Period A, then, is bracketed by this forceful combination of planets, drawing particular attention to what lies between. (The early months of Period A also marked the beginning of Mao Zedong's rise to tyrannical power, but this is beyond the scope of this article.)

There is another further astrological indication of great importance. Throughout Period A, Adolf Hitler was experiencing a once-in-a-lifetime transit: Uranus (as it was positioned during Period A) was in conjunction with his natal Sun. The influence of this aspect reached exact conjunction on three occasions during Period A. This transit brings an intense energy that must find expression somehow; it draws one on a new course and can make restrictions almost unbearable. We can well imagine how productive it could be when the one it influences is serving humanity with a gaze toward the future. In the case of Hitler, it availed his dark aims for a time.

What can be found if we look further back into the past, prior to Period A? We previously find Uranus along this eight-degree arc between July 1849 and April 1852. (For simplicity's sake, we will call this Period B.) Steiner referred to the middle of the nineteenth century as the time when materialism cast its longest shadow over our memory of our cosmic heritage. Should we continue on this trajectory, he warned, subearthly forces would begin to seep into our experience, attempting to direct our thinking, feeling, and willing from the dusky depths of the underworld. It is interesting that *Moby Dick* was published in 1851. Captain Ahab was consumed by his obsessive battle with the whale, the largest of all "subearthly" creatures, and, in the end, he was no match for its raw power. *Moby Dick* was a portent of what was in store should we continue to cast our gaze downward.

Less than two years before this period began, on February 21, 1848, Marx and Engels published *The Communist Manifesto*. On this day, the Sun was two degrees past Neptune in Aquarius: an ironic backdrop for the peddling of a system which provided only the illusion (Neptune) of fairness and equality (Aquarius); indeed, Neptune had been identified for the first time just seventeen months earlier. Marxism pays lip service to fairness by elevating the rights of the group over those of the individual—but once established, a simple majority can easily crush the rights of any minority, the right to freedom of speech paramount among them.

Communism is the political system that puts Marxist ideology into practice; through its doctrine of impossible equality, it maintains itself only through bloody tyranny. Close to 100 million souls have thus far been sacrificed on its altar:[1] the promise of an Edenic existence at "no cost to you" (cost in effort, sacrifice, and personal responsibility) continues to compel. And just as the publication of *The Communist Manifesto* came months before the start of Period B, so did the two-hundredth anniversary of the birth of Marx (May 5, 2018) closely precede the same eight-degree arc of Uranus that we find in 2019. These cosmic parallels deserve our attention.

In October of 1919, Rudolf Steiner had this to say about Marxism, which, he stated, had been plundering civilization and signified its downfall:

> Socialists suggest that the reality of all human history is to be sought only in economic processes, in the dynamics of economic life, in class warfare that arises from these economic processes. In this view, these economic realities are the foundation for the superstructure of law, ethics, cultural life altogether, thus also art, religion, science and so forth. In terms of the whole of humanity's history this is of course nonsense.[2]

In other words, Marxism views humanity in purely materialistic terms, and in presuming that any differences in personal economic health is solely the result of an inherent unfairness in the economic structure of society, seeds envy and unrest. Human beings are pitted against human beings.

Yet, in 1848, the cosmos was calling something forth that would shake up, even revolutionize societal and political structure: Uranus was conjunct Pluto in June of 1850 and March of 1851. The potential of this combination can be understood when we note that its next heavenly appearance occurred in the 1960s, facilitating great upheaval and violence in much of the West. (The opposition of Uranus and Pluto was present during the French Revolution—yet this need not have resulted in the gleeful slaughter of nobles and desecration of churches, as it did in the last decade of the eighteenth century. Both John the Baptist and the Nathan Jesus were born under this opposition; from the heliocentric perspective of each birth, the planets were less than two degrees apart. Their example as peaceful revolutionaries in the service of divine love will endure until the end of time. It was in evidence again in 1900, the year that marked the beginning of Steiner's teaching as well as the birth of Valentin Tomberg.)

---

[1] Courtois, et al., *The Black Book of Communism*.

[2] Steiner. *Understanding Society through Spiritual-Scientific Knowledge*, pp. 22, 58.

Before delving further into the particular historical events of Period A, it is important to look to the overarching cosmic script which serves as a foundational background to the unfolding of human evolution in the twentieth century. Indeed, a true understanding of events cannot be reached without this spiritual perspective. There are three rhythms associated with aspects of Christ that appear in remarkable synchronicity in the few years prior to Period A.

The rhythm of Christ's ether body is 33⅓ years. How can we understand this? Robert Powell reminds us in *The Christ Mystery*[1] that this is the length of time between the birth of Jesus and the Mystery of Golgotha, during which the events of his life were inscribed into his etheric body. Though the biography of each individual's life on Earth is inscribed in a similar way into his or her etheric body, ordinarily this life body dissolves back into the cosmos after physical death. This was not so in the case of Christ Jesus: his etheric body remained intact as a *time* organism, and has since been able to work throughout history through its 33⅓-year rhythm.

A brief summary of the thorough timeline found in *The Christ Mystery* can be stated as follows: Christ's descending etheric body left the realm of the Angeloi in 1899, coinciding with the beginning of the *Satya Yuga*. Though Steiner was able to perceive Christ's approach toward the aura of the Earth at this time, it would require another 33⅓-year period before this would be perceptible to others. Steiner's identification of this unfolding event as the primary purpose of the anthroposophic movement points to its enormous import. Therefore, the year 1933 marked the appearance of Christ in the etheric aura of the Earth.

Robert Powell explains:

> In 1899, the year that marks the end of the Hindu *Kali Yuga* [or, Dark Age, next followed by the 5,000-year Age of Light, or *Satya Yuga*], Rudolf Steiner had an intense, life-changing clairvoyant experience of Christ.... Steiner's inner experience involved what he termed the "Mystery of Golgotha"—the events of the Passion, Crucifixion, and Resurrection.... After this, Steiner became the "prophet" of Christ in his Second Coming, as John the Baptist was for Christ's first coming. Steiner often emphasized that his entire teaching of "Anthroposophy" (Spiritual Science) was to prepare for the Second Coming.[2]

In fact, Steiner began teaching in 1900. On January 12, 1910, while lecturing in Stockholm, he proclaimed the imminent return of the Risen One in etheric form, surrounding the Earth. Throughout his lectures on the return of Christ in the etheric, he pointed to the year 1933 as an important year in Christ's unfolding manifestation. Unfortunately, Steiner's premature death in 1925 prevented him from experiencing what he had foretold.[3] The year indicated by Rudolf Steiner as the key year in terms of Christ's return, 1933, was to be the year which saw the great teacher of humanity who followed Steiner begin to assume the role of the one who would lead us toward recognition and experience of Christ in the Etheric. This was the year in which this teacher, Valentin Tomberg, commenced work on his *Studies of the Old Testament*.[4]

In light of the indications cited above in reference to the 1933 appearance of the Etheric Christ, the actions of Stalin and Hitler during this very time period might appear to one as a counteroffensive against it.

Another path to communion with Christ is through the rhythm of his astral body, the bearer of the Eternal Apocalypse, through which the light of the Etheric Christ shines. This communion requires purification of our own astral natures, through the practice of the three sacred vows of obedience, chastity, and poverty. Through the Apocalypse Code, Dr. Powell reveals that humanity, since the Mystery of Golgotha, has been experiencing its unfolding through the cosmic footprints of the life of Jesus Christ (the cosmic being of divine love united with Jesus of Nazareth), who quite literally provides universal guidance to

---

1 Powell, *The Christ Mystery*, p. 8.

2 Powell, "The Apocalypse Code and the Year 2018," *Journal for Star Wisdom* 2018, pp. 34–35.

3 Powell, *The Christ Mystery*, p. 1.

4 See Tomberg, *Christ and Sophia*.

humanity until the end of time. The Apocalypse Code reveals that the period of 1,290 days which transpired between the Baptism in the Jordan on AD September 23, 29, and the Resurrection on April 5, 33, are the archetype for 1,290 "days" of earthly life, with each "day" lasting 29½ years. In other words, since the Resurrection, each 29½ years on Earth corresponds to one day in the ministry of Christ.

Many readers will recognize that twenty-nine and a half years is the average time needed for Saturn to circle the zodiac. It is the sphere marked by the orbit of Saturn through which we descend upon our return to Earth from spiritual realms, where each receives his or her spiritual mission—a unique task (in a given lifetime) through which each serves others as well as the evolution of humanity. Saturn is the planet of cosmic memory, so it is not surprising that it is through its 29½-year rhythm that we can remember each step taken by Jesus Christ. If we begin counting these earthly "days" in May of the year 33 (when the Ascension and Pentecost took place), we are taken to the year AD 38,000. This suggests that Earth evolution will be complete in AD 38,000, illuminating the profound significance of the closing words of the Gospel of Matthew: "Lo, I am with you always, even unto the end of the world" (28:20).

The timeline of this "clock" of humanity is supported and validated by the work of Rudolf Steiner, who described humanity's progression through seven Great Epochs that unfold according to the movement of the vernal point's regression through the zodiac. (This occurs at the rate of 1° every 72 years, or 30° every 2,160 years.) If we add to our current year (2019) the 5,875 years remaining in the post-Atlantean period *and* the subsequent 30,240 years of the two remaining Great Epochs yet to be experienced by humanity, we arrive at AD 38,134. In a span of so many thousands of years, we can regard this as corroboration.

So, where along humanity's "walk" through the life of Jesus Christ was humanity just prior to the start of Period A? The year 1929 corresponds to the start of our 29½-year experience of the First Temptation in the Wilderness, which occurred historically on November 27, 29. The first of the three temptations archetypal for all of humanity was the temptation to become a "prince of this world." Anne Catherine Emmerich describes it:

> Satan flew with the Lord to the highest peak of the mountain, and set him upon an overhanging, inaccessible crag much higher than the grotto. It was night, but while Satan pointed around, it grew bright, revealing the most wonderful regions in all parts of the world. The devil addressed Jesus in words something like these: "I know that thou art a great teacher, that thou art now about to gather disciples around thee and promulgate thy doctrines. Behold, all these magnificent countries, these mighty nations! Compare them to poor, little Judea lying yonder! Go rather to these. I will deliver them over to thee, if kneeling down thou wilt adore me!"
>
> As Satan pointed around, one saw first vast countries and seas, with their different cities into which kings in regal pomp and magnificence and followed by myriads of warriors were triumphantly entering.... One looked down upon all their details, every scene, every nation differing in customs and manners, in splendor and magnificence. Satan...showed him Palestine, but as a poor, little, insignificant place. This was a most wonderful vision, so extended, so clear, so grand, and magnificent! The only words uttered by Jesus were: "The Lord thy God shalt thou adore and him only shalt you serve!" Then I saw Satan in an inexpressibly horrible form rise from the rock, cast himself into the abyss, and vanish as if the earth had swallowed him.[5]

Humanity, then, began its encounter with the will-to-power in 1929. Obviously, human beings did not overcome this temptation when this 29½-year period ended in 1958, but 1929 and the chaos that followed Black Tuesday (Oct. 29, 1929) offered a unique set of circumstances through which the desire to exert the personal will at the expense of others was able to find expression in two individuals in particular. These two are largely regarded as the most evil of the

---

5 Emmerich, *Visions of the Life of Christ*, vol. 1, p. 370.

twentieth century—Joseph Stalin and Adolf Hitler. Followed by myriads of warriors, each eyed the mighty nations within his view.[1]

There exists one additional rhythm of the cosmic Christ, that of the "I" of Christ, which is also relevant to Period A; its twelve-year Jupiter cycle (representing the time required for Jupiter to circle the zodiac) has as its archetype the descent of Christ's "I" through the underworld following the Crucifixion. How did the unfolding of this twelve-year rhythm come to bear on the years leading up to Period A?

Steiner sought to reveal Christ's teachings to humankind through Anthroposophy; further, Powell reveals that the birth horoscope of Steiner is, in fact, the cosmic *indication* of the descent of Christ from the Sun, toward the Earth.[2] At this moment in time, Jupiter, from the perspective of the Sun, had just entered the Lion. What a beautiful picture this gives us, as it is through the heart forces, under the influence of Leo, that we can unite with the Christ Self. Each subsequent entry of heliocentric Jupiter into Leo marks a further stage of descent. Between June 15, 1920 and April 25, 1932, the Christ Self was in the realm of the Angels; between 1932 and 1945, in the earthly sphere of humanity. (The continuation of the path of the Christ "I" through the sub-earthly spheres toward the Mother began in 1945, and is beyond the scope of this article, and can be explored further in *The Christ Mystery*.)

## Stalin

Josef Stalin became General Director of the Soviet Communist Party in 1922, two years before the death of Lenin. This position had not been one of particular influence, but through it, Stalin was able to act as absolute ruler of the Soviet Union from 1928 and his death in 1953: all opposition had been, by then, crushed, and he was able to do as he pleased. What pleased him might constitute the most cruel, murderous, and bloodthirsty dictatorship in all of history. He seems to have drawn inspiration and support from the darkest places imaginable. It can be difficult for us today to fully understand the evil depths of this inspiration—as there still seems to be some difficulty in taking in and sorting through the breadth of his murderous accomplishments. (In Hitler's case, this became all too obvious.) The woven threads of the veil of deception continue to be spun around Josef Stalin today.

While Lenin's economic policy had tolerated some privatization, Stalin implemented collective farming (implicitly denying individual property rights) soon after coming to power. This effort, begun in 1928, was known as the First Five-Year Plan; through it, land, livestock, and grain were confiscated from the so-called "bread basket of Europe." The most successful farmers, or kulaks, were executed or sent to the gulags; they were demonized as bourgeois enemies and excluded from society. The State hoarded the grain and *kept it out of Ukraine*, even killing anyone who stole leftover morsels from the ground. Ukrainians were starved into submission and, furthermore, blocked from fleeing the famine. Under these dire circumstances, community and family suffered particularly: this was an early, brutal salvo intended to thwart the development of the coming Slavic Cultural Epoch that will be characterized by true concern for all of one's brothers and sisters.

Stalin banned the publication of census information during the 1932–33 famine, or *Holomodor*, and even exported precious grain to create the illusion of prosperity and health. In the 1950s, living victims of the *Holomodor* were discredited as anti-communist. Even the current Wikipedia page titled "Soviet Famine of 1932–33" does not establish the certainty of "killing by starvation" (*Holomodor*), but instead makes it sound as if it was the unintended result of economic policy. Thirteen percent of the Ukrainian populace perished. The famine continued for many years thereafter, and death estimates go as high as ten million.

---

1 The two tyrants joined forces for a time in August of 1939, when the Molotov-Ribbentrop Pact was signed. Consequently, Germany and Soviet Russia ostensibly established a policy of mutual nonaggression, which of course ended with the German invasion of the Soviet Union in 1941. But within the Pact there existed veiled protocols for the division of Northern and Eastern Europe between the two countries following the expected Axis victory of World War II.

2 Powell, Robert, *Hermetic Astrology*, vol. 2, p. 328.

The deliberate deceit put forth by Stalin was matched to a large extent by those of Western intellectuals, politicians, and journalists enamored by the promise of socialism. One journalist who stood out among the rest was Walter Duranty, chief correspondent in Moscow for *The New York Times* between 1922 and 1936. In 1932, he received a Pulitzer Prize for his propaganda, examples of which follow:

> November 15, 1931: There is no famine or actual starvation, nor is there likely to be.
> May 14, 1933: You can't make an omelet without breaking eggs.
> August 23, 1933: Any report of a famine in Russia is today an exaggeration of malignant propaganda.[3]

Reporting like this successfully cowed much of the West into buying into the utopian vision of collectivism, and arguably assisted Stalin's subjugation of Eastern Europe in the decades to follow. It may also be argued that President Roosevelt abetted Stalin, whom he chillingly called "Uncle Joe." Through the release of both the partially declassified information gathered through the Venona Project and the classified Russian State secrets made available for a short time after the fall of the Soviet Union, we are offered a glimpse of the scope of Soviet infiltration and sympathy in the US government.

Since the beginning of Stalin's absolute rule, there had been systematic purges of the clergy, wealthy peasants, and anyone engaged in private enterprise. These purges, intended to eliminate the bourgeoisie, came in hideous waves that varied in enormity: million were arrested, imprisoned, and sent to the hundreds of gulags ("corrective" labor camps) across the country. Countless others were killed before they reached the camps. In the twenties, men of religion were given the maximum sentence (at that time, ten years) and were prohibited from ever returning to their children and homes. Followers of religious societies (including the followers of Vladimir Solovyov) were "arrested and destroyed in passing."[4] During the wave of 1929 and 1930, anyone who'd had any capacity to earn was deemed guilty of having had the *ability* to hoard gold. But it was the tidal wave of dispossessed kulaks (the peasant landowners mentioned above) that raged over all the others: it bypassed prisons and went directly to the gulags, driving at least fifteen million peasants into the tundra. Solzhenitsyn writes:

> This wave poured forth, sank down into the permafrost, and even our most active minds recall hardly a thing about it. It is as if it had not even scarred the Russian conscience.[5]
>
> This wave was also distinct from all those that preceded it because no one fussed about with taking the head of the family first and then working out what to do with the rest...in this wave they burned out whole nests, whole families, from the start; they watched jealously to be sure that none of the children–fourteen, ten, even six years old–got away.[6]

By the end of 1934, just a few months into Period A, Stalin's Great Purge, also known as the Great Terror, began. This could be distinguished from those that preceded it by the imprisonment and/or execution of members of the Communist Party, the Red Army, and the Intelligentsia. Even association with a recognized enemy could bring one to the attention of the secret police, or NKVD, which served as the military wing of the government. Restraint was not required, as any charge could be cooked up and leveled against a political opponent. When it was not enough to associate with a perceived enemy or express thoughts critical of collectivism or its leadership, reasons for imprisonment (and even execution) could be fabricated. This Purge was set into motion after the December 1, 1934, assassination of Sergey Kirov; Stalin used the death of the Revolution leader at the hands of another communist as a pretext for some Party cleansing. In reality, Stalin likely had Kirov killed once he realized his formerly loyal protégé was acting outside his control.

Lenin had established the system of gulags, but it was under Stalin's direction that their maximal

---

3 Mayer, *Uncle Joe, FDR and the Deep State*, p. 21.
4 Solzhenitsyn, *The Gulag Archipelago*, p. 23.
5 Ibid., p. 19.
6 Ibid., p. 26.

terror was unleashed. Stalin's murderous purges exceeded the excesses of the French Revolution by several orders of magnitude.[1] Millions of political enemies were sent to these camps; needless to say, there was no legal recourse for the accused. Many remained in the gulags until Stalin's death. In 1973, Aleksandr Solzhenitsyn exposed the tragedy of the labor camps in *The Gulag Archipelago*, which resulted in his immediate expulsion from the Soviet Union—this, more than twenty years after the death of Stalin. Beginning in the forties, Solzhenitsyn had spent nearly a decade in a gulag over comments in a private letter that were critical of the State; it is rather touching to note that it was during these years that he abandoned Marxism, the fruits of which were laid bare in the camp, and became an Eastern Orthodox Christian.

The methods of arrest and interrogation as well as conditions within the labor camps are the subject of *The Gulag Archipelago*. It is not for the faint of heart. It seems unbelievable because, by and large, it is so far outside our own experience. But Solzhenitsyn warns in the introduction published in 1983: "If it were possible for any nation to fathom another people's bitter experience through a book, how much easier its future fate would become and how many calamities and mistakes it could avoid. But it is very difficult. There always is this fallacious belief: 'It would not be the same here; here such things are impossible.' Alas, all the evil of the twentieth century is possible everywhere on Earth."[2]

There is a story told of Stalin and three birds, with which he seeks to demonstrate political control. The underlings are told to imagine that the birds in their hands are the people; Stalin asks them how they would control them. The first fellow was so afraid that his bird would fly away that his tight grip crushed the bird to death. Seeing Stalin's disapproval, the second fellow neglected to hold on tightly enough, and the bird escaped and flew away. Stalin, impatient with the idiocy around him, ordered that the third bird be brought to him.

He slowly pulled out one feather at a time until the bird was completely naked, shivering in his hand. Stalin looked at the men and said something like, "You, see, he is even thankful for the warmth of my hand."

## Hitler

On January 30, 1933, a short time before the start of Period A, Hitler became Chancellor of Germany. Eighty-six days later, the Gestapo, led by Heinrich Himmler, was born: the Nazi secret police. Much like the NKVD in Soviet Russia, the Gestapo had broad authority, above judicial review, to investigate any and all threats to the Nazi Party. The establishment of the Gestapo made possible the fulfillment of Hitler's vision of concentration camps, set up and administered by Himmler. Before this, Himmler had been part of the rather helpful-sounding SS (*Schutzstaffel*, or "protection squadron"), the organization that was largely responsible for the genocidal killing during Hitler's Reich.

The German system of concentration camps began shortly after Hitler became Chancellor in 1933. They were designed to receive the masses of prisoners regarded as opponents to Hitler's rule. Originally the camps were established and operated locally by Stormtroopers (the SA) and local police. Gradually, there was a shift to larger, centrally organized camps that fell under the exclusive jurisdiction of the SS, thereby streamlining their killing. Dachau has the unfortunate distinction to have been the only camp that was large enough to remain in use between 1933 and the end of the war in 1945.

Two months after the establishment of the Gestapo, Germany experienced what became known as the Night of the Long Knives. Between June 30 and July 2, 1934, Hitler sought to permanently rid his own party of any whom he regarded as potentially disloyal. Estimates of the extrajudicial executions run in the hundreds, and many more enemies were arrested. Following this purge, all legal prohibition against this sort of killing had

---

1 Mayer, *Islamic Jihad, Cultural Marxism and the Transformation of the West*, p. 76.
2 Solzhenitsyn, *The Gulag Archipelago*, p. xxiii.

vanished within the Nazi Party, the only remaining political party in Germany. The result was the solidification of Hitler's power; exactly one month later, he would become Führer, the absolute dictator of Germany.

In early September, 1934, that year's Nuremberg Rally was held. It is largely through film that we are able to grasp the enormity, the pomp, and the effect of this particular event. Held annually by the Nazis since 1923, it was brimming with propaganda, intended to overwhelm the emotions and inspire awe for the Party. The 1934 rally was attended by nearly three quarters of a million people: there were fireworks, military displays, and Wagnerian music. Also notable in the 1934 rally was the introduction of a feat of stagecraft known as the cathedral of light; designed by Albert Speer, 152 antiaircraft (or Flak) searchlights pointed upward, surrounding the audience with glowing columns of light that reached far into the night sky, presenting a dark alternative to Christian worship.

March of 1935 saw the release of the mesmerizing propaganda film by Leni Riefenstahl, the *Triumph of the Will*, which records the Nuremberg Rally in artistic detail. The film answers any lingering questions one might have as to why so much of Germany followed Hitler. A more accurate title might have been *Triumph of the Personal Will*. We must look elsewhere for the true and elevated triumph of a will that is inspired by the divine: Beethoven overcoming his hearing loss and continuing to compose, or Jacques Lusseyran, who became a fearless leader of the French Resistance despite his blindness,[3] are two fine examples.

Early in 1936, Hitler violated the 1919 Treaty of Versailles as the German Army re-militarized the Rhineland. This region, west of the Rhine, had been demilitarized since 1919, thus serving as a sort of buffer against potential German aggression in the future. It can be argued that if the British and the French had summoned the will to oppose Hitler at that time, they would likely have easily succeeded. Hitler's generals had advised him against the move, as they deemed the likelihood of opposition so high. They even had plans to back off if opposed! We will never know how history might have been changed had Winston Churchill, then an MP, been in a position of significant power. He had been urging his fellow countrymen to wake up about Hitler since 1933, and had hoped for an Anglo-French alliance to oppose the re-militarization. In hindsight, it can be said that he knew exactly what Hitler was about. In April of 1936, the month that saw both the conjunction of Mars and Uranus as well as the transit of Uranus to Hitler's natal Sun, Churchill offered Britain this warning before the House of Commons: "When you are drifting, floating, down the stream of Niagara, it may easily happen that from time to time you run into a reach of quite smooth water, or that a bend in the river or a change in the wind may make the roar of the falls seem far more distant: but your position and your preoccupation are in no way affected thereby."[4]

After the re-militarization of the Rhineland, the balance of power was changed. Emboldened by the ease with which he was able execute his plan, Hitler's aggression intensified. Britain and France would pass up other chances to oppose him before it was too late.

### The Assault on Religion

Why did Marx label religion as the opiate of the masses? This question is a most serious one, for opium can ultimately kill, all the while lulling its users into a false sense of joy. Opium temporarily dulls pain, but its use interferes with one's ability to constructively work through one's karma. The continued use of opiates keeps our karma and our will impulses *in the dark*. According to Marx, then, religion acts as an opiate in that it keeps us from facing the true realities of life. It is critical that we look behind this smokescreen to seek a deeper understanding.

Religion cannot exist without a source: God, the Creator. And it is through this Creator that we receive our morality. Steiner said this in 1912:

---

3 See Lusseyran, *And There Was Light: The Extraordinary Memoir of a Blind Hero of the French Resistance in World War II*.

4 Winston Churchill, speech before the House of Commons, Apr. 6, 1936.

"Morality is an original, divine gift, part of the original content of human nature, just as spiritual power was part of human nature when humanity had not descended so far...thus we cannot speak about morality as if it were something that humanity first had to develop; morality is something that is at the foundation of the human soul."[1]

Deborah Tyler put it this way in 2017: "The highest moral achievement is service rendered from an appreciation of the divinity of the soul, in spite of perverseness of thought. Morality is comprehensive in scope, providing the true challenge to bigotry. Moral consciousness benefits all equally regardless of race, ethnicity, religion, sex.... Politically based valuation is inherently anti-moral. It worsens the stink of anger and division."[2]

Without God, then, morality is no more than what one wants to do, and, increasingly, we are seeing that "anything goes." The contemporary creep of Marxism in the West has added a further twist: when one denounces another's thoughts or behaviors as immoral, one is labeled intolerant. Of course, just what thoughts and behaviors are acceptable reflects the subjective beliefs of the elite: some "intolerance" is encouraged, while some is criminalized. It is a perverse irony that the only religion that much of the West unequivocally defends today is the one that requires submission and denies individual rights.

Furthermore, worshipping God requires the acceptance of a higher power which is therefore capable of divine judgment. Marxism fosters tyranny because within its worldview there is no higher power capable of passing judgment upon one's behaviors. It is no wonder that both Stalin and Hitler did everything they could to eradicate religion from their people. Alas, the sacred vow of obedience to God, which rivets will-to-power, was nowhere in their hearts. Solzhenitsyn had this to say:

Power is a poison well known for thousands of years.... But to the human being who has faith in some force that holds dominion over all of us, and who is therefore conscious of his own limitations, power is not necessarily fatal. For those, however, who are unaware of any higher sphere, it is a deadly poison. For them there is no antidote.[3]

Stalin, in addition to closing churches and targeting the clergy for the gulags, attempted to eradicate Christianity from education. Schoolteachers, for example, advised parents as to how to answer their children's questions about God. "Questions about the existence of God were to be answered with a simple 'There is no God.'"[4] Imagine a child of that time and place—running on a sunny hill covered with wildflowers or walking through a wood, zigzagging around shafts of light warming the soft forest floor, and drinking in the glory of God all around—being told emphatically by a parent or teacher, "There is no God!"

Hitler, too, did what he could to subvert the Judeo-Christian influence—mercy, love, and hope—in the society. The many pastors of protestant churches who publicly objected to Nazism were arrested.

The Nazis sought to gradually reform Christian celebrations and traditions by emphasizing the pagan, pre-Christian elements of its festivals; the birth of Jesus took a back seat to the winter solstice, and nationalistic hymns were sung 'round the tree at Christmas. Youth scouting, which was founded on Christian moral principles, was replaced with the Nazi Youth, requiring loyalty to the Party.

Himmler believed that a major task of the SS should be acting as the vanguard in overcoming Christianity and restoring a "Germanic" way of living. He said, "We live in an era of the ultimate conflict with Christianity. It is part of the mission of the SS to give the German people in the next half century the non-Christian ideological foundations on which to lead and shape their lives."[5]

Even with God out of the way, a tyrant needs a great deal of support to accomplish his or her

---

1 Steiner, *The Spiritual Foundation of Morality*, p. 38.
2 See http://www.americanthinker.com/articles/2017/09/morality_antimorality_and_the_leftwing_great_hatehustle.html.
3 Solzhenitsyn, *The Gulag Archipelago*, p. 69.
4 Kirschenbaum, *Small Comrades1*, p. 147.
5 Longerich, *Heinrich Himmler: A Life*, p. 270.

aims: namely, an iron fist around a corrupt, leviathan-scale government. With this control, the picture of the tyrant and those who support the tyrant as providers of all needs (safety, security, and spiritual sustenance) can be upheld. The aim of such a government is to suckle on the citizenry, amassing wealth and power until the last crumb of bread and the last drop of milk are gone. Through it, whole departments may endeavor to use their power to target political opponents.

One of the sharpest tools in the arsenal of bloated government is surveillance. Stalin and Hitler had to settle for loyal informants who had reason to fear for their lives if they failed. Perhaps the modern surveillance state was a gleam in their eyes. Though we are now being told incessantly that surveillance by the government, through its media and corporate allies, is intended to make our lives safer and easier, and to "bring us together," it is important to see it as the ahrimanic force that it is. Anyone left with lingering doubts on this point need only imagine what might have happened had this technology been in the hands of Stalin and Hitler. What might have been then is now a reality, and the position of Uranus can help illustrate the point. On February 21, 1848, the day *The Communist Manifesto* was published, Uranus moved from 23°6' Pisces to 23°8' Pisces. Uranus passed in front of these two zodiacal minutes on February 25, 2016, a full eight months after Trump had announced his run for US president. On this same day, *The New York Times* reported the following:

> The Obama administration is on the verge of permitting the National Security Agency to share more of the private communications it intercepts with other American intelligence agencies without first applying privacy protections to them.... The change would relax long-standing restrictions on access to the contents of the phone calls and email the security agency vacuums up around the world.[6]

---

6  Charlie Savage, "Obama Administration Set to Expand Sharing of Data That N.S.A. Intercepts," *The New York Times*. New York, Feb. 25, 2016.

## The Assault on Life

The enormity of the killing under the leadership of Stalin and Hitler offers us a stern reminder.

As Solzhenitsyn warned, it is very difficult indeed for those of us who live in relative safety and security to fully understand what creates the willingness to take a life. *The Gulag Archipelago* reveals that Stalin's intention was not only to kill, but also to take from the accused everything of value before doing so—family, dignity, property, and hope.

Yet we must be cautious about judging those who made the gulags run, as well as the informers who were so crucial to the gathering of prisoners for interrogation. Solzhenitsyn himself was recruited as a young man by the NKVD (he declined), and he wondered what he would have become if *he* had been the one wearing the NKVD officer's insignia.

> The NKVD school dangled before us special rations and double or triple pay...It was not our minds that resisted but something inside our breasts...
>
> If only there were evil people somewhere insidiously committing evil deeds, and it were necessary only to separate them from the rest of us...but the line dividing good and evil cuts through the heart of every human being.[7]

How will we judge ourselves when we consider, while in this life or after it, how we have treated the most innocent and/or helpless among us? When a great Western power allows medical doctors to terminate the lives of beloved children because their "quality of life" is deemed too poor? (May Charlie and Alfie rest in the arms of their Angels.) When we ration care to the elderly, while promoting assisted death "with dignity"? Does God's own plan lack dignity? When a high-ranking physician with a large superpower's primary (and government-funded) abortion provider *jokes* (on hidden camera) about saving up for a sports car through the sale of fetal tissue?[8] Are we too numb to summon outrage?

---

7  Solzhenitsyn, *The Gulag Archipelago*, pp. 74–75.
8  For access to this and similar videos, visit http://www.americanthinker.com/articles/2018/03/funding_the_planned_parenthood_chop_shop.html.

## The Assault on Children and Family

An extremely troubling aspect of the tyrannies of both Stalin and Hitler was the co-opting of children (and childhood) to further their aims. The motivation lay in molding the young into future soldiers of the cause through the exploitation of their typically intense and volatile feeling life (particularly true between the ages of 14 and 21). Ideally, this period of life is a time to take in as many points of view as one can while allowing them to sift through one's experience and one's developing higher faculties of reason and conscience. This simply cannot happen when one is only free to think or utter certain government-approved thoughts.

Meanwhile, Soviet propaganda idealized childhood and featured many illustrations of joyous children setting about their collective work. A poster that hung in every Soviet school proclaimed, "Thank you, Comrade Stalin, for our happy childhood."[1]

In the Stalinist schoolroom, teachers strived to educate the children in the "proper" manner and to separate them from their families. School teachers, in line with Marxist methods of child study, developed elaborate questionnaires to determine what sort of examples parents set for their children at home. Included in the inquiries was information about which reading materials were around the house, the presence of icons, the parents' relationship and sexual habits, and Party membership.[2] Soviet schools felt it was their job to protect children from their "backward" parents.[3] Communism was prioritized over family. Youth groups such as the Young Pioneers and the Little Octobrists (referring to the Julian calendar month of the Bolshevik Revolution) isolated all who would *not* join them, creating for the children a class enemy before they reached maturity. Sound familiar?

In Nazi Germany, children were reached in another way: the paramilitary Hitler Youth was the sole youth group in Germany once Hitler became Chancellor. It was about eight million strong by the start of World War II, and activities included hiking, singing, and drills—all mindful of the Nazi agenda. The seed for this organization lay in scouting and other established German youth associations, which Hitler infiltrated and twisted to his own aims, squeezing out of them every vestige of their Christian roots. The Hitler Youth concentrated their power by breaking up other youth gatherings such as church meetings and Bible study. A later development within the Hitler Youth was the formation of a patrol force that provided internal policing. Some children in this role turned over their parents, critical of Hitler, to their deaths in concentration camps.

At home in the United States, children are best reached and manipulated through the public education system, run almost entirely by self-proclaimed progressives who present a monolithic political worldview as the absolute, unchanging truth. Tomberg warned, "Truth is seen as a river whose spring must forever yield new water; otherwise the waters stagnate and die."[4] Yet Alan Bergstein described the towering worldview of the educational leadership in this way:

> Randi Weingarten, the [former] head of the millions-strong teachers unions, did not spend her hours in the White House "wasting time" discussing the educational deprivations of the current school system...Her time was well spent learning to politically organize her minions to psychologically prepare the kids of America to use their weaponry of youth, innocence, and fragility to overturn the freedoms their grandparents and forefathers fought so hard to secure.
>
> These kids...the teenage spokesmen for humanity and decency, were demanding that all licensed, trained, and law-abiding gun owners be deprived of their constitutional rights...[they] left no doubt that they will return in force whenever "democracy" is again threatened.[5]

---

1 Kirschenbaum, Lisa A., *Small Comrades*, p. 154.
2 Ibid., p. 143.
3 Ibid., p. 131.
4 Tomberg, *Christ and Sophia*, p. 38.
5 See http://www.americanthinker.com/blog/2018/03/obamas_civilian_army_it_was_the_students_all_along.html.

Some students who refused to participate in anti-gun protests in 2018 were suspended or physically punished. This is even worse than it sounds, as the marches, bus trips, and media interviews for the students were planned *by adults* to take place during school hours. As was suggested by one dear teenage friend who opted out of the protest, the revolutionaries could accomplish much more if they instead had a few kind words to say to the boys at the back of the room with their heads in their hands.

At the time of the birth of the US Department of Education in May of 1980, the country ranked first in education internationally. Under their care, we have sunk to twentieth, according to the World Top 20 Project,[6] behind Hungary and Estonia. Perhaps the minds at the Department of Education are on other things. Today's rather pathetic rates of rising illiteracy in the US are the result of willfully avoiding phonics in public education; a century ago, illiteracy in children was solely the result of too little schooling.[7]

Equally troubling in the recent decades is the insidious corruption of institutions for children with mandated sexual themes (public education and scouting paramount among them), all in the name of inclusivity. This agenda, devoid of moral righteousness, hollows out everything it enters, like a voracious worm in an apple. Even prekindergarteners are not spared. The rise in sexual crimes against children has risen accordingly, leading one to wonder if one motive for the agenda is, in fact, increased sexual access to our precious youngsters? Who will defend their innocence?

### The Assault on Freedom of Speech

Another compulsory tool in the service of tyranny is the handcrafting of information to convey whatever is wanted at the time, no matter how obviously this might contradict what people can see with their own eyes. This has several troubling facets: first, a large and powerful government has determined what may and may not be thought and said (there can be grave consequences for not doing so), and second, there are ready and willing governmental organs with the ability and inclination to spread that word.

The minds behind the push for totalitarian sameness in the West could be said to have found a point of entry with the identification of "hate speech." (Who can claim to support hate?) With it, a noose was put around the neck of the First Amendment of the US Constitution, the gold standard that applies protections equally to all. The identification of hate speech *ends* free speech, as not all hate is created equal: the elites decide what is offensive and what is not. Those who question, oppose, or are presumed to oppose the progressive agenda are regularly labeled, censored, ridiculed, fired, or even fired *at* (recall the Congressional baseball shooting of June 2017). Is violence against those with whom one disagrees beginning to become a moral imperative? A 2017 poll suggests it might, revealing that nineteen percent of US college students felt it was acceptable to use violence to disrupt a speaker who is saying "offensive and hurtful things," whereas nearly forty percent did not believe the First Amendment covers hate speech.[8]

Liberal bias in American media is nothing new (recall *The New York Times* in the 1930s). Throughout most of the twentieth century, it was very difficult indeed to find a contrary point of view. They were tolerated because they had no influence. Then came the twin earthquakes known as the Internet and talk radio: platforms through which the prevailing media worldview was challenged. The reaction of the dominant media was like that of a toddler whose mother has brought home infant twins: Take them back! I liked it better before.

In the twisted vocabulary of groupthink, opposing points of view are now "divisive" (another term reserved uniquely for "the opposition"). The original, Greek concept of dialectic described a meeting of friends, with the purpose of seeking the truth *together. Are we no longer able to simply*

---

6  See https://worldtop20.org.

7  See https://improve-education.org.

8  Catherine Rampell, "A Chilling Study Shows How Hostile College Students Are toward Free Speech," *The Washington Post*, Sept. 18, 2017.

*have an intelligent conversation about the issues of the day?*

Social media is becoming the primary purveyor of news, handpicking the items we're to see, completely omitting stories that are unflattering to those who share its views, and fabricating stories that can harm those who do not. We cannot afford to presume that it speaks the truth.

Where have we seen this before?

### The Assault on Self-Defense

Crippling the ability of the masses to defend themselves was a key objective of the Bolsheviks and the Nazis; an unarmed populace is an *absolute requirement* of tyranny.

The Bolsheviks quickly limited the availability of firearms among their citizens, criminalizing possession with few exceptions; *citizens* became *subjects*. The NKVD issued gun licenses, which made it easy for them to track and later confiscate weapons as they chose. By the time Stalin came to power, firearms were all but eliminated among the populace. Ukrainians had to defend themselves with farm implements. Stalin said, "If the opposition disarms, well and good. If it refuses to disarm, we shall disarm it ourselves."[1]

Nazi Germany also prepared well for the round up and extermination of Jews and other "undesirables" such as Gypsies, Christians, and Slavs. By the time the first major offensive was launched against the Jews, the police had revoked the gun licenses of those whom Hitler regarded as enemies of the State. The Jews, by then, had been thoroughly disarmed, making his work that much easier.[2]

Of all the possible planetary–zodiacal combinations, Uranus in Aries cries out for something new—moral thinking that benefits all of "one's flock." It is no small disappointment that we are witnessing modern iterations of the tired, failed tenets of Marxism, Communism, and the will of a small number of elites to rule from the shadows—"old water" indeed. Some resist this, seeking to expose these cabals to the purifying effect of air and light, as Hercules did as he arose and conquered the Lernean Hydra.

How *on Earth* will the future Slavic cultural epoch, the Age of Aquarius, manage to flower out of the soil of tyranny, decay, and violence? How do we break free of the tightening bonds of the barbed tendrils of technology?

We know that our Angels have brought us to the present incarnations so that we might witness exactly what is before our eyes. They did not place us here in hopes that we might recoil, bereft of faith. Nor can we "jump into the ring" and fight evil directly.

Rudolf Steiner, Valentin Tomberg, and Robert Powell have taught us well how to identify and name evil. Without doing so, we are powerless to create a better future; it is through the experience and assessment of evil that good is brought forward. However, once named, we need to remember to seek joy in the sunlight, in the majesty of nature, in every encounter and in every endeavor. As Claudia McLaren Lainson explains, we must focus our attention on what we want to see flourish in the world.[3] This has never been more important, as the systemic evil around us squabbles for our attention. Tomberg warns us that *occupying* oneself with evil can constitute *contact* with it, and even furnish arms to its powers.[4]

What new thoughts are the Angels trying to bring to our attention during dawn of the fortieth day? To what miracles will we be able to bear witness? Let us name evil, and then shout "Hallelujah!" loud enough for all the Angels to hear it.

---

1 The Political Report of the Central Committee, The Fifteenth Congress of the C.P.S.U.(B.), Dec. 7, 1927.

2 During *Kristallnacht* (night of crystal), Nov. 9–10, 1938, coordinated attacks of Jewish homes, synagogues, businesses, and hospitals occurred throughout Nazi Germany.

3 McLaren Lainson, "The Towers we Build: The Uranian Double Bind," *Journal for Star Wisdom* 2016, p. 64.

4 Anon., *Meditations on the Tarot*, pp. 402–403.

# THE RISING OF THE DHARMA SUN
## *A Hermetic Perspective*
## *Claudia McLaren Lainson*

*Hermeticism, as the aspiration to the totality of things, is neither a school, nor a sect, nor a community. It is the destiny of a certain class or group of souls. For there are souls who must necessarily aspire to the "totality of things," and who are impelled by the river current of thought, which never stops, flowing always forward and always further on, without cease.... There is no stopping for these souls; they cannot, without renouncing their own lives, leave this river of thought, which pours without cease—equally during youth, mature age, and old age—without halting, from one darkness needing to be illumined to another darkness needing to be penetrated.*[1]

The darkness we are now to penetrate is *the darkness of the lie*. It has fallen upon us like a cloak of shadow. And behind the lie lurks the danger of nationalism. Nationalism is a form of intoxication that drowns the conscience of the individuals concerned; it is egoism experienced in common by a group or a nation. Once formed, the collective enfolds and coagulates, sculpting a host body in which the common arrogance of the entity's members may flourish. Such groups then create self-generated demons. And from these enfolded organizations, hate "against" is easily fostered, causing divisiveness to flourish.

This is exactly the condition that asphyxiates any possibility for a group to cultivate a relationship to the "totality of things." In order for spiritual intelligence to enlighten a group, or nation, radiance must exist, which is the opposite of enfoldment. Radiance is the mark of communities wherein the individuals within the collective are humble, open-minded, and curious. Inversely, groups formed around their self-generated demons breed malignant masses, whether large or small, into which the "little self" can feel empowered, even justified, in self-righteousness, antipathies, and hate. Yet, it is exactly the little self that we must now outgrow. And therein lies the success of mass consciousness, for growth demands contact with the dark unknown—which is not only frightening, but is also threatening to the ignorance, passivity, and laziness of those who have fallen victim to the enshrouded light.

Radiance is the light born of freethinking. It is the signature of the intense activity generated in groups when seeking higher knowledge (i.e., *ultra*light). If we are to lift ourselves out of the mass graveyard of materialism, we will have to reclaim the Hermetic acumen of our forebears. "*O dry bones, hear the word of the Lord*" (Ez. 27:4).

Mystery wisdom was taught long ago by great teachers who spoke into an atmosphere alive with mystery. Their speech resounded as *living word*; thus were their cloaks light-filled. Words then had overtones that vibrated within them. And these overtones depended upon the atmosphere of the mysteries, for without this they would have died away unheard. The mysteries are now virtually silent, the spiritual qualities that were united with them having indeed perished. In their place we are left with abstract, mechanical thoughts, lacking all true measure of the insight that once radiated when numerous philosophers such as Pythagoras, Plato, and Chartres' *Alanus de insulis* expounded universal wisdom. They were Hermeticists of their time, who lived for the "river current of thought."

The inversion to resonating with such living thoughts is to resonate with the machine. While the former draws upon divine intelligence, the latter draws upon dead thinking—i.e., thinking separate from spirit. It is the plan of the evil one to set the human soul in resonance with the machine as well as in resonance with the malignant masses, for this is how he thwarts the possibility of spiritual awaking.

Hermeticism is a study beyond metaphysics and mysticism, for it saturates itself in the *totality of*

---

1  Anon., *Meditations on the Tarot*, pp. 264-265.

*things*. Its source is the great Book of the World, wherein are inscribed the sublime ideas of creation and destiny, and this is quietly expressed through the symbolism of facts. When one is devoted to the totality of things, one is in the process of opening the third-eye, the eye that sees with *world-interest*. Hermeticists work from the primacy of love's binding power, which unites all people in sisterhood and brotherhood. The inversion to world-interest is, of course, egoism, which has become a very dangerous and destructive force, for it is overripe. In the right era, it had its place; there was even a kind of goodness in it. As for now, however, "it is good in the wrong time"—which is characteristic of evil—and this is the tragic destiny of all forms of egoistic nationalism born out of mass consciousness.

The new Saturn/Pluto cycle of 2020 will occur in Sagittarius, which is ruled by the wise and benevolent Jupiter (the Jupiter chakra is connected with the third-eye). We too are wise when we practice seeing from a vantage above the fray of discordant divisiveness; for as we thereby resonate with divine intelligence—which yearns to think *with* us and *in* us—we gain access to the totality of things. In so doing, we also become practical idealists, shedding the constraints of our lower natures as we drink from the chalice of virtue. This ennobles the soul, allowing it to raise its frequency into concordance with the mysteries now being unveiled. We can then remember that the subtle governs the dense, that energy is primary to matter, and that light is eternal.

Although the battle of our time may appear to be physical, in realms of these energies it is a battle for the human soul. Current attempts to resonate the human soul to match the intensity of ubiquitous cell technology constitute, in effect, a blatant attack on the reverberating frequencies of divine intelligence. Awareness of the subtle energies will thus become ever more essential as we move forward. We must also maintain our faith in the emerging vigilance of our younger generations, for what the adversarial forces fear most is humanity's spiritual awaking. Indeed, they know full well it will be their ruin if ever more people tread a path of increasing knowledge of these realities.

Since 1899, we have left behind the necessity of *Kali* Yuga and entered into the 5,000-year period of *Satya* Yuga. Kali Yuga had the purpose of pointing us to material existence, thereby setting the stage for the development of the conscious ego. Satya Yuga, on the other hand, is like the dawn of a new Sun. As its light is now beginning to crown the horizon, it radiates forces of forgiveness, thus reinvigorating the now-developed ego to *again* set its compass towards spiritual realities. In doing so, human beings will overcome egoism. Whereas the signature of Kali Yuga is the guilt of denigration—i.e., unfair criticism of self or others, the signature of Satya Yuga is the restoration of the principle of cosmic order in the world. Many who choose to harmonize the broken relationship between their spiritual self and their personality find themselves increasingly inspired by this principle.

Although the past 120 years (i.e., since we entered Satya Yuga) may display little evidence of a turn towards spirit, we are not to be distracted. Change is notoriously slow, yet evidence abounds proving that the powers behind the great rhythms of time are breaking through. Such change reveals the goodness inherent in this new era. As a result of increasing spiritual understanding, ever more people are filled with *world-interest*. To this end, Rudolf Steiner brought reformation in many areas of life. And despite the fact that the forces against him were severe, the legacy of his life's work remains a foundation upon which the Dharma Sun of Satya Yuga[1] will continue to rise.

Self-absorption is boring. In self-absorption, the soul grasps incessantly for new diversions and entertainments to assuage the mendacity of its existence. Freedom requires *active* responsibility. Many of us, however, have become saturated with laziness, eventually succumbing to *world-weariness*—which either sparks action or else drives the soul into the loneliness of depression and hopelessness. Dangerous reasoning, so prevalent nowadays

---

1  *Dharma* refers to a time when the principle of cosmic order will be restored—i.e., when human beings again remember their spiritual heritage. *Dharma Sun* refers to the onset of this new age.

among the enfolded masses, increasingly molds itself to the past and is thus incapable of reaching into the future. Whether a global catastrophe is needed for more of us to acknowledge spiritual realities is something that still remains to be seen. Future evolution—the greatest deterrent to which is the narcissism of egoism—is dependent upon deeds carried out by individuals in freedom.

The resplendent light of Satya Yuga is now birthing from both above and below. And as the flame of spiritual awaking thereby grows ever brighter, we are not to be distracted by the menacing forces that will inevitably become stronger. The Book of Revelation gives us a similar concept for divinity's eternal flame. The fifth of the seven letters to the seven churches is addressed to the Church of Sardis—which refers to our current Piscean Age. In this letter we are told of the difference between the "name" and the "body of karma." The "name" is the ideal, and the "body of karma" is the state of the soul when separate from its ideal. When the soul has recognized its higher self, its true "name," it becomes clothed in white raiment—i.e., clothed in the divine archetype of its eternal self. The practice of discerning between the two, of separating the essential from the inessential, is a requirement for the spiritual aspirant:

> The progress of such practice requires insight into the difference between the "name" and the "body," in the sense that the "name" is the concrete meaning of the revelation of *manas* (spirit self) by means of the human soul, whereas the "body" is the life of the soul itself, aside from its connection with the spirit self, which guides one from incarnation to incarnation.[2]

Just as the clothed physical body is shielded from the eyes of the world, so also is our one true "name" clothed from being despoiled through the ignorance of the personality. The most important aspect of our age is to become aware of, and establish a relationship to, our spiritual *manas* principle. To this end, while also opening ourselves to the fact that intelligence must be spiritualized, we can imagine words again resounding with the power of the mysteries.

2  Tomberg, *Christ and Sophia*, p. 339.

The Dharma Sun of Satya Yuga is breaking through the dark grid of materialism, and this is exactly what is causing an even greater surging of ugliness from the ranks of evil beings—in the outer world and within us. As the old system continues to unravel, the death throes of desperation are evinced by the divisiveness, destructiveness, cynicism, cruelty, and greed that swirl around us. Mechanical, abstract, spiritless thinking—so typical in our time—is symptomatic of obsolete paradigms. We must find new imaginations.

It is a responsibility of education to move with the times, for only through balancing *destructive* technology by applying *constructive* technology will we be able to draw forth the mature spiritual capacities that many of our young people demonstrate so clearly. These "awakeed ones" are becoming aware of the harmful spell that technological glamour has woven into their lives, threatening to draw them unwittingly into addictive relationships with their dazzling electronic devices and with social media forums. Having allowed electromagnetic technology (i.e., the arbitrary magic of the fallen kingdoms) into our schools, must we not also invite the technologies of light—i.e., etheric technologies—as antidotes? This would necessitate that we teach our upper school children the realities of negative and positive subtle energies. Why would we avoid this curricular addition when so many of the younger generations now on Earth, aware of ever-impending darkness, have come into their current incarnation to join with others in the Michaelic battle for the human soul?

### New Imaginations

Something rarified is touching into earthly life and this is not going unnoticed. We are not to become mere machines that can be cyber-fashioned to live through an eternity *not* born of heaven, for such is the mark of the fatefully egoistic Transhumanists.[3]

3  "Transhumanist thinkers study the potential benefits and dangers of emerging technologies that could overcome fundamental human limitations, as well as the ethics of developing and using such technologies. They speculate that human beings

During the period of Jesus Christ's forty days in the desert, he was tempted in his human nature to enter Satan's world of magic. His victory will assuredly be echoed by all who choose to confront this temptation with spirit-awareness. Anne Catherine Emmerich depicts this trial:

> Then [Satan] showed him hanging on his hand a piece of apparatus that resembled a globe, or (perhaps still more) a bird cage. Jesus would not look at Satan, as this tempter desired; much less would he look into the globe. Instead, turning his back on him, he left the grotto. I saw that a look into Satan's trick-show disclosed the most magnificent scenes from nature: lovely pleasure gardens full of shady groves, cool fountains, richly laden fruit trees, luscious grapes, etc. All seemed to be within one's reach, and all was constantly dissolving into ever more beautiful, more enticing scenes. Jesus turned his back on Satan, and he vanished.[1]

It is frightening to glimpse into the one-sided danger of living in creation's caricature without simultaneously living into the inverse reality of *etheric magical truth*. Such truth is now radiating from the presence of the Etheric Christ. Learning how to receive these blessed radiations is the greatest challenge before us, and education regarding this is crucial. Indeed, our striving on the path of spiritual study can no longer be optional if we are to rise together into the Dharma Sun of Satya Yuga.

Given that the Earth is past the midpoint of its development, we will continue to live in its decaying processes for the remainder of our incarnations. It is therefore inevitable that eventually, whether in this life or those yet to come, we will realize that egoism becomes ever more dangerous as these death processes accelerate. And as these processes continue, the approaching descent of our "name" will draw those so striving into a closer relationship with the soul-spiritual forces being released[2]—for through the "name," we will remember that the source of all true intelligence is bestowed from worlds above. Spiritual cognitions are in fact increased through the very substance released by decay, and are the antidote to it. Moreover, we must see from the perspective of Hermeticism if we are to counteract the forces that would lead us to ahrimanic death (i.e., to the death of our *spiritual* self). Such death has two faces: abstraction and mechanization—the depersonalization of thinking as well as the depersonalization of our view of nature.

## Spiritual Effects of Deceit

Americans, perhaps most particularly, have for centuries been increasingly enveloped in webs of wretched lies and deceptions. Thus would it be tragically naïve to disregard warnings regarding the presence of evil beings and the deceptive practices of secret brotherhoods; for when a populace is manipulated into believing lies, it becomes surrounded by elemental beings that are actually forced into serving such deceits. These beings must weave in darkness as they spin cloaks of falsehood around us—creating murky, gloomy fields that refract all light.[3] Light alone can receive the soul-spiritual forces released in matter's decay; light alone can resonate with divine intelligence; light alone can receive the ministrations of angels who yearn to bring us truth.

Therefore, if we choose to believe the propaganda being fed to us by the ruthlessly insatiable world-elites, we will not experience the release of soul-spiritual energies that Steiner spoke of as the inevitable "byproduct" of degenerating matter. Instead, our destiny will find us *succumbing* to death processes (the abstract and the mechanical), whereby the oppressive, spiritless people standing behind materialism will continue to profit from

---

may eventually be able to transform themselves into beings with such greatly expanded abilities as to merit the label 'posthuman'" (Wikipedia entry on *Transhumanism*).

1 *The Visions of Anne Catherine Emmerich*, vol. 1, p. 369.
2 Steiner, *Understanding Society through Spiritual Scientific Knowledge*, p. 84: Everything physical is growing brittle; it is already in decline on the Earth, and we should not place our hope any longer in this physical level of things. Instead we can only expect something of what—to put it trivially—is sprinkling out precisely because the physical realm is in decline: the spirit and soul.
3 See Solari Report, Mar. 1, 2018: An interview with Thomas Meyer: https://constitution.solari.com/the-future-of-europe-with-thomas-meyer/.

their stupendous fabrications. These people would then achieve their intended goal of ensnaring Western populations through instigating uncertainty, confusion, and fear.

Nationalism, as the invisible intoxication resulting in the drowning of conscience, must be overcome. Hermeticists know this, and instead seek the spiritual air that has ever nurtured conscience. Of the three occult trials (fire, water, air)—especially as outlined in Steiner's *Knowledge of the Higher Worlds* and in Valentin Tomberg's *Inner Development*—we can easily imagine how the *air* trial is currently predominant. Without the air of spirit, we unwittingly think in accordance with the beast. Such is the delirium that incubates in isolated groups. "Folly [we could also say *deceit*] is a condition preventing that which is true from being grasped" (Plato, *Definitions*).

As we are in the second year of the twenty-nine-year unfolding of the fortieth day in the wilderness—the day angels came to minister to Jesus Christ—we must free ourselves from the fraudulent nationalistic agendas behind which our reality can be erroneously determined. In this regard, our greatest temptation is in our tendency to fall prey to false flag events. Much of the twenty-first century, for example, has thus far been shaped by the lie of 9/11. A closer view, however, shows many well-known accounts of this event to be preposterous. While the light recedes ever further from us, we must face the agonizing danger of an impending mass imprisonment engendered through duplicity. In fact, if we do not stand up and grasp hold of truth, we risk becoming pawns in a perilous game.

Economic tyranny has successfully overpowered our social and political systems, smothering any semblance of a threefold balance.[4] Powerfully wealthy people stand behind the arms industry and must continually feed themselves through the harvest of fresh conquests. New enemies are then sculpted through the blatant treacheries of false flag events; and such "events" serve to manipulate mass opinion according to the way power mongers need us to think. Thus are endless wars inevitable.

We need to face the fact that, for the most part, we have been sleeping—"distracted to death" by the spurious storylines of profiteers. Imagine how different things would look if we refused to go along with such schemes, while instead distancing ourselves from the misanthropic delusions that so often accompany them! We would then awake to the shocking degree of betrayal we suffer as a result of the deeds of immoral geniuses who have become Ahriman's people. In so awaking, we would liberate ourselves from mass deception, thereby regaining our ability to freely think in accordance with the principle of cosmic order. All of this is possible if we choose to participate in the rising of the Dharma Sun.

## The Gift of Sardis: The White Raiment of our Name

The coarseness of physical bodies makes it increasingly difficult for souls to fully inhabit them. In contrast, souls moving within etheric realms are aware of the archetypal realities that underlie all material substance. This is the world of the Hermeticist, where light holds sway. When we ingest this light, it stamps itself upon our etheric bodies. So enlivened, we become awake to the truth, and we resonate with the mysteries of divine intelligence. Through the taking in of light, we prepare ourselves to receive the mantle of the "name," which yearns to envelop us. Etheric subtle energies then cast away the menacing shadows of egoistic isolation.

Freedom is a choice. First, of course, we must realize the full measure of our slavery to the lie. The effort this requires will gradually divide us into two groups, which in turn will create two races, and eventually even two planets: one of these will be similar to the sci-fi scenarios so prevalent nowadays in Hollywood movies and virtual gaming; the other will be similar to the New Jerusalem of the Book of Revelation.

A *light-sheath* is descending upon all who practice spirit-awareness. We must be especially vigilant regarding the danger that lurks in the lies that

---

4   See Steiner, *Towards Social Renewal: Rethinking the Basis of Society.*

would obstruct this truth. Yet another kind of danger is that of compromise born of "political correctness"—which imposes agendas that have effectively silenced many. Valentin Tomberg equates such compromise with "defiling of the name."

> In the language of the Apocalypse, however, it [compromise] is called "defiling" the name's garment. Compromise is the principle of false peace between the two opposites in human life; it also leads to darkening the system of spiritual current that "sheathes" the personal like a garment.... The "light-sheath" ceases to radiate its beams and becomes darkened. This is the darkening that the Apocalypse calls defiling the garment of the name. Being "clothed in white raiment," by contrast, is the condition of being illumined by the light of the Spirit; thus, these whose activity is directed objectively outward stand with their impersonal, spiritual side toward the world. Strictly speaking, they do not merely "stand," but pursue a path laid down by Christ in the sense of the promise: "But thou hast a few names in Sardis that have not defiled their garments, and they shall walk with me in white, for they are worthy" (Rev. 3:4).[1]

In this age of the consciousness soul we must *not* abandon our task of awaking to our spirit self. The entire mission of our time is to confront the evil that is now upon us. "There are times when, through the aid of the starry beings, we are able to unveil the mystery of evil—beholding what evil is doing in our world and yet not faint in this beholding."[2] These are our times! And the Saturn/Pluto conjunction of 2020 bestows the blessings of aligning with the lofty guardians of truth who indwell the constellation of Sagittarius.

Sacred magic is *etheric white magic*. Its purpose is not the destruction of life, but rather the constructive collaboration between above and below. Tomberg names the acorn as an example of a constructive bomb—i.e., the slow explosion of the little acorn results in the growth of the mighty oak. It is a miracle!

> Yes, the miraculous does exist, for *life* is only a series of miracles, if we understand by "miracle" not the absence of cause (i.e., that it would not be caused by anyone or anything—which would be more the concept of "pure chance"), but rather the visible effect of an invisible cause, or the effect on a lower plane due to a cause on a higher plane.[3]

Miracles surround us in everyday life; yet unless we have reclaimed our freedom, such blessings will pass by unnoticed. We are born of seven spirits that constitute our totality in a *vertical* sense (i.e., physical, etheric, astral, "I," spirit self, life spirit, and spirit human). This insight—through which we remember the sacred origin of all life (the memory within)—gives us the power to overcome the abstraction of life forms born of subhuman realms. In a *horizontal* sense, we are in a process of evolution in time (i.e., of the seven stars of Saturn, Sun, Moon, Earth, future Jupiter, future Venus, and future Vulcan). This insight gives us the power to overcome the mechanizing of life forms, by means of which we remember the "biography" of the cosmos through great cycles of time (the memory of nature). In light of these insights, we find the ideal of the Cosmic Christ ("that hath the seven Spirits of God, and the seven stars"[4]) at the beginning of the letter to the church in Sardis:

> There are two kinds of memory: horizontal, temporal memory, which can be awakeed by nature, and vertical, spatial memory, through which we become aware of our own true character. As we can see from the "cross" of the fifth post-Atlantean culture, two kinds of memory arise from the force of spiritual opposition to the sub-natural mechanical sphere, in the one case, and in the other, to subhuman abstraction. It awakes higher inner activity in

---

1 Tomberg, *Christ and Sophia*, p. 339. An extensive endnote on this theme (see pp. 412–413), quoting what Rudolf Steiner wrote in the book *Theosophy* regarding this phenomenon, is introduced with this remark: "Rudolf Steiner describes this light sheath as 'the third kind of aura—the spiritual aura, side by side with the physical and the astral.'"
2 See Estelle Isaacson's article in this volume.
3 Anon., *Meditations on the Tarot*, p. 67.
4 Revelation 3:1.

opposition to the forces of death, both within and outside the human being.[5]

If we do not raise the cross upon which the vertical and the horizontal unite, we will not find the courage to meet evolution's turn—from destructive to constructive magic, from Kali Yuga to Satya Yuga. "A third of the stars in heaven" may indeed be cast down (i.e., our names will be blotted out of the Book of Life) if we avoid the spiritual mandate now upon us and live instead in adoration of our lower personal self. Vainglorious diversions will sweep us away into the "anti-river current of thought" in which we will fail to penetrate and illumine the world's darkness. And the totality of things will then elude us.

*The eye that constantly beholds what is ugly and fallen will become blind to the spiritual light.* What we devote our attention towards is of great consequence! Many will become lighthouses, illuminating the path that brings healing to our true sight, our *spiritual* sight. These will be people who, in freedom, speak forthrightly, despite the disturbance this may cause.

Taking full responsibility for the true meaning of freedom (thinking with the light) is a moral duty assigned to the human "I." Freedom is not "license." Rather does freedom give us the choice as to which burden we will pick up, which responsibility we will take upon ourselves in sacrifice for the future. In so doing we are noticed in worlds above. As we awake each day, knowing that we have purpose, our lives become noble. In this regard we can look back in gratitude to the great Hermeticists who have come before us, as well as seek inspiration from the many inspiring Platonists now among us. The Dharma Sun is rising and we are to turn our attention to this miracle.

## Abraham and Moses

The divine and flaming Word shines in the world of the silence of the soul and "moves" it. This movement is living faith—therefore real and authentic—and its light is hope, or illumination; whilst all springs from the divine fire that is love, or union with God. The three "ways" or stages of traditional mysticism—*purification, illumination, and union*—are those of the experience of divine breath, or faith; divine light, or hope; and divine fire, or love.

These three fundamental experiences of the revelation of the Divine constitute the triangle of *life*—for no spirit, no soul, and equally no body would be able to *live* if entirely deprived of all love, all hope, and all faith. They would then be deprived of all vital élan (the vital élan advanced by Henri Bergson as the general impulse behind evolution). But what else could this be but some form of love, hope, and faith operating at the basis of all life? It is because "in the beginning was the Word" and "all things were made through him" (John 1:1-3); and because the primordial Word still vibrates in all that lives, the *world* still lives and has the vital élan which is nothing other than love, hope, and faith inspired from the beginning by the creative Word.[6]

Through Valentin Tomberg we hear the voice of Abraham speaking, calling together the children of Eternal Israel; and we hear him through the voice of the Angel Jesus, who weaves the spirit of the stars into the body of the Earth.

What I have been telling you is merely one example. We must begin to bring this sense for the stars, this sense for the *beings* of the stars, into our present time. We must begin to help people understand anew that the Christ is a Sun Being. This is the fact that meets with the greatest opposition of all.[7]

Through Rudolf Steiner we hear the voice of Moses speaking. He calls us to remember the mission of our fifth cultural epoch in relation to Astrosophy. Through him the voice of Michael resounds, firing our will to act.

The spirits of the elements do indeed hear these things, and they pray that human beings will also listen.

---

5  Tomberg, *Christ and Sophia*, p. 335.

6  Anon., *Meditations on the Tarot*, pp. 71–72.

7  Steiner, *The Book of Revelation and the Work of the Priest*, p. 80.

# CLASSICS IN ASTROSOPHY, PART II
## *The Lunar Calendar, Concluded*
### Robert Powell, PhD

EDITOR'S NOTE: *In* Journal for Star Wisdom 2018, *I introduced readers to the first in a series of articles written more than forty years ago by Robert Powell. They were published originally in the* Mercury Star Journal, *whose previous editor was Robert's mentor Willi Sucher. Those articles have been virtually unavailable since their publication in the 1970s. The following is the second half of the series on the lunar calendar.*

These articles represent the earliest published works by Robert Powell. It is remarkable that the qualities that define Robert's work—clarity and thoroughness of description combined with a palpable devotional mood—were already present in those early articles. It is also remarkable that the subject of these articles (reestablishing our connection with the Lunar Sphere) has also carried through to the present day in his work (for example, see the brief article "Working with the *Star Wisdom* Calender" in the current volume). Why is this?

The Lunar Sphere is of particular importance in our time. It is the realm of the etheric; the realm of the life forces which flow into both biological development and the substance of thought itself. This realm is deeply connected to the realm in which Christ is appearing in our time, that is, in the Earth's etheric aura, just as he appeared in the physical realm approximately 2,000 years ago. Of the nine Spiritual Hierarchies at work between human beings and the Holy Trinity, the Lunar Sphere is the realm of activity of the Angels in particular, the Hierarchy standing just above humanity. This spiritual reality is of great consequence when we consider the moment in human development through which we are living. In a broad sense, it is the time of the advent of the etheric Christ (this advent occurs over a long period of time, for the entire Satya Yuga, from approximately AD 1899 to 4433). In a more specific sense, it is the end of the Cosmic Forty Days of Temptation in the Wilderness. Those Days of Temptation, which have tormented all of humanity in the same way Christ alone was tormented historically, began in 869. Only as of the year 2018 have we reached the start of the last "day" (each "day" lasts for one Saturn return of approximately 29½ years). On this day historically speaking (that is, for Christ as an individual) Angels came to minister to Christ after the previous thirty-nine days of torment and loneliness. As we experience the Cosmic amplification of this historical event between 2018 and 2047, all of humanity has a heightened possibility of attaining to direct relationship with the Angelic realm, of likewise being ministered unto by Angels. —JOEL PARK[1]

### The Use of the Lunar Calendar (*Christmas 1975*)

It is the endeavor of *Cosmology Reborn* to represent a twentieth-century perspective on the development of a new cosmic science, Astrosophy. Our intention is not only to present the results of research in this field, but also to establish a research methodology. From time to time, therefore, methods of research drawn from the domain of spiritual science will be presented for the attention of those striving to develop the path of knowledge leading from the spiritual in the human being to the spiritual in the universe. It is not intended that such methods should replace the usual meditative techniques outlined, for example, in *Guidance in Esoteric Training*,[2] for the basic exercises are a necessary foundation for any spiritual progress. The spiritual methods here described should be considered as an adjunct to the basic practices, offered with the specific aim of creating a

---

[1] These spiritual realities have been described by Robert Powell and others in many publications. See Powell, *The Christ Mystery*, for perhaps the most concise collection of such descriptions.

[2] Steiner, *Guidance in Esoteric Training*.

deepening relationship with the Cosmic Intelligences.³ It is through the creation of such a relationship that Astrosophy can flourish.

One of the great Buddhist maxims is, "All is change." Everything in the universe is in a perpetual process of transformation, of becoming. For one who becomes aware of this through following the meditative practices described, for example, in *How to Know Higher Worlds*,⁴ the feeling can arise that one has no support. It is as though the ground begins to slip away from under one's feet. And yet, just as those who are learning to swim find that they can do so in the moment they actually entrust themselves to the water, so does the soul find a new ground when it entrusts itself to the universal principle that "all is change"—i.e., when the soul lays aside the notion of rigidity that is the inherent characteristic of the physical world. The human soul can find itself at home when it truly lives in the manifold rhythms that underlie all existence.

Fiona Tweedale has described a way that the rhythm of the year may be spiritually experienced by meditating at a special time of the day—between dawn and sunrise—on the position of the Sun against the background of the constellations. Rudolf Steiner produced the first Soul Calendar⁵ in 1912/13 in collaboration with a young artist, Imma von Eckardstein. Under Rudolf Steiner's direction, she had practiced the meditations. During this process, she produced twelve zodiacal motifs consequent to the inner experiences she underwent. Rudolf Steiner had described to her how, if the meditation is practiced in mindfulness of the Mystery of Golgotha, the soul can become illumined from within and attain "inner perception" of the Zodiac.

Apart from meditating upon the Sun's yearly passage though the Zodiac, human beings may also become attuned to the other cosmic rhythms. Yet, as in the aforementioned meditation, the point of key significance is that the human being is enabled to enter the spiritual experience of these rhythms as a result of all that has ensued consequent to the Mystery of Golgotha—for it is indeed the "Christ Will in the encircling Round" that holds sway in regards to the movements of the starry heavens. This is beautifully expressed in the second verse of the Foundation Stone Meditation, which was given on the occasion of the founding of the General Anthroposophical Society.

> Human soul!
> You live in the beat of heart and lung,
> which leads you through time's rhythm
> into the feeling of your own soul's being.
> Practice spirit awareness
> in serenity of soul,
> where surging
> deeds of world becoming
> unite your "I"
> with the "I" of the world;
> then, you shall truly feel
> in the soul's inner working.
> For the Christ will reigns in the
>     spheres around us,
> shedding grace upon souls in the
>     world's rhythms.
> Spirits of light,
> let what is formed in the west
> be kindled from the east,
> saying:
> *In Christ, death becomes life.*⁶

In fact, the entirety of the Foundation Stone Meditation manifests the cosmic dialogue ever occurring between worlds above and worlds below. Thus Rudolf Steiner refers to this meditation as the "Foundation Stone of Love," thereby revealing the suprasensory reality that stands as the essential basis of all that may be described as "living with the events of the heavens."

One of this *Journal*'s central tasks is to help, in every way possible, all those who in the present times are seeking to live in "spirit-mindfulness" of the starry worlds. Moreover, in our astrosophical work we have found that the Foundation Stone Meditation leads to the *experience* of participation in the whole cosmos. For this reason

---

3   Powell, "Communion with the Cosmic Intelligences: the Macrocosmic Lord's Prayer," *Mercury Star Journal* i (1975), 81–86.
4   Steiner, *How to Know Higher Worlds*.
5   Steiner, *Kalendar 1912/13* (see *Calendar 1912–1913 Facsimile edition of the original book...*).
6   Steiner, *Start Now!*

(although other mantras such as the Macrocosmic Lord's Prayer[1] can bring the soul into a more conscious relationship with the beings of the higher worlds), the Foundation Stone Meditation is the touchstone, as well as the point of departure, for our work in Astrosophy.

More rapid than the yearly solar rhythm is the monthly lunar rhythm, which the soul can also gradually come to experience. The lunar rhythm is of overriding significance for the inner nature of the human being. (In women it even comes to expression in the physical body.) In following the lunar rhythm attentively from month-to-month, there grows a steadily increasing awareness of one's "inner soul nature": "During fourteen days, the part of the human being that is independent of the physical and etheric body is filled with productive forces. And during the next fourteen days, these forces work themselves out."[2] Indeed, awareness of the lunar cycle is accompanied by a feeling of bliss.

The soul can find an inestimable joy in discovering the cosmic world hidden within the Moon sphere. When this opening of the soul takes place, it is again important that an awareness of the Mystery of Golgotha is realized—for in this realization, human beings find their feet on the physical earth while at the same time being united with the Earth's spiritual mission.

Knowing the day of the lunar month (and therewith the phase of the moon) enables one to maintain a connection with the consciousness of the *physical* body, while at the same time opening to the oceanic realms of the Moon's *spiritual* existence. For this reason, knowledge of each particular day within the lunar rhythm provides an orientation for the soul's inner experience. What is of special importance in the practice of this exercise, however, is that it is carried through in full consciousness.

In the early stages of Initiation consciousness, an aspirant becomes aware that Moon forces are within one's being and that these forces always tend to develop a "second person" who is encased within oneself. A conflict now sets in. When the Moon forces begin to be *inwardly* active in this second person of whom I am speaking—not in waking consciousness, but during sleep—this second person is then released naturally by these *inner* Moon forces. Moreover, when this being is set free by the presence of the Moon at night and begins to awake towards consciousness in the passive condition of sleep, then that being (who is concealed *within* the first, the normal one) seeks to wander around in the light of the Moon and takes the other along. Such is the origin of the somnambulistic condition that is peculiar to sleepwalkers.

When the Moon is shining outside, it is thus possible to awake the second person, who then makes contact with magical forces (i.e., anomalous forces which differ in kind from those of nature) and begins to wander around. As a sleepwalker in a diminished state of consciousness, this entity behaves in a way that would be foreign to ordinary consciousness. Instead of lying in bed, as one would normally do, it wanders around and climbs on roofs, looking for the sphere that, in reality, ought to be experienced *outside* the physical body.

When this becomes a conscious inner experience and is directed into normal channels, we take the first step in Initiation-consciousness. In that case, however, we do not contact the actual, external Moon influences; instead, the Moon forces in our inner being enable the second person (or, second *being* within us) to develop consciousness. We must at all costs prevent this being from breaking loose, for there is always the danger that it might otherwise wander about, phantom-like, and stray along false paths. Indeed, it must be kept under control!

Inner stability and self-control are essential for the acquisition of Initiation-knowledge. Furthermore, these attributes serve to ensure that this potentially errant being stays *within* the body and remains linked to the ordinary, matter-of-fact consciousness associated with the physical body. We must perpetually struggle to prevent this creation of the strengthened inner Moon-nature from dissociating itself from us. It is strongly attracted to everything associated with metabolism, peristalsis, as well as the stomach and other organs. Thus it makes heavy demands upon these aspects of our physical nature.

---

[1] Ibid., pp 218ff, "Esoteric 'Our Father.'"
[2] Steiner, "The Moon," *Paths of Experience* (London, 1934), p. 123.

The first indication, the first experience, of an aspirant's dawning Initiation-knowledge is that of following one of the two paths that have to be traversed—the path that leads through the development, through the *conscious realization*, of the dream world.

And if, while in the dream state, one now becomes aware (which, as I have pointed out, is a necessary step), one realizes that though it is day without, one bears *within oneself* the night. In the daytime there thus awakes within oneself something like an "inner night."

When this Initiate-consciousness awakes, the day is still day to the outward eyes and for the external apprehension of things; but in the course of this day, the spiritual light of the Moon—with its refulgent beams—begins to invade and illumine all around. The spiritual begins to shine.

We know, therefore, that the aspirant brings the night consciousness into the day consciousness by means of inner effort. When this happens in full consciousness, just as other activities are performed consciously during the day—that is, when the vigilant aspirant is able to invoke the night activities of the Moon into the waking experiences of the daytime—then such a person is on the true path. If, however, one allows anything to enter oneself while not fully conscious, so that out of one's own inner momentum the night experiences arise in the day consciousness, then one finds oneself on the false path that ultimately leads to *mediumism*.

The essential point is, therefore, that we must be fully conscious—i.e., in full control of our experiences. The phenomena and experiences are not, however, decisive factors in and of themselves. Instead, it is a matter of *the way* in which we respond to them. If the ordinary sleepwalker could develop full consciousness at a time when he is climbing on the rooftop, he would at that moment experience an intimation of Initiation. Since he *fails* to develop this consciousness, he falls to the ground when we shout at him to awake him. If, on the other hand, he did not fall, but instead developed full waking consciousness and could maintain this condition, he would then be an Initiate. The task of Initiation-knowledge is to develop along sound lines—sound in *every* respect—that which is developed in the sleepwalker pathologically.

You will note, then, how a hair's breadth separates the true from the false in the spiritual world. There is no difficulty in distinguishing between the true and the false in the physical world, because a person can typically appeal to common sense and practical experience. As soon as an aspirant enters the spiritual world, however, it is exceedingly difficult to establish this distinction. The aspirant is then wholly dependent on inner control, inner awareness. Furthermore, when one has "awakeed the night in the day," moonlight gradually loses its character of external radiance. We experience it less externally; instead, it creates in us a general feeling of inner wellbeing. We become aware, however, of something else. The wonderful glowing light of Mercury illumines this spiritual night-sky. The planet Mercury actually rises in this night that has been wooed into the day. It is not a matter of the *physical* aspect of Mercury, for we realize that we are in the presence of something living. We cannot recognize immediately the living spiritual Beings who are the inhabitants of Mercury; but from the way in which Mercury appears to us, we have a general impression that we are in touch with a spiritual world.

When the spiritual moonlight becomes a universal life-giving force within us—i.e., one in which we *participate*—then the spiritual planet Mercury gradually rises in the night consciousness that has been wooed into the day consciousness. Out of this sparkling twilight in which Mercury appears, there then emerges the Being whom we call the Divine Being Mercury. We have absolute need of this Being, for otherwise confusion will set in. We must first of all find this Being—whom we know for certain belongs to Mercury—in the spiritual world. Through our knowledge of this Divine Being (Mercury) we are able to control at will the "second person" who is awakened within us. We no longer need to stumble along undefined paths like the sleepwalker. Instead, we can be led by the hand of Mercury—the messenger of the Gods—along the clearly defined paths that lead into the spiritual world.[3]

---

[3] Steiner, *True and False Paths in Spiritual*

Rudolf Steiner's description (which, because of its importance, has been quoted fully) makes it critically evident that one must enter the Moon sphere *while in full consciousness*. We live in the Moon sphere, the realm that is bounded by the orbit of the Moon, for this region interpenetrates our earthly world. Generally speaking, however, we are conscious *only* of that which is presented to our senses— namely, the physical world.

Under normal conditions, our consciousness is filled with the objects of the physical world. However, if we consciously extend our consciousness to the world that is bounded by the Moon—if, in fact, we *will* that world to enter our consciousness— then it can do so. It is here that the lunar calendar can be of assistance. If we choose an opportune moment in which to "woo the inner night of the Moon into the external day,"[1] we awake into the hidden knowledge of a particular day of the lunar month. This awareness establishes a connection between cosmic lunar worlds and the ordinary brain-bound consciousness of the physical body. The Moon sphere can then be entered into with full consciousness, wherein the individual is in full control. (Note that the "ordinary, matter-of-fact consciousness associated with the physical body" can be intensified through meditating upon gold).[2]

This *Journal* seeks to work with, and be guided by, the Divine Being Mercury so as to cultivate the safe—i.e., fully conscious, way towards knowledge of the higher worlds. The lunar calendar arose in antiquity at a time when human consciousness was becoming free of the Moon sphere to become more and more directed to the Earth sphere on the physical plane of existence. Through the lunar calendar a link was maintained with the Beings of the Moon sphere—the primeval Teachers of humankind. Now, in the twentieth century, the fully conscious use of the lunar calendar is a means of enabling the soul to orientate itself within the Moon sphere. This may be regarded as a "Mercury inspiration," one that can facilitate a safe entry into spiritual worlds through the exercise (and strengthening) of the faculty of thought. In this way, human beings remain free; they are always the sovereign initiators of their excursions into spiritual realms.

It is especially in the twentieth century that an awaking to the Moon sphere has assumed such importance for human beings. "For the Christ-Will in the encircling Round holds sway in Rhythms of Worlds bestowing Grace on the Soul."

Since the year 1933, the Risen Christ has been working in the etheric realm bordering the Earth, amongst the Beings of the Moon sphere.[3] The renewal of Christianity—striving toward *living* Christianity—is now taking place. This impulse seeks to be carried across the civilized world by an ever-increasing number of human beings in order that a truly Cosmic Christianity may hold sway in the world during the third millennium, and it can take hold of human hearts only through *experience*. Christ Jesus will not reappear on the physical plane to impose his presence upon humanity; for, above all, the Christ-Jesus Being leaves human beings free. We are left free to choose whether or not to raise ourselves to Christ Jesus in the etheric realm bordering the earthly realm.

Ways and means of expanding consciousness to the Moon sphere need to be found for those who are seeking the Risen Christ. The use of the lunar calendar, in conjunction with the spiritual practice here described by Rudolf Steiner as the "Evening Verse," is one such way.[4] Moreover, it is a way that is befitting modern individuals, for it unites the knowledge gained through the consciousness of the physical world (the knowledge of the natural science of astronomy) with the knowledge of higher worlds as the result of spiritual-scientific research. Thus the abyss separating the physical and spiritual realm may now be crossed. Furthermore, in the spiritual region known as Shambhala, Jesus Christ can also be found. "Once people are able

---

*Investigation* (tr. rev.).
1  Ibid., 196.
2  Ibid., 64-5, "...all that sustains our ordinary waking consciousness, all that keeps it 'normal'...is gold..."
3  Steiner, *The Reappearance of Christ in the Etheric*, ch. 2.
4  See also the *Evening Verse* included at the end of this article.

to penetrate Shambhala with their vision, they will also be able to understand the real meaning of much that is contained in the Gospels.... Thus, at a time when people have the least confidence in those documents [the Gospels], a new profession of faith in Jesus Christ will arise as we grow into the sphere where we shall encounter him—in the mysterious land of Shambhala."[5]

## Evening Verse

Words of meditation for those already more advanced, laying hold of the feeling:

Imagining oneself in the space illuminated by the Moon at night; therein one experiences with *feeling*

> In the Beginning was Jahve
> And Jahve was with the Elohim
> And Jahve was one of the Elohim
> And Jahve lives in me.

Then, in imagination, one lets the Moon-illumined space change into the space lit up by the Sun by day; therein one experiences with *feeling*

> And Christ lives in me
> And Christ is one of the Elohim
> And Christ is with the Elohim
> At the end, Christ will be."[6]

## Further Notes on the Lunar Calendar (*Easter 1976*)

The lunar calendar and its use has been discussed,[7] but clear rules have not yet been set forth regarding its determination. The general principle is referred to in the Babylonian "Creation Epic," wherein the Creator addresses the Moon as follows:

> At the beginning of the month, shine upon the land. Beam with thy horns, to make known the six days. On the seventh day, halve thy disc. On the fourteenth, thou shalt reach the half of thy monthly growth. (The rest is lost.)[8]

Thus the Moon's first quarter should fall on day seven of the lunar month, the Full Moon on day fourteen, and the last quarter Moon on day twenty-one. In addition, day 1 should coincide with the first sighting of the New Moon at dusk (on the western horizon); and day twenty-eight with the last appearance of the old Moon at dawn (on the eastern horizon). However, because of the Moon's highly variable rate of motion, it is not generally possible for a given lunar month to fulfill all these conditions. What is necessary is to fix one condition and hope that most of the remaining ones will be fulfilled. The system that the Babylonians eventually elaborated depended on fixing day one as the day of the New Moon's first appearance. Over centuries, they evolved a new method of calculating the moment of the first appearance of the New Moon,[9] taking account of the rate of motion of the Sun in relationship to the Moon, the Moon's latitude, the duration of daylight, and other factors.

However, the first appearance of the New Moon is dependent upon the location of the observer. For example, on a given date an observer in England may not be able to see the crescent Moon at sunset because of the Moon's proximity to the Sun, whilst his friend in California, viewing approximately eight hours later, may be able to see the thin crescent on the horizon if the Moon has separated sufficiently from the Sun, during the intervening time, to render it visible. The Babylonian priests, because they were concerned with observations made only in one place (Mesopotamia), did not face this problem. Hence they could take "first visibility" as the prime determinant of the lunar month, which began on the eve of first sighting and thus began the start of the Moon's day one. Thereafter, successive lunar days were counted. Using this method, it may occur that the Full Moon does not fall on the fourteenth day. Indeed, cuneiform texts indicate that the Full Moon could fall on the twelfth or thirteenth day, in which case the Full Moon was called "premature." If the Moon was not full by the fifteenth or sixteenth

---

5 Ibid., p. 91.
6 Steiner, *Guidance in Esoteric Training*, p. 44.
7 Powell, "Astronomical Notes: The Lunar Calendar," *Mercury Star Journal* i (1975), 58-67, 106-116.
8 Cf. F.H. Colson, *The Week* (Cambridge, 1926),

p. 120.
9 Cf. O. Neugebauer, *Astronomical Cuneiform Texts I* (London, 1955).

day, it was termed "retarded" (i.e., subnormal).[1] In this case, subsequent phases of the Moon would, accordingly, be premature or retarded.

The approach adopted by this *Journal* has been to make day fourteen the day on which the Moon becomes full, or rises full—therefrom *retrospectively* determining the remaining days of the lunar month. In such an approach, since the moment of Full Moon is independent of location, this criterion was deemed to be the most appropriate. It can happen, however, that this choice can lead to the anomaly of the crescent Moon becoming visible before day one of the lunar month commences!

An alternative procedure, and perhaps the simplest in practice, is to start from the astronomical New Moon (the *syzygy* or moment of conjunction with the Sun). Like the Full Moon, this is a phenomenon that is independent of place and is published well in advance by ephemerides, or even diaries. With this method, the date on which the conjunction of Sun and Moon occurs is noted.

Day one of the lunar month is then made to commence at sunset on the date following the syzygy, and the remaining lunar days are counted off thereafter. Note that the total number of days in the lunar month is at least twenty-nine (a "hollow" month) or at most thirty (a "full" month), since the shortest possible synodic month is 29.26 days and the longest 29.8 days (the average is 29.53059).

In ancient times, the lunar calendar was primarily of religious significance. The festivals and religious ceremonies were celebrated in the appropriate lunar month on special days of the month—notably the Sabbath (Saturday) or "seventh" days (sacred to Saturn) on which occurs the transition from one lunar phase to the next. Each lunar month was felt to bring a special quality. Thus the first lunar month of the year, commencing with the first New Moon of the year (the *neomenia*, or New Moon falling nearest the vernal equinox), was associated with the principle of creation. For example, the commentary on Nisan, the first lunar month in the Babylonian calendar, runs: "Nisan is the month of the constellation Iku (Aries), which is the throne-room of Anu. The king is lifted up, the king is installed. The blessed springing forth of vegetation of (by) Anu and Enlil. Month of the Moon-god, first born of Enlil."[2] Similarly, the second lunar month of the year is placed in correspondence with Taurus, and the rest of the lunar months with the remaining signs of the Zodiac.

In addition to observing the Sabbath days (seven, fourteen, twenty-one, twenty-eight), the birth of each lunar month was celebrated—hence the prime importance of the first appearance of the crescent Moon, which was experienced as the moment of birth. This is beautifully expressed on the Ptolemaic propylon of the temple of Khonsu in Karnak: "He (Khonsu, the Moon god) is conceived on *psdntyw*; is born on *sbd*; he grows old after *smdt*."[3] Making allowance for the slight difference between the reckoning of the Egyptian lunar month and that of the Babylonians, *psdntyw* corresponds to the day of conjunction (syzygy), *sbd* to day one (first appearance), and *smdt* to day fourteen (Full Moon).

In modern times, the lunar month can be of significance to one who is following a spiritual path. If the practice of certain spiritual exercises is to be carried out for the duration of one month,[4] it is helpful to follow the rhythm of the lunar month. All that is needed is a diary (or ephemeris) listing the occurrences of the New Moon (syzygy): 6 p.m. of the following day is then marked as the start of lunar day one. "The day begins in the occult sense at 6 p.m."[5] Subsequent lunar days are enumerated accordingly.

For the ancients who adhered to it, the lunar calendar was not only of theological significance, it was also of special importance in agriculture. The months had names such as "month of crops," "month of plucking fruit," "month of reaping," and "month of harvest."[6] Indeed, even certain

---

1 Cf. B.L. van der Waerden, *Science Awakening II* (Leyden, 1974), p. 116.

2 S. Langdon, *Babylonian Menologies and the Semitic Calendars* (London, 1935), p. 68.

3 R.A. Parker, *The Calendars of Ancient Egypt* (Chicago, 1950), p. 12.

4 Steiner, *Guidance in Esoteric Training* (London, 1972).

5 Ibid., p. 47.

6 Langdon, op. cit., p. 13.

secrets of the weather were known to follow the phases of the lunar month. Moreover, modern scientific methods are discovering that these laws still appear to hold true. Thus, it was known that changes in the weather occur on the days of transition from one lunar phase to the next. Both the US and Australian weather bureaus have discovered—independently by means of statistical research—that wide-spread precipitation of rainfall tends to occur immediately after the New or Full Moon. Modern science here confirms precisely the ancient Egyptian rule: "When the Moon is new, or full, the weather changes."[7]

From Babylonian sources, Dr. Balogh Barna has discovered a more comprehensive formulation of this ancient lunar weather law. He describes it as follows: "This old Assyrian-Babylonian Moon law is: the weather is in pulsation in two-week periods; certain types of weather can only change completely when the Moon is new or full, and this can be said more precisely (i.e., on the fourth day, counted from the day the Moon is new or full). The New Moon can only be seen one day later than the astronomical conjunction; so when we take this into account, the time is really five days. In these five days, the Moon moves the atmosphere—and this changes the weather. The second rule is: the weather which we get after the five-day period will usually last two weeks until the Moon is new or full again; and, if no change occurs before the end of another five-day interval, then the weather will remain the same for another two weeks."[8] Assuming its validity at the present time, this law could be of immense help to farmers in such instances as, for example, needing to know whether harvesting can be delayed for a few days. Here it is important that the farmer know precisely when a change in the weather might be expected.

Formulated in terms of the lunar calendar, it can be said that each lunar month may bring new weather conditions, or that a significant change in the weather may occur halfway through the month. The new weather conditions are conceived, as it were, at the time of conjunction, and grow to maturity from birth (day one) until day four. Once a certain kind of weather has come into being, within five days of the conception of the lunar month, it remains steady until the change of month occurs from the new towards the old, at the time of Full Moon. In the declining, waning part of the month, something new can come in; but if it does so, it will occur by day nineteen. Whatever is established by day nineteen of the lunar month will then last until a new lunar month is conceived at the next conjunction of Sun and Moon.

Balogh Barna maintains that even at the present time the weather is regulated in this way by phases of the Moon; and that the fundamental law of the changes in the weather occurring with the phases of the Moon "can be disturbed by only one exception—which is rare—and these are big solar protuberances and Sun-spots. Such solar events can make the weather very stormy and occasion cyclones lasting for a few days."[9]

In the light of this report, those farmers using the Biodynamic method of agriculture (who already pay attention to the movement of the Moon in the sowing of crops) may wish to test the lunar weather law for themselves, and thereby perhaps make a valuable contribution in this important area of astrosophical research. That there is a definite connection between weather conditions and planetary movements was known instinctively in antiquity. What is required in the modern scientific era are clearly formulated rules describing the inter-relationship between cosmos and earth. Astrosophical research seeks to discover such relationships and help to make them known so that humankind can begin to live once more in harmony with the cosmos.

As a footnote to "The Stars at the time of the Mystery of Golgotha,"[10] the Crucifixion took place on

---

7  B. Barna, "Vztahy medzi astronomiou a astrologiou v staroveku," *Kapiloty Z Vedeckej Astrologie* (Bratislava, 1969), 26-31.
8  Ibid.
9  Ibid.
10 An article by Adam Bittleston printed in the Easter, 1976 issue of the *Mercury Star Journal*, the same in which this article by Robert Powell appeared.

the day of preparation for the feast of the Passover, the festival traditionally celebrated on lunar day fourteen, the day of the full moon, in the first month (Nisan) of the year. According to the research of spiritual science, the date of the Crucifixion is April 3, 33, and the time at which the event took place is generally agreed to be 3 p.m.—shortly before the commencement of lunar day fourteen (the Sabbath). This is confirmed in the Gospels. For example, in the Gospel of St. Luke, after Joseph of Arimathea took the body of Jesus from the Cross and laid it in a tomb, it is said: "It was the day of Preparation, and the Sabbath was beginning." Now, on April 3, 33 (Julian) the Moon was full at about 5 p.m. Jerusalem time. It rose, partially eclipsed, at about 6:10 p.m. (sunset was about 6:15 p.m.) and the eclipse ended about 6:35 p.m.[1]

Thus the astronomical facts for April 3, 33 are in complete accordance with the description in the Gospels—that is, the Sabbath, lunar day fourteen, commenced at 6 p.m. on this date, when the Full Moon rose. Indeed, it should be noted throughout the Gospels that whenever the Sabbath is mentioned, it is the Sabbath days of the lunar month (days seven, fourteen, twenty-one, twenty-eight) that are referred to. For example, some authorities read, "On the second Sabbath after the first, while he was going through the grainfields" (Luke 6:1). In describing the Mystery of Golgotha, we can say that the Crucifixion occurred towards the end of lunar day 13 (sacred to Venus); that the Descent into the Underworld transpired on lunar day fourteen (sacred to Saturn); and that the Resurrection took place at dawn on lunar day fifteen (sacred to the Sun).

## The Lunar Calendar in 2019

### *Joel Park*

The essential piece of these articles on the Lunar Calendar points to the fact that the ancients followed the cycle of the Moon as an indication of the cosmic forces radiating to Earth at a given time. For example, during New Moon, First Quarter, Full Moon, and Last Quarter, the ancients saw the influence of Saturn radiating down to Earth via the Moon Sphere. In all, they took notice of twenty-eight distinct phases of the Moon, from one New Moon to the next. The first day of the lunar calendar (what would have been a "Sunday") occurred when the crescent moon first became visible in the night sky after the New Moon. Over the course of one lunar month, each of the seven planetary beings (Saturn, Sun, Moon, Mars, Mercury, Jupiter, and Venus) would have had rulership four times: once between New Moon and First Quarter, once between First Quarter and Full Moon, once between Full Moon and Last Quarter, and once between Last Quarter and New Moon.

Robert Powell's point is that we can resurrect this attention to the lunar cycle in conjunction with our meditative life. We can once again follow the phases of the Moon in their relationship to cosmic forces to come into closer relationship with Divine Sophia and the Etheric Christ, who are actively working in the Moon Sphere.

We can take this practice a step further, however. We can take up the indications of the anonymous author on page 458 of *Meditations on the Tarot*, in which he describes the traditional planetary rulers (the gods Saturn, Venus, etc.) as only being related to the psychophysical organism of the human being. If we wish to truly resurrect and christen the practice of following the lunar calendar, we must follow the daily rulerships that are related to the psycho-*spiritual* organism of the human being: rather than Saturn, the Virgin Mary; rather than Sun, the Risen Christ; rather than Moon, the Holy Trinity; rather than Mars, Archistrategist Michael; rather than Mercury, the Pastors and Healers of Humanity (the Ischim or Initiates); rather than Jupiter, the Holy Spirit; rather than Venus, Christ Crucified. If we follow the phases of the Moon, and in our inner and outer work invoke the guidance and assistance of the corresponding Spiritual Being, we have the possibility of "potentizing" our work.

Now, these seven rulers only account for the twenty-eight standard days of the lunar month, whereas any given lunar month is twenty-nine to

---

1 Calculation by James Hynes, Dublin, in a private communication to the author.

thirty days. What of the one or two extra days? They are like "eighth" days; they are octaves, which bring to mind Vulcan evolution (which is not normally represented in the days of the week). We can see these extra days as pauses, as openings in the spiral between lunar months. In light of these associations, it is the intuition and advice of this author that one would honor and invoke the Heavenly Father on the extra day(s), the day or two between months.

Last year, we tabulated the days of the lunar month and their corresponding rulerships for the month of January, as an aide to the reader. When we did so, we used the Full Moon as day fourteen, and calculated the rest of the month based around that. This time, we will use the alternative method suggested by Robert Powell in the above articles, that is, to find the day on which the New Moon occurs, and then to make the day following the New Moon day one of the lunar month. Keep in mind that, as indicated in the articles above, in esoteric practice the day begins at sundown, so when "January 1" is written, it means "from sundown December 31 until sundown January 1." The following list applies specifically to EST.

**January 6th** New Moon (Honoring the Heavenly Father)
———— 7th Day One (Honoring the Risen Christ)
———— 8th Day Two (Honoring the Holy Trinity)
———— 9th Day Three (Honoring the Archistrategist Michael)
———— 10th Day Four (Honoring the Ischim)
———— 11th Day Five (Honoring the Holy Spirit)
———— 12th Day Six (Honoring the Crucified Christ)
———— 13th Day Seven (Honoring the Virgin Mary)
———— 14th Day Eight (Honoring the Risen Christ)
———— 15th Day Nine (Honoring the Holy Trinity)
———— 16h Day Ten (Honoring the Archistrategist Michael)
———— 17th Day Eleven (Honoring the Ischim)
———— 18th Day Twelve (Honoring the Holy Spirit)
———— 19th Day Thirteen (Honoring the Crucified Christ)
———— 20th Day Fourteen (Honoring the Virgin Mary)
———— 21st Day Fifteen (Honoring the Risen Christ)
———— 22nd Day Sixteen (Honoring the Holy Trinity)
———— 23rd Day Seventeen (Honoring the Archistrategist Michael)
———— 24th Day Eighteen (Honoring the Ischim)
———— 25th Day Nineteen (Honoring the Holy Spirit)
———— 26th Day Twenty (Honoring the Crucified Christ)
———— 27th Day Twenty-One (Honoring the Virgin Mary)
———— 28th Day Twenty-Two (Honoring the Risen Christ)
———— 29th Day Twenty-Three (Honoring the Holy Trinity)
———— 30th Day Twenty-Four (Honoring the Archistrategist Michael)
———— 31st Day Twenty-Five (Honoring the Ischim)
**February 1st** Day Twenty-Six (Honoring the Holy Spirit)
———— 2nd Day Twenty-Seven (Honoring the Crucified Christ)
———— 3rd Day Twenty-Eight (Honoring the Virgin Mary)
———— 4th **New Moon** (Honoring the Heavenly Father)

One would then continue in the same way throughout the year.

# WORKING WITH THE *STAR WISDOM* CALENDAR

## Robert Powell, PhD

In taking note of the astronomical events listed in the Star Calendar, it is important to distinguish between long- and short-term astronomical events. Long-term astronomical events—for example, Pluto transiting a particular degree of the zodiac—will have a longer period of meditation than would the five days advocated for short-term astronomical events such as the New and Full Moon. The following describes, in relation to meditating on the Full Moon, a meditative process extending over a five-day period.

### Sanctification of the Full Moon

As a preliminary remark, let us remind ourselves that the great sacrifice of Christ on the Cross—the Mystery of Golgotha—took place at Full Moon. As Christ's sacrifice took place when the Moon was full in the middle of the sidereal sign of Libra, the Libra Full Moon assumes special significance in the sequence of twelve (or thirteen) Full Moons taking place during the cycle of the year. In following this sequence, the Mystery of Golgotha serves as an archetype for *every* Full Moon, since each Full Moon imparts a particular spiritual blessing. Hence the practice described here of *Sanctification of the Full Moon* applies to every Full Moon. Similarly, there is also the practice of *Sanctification of the New Moon*, as described in *Hermetic Astrology, Volume 2: Astrological Biography,* chapter 10.

During the two days prior to the Full Moon, we can consider the focus of one's meditation to extend over these two days as *preparatory days* immediately preceding the day of the Full Moon. These two days can be dedicated to spiritual reflection and detachment from everyday concerns, as one prepares to become a vessel for the in-streaming light and love one will receive at the Full Moon, something that one can then impart further—for example, to help people in need, or to support Mother Earth in times of catastrophe. During these two days, it is helpful to hold an attitude of dedication and service and try to assume an attitude of receptivity that opens to what one's soul will receive and subsequently impart—an attitude conducive to making one a true *servant of the spirit*.

The day of the Full Moon is itself a day of *holding the sacred space*. In doing so, one endeavors to cultivate inner peace and silence, during which one attempts to contact and consciously hold the in-streaming blessing of the Full Moon for the rest of humanity. One can heighten this silent meditation by visualizing the zodiacal constellation/sidereal sign in which the Moon becomes full, since the Moon serves to reflect the starry background against which it appears.

If the Moon is full in Virgo, for example, it reminds us of the night of the birth of the Jesus child visited by the three magi, as described in the Gospel of St. Matthew. That birth occurred at the Full Moon in the middle of the sidereal sign of Virgo, and the three magi, who gazed up that evening to behold the Full Moon against the background of the stars of the Virgin, witnessed the soul of Jesus emerge from the disk of the Full Moon and descend toward Earth. They participated from afar, via the starry heavens, in the Grail Mystery of the holy birth.

In meditating upon the Full Moon and opening oneself to receive the in-streaming blessing from the starry heavens, we can exercise restraint by avoiding the formulation of what will happen or what one might receive from the Full Moon. Moreover, we can also refrain from seeking tangible results or effects connected with our attunement to the Full Moon. Even if we observe only the date but not the exact moment when the Moon is full, it is helpful to find quiet time to reflect alone or to use the opportunity for deep meditation on the day of the Full Moon.

We can think of the two days following the Full Moon as a *time of imparting* what we have received from the in-streaming of the full disk of the Moon against the background of the stars. It is now possible to turn our attention toward humanity and the world and endeavor to pass on any spiritual blessing we have received from the starry heavens. Thereby we can assist in the work of the spiritual world by transforming what we have received into goodwill and allowing it to flow wherever the greatest need exists.

It is a matter of *holding a sacred space* throughout the day of the Full Moon. This is an important time to still the mind and maintain inner peace. It is a time of spiritual retreat and contact with the spiritual world, of holding in one's consciousness the archetype of the Mystery of Golgotha as a great outpouring of Divine Love that bridges Heaven and Earth. Prior to the day of the Full Moon, the two preceding days prepare the sacred space as a vessel to receive the heavenly blessing. The two days following the day of the Full Moon are a time to assimilate and distribute the spiritual transmission received into the sacred space we have prepared.

One can apply the process described here as a meditative practice in relation to the Full Moon to any of the astronomical events listed in *Star Wisdom*, especially as most of these *remember* significant Christ Events. Take note, however, whether an event is long-term or short-term and adjust the period of meditative practice accordingly.

---

*"The shadow intellect that is characteristic of all modern culture has fettered human beings to the Earth. They have eyes only for earthly things, particularly when they allow themselves to be influenced by the claims of modern science. In our age it never occurs to someone that their being belongs not to the Earth alone but to the cosmos beyond the Earth. Knowledge of our connection with the cosmos beyond the Earth—that is what we need above all to make our own.... When someone says 'I' to themselves, they experience a force that is working within, and the [ancient] Greek, in feeling the working of this inner force, related it to the Sun;...the Sun and the 'I' are the outer and inner aspects of one being. The Sun out there in space is the cosmic 'I.' What lives within me is the human 'I'.... Human beings are not primarily a creation of Earth. Human beings receive their shape and form from the cosmos. The human being is an offspring of the world of stars, above all of the Sun and Moon.... The Moon forces stream out from a center in the metabolic system.... [The] Moon stimulates reproduction.... Saturn works chiefly in the upper part of the astral body....Jupiter has to do with thinking...Mars [has] to do with speech.... The Mercury forces work in the part of the human organism that lies below the region of the heart...in the breathing and circulatory functions.... Venus works preeminently in the etheric body of the human being."* —RUDOLF STEINER, *Offspring of the World of Stars*, May 5, 1921

# SYMBOLS USED IN CHARTS

| | Planets | | Zodiacal Signs | | Aspects |
|---|---|---|---|---|---|
| ⊕ | Earth | ♈ | Aries (Ram) | ☌ | Conjunction 0° |
| ☉ | Sun | ♉ | Taurus (Bull) | ✶ | Sextile 60° |
| ☽ | Moon | ♊ | Gemini (Twins) | ☐ | Square 90° |
| ☿ | Mercury | ♋ | Cancer (Crab) | △ | Trine 120° |
| ♀ | Venus | ♌ | Leo (Lion) | ☍ | Opposition 180° |
| ♂ | Mars | ♍ | Virgo (Virgin) | | |
| ♃ | Jupiter | ♎ | Libra (Scales) | | |
| ♄ | Saturn | ♏ | Scorpio (Scorpion) | | |
| ♅ | Uranus | ♐ | Sagittarius (Archer) | | |
| ♆ | Neptune | ♑ | Capricorn (Goat) | | |
| ♇ | Pluto | ♒ | Aquarius (Water Carrier) | | |
| | | ♓ | Pisces (Fishes) | | |

| | Other | | |
|---|---|---|---|
| ☊ | Ascending (North) Node | ☌ | Sun Eclipse |
| ☋ | Descending (South) Node | ☍ | Moon Eclipse |
| P | Perihelion/Perigee | ☌̣ | Inferior Conjunction |
| A | Aphelion/Apogee | ☌̇ | Superior Conjunction |
| | Maximum Latitude | ⚷ | Chiron |
| | Minimum Latitude | | |

# TIME

The information relating to daily geocentric and heliocentric planetary positions in the sidereal zodiac is tabulated in the form of an ephemeris for each month, in which the planetary positions are given at 0 hours Universal Time (UT) each day.

Beneath the geocentric and heliocentric ephemeris for each month, the information relating to planetary aspects is given in the form of an aspectarian, which lists the most important aspects—geocentric and heliocentric/hermetic—between the planets for the month in question. The day and the time of occurrence of the aspect on that day are indicated, all times being given in Universal Time (UT), which is identical to Greenwich Mean Time (GMT). For example, zero hours Universal Time is midnight GMT. This time system applies in Britain; however, when summer time is in effect, one hour must be added to all times.

** In other time zones, the time has to be adjusted according to whether it is ahead of or behind Britain. For example, in Germany, where the time is one hour ahead of British time, an hour must be added; when summer time is in effect in Germany, two hours have to be added to all times.

Using the calendar in the United States, do the following subtraction from all time indications according to time zone:

- Pacific Time subtract 8 hours
  (7 hours for daylight saving time);
- Mountain Time subtract 7 hours
  (6 hours for daylight saving time);
- Central Time subtract 6 hours
  (5 hours for daylight saving time);
- Eastern Time subtract 5 hours
  (4 hours for daylight saving time).

This subtraction will often change the date of an astronomical occurrence, shifting it back one day. Consequently, since most of the readers of this calendar live on the American Continent, astronomical occurrences during the early hours of day *x* are sometimes listed in the Commentaries as occurring on days *x–1/x*. For example, an eclipse occurring at 03:00 UT on the 12th is listed as occurring on the 11/12th since in America it takes place on the 11th.[1]

## SIMPLIFYING THE PROCEDURE

The preceding procedure can be greatly simplified. Here is an example for someone wishing to know the zodiacal locations of the planets on Christmas Day, December 25, 2018. Looking at the December ephemeris, it can be seen that Christmas Day falls on a Tuesday. In the upper tabulation, the geocentric planetary positions are given, with that of the Sun indicated in the first column, that of the Moon in the second column, and so on. The position of the Sun is listed as 8°07' Sagittarius.

For someone living in London, 8°07' Sagittarius is the Sun's position at midnight, December 24/25, 2017—noting that in London and all of the United Kingdom, the Time Zone applying there is that of Universal Time/Greenwich Mean Time—UT/GMT.

For someone living in Sydney, Australia, which on Christmas Day is eleven hours ahead of UT/GMT, 8°07' Sagittarius is the Sun's position at 11 a.m. on December 25.

For someone living in California, which is eight hours behind UT/GMT on Christmas Day, 8°07' Sagittarius is the Sun's position at 4 p.m. on **December 24**.

For the person living in California, therefore, it is necessary to look at the entries for **December 26** to know the positions of the planets on December 25. The result is:

For someone living in California, which is eight hours behind UT/GMT on Christmas Day, the Sun's position at 4 p.m. on December 25 is 9°08' Sagittarius and, by the same token, the Moon's position on Christmas Day at 4 p.m. on December

---

1 See *General Introduction to the Christian Star Calendar: A Key to Understanding* for an in-depth clarification of the features of the calendar in *Star Wisdom*, including indications about how to work with it.

25 is 24°08' Pisces—these are the positions alongside December 26 at midnight UT/GMT—and eight hours earlier equates with 4 p.m. on December 25 in California.

From these examples it emerges that the **planetary positions as given in the ephemeris** can be utilized, but that according to the Time Zone one is in, **the time of day is different** and also for locations West of the United Kingdom **the date changes** (look at the date following the actual date).

Here is a tabulation in relation to the foregoing example of December 25 (Christmas Day).

### United Kingdom, Europe, And All Locations With Time Zones East Of Greenwich

Look at what is given alongside December 25—these entries indicate the planetary positions at these times:

- 12:00 a.m. (midnight December 24/25) in London (UT/GMT)
- 01:00 a.m. in Berlin (CENTRAL EUROPEAN TIME, which is one hour ahead of UT/GMT)
- 11:00 a.m. in Sydney (AUSTRALIAN EASTERN DAYLIGHT TIME, which is eleven hours ahead of UT/GMT)

### Canada, USA, Central America, South America, And All Locations With Time Zones West Of Greenwich

Look at what is given alongside December 26—these entries indicate the planetary positions at these times:

- 7:00 p.m. in New York (EASTERN STANDARD TIME, which is five hours behind UT/GMT)
- 6:00 p.m. in Chicago (CENTRAL STANDARD TIME, which is six hours behind UT/GMT)
- 5:00 p.m. in Denver (MOUNTAIN STANDARD TIME, which is seven hours behind UT/GMT)
- 4:00 p.m. in San Francisco (PACIFIC STANDARD TIME, which is eight hours behind UT/GMT)
- **IF SUMMER TIME IS IN USE,** add **ONE HOUR—FOR EXAMPLE:**
- 8:00 p.m. in New York (EASTERN DAYLIGHT TIME, which is four hours behind UT/GMT)
- 7:00 p.m. in Chicago (CENTRAL DAYLIGHT TIME, which is five hours behind UT/GMT)
- 6:00 p.m. in Denver (MOUNTAIN DAYLIGHT TIME, which is six hours behind UT/GMT)
- 5:00 p.m. in San Francisco (PACIFIC DAYLIGHT TIME, which is seven hours behind UT/GMT)

Note that in the preceding tabulation, the time given in Sydney on Christmas Day, December 25, is in terms of Daylight Time. Six months earlier, on June 25, for someone in Sydney they would look alongside the entry in the ephemeris for June 25 and would know that this applies (for them) to…

- 10:00 a.m. in Sydney (AUSTRALIAN EASTERN TIME, which is ten hours ahead of UT/GMT).

In these examples, it is not just the position of the Sun that is referred to. The same applies to the zodiacal locations given in the ephemeris for *all* the planets, whether geocentric (upper tabulation) or heliocentric (lower tabulation). *All that is necessary to apply this method of reading the ephemeris is to know the Time Zone in which one is and to apply the number of hours difference from UT/GMT.*

The advantage of using the method described here is that it greatly simplifies reference to the ephemeris when studying the **zodiacal positions of the planets**. However, for applying the time indications listed under "Ingresses" or "Aspects" it is still necessary to add or subtract the time difference from UT/GMT as described in the above paragraph denoted.**

# COMMENTARIES AND EPHEMERIDES
## JANUARY – DECEMBER 2019

*Commentaries and Ephemerides by Claudia McLaren Lainson, including Monthly Stargazing Previews & Astronomical Sky Watch by Julie Humphreys*

### STARGAZING

*There are human beings…who never look up to the stars their whole life long, who do not know where Leo is, or Aries or Taurus…Such people are born, in a next life on Earth, with a body that is somehow limp and flabby.*[1]

The following information is based on Eastern Standard Time and Eastern Daylight Time for the convenience of North American readers. Please adjust time zones accordingly.

Observing the apparent path of the planets (called the ecliptic) before the background of the fixed stars of the zodiac requires denizens of the northern hemisphere to look southward. On the days of our spring and autumn equinoxes, this path will begin directly in the east, arch over the southern horizon, and end directly due west. On the other 363 or 364 days of the year, you'll observe that the planets rise slightly north or south of east, culminate east or west of south, and set south or north of west—however, their east–south–west trajectory remains roughly the same. It is a wonderful exercise throughout the year to simply notice where the planet rise, culminate, and set in reference to your fixed surroundings: trees, steeples, mountains, and so on.

---
1 Steiner, *Karmic Relationships*, vol. 1, p. 86.

### JANUARY 2019

#### Stargazing Preview

Happy New Year, stargazers all! The year begins with Venus as a morning star. On the 1st you'll see her follow the waning Moon above the eastern horizon a few hours ahead of the Sun. Later that day, the Moon meets Venus in conjunction. Jupiter will be up two hours later (at about 0500), still an hour before sunrise.

Venus enters Scorpio on the 2nd. On the following day, the Moon moves past Jupiter from above, two days before it first finds Saturn and then the Sun for the January New Moon. And what a New Moon: it creates a Partial Solar Eclipse over Northeast Asia and the North Pacific. On the 6th, Venus reaches her greatest western elongation, meaning that the time between her rising and the Sun's is at its longest.

Sunset on the 12th will reveal Mars overhead, due south, above and slightly to the left of the Moon. By the time they set around midnight, the Moon will have passed Mars from below. The Full Moon in Cancer on the 21st brings a Total Lunar Eclipse to all of North America! The following morning, if you're up, you will be able to watch Venus and Jupiter rise in conjunction at around 0400. It's a great morning to get up early.

On the 30th, Venus moves into Sagittarius. The Moon will rise just ahead of Jupiter, hours away from their conjunction. On the last day of January, you'll be able to see the Moon pass above Venus as they reach their second conjunction of the month, this time in the first degree of Sagittarius. Look for Orion in the southeast at sunset—he sets at 0400.

## January Commentaries

NOTE: Rudolf Steiner gave a series of verse-meditations for deepening into the realities of the seven planets moving among the twelve constellations. We find this in the booklet titled *Twelve Cosmic Moods*. As planets ingress into different constellations, different moods are reflected in the human soul. In accord with such ingresses, the appropriate line of the relevant Cosmic Mood has been highlighted in bold.

**Jan 1: Sun 16° Sagittarius: Birth of the Nathan Jesus** (Dec/6/2 BC). At the turning point in time, following the death of Jesus Christ, the Nathan Jesus became the Angel Jesus. Through him, the fifth sacrifice of Christ is now occurring. Hence is the moral ether, the light of the Grail, radiating throughout the world. The human soul touches into the presence of the Etheric Christ through the Angel Jesus, and in so doing the soul is reciprocally touched. The moral ether dispels all polarities, asking us to lovingly *suffer* what appears as irreconcilable. We may thereby find solutions hitherto unimaginable. In suffering, Christ approaches us, comforting us, leading us to bear witness to what lies above duality. Only through overcoming our personal positions, opinions, and prejudice can we meet situations and others in true open-heartedness. The moral ether calls us to rise to the transpersonal. Without such openness, the moral ether would be inaccessible and Christ could not find us.

To rise to the transpersonal does not imply *depersonalization*, for the personality—the source of our tears when faced with mournful trials—is the sacred veil through which our "I" perceives the world. The transpersonal personality is devoted to truth over and above its own proclivities. It is therefore not distracted by itself when bearing witness to life. It does not take sides. Rather does it suffer to know the direct revelation it has lost.

In the letter to the church in Sardis, we hear of the "name," the garment of white raiment. The ultimate aim of our personality is to resonate with our one true "name." We suffer ourselves into silence so that we might unite with this garment. It is the Angel Jesus who bestows this raiment as his *manas* consciousness awakes within us, for each of our names is one irreplaceable note in the wondrous chorus of humanity:

> All the specific examples of future meetings with the Etheric Christ that Rudolf Steiner gives have one thing in common: the people (whether alone or in groups) who experience such meetings are, in every case, at their wits' end, not knowing which way to turn: the encounter takes place at the very moment when one's consciousness requires it. That need is felt once the soul has been prepared through great pain of inquiry to awake for that encounter. "Awake" in the soul means that it has experienced the questions of a conscience awakeed to the transpersonal; it is the condition needed to know "the hour of his coming."[1]

We can understand the concept of the Second Coming of Christ as the radiating presence of new ether, in-streaming Earth through the Angel Jesus. If we are to receive this light, however, we must make spiritual space available.

The moral ether (the *fifth ether*) finds its origins in human activity when the "I" is imbued with Christ:

> This moral ether, which comes into being when the Christ impulse permeates human volition and activities, is the "salt of the Earth" that allows the moral element to access nature in a way which has value for nature. The purpose of moral ether is to become an organ for the constructive influence of goodness in nature, just as salt may serve in the human organism as an organ of constructive "I" activity, which normally functions through the blood....
>
> The activity of the moral ether as nature's conscience is the secret of future white mechanical occultism.[2]

Humanity's communion with the Angel Jesus will awake a force through which we will call the beings of nature into free activity *with us*, wherein they will again be able to place their confidence in us. This is the essence of the work of sacred magic that brings about the liberation of nature. Through our union with the conscience of the Angel Jesus,

---

[1] Tomberg, *Christ and Sophia*, p. 337.
[2] *Christ and Sophia*, p. 225.

SIDEREAL GEOCENTRIC LONGITUDES : JANUARY 2019 Gregorian at 0 hours UT

| DAY | ☉ | ☽ | ☊ | ☿ | ♀ | ♂ | ♃ | ♄ | ♅ | ♆ | ♇ |
|---|---|---|---|---|---|---|---|---|---|---|---|
| 1 TU | 15 ♐ 15 | 17 ♎ 22 | 1 ♋ 53R | 28 ♏ 51 | 28 ♎ 29 | 4 ♓ 56 | 16 ♏ 46 | 16 ♐ 22 | 3 ♈ 37R | 19 ♒ 5 | 25 ♐ 35 |
| 2 WE | 16 16 | 0 ♏ 15 | 1 50 | 0 ♐ 19 | 29 29 | 5 36 | 16 58 | 16 29 | 3 36 | 19 6 | 25 37 |
| 3 TH | 17 17 | 12 54 | 1 48 | 1 47 | 0 ♏ 28 | 6 16 | 17 11 | 16 36 | 3 36 | 19 7 | 25 39 |
| 4 FR | 18 19 | 25 20 | 1 46 | 3 17 | 1 28 | 6 57 | 17 23 | 16 44 | 3 36 | 19 9 | 25 41 |
| 5 SA | 19 20 | 7 ♐ 35 | 1 44 | 4 46 | 2 29 | 7 37 | 17 36 | 16 51 | 3 36 | 19 10 | 25 43 |
| 6 SU | 20 21 | 19 41 | 1 43 | 6 16 | 3 29 | 8 18 | 17 48 | 16 58 | 3 36 | 19 11 | 25 45 |
| 7 MO | 21 22 | 1 ♑ 39 | 1 43 | 7 46 | 4 31 | 8 58 | 18 1 | 17 5 | 3 36D | 19 13 | 25 47 |
| 8 TU | 22 23 | 13 31 | 1 43D | 9 17 | 5 32 | 9 39 | 18 13 | 17 12 | 3 36 | 19 14 | 25 49 |
| 9 WE | 23 25 | 25 19 | 1 44 | 10 49 | 6 34 | 10 19 | 18 25 | 17 19 | 3 36 | 19 16 | 25 51 |
| 10 TH | 24 26 | 7 ♒ 6 | 1 45 | 12 21 | 7 37 | 11 0 | 18 37 | 17 26 | 3 36 | 19 17 | 25 53 |
| 11 FR | 25 27 | 18 55 | 1 45 | 13 53 | 8 40 | 11 40 | 18 49 | 17 33 | 3 36 | 19 19 | 25 55 |
| 12 SA | 26 28 | 0 ♓ 51 | 1 46 | 15 25 | 9 43 | 12 21 | 19 1 | 17 40 | 3 36 | 19 20 | 25 57 |
| 13 SU | 27 29 | 12 56 | 1 46 | 16 59 | 10 46 | 13 1 | 19 13 | 17 47 | 3 37 | 19 22 | 25 59 |
| 14 MO | 28 30 | 25 16 | 1 47 | 18 32 | 11 50 | 13 42 | 19 25 | 17 54 | 3 37 | 19 23 | 26 1 |
| 15 TU | 29 31 | 7 ♈ 55 | 1 47R | 20 6 | 12 54 | 14 23 | 19 37 | 18 1 | 3 37 | 19 25 | 26 3 |
| 16 WE | 0 ♑ 33 | 20 58 | 1 46 | 21 41 | 13 58 | 15 3 | 19 49 | 18 8 | 3 38 | 19 26 | 26 5 |
| 17 TH | 1 34 | 4 ♉ 26 | 1 46D | 23 16 | 15 2 | 15 44 | 20 0 | 18 15 | 3 38 | 19 28 | 26 7 |
| 18 FR | 2 35 | 18 22 | 1 46 | 24 51 | 16 7 | 16 24 | 20 12 | 18 22 | 3 39 | 19 30 | 26 9 |
| 19 SA | 3 36 | 2 ♊ 44 | 1 47 | 26 27 | 17 12 | 17 5 | 20 23 | 18 29 | 3 39 | 19 32 | 26 11 |
| 20 SU | 4 37 | 17 30 | 1 47 | 28 4 | 18 18 | 17 46 | 20 35 | 18 36 | 3 40 | 19 33 | 26 13 |
| 21 MO | 5 38 | 2 ♋ 32 | 1 47 | 29 41 | 19 23 | 18 26 | 20 46 | 18 43 | 3 41 | 19 35 | 26 16 |
| 22 TU | 6 39 | 17 43 | 1 47R | 1 ♑ 19 | 20 29 | 19 7 | 20 58 | 18 50 | 3 42 | 19 37 | 26 18 |
| 23 WE | 7 40 | 2 ♌ 53 | 1 46 | 2 57 | 21 35 | 19 48 | 21 9 | 18 57 | 3 42 | 19 39 | 26 20 |
| 24 TH | 8 41 | 17 53 | 1 46 | 4 36 | 22 42 | 20 28 | 21 20 | 19 3 | 3 43 | 19 40 | 26 22 |
| 25 FR | 9 42 | 2 ♍ 34 | 1 45 | 6 15 | 23 48 | 21 9 | 21 31 | 19 10 | 3 44 | 19 42 | 26 23 |
| 26 SA | 10 43 | 16 52 | 1 44 | 7 55 | 24 55 | 21 49 | 21 42 | 19 17 | 3 45 | 19 44 | 26 25 |
| 27 SU | 11 44 | 0 ♎ 45 | 1 43 | 9 36 | 26 2 | 22 30 | 21 53 | 19 24 | 3 46 | 19 46 | 26 27 |
| 28 MO | 12 45 | 14 12 | 1 43D | 11 17 | 27 9 | 23 11 | 22 4 | 19 30 | 3 47 | 19 48 | 26 29 |
| 29 TU | 13 46 | 27 16 | 1 43 | 12 59 | 28 16 | 23 51 | 22 14 | 19 37 | 3 48 | 19 50 | 26 31 |
| 30 WE | 14 47 | 9 ♏ 58 | 1 44 | 14 42 | 29 24 | 24 32 | 22 25 | 19 44 | 3 49 | 19 52 | 26 33 |
| 31 TH | 15 48 | 22 24 | 1 46 | 16 25 | 0 ♐ 32 | 25 13 | 22 35 | 19 50 | 3 51 | 19 54 | 26 35 |

INGRESSES :

| | |
|---|---|
| 1 ☿ → ♐ 18:49 | 20 ☽ → ♋ 19:58 |
| ☽ → ♏ 23:31 | 21 ☿ → ♑ 4:42 |
| 2 ♀ → ♏ 12:41 | 22 ☽ → ♌ 19:25 |
| 4 ☽ → ♐ 9: 6 | 24 ☽ → ♍ 19:45 |
| 6 ☽ → ♑ 20:40 | 26 ☽ → ♎ 22:41 |
| 9 ☽ → ♒ 9:32 | 29 ☽ → ♏ 5: 7 |
| 11 ☽ → ♓ 22:18 | 30 ♀ → ♐ 12:50 |
| 14 ☽ → ♈ 9: 2 | 31 ☽ → ♐ 14:53 |
| 15 ☉ → ♑ 11:14 | |
| 16 ☽ → ♉ 16:11 | |
| 18 ☽ → ♊ 19:29 | |

ASPECTS & ECLIPSES :

| | | | |
|---|---|---|---|
| 1 ☽ ☌ ♀ 22:25 | 11 ☽ ☌ ♆ 0:47 | ☿ ☌ ♇ 19:59 | 22 ☿ ☍ ☊ 6:54 |
| 2 ☉ ☌ ♄ 5:48 | ☉ ☌ ♇ 11:32 | 19 ☉ □ ♅ 1:28 | ♀ ☌ ♃ 12:25 |
| 3 ☽ ☌ ♃ 8:22 | 13 ☽ ☌ ♂ 0:10 | 20 ☽ ☍ ♄ 1:47 | 23 ☿ □ ♅ 11:11 |
| 4 ☽ ☌ ☿ 17:40 | ☿ ☌ ♄ 13:30 | ☽ ☍ ♇ 14: 0 | 24 ☽ ☍ ♆ 2:54 |
| 5 ☽ ☌ ♄ 18:31 | ♃ □ ♆ 19:45 | ☽ ☍ ☿ 18:55 | 26 ☽ ☍ ♂ 8:54 |
| 6 ☉ ☌ ☽ 1:27 | 14 ☉ □ ☽ 6:44 | ☽ ☌ ☊ 22:48 | 27 ☽ N□ ☊ 1:42 |
| ☉ ● P 1:40 | ☽ S□ ☊ 12:25 | 21 ♀ □ ♆ 4:22 | ☽ ☍ ♅ 5:19 |
| ☽ ☌ ♇ 12:10 | ☽ ☌ ♅ 15:54 | ☽ ☍● T 5:11 | ☉ □ ☽ 21: 9 |
| 7 ☽ ☌ ☋ 0: 7 | 17 ☉ ☍ ☊ 5: 1 | ☉ ☍ ☽ 5:15 | 30 ☉ S☋ ☿ 2:50 |
| 8 ☿ □ ♂ 10: 3 | ☽ ☍ ♀ 19:52 | ♂ □ ♄ 11:47 | 31 ☽ ☌ ♃ 0:22 |
| 9 ☽ ☌ A 4:39 | 18 ☽ ☍ ♃ 3: 9 | ☽ ☌ P 20: 6 | ☽ ☌ ♀ 17:33 |

SIDEREAL HELIOCENTRIC LONGITUDES : JANUARY 2019 Gregorian at 0 hours UT

| DAY | Sid. Time | ☿ | ♀ | ⊕ | ♂ | ♃ | ♄ | ♅ | ♆ | ♇ | Vernal Point |
|---|---|---|---|---|---|---|---|---|---|---|---|
| 1 TU | 6:41:27 | 20 ♎ 39 | 25 ♋ 18 | 15 ♊ 16 | 16 ♈ 40 | 11 ♏ 45 | 16 ♐ 29 | 6 ♈ 18 | 20 ♒ 47 | 25 ♐ 54 | 4 ♓ 59'42" |
| 2 WE | 6:45:23 | 23 35 | 26 55 | 16 17 | 17 14 | 11 49 | 16 31 | 6 19 | 20 47 | 25 54 | 4 ♓ 59'41" |
| 3 TH | 6:49:20 | 26 29 | 28 33 | 17 18 | 17 48 | 11 54 | 16 33 | 6 20 | 20 47 | 25 54 | 4 ♓ 59'41" |
| 4 FR | 6:53:16 | 29 21 | 0 ♌ 10 | 18 19 | 18 23 | 11 59 | 16 35 | 6 20 | 20 48 | 25 55 | 4 ♓ 59'41" |
| 5 SA | 6:57:13 | 2 ♏ 11 | 1 48 | 19 20 | 18 57 | 12 3 | 16 37 | 6 21 | 20 48 | 25 55 | 4 ♓ 59'41" |
| 6 SU | 7: 1: 9 | 5 0 | 3 25 | 20 22 | 19 31 | 12 8 | 16 38 | 6 22 | 20 48 | 25 55 | 4 ♓ 59'41" |
| 7 MO | 7: 5: 6 | 7 48 | 5 3 | 21 23 | 20 5 | 12 13 | 16 40 | 6 22 | 20 49 | 25 56 | 4 ♓ 59'41" |
| 8 TU | 7: 9: 2 | 10 35 | 6 40 | 22 24 | 20 39 | 12 18 | 16 42 | 6 23 | 20 49 | 25 56 | 4 ♓ 59'41" |
| 9 WE | 7:12:59 | 13 20 | 8 18 | 23 25 | 21 13 | 12 22 | 16 44 | 6 24 | 20 50 | 25 56 | 4 ♓ 59'41" |
| 10 TH | 7:16:56 | 16 6 | 9 55 | 24 26 | 21 47 | 12 27 | 16 46 | 6 24 | 20 50 | 25 56 | 4 ♓ 59'40" |
| 11 FR | 7:20:52 | 18 50 | 11 33 | 25 27 | 22 21 | 12 32 | 16 48 | 6 25 | 20 50 | 25 57 | 4 ♓ 59'40" |
| 12 SA | 7:24:49 | 21 35 | 13 10 | 26 29 | 22 54 | 12 36 | 16 49 | 6 25 | 20 51 | 25 57 | 4 ♓ 59'40" |
| 13 SU | 7:28:45 | 24 20 | 14 48 | 27 30 | 23 28 | 12 41 | 16 51 | 6 26 | 20 51 | 25 57 | 4 ♓ 59'40" |
| 14 MO | 7:32:42 | 27 5 | 16 25 | 28 31 | 24 2 | 12 46 | 16 53 | 6 27 | 20 51 | 25 58 | 4 ♓ 59'40" |
| 15 TU | 7:36:38 | 29 50 | 18 2 | 29 32 | 24 35 | 12 51 | 16 55 | 6 27 | 20 52 | 25 58 | 4 ♓ 59'40" |
| 16 WE | 7:40:35 | 2 ♐ 36 | 19 40 | 0 ♋ 33 | 25 9 | 12 55 | 16 57 | 6 28 | 20 52 | 25 58 | 4 ♓ 59'40" |
| 17 TH | 7:44:31 | 5 23 | 21 17 | 1 34 | 25 43 | 13 0 | 16 58 | 6 29 | 20 52 | 25 59 | 4 ♓ 59'39" |
| 18 FR | 7:48:28 | 8 11 | 22 55 | 2 35 | 26 16 | 13 5 | 17 0 | 6 29 | 20 53 | 25 59 | 4 ♓ 59'39" |
| 19 SA | 7:52:25 | 11 0 | 24 32 | 3 36 | 26 49 | 13 9 | 17 2 | 6 30 | 20 53 | 25 59 | 4 ♓ 59'39" |
| 20 SU | 7:56:21 | 13 50 | 26 9 | 4 37 | 27 23 | 13 14 | 17 4 | 6 31 | 20 54 | 25 59 | 4 ♓ 59'39" |
| 21 MO | 8: 0:18 | 16 43 | 27 47 | 5 38 | 27 56 | 13 19 | 17 6 | 6 31 | 20 54 | 26 0 | 4 ♓ 59'39" |
| 22 TU | 8: 4:14 | 19 37 | 29 24 | 6 39 | 28 29 | 13 24 | 17 7 | 6 32 | 20 54 | 26 0 | 4 ♓ 59'39" |
| 23 WE | 8: 8:11 | 22 34 | 1 ♍ 1 | 7 41 | 29 2 | 13 28 | 17 9 | 6 33 | 20 55 | 26 0 | 4 ♓ 59'39" |
| 24 TH | 8:12: 7 | 25 32 | 2 38 | 8 42 | 29 35 | 13 33 | 17 11 | 6 33 | 20 55 | 26 1 | 4 ♓ 59'38" |
| 25 FR | 8:16: 4 | 28 34 | 4 15 | 9 43 | 0 ♉ 8 | 13 38 | 17 13 | 6 34 | 20 55 | 26 1 | 4 ♓ 59'38" |
| 26 SA | 8:20: 0 | 1 ♑ 38 | 5 53 | 10 44 | 0 41 | 13 43 | 17 15 | 6 35 | 20 56 | 26 1 | 4 ♓ 59'38" |
| 27 SU | 8:23:57 | 4 46 | 7 30 | 11 45 | 1 14 | 13 47 | 17 16 | 6 35 | 20 56 | 26 2 | 4 ♓ 59'38" |
| 28 MO | 8:27:54 | 7 57 | 9 7 | 12 45 | 1 47 | 13 52 | 17 18 | 6 36 | 20 56 | 26 2 | 4 ♓ 59'38" |
| 29 TU | 8:31:50 | 11 12 | 10 44 | 13 46 | 2 20 | 13 57 | 17 20 | 6 37 | 20 57 | 26 2 | 4 ♓ 59'38" |
| 30 WE | 8:35:47 | 14 31 | 12 21 | 14 47 | 2 53 | 14 1 | 17 22 | 6 37 | 20 57 | 26 2 | 4 ♓ 59'38" |
| 31 TH | 8:39:43 | 17 54 | 13 58 | 15 48 | 3 26 | 14 6 | 17 24 | 6 38 | 20 58 | 26 3 | 4 ♓ 59'37" |

INGRESSES :

| |
|---|
| 3 ♀ → ♌ 21:29 |
| 4 ☿ → ♏ 5:27 |
| 15 ☿ → ♐ 1:27 |
| ⊕ → ♋ 11: 0 |
| 22 ♀ → ♍ 8:56 |
| 24 ♂ → ♉ 17:50 |
| 25 ☿ → ♑ 11:15 |

ASPECTS (HELIOCENTRIC +MOON(TYCHONIC)) :

| | | | | |
|---|---|---|---|---|
| 1 ☽ ☌ ☿ 7:51 | 8 ☽ □ ♂ 15:13 | 14 ☽ □ ♇ 1:19 | 20 ☽ ☍ ♇ 13:36 | 27 ☽ □ ☿ 9:15 |
| ☽ □ ♀ 16:50 | ☿ ☌ ♃ 15:20 | ☽ ☌ ♅ 21:15 | 21 ☿ ☌ ♄ 3:11 | ☽ ☍ ♅ 10:20 |
| ☿ ☌ ☋ 23:42 | 10 ☽ ☍ ♀ 6:38 | 15 ♂ ☌ ☊ 4:39 | ☽ □ ♅ 6:18 | ☿ □ ♅ 13:50 |
| 2 ⊕ ☍ ♄ 5:48 | ☽ □ ♃ 10:56 | 16 ☽ ☌ ♂ 7:52 | ⊕ □ ♅ 21: 2 | 29 ☽ ☍ ♂ 9:56 |
| ☽ ☌ ♃ 22: 5 | ☽ □ ☿ 23:46 | ♀ ☍ ♆ 17:52 | 22 ☽ □ ♂ 17:39 | 30 ☿ ☍ ⊕ 2:50 |
| 3 ☽ □ ♆ 15:11 | 11 ☽ ☌ ♆ 3:52 | 17 ♀ N□ ☊ 8:15 | 23 ☽ □ ♃ 16:59 | ☽ ☌ ♃ 7:48 |
| ⊕ ☌ P 22:32 | ⊕ ☍ ♇ 11:32 | ☽ ☍ ♃ 14:56 | 24 ☿ ☌ ♇ 3:46 | ☽ □ ♆ 21:11 |
| 4 ☿ □ ♀ 16: 5 | ♀ □ ♃ 15:17 | 18 ☽ □ ♆ 4:15 | ☽ ☍ ♆ 4:55 | |
| 5 ☽ ☌ ♄ 17:55 | ☿ □ ♆ 17:31 | ☽ □ ♀ 8:39 | 25 ☽ ☌ ♀ 3: 9 | |
| 6 ☽ ☌ ♇ 12:29 | 12 ☿ ☌ A 10:10 | 19 ☽ ☍ ☿ 16:42 | 26 ☽ □ ♄ 0:38 | |
| 7 ☽ □ ♅ 9:32 | 13 ☽ □ ♄ 7:41 | ☽ ☍ ♄ 23:18 | ☽ □ ♇ 15:44 | |

we may all become the "salt of the Earth," learning how to manifest morally inspired deeds that can penetrate nature with goodness.

Today asks us to comprehend the dilemma of the encapsulated personal element of our being in contrast to the freedom inherent in our transpersonal "name." The latter guides us to rise above discord; in doing so, we will experience untold miracles.

Tomorrow Saturn conjuncts the Sun, adding strength to our memory of the Angel Jesus.

**Mercury enters Sagittarius:** "Growth attains power of existence, in existence growth's power dies. **Attainment concludes joyful striving** in life's active force of will. World-activity matures in dying, forms vanish in reforming. May existence feel existence!" (Steiner, *Twelve Cosmic Moods*).

**Jan 2: ASPECT: Sun conjunct Saturn 16° Sagittarius: Birth of the Nathan Jesus** (Dec/6/2 BC). The Sun remains at the memory of this holy birth as it conjuncts Saturn. Thus is the Holy Virgin (Saturn) in communion with the powers of resurrection (Sun). Under this aspect the memory of the promises we made in heaven may quicken. Such promises are filled with the spiritual resolves we have carried into incarnation. In conjunction with the Sun, the Holy Virgin resurrects into consciousness that which otherwise may lie hidden. Since this occurs in Sagittarius, we can imagine ourselves as the Centaur, sublimating the lower impulses in order that the mantle of our higher self may shine upon us. Control of speech is our practice. Whence comes our word? Under whose authority?

Jesus always spoke the living word. He is our exemplar. How does our speech reveal the lack of discipline we may otherwise command over lower instinctual impulses? Are we obstructing the resurrecting power of our true "I" in denial of the mission to which we have pledged ourselves?

**Venus enters Scorpio:** "Existence consumes being, **yet in being existence endures**. In activity growth disappears, in growth activity persists. In chastising world-activation, in punishing self-formation, being sustains beings" (Steiner, *Twelve Cosmic Moods*). Venus rules Taurus which is opposite Scorpio. Therefore, Venus in Scorpio meets its detriment. Through endurance alone, Venus must rise out of the death-defying forces that could otherwise consume her. In so doing she becomes the "eagle," soaring into transpersonal realms wherein existence endures despite the consuming fire of consciousness.

**Jan 5: ASPECT: New Moon 20° Sagittarius and Partial Solar Eclipse over northeast Asia and the North Pacific; 8:33pm EST.** The Moon remembers its position as Peter and John were accosted by a lame man and petitioned for alms. The man lay outside the temple door as Peter said to him: "Look up!" When the man obeyed, Peter went on, "I have no silver nor gold, but what I have, I give to thee! In the name of Jesus Christ of Nazareth, arise and walk!" The man then stood up, joyfully leaping about (Jun/2/33).

Today marks the first New Moon of 2019, and the conjunction of Sun and Moon are cradled by Pluto and Saturn; and below Saturn stands Mercury. All five planets are in Sagittarius! When such a stellium gathers simultaneously with a new Moon, we are to take heed. This New Moon occurs conjunct the star Vega in the constellation of the Lyre, which is one of three points visible in the summer triangle; the other points are marked by Deneb and Altair. The Lyre was very important to the Greek god Apollo, son of Zeus. He was the god of music and was also known as the Archer. On this last night of the twelve holy days, we prepare to re-enter ordinary time. And under today's stellium, we can imagine bearing five gifts of truth: a truth-filled mind (Mercury); a truth-filled heart (Sun); a truth-filled will (Moon); a truth-filled love (Pluto/Phanes); and a truth-filled acceptance of the healing arms of the Virgin (Saturn).

The stars bequeath these gifts and ask us to hold fast to such treasures. Over the ensuing twelve months they will unfold, playing new harmonies born of Apollo's lyre (Vega). Will we recognize this? We can be assured that evil beings stalk such blessings with the intent of crushing them by the sheer weight of worry and fear. Such soul anxieties mark the eclipse of our one true "name," the white raiment the angels hold for us—waiting, *ever* waiting, to bestow this upon us. Without such protection, we are vulnerable to the voice in us that does not love us. This is the voice we are to denounce as we "look up, arise, and walk" toward the promise of the rising Dharma Sun, i.e., the restoration of cosmic harmony.

Attachments to guilt, blame, and denigration cast our eyes on the past, on the vanishing power of Kali Yuga. Instead, we are to see the grace of cosmic order that is breaking through the darkness of materialism, proclaiming a new time, a new 2,500-year period in history. The signature of the Satya Yuga is forgiveness of self and others; it is acceptance of our inevitable fall into the temptation of egoism and our willingness to rise out of it. The star beings invite us to stand as Archers, and walk toward the new light.

The gift of truth requires love, an *action* present wherever it lives; and this action is the science of love, i.e., sacred magic:

> Sacred or divine magic is the putting into practice of *mystical revelation*. The Master revealed to Peter what he had to do—inwardly and outwardly—to heal Aeneas at Lydda. It is here that the order of things in sacred magic is given: firstly, *real* contact with the Divine (mysticism), then the taking into *consciousness* of this contact (gnosis). and lastly *the putting into operation* or the execution of that which mystical revelation has made known as being the task to accomplish and the method to follow.[1]

First we are touched (mysticism), then we cognize the meaning within the touch (gnosis), and finally we act (sacred magic). If we reverse this process, we may encounter the formidable danger inherent in personal, arbitrary magic: action by the self, from the self. This denies the fact of higher worlds, endangering the personality by further separating it from its original status as having been born from the divine. In such circumstances we eclipse our Sun-self, and in its place we appoint the personal self. In so doing we lose our freedom. Freedom is the state of obedience in which the self follows what has been ordained in higher worlds. True freedom obeys. Are we believers? Even the devil believes and obeys the law. Human beings alone have been given the freedom to disobey, to fall into temptation.

We are all Jobs, proving to the devil that we remain true no matter the forces he may bring against us. This Sagittarius New Moon asks us to remember the holy gifts of truth, and to carry this memory in our hearts as the year before us unfolds.

**First quarter Moon**, January 14, 29° Pisces: Triumphant entrance into Jerusalem.

**Full Moon**, January 21, 6° Cancer: Jesus speaks to his mother regarding his approaching suffering.

**Last quarter Moon**, January 22, 12° Libra: Crucifixion.

**Lunar teachings of this cycle** begin with our resolve to free ourselves from the eclipse of egoistic darkness; rising instead to greet the new light. In so doing, we may find that we enter upon the path leading to the New Jerusalem, i.e., the future destiny of all humanity. Suffering creates a force that breaks through to revelation, thus granting that we, too, may find discourse with our Mother in the heart of the Earth. She patiently listens to all that troubles our soul, restoring our strength to take up our cross and carry the burdens that are ours to bear. We may thereby feel the hand of Jesus Christ resting upon our shoulder, bestowing comfort as we willingly help him carry the world's weight.

**Jan 6: Sun 21° Sagittarius: Commissioning of the Twelve Disciples** (Dec/10/30). Jesus commissioned the twelve while teaching on a high mountain. The commissioning occurred on a Sunday—a day forever representing the Resurrection of Christ. We can imagine him raising them above ordinary consciousness, uniting them with angelic realms of truth. Are we not all commissioned to raise our thoughts, cast out all that limits us, and thus prepare our souls to behold the daily miracles we too often ignore?

**Uranus stations direct 3° Aries.** Uranus was at this degree in the summer of 1849, as California, eighteen months after the discovery of gold at Sutter's Mill, experienced an influx of tens of thousands in search of riches. Many came east across the United States (twenty years before the Golden Spike established the Transcontinental Railroad), while others sailed around the treacherous waters of Cape Horn or to Panama, braving the ravages of tropical illness as they traversed the Isthmus. The untamed

---

[1] Anon., *Meditations of the Tarot*, p. 58.

nature of the panning and mining territory and the squalid and lawless conditions at the camps bred disease and crime. The vast majority of the money made went to shrewd suppliers to the "forty-niners." By the time the Rush was over in 1855, much damage had been done to the land (through mining practices) and to indigenous Californians (through displacement, servitude, or worse).

As the holy days and nights come to a close, and we enter ordinary time, we can remember the devastation that greed has caused throughout the world via the ravaging disease of gold-fever. The riches we seek are not material, they are spiritual. The five gifts we take from the holy nights (see above commentary) have been offered to nurture the opening of our spiritual eye. This necessitates that we find a spiritual relationship to worldly affairs—and especially to money.

Uranus in Aries focuses on the power of self-sacrifice. Moreover, Uranus carries messages directly from the center of the Milky Way, through which spiritual imaginations seek to illumine us. If our "I" can find a cause greater than itself, we may find that devotion turns us in the right direction, stimulating our readiness to receive the enlightened thoughts before which the thoughts of the brain-bound intellect seem but a ghostly shadow.

**Today is Epiphany, the festival of the three kings.** The door to the holy days and nights closes for another year. We are leaving the "high mountain" of this sacred time in the cycle of the year when the Christ draws so near to us. This is also the time of year when the archangels draw very close. It is as if their wings are touching while they encircle the Earth. Archangels watch over communities, bestowing gifts of healing to all members who may have fallen prey to divisive forces. Just as this is the celebration of the adoration of the baby Jesus by the Three Kings, so too does it remember the Baptism in the Jordan River, when Christ entered into the sheaths of the Nathan Jesus. And what event preceded the Baptism? It was the conversation between Jesus and Mary the night before. Jesus poured out his heart to Mary as he named all the evil he beheld in the world. In so naming, Christ, the comforter of all comforters, drew near to him. This the Blessed Virgin perceived, for only after Christ was first conceived into her immaculate heart could he enter the sheaths of Jesus the following day.

Epiphany is an ancient festival, celebrated throughout antiquity and pregnant with meaning:

> The 6th of January is the same date as that on which, in ancient Egypt, the Festival of Osiris was celebrated, the Festival of the re-finding of Osiris. As you know, Osiris was overcome by his enemy Typhon: Isis seeks and eventually finds him. This re-finding of Osiris, the Son of God, is represented in the Festival of the 6th of January. The Festival of the Three Kings is the same Festival, but in its Christian form. This Festival was also celebrated among the Assyrians, the Armenians, and the Phoenicians. Everywhere it is a Festival connected with a kind of universal baptism—a rebirth from out of the water. This in itself points to the connection with the re-finding of Osiris.[1]

Typhon/Ahriman stands ready to smother the spark of Osiris/Christ that we bring forth from these holy nights. Just as it was Isis-Sophia who found Osiris, so too is our soul commissioned to find and protect our star of hope as we leave extraordinary time and enter again into ordinary time. The magi lost sight of the star they were following when they approached Herod's castle. This is a warning to all, for we must guard our light as we begin our journey through ordinary time. We are to name Typhon and his hoards as did Jesus before his Baptism, for then shall the comforter find us.

In spring our star-seed will sprout, in summer it will flower, and in autumn it will come to fruition. Then, as winter again silences the mantle of Natura, this very same star will birth a new seed that we will carry into the Holy Nights yet to come. So precious is this gift! May we water it constantly, so that it may complete its seasons of growth.

We are still under the influence of the New Moon that occurred yesterday, reminding each of us to tune our soul's harp to the mighty cosmic harp of Apollo. Thus will we be prepared to enter fields wherein "truth" holds sway. We must follow our star!

---

1 Steiner, *The Festivals and Their Meaning*, "Christmas."

**Jan 8: ASPECT: Mercury 10° Sagittarius square Mars 10° Pisces.** Mars recalls two possessed men from Gergesa whose demons Jesus drove out into a herd of two thousand swine, which then plunged down into a lake and drowned (Dec/6/30).

The people of Gergesa were hostile toward Jesus after he drove their swine to their deaths. Nonetheless, in this healing we see that demons are far more perceptive than human beings, for it was the demons who cried out from the two possessed men, recognizing Christ and asking: "What have we to do with thee, Jesus, thou Son of God?" Ahriman stands behind such demons, still awaiting his final triumph. What was his plan for the people of Gergesa? Judith von Halle explicates this:

> The demons wished to be driven into pigs because they counted on reentering human bodies—in multiplied fashion even—when the latter ate slaughtered pig meat, or pork. By this means they hoped to get back into human bodies.[2]

Things are often *not* what they appear to be. If we can apply this to our everyday lives, we would unveil many mysteries. The return of the possessed swine to the watery element of the fallen ahrimanic-etheric was unavoidable. Furthermore, it was proof that evil must be held at bay, sentenced to its rightful place in the subearthly realm. As the people of Gergesa calculated their loses, greed caused hostility. Until we see money as the flow of spiritual blood—a substance working for fraternity among all people—it will ever deter us from what is right. If kept in the hands of a few, it will instead continue to *spill* blood, rather than being the heart's-blood of social-moral circulation. As Mars (the spoken word) is in Pisces, and square Mercury (mental energies) in Sagittarius, we can beware of restless speech that is driven aggressively from below, and instead fill our words with the power of Michaelic strength (Mars).

Dignity ensues when words are true, free from the magnetizing influences of the lower astral realms. Hate is stirred when dignity is lost. And with the loss of dignity comes abandonment of truth (Sagittarius).

---
2 von Halle, *Illness and Healing*, p. 135.

**Jan 11: ASPECT: Sun conjunct Pluto 26° Sagittarius.** The Sun was at this degree as Jesus, one Sabbath morning, healed the sick, the deaf, the blind, the palsied, and the lame. The Pharisees and Sadducees were scandalized but nonetheless left him to continue his work, for Jesus had written the secrets of their sins upon a wall (Dec/16/30).

This aspect increases intensity as it offers the potential for regeneration and rebirth. The secrets of our sins are also written upon a wall. This happens every night, as the angels inscribe all the many occurrences of our day upon the pages of the great "book of our life." Following our death, we will read this book, suffering or rejoicing in all that we caused in the souls of others. In bearing conscious witness to this kamaloka process, we receive all measure of goodness that will help us, in our next life, to overcome our deafness, blindness, lameness, and illness. As authors of this book, we determine what is written. Wise are those who live by day in such a manner that they author benevolence into the book of the night.

Today we can remember the third petition of the Lord's Prayer: Thy will be done.

**Jan 13: ASPECT: Jupiter 19° Scorpio square Neptune 19° Aquarius.** The Sun was at Jupiter's degree as Jesus healed (from afar) the servant of a Roman centurion. Later that day, the widowed mother of the youth of Nain begged Jesus to come and heal her twelve-year-old son (Nov/10/30).

This aspect occurs approximately every twelve years. The last occurrence was in 2006 and the next occurrence will be in 2025. The exact square between these two planets will occur three times this year: today, June 16, and September 21. Thus is this entire year under its influence. Individualism (Jupiter "I"-consciousness) must stand strong before the assault of mass consciousness (Neptune).

Healing from both near and afar is a capacity that can, and actually must, be taken up. The energy body has become a battleground upon which forces of good and evil rally for dominance. In this time of the Etheric Christ, it is the etheric body, the energy body, which is foremost in the targeted aim of the ahrimanic hordes. Neptune in its highest aspect represents the Goddess Night, i.e., Sophia's sanctifying grace through whom our life forces are vivified. Inversely, in its lowest aspect, Neptune represents the Woman of Babylon—the consort of Ahriman—who greedily feeds upon our life forces, causing them to wither.

Spiritual forces that once lived within us are no longer doing so. Over time our astral sheaths have contracted into closer union with our physical and etheric bodies, leaving behind the gods who once dwelt within us. Instead, we now have empty spaces—voids—that will be filled by one class of beings or another. And this is the mark of our age! If we are to reclaim our spiritual heritage, we must, through our own efforts, fill these voids with light.

Sophia/Neptune/Night awaits her invitation to regenerate our forces as we take up spiritual light; if we ignore her, however, the "other" woman happily usurps what has been divinely ordained, stealthily taking up her abode within us as she fills us with energetic viruses, systemic pathologies, and possession. The holes now constituting parts of our astral sheath must be filled with the fire of spirit:

> And now it was inevitable that something would wish to incorporate itself into these uninhabited sheaths within human astral bodies: something whose dwelling was doubtless in the spiritual spheres and was not human, but had fallen, and fallen out of the advancing evolution of the hierarchies who inhabit the planetary spheres. Into the empty sheaths of these places of the gods there entered the spirits which the Gospel refers to as demons.[1]

The demons we ingest through denying spirit—and by turning away from the toil inherent in seeking spirit—cast a shadow upon our etheric-energy bodies. Into such shadows creep the ahrimanic beings, magnetically luring us into subearthly realms resounding with anti-inspirations, i.e., dead sound. This inevitable situation demands that we learn new etheric-technologies; and these will allow us to clear out the usurping demons to regenerate our light and bring healing to our life forces. This can be done for ourselves, and this can also be done for others, regardless of whether they are in our presence or if they instead live afar. Such is the power of sacred magic in this time of the Satya Yuga, through which cosmic order is being restored. Recognizing our time, *in* our time, allows us to rediscover magical practices that have long lain hidden.

The Holy Spirit (Jupiter) in square to the Goddess Night (Neptune) can bring about a test of faith. For despite the delusions spawned from the Babylonian Woman, faith alone turns our mind's eye to Wisdom Sophia, through whom the Christ Light finds us—casting away all shadows.

**ASPECT 2: Mercury conjunct Saturn 18° Sagittarius.** Saturn remembers its position as Anne Catherine Emmerich received the stigmata (Dec/29/1812). The stigmata mark those who have been touched by Christ; thereby does his suffering become, to a certain extent, their suffering. At times this aspect may cause the mind to focus on negative thoughts; we then forget how the healing arms of the blessed Virgin (Saturn) ever hold us to guide us to fulfill on Earth the promises we have made in Heaven.

**Jan 14: 1st Quarter Moon 29° Pisces: Triumphant Entry into Jerusalem** (Mar/19/33). Today marks the first challenge to the new beginnings inaugurated at the New Moon one week ago. We are to manage the energy released by the New Moon to bring new structure to our personality, which necessitates letting go of the old and outworn.

A Pisces Moon asks us to engage enthusiastically with material existence; simultaneously allowing us to remain unfettered to forces lying in the subearthly depths. To love creation is to accept the mission of the Earth and humanity. To chain oneself to matter, on the other hand, grinds our soul to dust. Can we turn to the light, shedding at least some aspect of our egoism? Jesus Christ rode upon an ass as he entered Jerusalem. The ass represents our lower, instinctual nature. Our Sun-self commands over our lower impulses, girding us with love, while also inviting us to cooperate with the living being of our Mother Earth. Are we not often sleeping when the Self calls us to rise above the eclipse of materialism? Can we boldly step into "the darkness of an unknown future" (see next commentary)?

---

1 Ibid., pp. 65–66.

**Jan 15: Sun enters Capricorn: "May the future rest upon the past"** (Steiner, *Twelve Cosmic Moods*). The late William Bento illumines Steiner's mantra:

> Although this can be said to be a common sense statement, it touches on deeper mysteries within the stream of time. Implicit to this mood is how we all must bear the consequences and deeds of the past as seeds for the future. By being aware of this in the present, we can affect the stream of time with conscious intent and not relegate ourselves to the past. Instead, we step into and through the darkness of the unknown future.

**Jan 18: ASPECT: Mercury conjunct Pluto 26° Sagittarius.** Mercury was at this degree as Jesus, having endured forty days in the wilderness, descended from Mt. Attarus (Nov/30/29). This aspect propels the mind to penetrate into the depths of things, as did Jesus Christ during the time of his temptations. Never did he look at Satan or any of his magic tricks. He kept his eyes on the true kingdom, power, and glory of heaven.

**ASPECT 2: Sun 3° Capricorn square Uranus 3° Aries.** While the Sun was at this degree, Jesus taught in the synagogue with many friends and relatives in attendance, including the Holy Virgin. Jesus spoke of the light that should not be hidden under a bushel (Dec/23/29). This is a perfect memory for Uranus square Sun; for, Uranus brings illumination directly from the heart of the galaxy, turning the straw of the brain-bound intellect into the gold of spiritualized imaginations. Thus are we enabled to shine our light from the top of the hill, for all to see, rather than hiding it under the dark ceiling of our own skulls—under the bushel of materialistic, abstract intellectuality.

The inversion to this potential is the radicalism of the outliers, the geniuses as well as the revolutionaries, whose hearts are filled with a restlessness that is then externalized as a destructive force rising from subterranean spheres of influence. Revolution is like an earthquake; it throws that which is above into the below, and that which is below into the above. It is the inversion of the Hermetic axiom: *As above, so also below.*

Our hollow neural tubes are rightly to reflect spiritual thoughts, and to this end do those devoted to a harmonious future strive. Spirit's divine breath is not arbitrary or personal. It is the virginal water whence consciousness is reintegrated with its source.

**Jan 20: ASPECT: Venus 19° Scorpio square Neptune 19° Aquarius.** Venus remembers Jesus as he healed the dumb and paralyzed son of a Roman officer, Achias, who had begged Jesus to have pity on a child (Nov/6/30).

The New Moon of this month remembered Peter's healing of Achias (Aeneas), informing us of how we achieve sacred magic. Today's aspect reminds us of the sphere of the false Holy Spirit, the stolen waters, whence intoxication of the masses can swallow the sovereign authority of selfhood.

Venus (representing the crucifixion) in Scorpio, tends to reveal what lies hidden. And in square to the Goddess Night (Neptune) in Aquarius, it further reveals where we may be caught in the stolen waters; in the unchaste regions of desire, delusion, and fantasy. The chaste mind is not easily swept away by intoxications arising from the masses, i.e., from fallen Neptunian spheres of systemic pathologies. Thus must we hold fast to the crown of our sovereign "I," falling neither into a kind of fundamentalism nor into the ease that accompanies a lack of boundaries.

Fanatics are inwardly electrified, acting under the narcotic effect of feverish heat rising from their lower nature. Then there are those who accept anything, aligning themselves with the "great unity" of all natural and spiritual life. In this state, there is nothing to choose and nothing to lose. This results in diminishing the significance of individuality, for individuality requires strict and definite organization. Each of us has a path to tread that has not yet been cleared; it is our spiritual responsibility to forge this path. There *is* a definite choice, and everything to lose, if we instead forsake what our particular "I" is commissioned to uphold.

If we are to carry our Venus "cross," we must willingly bear the weight that has been placed upon our shoulders, understanding that the true measure of our earthly trials is decreed in higher realms. Our angel knows what we must endure if our heart is to open. Thus may we find the healing waters that continuously pour from the urns of Aquarius, cleansing our souls from all afflictions.

If we cannot love ourselves, we are limited in our ability to love others. This square can help unmask nonintegrated aspects of our personality.

**Mercury enters Capricorn: "To be strong in the present"** (Steiner, *Twelve Cosmic Moods*).

**Jan 21: ASPECT: Full Moon 6° Cancer opposite Sun 6° Capricorn and Total Lunar Eclipse, 12:13am EST, over the totality of the Americas.** The Moon at this degree remembers Jesus in Bethany, speaking at length to his mother about his approaching suffering (Feb/27/33).

The New Moon that inaugurated this lunar cycle remembered Apollo's lyre, ever resounding the harmony of our perfect self. The first quarter Moon called us to enter upon the path leading to the New Jerusalem, the holy city of the Lamb and his Bride, by awaking to the true mission of the Earth and humanity. Today the lunar cycle blossoms under the pall of a total lunar eclipse. A lunar eclipse allows evil thoughts to approach human beings who are desirous of being possessed by them. Materialists observe only the physical process of lunar phases; initiates, however, observe the spiritual element as well:

> But also in this case, the old initiates also knew that a spiritual reality was behind the physical fact. He knew that when there is an eclipse of the moon, thoughts stream through darkness down upon the earth; and that such thoughts have a closer relationship with the subconscious life than with the conscious life of the human being. The old initiates often made use of a certain simile when speaking to their pupils. It is, of course, necessary to translate their words into modern language, but this is the gist of what they said: "Visionaries and dreamers love to go for walks under the light of the Full Moon. There are, however, certain people who have no wish to receive the good thoughts coming to them from the cosmos, but who, on the contrary, are desirous of getting hold of evil, diabolical thoughts. Such people will choose the moment of a lunar eclipse for their nocturnal wanderings."[1]

The Moon remembers Jesus conversing with his mother regarding the suffering he would endure a mere six weeks in his future. He himself had no cause to suffer. It is unimaginable, however, to grasp the significance of how he freely bore the suffering of all humanity, throughout all time. To gain such understanding, we must advance in the process of evolution. The alternative is to unite with matter as it continues to decay. This is the grievous mistake of all who descend into the physical realm to such an extent they unite with the instinctive forces of the physical body—i.e., *they sensualize the spirit*. In Revelation, such persons are called "Nicolaitans."

Where we have allowed the lunar shadow-mind to eclipse our higher solar-mind, we are dead, paralyzed, and know this not. We are caught in regressive movement like the crab (Cancer), fleeing from one abstraction to another; and we mechanize creation as if it were one vast system operating under purely physical laws.

> What is most characteristic of this state [regression into facts drawn only from the sense world] is that *intelligence no longer moves forward but backward*. It looks to the least developed and the most primitive for the cause and explanation of what is most developed and most advanced in the process of evolution. Thus, it looks for the effective cause of the world not in the heights of creative consciousness but rather in the depths of the unconscious—instead of going forward and elevating itself toward God, it retreats into matter.[2]

Diminution, the principle of the eclipse, characterizes retrograde movement. The Moon reflects the light of the Sun; and when eclipsed, the Moon is reduced to materialistic intellectuality—mechanizing and abstracting what would otherwise be the ineffable purity of nature and the spiritual potential of the human being. At the beginning of the letter to the church of Sardis (in Revelation) we hear of the One who has the seven spirits and the seven stars. This is the message related to our cultural epoch.

When we remember the seven spirits, we awake to our spiritual potential from within; and when we remember the seven stars, we awake to the cosmic

---

[1] Steiner, *Human Questions and Cosmic Answers*, June 25, 1922, Dornach.

[2] *MOT*, p. 523.

biography of the Earth and to Nature in her wholeness. Regression arrests development, sloughing off those who are deaf to Apollo's lyre; such people are terrified of surrendering their lower ego-being to tread the path of the morning star, the path leading to the New Jerusalem.

Those who continue to choose the principle of the eclipse at this time in history, will find themselves bound to live the destiny of Narcissus, forever gazing at their own reflection while the process of evolution proceeds without them. In death they will be blind and deaf, for they must then live in a prison of their own making, suffering in loneliness despite the fact that they are surrounded by a multitude of the faithful.

The Sun, eclipsed by today's Full Moon, remembers the second conversion of Mary Magdalene. If we disallow our conversion, we will dig a hole in which we then must live.

> [This is] because the moon is the principle of *reflection*: just as it reflects the light of the Sun, so does human intelligence reflect the creative light of conscience—and the latter is eclipsed when "materialistic intellectuality" prevails.[3]

Seeing through the eyes of a Hermeticist, we find that esotericism is a way of seeing the profundity in ordinary and known things. The rule of synthesis overcomes intellectual rigidity, wherein the surface state of intelligence gives way to the soaring wings of moral conscience.

**ASPECT 2: Mars 19° Pisces square Saturn 19° Sagittarius.** Mars at its position today remembers Jesus having healed ten lepers. Later, a shepherd begged Jesus to come because his little daughter, about seven, had died. Looking up to heaven, Jesus placed one hand on her head and the other on her breast and prayed. The child then rose up (Jun/12/32).

The power of the Archangel Michael (Mars) is in dynamic tension with the Holy Virgin (Saturn). Another way of expressing this would be: What part of us fights against our appointed destiny? The shepherd in today's memory had a dying daughter. We are all shepherds, herding the unruly aspects of our personality. Our dying daughter is the aspect of our soul that has been deprived of spiritual air. Moreover, it is *air* that heals lesions on the skin, leprous lesions. In both cases, we deal with the breath of spirit and ask: Where am I directing, when instead I should be following?

Through the sphere of Mars comes the temptation (the fourth) to come in our own name. When the tempters were assaulting Jesus, the angels could not come to him, for his field was darkened by the demons and this would have caused the angels to faint. It was only after the 39th day, when the devils had left him, that the angels came to minister to him. This is an analogy for reconciling the square between Mars and Saturn. Where do we listen to our lower nature (Mars) at the expense of the resolves we have made in heaven (Saturn)? Saturn asks that we remain true. Mars asks that we cleanse ourselves from lower astral desires. When so cleansed, we may perceive the restraints laid upon us as the true gifts they are: they restrain to shepherd us to the spiritual air that is the promise of our intended destiny.

This aspect tempts us to give up, too easily overwhelmed by frustration. Yet, if we penetrate the inner dynamics of this creative tension, we may find that our frustrations are naught but embers longing to ignite into flames of gratification—into a loving acceptance of the truth we are destined to fulfill.

**Jan 22: Venus conjunct Jupiter 21° Scorpio.** Venus at this degree recalls Jesus delivering a powerful discourse, culminating with the words: "Come! Come to me, all who are weary and laden with guilt! Come to me, O sinners! Do penance, believe, and share the kingdom with me!" Mary Magdalene was deeply moved, and then converted. During the evening meal, she anointed the head of Jesus with ointment, as described in Luke 7:36-50 (Nov/8/30).

The two benefic planets, Venus and Jupiter, align in Scorpio. Thus are we blessed to see behind the veil of material appearances. The "cross" of Venus aligning with the Holy Spirit (Jupiter) brings the gift of insight, granted through patience. The infusion of life into that in us which is dead is what we call a *conversion*. Christ is the guarantor of this ever approachable miracle. And this aspect allows

---
3 Ibid., p. 494.

us to see into the realm of death (Scorpio), to look it in the face, and thereby hear Christ calling in a loud voice. Although he calls to us from worlds beyond, his voice awakes our inner memory that, in truth, we live from miracle to miracle.

The electromagnetic world threatens to reduce us, whereby we resonate with the machine of technology. Today's aspect, however, reminds us that we are to resonate with life! This is what restores the moral fabric to our social order, for when we resonate with life, we long to collaborate in sisterhood and brotherhood. Love (Venus) and wisdom (Jupiter) raise us from the deadening forces that would otherwise turn us to stone.

**Jan 23: ASPECT: Mercury 3° Capricorn square Uranus 3° Aries.** Retrograde Mercury stood at this degree as Philip (who would later travel to Ephesus for the death and assumption of the Virgin Mary in August of 44 AD) sought out Nathanael and said of Jesus, "We have found him of whom Moses in the law and also the prophets wrote, Jesus of Nazareth, the son of Joseph." Nathanael, having asked if anything good could come from Nazareth, was told, "Come and see" (Dec/25/29).

The healers and pastors (Mercury), in dynamic tension with imaginations streaming directly from the heart of the galaxy (Uranus), bid us to surrender to something greater than ourselves to recognize what good is coming from the Nazarene. He is with us and in us, imploring all to open their spirit-eye.

**Jan 27: 4th Quarter Moon 13° Libra: Crucifixion** (Apr/3/33). The first quarter Moon called for action, asking us to adjust to the energies released at the New Moon. The last quarter calls for consciousness. Will we awake to what has been granted during this lunar cycle? The New Moon asked us to free ourselves from the egoistic darkness of the eclipse, turning us toward the emerging new light. The first quarter Moon asked us to align with the path leading to New Jerusalem, the path of the morning star, whereby we awake to the presence of angels. The Full Moon asked us to suffer the death of our lower nature to receive the raiment of our higher self. Now we are asked to take up our cross.

Libra balances the scales, revealing all in us that must be laid aside. As we cull the inessential, we find acceptance of the fact that Christ is the Lord of Karma; it is he who strengthens us to remain faithful to the mission of the Earth and humanity, despite the burdens we must endure as the trials of our destiny. The inversion to expansion onto the spiritual measure of the cross is contraction, through which *measure* becomes *constriction*. Refusal to carry what is ours will cast us into a prison of our own making: the prison of egoistic loneliness. Within this prison are all souls who have refused to unite with the great purpose of human evolution. In accepting our cross, on the other hand, consciousness expands—it awakes. Thus do we increase our self as we prepare for the new lunar cycle before us.

**Jan 29: ASPECT: Superior conjunction of Sun and Mercury 15° Capricorn: Sun at the Death of John the Baptist** (Jan/4/31). A superior conjunction means that Mercury is on the far side of the Sun, gathering cosmic intelligence. At such times we can imagine ourselves offering a sacrifice to the gods. And what is the nature of this sacrifice? It is a time when we may humbly offer up our weaknesses, which then may return to us as strengths when Mercury later comes into inferior conjunction—blessing the Earth with all the wisdom gained while in communion with the mighty cosmos. Thus may we be raised to think with the gods (Capricorn).

An inferior conjunction occurs on March 14. The questions we offer today will fall upon us like rain at the time of cosmic response (inferior conjunction). John was beheaded. Must we not also remove the restraint of our brain-bound thinking if we are to receive holy wisdom?

**Jan 30: Venus enters Sagittarius:** "Growth attains power of existence, **in existence growth's power dies.** Attainment concludes joyful striving in life's active force of will. World-activity matures in dying, forms vanish in re-forming. May existence feel existence!" (Steiner, *Twelve Cosmic Moods*).

**Jan 31: ASPECT: Mars 26° Pisces square Pluto 26° Sagittarius.** Mars recalls the joyous day that Jesus healed three feeble-minded siblings who were particularly afraid of fire and believed others wanted to kill them. Jesus laid his hands on the children and returned them to normalcy; the children then awoke, as if from a dream (Jan/1/31).

We too must awake from the dream of feeble-mindedness that is the signature of our times, due to the quantity of distractions to which we've succumbed. History, however, may look back on this period as more of a nightmare. The Archangel Michael in dynamic tension with Pluto/Phanes brings steel to the will. This profound strengthening of the will is a signature of those who are prepared to courageously face evil—and in so doing, bring forth the good. Inversely, when one instead turns to Pluto/Hades, this aspect can ferment into perverse sexuality and violence.

Recognition of hierarchy humbles us, for we then realize that we are the lowest of all the ranks of spiritual beings. Discord is not due to differences as much as it is due to similarity. Cain and Abel worshiped the same God, yet this did not prevent Cain from slaying his brother. Wherever we are sworn to see others as mortal enemies, we are in fact slaying our brother. How can we be mortal enemies to one another when we together form the lowest rank? Does this not signify that ignorance can be assumed?

Negation of true hierarchy is the source of all violence, all wars, all strife. When we humble ourselves before the majesty of the heavenly hierarchies, we seek peace, we overcome our feeble-mindedness. And yes, we are indeed afraid of fire—the flame of the holy Word—for obedience is often perceived as a loss of freedom, when instead it is the complete restoration of Freedom. And, when we realize that freedom means we have surrendered the temporal on the altar of the eternal, we will effortlessly become who we truly are, who we ever have been, united with the One in whom we would willingly die to become.

# FEBRUARY 2019

## Stargazing Preview

February offers us a Capricorn New Moon on the 4th. When Mars enters Aries on the 6th, he'll be visible in the southwest for about five hours after sunset. On the evening of the 10th, you'll be able to see the Moon, nearly to its First Quarter, pass Mars from below. Venus on the 13th will rise just ahead of Saturn, and in five days' time these two will be in conjunction. February's Leo Full Moon on the 19th is a Supermoon, meaning that its proximity to the Earth makes it look bigger than usual.

Venus, now rising at 0430, moves into Capricorn on the 25th. On the 27th, the Moon will rise a little before Jupiter (around 0200), followed by Saturn and Venus—all before sunrise! Orion will be high in the south as the Sun sets.

## February Commentaries

**Feb 2: Candlemas.** The star-seed we are carrying from the Holy Nights now quickens with new life. We recall the five gifts of truth that marked Epiphany. Perhaps our star-seed is revealing its nature to us, becoming recognizable as a new gift. Soon this star-seed will sprout into the warmth of the Easter Sun, whereupon it will expand into the cosmic heights as a summer blossom; Michaelmas will then find it coming to fruition within us, as an inner capacity of strength. For now, we are tending to it and watering its promise.

**Feb 4: ASPECT: New Moon 21° Capricorn, 4:03 pm EST.** The Moon recalls the evening leading up to the Transfiguration on Mount Tabor. Jesus had earlier climbed along a footpath for two hours with Peter, John, and James the Greater. Anne Catherine described Tabor's peak thus: "On it was a large open place surrounded by a wall of shade trees. The ground was covered with aromatic herbs and sweet-scented flowers. Hidden in a rock was a reservoir, which upon the turning of a spigot poured forth water that was sparkling and very cold. The apostles washed Jesus's feet, and then their own" (Apr/3/31).

Today we begin a new lunar cycle. The Transfiguration was two years before the crucifixion. Throughout this entire period, Christ's greatest enemy, the Antichrist, would work against him. It was Ahriman who tortured Christ in the Garden of Gethsemane, showing him all the deeds human beings would do in his name. And it is this same being who now tortures all humanity. His aim is to strangle any possibility that the Second Coming may be recognized, as well as to destroy any possibility of transfiguration. The event of the Transfiguration of Jesus marked the enlightenment of his astral body. It is the destiny of the next cultural epoch, Philadelphia, that this will gradually occur within the *human* astral body. And the seeds for this potential are quickening in our age of the consciousness soul.

The prophesied birth of the Antichrist was February 5th, 1962.[1] He turns 57 this year. Rudolf Steiner foresaw that the School of Michael, which he was then founding, would stand against the School of Ahriman. Indeed, it has!

The Sun at the birth of this child was 21° Capricorn, just a few hours past a Capricorn New Moon. This New Moon kindles a fire proclaiming the task of our time as that of naming evil and calling forth the good. Regardless of whether the Antichrist has, or has not, incarnated, his signature is everywhere. Furthermore, we are to remember that standing witness to a new "force of hope" is paramount if we are to rise above the delusions parading upon the stage of Ahriman's theater.

The greater the ubiquity of technological grids, the more human nature is programmed to resonate with the machine, which in turn leads to the disintegration of our social organization—ultimately resulting in the moral decline of culture. When souls resonate with spirit, they seek companionship with others, knowing that when soul meets soul the universal sap of life flows. When human souls resonate with the machine, i.e., with electromagnetic cell towers and the like, they do not seek heart-to-heart or soul-to-soul togetherness, and this depletes the sap of life. Consequently, the fabric of the social order becomes brittle, then it tears, leaving lesions behind. Into these tears, these lesions, enters Ahriman. He replaces what is culturally invigorating with strip malls, banks, bars, gyms, and all manner of material convenience. Religious congregations diminish in number and significance, and true social longing for one another fades. Already we have seen family owned local stores being replaced by big box stores and Amazon, a phenomenon which most of us have by now bought into. The result is a tragic decline of town-centric community.

The family holds the child in the first seven years, the community in the second seven years, and the culture in the third seven years. We are turning our teens over to a torn and tattered culture. It can no longer protect them, elevate them, or inspire them. The main cause of our current addiction crisis may indeed be *the failure of culture*. Victims of the disease of addition are slipping through the cracks. We give them nothing to look up to that is worthy of the incredible spiritual capacities so many of them would have manifested in our society. We divide and fight over gun issues, drug issues, crime issues, poverty issues, and violence; but are these not symptoms of a much greater dilemma—one which we are each complicit in having somehow fashioned? "Cheaper, faster, easier" has led us down a road that is tearing us apart. Not only has the culture failed; community and family are also failing. How bad does it need to get before we decide to change?

Perhaps it is time to climb Mt. Tabor, to remember the light of spirit and our miraculous potential to re-establish our moral sensibility. A rainbow of peace is ours if we choose to restore our families, our communities, and our culture. The torrential forces of the death-culture will surely work against us. Indeed, it will take enormous courage and conviction to make the needed changes.

Hope moves and directs spiritual evolution in the world; it is a transfiguring light-force:

> Hope is for spiritual evolution what the instinct of reproduction is for biological evolution. It is the force and the light of the *final cause* of the world or, if you wish, the force and the light of

---

1  See Robert Powell's book *Prophecy-Phenomena-Hope*. Jean Dixon gave this birthdate for the one she called the "middle eastern child." This date (and place of birth) was later, in private conversation, confirmed by Willi Sucher.

SIDEREAL GEOCENTRIC LONGITUDES : FEBRUARY 2019 Gregorian at 0 hours UT

| DAY | ☉ | ☽ | ☊ | ☿ | ♀ | ♂ | ♃ | ♄ | ♅ | ♆ | ♇ |
|---|---|---|---|---|---|---|---|---|---|---|---|
| 1 FR | 16 ♑ 49 | 4 ♐ 36 | 1 ♋ 47 | 18 ♑ 9 | 1 ♐ 39 | 25 ♓ 53 | 22 ♏ 46 | 19 ♐ 57 | 3 ♈ 52 | 19 ♒ 56 | 26 ♐ 37 |
| 2 SA | 17 50 | 16 38 | 1 48 | 19 54 | 2 47 | 26 34 | 22 56 | 20 4 | 3 53 | 19 58 | 26 39 |
| 3 SU | 18 51 | 28 33 | 1 49 | 21 39 | 3 56 | 27 15 | 23 6 | 20 10 | 3 55 | 20 0 | 26 41 |
| 4 MO | 19 51 | 10 ♑ 24 | 1 48R | 23 25 | 5 4 | 27 55 | 23 16 | 20 17 | 3 56 | 20 2 | 26 43 |
| 5 TU | 20 52 | 22 12 | 1 47 | 25 11 | 6 12 | 28 36 | 23 27 | 20 23 | 3 58 | 20 4 | 26 45 |
| 6 WE | 21 53 | 4 ♒ 0 | 1 45 | 26 58 | 7 21 | 29 16 | 23 36 | 20 30 | 3 59 | 20 6 | 26 47 |
| 7 TH | 22 54 | 15 50 | 1 41 | 28 46 | 8 30 | 29 57 | 23 46 | 20 36 | 4 1 | 20 8 | 26 49 |
| 8 FR | 23 55 | 27 44 | 1 38 | 0 ♒ 34 | 9 39 | 0 ♈ 38 | 23 56 | 20 42 | 4 2 | 20 10 | 26 50 |
| 9 SA | 24 56 | 9 ♓ 44 | 1 34 | 2 22 | 10 48 | 1 18 | 24 6 | 20 49 | 4 4 | 20 12 | 26 52 |
| 10 SU | 25 56 | 21 53 | 1 30 | 4 11 | 11 57 | 1 59 | 24 15 | 20 55 | 4 6 | 20 14 | 26 54 |
| 11 MO | 26 57 | 4 ♈ 14 | 1 27 | 5 59 | 13 6 | 2 40 | 24 24 | 21 1 | 4 7 | 20 16 | 26 56 |
| 12 TU | 27 58 | 16 51 | 1 25 | 7 48 | 14 16 | 3 20 | 24 34 | 21 7 | 4 9 | 20 18 | 26 58 |
| 13 WE | 28 58 | 29 46 | 1 25D | 9 36 | 15 25 | 4 1 | 24 43 | 21 13 | 4 11 | 20 20 | 26 59 |
| 14 TH | 29 59 | 13 ♉ 4 | 1 25 | 11 24 | 16 35 | 4 41 | 24 52 | 21 19 | 4 13 | 20 23 | 27 1 |
| 15 FR | 1 ♒ 0 | 26 47 | 1 27 | 13 11 | 17 44 | 5 22 | 25 1 | 21 25 | 4 15 | 20 25 | 27 3 |
| 16 SA | 2 0 | 10 ♊ 55 | 1 28 | 14 57 | 18 54 | 6 2 | 25 9 | 21 31 | 4 17 | 20 27 | 27 5 |
| 17 SU | 3 1 | 25 30 | 1 29 | 16 42 | 20 4 | 6 43 | 25 18 | 21 37 | 4 19 | 20 29 | 27 6 |
| 18 MO | 4 1 | 10 ♋ 25 | 1 29R | 18 25 | 21 14 | 7 23 | 25 27 | 21 43 | 4 21 | 20 31 | 27 8 |
| 19 TU | 5 2 | 25 36 | 1 27 | 20 6 | 22 24 | 8 4 | 25 35 | 21 49 | 4 23 | 20 33 | 27 10 |
| 20 WE | 6 2 | 10 ♌ 52 | 1 23 | 21 45 | 23 34 | 8 44 | 25 43 | 21 55 | 4 25 | 20 36 | 27 12 |
| 21 TH | 7 3 | 26 4 | 1 19 | 23 20 | 24 45 | 9 25 | 25 51 | 22 0 | 4 27 | 20 38 | 27 13 |
| 22 FR | 8 3 | 11 ♍ 1 | 1 13 | 24 51 | 25 55 | 10 5 | 26 0 | 22 6 | 4 29 | 20 40 | 27 15 |
| 23 SA | 9 4 | 25 35 | 1 8 | 26 18 | 27 6 | 10 46 | 26 7 | 22 12 | 4 31 | 20 42 | 27 16 |
| 24 SU | 10 4 | 9 ♎ 41 | 1 3 | 27 40 | 28 16 | 11 26 | 26 15 | 22 17 | 4 34 | 20 45 | 27 18 |
| 25 MO | 11 5 | 23 18 | 1 0 | 28 57 | 29 27 | 12 6 | 26 23 | 22 23 | 4 36 | 20 47 | 27 20 |
| 26 TU | 12 5 | 6 ♏ 27 | 0 58 | 0 ♓ 7 | 0 ♑ 37 | 12 47 | 26 30 | 22 28 | 4 38 | 20 49 | 27 21 |
| 27 WE | 13 5 | 19 10 | 0 58D | 1 10 | 1 48 | 13 27 | 26 38 | 22 33 | 4 41 | 20 51 | 27 23 |
| 28 TH | 14 5 | 1 ♐ 33 | 0 59 | 2 6 | 2 59 | 14 8 | 26 45 | 22 39 | 4 43 | 20 54 | 27 24 |

INGRESSES :

| | |
|---|---|
| 3 ☽ → ♑ 2:55 | 21 ☽ → ♍ 6:16 |
| 5 ☽ → ♒ 15:51 | 23 ☽ → ♎ 7:25 |
| 7 ♂ → ♈ 1:42 | 25 ♀ → ♑ 11:18 |
| ☿ → ♒ 16:29 | ☽ → ♏ 12: 7 |
| 8 ☽ → ♓ 4:33 | ☿ → ♓ 21:36 |
| 10 ☽ → ♈ 15:49 | 27 ☽ → ♐ 20:58 |
| 13 ☽ → ♉ 0:25 | |
| 14 ☉ → ♒ 0:20 | |
| 15 ☽ → ♊ 5:32 | |
| 17 ☽ → ♋ 7:18 | |
| 19 ☽ → ♌ 6:55 | |

ASPECTS & ECLIPSES :

| | | |
|---|---|---|
| 2 ♂ □ ♇ 3:12 | ☽ ☌ ♅ 23:46 | ☉ ☍ ☽ 15:52 |
| ☽ ☌ ♄ 6:55 | 12 ☉ □ ☽ 22:25 | 20 ☽ ☍ ♆ 15:21 |
| ☽ ☌ ♇ 20:12 | 13 ♂ ☌ ♅ 6:17 | ☽ ☍ ☿ 19: 9 |
| 3 ☽ ☌ ☋ 6:35 | 14 ☽ ☍ ♃ 20:55 | 22 ☿ □ ♃ 20:38 |
| 4 ☉ ☌ ☽ 21: 2 | 16 ☽ ☍ ♀ 14:22 | 23 ♀ ☌ ♇ 3:47 |
| 5 ☽ ☌ ☿ 7: 9 | ☽ ☍ ♄ 17:38 | ☽ ☊ (N) ☊ 9:16 |
| ☽ ☌ A 9:34 | 17 ☽ ☍ ♇ 2:37 | ☽ ☍ ♅ 15: 9 |
| 7 ☽ ☌ ♆ 8:42 | ☽ ☌ ☊ 9:41 | 24 ☽ ☍ ♂ 3:11 |
| 9 ♂ □ ☊ 8:14 | 18 ♀ ☌ ♄ 10:51 | 26 ♀ ☍ ☊ 6:55 |
| 10 ☽ ☊ (S) ☊ 18:38 | 19 ☿ ☌ ♆ 6:41 | ☉ □ ☽ 11:26 |
| ☽ ☌ ♂ 20:47 | ☽ ☌ P 9:12 | 27 ☽ ☌ ♃ 14:32 |

SIDEREAL HELIOCENTRIC LONGITUDES : FEBRUARY 2019 Gregorian at 0 hours UT

| DAY | Sid. Time | ☿ | ♀ | ⊕ | ♂ | ♃ | ♄ | ♅ | ♆ | ♇ | Vernal Point |
|---|---|---|---|---|---|---|---|---|---|---|---|
| 1 FR | 8:43:40 | 21 ♑ 22 | 15 ♍ 35 | 16 ♋ 49 | 3 ♉ 58 | 14 ♏ 11 | 17 ♐ 25 | 6 ♈ 39 | 20 ♒ 58 | 26 ♐ 3 | 4 ♓ 59'37" |
| 2 SA | 8:47:36 | 24 55 | 17 12 | 17 50 | 4 31 | 14 16 | 17 27 | 6 39 | 20 58 | 26 3 | 4 ♓ 59'37" |
| 3 SU | 8:51:33 | 28 34 | 18 48 | 18 51 | 5 3 | 14 20 | 17 29 | 6 40 | 20 59 | 26 4 | 4 ♓ 59'37" |
| 4 MO | 8:55:29 | 2 ♒ 18 | 20 25 | 19 52 | 5 36 | 14 25 | 17 31 | 6 41 | 20 59 | 26 4 | 4 ♓ 59'37" |
| 5 TU | 8:59:26 | 6 8 | 22 2 | 20 53 | 6 8 | 14 30 | 17 33 | 6 41 | 20 59 | 26 4 | 4 ♓ 59'37" |
| 6 WE | 9: 3:23 | 10 5 | 23 39 | 21 54 | 6 41 | 14 35 | 17 34 | 6 42 | 21 0 | 26 5 | 4 ♓ 59'37" |
| 7 TH | 9: 7:19 | 14 9 | 25 16 | 22 55 | 7 13 | 14 39 | 17 36 | 6 43 | 21 0 | 26 5 | 4 ♓ 59'37" |
| 8 FR | 9:11:16 | 18 20 | 26 52 | 23 55 | 7 45 | 14 44 | 17 38 | 6 43 | 21 0 | 26 5 | 4 ♓ 59'36" |
| 9 SA | 9:15:12 | 22 38 | 28 29 | 24 56 | 8 17 | 14 49 | 17 40 | 6 44 | 21 1 | 26 6 | 4 ♓ 59'36" |
| 10 SU | 9:19: 9 | 27 5 | 0 ♎ 5 | 25 57 | 8 49 | 14 53 | 17 42 | 6 44 | 21 1 | 26 6 | 4 ♓ 59'36" |
| 11 MO | 9:23: 5 | 1 ♓ 40 | 1 42 | 26 58 | 9 22 | 14 58 | 17 43 | 6 45 | 21 2 | 26 6 | 4 ♓ 59'36" |
| 12 TU | 9:27: 2 | 6 23 | 3 18 | 27 58 | 9 54 | 15 3 | 17 45 | 6 46 | 21 2 | 26 6 | 4 ♓ 59'36" |
| 13 WE | 9:30:58 | 11 15 | 4 55 | 28 59 | 10 26 | 15 8 | 17 47 | 6 46 | 21 2 | 26 7 | 4 ♓ 59'36" |
| 14 TH | 9:34:55 | 16 17 | 6 31 | 0 ♌ 0 | 10 57 | 15 12 | 17 49 | 6 47 | 21 3 | 26 7 | 4 ♓ 59'36" |
| 15 FR | 9:38:52 | 21 27 | 8 7 | 1 0 | 11 29 | 15 17 | 17 51 | 6 48 | 21 3 | 26 7 | 4 ♓ 59'35" |
| 16 SA | 9:42:48 | 26 46 | 9 44 | 2 1 | 12 1 | 15 22 | 17 53 | 6 48 | 21 3 | 26 8 | 4 ♓ 59'35" |
| 17 SU | 9:46:45 | 2 ♈ 15 | 11 20 | 3 2 | 12 33 | 15 27 | 17 54 | 6 49 | 21 4 | 26 8 | 4 ♓ 59'35" |
| 18 MO | 9:50:41 | 7 52 | 12 56 | 4 2 | 13 5 | 15 31 | 17 56 | 6 50 | 21 4 | 26 8 | 4 ♓ 59'35" |
| 19 TU | 9:54:38 | 13 38 | 14 32 | 5 3 | 13 36 | 15 36 | 17 58 | 6 50 | 21 4 | 26 9 | 4 ♓ 59'35" |
| 20 WE | 9:58:34 | 19 31 | 16 9 | 6 3 | 14 8 | 15 41 | 18 0 | 6 51 | 21 5 | 26 9 | 4 ♓ 59'35" |
| 21 TH | 10: 2:31 | 25 32 | 17 45 | 7 4 | 14 39 | 15 45 | 18 2 | 6 52 | 21 5 | 26 9 | 4 ♓ 59'35" |
| 22 FR | 10: 6:27 | 1 ♉ 39 | 19 21 | 8 4 | 15 11 | 15 50 | 18 3 | 6 52 | 21 6 | 26 9 | 4 ♓ 59'34" |
| 23 SA | 10:10:24 | 7 51 | 20 57 | 9 4 | 15 42 | 15 55 | 18 5 | 6 53 | 21 6 | 26 10 | 4 ♓ 59'34" |
| 24 SU | 10:14:21 | 14 7 | 22 33 | 10 5 | 16 14 | 16 0 | 18 7 | 6 54 | 21 6 | 26 10 | 4 ♓ 59'34" |
| 25 MO | 10:18:17 | 20 25 | 24 8 | 11 5 | 16 45 | 16 4 | 18 9 | 6 54 | 21 7 | 26 10 | 4 ♓ 59'34" |
| 26 TU | 10:22:14 | 26 44 | 25 44 | 12 5 | 17 16 | 16 9 | 18 11 | 6 55 | 21 7 | 26 11 | 4 ♓ 59'34" |
| 27 WE | 10:26:10 | 3 ♊ 3 | 27 20 | 13 6 | 17 48 | 16 14 | 18 12 | 6 56 | 21 7 | 26 11 | 4 ♓ 59'34" |
| 28 TH | 10:30: 7 | 9 20 | 28 56 | 14 6 | 18 19 | 16 19 | 18 14 | 6 56 | 21 8 | 26 11 | 4 ♓ 59'34" |

INGRESSES :

| |
|---|
| 3 ☿ → ♒ 9:19 |
| 9 ♀ → ♎ 22:40 |
| 10 ☿ → ♓ 15:23 |
| 14 ⊕ → ♌ 0: 6 |
| 16 ☿ → ♈ 14:13 |
| 21 ☿ → ♉ 17:33 |
| 26 ☿ → ♊ 12:22 |
| 28 ♀ → ♍ 16: 4 |

ASPECTS (HELIOCENTRIC +MOON(TYCHONIC)) :

| | | | | |
|---|---|---|---|---|
| 1 ☿ ☊ (S) ☊ 14:49 | ☽ ☌ ♆ 10:26 | ☽ □ ♆ 14: 3 | ☽ ☍ ♆ 16: 6 | ☿ ☌ P 8:50 |
| 2 ☽ □ ♀ 1:16 | ♀ □ ♇ 12:18 | 15 ☿ □ ♇ 21: 7 | ☿ ☌ ☊ 16: 7 | 26 ☽ ☌ ♃ 18:21 |
| ☽ ☌ ♄ 1:38 | 8 ☿ ☌ ♆ 15: 1 | 16 ☽ ☍ ♄ 11:33 | 22 ☽ □ ♄ 11:32 | ☽ ☍ ♂ 21:15 |
| ♀ □ ♄ 3:56 | 9 ☽ □ ♄ 15:44 | 17 ☽ ☍ ♇ 1: 2 | 23 ☽ □ ♇ 0:58 | 27 ☽ □ ♆ 3:45 |
| ☽ ☌ ♇ 18:57 | 10 ☽ □ ♇ 8:14 | ☽ □ ☿ 17:28 | ☿ □ ⊕ 5:36 | |
| 3 ☽ □ ♅ 16:26 | ☽ ☍ ♀ 18:22 | ☽ □ ♅ 18:16 | ♂ ☍ ♃ 11:23 | |
| 5 ☿ □ ♂ 0: 0 | 11 ☽ ☌ ♅ 4:50 | ☿ ☌ ♅ 19:35 | ☽ ☍ ♅ 19:10 | |
| 6 ☽ □ ♂ 5:41 | 13 ☽ ☌ ♂ 20: 5 | 18 ☽ □ ♀ 4:28 | 24 ☿ ☍ ♃ 7:16 | |
| ☽ ☌ ☿ 18:45 | 14 ☽ ☍ ♃ 3:49 | 19 ☿ ☍ ♀ 5: 8 | ☿ ☌ ♂ 8:47 | |
| ☽ □ ♃ 21:35 | ♀ ☍ ♅ 4: 0 | 20 ☽ □ ♂ 5:18 | 25 ☽ ☌ ♀ 1:42 | |
| 7 ☿ □ ♃ 3: 0 | ☿ □ ♄ 7:15 | ☽ □ ♃ 7:36 | ☿ □ ♆ 2:37 | |

the ideal of the world—the magical radiation of the "Omega point," according to Teilhard de Chardin. This "Omega point" toward which spiritual evolution is tending—or that of the "noosphere," which surges triumphantly above the "barysphere" and "biosphere"—is the central point of the hope of the "personalizing world." It is the point of complete unity of the outer and inner, of matter and spirit, i.e., the God-Man, *the resurrected Jesus Christ*, just as the "Alpha point," the prime mover or the effective cause, is the Word which set in motion electrons, atoms, molecules, i.e., movement *directed* toward their association into planets, organisms, families, races, kingdoms.[1]

This is the hope that activates the marriage of opposites, inspiring us to rise above our differences to contemplate our sameness. We are all striving to arrive where our true self already awaits us. As is the hope of all mothers, we must believe that the future will be more glorious than the present. It is also the hope of Our Mother, who dwells in the heart of the Earth, praying that her children will turn to the School of Christ.

**First quarter Moon**, February 12, 28° Aries: the healing of Mary Cleophas.

**Full Moon**, February 19, 6° Leo: As enemies lay hands on him, Jesus speaks of his imminent departure.

**Last quarter Moon**, February 26, 13° Scorpio: Raising of the youth of Nain.

**Lunar teachings of this cycle** begin with the challenge to awake to the presence of evil. Joining a community devoted to spiritual endeavors is a modern-day equivalent to joining the circle of holy women. In such settings, healing becomes more possible. As we age, we begin preparation for crossing the threshold; and as we come to understand how we have let the enemies of Christ lay hold of us, we seek to reduce our karmic burdens. In the culminating quarter of this lunar cycle, we can then resurrect from negative energies that have held us captive. Thus do we become free to enter more consciously into the School of Christ and Sophia.

**Feb 6: Mars enters Aries:** "Arise, O shining light, take hold of growth's being, lay hold of forces weaving. **Ray out awaking life.** In face of resistance, succeed—in stream of time, recede. O shining light, abide!" (Steiner, *Twelve Cosmic Moods*). Mars is in rulership when in Aries, therefore its actions may be very positive as it "rays out awaking life."

**Feb 7: Mercury enters Aquarius:** "May the limited yield to the unlimited. What lacks boundaries should **found boundaries in its own depths**, and should arise in life's stream, as a flowing wave self-sustaining, in coming to existence self-shaping. Limit thyself, O unlimited!" (Steiner, *Twelve Cosmic Moods*).

**Feb 9: Sun 26° Capricorn: Cosmic memory of the Presentation in the Temple** (Jan/15/1 BC). As the Nathan Jesus was presented in the temple, the prophecy of Mary's pierced heart was given by Simeon. Estelle Isaacson bore witness to this event in the third volume of her Magdalene trilogy:

> Truly was the Blessed Mother's heart pierced, even as prophesied by the aged Simeon at the Presentation of the baby Jesus in the Temple. Because of this, her heart has become the domain of angels. She could converse freely with the angels, and they could work unhindered through her. This was so because she had willingly sacrificed her heart to become a vessel of compassion; and thereby for all coming time, she would bear humanity's suffering.

The Sun today reminds us that when our hearts break, angels may enter.

**Feb 12: First Quarter Moon 28° Aries: Healing of Mary Cleophas** (Nov/25/30). Mary Cleophas was one of the holy women as well as a niece of the Nathan Mary. At the beginning of Christ's ministry, she settled in the neighborhood of Capernaum, close to the house of the blessed Virgin. In November of AD 30, she lay desperately ill with fever and was healed by Christ. She died five years after the Ascension.

As we enter the first challenge of this lunar cycle, we open ourselves to perceive what must change within us if we are to participate in the transfiguring

---

[1] Anon., *Meditations on the Tarot*, p. 472.

of our culture. What must we do? Joining a community devoted to spiritual endeavors is a modern equivalent to joining the circle of holy women. Healing becomes more possible in such places; and through healing, the power of collaboration within community is strengthened.

As this Moon shines from the constellation of Aries, the sign of the Lamb and his Bride, we enter a process of *spiritualization* (Christ) and *interiorization* (Sophia). Devotion to principles higher than ourselves becomes ever more essential.

**Feb 13: ASPECT: Mars conjunct Uranus 4° Aries.** Mars remembers Jesus speaking in the synagogue of the institution of the Paschal Lamb. He said, "When the Sun and Moon are darkened, the mother brings the child to the temple to be redeemed." Many in attendance had an interior revelation of the death of John the Baptist (Jan/12/31).

Herod issued a threat to do away with Jesus as he had done away with John the Baptist. Thus did Herod display a warning that we must take seriously. Our cynical intellectualism has imprisoned us, as it imprisoned Herod, in the *maya* of the sense world. It requires a leap of faith to free ourselves from this barren desert, wherein we see no further than ourselves.

While imprisoned, John sent his disciples to question Christ. He was losing his vision, for at that time he was under grave attacks directed to him from Herod's black magicians. Before physically beheading him, they intended to *spiritually* behead him. In this way, they were attempting to thwart the possibility of John, following his death, becoming an overlighting presence in the circle of twelve. In this regard, Christ spoke of the darkening of Sun and Moon: the eclipse principle that ever accompanies the sense-bound world of abstract and mechanistic intellectuality.

The force of Michael (Mars) united with imaginations streaming from the the heart of our galaxy (Uranus) can effect rapid change. The will to break free from limitations is strong; and yet it must be disciplined, for this conjunction has an erratic nature that demands self-control. Uranus has a relationship with sixteenth Arcanum of the Tarot (The Tower), which addresses human evil, i.e., evil that comes from within. Thus does this aspect demand moral conscience. If we merely follow desire, we will act from presumptuous audacity; if, on the other hand, we act in accordance with the imaginations in-streaming from higher realms, we are obedient. Through obedience, we develop the patience to allow growth its proper time. We cultivate change over time:

> Here is the essence of the mission of Hermeticism, which is the memory working in the depths of our souls of the primordial and eternal mission of humankind: that of cultivating and maintaining the unforgettable garden of the dawn of humankind. There are "trees" to cultivate and maintain in this garden: the methods or ways of uniting Earth and Heaven—the rainbow of peace between that which is below and that which is above.[2]

Cultivating the garden of culture, community, and family can restore our hope that a brighter future is possible. Aries directs us to the lofty ideals hovering above all things; asking that we take hold of what is refined to sublimate that which is gross. We must not allow ourselves to be spiritually beheaded, for the generations coming after us will seek, and need, the light-thoughts we leave behind.

Since this aspect only occurs approximately every two years, it is wise to take advantage of its magnitude as we simultaneously pray that the unbridled passions of human evil, which constitute its lower nature, do not prevail.

**Sun enters Aquarius: "May the limited yield to the unlimited"** (Steiner, *Twelve Cosmic Moods*). The late William Bento explicates this mantra:

> All that finds its existence into forms, including all our thoughts, feelings and actions, remains bounded. The bounded are boundaries that too often confine and define who we are. Yielding to the boundless is not a given. It requires a willingness to let go and trust in the boundless, which is full of new possibilities. And the new possibilities, after all, are what allow us to continue our development and become free from the forms and patterns of our lives that tend to be static and inert.

---

2 Ibid., p. 440.

Discretion becomes silence, becomes meditative force, and then becomes power to perceive the imperceptible. The first decan of Aquarius is ruled by Mercury, the planet of movement, and is associated with the Southern Fish, whose main star Fomalhaut is 9° Aquarius.

**Sun 0° Aquarius: Healing of the paralyzed man at the pool of Bethesda (Jan/19/31).**

**Feb 18: ASPECT: Venus conjunct Saturn 22° Sagittarius.** At today's degree, Venus recalls Jesus teaching his disciples about adultery, divorce, and profanity.

The Venus cross stands with the Holy Virgin (Saturn). Where must we suffer our brokenness? The "I" of Christ broke into as many fragments as there are individuals in his Father's creation; yet, despite this fact, he was never separated from his wholeness. His crucifixion (Venus) bestowed the power of redemption upon each of us. This is proof of his enduring mercy. The redemptive power of mercy is a balm for our brokenness; it is an actual substance, for imperfections are *wounds* seeking the light. This realization gives us courage to accept ourselves exactly as we are. In so doing, our angel reveals where we have lost our patient faithfulness before the trials of our destiny.

The healing arms of the Virgin (Saturn) surround our karmic destiny, ever leading us to rise from all that is immoral and ugly. Venus longs for beauty, elegance, and all that is refined. When Saturn restrains her, she is granted introspective power. And when such isolation is freely accepted, we are granted glimpses into the deeper meaning of our life. When we fight against this, on the other hand, isolation becomes a constraining prison.

Venus and Saturn were conjunct as the Nathan Mary visited her cousin Elizabeth. Both were pregnant: Mary with Jesus; Elizabeth with John. The karmic bond between the two boys made possible the deepest mystery of Earth evolution, the Mystery of Golgotha. Karma preserves truth, guiding us toward the restoration of the cosmic order we know in the depths of our heart. Its underlying principle is naught but the birth pangs of conscience. When we take up our cross, our heart opens. Inversely, when our heart contracts into loneliness, this aspect can bring sadness and privation.

As this aspect occurs in Sagittarius, we are asked to mind our speech. *Ugly thoughts spill darkness. Beautiful thoughts open portals to the light.* This conjunction affords an opportunity to commune with interior love, strengthening our ability to love others.

**Feb 19: ASPECT: Full Moon 6° Leo opposite Sun 6° Aquarius, 10:53 am EST.** The Moon shone from this degree as Jesus went into the temple in Jerusalem and spoke of his departure, saying he was going to the Father. He described how the Fall into sin had begun in a garden and that it would end in a garden. Indeed, his enemies would soon lay their hands on him in the Garden of Gethsemane (Mar/28/33). The Sun illumining this Moon recalls the birth of the Nathan Mary (Jul/17/17 BC).

We reach the peak of the lunar cycle, which began at the New Moon of February 4th with the challenge to awake to evil. The first quarter Moon recalled the healing of one of the holy women, reminding us of the importance of being part of a community devoted to spiritual concerns. Now the Full Moon shines upon us from the constellation of Leo, inviting transformation, i.e., bringing the subconscious to consciousness as a transfiguring power.

Transfiguring is a process of redemption, from the state of the Fall to the reintegration of light that marks an ascent. It is a change of form into a more spiritual state. Unless we are locked in the illusion that we arose from a random primordial mist, void of celestial collaboration, we yearn to comprehend how the "finger of God" brought creation into form—and how we will continuously evolve into ever rarified manifestations of form. Thus does this Full Moon ask us to release ourselves from the endless repetition of a circle, and enter instead into the spiral of evolving growth. (The heart is the organ that leads us into the transfiguring spiral.) Evolution is the drama of a cosmic process playing out in time. It continuously offers possibilities of advancement through effort or grace. We were given freedom, and this is the key that liberates the soul, or else further entraps it in the illusion of *maya*. We are the authors of our biography.

The Sun today reminds us that an immaculate aspect of our being—the virginal aspect that was removed from us before the Fall—yearns to unite with us. The Moon reminds us of the One who went before us, paving the way, so that each of us could find the freedom inherent in the primacy of our destined future.

Sophia guards the memory of birth, the open portal in the circle. Through her, we birth ourselves into the spiral of grace. Yet we remember that hostility came between the woman and the serpent: the serpent seeks to hold us in his world of *maya*, whereas the woman seeks to liberate us through suffering. What is this suffering? It is birth. Whether via the birth of a child or the birth of an idea, we suffer against the mighty torrent of the serpent's world.

> The Woman-Virgin, who is the soul of the counter-movement to the serpent, and of suffering since the beginning of the world of the serpent, received, conceived and gave birth to the Word of the Father. "And the Word became flesh and dwelt amongst human beings in the world of the serpent, full of grace and truth." (John 1:14)[1]

The cosmic Sabbath is the opening in the closed circle. As the antechamber to eternity, it releases the soul into realms of unlimited growth and advancement.

Compassion is the virtue through which the soul finds the eternal Sabbath. For what we cannot love in the other serves to point us to what we do not love in our self. Thus does antipathy imprison us in the isolation of a soul enclosed within itself, endlessly lamenting its condition, while making no effort to love itself out of its confinement.

> The closed circle, in contrast, is in principle only a *prison*, whatever its extent may be. It is a wheel which turns on itself and therefore suggests no advancement beyond its circle. The idea that the closed circle—or wheel—suggests, is that of *eternal repetition*.[2]

Through the opening in the circle, we follow Christ; we transfigure into the light a portion of what the serpent has imprisoned. Then, through the power of compassion, we gradually evolve toward the freedom of eternity.

**ASPECT: Mercury conjunct Neptune 20° Aquarius: Healing of the Syrophoenician woman's daughter** (Feb/12/31). Tremendous powers of inspiration are possible under the influence of this aspect. It is short-lived, yet potent. Inversely, misconceptions, confusion, fear and paranoia result when the lower aspect of Neptune dominates, sweeping us away in the stolen waters of the Babylonian woman—Ahriman's consort.

**Feb 22: ASPECT: Mercury 26° Aquarius square Jupiter 26° Scorpio.** Mercury recalls the Flight into Egypt (Mar/2/5 BC). When the pastors and healers (Mercury) are in dynamic tension with the Holy Spirit (Jupiter), much may come to light. Jupiter's optimism illumines new imaginations. Such goodwill leads the humble soul toward new frontiers in thought.

**ASPECT 2: Venus conjunct Pluto 27° Sagittarius.** With Venus at this degree, we can remember Jesus withdrawing into the hills to pray after a day full of teaching and healing. That night, the disciples saw Jesus walking across the water toward them—although this is not to be confused with the fifth healing miracle of Christ (Dec/7/30).

The Venus cross in communion with Pluto/Phanes increases depth. Venus marks the sphere wherein dwell the archai, who govern over long epochs of time. Under this influence we can imagine karmic communities penetrating more deeply into their collective mission.

Every great wave of time brings groups of people to Earth who carry a common purpose. The mission of our time is to name evil and bring forth the good. This necessitates that we enter the secrets of "electrical fire" and the intoxication born of counter-intuition. Such fiery intoxications are to be feared when they arise in community as human-engendered demons, i.e., as egregores.

The Canaan Moloch who demanded the bloody sacrifice of the first born, mentioned so often in

---

1 Ibid., p. 240.
2 Ibid., p. 241.

the Bible, is not a hierarchical entity—either of good or of evil—but rather an evil *egregore*, i.e., a demon created artificially and collectively by human communities infatuated with the thrill of fear. The Mexican Quetzalcoatl is a similar instance of this. There, also, it was a matter of a demon created and worshipped collectively.[1]

With Venus conjunct Pluto, communities are given fair warning, for none are immune to the infiltration of these subtle organisms of ill will. The specter of communism that haunted Europe is another example of an egregore. It stole the future promise of the Aquarian age and thus beguiled the Slavic people into accepting, prematurely, a distorted Marxist caricature of the sisterhood and brotherhood yet to come. Indeed, this egregore made way for the terror of Stalin.

The West has its ideological superstructures as well, formed from human will and imagination to support a goal that benefits only a few. Nonetheless, such ghoulish ideologies become the obsession of the masses through the cunning manipulations of powerful organisms, with propaganda as their greatest weapon.

> The Word and idols, revealed truth and "ideological superstructures" of the human will, operate simultaneously in the history of the human race. Has there been a single century when the servants of the Word have not had to confront the worshippers of idols, *egregores*?[2]

No, not a single century. The idol of the West is money. How many people successfully avoid captivity by this demon? The tragedy of the egregore is that, once created, it enslaves the creator; thus locking the system into endless cycles of increasing greed. How do we stop creating these demons? First we must become aware of them.

> And having this knowledge, is it not time that we said to ourselves: let us be silent. Let us make our arbitrary will and imagination silent; let us impose on them the discipline of silence. Is this not one of the four traditional rules of Hermeticism: to dare, to will, to know, *to be silent!* To be silent is more than to keep things secret; it is more even than to guard oneself from profaning the holy things to which a respectful silence is owed. To be silent is, above all, *the great magical commandment of not engendering demons* through our arbitrary will and imagination; it is the task of silencing arbitrary will and imagination.[3]

The teaching offered by the Venus/Pluto conjunction is that, if we are to become free of the demons of *mass* will, we must employ silence in our *personal* will. This means: we must cease "wanting." What if we had enough? What if we slowed down? What if we spent more time with friends and family? Would not our riches grow? We have tasks appointed by very high beings. We are not here simply to amuse ourselves, we are here to serve the evolution of the Earth and humanity. We cannot just be spiritual, and not also religious. How can we say we are spiritual if we refuse to exert the effort necessary to understand what spirit is? Theology, and in particular *Christology*, is essential to the science of spirit.

Christ could walk on water because nothing pulled him under—no gravity held command over his being. Instead, he was aligned with all the stars in the heavens. Thus was he united with celestial gravitation. Demons create sucking pockets that pull us from the light, whereas light drives out darkness. Therefore, vigilance is needed if we are to protect our communities from the intoxication of mass-thought. A demon recognized is already rendered impotent.

Today's aspect offers penetrating depths into the mission, progress, and purity of community.

**Feb 23 and 24: Sun 10° Aquarius: The Feeding of the Five Thousand and the Walking on Water** (Jan/29-30/31). Christ exemplified the macrocosmic initiation at the Feeding of the Five Thousand, thereby bringing the twelve-fold power of the Zodiac through his heart and into the hearts of those there assembled. Thus were they amply fed from such a small quantity of bread. Only the twelve recognized Christ's eternal kingly nature, while the five thousand sought to crown him an earthly king.

---

1 Ibid., 405.
2 Ibid., p. 409.

3 Ibid., p. 409.

Later that evening, when Christ walked on water, he exemplified the fish initiation. He was held up by the force of warmth flowing from the heart of the Mother. It was she who bore his sinless countenance upon the water. Nothing stood between Jesus and the radiant power streaming from Shambhala.

There was nothing of the fish that remained after the miracle of the Feeding of the Five Thousand. This tells us that the fish initiation was something entirely new—it would find no response in human beings until after the death, the descent into Hell, and the resurrection of Christ.

Evil lies between the light substance of the Father and the condensed light that has become warmth in the Mother's kingdom—*and this is the misfortune of the world*. The effects of evil cause us to experience spirit as light, but as a *dead* light. They also cause us to experience warmth as life, but as a *dark* life.

When Christ descended into Hell, into the inner layers of the Earth, he brought the Father's light into the darkness of the Mother's realm. Since the time of this great deed, we have become able to experience this descent. Clothed in the living light, we will encounter the reciprocal forces of rising warmth. Thus have the paths through the darkness of death been redeemed for all who seek warmth and light as soul nourishment.

When the force of warmth ascends through the feet from below, we are able to descend through the light—far into the inner earthly realms. This descent will eventually reveal the mystery of resurrection. Yet, if this journey is undertaken without Christ, we are in danger of being torn to pieces by the disunity of evil.

**Feb 25: Venus enters Capricorn: "May the past feel the future"** (Steiner, *Twelve Cosmic Moods*). **Mercury enters Pisces: "In comprehending, seek to grasp"** (Steiner, *Twelve Cosmic Moods*).

**Feb 26: 4th Quarter Moon 13° Scorpio: Raising the Youth of Nain.** Jesus had called for a vessel of water and a little branch. When the lifeless boy's body was uncovered, Jesus sprinkled the dead youth with the branch, and with his hand made the sign of the cross over him. Anne Catherine then beheld a murky, black, cloud-like figure issuing from the body (Nov/13/30).

The lunar cycle today comes to its last phase. Now we must integrate and manifest what has been given. The transfiguring light inaugurated the cycle, calling for creative action; the first quarter called for communities to gather in devotion to spiritual work, asking us to find inspiration toward this goal; the Full Moon asked us to find our way out of the closed circle into the spiral, gathering the transformational light. Now we are asked if we can resurrect from any ensnarement the light has revealed to manifest the light.

The youth of Nain was an incarnation of the individuality who later became Parsifal, the Grail King. The transfiguring light is the Grail light. To find our way to the castle of the Grail, we must find the healing question. What ails us? What do we not know? How do we serve more and need less?

Moon in Scorpio reveals what is hidden. Angelic beings continuously seek vessels through whom the new imaginations can create a brighter future. Its highest manifestation is the Revelation of John. We may ask: What eclipses my ability to participate in the many revelatory imaginations that are manifesting everywhere?

# MARCH 2019

## Stargazing Preview

On the 1st of the month, if you're up early, catch a glimpse of the Moon and Saturn rising together at 0400. The following evening brings a Moon–Venus conjunction; this means that on the morning of the 3rd, Venus will rise just ahead of the Moon. It's worth getting up a little early to see (looking right-to-left) Jupiter, Saturn, Venus, and the Moon fanned out across the southern sky. It will be even easier to see them after the New Moon on the 6th! On the 11th, the Moon moves under Mars, which sets before 2300, about fifteen minutes ahead of our satellite. There's another Supermoon (Full Moon) on the 20th, positioned as it was (5° Virgo) at the onset of the present Age of Michael. Venus enters

SIDEREAL GEOCENTRIC LONGITUDES : MARCH 2019 Gregorian at 0 hours UT

| DAY | ☉ | ☽ | ☊ | ☿ | ♀ | ♂ | ♃ | ♄ | ♅ | ♆ | ♇ |
|---|---|---|---|---|---|---|---|---|---|---|---|
| 1 FR | 15 ♒ 6 | 13 ♐ 39 | 1 ♋ 1 | 2 ♓ 53 | 4 ♑ 10 | 14 ♈ 48 | 26 ♏ 52 | 22 ♐ 44 | 4 ♈ 46 | 20 ♒ 56 | 27 ♐ 26 |
| 2 SA | 16 6 | 25 35 | 1 2 | 3 33 | 5 21 | 15 28 | 26 59 | 22 49 | 4 48 | 20 58 | 27 27 |
| 3 SU | 17 6 | 7 ♑ 24 | 1 2R | 4 3 | 6 32 | 16 9 | 27 6 | 22 54 | 4 51 | 21 0 | 27 29 |
| 4 MO | 18 6 | 19 11 | 1 0 | 4 24 | 7 43 | 16 49 | 27 12 | 22 59 | 4 53 | 21 3 | 27 30 |
| 5 TU | 19 7 | 0 ♒ 58 | 0 55 | 4 36 | 8 54 | 17 29 | 27 19 | 23 4 | 4 56 | 21 5 | 27 31 |
| 6 WE | 20 7 | 12 49 | 0 49 | 4 38R | 10 6 | 18 9 | 27 25 | 23 9 | 4 59 | 21 7 | 27 33 |
| 7 TH | 21 7 | 24 45 | 0 40 | 4 31 | 11 17 | 18 50 | 27 31 | 23 14 | 5 1 | 21 10 | 27 34 |
| 8 FR | 22 7 | 6 ♓ 47 | 0 30 | 4 16 | 12 28 | 19 30 | 27 37 | 23 19 | 5 4 | 21 12 | 27 36 |
| 9 SA | 23 7 | 18 58 | 0 20 | 3 52 | 13 40 | 20 10 | 27 43 | 23 23 | 5 7 | 21 14 | 27 37 |
| 10 SU | 24 7 | 1 ♈ 17 | 0 10 | 3 19 | 14 51 | 20 50 | 27 49 | 23 28 | 5 9 | 21 16 | 27 38 |
| 11 MO | 25 7 | 13 48 | 0 2 | 2 40 | 16 3 | 21 30 | 27 54 | 23 33 | 5 12 | 21 19 | 27 39 |
| 12 TU | 26 7 | 26 30 | 29 ♊ 56 | 1 55 | 17 14 | 22 11 | 28 0 | 23 37 | 5 15 | 21 21 | 27 41 |
| 13 WE | 27 7 | 9 ♉ 27 | 29 52 | 1 5 | 18 26 | 22 51 | 28 5 | 23 41 | 5 18 | 21 23 | 27 42 |
| 14 TH | 28 7 | 22 41 | 29 51 | 0 11 | 19 38 | 23 31 | 28 10 | 23 46 | 5 21 | 21 25 | 27 43 |
| 15 FR | 29 6 | 6 ♊ 15 | 29 51D | 29 ♒ 15 | 20 49 | 24 11 | 28 15 | 23 50 | 5 24 | 21 28 | 27 44 |
| 16 SA | 0 ♓ 6 | 20 9 | 29 52 | 28 18 | 22 1 | 24 51 | 28 20 | 23 54 | 5 27 | 21 30 | 27 45 |
| 17 SU | 1 6 | 4 ♋ 26 | 29 52R | 27 20 | 23 13 | 25 31 | 28 24 | 23 58 | 5 30 | 21 32 | 27 47 |
| 18 MO | 2 6 | 19 3 | 29 50 | 26 24 | 24 25 | 26 11 | 28 29 | 24 2 | 5 33 | 21 34 | 27 48 |
| 19 TU | 3 5 | 3 ♌ 57 | 29 46 | 25 31 | 25 36 | 26 51 | 28 33 | 24 6 | 5 36 | 21 37 | 27 49 |
| 20 WE | 4 5 | 19 0 | 29 39 | 24 41 | 26 48 | 27 31 | 28 37 | 24 10 | 5 39 | 21 39 | 27 50 |
| 21 TH | 5 5 | 4 ♍ 5 | 29 30 | 23 55 | 28 0 | 28 11 | 28 41 | 24 14 | 5 42 | 21 41 | 27 51 |
| 22 FR | 6 4 | 19 1 | 29 20 | 23 13 | 29 12 | 28 51 | 28 44 | 24 17 | 5 45 | 21 43 | 27 52 |
| 23 SA | 7 4 | 3 ♎ 38 | 29 10 | 22 37 | 0 ♒ 24 | 29 31 | 28 48 | 24 21 | 5 48 | 21 46 | 27 53 |
| 24 SU | 8 3 | 17 51 | 29 0 | 22 7 | 1 36 | 0 ♉ 11 | 28 51 | 24 25 | 5 51 | 21 48 | 27 54 |
| 25 MO | 9 3 | 1 ♏ 35 | 28 53 | 21 43 | 2 48 | 0 51 | 28 54 | 24 28 | 5 54 | 21 50 | 27 55 |
| 26 TU | 10 2 | 14 50 | 28 48 | 21 25 | 4 0 | 1 30 | 28 57 | 24 31 | 5 57 | 21 52 | 27 55 |
| 27 WE | 11 2 | 27 39 | 28 45 | 21 13 | 5 12 | 2 10 | 29 0 | 24 35 | 6 0 | 21 54 | 27 56 |
| 28 TH | 12 1 | 10 ♐ 4 | 28 44 | 21 6 | 6 25 | 2 50 | 29 3 | 24 38 | 6 4 | 21 57 | 27 57 |
| 29 FR | 13 0 | 22 12 | 28 44D | 21 6D | 7 37 | 3 30 | 29 5 | 24 41 | 6 7 | 21 59 | 27 58 |
| 30 SA | 14 0 | 4 ♑ 8 | 28 44R | 21 11 | 8 49 | 4 10 | 29 8 | 24 44 | 6 10 | 22 1 | 27 59 |
| 31 SU | 14 59 | 15 56 | 28 43 | 21 22 | 10 1 | 4 49 | 29 10 | 24 47 | 6 13 | 22 3 | 27 59 |

INGRESSES :

| | |
|---|---|
| 2 ☽ → ♑ 8:56 | 20 ☽ → ♍ 17:29 |
| 4 ☽ → ♒ 22: 1 | 22 ♀ → ♒ 15:58 |
| 7 ☽ → ♓ 10:30 | ☽ → ♎ 17:58 |
| 9 ☽ → ♈ 21:30 | 23 ♂ → ♉ 17:35 |
| 11 ☊ → ♊ 6:49 | 24 ☽ → ♏ 21:11 |
| 12 ☽ → ♉ 6:31 | 27 ☽ → ♐ 4:29 |
| 14 ☿ → ♒ 4:53 | 29 ☽ → ♑ 15:39 |
| ☽ → ♊ 13: 0 | |
| 15 ☉ → ♓ 21:30 | |
| 16 ☽ → ♋ 16:36 | |
| 18 ☽ → ♌ 17:40 | |

ASPECTS & ECLIPSES :

| | | | |
|---|---|---|---|
| 1 ♀ □ ♅ 12:29 | 10 ☽ ☌ ♅ 7:29 | 19 ☽ ☌ P 19:55 | 29 ☽ ☌ ♄ 4:58 |
| ☽ ☌ ♄ 18:21 | 11 ☽ ☌ ♂ 15:25 | 20 ☽ ☍ ♆ 4:12 | ☽ ☌ ♇ 11:33 |
| 2 ☽ ☌ ♇ 3:47 | 14 ☉ □ ♃ 1:28 | ☽ ☍ ☿ 8:33 | ☽ ☌ ☋ 13: 7 |
| ☽ ☌ ☋ 11: 2 | ☽ ☍ ♃ 9:49 | 21 ☉ ☍ ☽ 1:41 | |
| ☽ ☌ ♀ 22: 1 | ☉ □ ☽ 10:26 | ♀ □ ♂ 8: 5 | |
| 4 ☽ ☌ A 11:27 | 15 ☉ ☌ ☿ 1:46 | 22 ☽ N ☊ 16:40 | |
| 6 ☉ ☌ ☽ 16: 2 | ☿ □ ♃ 23:15 | 23 ☽ ☍ ♅ 3:36 | |
| ☽ ☌ ♆ 16:47 | 16 ☽ ☍ ♄ 6:23 | 24 ☿ ☌ ♆ 17: 6 | |
| 7 ☉ ☌ ♆ 1: 7 | ☽ ☍ ♇ 12:52 | ☽ ☍ ♂ 22:36 | |
| ☽ ☌ ☿ 19: 7 | ☽ ☌ ☊ 16:22 | 27 ☽ ☌ ♃ 2:35 | |
| 9 ☽ S ☊ 21:51 | 18 ☽ ☍ ♀ 9:26 | 28 ☉ □ ☽ 4: 8 | |

SIDEREAL HELIOCENTRIC LONGITUDES : MARCH 2019 Gregorian at 0 hours UT

| DAY | Sid. Time | ☿ | ♀ | ⊕ | ♂ | ♃ | ♄ | ♅ | ♆ | ♇ | Vernal Point |
|---|---|---|---|---|---|---|---|---|---|---|---|
| 1 FR | 10:34: 3 | 15 ♊ 34 | 0 ♏ 32 | 15 ♌ 6 | 18 ♉ 50 | 16 ♏ 23 | 18 ♐ 16 | 6 ♈ 57 | 21 ♒ 8 | 26 ♐ 12 | 4 ♓ 59'33" |
| 2 SA | 10:38: 0 | 21 42 | 2 7 | 16 7 | 19 21 | 16 28 | 18 18 | 6 58 | 21 8 | 26 12 | 4 ♓ 59'33" |
| 3 SU | 10:41:56 | 27 45 | 3 43 | 17 7 | 19 52 | 16 33 | 18 20 | 6 58 | 21 9 | 26 12 | 4 ♓ 59'33" |
| 4 MO | 10:45:53 | 3 ♋ 41 | 5 18 | 18 7 | 20 23 | 16 38 | 18 21 | 6 59 | 21 9 | 26 12 | 4 ♓ 59'33" |
| 5 TU | 10:49:50 | 9 28 | 6 54 | 19 7 | 20 54 | 16 42 | 18 23 | 7 0 | 21 9 | 26 13 | 4 ♓ 59'33" |
| 6 WE | 10:53:46 | 15 7 | 8 30 | 20 7 | 21 25 | 16 47 | 18 25 | 7 0 | 21 10 | 26 13 | 4 ♓ 59'33" |
| 7 TH | 10:57:43 | 20 36 | 10 5 | 21 7 | 21 55 | 16 52 | 18 27 | 7 1 | 21 10 | 26 13 | 4 ♓ 59'33" |
| 8 FR | 11: 1:39 | 25 56 | 11 41 | 22 7 | 22 26 | 16 57 | 18 29 | 7 2 | 21 11 | 26 14 | 4 ♓ 59'33" |
| 9 SA | 11: 5:36 | 1 ♌ 7 | 13 16 | 23 8 | 22 57 | 17 1 | 18 30 | 7 2 | 21 11 | 26 14 | 4 ♓ 59'32" |
| 10 SU | 11: 9:32 | 6 8 | 14 51 | 24 8 | 23 27 | 17 6 | 18 32 | 7 3 | 21 11 | 26 14 | 4 ♓ 59'32" |
| 11 MO | 11:13:29 | 10 59 | 16 27 | 25 7 | 23 58 | 17 11 | 18 34 | 7 4 | 21 12 | 26 15 | 4 ♓ 59'32" |
| 12 TU | 11:17:25 | 15 40 | 18 2 | 26 7 | 24 29 | 17 16 | 18 36 | 7 4 | 21 12 | 26 15 | 4 ♓ 59'32" |
| 13 WE | 11:21:22 | 20 13 | 19 37 | 27 7 | 24 59 | 17 20 | 18 38 | 7 5 | 21 12 | 26 15 | 4 ♓ 59'32" |
| 14 TH | 11:25:19 | 24 37 | 21 12 | 28 7 | 25 30 | 17 25 | 18 39 | 7 5 | 21 13 | 26 16 | 4 ♓ 59'32" |
| 15 FR | 11:29:15 | 28 53 | 22 48 | 29 7 | 26 0 | 17 30 | 18 41 | 7 6 | 21 13 | 26 16 | 4 ♓ 59'32" |
| 16 SA | 11:33:12 | 3 ♍ 1 | 24 23 | 0 ♍ 7 | 26 30 | 17 35 | 18 43 | 7 7 | 21 13 | 26 16 | 4 ♓ 59'31" |
| 17 SU | 11:37: 8 | 7 1 | 25 58 | 1 7 | 27 1 | 17 39 | 18 45 | 7 7 | 21 14 | 26 16 | 4 ♓ 59'31" |
| 18 MO | 11:41: 5 | 10 54 | 27 33 | 2 6 | 27 31 | 17 44 | 18 47 | 7 8 | 21 14 | 26 17 | 4 ♓ 59'31" |
| 19 TU | 11:45: 1 | 14 40 | 29 8 | 3 6 | 28 1 | 17 49 | 18 48 | 7 9 | 21 15 | 26 17 | 4 ♓ 59'31" |
| 20 WE | 11:48:58 | 18 21 | 0 ♐ 43 | 4 6 | 28 31 | 17 54 | 18 50 | 7 9 | 21 15 | 26 17 | 4 ♓ 59'31" |
| 21 TH | 11:52:54 | 21 55 | 2 18 | 5 5 | 29 1 | 17 58 | 18 52 | 7 10 | 21 15 | 26 18 | 4 ♓ 59'31" |
| 22 FR | 11:56:51 | 25 24 | 3 53 | 6 5 | 29 31 | 18 3 | 18 54 | 7 11 | 21 16 | 26 18 | 4 ♓ 59'31" |
| 23 SA | 12: 0:48 | 28 48 | 5 29 | 7 4 | 0 ♊ 1 | 18 8 | 18 56 | 7 11 | 21 16 | 26 18 | 4 ♓ 59'30" |
| 24 SU | 12: 4:44 | 2 ♎ 7 | 7 4 | 8 4 | 0 31 | 18 13 | 18 58 | 7 12 | 21 16 | 26 19 | 4 ♓ 59'30" |
| 25 MO | 12: 8:41 | 5 23 | 8 39 | 9 3 | 1 1 | 18 17 | 18 59 | 7 13 | 21 17 | 26 19 | 4 ♓ 59'30" |
| 26 TU | 12:12:37 | 8 34 | 10 13 | 10 3 | 1 31 | 18 22 | 19 1 | 7 13 | 21 17 | 26 19 | 4 ♓ 59'30" |
| 27 WE | 12:16:34 | 11 41 | 11 48 | 11 2 | 2 1 | 18 27 | 19 3 | 7 14 | 21 17 | 26 19 | 4 ♓ 59'30" |
| 28 TH | 12:20:30 | 14 45 | 13 23 | 12 2 | 2 31 | 18 32 | 19 5 | 7 15 | 21 18 | 26 20 | 4 ♓ 59'30" |
| 29 FR | 12:24:27 | 17 47 | 14 58 | 13 1 | 3 0 | 18 36 | 19 7 | 7 15 | 21 18 | 26 20 | 4 ♓ 59'30" |
| 30 SA | 12:28:23 | 20 45 | 16 33 | 14 0 | 3 30 | 18 41 | 19 8 | 7 16 | 21 19 | 26 20 | 4 ♓ 59'29" |
| 31 SU | 12:32:20 | 23 41 | 18 8 | 15 0 | 4 0 | 18 46 | 19 10 | 7 17 | 21 19 | 26 21 | 4 ♓ 59'29" |

INGRESSES :

| |
|---|
| 3 ☿ → ♋ 9: 3 |
| 8 ☿ → ♌ 18:46 |
| 15 ☿ → ♍ 6:25 |
| ⊕ → ♍ 21:16 |
| 19 ♀ → ♐ 13: 2 |
| 22 ♂ → ♊ 22:56 |
| 23 ☿ → ♎ 8:35 |

ASPECTS (HELIOCENTRIC +MOON(TYCHONIC)) :

| | | | | | |
|---|---|---|---|---|---|
| 1 ☽ ☍ ☿ 7:52 | ☽ ☌ ♆ 16:49 | 13 ☿ ☍ ♆ 5:19 | 16 ☽ ☍ ♇ 10:21 | ☽ ☌ ☿ 13:35 | ☿ ☌ ☋ 22:52 |
| ☽ ☌ ♄ 9:15 | ☽ □ ♂ 18: 5 | ☽ ☍ ♃ 14:26 | 17 ☽ □ ♅ 4:27 | 23 ☽ ☍ ♅ 5:55 | 31 ♀ ☌ ♄ 16: 0 |
| ☿ ☍ ♄ 10:34 | 7 ⊕ ☍ ♆ 1: 7 | ☽ ☍ ♀ 20:58 | ♀ ☍ ♂ 23: 7 | 25 ☿ ☍ ♅ 13:49 | ☽ □ ☿ 20:56 |
| 2 ☽ ☌ ♇ 1:14 | ☿ N ☊ 13: 9 | ☽ □ ♆ 21:20 | 19 ☽ □ ♃ 22:13 | ♀ □ ⊕ 16:44 | |
| ⊕ □ ♃ 9:19 | 8 ⊕ □ ♂ 15:14 | 14 ♀ □ ♆ 0: 3 | 20 ☿ □ ♄ 3:19 | 26 ☽ ☌ ♃ 6:34 | |
| ☿ ☍ ♇ 17:48 | ☽ □ ♄ 23: 6 | ☽ □ ☿ 5: 5 | ☽ ☍ ♆ 3:33 | ☽ □ ♆ 11:59 | |
| ☽ □ ♅ 23: 6 | 9 ☽ □ ♇ 14:12 | ☽ ☌ ♂ 5:12 | ☽ □ ♂ 15:38 | 27 ☽ ☍ ♂ 8:42 | |
| 4 ☿ □ ♅ 13:39 | 10 ☽ ☌ ♅ 11: 6 | ☿ □ ♂ 5:29 | ☽ □ ♀ 20:49 | 28 ☽ ☌ ♀ 7:29 | |
| 5 ♂ □ ♆ 12:25 | 11 ♀ ☌ ♃ 11:42 | ♀ ☌ ☋ 9:37 | 21 ☽ □ ♄ 23:49 | ☽ ☌ ♄ 17:49 | |
| ☽ □ ♀ 13:54 | 12 ☿ □ ♃ 8:25 | 15 ☿ ☌ ⊕ 1:46 | 22 ☿ □ ♇ 6:17 | 29 ☽ ☌ ♇ 8:16 | |
| 6 ☽ □ ♃ 8: 3 | ☿ □ ♀ 19: 2 | ☽ ☍ ♄ 21:32 | ☽ □ ♇ 11:53 | 30 ☽ □ ♅ 6:21 | |

Aquarius on the 22nd, a day before Mars leaves Aries and finds Taurus.

The Moon rises just ahead of Jupiter on the 26th, the same day they will meet in conjunction at 29° Scorpio: the zodiacal longitude of the stinger of the Scorpion. You'll have more than five hours to see them before sunrise. On the 29th, the Moon and Saturn rise together, two hours ahead of the Sun. Orion will be in the southwest sky at sunset and will drop below the horizon shortly after midnight.

## March Commentaries

**Mar 1: ASPECT: Venus 5° Capricorn square Uranus 5° Aries.** Venus at this degree recalls Jesus being met by an old blind man led by two youths. Jesus took him to a nearby fountain, commanded him to wash his eyes, and then anointed his forehead, temples, and eyes with oil. The old man's sight was restored immediately (Dec/13/30).

The Venus cross in dynamic tension with Uranus may result in an *inner soul restlessness*. If we *externalize* this, we will seek satisfaction in the outer world. If, on the other hand, we *internalize* this, we may find incredible revelation. As always, the stars do not compel, they invite. Loving our brokenness turns our attention to the hearts of others, whereby we become vessels for higher imaginations. Morality alone determines the heart's focus.

This aspect occurred at the death of the Virgin Mary as well as at the Baptism of Jesus. These two events give ample evidence for the power of revelatory awaking such an aspect bestows.

As Venus is conjunct the south node, we can imagine great waves of energy streaming upward from the Mother in the heart of the Earth. When such energies are released, they quicken the spirit-eye, inviting us to wash away all trivial images to become witnesses to the mighty world-thoughts that surround us. Jesus took the blind man to a fountain. A fountain of healing waters streams upward from the Mother's realm below. These waters cleanse the soul of its petty thoughts, creating the emptiness into which the Mother's thoughts become our thoughts. With Venus in Capricorn we may long to think with the gods.

The north node points to the direction in which we are headed; the south node, on the other hand, tells us whence we have come. If we trace our past to its beginning, we find ourselves in the Garden of Paradise. This garden now abides in the inner earthly depths as the golden land of Shambhala.

**Mar 6: ASPECT: New Moon 21° Aquarius: Healing of the Nobleman's Son.** The Moon reached this degree shortly after midnight on the day that this miracle took place (Aug/3/30).

A new lunar cycle begins with the memory of the second archetypal healing by Jesus Christ. This healing is connected to the chakra in the region of the sacrum, the Venus chakra. The significance of this miracle at the turning point in time gives way to the question: What is the significance of this miracle at this time of the Second Coming?

When the Nobleman begged Jesus to heal his son, Jesus replied: "Unless you see signs and wonders, you will not believe." Such are our times. Hence do we go about our lives ignorant of the fact that we are constantly surrounded by signs and wonders. Digitalized thinking has not the power to behold great vistas, through which the miracle, the message, and the meaning of life can be discovered. Life itself is an "open secret," read by those who have developed effortless concentration, i.e., the ability to sustain uninterrupted attention to the great and wondrous arcana of our time. The word *arcanum* comes from the Latin *arcanus*, meaning "secret." This word entered into English as the Dark Ages gave way to the Renaissance. In like manner, the Dark Age of materialism has given way to the Renaissance of the Satya Yuga, the age of light. Each of us must now heal the dependent nobleman who dwells within us.

The nobleman had become a satellite, circling round the authority of his king. He had lost his verticality, his individual and sovereign "I." As a result, his son's blood was weak, and he lay dying. Such is the hereditary effect upon generations. Since the time of the Renaissance, this has played out as the gradual diminishment of humankind's relationship with their inner King: Christ. Thus have we lost touch with the vertical "I" that can read the signs of our times, and can stand before the false authorities to whom we have become satellites. Money and technology are the great kings of our era. Having surrendered our divine authority to these temporal idols, we risk weakening the blood-strength in the generations yet to come.

God made man "in his image and likeness" (Gen. 1:26). The divine image and the divine likeness coincided in the first man, before the original sin. But their coincidence did not persist after the Fall. The image has remained intact, but the initial likeness has been lost. Man is, following the original sin, in the "disfigurement of unlikeness," while conserving the image.

> Man was made in the image and likeness of God: in image he possesses freedom of will, and in likeness he possesses virtues. The likeness has been destroyed; however, man conserves the image. The image can be burnt in hell, but not consumed. It is damaged but not destroyed. Through fate as such it is not effaced, but subsists. Wherever the soul is, there also will be the image. It is not so with the likeness. This remains in the soul, which accomplishes the good; in the soul which sins it is wretchedly transformed. The soul which has sinned ranks with beasts devoid of intelligence. (St. Bernard of Clairvaux, *Sermon on the Annunciation of the Blessed Virgin Mary*)[1]

The word *sin* has become a "trip word," easily dismissed as part of a Christian doctrine few understand nowadays. If we substitute *missing the mark* for *sin*, we may find clearer access to the meaning of the effaced likeness. It is the likeness that we must restore to verticality, to morality, to operative function, and to the dignity of virtue. Moreover, without knowledge of higher worlds, the likeness can only continue to fall, becoming a satellite to one thing or another. Does this seem too harsh?

History informs us of certain things: A mere 600 years ago, humankind began to lose their faith in God, and instead placed their faith in themselves—i.e., in the human being. What has been the result? I believe this is obvious. The miracle of this healing, at this time of the Second Coming, is the miracle we are to render upon ourselves through the power given to us at the First Coming. This cannot be accomplished without turning to our Angel, who guards our image as well as our likeness:

> The Angel acquits his charge in five ways: he guards, cherishes, protects, visits, and defends. He is therefore a "flaming star," a luminous pentagram above the human being.
>
> He *guards* memory, i.e., the continuity of the great past in the present, which is the preparation for the great future. It is the guardian Angel who takes care that there is a connection between the great "yesterday, today, and tomorrow" of the human soul. He is a perpetual "memento" with regard to the primordial likeness, with regard to the eternal mission assigned to the soul in the cosmic symphony, and with regard to the special room for the soul "in my Father's house, where there are many rooms." (John 14:2)

Our subconscious, in its depths, is like a tomb wherein specters from the past chain us, obscuring not only the present, but also the future. When Jesus healed the nobleman's son, he made possible the healing of the hereditary lineage of all people for all time—for he restored the nobleman to the vertical power of his image. This is what sustains us, as it suffers no interference from the ghosts and specters of the past. In this light we can strive to heal that which is dead in us, and rise from the hereditary tombs into which we have placed ourselves.

It is the task of each of us to celebrate the fact that we now live in the 40th day, the day angels came to minister to Jesus Christ. Thus can we see signs and wonders if we simply disengage from our mistaken homage to the temporal self and its various idolatries. Instead we must turn our mind's eye to our perfect image, which is guarded by angels.

Aquarius is the constellation of the Angel-Human. Thus does this New Moon invite us to feel the wings of our divine advocate, our angel. And through this recognition, restore our vertical "I" to its rightful and sovereign relationship with the One it is eternally striving to become.

**First quarter Moon**, March 14, 29° Taurus: Jesus speaks of Melchizedek.

---

[1] Anon., *Meditations on the Tarot*, pp. 375-376.

**Full Moon,** March 20, 5° Virgo: Beginning of the Age of Michael.

**Last quarter Moon,** March 28, 12° Sagittarius: Jesus in Megiddo.

**Lunar teachings of this cycle** begin with the challenge to tend our vertical and sovereign "I." As the first quarter Moon calls for action, we may find that where we have freed ourselves from the binding ropes of idols we become more aware of the Sun mysteries. These are the mysteries guarded over by Melchizedek. Armed with Sun clarity, the Full Moon reminds us that we are to become Knights of Michael. He is the regent of the Sun and solar paladin of Melchizedek. As the last quarter ensues, we are to integrate the gifts bestowed by the New Moon, thus may we find our consciousness more willing to pierce deeper into the spiritual battle now raging, entering into the covenant of the new wine that aligns us with spiritual worlds.

Neptune conjunct this New Moon adds strength to the enduring influence of this lunar cycle.

**ASPECT 2: Sun conjunct Neptune 21° Aquarius.** The Sun recalls three secret disciples who came from Jerusalem to see Jesus in Bethany. They reported that the high priests and Pharisees wanted to send out spies, so that they could capture Jesus as soon as he came to Jerusalem (Feb/8/33).

Neptune's lower nature is associated with mass consciousness. And, this is exactly what has caused us to become satellites of false authorities. Mass consciousness operates through egregores, human-generated demons that are the driving force behind our collective idol worship. Nowadays, the god of money rules alongside the god of technology; together, they have become the idols of Western culture. They are perfect companions, as the desire for money is driven by consumerism and vice versa, a phenomenon that is all to evident in our time. Do not the "spies" of Google, Amazon, and Facebook know exactly how to tempt us into satisfying such desires? Are not many even going into debt due to this "dragnet," the result of which is often a kind of slavery? Thus do we too easily lose the verticality, our true authority, as we become part of the craving masses. Moreover, when the fire of desire is ignited in youth, before the "I" takes command, the ravaging flames have often spread too far for the "I" to manage—thus is the consumer born.

Yet today we hear of the secret disciples. Are these not readers of the arcana (secrets)? Are they not the antidote to the high priests and Pharisees of surveillance—of logarithms that are actually a form of black magic? Technology wields a terrible authority; all too easily, it overwhelms the spiritual author within.

In its highest manifestation, however, this aspect opens to us the mysteries, the arcana, that carry the potential for inner awakings; i.e., through its influence we may hear the gods speaking in us. Thus may we rise into communion with angels, archangels and archai—and in so doing, we would *participate* in beholding the Sophianic waves now instreaming from the future Aquarian age: the era of the Angel–Human. Indeed, this is the antidote to the stalking "inseeders" of the world's dangerous folly.

**Mar 13: ASPECT: Sun 28° Aquarius square Jupiter 28° Scorpio.** The Sun remembers Jesus as he preached in front of an inn in Kisloth. Thick rope, woven through stakes, was used to hold back the crowd. Among those listening were several rich merchants; Jesus taught them concerning the dangers attached to acquiring wealth. Pointing to one of the ropes, he said, "A rope like this would pass more easily through the eye of a needle than would a rich man into the kingdom of heaven" (Feb/16/30).

Again we are reminded of the pathology of our time: the pursuit of riches (and thereby its companion, debt) and our resultant slavery to the god of money. This aspect increases whatever it may be that occupies our heart. If that is consumerism, we will desire more things. If, on the other hand, it is spiritual treasure, then will revelation find us.

*Implantation* is a word that may better interpret the word "propaganda," which is far too overused to be any longer of use. Furthermore, implantation describes what is actually occurring when the spies of logarithms inflame desires. As the ropes that bind have been self-engendered, we look to Jupiter in Scorpio—for the beings in this constellation can inspire us to see what lies under the surface, giving us the information necessary if we are to untie the knots that bind us. Thus may we awake to the treasures of alchemical wealth, which none can steal.

Jupiter was at today's Sun degree at the first temptation of Jesus Christ. This gives due warning. We are to turn away from the *egregorian* authorities of our time.

**Mar 14: First Quarter Moon: 29° Taurus.** The Moon reached this degree as Jesus and the disciples met with seven philosophers who had received the baptism. Jesus spoke to them of Melchizedek as a true priest and king to whom they should turn their attention, adding that the sacrifice of bread and wine which Melchizedek had offered would be fulfilled and perfected, and would endure until the end of the world (May/11/31).

New Moon to first quarter was a time of action, asking us to rise above the world's false authorities to find the healing power of our own true "I." The period between the first quarter and the Full Moon is a time of inspiration. We seek to hear the voice within, consequent to the invigoration our actions have engendered.

Jesus Christ is the high priest of the Sun after the Order of Melchizedek. From him we receive the new wine that ignites our "I," as well as the bread of eternal life that strengthens our ability to perceive his presence now among us. These substances will indeed endure for all time.

**ASPECT: Inferior conjunction of Sun and Mercury 29° Aquarius.** Mercury was in superior conjunction with the Sun as Jesus and the disciples were again guests at the home of the Syrophoenician woman (whom he had healed four days earlier, along with her daughter). She begged Jesus to visit and help the people of Sarepta (where Elijah had resided during the drought), who were threatened with starvation: "Forgive me, a widow and once poor, to whom you have restored all, if I may be so bold as to plead also for Sarepta" (Feb/16/31).

The Syrophoenician woman had great faith; thus could both she and her daughter be healed. Sun conjunct Mercury (the healers and pastors of humankind) bestows forces of imagination. Inferior conjunctions mean that Mercury is between the Sun and the Earth, streaming potent revelation to the faithful. May we be among them as we enter the experience of this lunar phase.

**Mercury enters Aquarius:** "May the limited yield to the unlimited. What lacks boundaries should establish **boundaries in its own depths**, and should arise in life's stream, as a flowing wave self-sustaining, in coming to existence self-shaping. Limit thyself, O unlimited!" (Steiner, *Twelve Cosmic Moods*). Without boundaries, the mind (Mercury) will lose itself in the ocean of spiritual forces.

**Mar 15: Sun enters Pisces:** "**In losing, may loss be found**, in winning may gain be lost, in comprehending seek to grasp and maintain in maintaining. Through coming to existence upraised, through existing to become interlaced, may loss be gain in itself!" (Steiner, *Twelve Cosmic Moods*). The late William Bento illumines this mantra:

> Regardless of the nature of what has been released, there is a sense of accompanying loss. With those losses that have been treasured and valued (such as a loved one), there lives the hope that the object or being that is lost will not be forgotten or forlorn, but will find new life in an entirely new realm. The plea that states, "May the loss find itself" is really a statement of hope in the eternal cycle of life.

Above the first decan is the Square of Pegasus; hence the association of this decan with the body of Pegasus, the Winged Horse—also called the Horse of the Fountain. Saturn rules this decan. Pisces bestows Magnanimity born of Love. The challenge is to stay grounded in reality in the inclination toward the mystical.

**ASPECT: Mercury 28° Aquarius square Jupiter 28° Scorpio.** The Sun was at Jupiter's degree as Jesus taught first from the banks of the Sea of Galilee, and then from a ship that had been placed at his disposal. Around four that afternoon, he came ashore to a place of tax collectors where Matthew (then called Levi) lived. Levi cast himself down before Jesus; and Jesus said, "Arise, and follow me!" (Nov/19/30).

This aspect bestows a broad and positive perspective. Aquarian Mercury asks us to arise and follow the morning star. Through this star, we comprehend the future impulses already in-streaming. Thus do we also become early disciples of the Aquarian Age that is soon to come.

**Mar 20: ASPECT: Full Moon 5° Virgo opposite Sun 5° Pisces, 9:42 PM, EDT, and spring equinox.** With the Moon at 5° Virgo, we can recall the start of the current Age of Michael (Nov/10/1879). We are approximately half way through the Age of Michael. He is the Archistrategist working against the dragon and his hordes, fighting against the evil ones so that the wedding of the Lamb and his Bride may yet come to pass. This wedding is alchemical; it is the marriage between the lower and higher "I." It is *initiation*.

> And it is authentic victory that one must hope for and wait for in the conflict that tradition represents as the struggle between the Archistrategist Michael and the dragon. The day when it is achieved will be the day of a new festival—the festival of the coronation of the Virgin *on Earth*. For then the principle of opposition will be replaced on Earth by that of collaboration. This will be the triumph of life over electricity. And cerebral intellectuality will then bow before Wisdom (Sophia) and will unite with her.[1]

The principle of electricity is the opposite of the principle of the moral ether, which is the force "to overcome every subtle thing."

> The "subtle things" to overcome are the intellectual forces of temptation based on *doubt,* the psychic forces of temptation based on sterile *enjoyment,* and the electrical forces of temptation based on *power*.[2]

This Full Moon is the Moon of bread (Virgo) and fish (Pisces), the communion the Risen One gave to his disciples on the shores of the Galilee. Doubt, sterile enjoyment, and power constitute the "technology" of temptation. The inverse to this is faith, devotion, and powerlessness, i.e., the powerlessness of surrender to that which is higher, which measures the supreme accomplishment of true Power.

The Virgin (Virgo) carries an immaculate Force, one that indeed penetrates all solid substance. It is an *emollient action* that moves effortlessly through physical, psychic, and mental barriers. We become immaculate as our hearts open to the perfect self who dwells above our heads, like a star. As we grow into consciousness of this self, we diminish the effects issuing from all negative physical, psychic, and mental obstacles. We then engage in the "fish communion." *This communion weaves the binding power of love among community members, shielding them from the egregores that would otherwise cause harm.* (The intention of egregores is to destroy communities devoted to spiritual concerns, i.e., communities working to bring harmony between that which is above and that which is below.)

This Full Moon reveals the difference between the serpent and the Virgin. The serpent uses arbitrary and dark magic to lure humankind into his false kingdom. The Virgin, on the other hand, lures none. Rather do those who wield the sacred magic of her Force freely move between higher and lower worlds, uniting their consciousness with the phenomena of the archetypal world. We live in the winter of the Piscean age. In the brief second (from an evolutionary perspective) that human beings have occupied Earth, we have nearly destroyed the world. The Virgin tells us this does not need to be, for communion with her—as well as the *fish communion* that ignites sisterhood and brotherhood—are harbingers of the Aquarian age soon to come. From the ashes of the old, the new arises.

> The Virgin is the principle of springtime, i.e., that of creative spiritual élan and spiritual flourishing. The prodigious flourishing of philosophy and the arts in ancient Athens took place under the sign of the Virgin. Similarly, the flourishing of the Renaissance at Florence was under the vernal sign of the Virgin. Also, Weimar at the beginning of the nineteenth century was a place where the breath of the Virgin perceptibly moved hearts and minds.
>
> The sickness of the West today is that it is more and more lacking creative élan.[3]

The Age of Michael is one in which many are called to pick up the sword of truth, which is not

---
1 Anon., *Meditations on the Tarot*, pp. 282-283.
2 Ibid., p. 283.
3 Ibid., p. 291.

unlike the flaming sword of the Cherubim who guard the Tree of Life in Paradise. This is the sword of outer powerlessness—i.e., the sign of the crucifixion, which is at the same time the sign of true Power. The serpent's power binds us, creating obstacles to movement. Yes, we can move horizontally in his world, but vertical movement, *hermetic* movement, is arrested. The approaching age of Aquarius bestows the overlighting principle that guides spiritual communities—such communities manifest the fish communion given by the Risen One.

> Criticism and polemicism are mortal enemies of the spiritual life, for they signify the substitution of destructive electrical energy for constructive vital force. A complete change of the inspiring and motivating source takes place when a person or spiritual movement becomes engaged in the way of rivalry—with the criticism and polemicism that it comprises. Once carried away by electricity, "bearing witness against thy neighbor" will always be essentially and intrinsically false.[1]

We can remember the power of community into which the Virgin's Force weaves all together. The Michaelic battle, however, must not be waged *between* people. It is waged first in our own soul, then is it waged against the evil in the world. *Willingness to engage*, within and without, marks the fertile ground upon which stand the true knights of Michael—who unyieldingly unmask the beings of darkness.

Full Moon to last quarter Moon mark the time of transformation. Have we healed any tendency to be a satellite of false idols? Have we found the Melchizedek Sun shining into our strengthened "I"? To the degree to which this is true, we will pick up the sword offered to all who serve Michael in his battle with the dragon.

**Spring Equinox. Sun 5° Pisces**: Mother Earth is breathing out her soul. Her breath is half within the Earth and half without. The little seed of our future spiritual potential—which we carried out of the Holy Nights last January—is also breathing outward. Both microcosmically (in the human being) and macrocosmically (in the body of the Earth), an exhalation is taking place. The Earth Mother is going to sleep, and her dream body engenders the sprouting enlivening of Nature's springtide. *Nature is the soul of the Mother out-breathed in sleep. Just as our soul leaves our body in sleep, so too does the great Earth-soul leave her body in sleep, and this manifests as the beauty and majesty of Natura.* Our Christmas seed is preparing to take flight. It will begin its gradual ascent with the Earth-soul into the heights of summer. Here it will be infused with the creative forces necessary to develop into a full reality. This will come into form later, at Michaelmas. Today marks a sprouting quickening, both within and without. Not until the first Sunday after the first Full Moon following this equinox will the inner spirit of the Earth—Jesus Christ—begin the ascent to meet the warmth of the Sun.

We wait with expectant longing for the Full Moon and the Sunday that follows. The Full Moon is the spatial declaration announcing the triumph of solar forces over lunar forces. The first Sunday, however, marks the union of the spatial event with time. This restraint is the meaning behind the Lenten and Easter mysteries. *The Easter Sun is a benediction that marks the handing of the Earth over into the embrace of cosmic warmth and light.*

As we advance in our understanding of the festivals, we will come to realize that while we in the northern hemisphere are celebrating the vernal point at 5° Pisces, in six months' time (around Michaelmas), those who live in the southern hemisphere will celebrate their springtide—with their vernal point occurring at 5° Virgo. There is a balance: the southern hemisphere holding center, while the northern hemisphere expands to St. John's Tide. And with the northern hemisphere holding center as the southern peoples celebrate St. John's, the same balance is achieved. This is hygienic for the one consciousness of the one whole Earth in its yearly respiration.

**Mar 21: ASPECT: Venus 28° Capricorn square Mars 28° Aries.** Venus recalls Jesus at the start of the Sabbath, as he preached at a synagogue in Galilee. He was not well received by the learned teachers there, who criticized him for wandering

---

[1] Ibid., p. 300.

about the land instead of staying with his mother (Mar/3/30).

This aspect (also in cardinal signs, with Venus close to today's position) was present during the three temptation of Jesus Christ, as well as during the 40th day—when angels came to minister to him. Thus could we call this "the aspect of temptation."

We continue under the influence of yesterday's Full Moon, recalling *the Power of powerlessness* exemplified in the crucifixion, as the cross of Venus stands in dynamic tension with the Archangel Michael (Mars). The orbit of the planet Mars marks the sphere of old Moon evolution, when human beings were given their astral bodies. If lower astral forces are released, gentle Venus can be overwhelmed by disruptive domineering energies as well as lower sexual passions. This is not a good aspect when the world teeters on a precipice, all too ready to succumb to the temptation of violence. Inversely, however, this aspect resounds with the benevolence of the 40th day. Indeed, angels stand ready to deepen our devotion to the Word (Mars) and the love he brought to all creation (Venus).

Although Christ is not well received, many yet hear him and are aligning with him.

**Mar 22: Venus enters Aquarius:** "May the limited yield to the unlimited. **What lacks boundaries should found boundaries** in its own depths, and should arise in life's stream, as a flowing wave self-sustaining, in coming to existence self-shaping. Limit thyself, O unlimited!" (Steiner, *Twelve Cosmic Moods*).

**Mar 23: Mars enters Taurus:** "Become bright, radiant being, feel growth's power. Weave life's thread **into creative world existence**, in thoughtful revelation, in shining life-contemplation. O radiant being, appear!" (Steiner, *Twelve Cosmic Moods*). Mars finds it detriment in this sign, thus may its influence be misused or weakened.

**Mar 24: ASPECT: Mercury conjunct Neptune 22° Aquarius.** Mercury remembers the healing of the Syrophoenician woman and her daughter (Feb/12/31). Again we bask in tremendous powers of inspiration—if we are so inclined.

**Mar 28: Last Quarter Moon 12° Sagittarius.** The Moon shone from this degree as Jesus taught parables to the field workers east of Megiddo. Later on, Jesus cured a large group of variously afflicted individuals. He then praised John the Baptist to those who remained: "Among those born of women there has risen no one greater than John the Baptist" (Nov/15/30).

Today we enter the final phase of this lunar cycle. The period from the last quarter Moon to the New Moon is one of integration. The creative action of restoring our verticality at the New Moon has given way for new inspirations that can turn us toward the Sun mysteries of Melchizedek. The Full Moon asked for transformation, in that we are to surrender the serpent's kind of power for the true and selfless Power of Michaelic courage. All of this is now to become manifest *in* us. And, as this last quarter recalls Jesus in Megiddo, we are given ample warning, for Megiddo—"the valley of Jezreel"—is also known as the valley of Armageddon. Yet as we hear Jesus speaking of John, the witness of revelation, we can summon courage to willingly take up all challenges now set before us. This is the way of truth (Sagittarius).

John was last prophet born through the Abrahamic stream of blessing: a hereditary stream running throughout the community of ancient Israel. Following upon the miracle of turning water into wine at the wedding at Cana, a new revelation stream had opened. St. Paul would be blind for three days after encountering its light outside the gates of Damascus. May we too find the light of revelation as we meet the challenges of our time.

**Mercury stations direct 21° Aquarius.** Mercury again recalls the healing of the Syrophoenician woman and her daughter (Feb/12/31).

**Mar 31: Sun 15°46' Pisces: Birth of the Solomon Jesus (Mar/5/6 BC).** The Solomon Jesus was the reincarnation of the great teacher, Zarathustra, who was visited by the Three Kings. The kings brought the wisdom gathered by initiates in the three preceding cultural ages: myrrh from Ancient India, frankincense from Ancient Persia, and gold from Ancient Egypt. The influence of this great teacher, the Master Jesus, is always present on Earth. There is always an initiate who is working with him, even if he himself is not physically incarnated. The ideal of Pisces, the Sun sign at this birth, is "Not I, but Christ in me." To find this alignment is to surrender oneself to the force of "celestial gravitation," whereby the personal will follows the dictums of spiritual will.

We can pray that our will also learns how to lovingly follow the will of higher worlds (in Pisces, magnanimity becomes love).

**NOTE: Today marks the 94th anniversary of the death and transition of Rudolf Steiner into spiritual worlds.** Steiner's death Sun is conjunct the birth Sun of the Solomon Jesus, and his death Moon is conjunct the Sun's position at the Ascension of Christ. Furthermore, today remembers the Sun's location at the death and transition of Daniel Andreev (1959), author of the great work *The Rose of the World*, which is quoted earlier in this volume of *Star Wisdom*. This is a special day!

# APRIL 2019

## Stargazing Preview

As the month begins, you'll only have an hour or so to see Venus before sunrise; look for her conjunction with the Moon on the 2nd. April's New Moon happens on the 5th, and four days later the Moon catches up to Mars at 11° Taurus. You'll be able to see them in the southwest after sundown: they dip below the western horizon just before midnight, shortly before the rise of Jupiter in the east. On the 11th, Jupiter begins its seasonal retrograde movement from the last degree of Scorpio.

The 16th marks the ingress of Venus into Pisces; she's nearly too close to the Sun to be seen. Three days later, April's Full Moon shines from 4° Libra. The night of the 22nd will be the peak of the Lyrid meteor showers, which can be seen during the latter half of the month. The Lyrids are so-named because they appear to radiate from the constellation Lyra, high above Sagittarius (though they can appear anywhere in the night sky). Look to the NNE, below the upside-down pan of the Big Dipper, for your best shot of seeing the show. Unfortunately, the still-large waning Moon rises at about 2300 and will be visible throughout the rest of the night.

The Moon laps Jupiter on the 23rd (they rise around midnight) and Saturn on the 25th (rising at 0200). On the 30th, Saturn goes retrograde from 25° Sagittarius. You'll only have a few hours following sunset to catch a glimpse of Orion before he sinks below the western horizon.

## April Commentaries

**Apr 2: ASPECT: Mercury conjunct Neptune 22° Aquarius.** The Sun at Neptune's degree recalls Jesus teaching in the synagogue, and urging all to become baptized. The Pharisees again reproached him, saying that his disciples did not fast regularly. Jesus replied that they eat after long labor, and then only if others are supplied, referring to the Feeding of the Five Thousand that occurred twelve days earlier (Feb/10/31). This aspect is fleeting, yet beautiful. We can open to tremendous powers of inspiration so that we, too, may be baptized with light.

**Apr 5: ASPECT: New Moon 20° Pisces.** We enter a great and profound mystery if we contemplate the relationship between the movements of the Moon during the ten months of the embryonic period, which later play out in the unfolding of an individual's biography. Willi Sucher was the first to discover this principle of correspondence.

When the Solomon Jesus was seventeen years and one month old, the union in the temple between the two Jesus children occurred. Looking at the embryonic period that corresponds to this exact time, we see that the embryonic Moon was 20½° Pisces—conjunct where the Moon stands today. The union in the temple marked the *spiritual* death of the Solomon Jesus. His *physical* death would occur two months later. After his death, however, he continued to participate in the life of Jesus until Jesus died on the cross. Therefore, his biography continued to spiritually unfold although his physical body had died. At the time of the Crucifixion, the Solomon Jesus was (spiritually speaking) thirty-eight years old. The embryonic Moon that corresponds to this age was again 20½° Pisces.

In the case of a highly developed individuality such as Zarathustra, who was incarnated in the Solomon Jesus, death signifies merely a translation of activity from one realm to another. This individuality worked on, after the death of the body on June 5, AD 12, in union with the Nathan Jesus. Thus, the Solomon Jesus was active in preparing the way for the unfolding of the earthly mission of Jesus Christ—the mission which began with the baptism in the Jordan and culminated in the death on the cross on Golgotha.[1]

Thus does this New Moon remember the Moon's position (in the embryonic astrological biography of the Solomon Jesus) at the time of two great miracles: the Union in the Temple, and the Crucifixion of our Lord. Moreover, the Sun at today's degree is a mere 4° from its position at the birth of the Solomon Jesus, who became the Master Jesus.

At every moment of his biography, Jesus Christ was aligned with all the stars in the heavens. To a certain extent this is also true of initiates; and the more advanced they are, the more this applies.

Pisces is the constellation connected with the under-worldly mysteries of the Mother. Thus does this New Moon ask us to awake to the Mother and her fairy tale land of Shambhala, which rests at the Earth's center.

The Rosicrucians were committed to penetrating the inner Earth mysteries. They worked in caves and in the lower floors of castles—places with vaulted ceilings, painted blue and sprinkled with golden stars. When Valentin Tomberg entered the Catholic Church, he did this to plant Rosicrucian seeds into the sacred heart of Peter's Church.

These seeds continue to radiate a light, attracting forces from Shambhala. The awaking of this realm has been especially noticeable since 2014. Indeed, new organs of cognition are forming in response to the Mother's renewed activity. In South America it is said that children are exhibiting awareness of higher frequencies due to such new organs, and that nothing can destroy these organs once they have formed. In a sense we can say that these organs are the eyes of the Mother, seeing through her children. In North America it is different, for the entombment in materialism works against the forming of new organs.

The Mother offers gifts profusely, placing them at our feet. Lo, how we ignore these! On the first day of the Chymical Wedding of Christian Rosenkreutz, an old man spoke the following words:

If the poor human race
Were not so arrogant
It would have been given much good
From my mother's heritage,
But because the human race will not take heed
It lies in such straits
And must be held in prison.

Modern technologies are direct assaults against the Earth's new activity. The beings behind these technologies are grievously dark and foreign to the Earth proper. In the northern land of the Eagle, the death cult of materialism has so embedded itself that even the mention of developing new soul organs is easily dismissed, and the notion of the awaking of Shambhala would be considered equally absurd.

Christian Rosenkreutz (and the inner Earth mysteries) are nonetheless ever-present, as his etheric body is active regardless of whether he is incarnated or not. And he is very closely aligned with John the Baptist: the first Adam, the baptizer of Christ.

This New Moon thus remembers how the stars weave into us before we even take our first breath; and as this occurs in Pisces, it remembers the profundity of the inner Earth mysteries and the work of Rosicrucians.

**First quarter Moon,** April 12, 28° Gemini: Jesus speaks the parable of the overgrown weeds.

**Full Moon,** April 19, 4° Libra: Jesus Christ in the garden of Gethsemane.

**Last quarter Moon,** April 26, 11° Capricorn: Humble Philip is called into discipleship.

**Lunar teachings of this cycle** begin with the profundity of the star mysteries that weave into us from the moment of our conception to the moment of our birth. With the New Moon in Pisces, we are turned toward the surging forces radiating from Our Mother. While we joyfully celebrate Natura, we are asked to take action. As the first quarter Moon dawns, we may find new inspiration informing us

---

1 Powell, *Chronicle of the Living Christ*, p. 91.

of where the Pharisees indwell us; *these "Pharisees" infect us as the inhibiting weeds that overwhelm our Sun-self as well as our ability to cognize the rising inner Earth energies.* In the transformative time of the Full Moon, we remember Gethsemane and the agony of Christ. We also recall the power Christ would soon bequeath to us in order that we, too, may endure all temptation, which is the power of the enchristed "I" that indwells each of our hearts. The culminating last quarter Moon will remind us of humility, the first quality necessary to become a disciple.

**Apr 10: ASPECT: Venus conjunct Neptune 22° Aquarius: Healing of the Paralyzed Man.** Venus reached this zodiacal degree before midnight on the day of this healing miracle (Jan/19/31).

The healing of the paralyzed man occurred on a Friday—Venus day. The man's egoism in his past life was the cause of his paralysis in his current life. His patience, however, was extraordinary, as he had been waiting 38 years by the side of the healing pool of Bethesda for the One who would help him—Jesus Christ.

When the cross of Venus communes with the Goddess Night (Neptune) miracles indeed take place. For Neptune ever resounds Sophia's sanctifying grace, singing earthly souls into harmony with their own true self. When we accept ourselves exactly as we are, we begin to hear this cosmic symphony; it surrounds us as the divine anthem resounding from our eternal star.

At this time of the Second Coming we too are called to perform miracles. How do we begin to free ourselves from the paralyzing effects of our past lives? We may begin by taking up our cross, which opens our hearts, thus allowing us to hear what lives in the hearts of others. *Selfless love lifts us above the graveyard of the unconscious.* Today we listen to the Angel-Human (Aquarius).

This aspect (in Capricorn) occurred on the 40th day. Did not the angels sing their healing ministrations into the ravaged soul of Jesus?

**ASPECT 2: Sun 25° Pisces square Saturn 25° Sagittarius.** The Sun remembers the Sermon on the Mount, which signified the conclusion of Jesus's teaching of the Beatitudes. As Jesus took his leave, people shed tears of gratitude (Mar/15/31).

In dynamic tension with the Holy Virgin, the resurrecting powers of the Sun offer the challenge of accepting love's restraining benevolence. Where have we turned from the mission we promised to fulfill? Introspection may reveal the answer to this question. In hearing the response, we too may shed tears of gratitude, remembering that we are never alone, never unloved, and never without our angelic advocate.

**The Sun at this degree also remembers the feeding of the four thousand (Mar/15/31).** This is the miracle representing the unfolding of evolution in Time, i.e., the unfolding of the Earth's cosmic biography manifesting through the seven sacred days of creation (Saturn, Sun, Moon, Earth, future Jupiter, Venus, and Vulcan). In this remembering, we overcome all mechanistic thinking that would otherwise seek to exert control over nature, thus sublimating all her living beings to the law of the machine and the dangerous reasoning inherent in such blasphemy.

Time has torn asunder the "likeness of God" in which we were created. The eternal aspect of our "image," however, cannot be defiled. Our "likeness" must seek its "image" if we are to recreate the Paradisiacal Garden whence we have fallen.

**Apr 11: Jupiter stations retrograde 29° Scorpio.** Jupiter starts its retrograde movement in the foreground of the star *Lesath*, which marks the stinger of the Scorpion.

Death has lost its sting, however, when we understand how spiritual worlds receive each death in joyful celebration of our homecoming.

**Apr 12: First Quarter Moon 28° Gemini.** The Moon was between *Castor* and *Pollux*, as it is today, when Jesus taught in the temple in Jerusalem. He spoke there of the parable of the field overgrown with weeds that had to be carefully uprooted; thereby would the good grain ripen and not be uprooted with the weeds—meaning the Pharisees (Feb/26/33).

The beings indwelling the constellation of Gemini proclaim the commandment to follow our star and no one else's. We to weed our gardens of rigid,

## SIDEREAL GEOCENTRIC LONGITUDES : APRIL 2019 Gregorian at 0 hours UT

| DAY | ☉ | ☽ | ☊ | ☿ | ♀ | ♂ | ♃ | ♄ | ♅ | ♆ | ♇ |
|---|---|---|---|---|---|---|---|---|---|---|---|
| 1 MO | 15 ♓ 58 | 27 ♑ 43 | 28 ♊ 40R | 21 ♒ 37 | 11 ♒ 14 | 5 ♉ 29 | 29 ♏ 12 | 24 ♐ 50 | 6 ♈ 17 | 22 ♒ 5 | 28 ♐ 0 |
| 2 TU | 16 57 | 9 ♒ 32 | 28 34 | 21 58 | 12 26 | 6 9 | 29 13 | 24 52 | 6 20 | 22 7 | 28 1 |
| 3 WE | 17 57 | 21 27 | 28 25 | 22 24 | 13 38 | 6 48 | 29 15 | 24 55 | 6 23 | 22 9 | 28 1 |
| 4 TH | 18 56 | 3 ♓ 31 | 28 13 | 22 54 | 14 51 | 7 28 | 29 16 | 24 58 | 6 27 | 22 11 | 28 2 |
| 5 FR | 19 55 | 15 44 | 28 0 | 23 28 | 16 3 | 8 8 | 29 17 | 25 0 | 6 30 | 22 14 | 28 3 |
| 6 SA | 20 54 | 28 9 | 27 46 | 24 6 | 17 15 | 8 47 | 29 18 | 25 2 | 6 33 | 22 16 | 28 3 |
| 7 SU | 21 53 | 10 ♈ 44 | 27 33 | 24 48 | 18 28 | 9 27 | 29 19 | 25 5 | 6 37 | 22 18 | 28 4 |
| 8 MO | 22 52 | 23 31 | 27 21 | 25 34 | 19 40 | 10 6 | 29 20 | 25 7 | 6 40 | 22 20 | 28 4 |
| 9 TU | 23 51 | 6 ♉ 30 | 27 12 | 26 23 | 20 53 | 10 46 | 29 20 | 25 9 | 6 43 | 22 22 | 28 5 |
| 10 WE | 24 50 | 19 39 | 27 6 | 27 16 | 22 5 | 11 26 | 29 20 | 25 11 | 6 47 | 22 24 | 28 5 |
| 11 TH | 25 49 | 3 ♊ 1 | 27 3 | 28 11 | 23 18 | 12 5 | 29 20R | 25 13 | 6 50 | 22 26 | 28 6 |
| 12 FR | 26 48 | 16 36 | 27 2 | 29 10 | 24 30 | 12 45 | 29 20 | 25 15 | 6 53 | 22 28 | 28 6 |
| 13 SA | 27 47 | 0 ♋ 26 | 27 2 | 0 ♓ 11 | 25 43 | 13 24 | 29 20 | 25 16 | 6 57 | 22 30 | 28 6 |
| 14 SU | 28 46 | 14 31 | 27 2 | 1 15 | 26 55 | 14 3 | 29 19 | 25 18 | 7 0 | 22 31 | 28 7 |
| 15 MO | 29 44 | 28 50 | 27 0 | 2 21 | 28 8 | 14 43 | 29 19 | 25 19 | 7 4 | 22 33 | 28 7 |
| 16 TU | 0 ♈ 43 | 13 ♌ 22 | 26 55 | 3 30 | 29 20 | 15 22 | 29 18 | 25 21 | 7 7 | 22 35 | 28 7 |
| 17 WE | 1 42 | 28 2 | 26 48 | 4 41 | 0 ♓ 33 | 16 2 | 29 17 | 25 22 | 7 11 | 22 37 | 28 7 |
| 18 TH | 2 40 | 12 ♍ 44 | 26 38 | 5 55 | 1 45 | 16 41 | 29 15 | 25 23 | 7 14 | 22 39 | 28 8 |
| 19 FR | 3 39 | 27 22 | 26 27 | 7 11 | 2 58 | 17 20 | 29 14 | 25 25 | 7 17 | 22 41 | 28 8 |
| 20 SA | 4 38 | 11 ♎ 46 | 26 15 | 8 28 | 4 11 | 18 0 | 29 12 | 25 26 | 7 21 | 22 43 | 28 8 |
| 21 SU | 5 36 | 25 50 | 26 4 | 9 48 | 5 23 | 18 39 | 29 11 | 25 27 | 7 24 | 22 44 | 28 8 |
| 22 MO | 6 35 | 9 ♏ 31 | 25 56 | 11 10 | 6 36 | 19 18 | 29 9 | 25 27 | 7 28 | 22 46 | 28 8 |
| 23 TU | 7 33 | 22 46 | 25 49 | 12 34 | 7 48 | 19 57 | 29 6 | 25 28 | 7 31 | 22 48 | 28 8 |
| 24 WE | 8 32 | 5 ♐ 37 | 25 46 | 14 0 | 9 1 | 20 37 | 29 4 | 25 29 | 7 35 | 22 50 | 28 8 |
| 25 TH | 9 30 | 18 5 | 25 44 | 15 28 | 10 14 | 21 16 | 29 1 | 25 29 | 7 38 | 22 51 | 28 8R |
| 26 FR | 10 29 | 0 ♑ 16 | 25 44 | 16 58 | 11 27 | 21 55 | 28 59 | 25 30 | 7 42 | 22 53 | 28 8 |
| 27 SA | 11 27 | 12 14 | 25 44 | 18 29 | 12 39 | 22 34 | 28 56 | 25 30 | 7 45 | 22 55 | 28 8 |
| 28 SU | 12 25 | 24 5 | 25 43 | 20 3 | 13 52 | 23 13 | 28 53 | 25 30 | 7 48 | 22 56 | 28 8 |
| 29 MO | 13 24 | 5 ♒ 53 | 25 41 | 21 38 | 15 5 | 23 52 | 28 49 | 25 31 | 7 52 | 22 58 | 28 8 |
| 30 TU | 14 22 | 17 45 | 25 36 | 23 15 | 16 17 | 24 31 | 28 46 | 25 31 | 7 55 | 23 0 | 28 8 |

**INGRESSES :**

1 ☽ → ♒ 4:38
3 ☽ → ♓ 17: 2
6 ☽ → ♈ 3:33
8 ☽ → ♉ 12: 1
10 ☽ → ♊ 18:36
12 ☿ → ♓ 19:51
☽ → ♋ 23:15
15 ☽ → ♌ 1:56
☉ → ♈ 6:22
16 ♀ → ♓ 13: 9
17 ☽ → ♍ 3:12
19 ☽ → ♎ 4:22
21 ☽ → ♏ 7:13
23 ☽ → ♐ 13:24
25 ☽ → ♑ 23:28
28 ☽ → ♒ 12: 2

**ASPECTS & ECLIPSES :**

1 ☽ ☌ A 0:42
2 ☽ ☌ ♀ 6:30
☿ ☌ ♆ 9:57
3 ☽ ☌ ♆ 1:24
☽ ☌ ☿ 1:57
4 ♇ ☍ ☊ 19:41
5 ☉ ☌ ☽ 8:49
☽ □S ☊ 23:17
6 ☽ ☌ ♅ 16: 7
9 ☽ ☌ ♂ 8:14
10 ♀ ☌ ♆ 6:19
☉ □ ♄ 8:46
☽ ☍ ♃ 17:25
12 ☿ □ ♃ 4:17
☉ □ ☊ 5:52
☽ ☍ ♄ 15: 4
☽ ☌ ☊ 18: 9
☉ □ ☽ 19: 4
☽ ☍ ♇ 19:59
13 ☉ □ ♇ 8: 1
15 ♀ □ ♃ 23:14
16 ☽ ☍ ♆ 15: 8
☽ ☌ P 22:15
17 ☽ ☍ ♀ 4:28
☽ ☍ ☿ 11:50
18 ☽ N□ ☊ 22:30
19 ☉ ☍ ☽ 11:11
☽ ☍ ♅ 16:33
22 ☽ ☍ ♂ 18:33
☉ ☌ ♅ 23: 4
23 ☽ ☌ ♃ 11:42
25 ☽ ☌ ♄ 14:32
☽ ☌ ☋ 15: 0
☽ ☌ ♇ 19:46
26 ☉ □ ☽ 22:17
27 ♂ □ ♆ 13:17
28 ☽ ☌ A 18:34
30 ☽ ☌ ♆ 10:32
♄ ☍ ☊ 18:57

## SIDEREAL HELIOCENTRIC LONGITUDES : APRIL 2019 Gregorian at 0 hours UT

| DAY | Sid. Time | ☿ | ♀ | ⊕ | ♂ | ♃ | ♄ | ♅ | ♆ | ♇ | Vernal Point |
|---|---|---|---|---|---|---|---|---|---|---|---|
| 1 MO | 12:36:17 | 26 ♎ 35 | 19 ♐ 43 | 15 ♍ 59 | 4 ♊ 29 | 18 ♏ 51 | 19 ♐ 12 | 7 ♈ 17 | 21 ♒ 19 | 26 ♐ 21 | 4 ♓ 59'29" |
| 2 TU | 12:40:13 | 29 27 | 21 18 | 16 58 | 4 59 | 18 55 | 19 14 | 7 18 | 21 20 | 26 21 | 4 ♓ 59'29" |
| 3 WE | 12:44:10 | 2 ♏ 17 | 22 53 | 17 57 | 5 28 | 19 0 | 19 16 | 7 19 | 21 20 | 26 22 | 4 ♓ 59'29" |
| 4 TH | 12:48: 6 | 5 6 | 24 28 | 18 56 | 5 58 | 19 5 | 19 17 | 7 19 | 21 20 | 26 22 | 4 ♓ 59'29" |
| 5 FR | 12:52: 3 | 7 54 | 26 3 | 19 56 | 6 27 | 19 10 | 19 19 | 7 20 | 21 21 | 26 22 | 4 ♓ 59'29" |
| 6 SA | 12:55:59 | 10 40 | 27 37 | 20 55 | 6 57 | 19 14 | 19 21 | 7 21 | 21 21 | 26 22 | 4 ♓ 59'29" |
| 7 SU | 12:59:56 | 13 26 | 29 12 | 21 54 | 7 26 | 19 19 | 19 23 | 7 21 | 21 21 | 26 23 | 4 ♓ 59'28" |
| 8 MO | 13: 3:52 | 16 11 | 0 ♑ 47 | 22 53 | 7 55 | 19 24 | 19 25 | 7 22 | 21 22 | 26 23 | 4 ♓ 59'28" |
| 9 TU | 13: 7:49 | 18 56 | 2 22 | 23 52 | 8 24 | 19 29 | 19 26 | 7 23 | 21 22 | 26 23 | 4 ♓ 59'28" |
| 10 WE | 13:11:46 | 21 41 | 3 57 | 24 51 | 8 54 | 19 33 | 19 28 | 7 23 | 21 23 | 26 24 | 4 ♓ 59'28" |
| 11 TH | 13:15:42 | 24 25 | 5 32 | 25 50 | 9 23 | 19 38 | 19 30 | 7 24 | 21 23 | 26 24 | 4 ♓ 59'28" |
| 12 FR | 13:19:39 | 27 10 | 7 7 | 26 49 | 9 52 | 19 43 | 19 32 | 7 24 | 21 23 | 26 24 | 4 ♓ 59'28" |
| 13 SA | 13:23:35 | 29 56 | 8 41 | 27 47 | 10 21 | 19 48 | 19 34 | 7 25 | 21 24 | 26 25 | 4 ♓ 59'28" |
| 14 SU | 13:27:32 | 2 ♐ 42 | 10 16 | 28 46 | 10 50 | 19 53 | 19 35 | 7 26 | 21 24 | 26 25 | 4 ♓ 59'27" |
| 15 MO | 13:31:28 | 5 28 | 11 51 | 29 45 | 11 19 | 19 57 | 19 37 | 7 26 | 21 24 | 26 25 | 4 ♓ 59'27" |
| 16 TU | 13:35:25 | 8 16 | 13 20 | 0 ♎ 44 | 11 48 | 20 2 | 19 39 | 7 27 | 21 25 | 26 25 | 4 ♓ 59'27" |
| 17 WE | 13:39:21 | 11 6 | 15 1 | 1 42 | 12 17 | 20 7 | 19 41 | 7 28 | 21 25 | 26 26 | 4 ♓ 59'27" |
| 18 TH | 13:43:18 | 13 56 | 16 36 | 2 41 | 12 46 | 20 12 | 19 43 | 7 28 | 21 25 | 26 26 | 4 ♓ 59'27" |
| 19 FR | 13:47:15 | 16 49 | 18 11 | 3 40 | 13 14 | 20 16 | 19 45 | 7 29 | 21 26 | 26 26 | 4 ♓ 59'27" |
| 20 SA | 13:51:11 | 19 43 | 19 46 | 4 38 | 13 43 | 20 21 | 19 46 | 7 30 | 21 26 | 26 27 | 4 ♓ 59'27" |
| 21 SU | 13:55: 8 | 22 39 | 21 21 | 5 37 | 14 12 | 20 26 | 19 48 | 7 30 | 21 27 | 26 27 | 4 ♓ 59'26" |
| 22 MO | 13:59: 4 | 25 38 | 22 55 | 6 35 | 14 41 | 20 31 | 19 50 | 7 31 | 21 27 | 26 27 | 4 ♓ 59'26" |
| 23 TU | 14: 3: 1 | 28 40 | 24 30 | 7 34 | 15 9 | 20 35 | 19 52 | 7 32 | 21 27 | 26 28 | 4 ♓ 59'26" |
| 24 WE | 14: 6:57 | 1 ♑ 44 | 26 5 | 8 32 | 15 38 | 20 40 | 19 54 | 7 32 | 21 28 | 26 28 | 4 ♓ 59'26" |
| 25 TH | 14:10:54 | 4 52 | 27 40 | 9 31 | 16 7 | 20 45 | 19 55 | 7 33 | 21 28 | 26 28 | 4 ♓ 59'26" |
| 26 FR | 14:14:50 | 8 3 | 29 15 | 10 29 | 16 35 | 20 50 | 19 57 | 7 34 | 21 28 | 26 29 | 4 ♓ 59'26" |
| 27 SA | 14:18:47 | 11 18 | 0 ♒ 50 | 11 28 | 17 4 | 20 55 | 19 59 | 7 34 | 21 29 | 26 29 | 4 ♓ 59'26" |
| 28 SU | 14:22:44 | 14 37 | 2 25 | 12 26 | 17 32 | 20 59 | 20 1 | 7 35 | 21 29 | 26 29 | 4 ♓ 59'26" |
| 29 MO | 14:26:40 | 18 1 | 4 0 | 13 24 | 18 0 | 21 4 | 20 3 | 7 36 | 21 29 | 26 29 | 4 ♓ 59'25" |
| 30 TU | 14:30:37 | 21 29 | 5 35 | 14 23 | 18 29 | 21 9 | 20 4 | 7 36 | 21 30 | 26 30 | 4 ♓ 59'25" |

**INGRESSES :**

2 ☿ → ♏ 4:37
7 ♀ → ♑ 12: 5
13 ☿ → ♐ 0:38
15 ⊕ → ♎ 6: 7
23 ☿ → ♑ 10:27
26 ♀ → ♒ 11:17

**ASPECTS (HELIOCENTRIC +MOON(TYCHONIC)) :**

2 ☽ □ ♃ 19: 2
☽ ☌ ♆ 23:45
4 ☽ □ ♂ 5: 2
⊕ □ ♄ 8:46
5 ♀ ☌ ♇ 4:59
☽ □ ♄ 6:59
☽ □ ♇ 20:35
☽ □ ♀ 22:51
6 ☽ ☌ ♅ 17:34
9 ☿ ☌ ♃ 4:54
☿ □ ♆ 21:21
☽ ☍ ♃ 23:49
10 ☽ □ ♆ 3: 6
☽ ☍ ☿ 4:36
☿ ☌ A 9:21
11 ☽ ☌ ♂ 11:41
⊕ □ ♇ 14: 3
12 ♀ □ ♅ 4:34
☽ ☍ ♄ 5: 7
☽ ☍ ♇ 17: 3
13 ☽ □ ♅ 11:58
☽ ☍ ♀ 15:54
16 ☽ □ ♃ 10:59
☽ ☍ ♆ 13:11
17 ☿ ☍ ♂ 12: 5
18 ☽ □ ♂ 0: 2
☽ □ ☿ 2:25
♀ ☌ A 3:28
☽ □ ♄ 11:26
☽ □ ♇ 22:28
19 ☽ ☍ ♅ 16:50
20 ☿ ☌ ♄ 0:28
☽ □ ♀ 15:16
22 ☿ ☌ ♇ 6:31
☽ ☌ ♃ 19:58
☽ □ ♆ 21:34
⊕ ☍ ♅ 23: 4
24 ☽ ☍ ♂ 19:59
25 ☽ ☌ ♄ 3:35
☽ ☌ ♇ 16:28
☿ □ ♅ 20:17
26 ☽ □ ♅ 14:36
☽ ☌ ☿ 21:25
27 ☿ □ ⊕ 1:37
28 ☽ ☌ ♀ 19:34
30 ☽ □ ♃ 6:51
☽ ☌ ♆ 7:31
☿ □S ☊ 14: 2

dead thinking eclipsing our star's light. The New Moon that inaugurated this cycle reminded us of how—from the moment of our conception to the moment of our birth—the stars weave into us. *Star inscriptions*, recorded into our etheric bodies as we were formed in our mother's womb, may well be the origin of life's various trials and triumphs. Thus should we willingly accept all that comes to us on our biographical journeys.

Recognition of star wisdom turns us toward the mission of the West: cosmology. As this New Moon shone from the constellation of Pisces, a message to nurture and develop the inner Earth mysteries was heard. Having actively listened, we are now prepared to rid ourselves of all the weeds that tether us to the dying age of materialism and all its abstract, mechanical thinking. Indeed, when spiritual knowledge illumines us, we live from wonder to wonder.

Castor and Pollux represent two twins: one mortal, the other immortal. Uniting the two is key to uprooting the dormant weeds that constrict our progress.

**ASPECT 2: Mercury 29° Aquarius square Jupiter 29° Scorpio.** Mercury was at this degree as Jesus visited the sick in their homes to comfort them. At the start of the Sabbath, he taught in the synagogue, referring to the commandment "Honor thy parents" (Feb/24/30). The fourth commandment, "Honor thy father and thy mother," is the commandment of the continuity of tradition. In honoring our elders, we protect the threads that weave the future. This brings honor to the mission of the Earth as well as to the mission of humanity.

**Mercury enters Pisces:** "In losing may loss be found, in winning may gain be lost, **in comprehending seek to grasp** and maintain in maintaining. Through coming to existence upraised, through existing to become interlaced, may loss be gain in itself!" (Steiner, *Twelve Cosmic Moods*). Pisces is opposite Mercury's place of ruling in Virgo, therefore it is in its detriment when in this sign.

**Apr 13: Sun 28° Pisces: Peter receives the keys (Mar/19/31).** The Sun was at this degree as Jesus asked his disciples, "Who do men say that the Son of man is?" And they answered, "Some say John the Baptist, others say Elijah, and others Jeremiah or one of the prophets." Peter then called out: "Thou art Jesus the Christ, the Son of the living God." Jesus replied: "On this rock I will build my church, and the powers of death shall not prevail against it. And I will give you (Peter) the keys to the kingdom."

The Church was inaugurated when Peter received the keys: *Whatever is bound to the promise of Christ's heart is bound also in heaven; and whatsoever is loosed from this heart shall also be loosed in heaven*. This marked the beginning of the apostolic tradition in the first Christian Church, creating an eternal "place" wherein the heart of Christ rests. We have collectively loosed our hearts from Christ; and having done this, we have instead opened the gates of Hell—thus setting loose the dragon to prevail upon us. Peace will reign on Earth when we collectively recognize the original sanctity of Christ's *sacred heart*, from which each of us has received our individual ember. Fanning this ember ignites a fire, opening our heart to the revelation now pouring into the world as the light of the Dharma Sun[1] (Satya Yuga) grows ever stronger.

The Rosicrucian seeds that John was commissioned to plant in Peter's Church are flowering, and in this process a new light in-streams the Earth. Jesus decreed the emergence of these mysteries as part of his Second Coming. Perhaps the Risen One may also commission us to hear the new dispensations his etheric presence bestows.

**ASPECT: Sun 28° Pisces square Pluto 28° Sagittarius.** The Sun here recalls Jesus and the disciples as they journeyed to Sogane, where he taught and healed until late afternoon. Later, they traveled to a hill outside of town, and Jesus taught the disciples and listened to their accounts of the experiences they had undergone when on their missionary travels (Mar/18/31).

Intensity of one kind or another results from this influence. The resurrecting power of the Sun in dynamic tension with Phanes–Pluto can awake an inner knowing, a state wherein primal memories resurrect into the light. Like Peter, we can be the rock upon which the spiritual foundation of love

---

1 See the article, "The Rising of the Dharma Sun," in this volume of *Star Wisdom*.

triumphs over doubt, despair, and faithlessness. Improper use of power, however, sets loose intensely destructive forces that are currently "engineering" our planet. *Phanes is the divine love of the Father God, who fills us with an intuitive understanding of the seeds of eternity that underlie all creation.*

Awakening to nature inspires cooperation with her. Awakening to Hades–Pluto, on the other hand, justifies all the aggressive tactics we are presently directing against her. Righteousness is a force descending from above, which propels positive action. We can pray this is what triumphs in world events.

**Apr 14: Sun 29° Pisces: Palm Sunday and the beginning of Holy Week.** The days of Holy Week are the archetypal examples of what every day of the week signifies. Each Sunday marks the onset of a sevenfold process of change, expressing the unfolding of our inner work through *time*. During Holy Week, this process is uplifted, bestowing radiant life force as the Lenten season comes to its end.

- Sunday offers us a new sense of selfhood (Christ enters Jerusalem riding an ass).
- Monday offers us inner reflections through which we cast from us what will not serve the new solar forces we are birthing (the cleansing of the Temple).
- Tuesday we may find that the world, or our habit body, may fight against change (aggressive discourse from the Pharisees and scribes).
- Wednesday offers us the choice between restlessness (Judas/betrayal) and devotion (Magdalene/anointing).
- Thursday offers us the quiet of sacred space through which we may commune with the divine (the Last Supper).
- Friday offers us the opportunity to consciously bear the weight of our cross and to take up in us what is ours to transfigure (the Passion).
- Saturday offers us the opportunity to bear witness to what in us is caught in the snares of lower worlds (Entombment).
- Easter Sunday is the octave of today (Resurrection).

Thus do we rise to the light of the Easter Sun while carrying new resolves for our journey forward.

**Apr 15: Sun enters Aries:** "Arise, O shining light, take hold of growth's being, lay hold of forces weaving. Ray out awaking life. In face of resistance, succeed—in stream of time, recede. O shining light, abide!" (Steiner, *Twelve Cosmic Moods*). The Sun rules while in this sign.

The late William Bento illumines this mantra:

> A call is heard as the Sun enters the sign of Aries. It is a call to not merely arise, but to awake. The Sun effortlessly does this every morning, bestowing light upon us all. Should we not follow the Sun in this way? In the heart of every human being there lives this light that can be made available to others every day. It is our mandate to make it available to all, every day and in every way that aids an awaking to the many miracles taking place daily.

Aries, the sign of the Lamb and his Bride, calls us to devote ourselves to something greater than ourselves. Its worldview is *idealism*, wherein devotion becomes the power of self-sacrifice. It reflects the processes of spiritualization (Christ) and of interiorization (Sophia). The teachings of Hermes in ancient Egypt, in particular the teachings of Isis and Osiris, contained a pre-Christian understanding of the relationship between the Lamb and his Bride. The first decan is ruled by Mars and is associated with the Girdle of Andromeda, symbolizing the power of unity and purity worn by the Mystic Woman—who represents the soul of humanity.

**ASPECT: Venus 29° Aquarius square Jupiter 29° Scorpio.** Venus remembers Jesus as he again found vendors at the temple. Jesus admonished them more severely this time, and set about removing their tables to the outer court. The Pharisees, put to shame by Jesus's actions, were angered when the crowd identified him as the prophet of Nazareth. When Jesus left the temple, he healed a cripple (Apr/4/30).

The cross of Venus in dynamic tension with the Holy Spirit (Jupiter) graces the soul with wisdom, optimism, and concern for social justice. Inversely, there also exists the cross of temptation—the cross of Jezebel. This is the unholy cross dredged up from the muddy waters of the serpent. The Jezebel cross stimulates the electrical energy common to fanatics, who are driven by forces fomenting in the depths of the subconscious. If this is the cross we take up, cunning and manipulative behaviors will manifest, in total disregard for what may be best for those in our social milieu.

Angels have wisely decided the specific weight of burden we are to carry to turn our attention from self-absorption to world interest. When the "I" works downward from above, we overcome the Jezebel temptation, but when the "I" surrenders to seduction, we are overcome by intoxications rising from below. This aspect tests our moral development. Will loving wisdom inspire us to take up the cross of revelation, or will we instead opt for the electrifying cross of seduction?

Taking up the cross carried by the prophet from Nazareth leads us into realms filled with spiritual nourishment, especially with Venus in Aquarius. Thus do our burdens become light and our yokes easy.

Indeed, vendors have set up their tables everywhere, tempting us to want more of what we don't need. On this Monday of Holy Week, we may find a longing to restore our inner temple, the quiet place from which we contemplate mysteries far greater than the exchange of worldly goods.

**Apr 16: Sun 0° Aries: Cursing of the fig tree (3/20/33).** As Christ cursed the fig tree, he was giving warning that the time of the development of the "I" had dawned. No longer would it be safe to commune with spirit realms if consciousness was at all dimmed. Soon after he cursed the fig tree, Christ would arise from the grave as the Easter Sun crowned the horizon. Since this time, we are to ignite in our own heart the fire that we received from him; and in so doing, we are protected from the vaporous atavism that still seeks to envelop and drown the blessedness of his gift. Therefore, on the Monday before his crucifixion, Jesus Christ closed the door to the ancient practice of somnambulistic clairvoyance.

**Venus enters Pisces:** "In losing may loss be found, **in winning may gain be lost**, in comprehending seek to grasp and maintain in maintaining. Through coming to existence upraised, through existing to become interlaced, may loss be gain in itself!" (Steiner, *Twelve Cosmic Moods*). Venus is in exaltation in this sign, therefore Venus gains strength and energy.

**Apr 19: ASPECT: Full Moon 4° Libra opposite Sun 4° Aries: Gethsemane (Apr/2/33).** Today is Good Friday. The remembrance of Gethsemane—falling exactly on Good Friday of this year, when the Christian world commemorates this event—is profound.

The anguish of Gethsemane, which gave rise to perspiration of blood, was *eternal*. This night, the night of Gethsemane, was not measured in hours. It was—it is—immeasurable, therefore eternal. It is due to its eternity that he sweated blood, and not because of the temporary, and therefore passing, trial. He knew eternal Hell through experience, and as he came out of it, we have the "good news" that not only death is vanquished by the Resurrection, but also that Hell is—through Gethsemane.[1]

In the Garden of Gethsemane, Christ again encountered Ahriman, who showed him all the sins that would be done in his name throughout all time. Imagine Jesus being shown the inquisitions, not to mention all the other results of a Christology void of living spiritual wisdom. The antidote to Ahriman's alluring trick-show is rising within the light of the Dharma Sun, unmasking his pernicious stalking of all that is good. Satya Yuga is birthing etheric technologies that must become ordinary practices (sacred magic). In this way, we will gradually awake to the reality of energy fields and our responsibility to heal, cleanse, and effectively work in etheric realms. Then we will discover that we, too, can suffer darkness into light as a means of overcoming what could otherwise be the eternal Hell of victimhood.

Many now claim to be spiritual, but not religious. In truth, the two are inseparable. *To be spiritual*

---

1 Anon., *Meditations on the Tarot*, p. 181.

*turns the heart to higher worlds; to be religious, on the other hand, educates the heart in the theology of spirit.* Without understanding the theology of spirit, one cannot understand the true measure of spiritual worlds. To be spiritual suggests we have a sense that there is something other than the material world. To touch into this "something," however, we become religious as we fall on our knees in openhearted awe before the unimaginable profundities of the mysteries.

Humanity is now collectively experiencing the night in Gethsemane, as we collectively meet what Ahriman has perpetrated in the world. How do we cultivate light-filled energy fields to survive this encounter? Not only can we cultivate this around others and ourselves but we can also cultivate this around communities, schools, and even cities. If we do not work for the light, the darkness will continue to work unobstructed. It rests on our shoulders to respond to our times. Angels work with us when we engage in etheric technologies. To accomplish this, we must open the windows of a closed world:

> The sun shines on the good and wicked alike. But it is certainly necessary to open the windows of a dark room in order for light to be able to enter there. The *light* of the Sun is in no way created or merited by us. It is a gift, pure and simple—*gratia gratis data*. Nevertheless, it is necessary to open our windows in order for it to enter our abode, just as it is necessary to open our eyes to see it.[2]

If we choose to remain in darkness, we have no ground upon which we can voice our displeasure at the state of the world. Eternity marks the intensity experienced when a soul is separated from itself—when it is in a Hell of its own making. "Eternal hell is the state of a soul imprisoned within itself, where the *soul* has no hope of coming out. 'Eternal' means to say 'without hope.'"[3]

Opening a window means we are willing to respond to the light, announcing our readiness to achieve an eternal victory over the prison of passive hopelessness—i.e., Hell. This victory does not rest solely on wisdom, or even miracles; rather does it rest on the *power of love*. Those who love one another are Christians, regardless of what they may otherwise call themselves. And those who act on their love of one another are Christian Hermeticists.

Love holds the balance so that wisdom does not become cold theory, or miracles become passive expectation. Love acts, and this action is called sacred magic (etheric magic), i.e., the putting into practice of the science of love. Thus does the heart give warmth to gnosis as it reveals the invisible cause behind all miracles.

> We Hermeticists are theologians of that Holy Scripture revealing God, which is named "the world"; similarly, theologians of the Holy Scriptures revealing God are Hermeticists in so far as they dedicate their effort to the glory of God. And just as the world is not only a material body but is also soul and spirit, so is the Holy Scripture not simply the "dead letter" but is also soul and spirit.[4]

This Full Moon of Good Friday reminds us that we are all to become theologians of the Holy Scripture, i.e., Hermeticists, understanding the hallowed relationship between that which is above and that which is below. Through the science of sacred magic, we seek to *alter* what the dragon has caused. We are not only to protect the lamp of God's eternal love, we are further commissioned to *act* through the power of its illumination. If this light were to be extinguished, the entirety of humanity would plunge into the eternal Hell of hopelessness.

Spiritual air is cultivated through etheric technologies, as well as through worship, prayer, and benediction. This is what sustains life! Furthermore, it is the heart that engages in sacred magic, worships, and prays, ever longing for the resultant benediction of grace.

Have we enacted the New Moon's gift of awaking to the star mysteries that enter us from conception to death and beyond? Have we pulled the weeds of doubt from our souls? Are we willing to engage in the etheric technologies of sacred magic that free the world from the Hell of despair? If so, we will integrate the principle of humility as this lunar phase concludes. Indeed, *humility is the gift*

---

2   Ibid., p. 179.
3   Ibid., p. 180.
4   Ibid., p. 188.

*bestowed when the heart awakes to the theology of love.*

**Sun 4° Aries: Cosmic memory of Jesus speaking the "woe upon the Pharisees" (3/24/33).** Less than a month before his crucifixion, Jesus spoke of his kingdom that is to come, and reprimanded the Pharisees for their hypocrisy: "You snakes! You brood of vipers! How will you escape being condemned to hell? Therefore, I am sending you prophets and sages and teachers. Some of them you will kill and crucify; others you will flog in your synagogues and pursue from town to town" (Matt. 23:33–34).

And yet the Pharisees of the modern world continue to crucify the prophets who threaten their authority. Valentin Tomberg is one among those who was slandered and misrepresented. The erudite are too often the last to recognize new dispensations. Yet, there are those who have been sent to be guardians of the spiritual guidance of humanity whether heard or not, and they speak their own kind of woe unto the Pharisees—who cling too long onto tradition and therefore mummify:

> To be a guardian signifies two things: firstly, the study of and practical application of the heritage of the past; and secondly, *continuous creative effort* aiming at the advancement of the work. For the tradition lives only when it is deepened, elevated and increased in size. Conservation alone does not suffice at all. It is only a corpse which lends itself to conservation by means of mummification.[1]

What do we not only cherish, but also unwisely cling to—even to the degree of *mummification?*

**Apr 21: Christian Celebration of Easter Sunday.** Today remembers Christ's Resurrection. As we gain wisdom, we become wise as serpents; and as our hearts open, we become innocent as doves. Thus do we ever so gradually approach the springtide of *our* resurrection. It already awaits us at the *omega point* of evolution's end, for we are each one golden thread in the One Resurrection body of Christ. As spiritual human beings who have descended into the material world, we are born of spirit. Furthermore, as we must incarnate into our destined stream of heredity, we are also born of our ancestors. As we mature spiritually, however, we will take less and less from the horizontal stream of heredity and become ever more aligned with the vertical descending stream of spirit, for this stream bears the divine image and likeness of our true being—in Christ.

The physical body we are given arises from an immortal kernel of indestructible will, and is eternal in its nature. The elemental substance of the physical body may decompose at death, but the spiritual force that created it lives on:

> Death—disincarnation—signifies the separation of the soul and spirit from the physical body, including its indestructible kernel or resurrection body. Whilst the soul and spirit ascend to the spiritual world—accompanied by the forces of vitality (the "etheric" or "vital body") and psychic forces (the "astral body," i.e., psychic habits, desires, character and psychic dispositions)—the resurrection body descends in the opposite sense, i.e., below, toward the center of the Earth. As it is active will during life, its descent is due to progressive relaxing of the will. The latter withdraws more and more within itself, [as it is released from] the effort concentrated previously on the task of rendering and maintaining the physical body in conformity with the soul and spirit of the incarnated individuality. *This withdrawal of the Resurrection body within itself after death amounts to what one understands by "peace" in speaking of the peace of the dead.*[2]

The Resurrection body is a body of perfect freedom, expressive of the manifestation of the eternal individuality itself. *It is the fundamental will underlying all matter.* It is also the fruition of the vertical line of spiritual descent, the result of the unification of both its upper and lower points. Indeed, freedom is the realization of the individualized will—free of all impediments in the horizontal line of heredity as well as in the horizontal realm of mass consciousness.

---

1 Anon., *Meditations on the Tarot*, p. 608 (italics added).

2 Anon., *Meditations on the Tarot*, p. 580. (Emphasis in italics by CML.)

Furthermore, the Resurrection body is born from the heart of the Earth and soars on wings feathered from the heart of the Galaxy. It can manifest as light (as happened to Paul at the gates of Damascus), or as a current of warmth, or as a breath of vivifying freshness, or even as a luminous human form (such as when Christ appeared soon after his Resurrection). Tomberg calls it a "synthesis of life and death, i.e., capable of acting here below as a living person and at the same time enjoying freedom from terrestrial links like a deceased person." Yet the descent of Christ, the purpose of which was to unite the resurrection force as a possibility for *all* of humanity, was a deed incomprehensible to the spiritual beings who stood witness. The spiritual worlds held their breath at the descent of Christ into Hell—a world unknown to the higher hierarchies was being penetrated by Jesus Christ.

The resurrection of our Savior takes place as an actual rhythm of the Earth and as a spiritual power, creating substance every Sunday anew in every single human being. At the moment the Christ-Sun arose from the grave in the first Resurrection body, he merged into the innermost heart of every human soul, including those not incarnated at that time. It is now up to us—in humility, in devotion, and in joy—to celebrate daily this inner core of holiness. We are to become aware that we ourselves bear *him,* the highest and most precious, within *us.*

Today we celebrate the Risen One and our work of reaching the omega point, where we already wait for ourselves to arrive.

**Sun 6° Aries: Cosmic memory of Jesus teaching regarding his Second Coming (3/26/33); also, cosmic memory of the "enmity of the Pharisees" (3/26/31).** Jesus told the Pharisees that penitence was the way forward, but they were too immersed in their own hardened beliefs to understand his meaning. Their enmity then increased, for they found no entrance into the new imaginations Jesus was bringing. True imaginations unite, whereas ahrimanic imaginations divide, bringing a conviction of knowing—but without being connected to the source of true knowing. Ahrimanic knowing, on the other hand, is mere cunning in disguise. Self-will is an obstacle to the brotherhood and sisterhood our times call us to manifest; and this, unfortunately, is the quality of will that underlies all divisiveness. *If our imaginations do not contribute to unification, their origins are to be suspect.*

**Apr 22: ASPECT: Sun conjunct Uranus 7° Aries.** The Sun recalls the rage of the Pharisees as they learned that the healing of the paralyzed man had occurred on the Sabbath. As the temple guards endeavored to take Jesus into custody, the sky suddenly grew dark; a heavenly voice then proclaimed, amid a noise like thunder: "This is my beloved son in whom I am well pleased!" (Mar/28/31). Each year, on the day after Easter, the resurrection power of the Sun meets the scintillating brilliance of holy imaginations. We remember the theophany: the voice of the Father calling to his Son. May we also continue to hear a chorus of angels awaking our Sun-hearts to possibilities previously unimaginable. Thus will the raging forces of opposition be brought to silence.

**Apr 25: Pluto stations retrograde 28° Sagittarius.** Pluto stood at this degree in the summer of 1772, directly between the Boston Massacre and the Boston Tea Party (Pluto was less than three degrees from its position today at both events). British soldiers were stationed to enforce unpopular taxes and crown rule. On the day of the Massacre in March of 1770, disgruntled Americans were attacking the soldiers with snowballs and other deadlier objects; the situation escalated and the soldiers fired into the crowd, killing three on the spot and wounding three others who would die later. The British attempted to tighten the leash further on the Americans through the Tea Act in May of 1773, which sought to give the East India Company a tea monopoly throughout the colonies, but this only stoked the flames of independence; the Tea Party took place on December 16, 1773.

May rebellion instead become *re-evolution,* sublimating all violent tendencies. Each Easter Sun bequeaths a yearly benediction, guiding us to find a peaceful approach to forward progress; and the message of this year's Easter Sun, which dawned four days ago, is still being integrated. The dragon who works against this has seven heads. If we cut off one, will ten more grow? Our abuse of freedom will find its restitution in revolution, for such events mask the fact that we are naught but slaves caught up in a mass thought, intoxicated with poison wine. Obedience alone restores the good that evil has splintered and thus denigrated, and obedience results in harmlessness. We must not generate more giants, more heads on the dragon. Instead we must find solutions by suffering our differences to such an extent that spirit draws near to us, revealing reconciliations previously unimaginable.

**Sun 10° Aries: Cosmic memory of the "Visitation" (3/30/2 BC).** The Nathan Mary, pregnant with Jesus, visited her cousin Elizabeth, who was pregnant with John the Baptist. During that meeting, all four of them were filled with holy awe as the Old Adam, John the Baptist in Elizabeth's womb, was quickened by the presence of the New Adam, the Jesus child in Mary's womb.

**Apr 26: Last quarter Moon 11° Capricorn.** The Moon was at this degree as Jesus and his disciples went for a little walk following Jesus's afternoon teaching in the synagogue. Philip, who was modest and humble, hung back. Jesus turned and said, "Follow me," whereupon Philip, filled with joy, joined the other disciples (Dec/24/29).

Humility is the prerequisite for discipleship. In the preceding lunar phases, we have remembered star mysteries, we have weeded our gardens, and we have prayed in Gethsemane. Now we are to integrate humility as Capricorn commissions us to bless the Earth with the grandeur of new imaginations. We are wise to not underestimate the courage necessary if we are to represent the hitherto unknown. If we retreat from such a task, we may find cowardice engulfing us in doubt and despair. It is better to prudently act than to endlessly wait for confirmation, for the act itself reveals the next step forward.

**Apr 27: Sun 12° Aries: The last anointing of Jesus by Mary Magdalene (4/1/33).** This began the grievous Passion of our Lord. He would be mocked, scorned, scourged, crowned with thorns, carry the great burden of his cross, and finally be nailed to it and crucified. His death, resurrection, and ascension constitute the greatest mystery in all Earth evolution.

Mary Magdalene's last anointing of Christ set the betrayal by Judas in motion. "Truly, I say to you, wherever this gospel is proclaimed in the whole world, what she has done will also be told in memory of her" (Matt. 26:13).

Magdalene's devotional understanding of Christ had stood in opposition to how Judas thought of him. Judas could not see what was right before his eyes. Magdalene exemplified the courage necessary for those who would be representatives of higher thoughts (Aries). This must often be done, despite those who mutter against such truths. Indeed, the inner restlessness of Judas was projected upon the world as he stood against her anointing of Christ with costly oil.

Today our hearts may find an openness to a new Gospel—the Gospel of the Second Coming. *The revelations therein will inevitably shatter belief systems built on subservience to some outer authority, as well as those based simply on the arrogance of one's pride, or merely the quantitative measure of all things.*

What is devotion? It is the substance of restlessness that has been taken hold of and interiorized. The passive person lacks devotion; and the restless person refrains from the efforts of interiorization.

**ASPECT: Mars 23° Taurus square Neptune 23° Aquarius.** Mars at Neptune's position remembers Jesus as he prepared for the Sermon on the Mount. He sent out his disciples to make it known that he would be giving instruction on the mountain beyond Gabara. Some sixty disciples, friends, and relatives came in expectation of the occasion; among them was Mary Magdalene, whose sister Martha had persuaded her to come (Nov/7/30).

Archangel Michael in dynamic tension with the Goddess Night heightens the inspirational power (Neptune) of the word (Mars). Inversely, the lower astral nature in dynamic tension with the Woman of Babylon (lower Neptune) arouses suspicion, deceitfulness, and doubt. From which cup will we sup? When benefic inspirations fall into unholy realms, they tangle into knots of confusion. This is a state common to the masses. One then loses discernment between one's own thoughts and the broiling field of collective thoughts.

The mountain upon which the Beatitudes and the Lord's Prayer were spoken recalls the miracle of words filled with inspiration to such an extent that they will endure for all time. Words form chalices into which an energy is drawn from one source or another. When words are beautiful, benevolent energies incarnate. When words are ugly, on the other hand, malevolent energies incarnate. We are each responsible for the chalices we create and the subsequent energies we call into being.

The eternity of goodness is juxtaposed by the relative eternity of evil, which will eventually come to an end, but until that time it endures. The evil we create tethers us to subearthly layers of the Earth, while the goodness we create also tethers us to suprasensory realms. Thus do we bind ourselves to one specific energy source or another by the quality of the words we speak.

Like Mary Magdalene, we are to heal our souls through our union with the benevolence of the living Word.

**Apr 29: Saturn stations retrograde 25° Sagittarius.** Saturn's degree was rising as John the Baptist beheld Jesus across the Jordan River and spoke to those assembled: "Behold the Lamb of God!" (Dec/1/29).

**Apr 29: Sun 14° Aries: Cosmic memory of the death of Jesus Christ on the Cross (4/3/33).** The Sun today remembers the most wretched moments in the life of Christ, as he achieved his final victory on the hill of Golgotha. All that Christ then experienced *from* humanity allows him now to give *to* humanity. The deeds done to him during the Passion created the opening in the laws of karma that allows him to now spiritually touch us in this time of the Second Coming. Christ gives all his love to humanity, as humanity once gave all of its hatred to him. Each step of the way must be contemplated as a part of Earth evolution's greatest mystery. The Passion of Christ is the path of the initiate. We may pray for the strength to willingly carry the cross of our own burdens, for this lightens the Cross of Christ. In the words of Judith von Halle:

There can be no fantasy or even wish on the part of the spiritual pupil of entering upon a path of cognition that would be broad and well trodden, easy and without effort. The path of cognition that one takes is one's own. Hence no one has entered upon it before. At the beginning of the journey, at the time of one's decision to commit, it actually does not exist at all. It is one's task to direct oneself through the morass of one's soul urgings, and to direct one's I through the "soul emptiness of space," through the "time-destroying stream."[1]

The sacred freedom that Christ brought to all humanity is a force of guidance directing each of us to find our own way—upon our own untrodden path—to realize our own initiation.

**Apr 30: Sun 14°57′: The Descent into Hell** (Friday, Apr/3/33). At sunset, three hours after the crucifixion the Moon was just rising in the east, and Saturn was directly overhead. Christ had entered into the subearthly realms to squarely face his archenemy, Ahriman, and to find his Mother in the deepest depths.

The way to the Earth Mother leads through the subearthly spheres. There one finds her, as well as eternal life. After encountering the Mother, one can resurrect. Christ, the Son, reconnected the Father and the Mother—who are separated by substance and by evil, the belt of lies. Moreover, human beings have the task of bringing about the connection once again.

Through Christ's descent into hell, whereby he encountered the Mother and thus made possible the Resurrection and Ascension, Sacred Magic arose via the connection of above and below. One cannot rule substance; one can only master it from within.

The Mother has hidden herself; she has fled into the interior of the Earth. Therefore, she was actually forgotten for a time. And now a gradual understanding and seeking of the Earth Mother—the remembrance of her name—is resurrecting.

The human soul has no place on Earth and also not in the spiritual world. There [we find]

---

1 von Halle, *The Descent into the Depths of the Earth*, p. 20.

the *spirit*, not the soul. Paradise was the realm of the soul; it has disappeared into the interior of the Earth with the Mother. Paradise, Shambhala, is our home; without Shambhala, we are homeless wanderers. However, Christ—after his death—encountered the Tree of Life.[1] One may thus hope that Shambhala will appear again on Earth. Shambhala is not something spatial. It is not a place, but a state of consciousness that is present always and everywhere. It is the Earth's etheric body, permeated with the breath of Buddhi. Furthermore, in the coming kingdom one will experience how the Mother warms the homeless souls. One will then become capable of being truly faithful from within, organically. Whereas we are currently still unfaithful in this "organic" sense. In the coming kingdom we will have in our hearts a stream of daily bread—daily memory/thought of the Name of the Mother.[2]

# MAY 2019

## Stargazing Preview

There's a New Moon on the 4th; once the Sun and Moon set, you'll have a clear view of Mars in the southwest. The opposition of Mars and Jupiter falls on the 5th, so don't forget to look for Jupiter on the eastern horizon as Mars is setting at 2300. The night of the 6th will be the best chance to see the Eta Aquarid meteor showers this year, made even better by the fact that the waxing crescent Moon will be visible for only a few hours after sunset. Look due north, below Cassiopeia, for your best opportunity to see them. On the 7th, the day before Mars enters Gemini, you'll see Mars set at 2300, just before the Moon does so.

May's Full Moon shines from 3° Scorpio on the 18th. The conjunction of the Moon and Jupiter occurs on the 20th: you'll be able to see Jupiter rise first at around 2200. If you're up before sunrise on the 22nd, watch for Saturn, slightly to the left of the Moon in the southwest.

## May Commentaries

**May 1: Sun 15°39′: Cosmic memory of the Resurrection (4/5/33).** The depth of this mystery holds the promise that each human being may become a Christ Bearer. The words of the Risen Christ to Mary Magdalene sound throughout time: "Touch me not, for I am not yet ascended unto the Father; but go unto my brethren, and say to them, 'I ascend unto my Father and your Father, unto my God and your God'" (John 20:17). These words contain the powerful fact that Christ—following his descent to the Mother on Holy Saturday, and following his resurrection soon thereafter—would then ascend to his Father, thereby restoring the unity between the Mother in the depths and the Father in the heights.

The Ascension (forty days from this memory of the Resurrection) was a deed that would also unite fallen humanity with its divine archetype, which had been sacrificed at the time of the Fall. From the moment of the Resurrection onward, Christ has been within us. This eternal oneness with Christ interconnects the whole of humanity into sacred brotherhood and sisterhood. The actual awaking of the disciples to the reality of this oneness came only later at the Holy Whitsun Festival.

During the forty days between the Resurrection and the Ascension, the disciples were in a kind of sleep. Etheric images from their daily life with Christ during his three and one-half years on Earth rose into their consciousness, helping them to understand the cosmic teachings Christ was giving during the forty days after the Resurrection. These cosmic teachings were culled from main-stream Christianity; they are resurrecting in this time of the Second Coming, emerging especially through the ambassadors of Christ who are now working with us. Indeed, the Gospel of the Second Coming is currently being written to *reveal* these teachings.

Valentin Tomberg, in his summary of the last four stages of the Passion (the carrying of the cross, the crucifixion, the entombment, and the resurrection) brought the image of the Rose Cross:

---

1 We can recall that the Cosmic Christ *is* the Tree of Life, and this is what Christ Jesus encountered in Shambhala.
2 See Estelle Isaacson's article in *Starlight,* Easter/Pentecost 2015.

This picture is the Rose Cross, which epitomizes not only the higher stages of the Passion but also, in fact, the whole path of Christian initiation. It is the symbol of the narrow way of sacrifice and the forces of resurrection that flower on this path. Death and resurrection are the two fundamental themes of the Christian spiritual path, and the two were united in the symbol of the Rose Cross.

Thus the black cross with the glowing red roses can summarize all we have said here about Christian initiation; it can stand, if only for a moment, before the inner eye of the reader's soul as a token of the solemn spirit world and, at the same time, as the author's Easter greeting to his readers.[3]

The Sun at this degree sends strengthening forces to anyone whose heart opens to receive the unfathomable mercy of Christ in their devotion to a path of initiation.

**ASPECT: Mercury 25° Pisces square Saturn 25° Sagittarius.** The Sun at Mercury's degree remembers Jesus as he celebrated the beginning of the Feast of the Dedication of the Temple of Zorobabel. It was Zorobabel—of the house of David—who had laid the foundation stone of the temple around 519 BC (Mar/15/30). We are all to lay a foundation stone for the future impulses now in-streaming. To this end, our thinking must be such that it contributes to the well-being of humanity. Negative thinking contributes, instead, to frequencies of unrest. The power of a truthful mind (Mercury in Sagittarius) will, however, also bring sorrow—as we come to understand how often our thoughts are destructive. *Positive thoughts attract benevolence.*

**May 2: ASPECT: Mercury 28° Pisces square Pluto 28° Sagittarius.** Mercury was at this degree as a crowd of people sought out Jesus on the mountain (outside of Regaba). He taught them about the Lord's Prayer, and healed many of the sick who were there. Afterward he continued on his way with the disciples, speaking about the great trials that the future would bring (Mar/3/31). This aspect represents a brief, but intense, transit. The darker sides of human nature are like locked vaults; they can only be opened when our mind penetrates our inner darkness without losing focus on the light. In so doing, rich experiences are gained. Great trials are indeed before us, yet above all discord shines the eternal light of goodness, which protects us as we retrieve our light.

**May 3: Sun 17° Aries: Christ appears to two disciples on the way to Emmaus (4/6/33).** The day after the Resurrection, the disciples Luke and Cleophas were wavering in faith. Anne Catherine Emmerich describes them as anxious and doubting—they could not understand how the Messiah could have been so shamefully mistreated (i.e., crucified).

Doubt is a dangerous adversary. It renders the art of sacred magic powerless. If indeed Christ rose from the dead and promised that even more would *we* do in his name, then doubt must be conquered. Not only does doubt imprison freedom, it also breeds fear, hate, apathy, and despair. These are the neuroses of obsession, causing the endless circle of worry. The devil we fear most lives not in the outer world. It lives within us. Doubt announces its presence.

We are all under the temptations suffered by Job in the Bible. The devil tempting him was not an atheist—no, *he* had no doubt in God. What he doubted, though, was Job's faith in God.

Under the solar influence of this memory, we are wise to understand that if we can resist the devil, the devil becomes our friend. Thus may we find that there is one walking with us, whose touch we long to feel.

**Mercury enters Aries:** "Arise, O shining light, take hold of growth's being, lay hold of forces weaving. Ray out awaking life. In face of resistance, succeed—in stream of time, recede. O shining light, abide!" (Steiner, *Twelve Cosmic Moods*).

**May 4: ASPECT: New Moon 19° Aries. The Sun remembers the conversation with Nicodemus in the night (4/9/30).** This conversation depicts the reintegration of consciousness, i.e., the baptism of water and the spirit. This baptism prepares us to become conscious during the night, when our astral body and ego have temporarily departed from the sleeping etheric and physical body. Imagine the etheric

---

[3] Tomberg, *Christ and Sophia*, p. 290.

| SIDEREAL GEOCENTRIC LONGITUDES : MAY 2019 Gregorian at 0 hours UT | | | | | | | | | | | |
|---|---|---|---|---|---|---|---|---|---|---|---|
| DAY | ☉ | ☽ | ☊ | ☿ | ♀ | ♂ | ♃ | ♄ | ♅ | ♆ | ♇ |
| 1 WE | 15 ♈ 20 | 29 ♒ 45 | 25 ♊ 29R | 24 ♓ 54 | 17 ♓ 30 | 25 ♉ 10 | 28 ♏ 42R | 25 ♐ 31R | 7 ♈ 59 | 23 ♒ 1 | 28 ♐ 8R |
| 2 TH | 16 19 | 11 ♓ 55 | 25 19 | 26 34 | 18 43 | 25 50 | 28 39 | 25 30 | 8 2 | 23 3 | 28 8 |
| 3 FR | 17 17 | 24 19 | 25 8 | 28 17 | 19 56 | 26 29 | 28 35 | 25 30 | 8 6 | 23 4 | 28 7 |
| 4 SA | 18 15 | 6 ♈ 58 | 24 56 | 0 ♈ 1 | 21 9 | 27 8 | 28 31 | 25 30 | 8 9 | 23 6 | 28 7 |
| 5 SU | 19 13 | 19 51 | 24 45 | 1 47 | 22 21 | 27 47 | 28 26 | 25 29 | 8 12 | 23 7 | 28 7 |
| 6 MO | 20 11 | 2 ♉ 58 | 24 35 | 3 35 | 23 34 | 28 26 | 28 22 | 25 29 | 8 16 | 23 9 | 28 6 |
| 7 TU | 21 10 | 16 19 | 24 27 | 5 25 | 24 47 | 29 5 | 28 17 | 25 28 | 8 19 | 23 10 | 28 6 |
| 8 WE | 22 8 | 29 50 | 24 22 | 7 17 | 26 0 | 29 43 | 28 12 | 25 27 | 8 22 | 23 11 | 28 6 |
| 9 TH | 23 6 | 13 ♊ 30 | 24 20 | 9 10 | 27 13 | 0 ♊ 22 | 28 8 | 25 27 | 8 26 | 23 13 | 28 5 |
| 10 FR | 24 4 | 27 20 | 24 20D | 11 6 | 28 26 | 1 1 | 28 3 | 25 26 | 8 29 | 23 14 | 28 5 |
| 11 SA | 25 2 | 11 ♋ 17 | 24 20 | 13 3 | 29 38 | 1 40 | 27 57 | 25 25 | 8 33 | 23 16 | 28 4 |
| 12 SU | 26 0 | 25 21 | 24 21R | 15 2 | 0 ♈ 51 | 2 19 | 27 52 | 25 24 | 8 36 | 23 17 | 28 4 |
| 13 MO | 26 58 | 9 ♌ 31 | 24 20 | 17 2 | 2 4 | 2 58 | 27 47 | 25 22 | 8 39 | 23 18 | 28 3 |
| 14 TU | 27 56 | 23 47 | 24 18 | 19 5 | 3 17 | 3 37 | 27 41 | 25 21 | 8 43 | 23 19 | 28 3 |
| 15 WE | 28 53 | 8 ♍ 4 | 24 13 | 21 9 | 4 30 | 4 16 | 27 35 | 25 20 | 8 46 | 23 20 | 28 2 |
| 16 TH | 29 51 | 22 20 | 24 6 | 23 14 | 5 43 | 4 54 | 27 29 | 25 18 | 8 49 | 23 22 | 28 2 |
| 17 FR | 0 ♉ 49 | 6 ♎ 31 | 23 58 | 25 21 | 6 56 | 5 33 | 27 23 | 25 17 | 8 52 | 23 23 | 28 1 |
| 18 SA | 1 47 | 20 30 | 23 49 | 27 30 | 8 8 | 6 12 | 27 17 | 25 15 | 8 56 | 23 24 | 28 1 |
| 19 SU | 2 45 | 4 ♏ 14 | 23 41 | 29 39 | 9 21 | 6 51 | 27 11 | 25 13 | 8 59 | 23 25 | 28 0 |
| 20 MO | 3 42 | 17 40 | 23 35 | 1 ♉ 49 | 10 34 | 7 29 | 27 5 | 25 11 | 9 2 | 23 26 | 27 59 |
| 21 TU | 4 40 | 0 ♐ 45 | 23 31 | 4 0 | 11 47 | 8 8 | 26 58 | 25 9 | 9 5 | 23 27 | 27 59 |
| 22 WE | 5 38 | 13 30 | 23 28 | 6 11 | 13 0 | 8 47 | 26 52 | 25 7 | 9 8 | 23 28 | 27 58 |
| 23 TH | 6 36 | 25 56 | 23 28D | 8 23 | 14 13 | 9 25 | 26 45 | 25 5 | 9 12 | 23 29 | 27 57 |
| 24 FR | 7 33 | 8 ♑ 7 | 23 29 | 10 35 | 15 26 | 10 4 | 26 38 | 25 3 | 9 15 | 23 30 | 27 56 |
| 25 SA | 8 31 | 20 6 | 23 30 | 12 46 | 16 39 | 10 43 | 26 31 | 25 1 | 9 18 | 23 31 | 27 55 |
| 26 SU | 9 29 | 1 ♒ 59 | 23 31 | 14 56 | 17 52 | 11 21 | 26 24 | 24 59 | 9 21 | 23 32 | 27 55 |
| 27 MO | 10 26 | 13 49 | 23 31R | 17 6 | 19 5 | 12 0 | 26 17 | 24 56 | 9 24 | 23 33 | 27 54 |
| 28 TU | 11 24 | 25 43 | 23 30 | 19 15 | 20 18 | 12 38 | 26 10 | 24 54 | 9 27 | 23 33 | 27 53 |
| 29 WE | 12 21 | 7 ♓ 45 | 23 27 | 21 22 | 21 31 | 13 17 | 26 3 | 24 51 | 9 30 | 23 34 | 27 52 |
| 30 TH | 13 19 | 20 0 | 23 22 | 23 28 | 22 44 | 13 55 | 25 56 | 24 48 | 9 33 | 23 35 | 27 51 |
| 31 FR | 14 16 | 2 ♈ 30 | 23 17 | 25 31 | 23 57 | 14 34 | 25 48 | 24 46 | 9 36 | 23 36 | 27 50 |

INGRESSES :

| | |
|---|---|
| 1 ☽ → ♓ 0:29 | ☽ → ♎ 12:56 |
| 3 ☽ → ♈ 10:50 | 18 ☽ → ♏ 16:32 |
| ☿ → ♈ 23:43 | 19 ☿ → ♉ 3:54 |
| 5 ☽ → ♉ 18:35 | 20 ☽ → ♐ 22:36 |
| 8 ☽ → ♊ 0:18 | 23 ☽ → ♑ 7:57 |
| ♂ → ♊ 10:11 | 25 ☽ → ♒ 19:59 |
| 10 ☽ → ♋ 4:37 | 28 ☽ → ♓ 8:34 |
| 11 ♀ → ♈ 7: 7 | 30 ☽ → ♈ 19:14 |
| 12 ☽ → ♌ 7:53 | |
| 14 ☽ → ♍ 10:27 | |
| 16 ☉ → ♉ 3:35 | |

ASPECTS & ECLIPSES :

| | | | |
|---|---|---|---|
| 1 ☿ □ ☊ 7:45 | ☽ ☍ ♃ 21: 9 | 17 ☽ ☍ ♀ 0:46 | 25 ☉ □ Π 23:40 |
| ☿ □ ♄ 8:49 | ☽ ☌ ♂ 23:48 | ☽ ☍ ♅ 4: 2 | 26 ☽ ☌ A 13:46 |
| 2 ☽ ☌ ♀ 14:38 | 8 ☿ ☌ ♅ 14:20 | 18 ☽ ☍ ☿ 14:24 | ☉ □ ☽ 16:32 |
| ☿ □ ♇ 21:47 | 9 ♀ □ ♇ 17:15 | ♀ ☌ ♅ 16:14 | 27 ☽ ☌ ♆ 19:38 |
| 3 ☽ ⚼ ☊ 1:32 | ☽ ☌ ☊ 18:48 | ☉ ☍ ☽ 21:10 | 30 ☿ □ ♆ 1:25 |
| ☽ ☌ ☿ 8:46 | ☽ ☍ ♄ 20:43 | 20 ☽ ☌ ♃ 17: 3 | ☽ ⚼ ☊ 6:28 |
| 4 ☽ ☌ ♅ 2:14 | 10 ☽ ☍ ♇ 1:18 | 21 ☉ S☌ ☿ 13: 5 | 31 ☿ ☍ ♃ 3:10 |
| ☉ ☌ ☽ 22:44 | 12 ☉ □ ☽ 1:11 | ☽ ☍ ♂ 14:34 | ☽ ☌ ♅ 13:25 |
| 5 ♂ ☍ ♃ 21:56 | 13 ☽ ☌ P 21:42 | 22 ☽ ☌ ☋ 19:11 | |
| 6 ♀ □ ☊ 18: 3 | ☽ ☍ ♆ 23:14 | ☽ ☌ ♄ 22:21 | |
| 7 ♀ □ ♄ 13:25 | 16 ☽ N□ ☊ 2:56 | 23 ☽ ☌ ♇ 3:56 | |

| SIDEREAL HELIOCENTRIC LONGITUDES : MAY 2019 Gregorian at 0 hours UT | | | | | | | | | | | |
|---|---|---|---|---|---|---|---|---|---|---|---|
| DAY | Sid. Time | ☿ | ♀ | ⊕ | ♂ | ♃ | ♄ | ♅ | ♆ | ♇ | Vernal Point |
| 1 WE | 14:34:33 | 25 ♑ 2 | 7 ♒ 10 | 15 ♎ 21 | 18 ♊ 57 | 21 ♏ 14 | 20 ♐ 6 | 7 ♈ 37 | 21 ♒ 30 | 26 ♐ 30 | 4 ♓ 59'25" |
| 2 TH | 14:38:30 | 28 41 | 8 45 | 16 19 | 19 26 | 21 18 | 20 8 | 7 38 | 21 30 | 26 30 | 4 ♓ 59'25" |
| 3 FR | 14:42:26 | 2 ♒ 25 | 10 21 | 17 18 | 19 54 | 21 23 | 20 10 | 7 38 | 21 31 | 26 31 | 4 ♓ 59'25" |
| 4 SA | 14:46:23 | 6 16 | 11 56 | 18 16 | 20 22 | 21 28 | 20 12 | 7 39 | 21 31 | 26 31 | 4 ♓ 59'25" |
| 5 SU | 14:50:19 | 10 13 | 13 31 | 19 14 | 20 50 | 21 33 | 20 13 | 7 40 | 21 32 | 26 31 | 4 ♓ 59'25" |
| 6 MO | 14:54:16 | 14 17 | 15 6 | 20 12 | 21 18 | 21 38 | 20 15 | 7 40 | 21 32 | 26 32 | 4 ♓ 59'24" |
| 7 TU | 14:58:13 | 18 28 | 16 41 | 21 10 | 21 47 | 21 42 | 20 17 | 7 41 | 21 32 | 26 32 | 4 ♓ 59'24" |
| 8 WE | 15: 2: 9 | 22 47 | 18 16 | 22 8 | 22 15 | 21 47 | 20 19 | 7 42 | 21 33 | 26 32 | 4 ♓ 59'24" |
| 9 TH | 15: 6: 6 | 27 13 | 19 52 | 23 6 | 22 43 | 21 52 | 20 21 | 7 42 | 21 33 | 26 32 | 4 ♓ 59'24" |
| 10 FR | 15:10: 2 | 1 ♓ 48 | 21 27 | 24 4 | 23 11 | 21 57 | 20 22 | 7 43 | 21 33 | 26 33 | 4 ♓ 59'24" |
| 11 SA | 15:13:59 | 6 32 | 23 2 | 25 2 | 23 39 | 22 1 | 20 24 | 7 44 | 21 34 | 26 33 | 4 ♓ 59'24" |
| 12 SU | 15:17:55 | 11 24 | 24 37 | 26 0 | 24 7 | 22 6 | 20 26 | 7 44 | 21 34 | 26 33 | 4 ♓ 59'24" |
| 13 MO | 15:21:52 | 16 26 | 26 13 | 26 58 | 24 35 | 22 11 | 20 28 | 7 45 | 21 34 | 26 34 | 4 ♓ 59'23" |
| 14 TU | 15:25:48 | 21 37 | 27 48 | 27 56 | 25 3 | 22 16 | 20 30 | 7 45 | 21 35 | 26 34 | 4 ♓ 59'23" |
| 15 WE | 15:29:45 | 26 56 | 29 23 | 28 54 | 25 31 | 22 21 | 20 31 | 7 46 | 21 35 | 26 34 | 4 ♓ 59'23" |
| 16 TH | 15:33:42 | 2 ♈ 25 | 0 ♓ 59 | 29 52 | 25 58 | 22 25 | 20 33 | 7 47 | 21 36 | 26 35 | 4 ♓ 59'23" |
| 17 FR | 15:37:38 | 8 2 | 2 34 | 0 ♏ 50 | 26 26 | 22 30 | 20 35 | 7 47 | 21 36 | 26 35 | 4 ♓ 59'23" |
| 18 SA | 15:41:35 | 13 48 | 4 9 | 1 48 | 26 54 | 22 35 | 20 37 | 7 48 | 21 36 | 26 35 | 4 ♓ 59'23" |
| 19 SU | 15:45:31 | 19 42 | 5 45 | 2 45 | 27 22 | 22 40 | 20 39 | 7 49 | 21 37 | 26 35 | 4 ♓ 59'23" |
| 20 MO | 15:49:28 | 25 43 | 7 20 | 3 43 | 27 49 | 22 44 | 20 41 | 7 49 | 21 37 | 26 36 | 4 ♓ 59'22" |
| 21 TU | 15:53:24 | 1 ♉ 50 | 8 56 | 4 41 | 28 17 | 22 49 | 20 42 | 7 50 | 21 37 | 26 36 | 4 ♓ 59'22" |
| 22 WE | 15:57:21 | 8 2 | 10 31 | 5 39 | 28 45 | 22 54 | 20 44 | 7 51 | 21 38 | 26 36 | 4 ♓ 59'22" |
| 23 TH | 16: 1:17 | 14 18 | 12 7 | 6 36 | 29 12 | 22 59 | 20 46 | 7 51 | 21 38 | 26 37 | 4 ♓ 59'22" |
| 24 FR | 16: 5:14 | 20 36 | 13 42 | 7 34 | 29 40 | 23 4 | 20 48 | 7 52 | 21 38 | 26 37 | 4 ♓ 59'22" |
| 25 SA | 16: 9:11 | 26 55 | 15 18 | 8 32 | 0 ♋ 8 | 23 8 | 20 50 | 7 53 | 21 39 | 26 37 | 4 ♓ 59'22" |
| 26 SU | 16:13: 7 | 3 ♊ 14 | 16 53 | 9 29 | 0 35 | 23 13 | 20 51 | 7 53 | 21 39 | 26 38 | 4 ♓ 59'22" |
| 27 MO | 16:17: 4 | 9 31 | 18 29 | 10 27 | 1 3 | 23 18 | 20 53 | 7 54 | 21 40 | 26 38 | 4 ♓ 59'22" |
| 28 TU | 16:21: 0 | 15 44 | 20 5 | 11 24 | 1 30 | 23 23 | 20 55 | 7 55 | 21 40 | 26 38 | 4 ♓ 59'21" |
| 29 WE | 16:24:57 | 21 53 | 21 40 | 12 22 | 1 58 | 23 28 | 20 57 | 7 55 | 21 40 | 26 38 | 4 ♓ 59'21" |
| 30 TH | 16:28:53 | 27 55 | 23 16 | 13 20 | 2 25 | 23 32 | 20 59 | 7 56 | 21 41 | 26 39 | 4 ♓ 59'21" |
| 31 FR | 16:32:50 | 3 ♋ 50 | 24 52 | 14 17 | 2 52 | 23 37 | 21 0 | 7 57 | 21 41 | 26 39 | 4 ♓ 59'21" |

INGRESSES :

| |
|---|
| 2 ☿ → ♒ 8:32 |
| 9 ☿ → ♓ 14:38 |
| 15 ♀ → ♓ 9:15 |
| ☿ → ♈ 13:29 |
| 16 ⊕ → ♏ 3:19 |
| 20 ☿ → ♉ 16:51 |
| 24 ♂ → ♋ 17:24 |
| 25 ☿ → ♊ 11:41 |
| 30 ☿ → ♋ 8:22 |

ASPECTS (HELIOCENTRIC +MOON(TYCHONIC)) :

| | | | | | |
|---|---|---|---|---|---|
| 2 ☽ □ ♂ 15: 9 | ☿ ☌ ♆ 17:12 | ☽ □ ♃ 21:26 | 19 ☿ ☌ ☊ 15:24 | ☿ ☍ ♃ 9:27 | 31 ☽ □ ♂ 0:43 |
| ☽ □ ♄ 15:58 | ☿ □ ♃ 18:26 | 14 ☽ ☍ ♀ 7:35 | 20 ☽ □ ♆ 7:11 | 27 ☽ ☌ ♆ 15:50 | ☽ □ ☿ 4:40 |
| 3 ☽ □ ♇ 4:11 | 9 ☽ ☍ ♄ 11:55 | ☿ □ ♂ 17: 1 | ☽ ☌ ♃ 9:18 | ☽ □ ♃ 19:15 | ☽ ☌ ♅ 10:16 |
| ♂ ☍ ♄ 14:30 | ☽ ☌ ♂ 16:34 | ☿ □ ♇ 22:22 | 21 ☿ ☍ ⊕ 13: 5 | 28 ♀ □ ♄ 12:53 | ☿ □ ♅ 16:59 |
| 4 ☽ ☌ ♅ 1:17 | ☽ ☍ ♇ 22:39 | 15 ☽ □ ♄ 20:59 | ☽ □ ♀ 17:31 | ☿ ☍ ♄ 20:18 | |
| ♃ □ ♆ 17:45 | 10 ♀ ☌ ♆ 1:40 | 16 ☽ □ ♂ 6:20 | 22 ☽ ☌ ♄ 13:56 | ☿ □ ♀ 22:53 | |
| 6 ☿ ☌ ♀ 7:43 | ♀ ⚼ ☊ 6: 1 | ☽ □ ♇ 7: 9 | 23 ☽ ☌ ♇ 1:19 | 29 ☿ ☍ ♇ 18:54 | |
| 7 ☽ □ ♀ 0:45 | ♀ □ ♃ 7:55 | ☿ ☌ ♅ 22:56 | ☽ ☍ ♂ 6:39 | 30 ☽ □ ♄ 1:53 | |
| ☽ □ ☿ 5:37 | ☽ □ ♅ 17:54 | 17 ☽ ☍ ♅ 2:11 | ☽ □ ♅ 23:30 | ☽ ☌ ♀ 7:14 | |
| ☽ □ ♆ 9:19 | 13 ☿ □ ♄ 18:51 | ☽ ☍ ☿ 4:23 | 24 ☿ □ ♆ 3:57 | ☽ □ ♇ 12:49 | |
| ☽ ☍ ♃ 9:40 | ☽ ☍ ♆ 20:18 | ♂ ☍ ♇ 7:34 | ☿ ☌ P 8: 8 | ☿ ☌ ♂ 19:42 | |

body awake to what is occurring, being imprinted by our activity in the night. As the etheric is our memory body, we would be able to recall these nighttime encounters. This is what happened to Nicodemus: he *consciously* conversed with Christ in the night and remembered his conversation.

Later, when Nicodemus would receive the body of Christ from the cross, he would be shattered by what had happened to Jesus. His broken heart then became the iron will that would support him in the work he would do in his later incarnations. Nicodemus thereby became one of the first to swallow the New Testament—i.e., he internalized love. Thus was it written into the great Book of Life that he would be given the destiny task of awaking to the wisdom of the stars as well as the task of guiding others to these mysteries. For the stars are held together by the binding power of love, and each star being is in continual communion with the Being of Love, Christ.

The disciples of the night engaged in a journey of self-discovery. That in them which needed to die away, such as egoism and rigidity, would be illumined. Furthermore, to maintain consciousness in the night they would have to establish a new orientation. Day-consciousness is anchored by spatial orientation. In the night, however, *moral* orientation is necessary, for the ground is no longer firmly beneath our feet. Moral orientation can be practiced by day, as we learn to experience the simultaneity of spiritual dimensions that co-exist in every moment. Even the most minor circumstance may represent a significant spiritual event.

Each of us is one irreplaceable portal leading into the one eternal community of humankind. In like manner, each of the seven sacraments of the Church represents a different portal into one reality—the Great Initiation. Passing through these portals will be the Great Initiation that lies in our future. The Initiator stands above us as the sole Master of Masters. Thus do we not strive to rise above any other in community; rather do we strive to recognize what the other does better than we do. *This practice culls the weight of egoism from us, which would otherwise render the night dark and and the spirit silent.*

The seven sacraments of the Church are the prismatic colors of the white light of one sole Mystery or Sacrament, known as that of the Second Birth, which the Master pointed out to Nicodemus in the nocturnal initiation conversation that He had with him. It is this which Christian Hermeticism understands by the *Great Initiation*.

It goes without saying that nobody initiates anyone else, if we understand by "initiation" the Mystery of the *second birth* or the Great Sacrament. This Initiation is operative from above and has the value and the duration of eternity. The Initiator is above, and here below one meets only the fellow pupils; and they recognize each other by the fact that they "love one another" (John 13:34–35).[1]

The second birth is the birth of water and the spirit. Through this birth, we experience the integration of consciousness, which allows us to awake into nighttime communion—that is, day consciousness unites with night consciousness. This integration is the re-establishment of the state of consciousness that was ours prior to the Fall. Moreover, we are then able to read secrets, i.e., understand the rarified influences that stream from ideals, archetypes, symbols, and arcana. To reach into the Great Initiation, however, we must overcome the trial of our time: the trial of satisfied desires. Where does this end? What can actually satisfy desires born of Mammon?

Everyone will have well-furnished accommodation with a telephone, a radio, a television set, a refrigerator, a washing machine....And what then? Yes, cinema, theatre, concerts, ballet, sport....And what then? Yes, science will furnish new occasions and directions for activity, for the imagination and for desire. One will visit the moon, the planets...And what then? There will be unparalleled adventures to experience and to know about, which as yet we cannot imagine—as, for example, the discovery of the existence of other intelligent beings, other "humankinds" on the planets....And what then? No answer.

No, there is certainly an answer: it is given by the parable of the prodigal son. What is the

---

1 Anon., *Meditations on the Tarot*, p. 4.

value of television sets, washing machines, supersonic aircraft, spaceships, flights to the planets and galactic exploration in comparison with the loving embrace of the Father upon the return of his son to the parental home?[1]

The loneliness of the endless search to satisfy our desires will eventually turn us in a new direction. Already we are experiencing the barrenness of illusion into which we have fallen. This New Moon asks us to reevaluate all things.

**First quarter Moon, May 11, 26° Cancer: Death of the Nathan Mary.**

**Full Moon, May 18, 3° Scorpio: The Resurrection.**

**Last quarter Moon, May 26, 10° Aquarius: The third temptation.**

**Lunar teachings of this cycle** begin with the conversation in the night, seeding new possibilities to those who practice entering consciously into sleep. The first quarter Moon will ask us to act in remembrance of the Death of the Nathan Mary. Her immaculate soul was one with the Angel Jesus and thus was she ever in communion with the night. We too may commend our souls into the waiting arms of angels as we prepare to enter the great School of the Night. The Full Moon remembers the Resurrection of Christ. Are we willing to enter the transformational experience of remembering, each morning, the content of our activity during sleep—i.e., will we resurrect the night into day? The last quarter Moon—as it recalls the third temptation in the wilderness—marks the period of integrating what this lunar cycle has offered. This was the temptation of materialism, of turning life into a caricature of itself (i.e., bread into stone). As we awake to how mechanical and abstract thinking has depersonalized our experience of life, we will turn from the rigidifying "wonders" of virtual imitations and remember what truly sustains us as the Bread of Life

**May 5: ASPECT: Mars 28° Taurus opposite Jupiter 28° Scorpio.** Mars was at this same degree when Jesus spoke with about seventy disciples after their return from their missionary journeys. As Jesus helped at the reception, Peter said, "Lord, do you want to serve? Let us serve!" Jesus replied that he had been sent to serve; he spoke of humility and said that whoever would be first must be the servant of all. He then said that his conception had not been human, but divine—from the Holy Spirit. He spoke with great reverence of his mother, calling her the purest vessel and the holiest of created beings. Also, he referred to the Fall and the ensuing separation from God, adding that he had come to restore the relationship with God (Apr/7/31).

The Archangel Michael standing across from the Holy Spirit bequeaths a benediction on all who dare to act as knights in the great battle of our time—the battle for the human soul. In the Pythagorean school, one was sentenced to five years of silence before one dared to speak. As Mars represents the power of the Word, such a practice ensures that we do not spill arbitrary, meaningless words that compulsively rise from our lower natures. Mars opposite Jupiter is a benevolent influence when we are able to exert self-control, patience, and humility. Inversely, rash and undisciplined actions increase the potential for destructive energies.

Mars in Taurus asks that we practice verbal restraint to listen. In so doing, insights are gained. In exercising "right speech," the earthly Bull nature is elevated so that it can fly with the revelatory gifts of the Eagle (Jupiter in Scorpio).

**May 7: ASPECT: Venus 25° Pisces square Saturn 25° Sagittarius.** Venus remembers the Last Anointing. Mary Magdalene entered the room bearing a costly ointment; she cast herself down at Jesus's feet, weeping as she anointed them. She then dried his feet with her hair. Some of the disciples were irritated with this interruption, but Jesus commanded: "Do not take offense at this woman!" Then he spoke quietly with her, after which she took the remaining ointment and poured it upon his head. Fragrance filled the room. As she attempted to leave them, Judas held out his arm and blocked the way, scolding her for wasting money on the ointment. Later, Judas betrayed Jesus to the Pharisees for thirty pieces of silver (Apr/1/33).

The cross of Venus in dynamic tension with the Holy Virgin (Saturn) calls us into introspective moods of soul. We are so deprived of knowing

---

1 Ibid., p. 597.

how to do this, however, that we often confuse introspection with depression. Thus do we reach for pharmaceuticals when, instead, we could enter contemplation—i.e., devotion to our true destiny. The Holy Virgin leads us from self-absorption to world-interest. Thus do we serve in the outer world that which we are mourning in our inner world. For example: if we find we cannot love ourselves, we are to love others more, for this is the healing counteraction.

Introspection is a powerful state wherein we may discover where we have separated from love, put down our cross, and enfolded within ourselves. What do we need to let die if we are to extend our arms into the world widths by taking up our cross? Magdalene anointed Christ, recognizing him as the Redeemer. We are to find the Christ in all others despite the Judas in us, who would rather mutter and complain against the world's imperfection.

**May 8: Sun 22° Aries: Christ appears to eleven disciples (4/11/33).** The Risen One's first words to those assembled were "Peace be to you." Thomas was among the apostles, and this was when Jesus showed him his wounds. Anne Catherine Emmerich saw the wounds as radiant Suns. Afterward Jesus gave communion to Peter, gracing him with strength and vigor as he breathed upon him. Emmerich witnessed this:

> Jesus put his mouth to Peter's mouth, then to his ears, and poured that strength into each of the three. It was not the Holy Spirit himself, but something that the Holy Spirit was to quicken and vivify in Peter at Pentecost. Jesus laid his hands on him, gave him a special kind of strength, and invested him with chief power over the others.[2]

The sense of hearing is precious beyond measure. We can imagine the Eustachian tubes rising from the larynx, forming the sense of hearing—which in its highest manifestation is able to listen into the inaudible silence whence inspiration resounds. Thus does one hear the beating of the world heart. Now that we are living in the time of the 40th day, the day angels came to minister to Christ, our sense of hearing needs to be protected from the onslaught of continuous noise. For in the silence of the quiet mind we receive angelic messages.

Jesus seemed to bless Peter with the capacity of inspiration, i.e., comprehension of the inaudible. When he breathed into Peter's ears and into his mouth, we can imagine Peter being joined to a larger community—overseen by an Archangel—representing the community of Christians being formed at that time.

We must find reprieve from the serpent's closed circle, in which increasing decibels of ubiquitous noise sentence a deaf humanity to a spiritually silent world. Silence lifts us out of this hellish isolation, opening our ears to realms of inspiration. In this silence we too may hear the greeting of the Risen One: "Peace be to you."

**Mars enters Gemini:** "Reveal thyself, Sun life, set repose in movement, embrace joyful striving **toward life's mighty weaving,** toward blissful world-knowing, toward fruitful ripe-growing. O Sun life, endure!" (Steiner, *Twelve Cosmic Moods*).

**ASPECT: Mercury conjunct Uranus 8° Aries.** Mercury remembers Jesus teaching the disciples on a hill, speaking of the lost sheep, the lost coin (in which Jesus speaks of the importance of searching for a single lost sheep or coin—even if one has many times that), and the ten virgins (of whom five had not brought enough oil to light the way to their bridegrooms). Some Jews from Cyprus came to Jesus to tell him how much they longed to hear him (Apr/21/31).

The pastors and healers (Mercury) are conjunct the mighty revelations in-streaming from the center of our Galaxy (Uranus). This same aspect (also in Aries) occurred at the conception of the Nathan Jesus. Is there a finer example of direct revelation? No, for the Nathan Jesus was an immaculate soul, i.e., formed purely of spiritual substance and free from all aspects of the Fall. He continues to mourn every lost sheep, and he is the oil in all lamps. Do we not long to work with him as ministers of our brothers and sisters? Today, revelation is strengthened.

**May 9: ASPECT: Venus 28° Pisces square Pluto 28° Sagittarius.** Venus shone from this degree as the

---

2 *ACE Complete*, p. 1350.

apostles brought bread and clothing from Sarepta to be distributed to the poor Jews in the settlements (Feb/18/31).

The Venus cross stands in dynamic tension with the ruler of the underworld: Hades/Pluto. From a different vantage, however, we would say the Venus cross stands in dynamic tension with the highest world: Phanes–Pluto, the divine love of the Father.

Venus was in Pisces throughout the entire Passion of Christ. Venus represents the sacred beauty of Love's birth. When she aspects Pluto, she also unmasks the particular quality of love we carry in our hearts, for love has various manifestations. Beauty is the result of light coming to consciousness; when this occurs, the element of constraint lifts from the heart and the cross is taken up. The greater our willingness to take up our cross, the greater is the quality of our love. Love is the vocation of all humanity, and it is active wherever it exists.

The crucifixion exemplified the beauty of love in action. From the cross, Jesus Christ forgave the trespasses of his persecutors. It was due to his purity of soul that he could bear the *world* cross. We are only asked to take up our own cross—to work toward healing our brokenness so that we may serve the world cross.

The "I" of Christ broke into as many fragments as there are individuals in his Father's creation; yet, despite this fact, he was never separated from his wholeness. This applies also to us in our brokenness. *Our imperfections are wounds seeking the light, and we must remember that we are never separate from our creator.* This realization gives us courage to accept ourselves exactly as we are. In so doing, our angel leads us to all that prevents us from taking up our beds (i.e., our karma) and walking forward.

When Venus squares Pluto, a choice stands before us: Will we gather *darkness* from Hades, or *light* from Phanes? The former choice will further fracture our emotional life, while the latter will reveal to us the actions necessary if we are willing to tread the path toward the Way, the Truth, and the Life that destiny has prepared for us. We can pray that we will not be abandoned unto temptation, but that we will instead be delivered from our soul's estrangement from itself.

Venus in Pisces inspires love of our neighbors as well as of our enemies; most poignantly, it also inspires love for oneself. In such magnanimity we are willing to "suffer with the world."

**May 11: Sun 25° Aries: Christ appears to seven disciples (4/15/33). Feed my sheep.** This occurred at the northeast end of the Sea of Galilee (John 21:1–23). Here Peter is bid three times to "feed my sheep." In his three responses, Peter is healed from his three denials of Jesus. He is given the task to be the spiritual leader of the exoteric Church, to ensure that the sacraments, Holy Communion above all, continue to be celebrated for all time. Peter asks what will become of John, and the Risen One answers: "If it is my will that he remain until I come, what is that to you?" Implicit here is the task of the esoteric Church of John, which was to await the Second Coming of Christ in the etheric realm. The Church of Peter has the task to lead human beings *to* the threshold of the spiritual world, and the Church of John has the task of leading them *across* the threshold into the spiritual world. We are living in a time when all of humanity is crossing the threshold, a time when the Angel Jesus is so very near to us. For we are entering into the new mysteries of the Holy Grail: the mystery of the fifth light, of the moral ether. Corresponding to the Mass in the exoteric church of Peter is the Grail Mystery in the esoteric church of John— both of which always work together.

At this appearance, the Risen One offered the fish communion to his disciples. *The Fish Communion opens a pathway that streams upward by way of the feet, representing a communion with the interior of the Earth.*

The Risen One introduced the "Fish Communion" on the shores of the Galilee, opening communion with the mysteries of the inner Earth. He had already passed through the nine evil subearthly layers of the inner Earth during his descent into Hell. Thus could he now manifest the communion of fish as the antidote to the evil influences rising from these realms. The Fish Communion is especially beneficial for communities, for it weaves the protective forces of love around the circle.

Evil always seeks entrance into communities whose mission is awaking to the new light. It is able to enter through its weakest link. Judas was the weakest link in the circle of disciples. Not only must we guard against the Judas without, we must also take care that we ourselves do not become the Judas from within.

John's task is to protect communities gathering in awareness of the Second Coming. This fact signals the importance of maintaining harmony in community regardless of how cunningly divisive forces storm around us. When communities are committed to loving each other, they swim together in a sea of warmth directly streaming from the Angel Jesus.

**Venus enters Aries: "Take hold of growth's being"** (Steiner, *Twelve Cosmic Moods*).

**First Quarter Moon, 26° Cancer: Death of the Nathan Mary (Aug/5/12).** On this day, the Moon, Mars, and Mercury were conjunct.

The seeds planted at the New Moon are to be acted upon. Have we practiced entering more consciously into sleep, in devotion to the conversations we will enter there? Awaking to the night is tantamount to awaking into Kamaloka, for sleep is the little brother of death.

The Nathan Mary was continuously in conversation with the night, for her immaculate heart knew no sin. *Sin is what shatters the integration of consciousness.* Yet, as we live in the time where *dharma* triumphs over *karma*—as we have entered into the Satya Yuga—we are not to fear the separateness our errors have caused; rather are we to celebrate the victory achieved when the darkness of sin rises into the light of consciousness.

**May 12: Sun 26°50' Aries: Christ appears to five hundred (4/16/33).** The Risen One appeared to the five hundred two weeks after the Last Supper. This was one of approximately ten appearances (following the Resurrection) recorded in the Gospels.

Peter and many disciples were together. Many people came to hear from them regarding the death and resurrection of Jesus Christ. As Peter was addressing the crowd, a radiant figure passed through their midst. Peter moved aside and the Lord took his place. Jesus spoke of the persecutions that would befall his followers, and he also spoke of the promised rewards in heaven that would result.

We can remember that persecutions do befall many of those daring to speak truths. We do not, however, work for personal reward. Rather do we ceaselessly work on behalf of spiritual necessity. Thus are we called to bring the new mysteries to light, regardless of those who spurn them. Indeed, Christ stands in the midst of both believers and non-believers.

The age of the consciousness soul must become *the age of the soul's conscience* if we are to maintain faith in our eventual encounter with the Risen One.

**May 15: Sun enters Taurus: "Become bright, radiant being,** feel growth's power. Weave life's thread in creative world existence, in thoughtful revelation, in shining life-contemplation. O radiant being, appear!" (Steiner, *Twelve Cosmic Moods*). The late William Bento illumines this mantra:

> The shining light is here defined as a glorious being. It is not a phenomenon dissected as a scientific empirical fact. It is alive with beingness. And surrounding this being is an aura of glory. Can you now gaze at the Sun with new eyes? Can you now look into another's eyes and see a glimmer of this glorious being? When this indeed occurs in our seeing, we can experience the awe, wonder and reverence of the sacredness of the "I/Thou" consciousness out of which each human being shines forth.

In Taurus, Inner Balance becomes Progress. The work of transforming the will is paramount. The first decan is ruled by Venus and is associated with Perseus, who was helped by Athena to overcome the Medusa.

**May 18: ASPECT: Full Moon 3° Scorpio opposite Sun 3° Taurus: the Moon recalls the Resurrection of Jesus Christ (Apr/5/33).** The fullness of this lunar cycle rests upon the seeds planted at the New Moon, which directed us to the conversation in the night between Nicodemus and Jesus. We were guided to contemplate the loneliness of a soul whose barren desires render the night empty. Did we reevaluate what is important in our life? Did the first quarter Moon set action in motion, whereby we heightened our conscious approach to sleep in memory of the immaculate soul of the Nathan Mary? She is a primary example of one whose consciousness was integrated.

As the Full Moon illumines the night sky, we remember the Resurrection. Moreover, as this Moon is in Scorpio, we can ask ourselves: What is hidden? Where are we ensnared in regions that imprison our light? To regain this light, we must raise ourselves from three different regions of unconsciousness: forgetting, sleep, and death. Juxtaposed to these areas of unconsciousness are remembering, awaking, and rebirth (i.e., resurrection). We resurrect memory, we resurrect from sleep, and we resurrect into a life in spirit upon our physical death. Yet beyond physical death are the dead regions to which we have relegated our consciousness, resulting in a kind of psychic and even moral layer of entombment.

> Similarly, beyond clinical death there is a psychic death and a moral death. During our seventy or eighty years of life, we bear within us layers of death in our psychic being. There are things which are missing from our psychic and moral being. The *absence* of faith, hope, and love cannot be remedied either by arguments or by exhortations or even by a living example. An act of divine magic—or grace—is necessary to accomplish the *infusion* of life into that which is dead. And if Christ is worshipped as the Risen One, it is because those who bear death within them know that it is only divine magic that can raise what is dead within them, and that the risen Christ is the guarantor of this.[1]

As we enter sleep each night, only free consciousness can participate in Night School. The aspects of the self that have been subtracted from our consciousness inevitably reduce our ability to engage in conversations of the night. We must continually ask: What do we *not* know? What lies hidden? We must seek to understand these things. To find the answer to such questions turns us from *ordinary* memory, working in the horizontal stream of time, to *extraordinary* memory, working within the vertical stream of time. The former marks the life of day-consciousness; the latter marks the life of night-consciousness, i.e., in suprasensory realms. Vertical consciousness remembers everything, inclusive of all the light we have buried as well as all the light we bore to Earth as we descended into matter. Thus is vertical memory a *moral* memory:

> The following reveals it to its highest conceivable degree—other degrees being only its analogous, weakened manifestations:
>
>> Now Jesus *loved* Martha and her sister and Lazarus...when Jesus came, he found that Lazarus had already been in the tomb four days....Jesus wept....Then Jesus, deeply moved again, came to the tomb; it was a cave, and a stone lay upon it. Jesus said: *Take away the stone*....So they took away the stone...Jesus *cried with a loud voice: Lazarus, come out*. The dead man came out, his hands and feet bound with bandages, and his face wrapped with a cloth. (John 11:5–44)
>
> Here is the *force of recall* in its most complete, most strong and most elevated manifestation. It is *love,* for "Jesus loved Martha and her sister and Lazarus."[2]

The power of this recall is the power of resurrection. It comprises three stages: Jesus came, he removed the stone from the tomb, and he cried out in a loud voice. If we consciously approach the threshold between day and night, we have come. Furthermore, if we vanquish the force of doubt, cynicism, and fear, we remove the stone, allowing night's door to open. Moreover, if we cry out in a loud voice, the reverberations engender a response from our angel: we are greeted. The question remains: Can we remember? Recall of our night activity is the miracle of resurrection, in that it is a manifestation of this world of *invisible suprasenible causation.*

> All that is not mechanical—physical, psychic and intellectual—is miraculous, and all that is not miraculous is only mechanical—physical, psychic and intellectual. Freedom is a miracle, and the human being is only free in so far as he or she is not a machine—physical, psychic and intellectual. We have no other choice than between the machine and slavery, on the one

---

1  Anon., *Meditations on the Tarot*, p. 343.

2  Ibid, 348.

hand, and the miracle and freedom, on the other hand.[3]

How clearly this expresses the magnitude of effort required if we are to resurrect from the tomb all in us that we have subtracted from consciousness! For, what we have subtracted will be needed if we are to cross the threshold and resurrect our consciousness from night into day. The threads that bind us to the darkness of the unconscious tether us in such a way that we can be cruel, aggressive, pathetic, or ignorant toward those we fear are our enemies. We recall, however, the teaching of the Master: We are to love our enemies, do good to those who hate us, and bless those who curse us, and even pray for those who persecute us. Thus, he tells us, we become sons and daughters of our Father in Heaven.

This Full Moon flowers in the transformative experience of remembering that our consciousness was once integrated, and we did not know death. It is Lucifer who tore time's continuity to pieces. We must reestablish this. Our one mission on Earth is to love one another as well as love the mission of the Earth. Indeed, this is the power behind all resurrection.

Death is the guardian of the threshold, who assures that those unworthy will not gain conscious entrance into its sanctuary. The guardian causes forgetting, sleep, and—if necessary—death. For no one can storm the gates of heaven! Moral endeavor, *by day*, is the key that opens the secrets of the night.

The Scorpio Moon asks us to open the night and read the Book. As we gather manna from the night, we elevate the scorpion to the rank of eagle.

**ASPECT 2: Venus conjunct Uranus 9°Aries.** Venus remembers the Ascension of Jesus Christ (May/14/33). When the cross of Venus communes with Uranus, the soul yearns for something new. If this yearning turns to the material world for satisfaction, it will find a thirst that cannot be quenched. If, on the other hand, the yearning soul turns to spiritual worlds for satisfaction, it will find freedom from all thirst. From the cross, Jesus spoke: "Behold thy son, behold thy mother." Not only was he referring to Lazarus (who was Cain), and Mary (who was Eve), who stood at the foot of the cross. No, he was also referring to the dead entombed within us, to whom we are both mother and son, as well as father and daughter. Ahriman stands as the surrogate guardian of the inner Earth graveyard. Love raises the dead, freeing the ahrimanic—after which we gladly pick up our cross. Then can we be assured that the new imaginations Uranus bestows are pure, and not the inflating illusions of the serpent.

The Ascension of Christ opened the gates of heaven for all time. And the light thus released illumines even the ahrimanic graveyards within the inner Earth. Therefore, we behold what seeks to be unmasked to receive undistorted revelation.

**Mercury enters Taurus:** "Become bright, radiant being, feel growth's power. **Weave life's thread** in creative world existence, in thoughtful revelation, in shining life-contemplation. O radiant being, appear!" (Steiner, *Twelve Cosmic Moods*).

**May 21: ASPECT: Superior conjunction of Sun and Mercury 5° Taurus: the *Pleiades*.** Mercury recalls Jesus spending the whole day at Lazarus's castle in Bethany. The Pharisees, thinking he was at the home of Mary Mark, went there to take him into custody. There they found only his mother, Mary, and the holy women. After telling them to leave the city, the Pharisees went away. The women hurried to Bethany, where they found Martha together with Silent Mary. A few hours later, Silent Mary died in the presence of the Holy Virgin. That same evening Nicodemus came to Bethany and talked privately with Jesus through the night (Apr/8/30).

Five days before the last quarter Moon, we again hear of Nicodemus and the nighttime conversations that inaugurated this lunar cycle.

The Pleiades are the seven sisters of harmony. Mercury, on the far side of the Sun, is gathering cosmic forces of intuition that will fall upon us like rain as the inferior conjunction occurs July 21st.

There will always be Pharisees of one kind or another who work against the light of revelation, which is the main characteristic of Sun conjunct Mercury. The ones we are to fear most, however, are the ones that live *in* us. Once we have silenced

---

3 Ibid., pp. 349–350.

them within, they are rendered impotent in the outer world.

When we open to the healing ministrations of Mercury, we become healers. Thus does our work begin as we oppose the dark knights of depersonalization: the abstract and mechanical thinking so prevalent today. We are to hold fast to the crown of our enchristed self so as to gather the cosmic secrets this aspect bestows.

**May 26: Last Quarter Moon 10° Aquarius:** *Deneb*. The Moon was at this zodiacal longitude early on the day of the third temptation in the wilderness (Nov/29/29). We enter the conclusion of this lunar cycle with the temptation of Ahriman, who wanted Christ to turn stones to bread. This temptation has everything to do with money, greed, and the enormity of the economic reductionism that currently rules the world.

Deneb is a mega star marking the tail of the Swan at the head of the Northern Cross. This star is visible in the summer triangle along with Vega and Altair in the constellation of the Eagle. The Sun was conjunct Deneb at the feeding of the five thousand: this was a miracle expressing the course of evolution in space, i.e., the vertical evolution of human consciousness from its present focus on the physical world to its future focus in ever higher realms of spirit. The Sun remained in conjunction with Deneb at the walking on water, which occurred after sundown following the feeding of the five thousand. Obviously this is a very powerful mega star.

The Moon conjunct Deneb asks us where egoism is eclipsing receptivity to our higher self. Moreover, this conjunction asks what ghosts and specters have seized hold of us, dragging us into lower realms of consciousness that ensnare us in under-worldly fixations.

Have we re-evaluated all things so that we might approach the night with some measure of consciousness? Have we gathered the courage to meet death, i.e., the guardian of the threshold between day and night? Have we resurrected any measure of light that has been subtracted from us? These were the questions of the New Moon, the first quarter Moon, and the Full Moon. All our efforts now allow us to meet an aspect of our ahrimanic double—the part of us that has turned its back on spirit. For there is our spiritual brother, i.e., the Lesser Guardian of the Threshold, and then there is the guardian of the graveyard, the *surrogate* guardian, who lures us to believe in matter over and above spirit. *"O dry bones, hear the word of the Lord"* (Ez. 27:4).

**May 29: ASPECT: Mercury 23° Taurus square Neptune 23° Aquarius.** Mercury was at Neptune's degree as Jesus healed in a town marketplace. Jesus cured one man suffering from a crippled arm and deaf-and-dumbness. The man then turned to the pagans and Jews and began to speak prophetically: "The food that you, the children of the house, reject, we outcasts shall gather up. We shall live upon it and give thanks. What you allow to go to waste of the bread of heaven will be to us the fruit of the crumbs that we gather up" (Feb/13/31). Neptune illumines the quiet mind, while confusing the restless mind.

**May 30: ASPECT: Mercury 26° Taurus opposite Jupiter 26° Scorpio.** The Sun at Jupiter's degree recalls the day Jesus went to the home of a leper and healed him. Jesus and the disciples then walked to Capernaum, where Jesus taught in the synagogue. As he was leaving, two lepers came to him. Trembling, they sank down on their knees before him. Jesus then laid his hands upon them, breathed upon the face of each, and said: "Your sins are forgiven!" The Pharisees questioned by what right he was able to forgive sins (Nov/17/30). Benevolent Jupiter across the heavens from Mercury brings optimism to the humble and meek, while perhaps inflating those less disciplined. Under the influence of this aspect, forgiveness comes easily.

# JUNE 2019

## Stargazing Preview

This month begins with the Moon rising just ahead of Venus at 0430; they reach conjunction later on the 1st. The Moon catches up with the Sun on the 3rd, the day before Venus enters Taurus. After sunset on the 5th, look for Mars in the southwest, slightly to the right of the Moon: they set at 2200.

Jupiter will be "Full" on the 10th, meaning that the Sun at 24° Taurus will be directly opposite Jupiter. You'll be able to watch Jupiter rise at 2000. On the 14th, Mars will be opposite Saturn! You can imagine them at contrary ends of a seesaw: as Mars again sets at 2200, Saturn will rise in the east.

The Moon becomes Full on the 17th in the first degree of Sagittarius, then conjuncts Saturn the following day. The 23rd brings us another opposition–this time between Venus and Jupiter. Venus crests the eastern horizon an hour ahead of the Sun, and you'll be able to see Jupiter low in the east after sunset. And don't forget to look above the western horizon for a glimpse of Mars as he enters Cancer–you'll have about and hour and a half to see him before he sets. Venus, getting ever closer to the Sun, enters Gemini on the 29th.

## June Commentaries

**Jun 2: Mercury enters Gemini:** "Reveal thyself, Sun life; set repose in movement; **embrace joyful striving** toward life's mighty weaving, toward blissful world-knowing, toward fruitful ripe-growing. O Sun life, endure!" (Steiner, *Twelve Cosmic Moods*). Mercury rules in this sign.

**Jun 3: ASPECT: New Moon 18° Taurus: Healing of three blind boys.** Three blind boys playing flutes were led into the room where Jesus and the disciples were eating their midday meal. Jesus asked them if they would like to see the light; and then, much to their joy, he healed them (May/10/31).

A new lunar cycle begins, remembering the restoration of sight to the blind. The boys needed only to answer one simple question: *Would you like to see the light?* Imagine the Angel Jesus, as he radiates the light of the fifth sacrifice upon all humanity, asking us this same simple question.

Indwelling the constellation of Taurus are star beings who form the larynx: the fifth chakra. This lotus flower is related to the "Good Shepherd." It is he who walks upon the etheric watery element without fear, for he knows not any soul agitation. He is the sinless one, guiding us to calm shores of peace. The Good Shepherd speaks: "Be not afraid, it is I."

The Taurus beings remind us that the Good Shepherd eternally lives as the source of all courage. Every time we call a lost part of ourselves into consciousness, we walk on water. For it is only the true "I" that can do this, and every "I" is a spark from the divine "I" of the Good Shepherd. Thus are the beings of this constellation related to the Word—a creative substance that actually creates new "I"-forces. Yet if one speaks, one must also be able to hear; therefore do these mighty beings also teach us to listen.

The Good Shepherd walks with us when we overcome our fear. Moreover, he is the force that works into us when we call our soul's darkness into the light, i.e., when we resurrect our dead.

> There is no idea and ideal more bold, more contrary to all empirical experience, and more shocking to common sense than that of resurrection. Indeed, the idea and ideal of resurrection presupposes a force of soul which renders it capable: not only of emancipation from the hypnotizing influence of the totality of empirical facts, i.e., of breaking away from the world; not only of deciding to take part in the evolution of the world—that is to say, no longer in the capacity of an object of the world but also, and rather, as a subject, i.e., of becoming a motivating spirit instead of a "moved" spirit; not only of participating actively in the process of world evolution; but also of raising oneself to conscious participation in the work of divine magic—the magical operation on a cosmic scale whose aim is resurrection.[1]

The work of resurrection presupposes the union of divine will with human will, for this is the formula that births sacred magic; *it is the miracle of becoming an active instrument of the divine*. Thus do we matriculate from a "moved spirit," to a "motivating spirit."

Affirmatively answering the simple question not only opens our spiritual eye, it also appoints us the task of creating new "I" forces. This we do when we fearlessly engage in right speech. Creating "I"

---

1 Anon., *Meditations on the Tarot*, p. 558.

forces is the solution to the social trials of our time. When our speech creates vessels into which the Good Shepherd may enter, we rise above social discord—i.e., we walk on water.

Where are the forces supporting us to be found? They are twofold. From above, rays of light descend, pregnant with the fire of our divine "I." And from below, waves of warmth ascend, pregnant with the power of the Mother. Thus, from the crown of our heads and from the bottom of our feet, forces support us when we take responsibility for the fact that we are creative beings who determine social well-being. Accepting this, however, means that we are willing to swallow the Book wherein all our errors have been recorded. It is so sweet on the tongue, for we realize that we are "born from the divine"; yet it is so bitter in our stomachs, for we must digest the sorrowful abuses that we have rendered against our divinity. In this Book are inscribed our transgressions, which appear quite fixed due to the blackness of the ink. Yet we must fear not, for all that has been recorded constitutes that which is worthy of resurrection—i.e., that which sustains the *world memory*. Thus have been preserved the precious—and still living—dead, assuring that they will not disappear from the chronicle of the world. "Fear not," proclaims the Good Shepherd, for the dead letters scribed in the black ink are naught but the temporary paralysis of mortal sin at rest. As we resurrect the karma we have contributed to this Book, we change the world—we become authors of the world's becoming—we become "motivators."

This New Moon reminds us that during this time of the Satya Yuga, the karma we have inscribed into the Book of Life (representing the moral chronicle) is not a judgment against us; rather is it the means of our salvation. For, in raising error to the light of day, we activate our inherent ability to recall our dead to life. *This* is resurrection. What previously contributed to the anxiety of the world is then erased, as mercy enters our redeeming deeds into the Book. And what is the cause of world anxiety if not the agitating forces released as the dead cry out for salvation? "Resurrection is not an all-powerful divine act, but rather the effect of the meeting and union of divine love, hope, and faith with human love, hope, and faith."[1]

This New Moon reminds us that we have the creative power to work with the Good Shepherd to restore the holy waters that constitute the collective soul of humankind.

**First quarter Moon, 24° Leo: Healing of the Essenes daughter.**

**Full Moon, 1° Sagittarius: Healing of Theokeno.**

**Last quarter Moon, 9° Pisces: Jesus converses with some of his disciples regarding his entry into Jerusalem.**

**Lunar teachings of this cycle** begin with the healing of three blind boys under the mighty influence of the star beings indwelling the constellation of Taurus. We are asked to unite our will with divine will, to create "I" forces through the power of the cosmic Word, and to practice using this force to raise the dead in us. As the first quarter Moon dawns, and as we contemplate the raising of the daughter of the Essene, what we have put into action will return as inspiration. She is a symbol for our mortal sin becoming effaced from the Book of Life—i.e., being raised from the dead. The transforming powers of the Full Moon remind us of Mensor, the Gold King, and the treasures of ancient star wisdom he represents. For when we work with the Book of Life, we enter the mysteries of the starry heavens. As the final quarter Moon dawns, we prepare to enter the path leading to the new Jerusalem—i.e., to join the congregation of the faithful who have severed their bondage to *maya* and have thus opened their spiritual eye.

**Jun 4: Venus enters Taurus:** "Become bright, O Radiance of Being. **Feel growth's power.** Weave life's thread in creative world existence, in thoughtful revelation, in shining life-contemplation. O Radiance of Being, appear!" (Steiner, *Twelve Cosmic Moods*). Venus is in rulership in this sign.

**Jun 9: Christian celebration of Pentecost.** See commentary for June 18 (cosmic Pentecost).

**ASPECT: Sun 23° Taurus square Neptune 23° Aquarius: Ascension of Jesus Christ** (May/14/33). The Sun remembers the Ascension of Christ. The

---
1 Ibid., pp, 571-572.

SIDEREAL GEOCENTRIC LONGITUDES : JUNE 2019 Gregorian at 0 hours UT

| DAY | ☉ | ☽ | ☊ | ☿ | ♀ | ♂ | ♃ | ♄ | ♅ | ♆ | ♇ |
|---|---|---|---|---|---|---|---|---|---|---|---|
| 1 SA | 15 ♉ 14 | 15 ♈ 19 | 23 ♊ 11R | 27 ♉ 33 | 25 ♈ 10 | 15 ♊ 12 | 25 ♏ 41R | 24 ♐ 43R | 9 ♈ 39 | 23 ♒ 36 | 27 ♐ 49R |
| 2 SU | 16 12 | 28 26 | 23 4 | 29 33 | 26 23 | 15 51 | 25 34 | 24 40 | 9 42 | 23 37 | 27 48 |
| 3 MO | 17 9 | 11 ♉ 52 | 22 59 | 1 ♊ 30 | 27 36 | 16 29 | 25 26 | 24 37 | 9 45 | 23 38 | 27 47 |
| 4 TU | 18 7 | 25 34 | 22 55 | 3 25 | 28 49 | 17 8 | 25 19 | 24 34 | 9 48 | 23 38 | 27 46 |
| 5 WE | 19 4 | 9 ♊ 30 | 22 53 | 5 18 | 0 ♉ 2 | 17 46 | 25 11 | 24 31 | 9 51 | 23 39 | 27 45 |
| 6 TH | 20 2 | 23 36 | 22 52 | 7 8 | 1 15 | 18 25 | 25 4 | 24 28 | 9 53 | 23 39 | 27 44 |
| 7 FR | 20 59 | 7 ♋ 49 | 22 53D | 8 55 | 2 28 | 19 3 | 24 56 | 24 24 | 9 56 | 23 40 | 27 43 |
| 8 SA | 21 56 | 22 4 | 22 54 | 10 40 | 3 41 | 19 42 | 24 48 | 24 21 | 9 59 | 23 40 | 27 42 |
| 9 SU | 22 54 | 6 ♌ 20 | 22 56 | 12 22 | 4 54 | 20 20 | 24 41 | 24 18 | 10 2 | 23 41 | 27 41 |
| 10 MO | 23 51 | 20 34 | 22 56 | 14 2 | 6 8 | 20 59 | 24 33 | 24 14 | 10 4 | 23 41 | 27 40 |
| 11 TU | 24 49 | 4 ♍ 43 | 22 56R | 15 39 | 7 21 | 21 37 | 24 25 | 24 11 | 10 7 | 23 41 | 27 38 |
| 12 WE | 25 46 | 18 46 | 22 54 | 17 13 | 8 34 | 22 15 | 24 18 | 24 7 | 10 10 | 23 42 | 27 37 |
| 13 TH | 26 43 | 2 ♎ 40 | 22 52 | 18 45 | 9 47 | 22 54 | 24 10 | 24 3 | 10 12 | 23 42 | 27 36 |
| 14 FR | 27 41 | 16 25 | 22 48 | 20 14 | 11 0 | 23 32 | 24 2 | 24 0 | 10 15 | 23 42 | 27 35 |
| 15 SA | 28 38 | 29 57 | 22 45 | 21 40 | 12 13 | 24 10 | 23 55 | 23 56 | 10 18 | 23 42 | 27 34 |
| 16 SU | 29 35 | 13 ♏ 16 | 22 42 | 23 3 | 13 26 | 24 49 | 23 47 | 23 52 | 10 20 | 23 43 | 27 32 |
| 17 MO | 0 ♊ 32 | 26 19 | 22 39 | 24 23 | 14 40 | 25 27 | 23 40 | 23 48 | 10 23 | 23 43 | 27 31 |
| 18 TU | 1 30 | 9 ♐ 7 | 22 38 | 25 41 | 15 53 | 26 5 | 23 32 | 23 45 | 10 25 | 23 43 | 27 30 |
| 19 WE | 2 27 | 21 40 | 22 37D | 26 55 | 17 6 | 26 44 | 23 25 | 23 41 | 10 27 | 23 43 | 27 29 |
| 20 TH | 3 24 | 3 ♑ 59 | 22 38 | 28 7 | 18 19 | 27 22 | 23 17 | 23 37 | 10 30 | 23 43 | 27 27 |
| 21 FR | 4 21 | 16 5 | 22 39 | 29 15 | 19 32 | 28 0 | 23 10 | 23 33 | 10 32 | 23 43 | 27 26 |
| 22 SA | 5 19 | 28 3 | 22 40 | 0 ♋ 21 | 20 46 | 28 38 | 23 2 | 23 29 | 10 34 | 23 43R | 27 25 |
| 23 SU | 6 16 | 9 ♒ 56 | 22 42 | 1 23 | 21 59 | 29 17 | 22 55 | 23 24 | 10 37 | 23 43 | 27 23 |
| 24 MO | 7 13 | 21 47 | 22 43 | 2 22 | 23 12 | 29 55 | 22 48 | 23 20 | 10 39 | 23 43 | 27 22 |
| 25 TU | 8 10 | 3 ♓ 41 | 22 43 | 3 18 | 24 26 | 0 ♋ 33 | 22 41 | 23 16 | 10 41 | 23 43 | 27 21 |
| 26 WE | 9 8 | 15 44 | 22 43R | 4 10 | 25 39 | 1 11 | 22 34 | 23 12 | 10 43 | 23 43 | 27 19 |
| 27 TH | 10 5 | 27 58 | 22 42 | 4 59 | 26 52 | 1 49 | 22 27 | 23 8 | 10 45 | 23 43 | 27 18 |
| 28 FR | 11 2 | 10 ♈ 30 | 22 41 | 5 44 | 28 5 | 2 28 | 22 20 | 23 3 | 10 48 | 23 42 | 27 16 |
| 29 SA | 11 59 | 23 22 | 22 40 | 6 25 | 29 19 | 3 6 | 22 13 | 22 59 | 10 50 | 23 42 | 27 15 |
| 30 SU | 12 56 | 6 ♉ 35 | 22 39 | 7 2 | 0 ♊ 32 | 3 44 | 22 6 | 22 55 | 10 52 | 23 42 | 27 14 |

INGRESSES :

| | |
|---|---|
| 2 ☽ → ♉ 2:49 | 19 ☽ → ♑ 16:12 |
| ☿ → ♊ 5:32 | 21 ☿ → ♋ 16:14 |
| 4 ☽ → ♊ 7:40 | 22 ☽ → ♒ 3:55 |
| ♀ → ♉ 23:18 | 24 ♂ → ♋ 3:16 |
| 6 ☽ → ♋ 10:49 | ☽ → ♓ 16:35 |
| 8 ☽ → ♌ 13:20 | 27 ☽ → ♈ 3:55 |
| 10 ☽ → ♍ 15:59 | 29 ☽ → ♉ 12: 7 |
| 12 ☽ → ♎ 19:22 | ♀ → ♊ 13:27 |
| 15 ☽ → ♏ 0: 5 | |
| 16 ☉ → ♊ 10:25 | |
| 17 ☽ → ♐ 6:51 | |

ASPECTS & ECLIPSES :

| | | | |
|---|---|---|---|
| 1 ☽ ☌ ♀ 19:54 | ☉ □ ☽ 5:58 | 17 ☉ ☍ ☽ 8:29 | 24 ☽ ☌ ♆ 3:55 |
| 3 ☉ ☌ ☽ 10: 0 | ☉ ☍ ♃ 15:27 | 18 ☿ ☌ ♂ 16: 3 | ♀ □ ♆ 10: 4 |
| ☽ ☍ ♃ 23:33 | 12 ☽ ⊓N ☊ 7: 6 | 19 ☽ ☌ ☋ 1:51 | 25 ☉ □ ☽ 9:45 |
| 4 ☽ ☌ ☿ 15:40 | ♂ ☌ ☊ 22:51 | ☽ ☌ ♄ 3:52 | 26 ☽ ⊓S ☊ 13:44 |
| 5 ☽ ☌ ♂ 14:46 | 13 ☽ ☍ ♅ 13: 9 | ☽ ☍ ♂ 10:21 | 28 ☽ ☌ ♅ 0:33 |
| ☽ ☌ ☊ 22:45 | 14 ♂ ☍ ♄ 15:49 | ☿ ☍ ♇ 10:51 | |
| 6 ☽ ☍ ♄ 1:26 | 15 ☿ ☌ ☊ 18: 1 | ☽ ☌ ♇ 11:15 | |
| ☽ ☍ ♇ 6:59 | 16 ☽ ☍ ♀ 0:21 | ☽ ☍ ☿ 11:18 | |
| 7 ☽ ☌ P 23:13 | ☿ ☍ ♄ 13:59 | 20 ♂ ☍ ♇ 3:18 | |
| 9 ☉ □ ♆ 19:42 | ♃ □ ♆ 14:13 | 23 ☽ ☌ A 8:18 | |
| 10 ☽ ☍ ♆ 5:16 | ☽ ☌ ♃ 19: 7 | ♀ ☍ ♃ 16:44 | |

SIDEREAL HELIOCENTRIC LONGITUDES : JUNE 2019 Gregorian at 0 hours UT

| DAY | Sid. Time | ☿ | ♀ | ⊕ | ♂ | ♃ | ♄ | ♅ | ♆ | ♇ | Vernal Point |
|---|---|---|---|---|---|---|---|---|---|---|---|
| 1 SA | 16:36:46 | 9 ♋ 38 | 26 ♓ 27 | 15 ♏ 15 | 3 ♋ 20 | 23 ♏ 42 | 21 ♐ 2 | 7 ♈ 57 | 21 ♒ 41 | 26 ♐ 39 | 4 ♓ 59'21" |
| 2 SU | 16:40:43 | 15 16 | 28 3 | 16 12 | 3 47 | 23 47 | 21 4 | 7 58 | 21 42 | 26 40 | 4 ♓ 59'21" |
| 3 MO | 16:44:39 | 20 45 | 29 39 | 17 10 | 4 14 | 23 52 | 21 6 | 7 59 | 21 42 | 26 40 | 4 ♓ 59'21" |
| 4 TU | 16:48:36 | 26 5 | 1 ♈ 15 | 18 7 | 4 42 | 23 56 | 21 8 | 7 59 | 21 42 | 26 40 | 4 ♓ 59'20" |
| 5 WE | 16:52:33 | 1 ♌ 15 | 2 51 | 19 5 | 5 9 | 24 1 | 21 9 | 8 0 | 21 43 | 26 41 | 4 ♓ 59'20" |
| 6 TH | 16:56:29 | 6 16 | 4 26 | 20 2 | 5 36 | 24 6 | 21 11 | 8 1 | 21 43 | 26 41 | 4 ♓ 59'20" |
| 7 FR | 17: 0:26 | 11 7 | 6 2 | 21 0 | 6 3 | 24 11 | 21 13 | 8 1 | 21 44 | 26 41 | 4 ♓ 59'20" |
| 8 SA | 17: 4:22 | 15 48 | 7 38 | 21 57 | 6 31 | 24 15 | 21 15 | 8 2 | 21 44 | 26 42 | 4 ♓ 59'20" |
| 9 SU | 17: 8:19 | 20 21 | 9 14 | 22 54 | 6 58 | 24 20 | 21 17 | 8 3 | 21 44 | 26 42 | 4 ♓ 59'20" |
| 10 MO | 17:12:15 | 24 44 | 10 50 | 23 52 | 7 25 | 24 25 | 21 18 | 8 3 | 21 45 | 26 42 | 4 ♓ 59'20" |
| 11 TU | 17:16:12 | 29 0 | 12 26 | 24 49 | 7 52 | 24 30 | 21 20 | 8 4 | 21 45 | 26 42 | 4 ♓ 59'19" |
| 12 WE | 17:20: 8 | 3 ♍ 7 | 14 2 | 25 46 | 8 19 | 24 35 | 21 22 | 8 5 | 21 45 | 26 43 | 4 ♓ 59'19" |
| 13 TH | 17:24: 5 | 7 7 | 15 38 | 26 44 | 8 46 | 24 39 | 21 24 | 8 5 | 21 46 | 26 43 | 4 ♓ 59'19" |
| 14 FR | 17:28: 2 | 11 0 | 17 14 | 27 41 | 9 13 | 24 44 | 21 26 | 8 6 | 21 46 | 26 43 | 4 ♓ 59'19" |
| 15 SA | 17:31:58 | 14 47 | 18 50 | 28 38 | 9 40 | 24 49 | 21 28 | 8 6 | 21 46 | 26 44 | 4 ♓ 59'19" |
| 16 SU | 17:35:55 | 18 27 | 20 26 | 29 36 | 10 7 | 24 54 | 21 29 | 8 7 | 21 47 | 26 44 | 4 ♓ 59'19" |
| 17 MO | 17:39:51 | 22 1 | 22 3 | 0 ♐ 33 | 10 34 | 24 59 | 21 31 | 8 8 | 21 47 | 26 44 | 4 ♓ 59'19" |
| 18 TU | 17:43:48 | 25 30 | 23 39 | 1 30 | 11 1 | 25 3 | 21 33 | 8 8 | 21 48 | 26 45 | 4 ♓ 59'18" |
| 19 WE | 17:47:44 | 28 54 | 25 15 | 2 28 | 11 28 | 25 8 | 21 35 | 8 9 | 21 48 | 26 45 | 4 ♓ 59'18" |
| 20 TH | 17:51:41 | 2 ♎ 13 | 26 51 | 3 25 | 11 55 | 25 13 | 21 37 | 8 10 | 21 48 | 26 45 | 4 ♓ 59'18" |
| 21 FR | 17:55:37 | 5 28 | 28 27 | 4 22 | 12 22 | 25 18 | 21 38 | 8 10 | 21 49 | 26 45 | 4 ♓ 59'18" |
| 22 SA | 17:59:34 | 8 39 | 0 ♉ 4 | 5 19 | 12 49 | 25 23 | 21 40 | 8 11 | 21 49 | 26 46 | 4 ♓ 59'18" |
| 23 SU | 18: 3:31 | 11 47 | 1 40 | 6 16 | 13 16 | 25 28 | 21 42 | 8 12 | 21 49 | 26 46 | 4 ♓ 59'18" |
| 24 MO | 18: 7:27 | 14 51 | 3 16 | 7 14 | 13 42 | 25 32 | 21 44 | 8 12 | 21 50 | 26 46 | 4 ♓ 59'18" |
| 25 TU | 18:11:24 | 17 52 | 4 53 | 8 11 | 14 9 | 25 37 | 21 46 | 8 13 | 21 50 | 26 47 | 4 ♓ 59'18" |
| 26 WE | 18:15:20 | 20 51 | 6 29 | 9 8 | 14 36 | 25 42 | 21 47 | 8 14 | 21 50 | 26 47 | 4 ♓ 59'17" |
| 27 TH | 18:19:17 | 23 47 | 8 6 | 10 5 | 15 3 | 25 47 | 21 49 | 8 14 | 21 51 | 26 47 | 4 ♓ 59'17" |
| 28 FR | 18:23:13 | 26 40 | 9 42 | 11 3 | 15 30 | 25 52 | 21 51 | 8 15 | 21 51 | 26 48 | 4 ♓ 59'17" |
| 29 SA | 18:27:10 | 29 32 | 11 19 | 12 0 | 15 56 | 25 56 | 21 53 | 8 16 | 21 52 | 26 48 | 4 ♓ 59'17" |
| 30 SU | 18:31: 6 | 2 ♏ 23 | 12 55 | 12 57 | 16 23 | 26 1 | 21 55 | 8 16 | 21 52 | 26 48 | 4 ♓ 59'17" |

INGRESSES :

| |
|---|
| 3 ♀ → ♈ 5:17 |
| 4 ☿ → ♌ 18: 6 |
| 11 ☿ → ♍ 5:45 |
| 16 ⊕ → ♐ 10:10 |
| 19 ☿ → ♎ 7:54 |
| 21 ♀ → ♉ 23: 3 |
| 29 ☿ → ♏ 3:53 |

ASPECTS (HELIOCENTRIC +MOON(TYCHONIC)) :

| | | | | |
|---|---|---|---|---|
| 1 ♀ □ ♇ 3: 1 | 8 ♀ ☌ ♅ 5:58 | 13 ☽ ☍ ♅ 9:25 | ☽ ☍ ♂ 16:17 | 29 ☽ ☍ ☿ 14:22 |
| 3 ☿ ⊓N ☊ 12:29 | 9 ☿ ☍ ♆ 7:31 | ☽ □ ♂ 10:58 | 21 ☿ ☍ ♅ 20:25 | 30 ☽ ☌ ♀ 12:45 |
| ☽ □ ♆ 17:16 | ☿ □ ⊕ 17:46 | 14 ☽ ☍ ♀ 1:38 | 22 ☽ □ ♀ 4:41 | |
| ☽ ☍ ♃ 21: 9 | ☿ □ ♃ 22:10 | 16 ☽ □ ♆ 15:36 | 23 ☿ □ ♂ 13:30 | |
| 5 ☽ ☍ ♄ 19:54 | 10 ☽ ☍ ♆ 2: 0 | ☿ □ ♄ 20:34 | 24 ☽ ☌ ♆ 0: 6 | |
| 6 ☽ ☍ ♇ 5:13 | ☽ □ ♃ 6:33 | ☽ ☌ ♃ 21:30 | ☽ □ ♃ 7:38 | |
| ☽ □ ♀ 20:38 | ☽ ☌ ☿ 10: 9 | 18 ☿ □ ♇ 8:43 | 26 ☽ □ ♄ 11:58 | |
| ☽ ☌ ♂ 20:56 | ⊕ ☌ ♃ 15:12 | ☽ ☌ ♄ 23:50 | ☽ □ ♇ 21:41 | |
| 7 ☽ □ ♅ 0:21 | 11 ♂ □ ♅ 10:45 | 19 ☽ ☌ ♇ 9:51 | ☿ ☌ ☋ 22: 8 | |
| ♀ □ ♂ 0:23 | 12 ☽ □ ♄ 4:29 | ☽ □ ☿ 19:16 | 27 ☽ ☌ ♅ 19:43 | |
| ⊕ □ ♆ 18:29 | ☽ □ ♇ 13:41 | 20 ☽ □ ♅ 8:15 | 28 ☽ □ ♂ 9:44 | |

Ascension was possible only consequent to the Descent into Hell; for, in his descent, Christ encountered the source of life within everything living—the Divine Mother. He brought from her depths the living stream that once was known as Paradise, and this lost remnant of humanity's perfection changed even the worlds above.

When the Mother long ago withdrew into the heart of the Earth, Paradise went with her. Where Paradise once existed, the place of Kamaloka now exists. It is the sphere we enter after death to make right our wrongs. Here resides moral memory: a tableau comprising that which has eternal value and meaning.

As we remember our Mother's Name, we recall not only the etheric purity in which we once dwelled before the time of the Fall, but also the record of our soul's transgressions.

The immaculate heart of Mary bore witness to Christ's descent into the depths of the inner Earth, while the beloved disciple John bore witness to the majesty of the Father in the heights. Christ unites the heights and the depths. *Thus John does not soar off into spiritual oblivion, and Mary does not sink down into subearthly bondage.*

The Ascension reminds us that we too will eventually know what John and Mary experienced. When Christ spoke the words from the cross: "Behold, this is your son; behold, this is your mother," he was uniting the separation between his Mother and his Father, as well as that which lies between our higher and lower natures. Indeed, he was birthing the initiation path of the Rose Cross, wherein one's heart experiences the middle point between two extremes. This is where the seven roses flower.

The disciples were bereft after the Ascension, having experienced the sudden loss of their beloved Jesus Christ. In a suffering of separation that prepared them for Pentecost, they entered into the soul's dark night, which would enclose them in misery for ten days. The Rose Cross bids us to suffer ourselves into completeness; and in this noble state of soul, we find the comforter—the force of union.

Not only was the effect of the Ascension monumental for earthly humankind, it was also a deed that was carried into all the hierarchies of heaven:

If Jacob had been there to watch the Ascension (and I am certain that in some form he was), he surely would have seen again the "ladder," reaching into heaven, upon which the angels ascend and descend.

This ladder is symbolic of the various levels of heaven attained and surpassed as one ascends to Heaven either through initiation or death. Christ was now to ascend through the hierarchies as he returned to his Father, and at each stage of his Ascension there was an important work to be done.[1]

The fact that Christ's Ascension created a profound change in the different hierarchical spheres is incredible to contemplate. One can imagine the beings indwelling these spheres experiencing new revelation as Christ resurrected into their realms; and in bringing to them the new Gospel, he changed these beings for all time.

The transfigured higher worlds seek to transfigure also our *earthly* world; and this will come to pass when human beings turn to the ever-present guidance that surrounds us in our daily lives. Singing their hymns of praise, angelic choirs resound from the grounds of eternity, glorifying the renewal of Grace that was delivered via the Ascension into their holy spheres.

**Jun 10: First Quarter Moon 24° Leo.** The Moon remembers a messenger coming to tell Jesus that the daughter of Jairus, an Essene, had died. Jesus left the disciple and went to the girl, who was wrapped for burial. Jesus ordered the bindings to be loosened, then took the girl's hand and told her to rise. She sat up and stood before him. Jesus warned those present not to speak of what they had witnessed (Feb/7/30).

This girl was approximately sixteen years of age and had no love for her father. She was vexed at him because of his regard for the poor; she despised his charitable disposition and his pious nature. After Jesus raised her from the dead, she reformed and later joined the circle of holy women.

This miracle begs the question as to why Christ Jesus brought back to life such a disobedient

---

1 Isaacson, *Through the Eyes of Mary Magdalene*, vol. III, p. 252.

daughter. Was this done in honor of her pious father? This may be a very good example of the difference between "natural selection" and "spiritual election." The latter serves a higher mandate that may not be visible to the non-initiated; the former marks self-elevation.

Much is demanded of those who would be students of the mysteries. A "field of understanding" must be created through which ever-more complex expressions of the sacred truths become comprehensible. Furthermore, where a matrix of spiritual reality has collectively been created, students find themselves engaged in *experiences of truth*—rather than simply gathering and logging facts.

This Leo Moon brings us to the heart of the matter, asking us to look deeper than we may otherwise attempt to do. We must remember that things are often not what they appear to be. Miracles and mysteries surround us. We now face the challenge of adapting to the gifts of the New Moon: *summoning the courage to resurrect our dead.*

**ASPECT: Sun 24° Taurus opposite Jupiter 24° Scorpio.** The Sun shone from this degree as Jesus taught about the Feast of Weeks, about the giving of the Law on Mount Sinai, and about baptism. The Fest of Weeks, which marked the wheat harvest in Israel, began that evening; there was a torchlight procession, which Jesus joined. Later, he retired to pray alone (May/16/31).

Jupiter increases what it aspects. It offers benevolent gifts to the humble; inversely, it inflates greed in the egotistical. The resurrecting powers of the Sun, standing across the heavens from the hallowed spheres of the Holy Spirit, pose the question: *What air do you breathe?* Is it the spiritual air of the aspirant, or the polluted air of Mammon? As this aspect occurs under the influence of the first quarter Moon in Leo, we search in our heart for the answer to this question. Are we ready to open our spirit-eye and breathe spiritual air?

**Jun 14: ASPECT: Mars 24° Gemini opposite Saturn 24° Sagittarius.** Mars recalls its position as Jesus took part in the Feast of Weeks in the synagogue. He walked at the head of the column of rabbis as they proceeded around the synagogue while blessing the land, the sea, and all regions of the earth. There then followed a reading which had to do with the period between the exodus from Egypt and the giving of the Law on Mount Sinai on the fiftieth day after Passover (May/17/31).

The first fruits of spring are a reminder of the primal forces of resurrection that rise from the inner Earth after having incubated in the isolation of a cold and dark winter season. As the cold gives way to the warmth of solar in-streaming, all life meets the Sun with a renewed sense of hope.

This is a poignant memory for this aspect. The cold darkness of winter has captured parts of our consciousness. From this isolation ghosts and specters speak through us. They are *our* self-generated ghosts and specters, yet we often fall into the temptation of happily projecting them onto others—for our convenience.

When the Archangel Michael (Mars) stands opposite the Holy Virgin (Saturn), lies are unmasked. What is the quality of virtue in our words? If we speak through the cold mouths of our dead—i.e., through our lower astral nature, we will find frustration and disappointment. Inversely, if we call down the fire of the holy Word, we will find an enthusiasm to meet—and to redeem—the fallen aspects of ourselves.

Under this influence, Marcian bullies will feel like people are standing in their way, and this will anger them. We can pray this does not play out in world events as reckless action.

This aspect was present at the Baptism in the Jordan River as well as at the start of the forty days of temptation. Indeed, the bully Satan despised the fact that Christ was born, knowing as he did that Christ would always stand in his way. On the Mt. of Temptation, Satan attempted to defeat him, but he underestimated the power of Love that will forever stand in his way. Our task is to stand with Christ and his solar advocate, Michael.

The awaking apposition between the human soul and the secrets of its deepest spiritual resolve asks if we have the necessary persevering faithfulness to stand against the temptation of the lower astral world. Will we surrender what lacks nobility to accept the healing arms of the Holy Virgin? Resurrection—or aggression?

**Jun 16: Sun enters Gemini:** "Reveal thyself, Sun life, set repose in movement, embrace joyful striving toward life's mighty weaving, toward blissful world-knowing, toward fruitful ripe-growing. O Sun life, endure!" (Steiner, *Twelve Cosmic Moods*).

The late William Bento characterized this mantra:

> Within this phrase there is a hidden mystery. How does the Sun hide from our view? It is certainly not the physical Sun we see daily that is being referred to here—but the living, etherically-permeated Sun, felt and experienced, though rarely perceived. Within this Sun exist the threefold sources of health, life and goodness. *How easily we forget to place our trust in this ever-present stream of divinity when we are faced with illness, death, and evil!* For this reason alone it is well worth reminding ourselves to see beyond appearances and to behold the true revelation of the Sun—which reveals itself to our hearts, where its life resides.

The first decan of Gemini is ruled by Jupiter and associated with Orion, whose bright star Betelgeuse is located at 4° Gemini.

**ASPECT: Jupiter 24° Scorpio square Neptune 24° Aquarius.** The Sun at Neptune's degree remembers many sick and possessed people being brought to Jesus at the close of the Sabbath. In public, before a large crowd, Jesus then healed the sick and cast out devils (Feb/11/30).

This is one of the major planetary aspects occurring in 2019. The first exact square was on January 13th. This is its second occurrence, and the last exact square will occur on September 21st. The January square reminded us of Christ healing from afar. Today we are reminded of the possessed and the casting out of demons.

There are three main levels to the sickness of soul: catching a negative energy virus; being implanted with a systemic worm—i.e., an "inseeded" thought not created by the soul; and, lastly, an actual possession.

This transit can bring up thoughts that can shatter our illusion of wellness. Suspicions, deceptions, and even paranoia may arise. Such are the accoutrements of the Woman of Babylon (lower Neptune influences). Inversely, the Goddess Night (higher Neptune influences) bestows a wealth of inspiring insights, parting the veil that has long obscured Sophianic realms of wonder.

The demons that quietly indwell us may go unnoticed for a long time, until an opposite influence enters our field. Then will they rail against the light this opposite influence exerts, for the demons know that light unmasks their secrets. Lured from their hidey-holes, they spit gall and poison, shocking the soul who unwittingly bears their messages of hate.

When Christ performed an exorcism (i.e., cast out demons), he would stand at a safe distance from the one infected: he knew that if he met the demon while it was still operating within the physical body of the one he was healing, it could possibly tear the soul apart. Christ did not speak softly or gently when casting out demons; rather would he speak in a mighty and thunderous voice. It was thus the power of the spirit resounding in his fullness of voice that would drive out the demon, for evil can only flee when facing the power of the living Word.

Despite the fact that many failed to recognize Christ, this was not the case with the demons. They immediately recognized him, and would often shout at him through the being they had possessed. It would be foolish of us to imagine that we have no demons. If that were true, we would have reached our enlightenment, following in the footsteps of Gautama.

Demons have been given free access to us through technological gadgets, as well as through the egregores of mass consciousness. How much of what we think has actually been implanted rather than created? It has become a dire necessity that we learn new etheric technologies for clearing demons from our personal energy fields, from the energy fields of others, and even from the energy fields of organizations. This is the work of sacred magic.

This aspect was present (although in different signs) at the death of the Nathan Mary as well as at the Transfiguration. In both instances we witness the power of the Holy Spirit (Jupiter) in dynamic tension with the Goddess Night (Neptune), who parts the veil between worlds and thereby causes demons to flee.

In the two examples (Mary's death and the Transfiguration), we see how Mary's soul departed in radiant glory; we also see how her Son received the mantle of the enlightened astral body. These events reveal what this aspect can achieve for those bearing the revelatory gaze of the *apocalyptist* (Scorpio as the Eagle), and for those who commune with angels (Aquarius).

It will be interesting, or perhaps unsettling, to see how this influence may play out in world events throughout this year.

**ASPECT 2: Mercury 24° Gemini opposite Saturn 24° Sagittarius.** Mercury recalls four Pharisees, not far from Jericho, as they warned Jesus not to come to Jerusalem—for Herod sought to kill him. Jesus replied: "Go and tell that fox, 'Behold, I cast out demons and perform cures today and tomorrow, and the third day I finish my course….it cannot be that a prophet should perish away from Jerusalem.' O Jerusalem, Jerusalem, killing the prophets and stoning those who are sent to you!" (May/29/32). Is this not a recurring theme in the history of esoteric traditions? The mind that hates, kills, as does the mind that lies. Murderous—or merciful?

**Jun 17: ASPECT: Full Moon 1° Sagittarius opposite Sun 1° Gemini: Healing of Theokeno.** The Moon recalls Jesus as he went with Mensor (the gold king) to Theokeno (the king of frankincense), who was very ill (Sair, the third king who had been guided to the birth of the Solomon Jesus, had already died). Jesus commanded that Theokeno rise and accompany him to the temple. Theokeno, not doubting, rose up at once, able to walk (Sep/28/32).

The transformational time of the Full Moon has come. What have we done to better align our speech with the creative power of the living Word? Do we feel the resurrecting presence of the Good Shepherd? Have we raised any aspects of our unconsciousness to the light? The efforts thus exerted empower us to receive the benediction of this Sagittarius Moon.

The Sun at 2° Sagittarius remembers the healing of the man born blind. The Sun at 2° Gemini remembers Pentecost. This Full Moon, cradled between two powerful events, may quicken the spiritual eye to experience the descent of the Holy Spirit. And today we also remember the Gold King and the riches of star wisdom we must now comprehend.

It takes an initiate to model new capacities that will only later become the capacities of ordinary human beings. They come before their time, and they are thus often unrecognized. Recognition is a powerful force, one that protects advanced souls from the onslaught of demons who strive unceasingly to destroy them. Most initiates have at least a small circle around them, which serves to assure that what they have brought will be entered into the annals of history. Most of them are like hermits, living alone in their souls, communing with higher worlds, growing ever less desirous of normal human relationships. "For the gate is narrow and the way is hard, that leads to life. And those who find the way are few" (Matthew 7). Yes, the world's hermits must seek the narrow gate, forging an as yet unpaved path to worlds above. They carry the lamp of Trismegistus; they wear the mantle of Apollonius; and they touch into existence through the staff of the patriarchs.

The continuation of progressive humanity is due to the light such hermits shine into the world's darkness. And although their lamps may separate them from the collective, they nonetheless have audience in higher abodes. The three kings were hermits of their time. They brought the initiate wisdom gathered in the three preceding cultural ages: myrrh from ancient India, frankincense from ancient Persia, and gold from ancient Eygpt.

Theokeno was the king who brought frankincense to the cradle of the Solomon Jesus. He represented the ancient Persian cultural epoch. Just as our current cultural epoch stands opposite the ancient Egyptian cultural epoch, so will the future Slavic cultural epoch stand opposite the ancient Persian cultural epoch. Thus do we see that the healing of Theokeno was more than simply the healing of an initiate; it was, symbolically, the healing of the future.

Sagittarius holds the fullness of today's Moon, representing the Centaur—who rides the intellect in absolute control over lower passions and instincts. He seeks but one thing: *truth*. This is the exercise of this lunar phase.

The world was created through one source: the Word. The intellect is the mirror upon which the light of the Word illumines that which has been created to those who are capable of seeing. Although the light of truth shines continually into the world, the world darkness comprehends it not. All who dwell in darkness, therefore, are blind to the light.

> But the darkness of the world that is not penetrated by the Word is not the source of consciousness, and the human intellect that is not illumined by the Word is not the principle of the world. In the phenomenal world there are "objective illusions," i.e., "things which are *not real*," and which have not been made by the Word, but which have arisen for an ephemeral existence from the sub-strata of darkness. In the domain of subjective consciousness there are illusions, i.e., notions, ideas and ideals which are *not real*, which have not been engendered by the light of the Word, but which have arisen for an ephemeral existence from the depths of darkness in the subconscious.[1]

For the most part our intellects have been take up in the ruse of the serpent. For there is the Word and the word, and there is the World and the world. The creative force of the Father permeates the Word and the World; the word and the world, on the other hand, have been fractured into puzzle pieces that can be reordered to suit the temporal convenience of the intellect.

Darwin's law, claiming the "struggle for existence," will in the the future give way to the new law, the "law of cooperation." The law of struggle rendered Theokeno ill—he lay dying. When the Word entered into his tent, he was healed, having rescued his gift of frankincense in service to the future to which it was destined.

> Thus the "law" of the *struggle for existence* that Darwin observed in the domain of biology will one day cede its place to the law of *cooperation for existence*, which exists already in the cooperation of flowering plants and bees, in the cooperation of different cells in an organism, and in cooperation in the human social organism. The end of the "law" of the struggle for existence and the future triumph of the law of cooperation for life has been foretold by the prophet Isaiah: "The wolf shall dwell with the lamb, And the leopard shall lie down with the kid. And the calf and the lion and the fatling together. And a little child shall lead them" (Is. 11:6).
>
> This will be, because the new "law"—i.e., a profound change in the psychic and physical structure of beings—will replace the old "law," firstly in consciousness, then in desires and affections, then lastly in the organic structure of beings.[2]

The New Moon recalled the healing of the blind; it also recalled the task to create new "I" forces through the power of the Word. The first quarter Moon recalled the raising of the daughter of Jairus: our commission to raise the dead in us. The transformational influences of the Full Moon now offer a benediction upon all efforts we have exerted to fulfil what this lunar phase inaugurated—bearing witness to the future through recognition of star wisdom.

Tomorrow is Cosmic Pentecost, which strengthens the light of this Full Moon.

**Jun 18: Sun 2°35' Gemini: Cosmic Pentecost (May/24/33).** Late tonight the Sun reaches the exact degree of Pentecost (11:12 pm EDT). At Pentecost, Sophia descended through the Holy Spirit and entered into the being of the Blessed Virgin Mary. Thus was Mary-Sophia born. At this degree the Sun is directly opposite the Galactic Center (2° Sagittarius). The Galactic Center (also known as the Central Sun) is the Divine Heart of the galaxy, which is the source of the Holy Spirit. At Pentecost, the Blessed Virgin Mary—who was presented by Jesus Christ as the center of the community—served as this heart-center and as the bearer of Divine Sophia:

> Because of extremely complicated influences and experiences coming from the spiritual world, *Mary had an astral body that was so purified it could receive the revelations of Sophia and pour them out again as inspirations of the soul.* This faculty was the very reason

---

1 Anon., *Meditations on the Tarot*, p. 203.

2 Ibid., p. 208.

why, at the time of Pentecostal revelation, the Virgin Mary occupied the central position in the circle of the twelve. Without her, the revelation would have been only spiritual; there would have been twelve prophets, united in the Holy Spirit as was ancient prophecy. Through the cooperation of Mary, however, something more could happen; the disciples' hearts beat in harmony with hers while they experienced the Pentecostal revelation as personal human conviction. Through this experience, they became not prophets but specifically apostles.[3]

The difference between prophets and apostles is that prophets proclaim revelations impersonally, whereas apostles reveal the Holy Spirit as it lives within their own souls. This was possible only because the Virgin Mary transmitted *ensouled revelation* to the disciples. Through her, revelation became personal and yet maintained its objective spiritual truth.

From the moment of Pentecost onward, the silence imposed on Sophia through Lucifer's intervention in human destiny was released. Sophia became free to reach down into groups of earthly human beings. This was a great event for both the earthly and spiritual worlds.

*The sparks of fire that issued from her blessed being were the ensouled manifestation of Christ's cosmic I Am.* This eternal "I" of the world was born into the disciples through the immaculate heart of the divine Mary-Sophia, who was standing at the very heart of their community. Since that first Pentecost, the Christ spirit has lived within human souls on Earth. Pentecost was the awaking of Christ's disciples from a dreamlike state, whereby they united with the principle of Christ's love as an experience within their own being. *We also* are to awake from our dreamlike sleep, to meet the challenge of our time with hearts attuned in wakeful spirit-awareness.

Emanations from the heart of the galaxy are increasing in our time, leading us ever forward. Sun in Gemini asks that we revere the "I" in others, that we follow our star and find our way to the manger of our heart's center.

**ASPECT: Mercury conjunct Mars 26° Gemini.** Mars recalls its degree at the First Crusade in Jerusalem (Jul/15/1099). Healers (Mercury) speak words in such a manner that goodness is created in this world. Under the influence of the Pentecost Sun, it is wise to watch our speech. *Aggression reveals where we are bound to the ruse of the serpent's world.*

**Jun 19: ASPECTS: Mercury and Mars 27° Gemini opposite Pluto 27° Sagittarius.** The Sun was at Pluto's degree as Jesus healed by word of command several people who had been carried to a place in front of the synagogue (Dec/17/29). The Archangel Michael (Mars) joins with the pastors and healers (Mercury) as they both stand in opposition to Pluto. We pray that this does not result in an anti-Pentecost event. Intensity, primal energies, aggression, violence, and domination may rise from the lower levels of consciousness when it is Pluto/Hades who commands. Inversely, when Pluto–Phanes rules, moral courage enthuses the will to act in defense of righteousness.

This same aspect (in these same constellations) occurred during the entire Passion of Christ. Indeed, violence held sway. Nonetheless, the power of Love was victorious.

The faithfulness emanating from Gemini measures our steps, readying all whose task is to take up the battle with the dragon. First we must know the dragon within; and then, through the power of our "I," we must cast him into his proper place.

This is the true Michaelic battle that must today generally be waged within us. The prime thing here is not so much to accuse others of their un-Michaelic conduct, but rather to examine ourselves. The battle should not be waged *between* people—irrespective of how misguided or jeopardized one person may consider another. First and foremost, this battle takes place in our own soul, and it is there that it may and must be waged in the most stringent and unwavering way, day after day. Thus Michael helps us to fulfill Christ's mission to the world.[4]

---

3 Tomberg, *Christ and Sophia*, p. 306.

4 von Halle, *Illness and Healing and the Mystery Language of the Gospels*, p.86.

Such are sobering words for a sobering aspect.

**Jun 21: Summer Solstice 7:54 AM EDT.**

> At the times of the solstices and equinoxes, it was experienced [in the massive temple at Karnak] that unique conditions prevailed by virtue of the Sun and the Earth entering into a special relationship with one another. At such times it was felt that the possibility arose for impulses and revelations from the cosmos to be transmitted to receptive human minds below. This was felt especially to be so at the time of the summer solstice. In the hermetic tradition of ancient Egypt it was imagined that at this time the Sun became enthroned. The Sun was pictured as ascending through the Zodiac to reach its place of enthronement on the day of the summer solstice, when the Sun stands highest in the heavens. According to this imaginative picture, the sublime Sun god, ascending his throne, would send down true being (i.e., light and life) from above.[1]

Today blesses us with the exaltation of the Sun.

The summer solstice is the flowering time in the cycle of the seasons. The seeds we carried from the Mother's manger during the Holy Nights now flower, as they soar into the heights of heaven. Here they will gather the creative forces necessary to become earthly deeds at the time of Michaelmas. We were given these seeds of our future spiritual potential; now we let them expand beyond us, as we tether our will to the demands of tending our earthly gardens. The intensity of cosmic forces brings the warmth that will ripen the seeds within these flowers—so they may come to fruition as they return to us when the Earth's soul inbreathes in autumn. Then will the dragons rise against the light, and we will pick up St. Michael's sword to sever the old while making room for the new. Thus is a space created as the womb of conception into which new seeds will be planted in the Holy Nights to come.

The constellation of Gemini forms a *spiritual corridor* between the above and the below. Through perseverance, we faithfully maintain our concentration so that this vertical path of revelation maintains its integrity. *It is the "narrow way" through which spirit and matter converse.*

Gemini calls us to follow our star, that we may again find the manger within as we rest into winter's dark nights during this time when the year comes to its end. Will we have oil in our lamps?

**Neptune stations retrograde 23° Aquarius.**

**Mercury enters Cancer:** "Thou resting, glowing light, create life warmth, **warm soul life** to gain strength in test of trial, to become spirit-permeated, in peaceful light created. Thou glowing light, become strong!" (Steiner, *Twelve Cosmic Moods*).

**Jun 23: ASPECT: Venus 23° Taurus opposite Jupiter 23° Scorpio.** Venus recalls its degree as Jesus went to a house where ten lepers lay. He healed them, instructing them to bathe in a nearby pool and to present themselves to the priests to show that they were healed. As Jesus left them, one of the lepers cast himself down and gave thanks (May/18/32). Love and Wisdom stand across from each other, exchanging their respective gifts.

The Venus cross becomes lighter when facing the Holy Spirit (Jupiter). Benevolent Jupiter expands consciousness, uplifting the soul to bear witness to the greater story. After healing lepers, Christ would speak the sixth commandment: Thou shall not kill. Lies are murders in spiritual worlds, and must have something to do with leprous conditions.

Human beings alone are capable of lies. With Jupiter in Scorpio, the part of us that is willing to lie may be unmasked, restoring our commitment to truth. And, with Venus in Taurus, the true nature of the life within our words may come to consciousness:

> If we speak the truth about our neighbor, we are creating a thought that the seer can recognize by its color and form, and it will be a thought that gives strength to our neighbor. Any thought containing truth finds its way to the being whom it concerns and lends him strength and vigor. If I speak lies about him, I pour out a hostile force that destroys and may even kill him. In this way every lie is an act of murder. Every spoken truth creates a life-promoting element; every lie, an element hostile to life. Anyone who knows this will take much greater care to speak the truth

---

[1] *HA I*, pp. 12-13.

and avoid lies than if he is merely preached at and told he must be nice and truthful.[2]

May the grace of this aspect illumine us.

**Mars enters Cancer:** "Thou resting, glowing light, create life warmth, warm soul life **to gain strength in test of trial**, to become spirit-permeated, in peaceful light created. Thou glowing light, become strong!" (Steiner, *Twelve Cosmic Moods*). Mars is in its fall in this sign as Cancer is opposite it place of exaltation (Capricorn); therefore strength must indeed hold sway in all trials.

**Jun 24: ASPECT: Venus 23° Taurus square Neptune 23° Aquarius.** Venus was at its degree during the solar eclipse of July 21, 2009. (There will not be a longer eclipse in the 21st century.)

In memory of this longest eclipse, we find the cross of Venus in dynamic tension with the Goddess Night (Neptune). As this aspect also occurred at the summons of Judas, however, we must be watchful of deceptive influences emanating from the unholy waters of fallen Neptune, which are indicative of the tendency of mass consciousness to "inseed" foreign thoughts.

Since 2009 we have been constantly at war; divisiveness has escalated at an alarming rate; and systemic social pathologies have led to stunning increases in addictions. As Venus transits the memory of this longest eclipse of the entire 21st century, we must be wise as serpents and innocent as doves—i.e., we must know the intelligence of the serpent and in openheartedness restore innocence. Moreover, it is of utmost importance that we *protect the innocence of our children*. Thus will we find the healing waters of the Goddess washing us clean of all affliction.

**Jun 25: Last Quarter Moon 9° Pisces.** The Moon remembers a basement room in Lazarus's house, when Jesus told Lazarus, Peter, James, and John that tomorrow would be the day of his triumphant entry into Jerusalem. This event was accompanied by a total eclipse of the Sun (Mar/18/33). Today we enter the last phase of this lunar cycle. Have we turned to the Good Shepherd in fearlessness? Have we raised the dead from the darkness of our lower nature? Did we meet the transfiguring forces of the Full Moon in homage to the future age of Aquarius that we now must serve? The phase of integration has dawned, and the spiritual response of benediction will befall us due to the efforts we have exerted. Will we enter community with the congregation of the faithful who are committed to Eternal Jerusalem, i.e., the holy city of the Lamb and his Bride?

Just as a total eclipse occurred on this night in Lazarus's basement, so too do we remember how evil finds its abode in us when we allow our Sun-self to be eclipsed.

**Jun 29:** Sun 12° Gemini: Birth of John the Baptist (6/4/2 BC).

**Venus enters Gemini:** "Reveal thyself, Sun life, **set repose in movement**, embrace joyful striving toward life's mighty weaving, toward blissful world-knowing, toward fruitful ripe-growing. O Sun life, endure!" (Steiner, *Twelve Cosmic Moods*).

# JULY 2019

## Stargazing Preveiw

The New Moon on the 2nd brings a Total Solar Eclipse to lower South America; may the condors keep watch over the guanaco until it's over! On the 4th, an hour or so after sunset, Mars will set moments before the Moon. Saturn, rising at 2100, will be at its most brilliant on the 9th, when it is opposite the Sun. The Moon laps Jupiter again on the 13th; look for them in the southeast at sunset.

On the 16th, Saturn will rise just ahead of the Full Moon, so you'll be able to watch them throughout the night as they move along the ecliptic, from east to west. July's second New Moon takes place on the 31st. Orion will be low in the east for about four hours before dawn.

## July Commentaries

**Jul 1:** Sun 14° Gemini: Death of the Solomon Jesus (6/5/12 BC).

---

[2] Steiner, *Founding a Science of the Spirit*, lect. 2.

**Jul 2: ASPECT: New Moon 15° Gemini and Total Solar Eclipse over Chile, Argentina, and the South Pacific (3:15 pm EDT).** The Moon was at this degree on the evening following the second conversion of Mary Magdalene. Turning to different parts of the assembled crowd, Jesus commanded the devils to depart from all those who sought freedom from their possession. Many, including Mary Magdalene, sank to the ground as the dark forces left them. This happened to Mary Magdalene three times. As Jesus spoke to her for the third time, she fell unconscious again as another devil departed from her. She cast herself at his feet and begged for salvation (Dec/26/30).

This New Moon is cradled by the Sun's memory of the death of the Solomon Jesus (yesterday) and by his conception (tomorrow). Thus are the Master Jesus and the virtue of faith foundational for the beginning of this new lunar cycle.

The mighty star beings indwelling the constellation of Gemini represent faithfulness and the perseverance this requires. There are different types of faith. Some find it in the conviction that there is ultimate goodness and beauty in the world. Others find it as something founded on one's intimate inner experience of a divine breath, i.e., a presence that weaves in all things. Faith born of inner experience bestows an intrinsic authority through which one believes without any support either from without or from within. *The strength of faith is a knowingness greater than all intellectual assumptions. It can only be found in the inner chamber of the heart.* Mary Magdalene would come to know this experience of faith—faith at first hand!

Faith fills the gaps in our intelligence, forming a bridge; and crossing over this bridge opens the possibility of soaring beyond the confines of sense-based intelligence. For, at the edge of the intellect's boundary we must leap if we are to enter realms teeming with the pure spontaneity of intuition. Thus does faith grant us transcendence into realms of wonder.

Spontaneity marks the child-like world of innocence. We can imagine how Magdalene may have become child-like when the demons left her, the innocence of faith having freed her from all darkness. Being naturally loving and spontaneously wise, children faithfully return to Earth. Their highest hope is that they will learn to follow their star and that life's disruptions will not rob them of this heavenly light.

> Just as the mages from the East made a long journey and brought presents to the [Solomon Jesus] Child, in following the "star," so also Hermeticism is on the way from century to century to arrive at the manger—not to arrive there with empty hands, but to place there the presents which are the fruit of the millennial-old effort of human intelligence which follows the "star."[1]

The star we follow will eventually lead us to the center of evolution's heart, to the center of our individual heart, and to the center of our destination. Therein is the heart of the Omega point, where we will celebrate the final victory of our resurrection in Jesus Christ. Yet, every time we reclaim our light we are resurrecting—i.e., we bring latent energies into activity as our child-like wholeness is restored.

> But those who follow the "star" must learn a lesson once and for all: not to consult Herod and the "chief priests and scribes of the people" at Jerusalem, but to follow the "star" that they have seen "in the East" and which "goes before them," without seeking for indications and confirmation on the part of Herod and his people. The gleam of the "star" and the effort to understand its message ought to suffice. Because Herod, representing the anti-revelatory force and principle, is also eternal.[2]

Herein lies the warning we are all to heed. The new mysteries require the leap of faith that leads to intuition, and this is exactly what the Herods in the world fight against. Relying solely on their own personal authority, they find the concept of suprasensory authority threatening. Had the disciples of Jesus ignored his miracles, they would not have experienced the depth of faith that needed no affirmation from outer authorities. *How many miracles are we passing by due to our faithless need to confirm suprasensory realities by using the logic of the eclipsed intellect?*

---

1 Anon., *Meditations on the Tarot*, pp. 530-531.
2 Ibid., pp. 533-534.

## SIDEREAL GEOCENTRIC LONGITUDES : JULY 2019 Gregorian at 0 hours UT

| DAY | ☉ | ☽ | ☊ | ☿ | ♀ | ♂ | ♃ | ♄ | ♅ | ♆ | ♇ |
|---|---|---|---|---|---|---|---|---|---|---|---|
| 1 MO | 13 ♊ 54 | 20 ♉ 12 | 22 ♊ 38R | 7 ♋ 36 | 1 ♊ 46 | 4 ♋ 22 | 21 ♏ 59R | 22 ♐ 51R | 10 ♈ 54 | 23 ♒ 42R | 27 ♐ 12R |
| 2 TU | 14 51 | 4 ♊ 11 | 22 37 | 8 5 | 2 59 | 5 0 | 21 53 | 22 46 | 10 56 | 23 41 | 27 11 |
| 3 WE | 15 48 | 18 28 | 22 37 | 8 30 | 4 12 | 5 39 | 21 46 | 22 42 | 10 57 | 23 41 | 27 9 |
| 4 TH | 16 45 | 2 ♋ 59 | 22 37D | 8 50 | 5 26 | 6 17 | 21 40 | 22 37 | 10 59 | 23 41 | 27 8 |
| 5 FR | 17 43 | 17 37 | 22 37 | 9 7 | 6 39 | 6 55 | 21 34 | 22 33 | 11 1 | 23 40 | 27 7 |
| 6 SA | 18 40 | 2 ♌ 18 | 22 37 | 9 18 | 7 53 | 7 33 | 21 28 | 22 29 | 11 3 | 23 40 | 27 5 |
| 7 SU | 19 37 | 16 54 | 22 38 | 9 25 | 9 6 | 8 11 | 21 22 | 22 24 | 11 5 | 23 39 | 27 4 |
| 8 MO | 20 34 | 1 ♍ 21 | 22 38 | 9 27R | 10 20 | 8 49 | 21 16 | 22 20 | 11 6 | 23 39 | 27 2 |
| 9 TU | 21 31 | 15 35 | 22 38R | 9 25 | 11 33 | 9 27 | 21 10 | 22 15 | 11 8 | 23 38 | 27 1 |
| 10 WE | 22 29 | 29 33 | 22 38 | 9 17 | 12 47 | 10 6 | 21 4 | 22 11 | 11 10 | 23 38 | 26 59 |
| 11 TH | 23 26 | 13 ♎ 15 | 22 38D | 9 6 | 14 0 | 10 44 | 20 59 | 22 7 | 11 11 | 23 37 | 26 58 |
| 12 FR | 24 23 | 26 41 | 22 38 | 8 49 | 15 14 | 11 22 | 20 54 | 22 2 | 11 13 | 23 36 | 26 56 |
| 13 SA | 25 20 | 9 ♏ 52 | 22 38 | 8 29 | 16 28 | 12 0 | 20 48 | 21 58 | 11 14 | 23 36 | 26 55 |
| 14 SU | 26 17 | 22 47 | 22 38 | 8 4 | 17 41 | 12 38 | 20 43 | 21 53 | 11 15 | 23 35 | 26 54 |
| 15 MO | 27 15 | 5 ♐ 29 | 22 39 | 7 35 | 18 55 | 13 16 | 20 38 | 21 49 | 11 17 | 23 34 | 26 52 |
| 16 TU | 28 12 | 17 58 | 22 39 | 7 3 | 20 8 | 13 54 | 20 34 | 21 45 | 11 18 | 23 34 | 26 51 |
| 17 WE | 29 9 | 0 ♑ 16 | 22 39R | 6 28 | 21 22 | 14 32 | 20 29 | 21 40 | 11 19 | 23 33 | 26 49 |
| 18 TH | 0 ♋ 6 | 12 24 | 22 39 | 5 50 | 22 36 | 15 10 | 20 25 | 21 36 | 11 21 | 23 32 | 26 48 |
| 19 FR | 1 4 | 24 25 | 22 38 | 5 11 | 23 49 | 15 48 | 20 20 | 21 31 | 11 22 | 23 31 | 26 46 |
| 20 SA | 2 1 | 6 ♒ 19 | 22 37 | 4 31 | 25 3 | 16 26 | 20 16 | 21 27 | 11 23 | 23 30 | 26 45 |
| 21 SU | 2 58 | 18 11 | 22 35 | 3 49 | 26 17 | 17 5 | 20 12 | 21 23 | 11 24 | 23 30 | 26 43 |
| 22 MO | 3 55 | 0 ♓ 2 | 22 34 | 3 8 | 27 31 | 17 43 | 20 8 | 21 19 | 11 25 | 23 29 | 26 42 |
| 23 TU | 4 52 | 11 56 | 22 33 | 2 28 | 28 44 | 18 21 | 20 5 | 21 14 | 11 26 | 23 28 | 26 40 |
| 24 WE | 5 50 | 23 57 | 22 31 | 1 50 | 29 58 | 18 59 | 20 1 | 21 10 | 11 27 | 23 27 | 26 39 |
| 25 TH | 6 47 | 6 ♈ 11 | 22 31 | 1 14 | 1 ♋ 12 | 19 37 | 19 58 | 21 6 | 11 28 | 23 26 | 26 38 |
| 26 FR | 7 44 | 18 39 | 22 31D | 0 41 | 2 26 | 20 15 | 19 55 | 21 2 | 11 29 | 23 25 | 26 36 |
| 27 SA | 8 42 | 1 ♉ 28 | 22 32 | 0 11 | 3 40 | 20 53 | 19 52 | 20 58 | 11 30 | 23 24 | 26 35 |
| 28 SU | 9 39 | 14 40 | 22 33 | 29 ♊ 46 | 4 53 | 21 31 | 19 49 | 20 54 | 11 30 | 23 23 | 26 33 |
| 29 MO | 10 36 | 28 18 | 22 34 | 29 25 | 6 7 | 22 9 | 19 47 | 20 49 | 11 31 | 23 22 | 26 32 |
| 30 TU | 11 34 | 12 ♊ 22 | 22 35 | 29 10 | 7 21 | 22 47 | 19 44 | 20 46 | 11 32 | 23 20 | 26 30 |
| 31 WE | 12 31 | 26 50 | 22 35R | 29 0 | 8 35 | 23 25 | 19 42 | 20 42 | 11 32 | 23 19 | 26 29 |

### INGRESSES :

| | |
|---|---|
| 1 ☽ → ♊ 16:53 | 24 ♀ → ♋ 0:36 |
| 3 ☽ → ♋ 19: 6 | ☽ → ♈ 11:55 |
| 5 ☽ → ♌ 20:14 | 26 ☽ → ♉ 21:16 |
| 7 ☽ → ♍ 21:44 | 27 ☿ → ♊ 10: 8 |
| 10 ☽ → ♎ 0:46 | 29 ☽ → ♊ 2:56 |
| 12 ☽ → ♏ 5:59 | 31 ☽ → ♋ 5:10 |
| 14 ☽ → ♐ 13:35 | |
| 16 ☽ → ♑ 23:28 | |
| 17 ☉ → ♋ 21:21 | |
| 19 ☽ → ♒ 11:14 | |
| 21 ☽ → ♓ 23:56 | |

### ASPECTS & ECLIPSES :

| | | | | |
|---|---|---|---|---|
| 1 ☽ ☍ ♃ 3: 4 | 7 ☽ ☍ ♆ 11:10 | ☽ ☌ ♄ 7:17 | ☽ ☌ ♆ 10:45 | 31 ☽ ☌ ☿ 3:31 |
| ☽ ☌ ♀ 21:47 | 8 ☿ ☌ ♂ 22:25 | ☽ ☌ ☋ 9: 5 | ☉ ☌i ☿ 12:32 | ☽ ☌ ♀ 20:49 |
| 2 ☉ ☌ ☽ 19:15 | 9 ☉ □ ☽ 10:53 | ☽ ☌ ♇ 17:14 | 23 ☽ S ☊ 21: 9 | |
| ☉ ● T 19:21 | ☽ N ☊ 12: 3 | ☽ •–• P 21:29 | 25 ☿ ☌ ♀ 0:25 | |
| 3 ☽ ☌ ☊ 6:53 | ☉ ☍ ♄ 17: 6 | ☉ ☍ ☽ 21:37 | ☉ □ ☽ 1:17 | |
| ☽ ☍ ♄ 7: 0 | 10 ☉ ☌ ☊ 3:48 | 17 ♀ ☍ ♄ 5:33 | ☽ ☌ ♅ 10:15 | |
| ☽ ☍ ♇ 14:23 | ☽ ☍ ♅ 20:19 | ☽ ☍ ☿ 11:37 | 28 ☽ ☍ ♃ 9: 7 | |
| 4 ♄ ☍ ☊ 3:23 | 11 ♂ □ ♅ 17:57 | 18 ♀ ☌ ☊ 0:57 | 29 ☉ □ ♅ 23:11 | |
| ☽ ☌ ♂ 5:40 | 13 ☽ ☌ ♃ 20: 9 | ☽ ☍ ♂ 5:48 | 30 ☽ ☍ ♄ 13:55 | |
| ☽ ☌ ☿ 9:49 | 14 ☉ ☍ ♇ 14:45 | 21 ☽ ☌ A 0:20 | ☽ ☌ ☊ 17: 1 | |
| 5 ☽ ☌ P 5: 7 | 16 ☽ ☍ ♀ 4:40 | ♀ ☍ ♇ 8:27 | ☽ ☍ ♇ 23:25 | |

## SIDEREAL HELIOCENTRIC LONGITUDES : JULY 2019 Gregorian at 0 hours UT

| DAY | Sid. Time | ☿ | ♀ | ⊕ | ♂ | ♃ | ♄ | ♅ | ♆ | ♇ | Vernal Point |
|---|---|---|---|---|---|---|---|---|---|---|---|
| 1 MO | 18:35: 3 | 5 ♏ 11 | 14 ♉ 32 | 13 ♐ 54 | 16 ♋ 50 | 26 ♏ 6 | 21 ♐ 56 | 8 ♈ 17 | 21 ♒ 52 | 26 ♐ 48 | 4 ♓ 59'17" |
| 2 TU | 18:39: 0 | 7 59 | 16 8 | 14 52 | 17 16 | 26 11 | 21 58 | 8 18 | 21 53 | 26 49 | 4 ♓ 59'17" |
| 3 WE | 18:42:56 | 10 45 | 17 45 | 15 49 | 17 43 | 26 16 | 22 0 | 8 18 | 21 53 | 26 49 | 4 ♓ 59'16" |
| 4 TH | 18:46:53 | 13 31 | 19 22 | 16 46 | 18 10 | 26 20 | 22 2 | 8 19 | 21 53 | 26 49 | 4 ♓ 59'16" |
| 5 FR | 18:50:49 | 16 16 | 20 58 | 17 43 | 18 36 | 26 25 | 22 4 | 8 20 | 21 54 | 26 50 | 4 ♓ 59'16" |
| 6 SA | 18:54:46 | 19 1 | 22 35 | 18 40 | 19 3 | 26 30 | 22 6 | 8 20 | 21 54 | 26 50 | 4 ♓ 59'16" |
| 7 SU | 18:58:42 | 21 46 | 24 12 | 19 38 | 19 30 | 26 35 | 22 7 | 8 21 | 21 54 | 26 50 | 4 ♓ 59'16" |
| 8 MO | 19: 2:39 | 24 31 | 25 48 | 20 35 | 19 56 | 26 40 | 22 9 | 8 22 | 21 55 | 26 51 | 4 ♓ 59'16" |
| 9 TU | 19: 6:35 | 27 16 | 27 25 | 21 32 | 20 23 | 26 44 | 22 11 | 8 22 | 21 55 | 26 51 | 4 ♓ 59'16" |
| 10 WE | 19:10:32 | 0 ♐ 1 | 29 2 | 22 29 | 20 49 | 26 49 | 22 13 | 8 23 | 21 55 | 26 51 | 4 ♓ 59'15" |
| 11 TH | 19:14:29 | 2 47 | 0 ♊ 39 | 23 26 | 21 16 | 26 54 | 22 15 | 8 24 | 21 56 | 26 51 | 4 ♓ 59'15" |
| 12 FR | 19:18:25 | 5 34 | 2 16 | 24 24 | 21 42 | 26 59 | 22 16 | 8 24 | 21 56 | 26 52 | 4 ♓ 59'15" |
| 13 SA | 19:22:22 | 8 22 | 3 53 | 25 21 | 22 9 | 27 4 | 22 18 | 8 25 | 21 57 | 26 52 | 4 ♓ 59'15" |
| 14 SU | 19:26:18 | 11 11 | 5 30 | 26 18 | 22 35 | 27 9 | 22 20 | 8 26 | 21 57 | 26 52 | 4 ♓ 59'15" |
| 15 MO | 19:30:15 | 14 2 | 7 7 | 27 15 | 23 2 | 27 13 | 22 22 | 8 26 | 21 57 | 26 53 | 4 ♓ 59'15" |
| 16 TU | 19:34:11 | 16 54 | 8 44 | 28 12 | 23 28 | 27 18 | 22 24 | 8 27 | 21 58 | 26 53 | 4 ♓ 59'15" |
| 17 WE | 19:38: 8 | 19 49 | 10 21 | 29 10 | 23 55 | 27 23 | 22 25 | 8 28 | 21 58 | 26 53 | 4 ♓ 59'14" |
| 18 TH | 19:42: 4 | 22 45 | 11 58 | 0 ♑ 7 | 24 21 | 27 28 | 22 27 | 8 28 | 21 58 | 26 54 | 4 ♓ 59'14" |
| 19 FR | 19:46: 1 | 25 44 | 13 35 | 1 4 | 24 48 | 27 33 | 22 29 | 8 29 | 21 59 | 26 54 | 4 ♓ 59'14" |
| 20 SA | 19:49:58 | 28 46 | 15 12 | 2 1 | 25 14 | 27 38 | 22 31 | 8 29 | 21 59 | 26 54 | 4 ♓ 59'14" |
| 21 SU | 19:53:54 | 1 ♑ 51 | 16 49 | 2 59 | 25 40 | 27 42 | 22 33 | 8 30 | 21 59 | 26 54 | 4 ♓ 59'14" |
| 22 MO | 19:57:51 | 4 59 | 18 26 | 3 56 | 26 7 | 27 47 | 22 34 | 8 31 | 22 0 | 26 55 | 4 ♓ 59'14" |
| 23 TU | 20: 1:47 | 8 10 | 20 3 | 4 53 | 26 33 | 27 52 | 22 36 | 8 31 | 22 0 | 26 55 | 4 ♓ 59'14" |
| 24 WE | 20: 5:44 | 11 25 | 21 41 | 5 50 | 27 0 | 27 57 | 22 38 | 8 32 | 22 1 | 26 55 | 4 ♓ 59'14" |
| 25 TH | 20: 9:40 | 14 44 | 23 18 | 6 48 | 27 26 | 28 2 | 22 40 | 8 33 | 22 1 | 26 56 | 4 ♓ 59'13" |
| 26 FR | 20:13:37 | 18 8 | 24 55 | 7 45 | 27 52 | 28 6 | 22 42 | 8 33 | 22 1 | 26 56 | 4 ♓ 59'13" |
| 27 SA | 20:17:33 | 21 36 | 26 32 | 8 42 | 28 19 | 28 11 | 22 43 | 8 34 | 22 2 | 26 56 | 4 ♓ 59'13" |
| 28 SU | 20:21:30 | 25 9 | 28 10 | 9 40 | 28 45 | 28 16 | 22 45 | 8 35 | 22 2 | 26 57 | 4 ♓ 59'13" |
| 29 MO | 20:25:27 | 28 48 | 29 47 | 10 37 | 29 11 | 28 21 | 22 47 | 8 35 | 22 2 | 26 57 | 4 ♓ 59'13" |
| 30 TU | 20:29:23 | 2 ♒ 33 | 1 ♋ 24 | 11 34 | 29 38 | 28 26 | 22 49 | 8 36 | 22 3 | 26 57 | 4 ♓ 59'13" |
| 31 WE | 20:33:20 | 6 24 | 3 2 | 12 32 | 0 ♌ 4 | 28 31 | 22 51 | 8 37 | 22 3 | 26 57 | 4 ♓ 59'13" |

### INGRESSES :

| |
|---|
| 9 ☿ → ♐ 23:51 |
| 10 ♀ → ♊ 14:20 |
| 17 ⊕ → ♑ 21: 7 |
| 20 ☿ → ♑ 9:39 |
| 29 ♀ → ♋ 3:11 |
| ☿ → ♒ 7:44 |
| 30 ♂ → ♌ 20:26 |

### ASPECTS (HELIOCENTRIC +MOON(TYCHONIC)) :

| | | | | | |
|---|---|---|---|---|---|
| 1 ☽ □ ♆ 2:53 | ☿ ☌ A 8:35 | 11 ☽ □ ♂ 14:43 | 19 ☽ ☍ ♂ 0:47 | ☽ □ ☿ 22:37 | ☽ □ ♅ 19: 9 |
| ☽ ☍ ♃ 10:15 | ☽ □ ☿ 9:55 | 13 ☽ □ ♆ 22:26 | ☿ ☌ ♇ 9:14 | 26 ☽ □ ♂ 17:56 | |
| 3 ☽ ☍ ♄ 5:53 | ☽ □ ♀ 13:35 | 14 ☽ ☌ ♃ 8:14 | 21 ☽ ☌ ♆ 7:43 | ⊕ □ ♅ 20:31 | |
| ☽ ☍ ♇ 13:51 | ☽ □ ♃ 16: 7 | ⊕ ☌ ♇ 14:28 | ☿ ☌ ⊕ 12:32 | 27 ♀ ☍ ♇ 5:54 | |
| 4 ☽ □ ♅ 8:46 | 8 ♀ ☍ ♃ 13:21 | 15 ☽ ☍ ♀ 3:34 | ☽ □ ♃ 19:26 | ☿ S ☊ 13:13 | |
| 5 ☽ ☌ ♂ 1:39 | ☿ ☌ ♃ 19:20 | ☽ ☌ ☿ 21:19 | 23 ☿ □ ♅ 2:41 | 28 ☽ □ ♆ 13: 3 | |
| ♀ ☌ ☊ 12:59 | 9 ☿ ☍ ♀ 3:24 | 16 ☽ ☌ ♄ 8:36 | ☽ □ ♀ 18:46 | 29 ☽ ☍ ♃ 0: 4 | |
| ⊕ ☌ A 13:36 | ☽ □ ♄ 11:18 | ☽ ☌ ♇ 17:22 | ☽ □ ♄ 21:22 | ☿ ☍ ♂ 2:49 | |
| ♀ □ ♆ 13:48 | ⊕ ☌ ♄ 16:50 | 17 ☽ □ ♅ 16:10 | 24 ☽ □ ♇ 5:52 | 30 ☽ ☍ ♄ 17:25 | |
| 7 ☿ □ ♆ 1:14 | ☽ □ ♇ 19:19 | ☿ ☌ ♄ 21:31 | ♀ ☍ ♄ 14:26 | 31 ☽ ☍ ♇ 0:12 | |
| ☽ ☍ ♆ 8:16 | 10 ☽ ☍ ♅ 15:25 | 18 ♂ N ☊ 18:43 | 25 ☽ ☌ ♅ 4:36 | ☽ ☌ ♀ 11:21 | |

Therefore, it is not thanks to the suppression of intelligence, or by becoming less intelligent, that intuition is attained; but rather, on the contrary, it is thanks to its intensification—until it becomes creative and is thus united to its higher, transcendental aspect, *after which* it is united to wisdom.[1]

The spiritual exercise of this New Moon is to practice seeing ordinary and simple things through the eyes of a child. For in *not knowing*, knowingness may then move through us—giving us the experience of the divine breath that then lives as the certainty of faith. As this New Moon is also a total eclipse of the Sun, we are reminded of the intellect's dark power, which prides itself on dismissing transcendent and childlike wisdom.

**First quarter Moon, 22° Virgo: The last anointing of Jesus Christ by Magdalene.**

**Full Moon, 29° Sagittarius: The death of Thomas.**

**Last quarter Moon, 7° Aries: Jesus teaches the way to the cross as he inwardly suffers humanity's corruption. He also speaks of his triumphant entry into Jerusalem.**

**Lunar teachings of this cycle** begin with the memory of faithful innocence and how demons seek to devour what is child-like in the human soul. As we put into action the ability to leap beyond our sense-bound limitations, we again encounter Magdalene as the first quarter Moon dawns, recalling the courage she exemplified when she anointed Christ. During the transformational period of the Full Moon, we may find our courage has increased consequent to overcoming our doubt—as did Thomas. He exemplifies the victory of faith over the eclipsing darkness of the intellect. In the integrative period of the last quarter Moon, we may find we enter more fervently onto the narrow way of the cross, ever seeking the freedom born within those who willingly accept the new light, the new intelligence, and the new way forward—toward the future city of the Lamb and his Bride.

**Jul 3: Sun 16° Gemini: Conception of the Solomon Jesus (6/7/7 BC).** Still under the influence of yesterday's New Moon, we recall the conception of wisdom, the Solomon Jesus, and the magi who followed the star to find him. This is the Jesus child described in the Gospel of St. Matthew, whose lineage is traced back to Abraham.

The Solomon Jesus, also referred to as the Master Jesus, was the reincarnation of the mighty individuality who once lived on Earth as Zarathustra. At his conception, a mighty flow of cosmic forces streamed into the hereditary lineage of ancient Israel, potentially redeeming in its wake all that had gone astray. This lineage had begun at the blessing of Abraham, and it continued as the Yahweh stream in the blood of all future generations of Israel.

The conception Sun of the Master Jesus is very close to the star Sirius (19° Gemini), which is sometimes referred to as the star of the Master Jesus. In contemplating transits to the conceptions, births, and deaths of the great initiates, we gain the possibility of communing with them via the portals that are opened when the stars remember their transitions between earthly and spiritual worlds. Reawaking to the potential of these star memories is part of the mystery tradition inherent in a new star wisdom.

**Jul 8: ASPECT: Mercury stations retrograde and conjuncts Mars 9° Cancer.** Mercury remembers Jesus as he taught and healed and also drove out demons from those possessed. Sinners and publicans encompassed him on all sides; and on the roads by which he had to pass lay the sick, sighing and imploring help. He taught and cured without intermission, and was eminently gentle, earnest, and tranquil (Jun/8/32).

**Jul 9: 2nd Quarter Moon 22° Virgo: Last Anointing (Apr/1/33).** The New Moon recalled Magdalene's conversion and the restoration of faithful innocence. Now we are asked to change our ways, which takes courage. This is exactly what Magdalene exemplified as she walked into a room filled with Jewish men, who were stunned by her audacity, to anoint Jesus. Is there not always an innocence in true courage?

**ASPECT: Sun 22° Gemini opposite Saturn 22° Sagittarius.** The Sun recalls Jesus and the disciples after they had dined together; they all went to

---
1 Ibid., p. 542.

Andrew's house, where accounts were given of the missionary journeys undertaken by each. That evening, Jesus returned to his mother's house, where he introduced the newly converted disciples to her. This was so that she, as their "spiritual mother," could find a place for each in her heart and in her prayers and bestow her blessings upon them (Jun/14/31).

The resurrecting powers of the Sun standing across the heavens from the Holy Virgin (Saturn) lend vigor to our "I," calling it to rise to its full dignity—not only to meet our own destiny resolves, but also to more consciously serve the mission of the Earth and humanity.

If we are to restore the world's innocence, we are wise to recognize our spiritual Mother and to accept the loving embrace of the Holy Virgin.

**Jul 11: ASPECT: Mars 11° Cancer square Uranus 11° Aries.** The Sun was where Uranus is today as Jesus taught for the last time in the temple. Before leaving his disciples, he wished to bestow on them all that he had—not money and property, which he did not have, but his power and his forces. He also wanted to establish an intimate union with them, a more perfect union than the present one, that would endure until the end of the world. He asked them to become united with one another *as limbs of one body* (Mar/31/33).

In an immoral soul, the effects of this influence would cause agitation, restlessness, and recklessness. It is unsettling to imagine how this aspect may release lower energies and then play out in world events. When influencing the spiritually mature, however, the power of Michael—in dynamic tension with the Uranian force of lightning quick change—is the signature of those who change the world.

John the Baptist was born under this aspect (i.e., with Mars also in Cancer). He is a perfect example of one who stood at the turning point in time as an eccentric idealist determined to change the world.

The "power and forces" that Jesus wanted to bestow upon his disciples can be thought of as Mars/Uranus forces, i.e., the lightning of direct revelation and the forceful powers upon which such revelation come to manifestation. As this last teaching in the Temple was before his death, before he bestowed the Pentecostal fire upon the disciples, he could not yet transmit to them as he wished. Asking them to unite with one another, however, was the teaching he could give, preparing them to become a group vessel that would, ever again, receive his teachings until the end of time. Such united groups must continue to form if we are to serve the radical change the Satya Yuga is bringing to spiritually-focused communities. Indeed, the time of the dominance of the sense-bound intellect is over. Beware, however, those who claim they stand in the revelation stream. Those who do stand in this stream, would *not* speak of this. Instead, they would selflessly serve the community's awaking—at the expense of being recognized themselves. The way is so painfully narrow, and so poignantly void of egoism!

**Jul 14: ASPECT: Sun 27° Gemini opposite Pluto 27° Sagittarius.** The Sun shone from Pluto's degree as Jesus went to Carianthaim after healing people on the outskirts of Saphet. Before entering the town, he blessed a group of children. Later, in synagogue, Jesus taught again on the Beatitudes and interpreted a passage regarding Solomon's temple from 1 Kings 6:15–19: "He lined the walls of the house on the inside with boards of cedar; from the floor of the house to the rafters of the ceiling, he covered them on the inside with wood; and he covered the floor of the house with boards of cypress. He built twenty cubits of the rear of the house with boards of cedar from the floor to the rafters, and he built this within as an inner sanctuary, as the most holy place" (Dec/17/30).

No matter how well we construct walls of protection, we are wise to find our resilience when Phanes faces us with the need to change. The inner sanctuary of our temple, our heart, commends our spirit to obey our Father. Friedrich Nietzsche was born under this aspect. He beheld the "superman" when he could instead have become a spirit-messenger.

**Jul 16: ASPECT: Full Moon 29° Sagittarius opposite Sun 29° Gemini and Partial Lunar Eclipse over Africa, western India, Australia, and southernmost South America, 5:37 EDT.** The Moon reached this zodiacal degree on the evening of the day when

Jesus healed ten lepers, and later raised from the dead the young daughter of one of the healed men (Jun/12/32). The Sun at this degree remembers the death of Thomas (12/18/72).

As Sun and Moon unite in the last degree of Sagittarius, we bid farewell to the Archer and his razor thin focus on truth. Early next year, in January of 2020, Saturn will enter Capricorn. Are our quivers filled with truth's arrows, in readiness to climb the high mountain to realms where the thinking of the gods holds sway (Capricorn)? This Moon tests us as it brings with it the shadow of a lunar eclipse. Will the sense-bound intellect obscure the high peaks wherein the faithful gather?

Mystical revelation bestows its riches upon the humble. From humility we begin the arduous ascent toward the restoration of our freedom. The means by which this is achieved is through the burgeoning power of sacred magic. For when we acknowledge that we are but the lowest rung in the hierarchies of heaven, we fall on our knees in homage to what we do *not* yet know. Thus does the magical remedy fall into our hands as the means through which we rediscover the fact that we have imprisoned ourselves in the "dangerous reason of our time." Thus do we seek the liberating action that sets the soul free, granting movement to the enslaved, healing to the sick, and flight to the wings of spirit. As we soar into realms of spirit thinking, we leave behind doubt, fear, hate, apathy, and despair. Rising above the trivial, we enter the profundity of new sight; we bow to the hierarchies upon whose ladder we begin our ascent. During an eclipse, we remember that we are not to fear the devil; *rather are we to expose the perverse tendencies in ourselves.*

> Humankind, with the possible perversity of their warped imagination, is far more dangerous than the devil and his legions. For human beings are not bound by the convention concluded between Heaven and Hell; they can go beyond the limits of the law and engender *arbitrarily* malicious forces whose nature and action are *beyond* the framework of the law.[1]

Indeed, we are the most dangerous species upon the Earth, for we negate the truth of hierarchy—and this is the primal cause behind all violence. Thus do we, without regret, manipulate, engineer, and abuse the sacred creation that has been given to us. Our sorrowful Mother mourns our ignorance as she bears witness to the fact that we are choosing to fall even further from our paradisiacal home.

St. Paul, who was blinded outside the gates of Damascus, received the Grail light directly from the Risen Christ—i.e., he awakeed *in* truth as he awakeed to the One who bore the light of truth in sacrifice to the all of humanity. Must we not "re-cognize" our place in the holy order of things? Nature is the ground upon which the future will rise into a new manifestation of being. Thus is the ground upon which we walk the holiest of holies. Yet, time and time again, we set ourselves against her.

> For the creation waits with eager longing for the revealing of the sons [and daughters] of God; for the creation was subjected to futility, not of its own will but by the will of him who subjected it in hope; because the creation itself will be set free from its bondage to decay and obtain the glorious liberty of the children of God. We know that the whole creation has been groaning in travail together until now; and not only the creation, but we ourselves, who have the first fruits of the Spirit, groan inwardly as we wait for adoption as sons [and daughers], the redemption of our bodies. (Rom. 8:19–23)

This Full Moon is the transformational fulfillment of what was set in action at the New Moon: our remembrance of innocent faithfulness, through which we restore the childlike heart. Such purity of soul renders demons no abode within us. The first quarter Moon set us the task of recognizing the Christ, "anointing" him as we gain the courage to behold him in all others. Now we remember Thomas, who overcame all doubt to enter the community then forming: the community of Eternal Israel. The integrating period of the last quarter Moon soon to come will challenge us to suffer our way into the new light.

**Jul 17: ASPECT: Venus 21° Gemini opposite Saturn 21° Sagittarius.** Venus was at this exact degree as Jesus restored sight to two blind people sitting

---

1 Ibid., p. 62.

by the roadside about an hour from Jericho. They had cried out, "Have mercy on us, Son of David!" When Jesus asked them what they wanted him to do for them, they replied: "Lord, let our eyes be opened" (Jun/10/32).

The holy cross of Venus stands opposite the loving embrace of the Holy Virgin (Saturn). The Blessed Virgin bore witness to every moment in the agony of her son's Passion. This was eternally inscribed into the memory of the world. On that fateful Friday, as her son hung dying upon the cross, her heart beat with his sacred heart—thereby gracing the world with the meaning of love.

Our willingness to carry our cross helps Christ carry his cross—in whatever small measure. For this he will continue to do until each of us have fully taken up our own.

This aspect occurred as the forty days in the wilderness began, informing us that *trial precedes victory*. Inversely, if we refuse to carry the weight that is ours alone, we will find the cross too heavy and we will instead lay it down. In so doing, our heart will remain hardened against the promise of an awaiting victory. Love is the way, and without an open heart, the Holy Virgin cannot show us that which is ours to see.

**Sun enters Cancer:** "**Thou resting, glowing light**, create life warmth; warm soul-life to gain strength in test of trial, to become spirit-permeated, in peaceful light created. Thou glowing light, become strong!" (Steiner, *Twelve Cosmic Moods*).

The late William Bento illumines this mantra:

> As the Sun reaches its zenith in the summer sky, it appears to rest and emit a luminous glow of warmth and light. This high point of the yearly cycle offers us the opportunity to express our gratitude for all the life we see around us, knowing that its existence is due to the Sun's luminosity. This phase opens the breast and allows our heart to enter dialogue with the mighty orb of warmth and light that bestows life to all.

In Cancer, "Selflessness becomes Catharsis." (The Cathars were the pure ones.) The instinct to purify oneself is now amplified. The first decan is ruled by Mercury and is associated with the constellation of Argo the Ship—in which, according to Greek mythology, Jason and the Argonauts recovered the Golden Fleece.

**Jul 21: ASPECT: Venus 27° Gemini opposite Pluto 27° Sagittarius.** Venus remembers Jesus as he visited an iron mine and spoke the words: "And as you wish that men would do to you, do so to them (May/4/31). The cross, again, is our contemplation. Today, however, Venus stands opposite Pluto. O Phanes, how we long to hear your refrains of peace—yet our hearts have grown cold and our wills lack the iron of courage!

Where we have turned from obedience to Pluto–Phanes, we encounter a need to control others and situations, to become obsessed, and even to experience violence that otherwise would remain beneath the surface—in both the world and in ourselves.

A simple remedy is given: to do unto others as we would have them do unto us. As we practice this, we heal our brokenness by taking up the cross of love.

**ASPECT 2: Inferior conjunction of Sun and Mercury 3° Cancer.** The Sun recalls Jesus as he ended his morning teaching with a talk on the significance of the word *Amen*. The Holy Virgin begged Jesus not to go to Jerusalem, fearing for his safety. Jesus comforted her, but he also told her that she should be courageous and should strengthen and encourage the others (Jun/25/31).

The superior conjunction of May 21st remembered the seven sisters of harmony: the Pleiades. We then gathered intuitions from the cosmic beings of the zodiac. Today the inferior conjunction pours upon us the images that light our way to the great Amen, the Cosmic Christ who leads us where it is we need to go.

**Jul 23: Venus enters Cancer:** "Thou resting, glowing light, **create life-warmth**; warm soul life to gain strength in test of trial, to become spirit-permeated, in peaceful light created. Thou glowing light, become strong!" (Steiner, *Twelve Cosmic Moods*).

**Jul 24: ASPECT: Mercury conjunct Venus 1° Cancer.** Venus enlivened the memory of Jesus as he continued to teach near the well at Chytroi while the disciples baptized. Later he went to the village of Mallep, where he was received with joy and celebration. In the synagogue there he taught concerning the Lord's Prayer petition "Thy Kingdom Come" (May/9/31). Heart and mind find harmony at the onset of the last period in this lunar cycle.

**4th Quarter Moon 7° Aries.** This Moon remembers Jesus in the temple in Jerusalem, teaching from the teacher's chair in the portico of Solomon, where he had taught at age twelve. Jesus spoke with great seriousness of the way leading to the Cross. Inwardly, he was torn with sorrow at humanity's corruption (Feb/20/33). The integration of the lunar cycle is upon us. This cycle began with the memory of innocence and faithfulness, as we recalled the conversion of Magdalene. The first quarter Moon challenged us to gather courage. The Full Moon confronted us with the trial of overcoming doubt, and of remembering the sacred ground of our Mother. Now all must be integrated if we are to strengthen our relationship to angelic worlds. As we suffer our corruption, and the corruption of all humanity, we are never to lay down the burden that is ours to carry. For, the cross represents the measure of our spiritual weight. When carried, it leads us to the future that is ours alone to discover. The heart knows the way; thus must it remain open, willingly suffering in silent devotion to something higher than itself.

**Jul 27: Mercury enters Gemini:** "Reveal thyself, Sun life; set repose in movement; **embrace joyful striving** toward life's mighty weaving, toward blissful world-knowing, toward fruitful ripe-growing. O Sun life, endure!" (Steiner, *Twelve Cosmic Moods*). Mercury rules in this sign.

**Jul 29: ASPECT: Sun 11° Cancer square Uranus 11° Aries.** The Sun at Uranus's degree recalls Jesus and Obed as they entered the inner court of the temple in Jerusalem, where the priests and Levites were holding a discourse concerning the Passover festival. Jesus threw the assembly into consternation by telling them that the sacrifice of the paschal lamb (meaning the Lamb of God) would soon be fulfilled, so that the temple and its services would then come to an end (Apr/1/30).

The resurrecting power of the Sun, in dynamic tension with Uranus, is the harbinger of change. The soul trembles as the unknown approaches. Where do we find solace? Imagine being faced with a blinding light, unknowable in its radiance. We see it coming toward us. Does fear arise? Anger? Such emotions inform us of our unwillingness to meet change. Yet, this same aspect occurred (in different signs) at the Ascension of Christ. This event is the perfect example of the power inherent in this cosmic signature: we are to rise into the light and sacrifice whatever in us fears what the light brings.

**Jul 31: ASPECT: New Moon 13° Cancer.** The Moon stands before the mystery of the Cosmic Beehive. This new lunar cycle occurs in what is known as the Beehive (Greek: *Praesepe*). The Beehive marks the cluster of stars at the center of the two spiraling arms of the constellation of Cancer. This area is also what is known in Hinduism as the lunar *nakshatra Pushya* (4°-17° Cancer). Through this divine portal, Greek legend tells us, human souls enter creation to gather the nectar of earthly experience. This they will later return to the Queen of Heaven: Sophia.

Furthermore, the prophesied incarnation of the Kalki Avatar (Hinduism)—also known as the Maitreya Buddha (Buddhism)—will occur when Sun, Moon, and Jupiter are in this region of the heavens.

> When the Supreme Lord has appeared on Earth as Kalki, the maintainer of religion, Satya Yuga will begin, and human society will bring forth progeny in the mode of goodness....When the Moon, the Sun, and Brhaspati (Jupiter) are together in the constellation Karkata (Cancer), and all three enter simultaneously into the lunar mansion Pushya—at that exact moment the age of Satya, or Krita, will begin. (*Gautama Buddha's Successor*, chapter one: 2014 and the Coming of the Kalki Avatar.)

Rudolf Steiner spoke of cultural rhythms, which occur every 600 years. The cultural age of Pisces began in the year 1414, signifying the onset of a new cultural rhythm. Moving 600 years into the future, the next onset of a cultural rhythm began in the year 2014. Steiner also spoke of Satya Yuga as a period he called the "New Age of Light," which began, according to him, at the close of the 20th century. Furthermore, he foresaw that a new turning point would enter human consciousness around 1933—which marked the onset of the Second Coming of Christ in the etheric realm.

As we entered into the new millennium in the year 2000, we began to mirror the time period before Christ (2000 BC) when Abraham was leading his people out of atavistic clairvoyance into clear day-waking consciousness. The Age of Light has the mission to lead clear day-waking consciousness into realms of imagination, i.e., into a conscious "I"-imbued clairvoyance wherein human beings are able to reconnect with angelic spheres. *In the time of Abraham, we suffered night consciousness into day, and now we must suffer day consciousness into night—i.e., we long ago lost our effortless union with the Divine, and now we must reclaim this through overcoming our moribund brain-bound thinking.* This alone assures that we will gather nectar from higher beings.

Dr. Steiner was very clear that the individuality in the process of becoming the Maitreya Buddha had incarnated at the beginning of the 20th century (just after the beginning of Satya Yuga) and would become noticeable in the 1930s. Furthermore, he stated that the main mission of this person (who has been identified by many as Valentin Tomberg) would be to proclaim the advent of the Second Coming of Christ.

The prophecy of the Kalki–Maitreya's reincarnation—which was to occur when Sun, Moon, and Jupiter come together in the Beehive—perhaps took place in 2014 as these three heavenly bodies indeed lined up at the center of the spiraling arms of the constellation of Cancer. The state of the world as Kali Yuga (i.e., the age of darkness) concluded was prophesied as a time when goodness would be painfully needed in the community of humanity.

> By the time the age of Kali ends... religious principles will be ruined... So-called religion will be mostly atheistic... the occupations of men will be stealing, lying, and needless violence, and all the social classes will be reduced to the lowest level... Family ties will extend no further than the immediate bonds of marriage... homes will be devoid of piety, and all human beings will have become like assess. At that time, the Supreme personality of the Godhead will appear on the Earth. Acting with the power of pure spiritual goodness, he will rescue eternal religion... Lord Kali will appear in... the great soul of *Vishnuyasha*... When the Supreme Lord has appeared on Earth as Kalki, the maintainer of religion, *Satya Yuga* will begin, and human society will bring forth progeny in the mode of goodness. (*S'rimad Bhagavatam* 12; 2:16–23)

Most would agree that our times are very much like the above description. We are five years into the new cultural rhythm that began in 2014. Moreover, we are living in the historic unfolding of the 40th day in the wilderness, the day when angels came to minister to Jesus Christ. They long to minister also to us.

This New Moon asks us: Are we ready to see? Can we take the leap into realms of light that are now filled with new dispensations? Are we prepared to live into an Age of Light: the Satya Yuga?

**First quarter Moon, 20° Libra: Guards seize Jesus as his Father speaks (Theophany): "This is my beloved Son."**

**Full Moon, 27° Capricorn: Vision of Ezekiel regarding the breath of the Holy Spirit breathed into the dead.**

**Last quarter Moon, 5° Taurus: Healing of the paralyzed man.**

**Lunar teachings this cycle** begin with the memory of the Age of Light and the necessity of reestablishing our communion with angelic beings. As the first quarter Moon dawns, we recall the furious power of envy as the Pharisees attempted to take Jesus into custody. The Full Moon reminds us to raise the dead within, for they are naught but the binding power of guilt that turn us from the light. In the integrating phase of the last quarter, we also remember the paralyzed man, who suffered in this life what he bound himself to in his former life.

# AUGUST 2019

## Stargazing Preview

Following sunset on the 1st you might get a momentary glimpse of the Moon-Mars conjunction; the Moon by now will appear as a silvery edge of light. At sunset on the 9th, Jupiter will be overhead, due south, slightly to the right of the Moon; you'll see Saturn lower in the east, to their left. Two days later, Jupiter will station direct.

The 12th is a big day for stargazing! Once the Sun is down, you'll be able to see Jupiter high in the southeastern sky. From there, if you follow the ecliptic toward the eastern horizon, you'll find the Moon and Saturn. Now you'll be ready for the main event: the peak of the Perseid meteor showers! They are so-named because they appear to radiate from the constellation Perseus, seen above the Ram and the Bull. Your best viewing time frame will be between moonset (0330) and sunrise (0630); bundle up with a friend and look for the radiant in the NNE, below Cassiopeia. Good luck!

Invisible to the eye but important to be aware of is the August 14th superior conjunction of the Sun and Venus. For the rest of the year, Venus will be an evening star, though she won't be visible for a while yet. August's Capricorn Full Moon takes place on the 15th.

The 30th will bring us the Leo New Moon; in fact, Mercury, the Sun and Moon, Mars, *and* Venus will all be nestled in Leo, no more than 9° apart. I can feel the heat from here! You'll be able to see Orion high in the southern sky just before sunrise.

## August Commentaries

**Aug 2: ASPECT: Venus 11° Cancer square Uranus 11° Aries.** Venus remembers Jesus teaching all day, expounding again upon the theme of the persecution of the prophets that is summarized in Matthew 21:33-43. In this passage, Jesus says, "The very stone which the builders rejected has become the head of the corner; this was the Lord's doing" (Jul/27/30).

The lovely cross of Venus, in dynamic tension with the light-bringer (Uranus), challenges us to discern between the holy light of spirit and the unholy light of Lucifer. When the holy light illumines our karmic communities, we face the challenge of having to change our ways and adjust to what the new light asks of us. This assures continuity of growth.

Venus marks the orbit wherein dwell the mighty archai, the Spirits of Time. These lofty beings send waves of human beings into creation to carry out what must be developed in evolution's unfolding in time. Thus do they sound us together into groups. Sometimes the sound is a cacophony of negative karma seeking *resolution* (Moon karma); sometimes it is the harmony of good karma seeking to continue its *blessedness* (Sun karma). In either case, we are shown how to align with the primal essence of love as it resounds continuously in the "wave" of our destiny.

The prophets who come into incarnation to model new capacities, i.e., new relationships to higher worlds, are too often persecuted. Nonetheless, few go completely unnoticed as they represent the center around which karmic communities form.

This aspect occurred at the death of the Solomon Mary, with Venus also in Cancer. Her death was an assumption into heaven, for she left no footprints in the sands of ordinary time. Instead, she paved the way for each of us to find our way into Earth's future manifestation. Therefore, we see that this dynamic tension serves to reveal where we have turned from the light, building false structures upon a cornerstone fashioned in the "Belt of Lies"—Lucifer's kingdom.

What footsteps are we leaving behind us? Would we not rather face them now, so as to lessen the burden we will meet as we cross the threshold?

**Aug 5: Mercury enters Cancer:** "Thou resting, glowing light; create life-warmth; **warm soul-life** to gain strength in test of trial, to become spirit-permeated, in peaceful light created. Thou glowing light, become strong!" (Steiner, *Twelve Cosmic Moods*).

**Aug 7: First Quarter Moon 20° Libra.** The Moon shone from this degree as the temple guards took custody of Jesus after they learned that he'd been healing on the Sabbath. At the height of the uproar,

## SIDEREAL GEOCENTRIC LONGITUDES : AUGUST 2019 Gregorian at 0 hours UT

| DAY | ☉ | ☽ | ☊ | ☿ | ♀ | ♂ | ♃ | ♄ | ♅ | ♆ | ♇ |
|---|---|---|---|---|---|---|---|---|---|---|---|
| 1 TH | 13 ♋ 29 | 11 ♋ 37 | 22 ♊ 35R | 28 ♊ 56R | 9 ♋ 49 | 24 ♋ 3 | 19 ♏ 40R | 20 ♐ 38R | 11 ♈ 33 | 23 ♒ 18R | 26 ♐ 28R |
| 2 FR | 14 26 | 26 37 | 22 33 | 28 58D | 11 3 | 24 41 | 19 38 | 20 34 | 11 34 | 23 17 | 26 26 |
| 3 SA | 15 23 | 11 ♌ 41 | 22 31 | 29 7 | 12 17 | 25 19 | 19 36 | 20 30 | 11 34 | 23 16 | 26 25 |
| 4 SU | 16 21 | 26 40 | 22 28 | 29 21 | 13 31 | 25 58 | 19 35 | 20 26 | 11 34 | 23 15 | 26 24 |
| 5 MO | 17 18 | 11 ♍ 25 | 22 25 | 29 43 | 14 45 | 26 36 | 19 34 | 20 22 | 11 35 | 23 13 | 26 22 |
| 6 TU | 18 16 | 25 51 | 22 22 | 0 ♋ 10 | 15 59 | 27 14 | 19 32 | 20 19 | 11 35 | 23 12 | 26 21 |
| 7 WE | 19 13 | 9 ♎ 55 | 22 21 | 0 45 | 17 13 | 27 52 | 19 31 | 20 15 | 11 35 | 23 11 | 26 20 |
| 8 TH | 20 11 | 23 35 | 22 21D | 1 25 | 18 27 | 28 30 | 19 31 | 20 12 | 11 36 | 23 9 | 26 18 |
| 9 FR | 21 8 | 6 ♏ 52 | 22 21 | 2 12 | 19 41 | 29 8 | 19 30 | 20 8 | 11 36 | 23 8 | 26 17 |
| 10 SA | 22 6 | 19 49 | 22 23 | 3 6 | 20 55 | 29 46 | 19 30 | 20 5 | 11 36 | 23 7 | 26 16 |
| 11 SU | 23 3 | 2 ♐ 29 | 22 25 | 4 6 | 22 9 | 0 ♌ 24 | 19 30 | 20 1 | 11 36 | 23 5 | 26 14 |
| 12 MO | 24 1 | 14 54 | 22 26 | 5 11 | 23 23 | 1 2 | 19 30D | 19 58 | 11 36 | 23 4 | 26 13 |
| 13 TU | 24 58 | 27 8 | 22 26R | 6 23 | 24 38 | 1 40 | 19 30 | 19 55 | 11 36R | 23 3 | 26 12 |
| 14 WE | 25 56 | 9 ♑ 13 | 22 25 | 7 40 | 25 52 | 2 18 | 19 30 | 19 52 | 11 36 | 23 1 | 26 11 |
| 15 TH | 26 53 | 21 12 | 22 22 | 9 3 | 27 6 | 2 56 | 19 31 | 19 49 | 11 36 | 23 0 | 26 9 |
| 16 FR | 27 51 | 3 ♒ 6 | 22 17 | 10 30 | 28 20 | 3 35 | 19 31 | 19 46 | 11 36 | 22 58 | 26 8 |
| 17 SA | 28 49 | 14 58 | 22 11 | 12 3 | 29 34 | 4 13 | 19 32 | 19 43 | 11 35 | 22 57 | 26 7 |
| 18 SU | 29 46 | 26 49 | 22 4 | 13 39 | 0 ♌ 48 | 4 51 | 19 33 | 19 40 | 11 35 | 22 55 | 26 6 |
| 19 MO | 0 ♌ 44 | 8 ♓ 41 | 21 57 | 15 20 | 2 3 | 5 29 | 19 35 | 19 37 | 11 35 | 22 54 | 26 5 |
| 20 TU | 1 42 | 20 37 | 21 50 | 17 5 | 3 17 | 6 7 | 19 36 | 19 34 | 11 34 | 22 52 | 26 4 |
| 21 WE | 2 39 | 2 ♈ 40 | 21 45 | 18 52 | 4 31 | 6 45 | 19 38 | 19 32 | 11 34 | 22 51 | 26 3 |
| 22 TH | 3 37 | 14 52 | 21 41 | 20 43 | 5 45 | 7 23 | 19 39 | 19 29 | 11 34 | 22 49 | 26 1 |
| 23 FR | 4 35 | 27 18 | 21 40 | 22 36 | 7 0 | 8 1 | 19 41 | 19 27 | 11 33 | 22 48 | 26 0 |
| 24 SA | 5 33 | 10 ♉ 2 | 21 39D | 24 31 | 8 14 | 8 40 | 19 44 | 19 24 | 11 33 | 22 46 | 25 59 |
| 25 SU | 6 31 | 23 8 | 21 40 | 26 27 | 9 28 | 9 18 | 19 46 | 19 22 | 11 32 | 22 45 | 25 58 |
| 26 MO | 7 29 | 6 ♊ 40 | 21 41 | 28 24 | 10 42 | 9 56 | 19 49 | 19 20 | 11 31 | 22 43 | 25 57 |
| 27 TU | 8 26 | 20 38 | 21 42R | 0 ♌ 23 | 11 57 | 10 34 | 19 51 | 19 18 | 11 31 | 22 42 | 25 56 |
| 28 WE | 9 24 | 5 ♋ 4 | 21 41 | 2 22 | 13 11 | 11 12 | 19 54 | 19 16 | 11 30 | 22 40 | 25 55 |
| 29 TH | 10 22 | 19 54 | 21 39 | 4 21 | 14 26 | 11 50 | 19 57 | 19 14 | 11 29 | 22 38 | 25 54 |
| 30 FR | 11 20 | 5 ♌ 2 | 21 34 | 6 20 | 15 40 | 12 29 | 20 1 | 19 12 | 11 28 | 22 37 | 25 53 |
| 31 SA | 12 18 | 20 18 | 21 27 | 8 18 | 16 54 | 13 7 | 20 4 | 19 10 | 11 27 | 22 35 | 25 53 |

### INGRESSES :

2 ☽ → ♌ 5:22
4 ☽ → ♍ 5:23
5 ☿ → ♋ 15:45
6 ☽ → ♎ 7: 0
8 ☽ → ♏ 11:30
10 ♂ → ♌ 8:48
☽ → ♐ 19:16
13 ☽ → ♑ 5:40
15 ☽ → ♒ 17:44
17 ♀ → ♌ 8:21
18 ☉ → ♌ 5:39
☽ → ♓ 6:26
20 ☽ → ♈ 18:43
23 ☽ → ♉ 5: 7
25 ☽ → ♊ 12:16
26 ☿ → ♌ 19:23
27 ☽ → ♋ 15:39
29 ☽ → ♌ 16: 4
31 ☽ → ♍ 15:14

### ASPECTS & ECLIPSES :

1 ☉ ☌ ☽ 3:10
☽ ☌ ♂ 20:46
2 ☽ ☌ P 7:12
♀ □ ♅ 9:58
3 ☽ ☍ ♆ 18:29
5 ☽ N□ ☊ 18: 9
7 ☽ ☍ ♅ 2:54
☉ □ ☽ 17:29
9 ☽ ☌ ♃ 23:23
12 ☽ ☌ ♄ 9:52
☽ ☌ ☋ 14:45
☽ ☌ ♇ 22:10
13 ☽ ☍ ☿ 20:31
14 ☉ S☌ ♀ 6: 6
15 ☉ ☍ ☽ 12:28
☽ ☍ ♀ 13:15
16 ☽ ☍ ♂ 1: 0
☿ □ ♅ 17: 5
17 ☽ ☌ A 11:13
☽ ☌ ♆ 16: 8
20 ☽ □S ☊ 2:25
21 ☽ ☌ ♅ 17:32
23 ☉ □ ☽ 14:55
24 ♀ ☌ ♂ 17: 3
☽ ☍ ♃ 17:52
26 ☽ ☍ ♄ 21:44
27 ☽ ☌ ☊ 1:47
☽ ☍ ♇ 8:53
30 ☽ ☌ ☿ 2:21
☉ ☌ ☽ 10:36
☽ ☌ ♂ 12:13
☽ ☌ P 15:50
☽ ☌ ♀ 18:11
31 ☽ ☍ ♆ 3:34

## SIDEREAL HELIOCENTRIC LONGITUDES : AUGUST 2019 Gregorian at 0 hours UT

| DAY | Sid. Time | ☿ | ♀ | ⊕ | ♂ | ♃ | ♄ | ♅ | ♆ | ♇ | Vernal Point |
|---|---|---|---|---|---|---|---|---|---|---|---|
| 1 TH | 20:37:16 | 10 ♒ 21 | 4 ♋ 39 | 13 ♑ 29 | 0 ♌ 30 | 28 ♏ 35 | 22 ♐ 53 | 8 ♈ 37 | 22 ♒ 3 | 26 ♐ 58 | 4 ♓ 59'12" |
| 2 FR | 20:41:13 | 14 25 | 6 17 | 14 27 | 0 56 | 28 40 | 22 54 | 8 38 | 22 4 | 26 58 | 4 ♓ 59'12" |
| 3 SA | 20:45: 9 | 18 36 | 7 54 | 15 24 | 1 23 | 28 45 | 22 56 | 8 39 | 22 4 | 26 58 | 4 ♓ 59'12" |
| 4 SU | 20:49: 6 | 22 55 | 9 31 | 16 21 | 1 49 | 28 50 | 22 58 | 8 39 | 22 5 | 26 59 | 4 ♓ 59'12" |
| 5 MO | 20:53: 2 | 27 22 | 11 9 | 17 19 | 2 15 | 28 55 | 23 0 | 8 40 | 22 5 | 26 59 | 4 ♓ 59'12" |
| 6 TU | 20:56:59 | 1 ♓ 58 | 12 46 | 18 16 | 2 42 | 29 0 | 23 2 | 8 41 | 22 5 | 26 59 | 4 ♓ 59'12" |
| 7 WE | 21: 0:56 | 6 42 | 14 24 | 19 14 | 3 8 | 29 4 | 23 3 | 8 41 | 22 6 | 27 0 | 4 ♓ 59'12" |
| 8 TH | 21: 4:52 | 11 34 | 16 1 | 20 11 | 3 34 | 29 9 | 23 5 | 8 42 | 22 6 | 27 0 | 4 ♓ 59'11" |
| 9 FR | 21: 8:49 | 16 36 | 17 39 | 21 9 | 4 0 | 29 14 | 23 7 | 8 43 | 22 6 | 27 0 | 4 ♓ 59'11" |
| 10 SA | 21:12:45 | 21 47 | 19 16 | 22 6 | 4 27 | 29 19 | 23 9 | 8 43 | 22 7 | 27 1 | 4 ♓ 59'11" |
| 11 SU | 21:16:42 | 27 7 | 20 54 | 23 4 | 4 53 | 29 24 | 23 11 | 8 44 | 22 7 | 27 1 | 4 ♓ 59'11" |
| 12 MO | 21:20:38 | 2 ♈ 36 | 22 31 | 24 1 | 5 19 | 29 29 | 23 12 | 8 45 | 22 7 | 27 1 | 4 ♓ 59'11" |
| 13 TU | 21:24:35 | 8 14 | 24 9 | 24 59 | 5 45 | 29 33 | 23 14 | 8 45 | 22 8 | 27 1 | 4 ♓ 59'11" |
| 14 WE | 21:28:31 | 14 0 | 25 46 | 25 56 | 6 11 | 29 38 | 23 16 | 8 46 | 22 8 | 27 2 | 4 ♓ 59'11" |
| 15 TH | 21:32:28 | 19 54 | 27 24 | 26 54 | 6 38 | 29 43 | 23 18 | 8 47 | 22 9 | 27 2 | 4 ♓ 59'11" |
| 16 FR | 21:36:25 | 25 55 | 29 1 | 27 52 | 7 4 | 29 48 | 23 20 | 8 47 | 22 9 | 27 2 | 4 ♓ 59'10" |
| 17 SA | 21:40:21 | 2 ♉ 2 | 0 ♌ 39 | 28 49 | 7 30 | 29 53 | 23 21 | 8 48 | 22 9 | 27 3 | 4 ♓ 59'10" |
| 18 SU | 21:44:18 | 8 14 | 2 16 | 29 47 | 7 56 | 29 58 | 23 23 | 8 49 | 22 10 | 27 3 | 4 ♓ 59'10" |
| 19 MO | 21:48:14 | 14 30 | 3 54 | 0 ♒ 45 | 8 23 | 0 ♐ 2 | 23 25 | 8 49 | 22 10 | 27 3 | 4 ♓ 59'10" |
| 20 TU | 21:52:11 | 20 48 | 5 31 | 1 42 | 8 49 | 0 7 | 23 27 | 8 50 | 22 10 | 27 4 | 4 ♓ 59'10" |
| 21 WE | 21:56: 7 | 27 7 | 7 9 | 2 40 | 9 15 | 0 12 | 23 29 | 8 51 | 22 11 | 27 4 | 4 ♓ 59'10" |
| 22 TH | 22: 0: 4 | 3 ♊ 26 | 8 46 | 3 38 | 9 41 | 0 17 | 23 31 | 8 51 | 22 11 | 27 4 | 4 ♓ 59'10" |
| 23 FR | 22: 4: 0 | 9 43 | 10 24 | 4 36 | 10 7 | 0 22 | 23 32 | 8 52 | 22 11 | 27 4 | 4 ♓ 59' 9" |
| 24 SA | 22: 7:57 | 15 56 | 12 1 | 5 33 | 10 34 | 0 27 | 23 34 | 8 52 | 22 12 | 27 5 | 4 ♓ 59' 9" |
| 25 SU | 22:11:54 | 22 4 | 13 39 | 6 31 | 11 0 | 0 32 | 23 36 | 8 53 | 22 12 | 27 5 | 4 ♓ 59' 9" |
| 26 MO | 22:15:50 | 28 6 | 15 16 | 7 29 | 11 26 | 0 36 | 23 38 | 8 54 | 22 13 | 27 5 | 4 ♓ 59' 9" |
| 27 TU | 22:19:47 | 4 ♋ 1 | 16 54 | 8 27 | 11 52 | 0 41 | 23 40 | 8 54 | 22 13 | 27 6 | 4 ♓ 59' 9" |
| 28 WE | 22:23:43 | 9 48 | 18 31 | 9 25 | 12 18 | 0 46 | 23 41 | 8 55 | 22 13 | 27 6 | 4 ♓ 59' 9" |
| 29 TH | 22:27:40 | 15 26 | 20 9 | 10 23 | 12 44 | 0 51 | 23 43 | 8 56 | 22 14 | 27 6 | 4 ♓ 59' 9" |
| 30 FR | 22:31:36 | 20 55 | 21 46 | 11 21 | 13 11 | 0 56 | 23 45 | 8 56 | 22 14 | 27 7 | 4 ♓ 59' 8" |
| 31 SA | 22:35:33 | 26 14 | 23 23 | 12 19 | 13 37 | 1 1 | 23 47 | 8 57 | 22 14 | 27 7 | 4 ♓ 59' 8" |

### INGRESSES :

5 ☿ → ♓ 13:50
11 ☿ → ♈ 12:42
16 ♀ → ♌ 14:25
☿ → ♉ 16: 5
18 ⊕ → ♒ 5:25
♃ → ♐ 11:45
21 ☿ → ♊ 10:56
26 ☿ → ♋ 7:38
31 ☿ → ♌ 17:23

### ASPECTS (HELIOCENTRIC +MOON(TYCHONIC)) :

2 ☽ ☌ ♂ 7: 5
3 ♀ □ ♅ 11: 5
☽ ☍ ☿ 15:29
☽ ☍ ♆ 16:36
☿ ☌ ♆ 19:20
4 ☽ □ ♃ 3:31
5 ☿ □ ♃ 8:17
☽ □ ♄ 19:14
6 ☽ □ ♇ 1:54
☽ ☍ ♅ 21:52
7 ☽ □ ♀ 8:50
8 ♀ ☌ P 11:52
☽ □ ♂ 18:35
10 ☽ □ ♆ 4:18
☿ □ ♄ 6:14
☽ ☌ ♃ 18: 4
☿ □ ♇ 23:33
12 ☽ ☌ ♄ 16:18
☽ ☌ ♇ 23:47
13 ☿ ☌ ♅ 2:13
☽ □ ♅ 23: 6
14 ♀ ☍ ⊕ 6: 6
☽ □ ☿ 18:47
15 ☽ ☍ ♀ 14:27
☿ ☌ ☊ 14:38
16 ☽ ☍ ♂ 8:18
☿ □ ⊕ 9: 8
☿ □ ♀ 16:41
17 ☽ ☌ ♆ 14:34
☿ □ ♂ 22:47
18 ☽ □ ♃ 6:24
20 ☿ □ ♆ 5:13
☽ □ ♄ 5:40
☿ ☌ P 7:23
☽ □ ♇ 12:52
21 ☿ ☍ ♃ 11:51
☽ ☌ ♅ 12:12
22 ♀ ☌ ♂ 18:24
24 ☽ □ ♂ 0:59
☽ □ ♀ 4:12
☽ □ ♆ 22:18
25 ☿ ☍ ♄ 6: 5
☽ ☍ ♃ 13:17
☿ ☍ ♇ 19:56
♂ ☌ A 22:41
27 ☽ ☍ ♄ 5: 6
☽ ☍ ♇ 10:50
☿ □ ♅ 20:18
28 ☽ □ ♅ 6:18
☽ ☌ ☿ 12:31
30 ♀ N□ ☊ 1: 8
♀ ☍ ♆ 6:55
☿ N□ ☊ 11:46
☽ ☌ ♂ 13:11
31 ☽ ☍ ♆ 3: 2
☽ ☌ ♀ 5:25
☽ □ ♃ 16:55

the sky grew dark and Jesus looked to heaven and said: "Father, render testimony to thy Son!" The thunderous voice that replied, calling Jesus his beloved son, terrified his enemies; the disciples were then able to escort Jesus from the temple in safety (Mar/28/31).

The New Moon reminded us of the Age of Light, Satya Yuga. Those who dare perceive this will inevitably threaten the status quo, and the enemies of this light will want to silence them. Nonetheless, the theophany of the Father can be heard by turning to his Son. This strikes fear into the spiritless hearts of those who guard the grave of Kali Yuga—the "dark age."

Later today the Moon will reach 23° Libra, its position at the descent into Hell. And as the impending Full Moon reminds us of the dead being given life, we are wise to stand with the beloved Son and prepare to raise our own dead. Where do we cling to the old?

**Aug 10: Sun 22°43' Cancer: Death of Lazarus (7/15/32).** We can imagine Lazarus journeying with the dead until his raising, eleven days from now.

**Mars enters Leo:** "Invigorate with senses' might, existing ground of worlds, the essence of feeling beings toward **firmly-willed existence**. In stream of life flowing, in weaving pain of growing, with senses' might, arise!" (Steiner, *Twelve Cosmic Moods*).

**Aug 11: Jupiter stations direct 19° Scorpio.** The Sun at Jupiter's degree again remembers Jesus as he healed from afar the servant of a Roman centurion. Later that day, the widowed mother of the youth of Nain begged Jesus to come and heal her twelve-year-old son (Nov/10/30).

The youth of Nain had two subsequent incarnations of extreme importance: Mani (3rd century AD), and the Grail King: Parsifal (9th century AD). This being is in the process of becoming the first human Manu, which is the rank of a Sun initiate.

The raising of the youth of Nain was done as preparation for this being's future incarnations. During his life as Mani he worked to bring about the reconciliation of all religions. He traveled far and wide, teaching a kind of unity that eventually became known as Manichaeism. This doctrine holds that evil is just as eternal as is good, and thus will continue forever. Yet evil must be transformed, for originally it *was* good. Furthermore, overcoming darkness comes through mildness, not aggression. Manichaeans believed that one can redeem evil by uniting with it, although this is not a task to be undertaken unless one has been specifically directed to this kind of work.

The youth of Nain was called the "son of the widow." Are we not all widowed souls, having long ago been separated from our divine nature?

**Uranus stations retrograde 11° Aries.** Uranus reached this degree in April of 1936, three years into the Chancellorship of Adolf Hitler. Winston Churchill's early intuitions of the ambitions of Hitler were summarily ignored, in part due to his leonine reputation as a ready warrior (indeed, he was born under a Leo Moon, with the Sun at *Antares*, the star that marks the heart of the Scorpion). Churchill, during one of his April speeches before the House of Commons (when Mars was conjunct Uranus), thus described Britain's relations to Nazi Germany: "When you are drifting, floating, down the stream of Niagara, it may easily happen that from time to time you run into a reach of quite smooth water, or that a bend in the river or a change in the wind may make the roar of the falls seem far more distant: but your position and your preoccupation are in no way affected thereby."

These are sobering thoughts, in view of the current world situation.

**Aug 13: Sun 25° Cancer: Birth of the Nathan Mary (7/17/17 BC).** The Nathan Mary was connected with the spiritual stream of love and compassion that attained its high point in Hinduism as well as in Buddhism. As the mother of the Nathan Jesus (the Angel Jesus), her immaculate heart is one with the heart of Jesus. Together they are birthing a new stream: the stream of Christianized Buddhism. This is the Christianity of love we hear in the Gospel of St. Luke. In carefully listening, however, we will discern the octave of this Gospel resounding also in our time.

**Aug 14: ASPECT: Superior conjunction of Sun and Venus 26° Cancer.** Venus recalls Jesus and some Levites visiting the birthplace of Elizabeth. Afterward, Jesus went to heal the sick in their homes. While teaching at the synagogue, he spoke of Samson and his deeds—as an example of a forerunner of the Messiah (Jun/2/31).

Samson had retained forces of the old cosmic vision, symbolized by his long hair. When his hair was cut off, this capacity vanished from him. Like Hercules, Samson too vanquished a lion and made its strength his own. In the carcass of the lion, Samson found a swarm of bees and he nourished himself from their honey. This gives us a picture of the Sun-corporeality Samson gained, which did not consume the suprasensory visionary capacity that was alive in him. This capacity continued in a few of the Israelites as a lamp reminding them of their highest mission: recognition of the Messiah.

The alleged defeat of Samson was actually a victory. For through Samson, Israel's awaking consciousness struck its first blow against the dark magical practices of the Philistines. Thus is Samson a figure who preserved Sun-consciousness as a forerunner of the promised Messiah.

The ass's jawbone—used by Samson to kill a thousand men—represents the constellation of Cancer and the secrets of evolution. For, two stars stand in this constellation—the Northern Ass (*Asellus borealis*) and the Southern Ass (*Asellus australis*). Cancer is the sign under which the old is replaced by the new, ever and ever again.

Under the beautiful influences of Sun conjunct Venus in Cancer, and through the catharsis gained by taking up our cross, we find forces of renewal calling us into a new future. Freedom means taking responsibility, i.e., taking up a burden on behalf of the future. This requires selfless service to something greater than oneself, which is a lovely reflection of the cross Christ carried.

**Aug 15: ASPECT: Full Moon 27° Capricorn opposite Sun 27° Cancer.** The Sun remembers Jesus as he went to a place not far from a battlefield, where, in a vision Ezekiel had beheld the bones of the dead that were gathered together and restored to life. Jesus taught and consoled the people living there, teaching them that Ezekiel's vision was about to be fulfilled—meaning that the breath of new life into the dead was a vision referring to the sending of the Holy Spirit (Jul/20/29).

The Beehive, which we remembered at the New Moon, recalled the Age of Light (Satya Yuga). The first quarter Moon reminded us that there are always enemies to battle when the new is incarnating into time. Now we encounter the transformational forces of the Full Moon by remembering the dead who are redeemed by the breath of the Holy Spirit.

The teaching referred to today occurred two months before the Baptism of Jesus. These were the last weeks that the Master Jesus would indwell the physical body of Jesus, for he would soon depart from him as the dove descended upon Jesus on the shores of the Jordan River. The descent of the Holy Spirit marked the beginning of the incarnation of Christ into Jesus, and this would eventuate in Jesus bringing the Holy Spirit to all people. Thus will this force bring the breath of life into the realms wherein the bones of our dead are gathered. Is this not what Ezekiel foresaw?

Capricorn represents continuity of growth—i.e., the sap of life ever flowing. And from where do these nourishing waters originate? There are two sources, the holy waters above, and the muddy waters of the serpent below.

> Just as there is Fire and fire, i.e., the celestial Fire of divine love and the fire of electricity due to friction, so there is also Water and water, i.e., the celestial Water of the sap of growth, progress, and evolution, and the lower water of instinctivity—the "collective unconscious," engulfing collectivity—which is the water of floods and drowning.[1]

Will our gathered bones find the breath of the Holy Spirit? All depends on the kind of growth we desire. For the process of continuity demands that we choose between the two waters. Both of these waters flow in our veins: one stream we must draw upward and cleanse; the other is already godly. Here the principle of dualism lives inside us.

---

1 Anon., *Meditations on the Tarot*, p. 469.

When we climb, however, to the summit of the mountain (Capricorn), we see far—we rise above what dualism would otherwise tear asunder. In a sense, we could say that we rise closer to our star, which ever shines above our head. From this vantage we gain the ability to "nail opposites together." The artistry of this capacity necessitates the union of light and will; i.e., not only must we see far, we must also act. *We must suffer duality until a third light breaks through, illumining the rainbow of reconciliation that streams from the holy Waters of spirit.* This opens possibilities hitherto unimaginable. If we cannot sustain the intensity of suffering duality, however, we will instead find the unholy mud of the serpent rising, demanding that we take one side or the other. Thus will we remain on the tarmac—when instead we could have taken flight! Are we willing to rise above the divisiveness and noise caused by one duality fighting against another? Senselessness has become the norm, for the mud seems so much more satisfying, and requires no effort.

Knowing that there is a choice, however, can inspire us to await the emergence of the rainbow as it arches across the heavens. This requires that we muster a sense of hope.

> Hope is not something subjective due to an optimistic or sanguine temperament, or to a desire for compensation in the sense of modern Freudian and Adlerian psychology. It is a light-force which radiates objectively and which directs creative evolution toward the world's future. It is the celestial and spiritual counterpart of the terrestrial and natural instinct of biological reproduction—which, with mutation, produces natural selection, which later, in its turn, produces with time biological progress. In other words, hope is what moves and directs *spiritual evolution* in the world. In so far as it moves, it is an objective force, and in so far as it orientates and directs, it is a subjective light. This is why we may speak of it as a "light-force."[1]

From a certain vantage, the choice is simple: Do we or do we not want to evolve? If we answer affirmatively, we choose the holy Water over the mud of the serpent. Having made this choice, we will gradually (or even suddenly) find ourselves enveloped in an atmosphere of grace.

This light of Satya Yuga founded this lunar cycle. Did we manage to silence the furious envy of enemies (both within and without) who work against change? Now we enter the transformational phase. We must not become dualistic; nor must we be of the "little" people, who fight for position, turf, and all such trivialities. Instead, we must transform *by ridding ourselves of our own mud.*

Having done some measure of work, we may find this Full Moon bestows the breath of the Holy Spirit upon our dry bones, gathering them into the springtide of life as we lift above the cacophony of world discord to serve the hope of spiritual evolution.

**Aug 16: ASPECT: Mercury 11° Cancer square Uranus 11° Aries.** Mercury was at the eleventh degree of the Crab as Jesus taught the disciples about their mission, work, attitudes, and errors. He mentioned their future persecution and spoke at length about the parable of the workers in the vineyard, in which a householder paid some workers—those who had worked only an hour—no less than those who had toiled all day. The vineyard owner explained: "Friend, I am doing you no wrong; did you not agree [to work] with me for a denarius? Take what belongs to you, and go....So the last will be first, and the first last" (Jun/17/31).

Still under the influence of yesterday's Full Moon, this fleeting aspect readies the mind to choose the holy Waters of hope—despite the unknowable forces of change (Uranus) now upon us: "Leap, and the net will appear " (Goethe).

**Aug 17: Venus enters Leo:** "Invigorate with senses' might **existing ground of worlds**, the essence of feeling beings toward firmly willed existence. In stream of life flowing, in weaving pain of growing, with senses' might, arise!" (Steiner, *Twelve Cosmic Moods*).

**Aug 18: Sun enter Leo:** "Irradiate with senses' might existing ground of worlds, the essence of feeling beings toward firmly willed existence. In stream of life flowing, in weaving pain of growing,

---

1 Ibid., pp. 471-472.

with senses' might, arise!" (Steiner, *Twelve Cosmic Moods*).

The late William Bento explicates this mantra:

> One of the most primal gifts we received from the Cosmos was the possibility to be endowed with senses, to have the capacity to witness the creation of all things upon the Earth. It is a gift we can too easily take for granted. Yet, when we ponder how the Sun being has gathered the forces of the entire Zodiac and poured them down upon our uprightness in such a way as to create portals into the external world, we can sensitize ourselves to feel how this in-streaming of forces has never ceased. *In the infusion and invigoration of our senses' activity, these forces enable us to behold the world in all its beauty.*

The first decan, ruled by Saturn, is associated with the faint constellation of Leo Minor, the Lesser Lion, above Leo and below the Great Bear. The virtue: *Compassion becomes Freedom*. This freedom is the foundation of the spiritualized "I."

**Aug 21: Sun 3° Leo: The raising of Lazarus (7/26/32).** This is the last of the seven healing miracles of Christ. At Lazarus' death, his angel placed him in the custody of John the Baptist, who was then indwelling angelic realms and was commissioned to guide Lazarus as he traversed the dark regions of the underworld. A contemporary Christian mystic beheld the mystery of the descent of Lazarus into the sub-earthly spheres, wherein she experienced the pain of fallen Nature:

> Here we paused. We were at the threshold of Hell. John the Baptist held his hands over Lazarus' head, whereupon a radiant garment of light spilled from his hands. It was like water pouring out. The light completely enveloped Lazarus, and the garment of his being grew ever more luminous. Then John told him that he was going to escort him on a further descent, a descent into the Earth, and that he was to experience a "burial" in the Heart of the Mother. The garment of light he was being provided was to protect him as they passed further through the sub-earthly spheres—the realms of darkness.
>
> And so the descent began. As we proceeded through the sub-earthly spheres, Lazarus heard the cries of souls that had become trapped in the bowels of Hell. They cried out to him for release. John, however, was not moved by these cries.
>
> When Lazarus looked to John for solace, John said, "One who is mightier than both of us shall come to save these souls. Turn your ears away; heed not their cries, lest you lose yourself in the darkness!"
>
> A golden sphere came into view. Peace and warmth emanated from this sphere. We were enveloped in its golden light, light of a different quality than that of the sunlight at the surface of the Earth. This light seemed to have more substance to it. I felt pulled more and more deeply into the light, as if the light wished to receive us into its midst.
>
> Whereas the light of the Sun is expansive, offering itself magnanimously to all, touching us wherever we may be, the light at the center of the Earth has a quality of "drawing in," of enfolding. I felt the golden light all through my being as we journeyed into it, drawn toward its center. Lazarus and John appeared completely golden, as though turned to gold.
>
> Then I heard a whispering voice saying, O My son Lazarus! O My Son!
>
> Beings in service to the Mother encircled us. They made a sound like delicate chimes and the soft unfolding of wings. They were winged creatures, each with many wings. Upon their faces was the smile of eternity. We were as though enveloped in the sweet smile of the Mother, who smiles into your soul![2]

Each of us will at some time be called to experience *the earth trial*—whereby we must inwardly behold our fallen nature and endure all that we must suffer into goodness. At the same time, we are to respect John's warning: not to see our ghosts nor hear their cries—for these are naught but chimeras we ourselves have created. We have successfully withstood the earth trial when our heart instead follows the light *through* the darkness. The light is the healer, and the cries of the lost are distractions. The light we are to follow is born of Christ, who meets us as we complete our journey through the miasmic specters of temptation. Christ's light

---

[2] Isaacson, *Through the Eyes of Mary Magdalene*, vol. 1, p. 188.

will bring solace to anguished souls, and it will cast out ghosts who inhabit the shadows we have self-engendered.

What is fallen in us contributes to the entire paradigm of fallen Nature. The forces in the inner Earth—which pull us toward the Earth's center—represent what we call "gravity." Seen in another light, however, gravity is the binding power of love *emanating* from the womb of the Earth, where dwells the inner Earth-Sun. In Christ's light, we can contemplate our ability to face in us—until we transform ourselves—what contributes to the ongoing enchainment of our Mother.

**Aug 23: Last Quarter Moon 5° Taurus: Healing of the Paralyzed man at the Pool at Bethesda** (Jan/19/31). We arrive at the final phase of this lunar cycle with the third healing miracle of Jesus Christ. This miracle represents the healing of all deeds of our past to which, without the Christ, we would continually be bound. Releasing the past allow us to create a new future.

This miracle is connected to the third chakra—in the region of the solar plexus—the chakra which, along with governing movement, serves to guard the individual's consciousness. *Indecision weakens this chakra.*

> "I" consciousness of the past, which preserves its activity from the previous incarnation and in which many human beings live and act, is called consciousness of the "dead" in the Gospels, and those who live under the "I" impulse of the past are simply called "the dead." Thus, healing the paralyzed man involved more than merely the present "I"; the "dead," in particular, heard the "voice of the son" and experienced a conversion in his past consciousness.[1]

The paralyzed man had used excessive personal force in his past incarnation, selfishly ignoring both others and the angels. Now, in the time of Christ's ministry, he was ignored by others—as well as by the angel at the pool of Bethesda. He had lain there for 38 years, asking for help, but to no avail, until Christ visited this pool and asked: "Wilt thou be made whole?"

---

1 Tomberg, *Christ and Sophia*, p. 251.

The lunar cycle enters into its concluding phase. We began with the light of the Satya Yuga, moved through the challenge of enemies to the new, and then proceeded on to the breath of the Holy Spirit—thereby enlivening the dead. Now we remember the dead *in us*. Are we willing to face the trial of our own descent into the unknown realms of our subconscious? There we will find the graveyard. The dead absorb the light we would otherwise use to increase our perceptions in this time of the historic unfolding of the 40th day. Oh, how the angels rejoice when their light awakes in us!

**Aug 24: ASPECT: Venus conjunct Mars 9° Leo.** Venus recalls Jesus in Capernaum on the Sabbath. A man possessed of an unclean spirit approached him. Jesus commanded: "Be silent, and come out of him!" Then the unclean spirit, convulsing the man, cried with a loud voice and came out of him (Aug/19/30).

The cross of Venus stands with the Archangel Michael, close to the heart of the Lion. What courage this inspires in our soul! Taking up our cross represents our willingness to repair our brokenness, i.e., where we have separated ourselves from spirit. Indeed, such brokenness is the cause of both personal and global suffering. Leo asks that we have compassion for others, thus turning our focus away from ourselves. In so doing—and as we accept the full measure of the world's sorrow—we begin to radiate. We may find that it is easier to suffer what is done unto us than it is to witness the suffering done unto others. This is a shift that will bear fruit in the Aquarian age to come.

This aspect occurred, also in Leo, at the birth of the Nathan Mary. Is there a finer example of one who bore the full weight of her cross? Mary is ever united to the World Soul; and as we repair our separateness, we draw ever closer to her.

The "unclean spirits" (the negative beings and energies within us) may be commanded to vanish by the power of sacred magic, which comprises skills we must learn as the new etheric technologies of our time.

**Aug 26: Mercury enters Leo:** "Invigorate with senses' might, existing ground of worlds, **the**

**essence of feeling being** toward firmly-willed existence. In stream of life flowing, in weaving pain of growing, with senses' might, arise!" (Steiner, *Twelve Cosmic Moods*).

**Aug 29: Sun 11° Leo: Healing of the Nobleman's Son (Aug/3/30).** The nobleman begged Jesus to come to heal his son. Jesus replied, "Unless you see signs and wonders, you will not believe."

This was the second of the seven healing miracles of Christ. The Nobleman had given his "I" in service to his king, as was commonplace in these times. His "I" had become a satellite, circling the "I" of the sovereign Sun of his king. He had lost the *verticality* of his "I"; as a consequence, his son suffered a physical ailment—his blood was not strong enough to carry the "I"—and now he lay dying.

The stream of heredity flows from past to future. Indeed, the past is carried in such a way that the "I" and the physical body of the father, as well as the astral and the etheric bodies of the mother, represent the material of heredity—which is passed on to the children. This occurs in reverse, however: the father's *I* influences the child's physical organism, and the father's *physical body* influences the child's "I." Similarly, the mother's *astral body* provides the heredity model for the child's etheric body, while her *etheric body* is the model for the child's astral organism. Thus, when the Bible tells us that the "sins of the fathers" will be visited upon the children (never mentioning the "sins of the mothers"), we should understand this to mean that one's "I"-being "sins"; furthermore, that it is the father's "I" (not the mother's) which has more influence on the physical blood.

In this miracle, Christ healed heredity that was based on the blood connection between generations. He healed the past, and in so doing this principle became possible for all humanity. How do we heal the past? By becoming more human, more "I-strong," we direct healing into the hereditary lineage for all generations still to come.

It is becoming ever more important for each of us to align our "I" with the vertical force of spiritual generation—as a *rejuvenating force* that nourishes the weakened state of hereditary blood.

**Aug 30: ASPECT: New Moon 12° Leo.** The Moon shone from this degree on the evening of the day that one of the holy women, Joanna Chuza, had succeeded in retrieving the head of John the Baptist. Earlier that day, the Pharisees had labelled Jesus a "disturber of the peace" for continuing to preach his "innovations" (Apr/19/31).

The Moon recalls the retrieval of John's head, and the Sun remembers the death of the Nathan Mary (Aug/5/12). She died four months after the union in the temple between the two Jesus children. Thus could we say that this New Moon asks us to overcome the limitations posed by the intellect to enter spheres wherein dwell angels. Goethe said: "Leap and the net will appear." Thus do we overcome captivity in the serpent's closed circle. Mary was an immaculate soul in constant communion with angelic realms, and John's beheading resulted in his becoming the angelic guardian of the circle of twelve. Mary and John took the leap—and most certainly the net appeared!

Leo is the constellation that forms the heart, from which we spiritualize our "I." This occurs as we enter the transformational experience of moving from "enfoldment" to "unfolding," as we do every night; we *in*volve ourselves with matter by day, and we *e*volve into spirit by night. Thus do we enter the enfolded circle to gain the experience of becoming human, and we unfold from the circle to gain the experience of becoming spirit. We come and we go.

Yet for some the circle has no entrance, nor does it have an exit. They feel they are caught in endless appearances and disappearances, wherein they meet the same thing over and over again. On the other hand, however, some are "spiritual athletes," who see that there is a thin passage in the circle through which one may leap into worlds of eternity, i.e., take hold of the fact that the serpent's closed circle is naught but the illusion to which the less gifted cling. To the athlete, nothing is finite—there is always greater skill to be attained. Yes, to these few, the limitless grants something new each day.

According to Genesis, the Father finished the work of creation in seven days, after which he rested. Did not this rest infer that there was a resting place outside the boundaries of creation? A place beyond the eternal circling? Where is the Father's place of rest? Where do we find the passageway to this boundless eternity? Yes, indeed there was a portal, but this the serpent sought to close. For according to the serpent, freedom was the gamble of the gods that would deliver created beings into his hands. The serpent realized that the circle *must* be closed lest the beings the Father created remain bound to him. So he took matters into his own hands. Legend tells us of such things:

> And the serpent took his tail into his mouth and thus formed a closed circle. He turned himself with great force and thus created in the world the great swirl which caught hold of Adam and Eve. And the other beings, upon whom Adam had impressed the names that he gave them, followed them.
>
> And the serpent said to the beings of the world moving on this side of the closed circle, that he formed by taking his tail into his mouth and setting himself in rotation: "Here is your way—you will commence by my tail and you will arrive at my head. Then you will have traversed the length of the circle of my being and you will have within you the entire closed circle, and thus you will be free as I am free." [1]

We know, of course, that this is not true freedom, for it has no means through which it may increase itself. It simply depicts the monotony of endless horizontal expansion, where we circle from head to tail, finding the same problems, in different costumes, endlessly reappearing. Something else had to happen. Yes, and this was offered by the woman! For, if she was to give birth, she would of course require access to the spirit ocean wherein all souls waiting to enter the circle are at rest with the Father. She required a *Sabbath door*, i.e., a portal to the resting place.

> But woman guarded the memory of the world opened toward the Father and the holy Sabbath. And she offered herself for the rending of the closed circle in herself to give birth to children issuing from the world beyond it, from the world where there is the Sabbath. Thus originated the suffering of her pregnancy, and thus originated sorrow on this side of the world of the serpent. [2]

Thus also did hostility come between the woman and the serpent, for she brought to ruin his plan—she set up a countercurrent to his endless and monotonous swirling. To make matters worse, prophets came, proclaiming not only the *fact* of transformational forces living within each soul, but also the prophecy of a Messiah—one who would hold open the Sabbath door in the serpent's closed circle *until the very end of time.*

On the hill of Golgotha, time indeed turned! Now we all must create a countercurrent in the serpent's circle so that we too may find our entrance and exit. We must take the leap of faith, believing that the net will appear. We must follow the woman and the prophet if we are to find the Messiah.

Thus does the foundation of this new lunar cycle rest upon the "woman" who kept open the closed circle: the Nathan Mary. And John, the first Adam, represented the first to enter the closed circle, which he did as he experienced the Fall from Paradise.

**First quarter Moon, 18° Scorpio: Jesus and two of his "night disciples" meet at the home of Lazarus.**

**Full Moon, 26° Aquarius: The healing of the nobleman's son.**

**Last quarter Moon, 4° Gemini: Jesus explains his mission, his imminent withdrawal from his physical body, and asks his disciples to separate themselves from the consequences of the Fall.**

**Lunar teachings of this cycle** begin with understanding the closed circle of the serpent's world, as well as with finding the key to infinity's door—the *Sabbath door.* As the time of action dawns at the first quarter Moon, we are asked to meet in secret places, where Lazarus, the spiritual brother of Christ, awaits us. The term *secret places* refers to communities reading the arcana, i.e., reclaiming mystery wisdom. The Full Moon remembers the healing of heredity forces, which signifies the regaining of the sovereignty of our true "I." If we are to take the leap through the Sabbath door, we will need full awareness of the "I" within us. As the last quarter comes to pass, we are to integrate

---

1 Anon., *Meditations on the Tarot*, p. 239.

2 Ibid., 239.

these phases by comprehending the presence of the etheric Christ—who, though no longer physically with us, gave us the power to find him.

Unbinding our souls from fallen realms of error is key. We leap, we read arcana, we hold fast the crown of our "I," and we heal.

# SEPTEMBER 2019

## Stargazing Preview

With so many planets near the Sun, it's a quiet month for stargazing. However, between the 6th and the 8th, you'll see the first quarter Moon overhead at sundown, moving past (and above) Jupiter on the 6th, and in front of Saturn on the 8th. The Aquarius Full Moon occurs on the 14th. Four days later, Saturn stations direct; look for it high in the southeast after sunset.

On the 29th, one day following the New Moon, you might be able to catch a glimpse of the barest sliver of Moon in conjunction with Venus at 23° Virgo; they set thirty minutes after the Sun. By the end of the month, Orion will rise at 2200.

## September Commentaries

**Sep 2: ASPECT: Sun conjunct Mars 15° Leo.** Mars recalls Jesus teaching at a place used by the Essenes that went back to the days of the prophets (Aug/24/29).

A courageous heart is gentle; a cowardly heart is aggressive. This aspect (in Gemini) was also present at the death of the Solomon Jesus. Imagine the incredible courage of this gentle being, who sacrificed himself so that the birth of Christ into Jesus could occur: he gave even his life to make way for love!

The resurrecting power of the Sun, in communion with the Archangel Michael, bestows forces of enthusiastic energy. The direction to which this may be applied, however, reveals one's moral development.

Abraham was the first prophet. We hear his new teachings in the book *Meditations on the Tarot*. He was also the teacher of the Essenes in Qumran, one hundred years before Christ, whose wisdom we find in the Dead Sea Scrolls (which were discovered in 1947). The Essenes knew this teacher as Jeshu ben Pandira, the teacher of righteousness, who was later stoned to death and hung from a tree. Qumran is located a few miles from the place in the Jordan River where Christ was baptized by John. Jeshu ben Pandira prepared the ground for what was to become the greatest event in all of Earth evolution.

With Sun and Mars in conjunction, we may live into the power of the living word that issued forth from all the prophets who have guarded the sacred mysteries throughout time. When the word descends from our higher "I," our speech, too, is righteous. Inversely, when the word ascends from the darkness of the blood, it tends to be full of Martian egoism.

**ASPECT 2: Venus 20° Leo square Jupiter 20° Scorpio.** Venus recalls a morning before daybreak, when Jesus, John, and Matthew went to the house on Mount Zion where the last supper would take place. This house belonged to Nicodemus, and Jesus remained there through the night. A meeting of the Pharisees and high priests was held to discuss the raising of Lazarus, for the Pharisees feared that Jesus might awake all the dead and that this would lead to great confusion. In Bethany, a great tumult arose, and Lazarus was forced to hide (Jul/27/32).

How terribly dangerous were these last months! Imagine Jesus awaking all the dead. Yet this is exactly what would later occur on the hill of Golgotha, as the dead arose from their graves and walked through the city. Still, we are not to imagine this as a resurrection *per se*. No, these were ghosts and specters arising from former times. They were the dead that had long ago fallen prey to death, i.e., they fell prey to time's passing into the static tomb of yesterday. All events in time are recorded in a memory that lives within the inner layers of the Earth. These memories have become "the dead" dead (or the psychic geological memory). When this memory rises from the past into the present, it alarms—for its shattering effect confuses the order of time.

SIDEREAL GEOCENTRIC LONGITUDES : SEPTEMBER 2019 Gregorian at 0 hours UT

| DAY | ☉ | ☽ | ☊ | ☿ | ♀ | ♂ | ♃ | ♄ | ⛢ | ♆ | ♇ |
|---|---|---|---|---|---|---|---|---|---|---|---|
| 1 SU | 13 ♌ 16 | 5 ♍ 33 | 21 ♊ 20R | 10 ♌ 16 | 18 ♌ 9 | 13 ♌ 45 | 20 ♏ 8 | 19 ♐ 8R | 11 ♈ 26R | 22 ♒ 33R | 25 ♐ 52R |
| 2 MO | 14 14 | 20 34 | 21 12 | 12 14 | 19 23 | 14 23 | 20 11 | 19 7 | 11 25 | 22 32 | 25 51 |
| 3 TU | 15 13 | 5 ♎ 15 | 21 6 | 14 11 | 20 38 | 15 2 | 20 15 | 19 5 | 11 24 | 22 30 | 25 50 |
| 4 WE | 16 11 | 19 29 | 21 1 | 16 7 | 21 52 | 15 40 | 20 19 | 19 4 | 11 23 | 22 29 | 25 49 |
| 5 TH | 17 9 | 3 ♏ 14 | 20 58 | 18 2 | 23 6 | 16 18 | 20 24 | 19 2 | 11 22 | 22 27 | 25 48 |
| 6 FR | 18 7 | 16 32 | 20 57 | 19 56 | 24 21 | 16 56 | 20 28 | 19 1 | 11 21 | 22 25 | 25 48 |
| 7 SA | 19 5 | 29 24 | 20 57D | 21 49 | 25 35 | 17 35 | 20 33 | 19 0 | 11 20 | 22 24 | 25 47 |
| 8 SU | 20 3 | 11 ♐ 57 | 20 58 | 23 40 | 26 50 | 18 13 | 20 38 | 18 59 | 11 19 | 22 22 | 25 46 |
| 9 MO | 21 2 | 24 13 | 20 58R | 25 31 | 28 4 | 18 51 | 20 43 | 18 58 | 11 17 | 22 20 | 25 45 |
| 10 TU | 22 0 | 6 ♑ 18 | 20 57 | 27 21 | 29 19 | 19 29 | 20 48 | 18 57 | 11 16 | 22 19 | 25 45 |
| 11 WE | 22 58 | 18 15 | 20 54 | 29 9 | 0 ♍ 33 | 20 8 | 20 53 | 18 56 | 11 15 | 22 17 | 25 44 |
| 12 TH | 23 56 | 0 ♒ 7 | 20 47 | 0 ♍ 56 | 1 48 | 20 46 | 20 58 | 18 56 | 11 13 | 22 15 | 25 43 |
| 13 FR | 24 55 | 11 58 | 20 38 | 2 43 | 3 2 | 21 24 | 21 4 | 18 55 | 11 12 | 22 14 | 25 43 |
| 14 SA | 25 53 | 23 50 | 20 27 | 4 28 | 4 17 | 22 3 | 21 10 | 18 55 | 11 10 | 22 12 | 25 42 |
| 15 SU | 26 52 | 5 ♓ 43 | 20 15 | 6 12 | 5 31 | 22 41 | 21 16 | 18 54 | 11 9 | 22 10 | 25 42 |
| 16 MO | 27 50 | 17 40 | 20 2 | 7 54 | 6 46 | 23 19 | 21 22 | 18 54 | 11 7 | 22 9 | 25 41 |
| 17 TU | 28 48 | 29 41 | 19 50 | 9 36 | 8 0 | 23 58 | 21 28 | 18 54 | 11 5 | 22 7 | 25 41 |
| 18 WE | 29 47 | 11 ♈ 50 | 19 40 | 11 17 | 9 15 | 24 36 | 21 34 | 18 54 | 11 4 | 22 5 | 25 40 |
| 19 TH | 0 ♍ 45 | 24 7 | 19 32 | 12 57 | 10 29 | 25 14 | 21 41 | 18 54D | 11 2 | 22 4 | 25 40 |
| 20 FR | 1 44 | 6 ♉ 35 | 19 27 | 14 35 | 11 44 | 25 53 | 21 47 | 18 54 | 11 0 | 22 2 | 25 40 |
| 21 SA | 2 43 | 19 18 | 19 25 | 16 13 | 12 58 | 26 31 | 21 54 | 18 54 | 10 59 | 22 1 | 25 39 |
| 22 SU | 3 41 | 2 ♊ 20 | 19 24 | 17 50 | 14 13 | 27 10 | 22 1 | 18 54 | 10 57 | 21 59 | 25 39 |
| 23 MO | 4 40 | 15 43 | 19 24 | 19 25 | 15 27 | 27 48 | 22 8 | 18 55 | 10 55 | 21 57 | 25 38 |
| 24 TU | 5 39 | 29 31 | 19 24 | 21 0 | 16 42 | 28 27 | 22 16 | 18 55 | 10 53 | 21 56 | 25 38 |
| 25 WE | 6 37 | 13 ♋ 45 | 19 22 | 22 34 | 17 56 | 29 5 | 22 23 | 18 56 | 10 51 | 21 54 | 25 38 |
| 26 TH | 7 36 | 28 24 | 19 18 | 24 6 | 19 11 | 29 44 | 22 30 | 18 57 | 10 49 | 21 53 | 25 38 |
| 27 FR | 8 35 | 13 ♌ 24 | 19 11 | 25 38 | 20 26 | 0 ♍ 22 | 22 38 | 18 57 | 10 47 | 21 51 | 25 37 |
| 28 SA | 9 34 | 28 36 | 19 1 | 27 9 | 21 40 | 1 1 | 22 46 | 18 58 | 10 45 | 21 49 | 25 37 |
| 29 SU | 10 33 | 13 ♍ 51 | 18 50 | 28 39 | 22 55 | 1 39 | 22 54 | 18 59 | 10 43 | 21 48 | 25 37 |
| 30 MO | 11 32 | 28 58 | 18 39 | 0 ♎ 8 | 24 9 | 2 18 | 23 2 | 19 0 | 10 41 | 21 46 | 25 37 |

INGRESSES :

| | |
|---|---|
| 2 ☽ → ♎ 15:20 | 21 ☽ → ♊ 19:45 |
| 4 ☽ → ♏ 18:16 | 24 ☽ → ♋ 0:49 |
| 7 ☽ → ♐ 1: 7 | 26 ☽ → ♌ 2:34 |
| 9 ☽ → ♑ 11:26 | ♂ → ♍ 10:13 |
| 10 ♀ → ♍ 13:19 | 28 ☽ → ♍ 2:11 |
| 11 ☿ → ♍ 11:20 | 29 ☿ → ♎ 21:46 |
| ☽ → ♒ 23:44 | 30 ☽ → ♎ 1:39 |
| 14 ☽ → ♓ 12:28 | |
| 17 ☽ → ♈ 0:36 | |
| 18 ☉ → ♍ 5:21 | |
| 19 ☽ → ♉ 11:22 | |

ASPECTS & ECLIPSES :

| | | | | |
|---|---|---|---|---|
| 2 ☽ N□ ☊ 1: 0 | 8 ☽ ☌ ♄ 13:41 | ♂ ☍ ♆ 5:38 | ☽ ☌ ☊ 6:29 | ☽ ☌ ♀ 15:37 |
| ☉ ☌ ♂ 10:41 | ☉ □ ♃ 15:25 | ☽ ☍ ♀ 23:33 | ☽ ☍ ♇ 17:19 | 30 ☽ ☌ ☿ 2: 4 |
| ♀ □ ♃ 16:25 | ☽ ☌ ☋ 17:36 | 15 ☽ ☍ ☿ 1: 7 | 25 ♀ □ ♄ 19:19 | ☽ ☍ ⛢ 18:54 |
| 3 ☽ ☍ ⛢ 10:16 | 9 ☽ ☌ ♇ 3: 2 | 16 ☽ □S ☊ 4:40 | 26 ♀ □ ☊ 2: 0 | |
| ☿ ☌ ♂ 15:39 | 10 ☉ ☍ ♆ 7:32 | 17 ☽ ☌ ⛢ 22:29 | ☿ □ ♇ 23:47 | |
| 4 ☉ S☋ ☿ 1:39 | 12 ♂ □ ♃ 9: 5 | 21 ☽ ☍ ♃ 4:52 | 27 ☽ ☍ ♆ 13:20 | |
| ♀ ☍ ♆ 11:32 | 13 ☽ ☌ A 13:44 | ♃ □ ♆ 17:45 | 28 ☽ ☌ P 2:19 | |
| 6 ☉ □ ☽ 3: 9 | ☿ ☌ ♀ 15: 9 | 22 ☉ □ ☽ 2:39 | ☽ ☌ ♂ 3:56 | |
| ☿ □ ♃ 7:10 | ☽ ☍ ♂ 20:11 | ☿ □ ♄ 16:17 | ♄ ☍ ☊ 6:15 | |
| ☽ ☌ ♃ 7:18 | ☽ ☌ ♆ 20:42 | ☿ □ ☊ 23:44 | ☉ ☌ ☽ 18:25 | |
| 7 ☿ ☍ ♆ 7:22 | 14 ☉ ☍ ☽ 4:31 | 23 ☽ ☍ ♄ 5:37 | 29 ☽ N□ ☊ 7:46 | |

SIDEREAL HELIOCENTRIC LONGITUDES : SEPTEMBER 2019 Gregorian at 0 hours UT

| DAY | Sid. Time | ☿ | ♀ | ⊕ | ♂ | ♃ | ♄ | ⛢ | ♆ | ♇ | Vernal Point |
|---|---|---|---|---|---|---|---|---|---|---|---|
| 1 SU | 22:39:29 | 1 ♌ 24 | 25 ♌ 1 | 13 ♒ 17 | 14 ♌ 3 | 1 ♐ 5 | 23 ♐ 49 | 8 ♈ 58 | 22 ♒ 15 | 27 ♐ 7 | 4 ♓ 59' 8" |
| 2 MO | 22:43:26 | 6 24 | 26 38 | 14 15 | 14 29 | 1 10 | 23 50 | 8 58 | 22 15 | 27 7 | 4 ♓ 59' 8" |
| 3 TU | 22:47:23 | 11 15 | 28 15 | 15 13 | 14 55 | 1 15 | 23 52 | 8 59 | 22 15 | 27 8 | 4 ♓ 59' 8" |
| 4 WE | 22:51:19 | 15 56 | 29 53 | 16 11 | 15 22 | 1 20 | 23 54 | 9 0 | 22 16 | 27 8 | 4 ♓ 59' 8" |
| 5 TH | 22:55:16 | 20 28 | 1 ♍ 30 | 17 9 | 15 48 | 1 25 | 23 56 | 9 0 | 22 16 | 27 8 | 4 ♓ 59' 8" |
| 6 FR | 22:59:12 | 24 52 | 3 7 | 18 8 | 16 14 | 1 30 | 23 58 | 9 1 | 22 17 | 27 9 | 4 ♓ 59' 7" |
| 7 SA | 23: 3: 9 | 29 7 | 4 44 | 19 6 | 16 40 | 1 35 | 23 59 | 9 2 | 22 17 | 27 9 | 4 ♓ 59' 7" |
| 8 SU | 23: 7: 5 | 3 ♍ 14 | 6 21 | 20 4 | 17 7 | 1 39 | 24 1 | 9 2 | 22 17 | 27 9 | 4 ♓ 59' 7" |
| 9 MO | 23:11: 2 | 7 14 | 7 58 | 21 2 | 17 33 | 1 44 | 24 3 | 9 3 | 22 18 | 27 10 | 4 ♓ 59' 7" |
| 10 TU | 23:14:58 | 11 7 | 9 35 | 22 0 | 17 59 | 1 49 | 24 5 | 9 4 | 22 18 | 27 10 | 4 ♓ 59' 7" |
| 11 WE | 23:18:55 | 14 53 | 11 12 | 22 59 | 18 25 | 1 54 | 24 7 | 9 4 | 22 18 | 27 10 | 4 ♓ 59' 7" |
| 12 TH | 23:22:52 | 18 33 | 12 49 | 23 57 | 18 51 | 1 59 | 24 9 | 9 5 | 22 19 | 27 10 | 4 ♓ 59' 7" |
| 13 FR | 23:26:48 | 22 7 | 14 26 | 24 55 | 19 18 | 2 4 | 24 10 | 9 6 | 22 19 | 27 11 | 4 ♓ 59' 7" |
| 14 SA | 23:30:45 | 25 36 | 16 3 | 25 54 | 19 44 | 2 9 | 24 12 | 9 6 | 22 19 | 27 11 | 4 ♓ 59' 6" |
| 15 SU | 23:34:41 | 28 59 | 17 40 | 26 52 | 20 10 | 2 13 | 24 14 | 9 7 | 22 20 | 27 11 | 4 ♓ 59' 6" |
| 16 MO | 23:38:38 | 2 ♎ 19 | 19 17 | 27 51 | 20 36 | 2 18 | 24 16 | 9 8 | 22 20 | 27 12 | 4 ♓ 59' 6" |
| 17 TU | 23:42:34 | 5 34 | 20 54 | 28 49 | 21 3 | 2 23 | 24 18 | 9 8 | 22 20 | 27 12 | 4 ♓ 59' 6" |
| 18 WE | 23:46:31 | 8 44 | 22 31 | 29 48 | 21 29 | 2 28 | 24 19 | 9 9 | 22 21 | 27 12 | 4 ♓ 59' 6" |
| 19 TH | 23:50:27 | 11 52 | 24 7 | 0 ♓ 46 | 21 55 | 2 33 | 24 21 | 9 10 | 22 21 | 27 13 | 4 ♓ 59' 6" |
| 20 FR | 23:54:24 | 14 56 | 25 44 | 1 45 | 22 22 | 2 38 | 24 23 | 9 10 | 22 22 | 27 13 | 4 ♓ 59' 6" |
| 21 SA | 23:58:21 | 17 57 | 27 21 | 2 43 | 22 48 | 2 43 | 24 25 | 9 11 | 22 22 | 27 13 | 4 ♓ 59' 5" |
| 22 SU | 0: 2:17 | 20 55 | 28 57 | 3 42 | 23 14 | 2 47 | 24 27 | 9 12 | 22 22 | 27 13 | 4 ♓ 59' 5" |
| 23 MO | 0: 6:14 | 23 51 | 0 ♎ 34 | 4 41 | 23 40 | 2 52 | 24 28 | 9 12 | 22 23 | 27 14 | 4 ♓ 59' 5" |
| 24 TU | 0:10:10 | 26 45 | 2 10 | 5 39 | 24 7 | 2 57 | 24 30 | 9 13 | 22 23 | 27 14 | 4 ♓ 59' 5" |
| 25 WE | 0:14: 7 | 29 37 | 3 47 | 6 38 | 24 33 | 3 2 | 24 32 | 9 14 | 22 23 | 27 14 | 4 ♓ 59' 5" |
| 26 TH | 0:18: 3 | 2 ♏ 27 | 5 23 | 7 37 | 24 59 | 3 7 | 24 34 | 9 14 | 22 24 | 27 15 | 4 ♓ 59' 5" |
| 27 FR | 0:22: 0 | 5 16 | 7 0 | 8 36 | 25 26 | 3 12 | 24 36 | 9 15 | 22 24 | 27 15 | 4 ♓ 59' 5" |
| 28 SA | 0:25:56 | 8 3 | 8 36 | 9 35 | 25 52 | 3 17 | 24 38 | 9 16 | 22 24 | 27 15 | 4 ♓ 59' 4" |
| 29 SU | 0:29:53 | 10 50 | 10 12 | 10 33 | 26 18 | 3 22 | 24 39 | 9 16 | 22 25 | 27 16 | 4 ♓ 59' 4" |
| 30 MO | 0:33:50 | 13 36 | 11 49 | 11 32 | 26 45 | 3 26 | 24 41 | 9 17 | 22 25 | 27 16 | 4 ♓ 59' 4" |

INGRESSES :

| |
|---|
| 4 ♀ → ♍ 1:51 |
| 7 ☿ → ♍ 5: 4 |
| 15 ☿ → ♎ 7:14 |
| 18 ⊕ → ♓ 5: 6 |
| 22 ♀ → ♎ 15:34 |
| 25 ☿ → ♏ 3:13 |

ASPECTS (HELIOCENTRIC +MOON(TYCHONIC)) :

| | | | | |
|---|---|---|---|---|
| 2 ☽ □ ♄ 5:17 | 7 ☽ ☌ ♃ 4: 7 | 14 ☿ □ ♇ 11:10 | ⊕ □ ♃ 23:42 | ☽ ☌ ♂ 19:34 |
| ☽ □ ♇ 10:38 | ☽ □ ♀ 11:37 | ☽ □ ♃ 16:54 | 21 ☽ □ ♆ 5:41 | 28 ☽ □ ♃ 7:23 |
| ⊕ ☍ ♂ 10:42 | ☿ □ ♃ 14:30 | 16 ☽ ☍ ♀ 3:44 | ☽ □ ♂ 6:43 | ♀ ☍ ⛢ 9:54 |
| 3 ☽ ☍ ⛢ 6:13 | 8 ☽ ☌ ♄ 23:40 | ☽ □ ♄ 13:13 | 22 ☽ ☍ ♃ 0:50 | 29 ☽ □ ♄ 17: 8 |
| ☿ ☌ ♂ 20:41 | 9 ☽ ☌ ♇ 5:48 | ☽ □ ♇ 19: 2 | ☿ ☌ ☋ 21:28 | ☽ □ ♇ 21:16 |
| 4 ☿ ☍ ⊕ 1:39 | ☿ ☌ ♀ 7:41 | 17 ☽ ☍ ☿ 15:46 | 23 ☽ ☍ ♄ 15:20 | 30 ☽ ☍ ⛢ 16:39 |
| ♀ □ ♃ 22:44 | 10 ☽ □ ⛢ 5:32 | ☽ ☌ ⛢ 18:43 | ☽ ☍ ♇ 20: 4 | ☽ ☌ ♀ 23:20 |
| 5 ☿ ☍ ♆ 9:43 | ⊕ ☌ ♆ 7:15 | 18 ☿ ☍ ⛢ 3: 7 | 24 ☽ □ ♀ 5: 7 | |
| ☽ □ ♂ 23:26 | 13 ☿ □ ♄ 14:14 | 19 ♀ □ ♄ 3:29 | ☽ □ ⛢ 16:26 | |
| 6 ☽ □ ♆ 10:37 | ☽ ☍ ♂ 15:23 | 20 ♂ ☍ ♆ 0: 4 | 26 ☽ □ ☿ 8: 3 | |
| ☽ □ ☿ 23:10 | ☽ ☌ ♆ 20:57 | ♀ □ ♇ 22: 6 | 27 ☽ ☍ ♆ 14:14 | |

The fear-filled thinking in the hardened souls of the Pharisees was like the rising of such ghosts. They dragged the dead corpses of old traditions along with them, unchanged since the time of Moses. At the turning point in time, however, these rigid concepts rose as "the dead" dead that obstructed their ability to understand what was right before their eyes.

While Sun and Mars are today conjunct in Leo, the cross of Venus stands nearby in dynamic tension with the Holy Spirit (Jupiter). Throughout the Passion of Christ this same aspect (in different signs) was active. Love (Venus), in creative discourse with wisdom (Jupiter), indeed midwifed the greatest deed of all Earth evolution. Christ has never given up his cross; he will carry it until each of us have picked up our own. And as he hung in the agony of death, he forgave all who were reviling him. *Wisdom inclines us to seek the way of forgiveness as the highest manifestation of love.*

If lower Venus forces are increased, we turn our back on the cross, feeling it too inconvenient to carry. Inversely, when the cross is taken up, the heart opens, and wisdom breaths the fire of the spirit into our brokenness. Thus does this aspect ask us to love ourselves exactly as we are, so that we may freely love all others. *This* is how we receive the fiery breath of the Holy Spirit! The dead thoughts of past wisdom must not rise from the dead, for such ghosts will compromise our spirit-awareness and deaden us to the living currents that are with us in every single moment of time.

**Sep 3: ASPECT: Mercury conjunct Mars 15° Leo.** The Sun at this degree marked the first time that Jesus taught in the synagogue at Capernaum. Among the large crowd were the future disciples Peter and Andrew (Aug/8/29). A short time before his Baptism, Jesus was teaching to men who would later become his disciples. His words must have been a healing balm to their souls. When we refuse to receive the healer (Mercury), however, our words tend to become aggressive (Mars).

**ASPECT 2: Superior conjunction of Sun and Mercury 16° Leo.** Uranus was at the degree of this conjunction as Jesus visited a village near Jericho. On the way, he passed two blind people sitting at the roadside who called out to him, "Have mercy on us, Son of David!" Jesus touched their eyes, and their sight was immediately restored to them (Jun/10/32).

This aspect bestows mighty healing forces into the will of all who open to receive such blessing. Intuitions gained during a superior conjunction, however, may not come to consciousness until the time of the inferior conjunction. For when Mercury is on the far side of the Sun, it communes with the mighty beings of the Zodiac; when on the near side, i.e., between the Sun and the Earth, it gathers solar imaginations and bestows these upon human beings. As this conjunction occurs in Leo, we may find that our hearts are unusually open to such imaginal gifts.

The consequent inferior conjunction will occur on November 11th.

**Sep 4: ASPECT: Venus 22° Leo opposite Neptune 22° Aquarius.** Venus remembers Jesus and the disciples visiting a school for orphans, where he told the children the story of Job as it *actually* took place. (According to Anne Catherine, Job was Abraham's great-great-great-grandfather.) Jesus spent the whole day with the children and took an evening walk with them (Aug/29/30).

The crucifying cross of love stands opposite the Goddess Night. We normally think of the crucifixion as something horrible, and indeed it was. When we speak of the cross of Venus, however, we are not speaking of a physical crucifixion; rather are we invited into an eternal archetype of the Rose Cross, which represents the stream of time coming from the future. And, due to its specific focus on the future, it is the apocalyptic stream of time; it bears within it the occult knowledge of the Grail.

Beyond the veil of the physical world weave realms wherein each soul has a divinely appointed weight (vertical) as well as a divinely appointed measure (horizontal). This is our cross. Carrying this suprasensory cross opens the heart to serve the apocalyptic revelations of the future. Cross-bearing means to fully extend our arms onto the horizontal beam, and to nail our feet onto the depths of the vertical beam. Then do we *feel* not only the full measure of our brokenness (i.e., our separateness from our true self), we also enter the sorrow of the world. And then do we accept the full weight of our *will's* work in the world, *our fidelity to the future*. From this stance, nobility is born.

This was Job's lot in life, to be tempted egregiously by Satan until he proved to the evil one that his love of God was unshakable. In so doing, Job created a portal between worlds that will never close.

When we say "yes" to serving the mission of the Earth and humanity, we have the *verticality* of spiritual weight. Furthermore, when we say "yes" to the trials we will meet along the way, we have the *horizontality* of spiritual measure. Thus do we become collaborators in bringing the future to birth; for we, too, create portals between worlds, creating star seeds of light that break through the endless monotony of life in the serpent's closed circle.

Much too often, souls are captured in the trivialities of life, thereby masking the great purpose of our existence. Venus represents the cross that Love bears for the betterment of the world. For Venus is love, and love is Christ, and loving each other was the sole commandment given to us in the New Testament. Love opens the heart—just as unlovingness closes it. When Venus aspects a planetary body, she is asking us to weigh and measure the quality of our love.

When the Venus cross stands opposite Neptune, great inspirations are possible—great deceptions are too. This aspect was present (although in different constellations) at the death of the Solomon Jesus. As the death horoscope is a spiritual judgment of the life we have concluded, we can imagine how strongly the inspiring powers of Neptune strengthened the Master Jesus when he took up the cross of his divine mission—on behalf of the betterment of all humanity.

Do we invite inspirations—or deceptions? All rests on how we use freedom, for freedom is inescapably tied to responsibility, asking us what measure of the world's sorrow we will take upon ourselves—which then determines our spiritual weight. This requires patient suffering, willing service, and faith before the trials that have been given to us.

Venus in Leo summons us to open our heart. Neptune in Aquarius reminds us of the Angel Human we long to become.

**Sep 5: First Quarter Moon 18° Scorpio.** This Moon recalls Jesus and Nicodemus before daybreak, as they set off for Lazarus' house on Mount Zion in Jerusalem. Joseph of Arimathea joined them there (Apr/9/30). The New Moon reminded us of the open portal in the closed circle that the woman guards. Now we must act. The Sabbath door marks the passageway through which we enter night consciousness, and through which we again pass as we awake each morning. The "night disciples" of Christ used this door. To take this seriously means that we also are to approach the night as disciples, humbling ourselves as we pray for mercy before the fact of our transgressions, and praying to remember all the miracles that take place each night. As the Moon shines from Scorpio, we can pray that we be given the wings of the eagle—so that we may peer into realms of revelatory wonder. To read revelation, however, means that tasks will be assigned. *Once we have thus truly seen, it becomes a "fall" to vanquish what was revealed*—although, in the short run, it is easier by far to remain passive victims in the endless repetition of a closed circle.

With the upcoming Full Moon occurring in Aquarius, we are wise to strengthen our relationship with the night, wherein our angel awaits us.

**Sep 6: ASPECT: Mercury 20° Leo square Jupiter 20° Scorpio.** Mercury was at this degree as Jesus arrived at Gathhepher, where he continued his healing work. He and some disciples then went on to Capernaum to the house of Jesus' mother, where about seven holy women and many others (including Lazarus) awaited them. They discussed John's imprisonment. Jesus spoke of it as a sign, marking the beginning of his public work (Jul/18/30). In dynamic tension with the Holy Spirit (Jupiter), our minds (Mercury) must settle, listen, and focus if we are to recognize the messages of the Holy Spirit that Jupiter today bestows.

**Sep 7: ASPECT: Mercury 22°Leo opposite Neptune 22° Aquarius.** Mercury recalls Jesus as he comforted Mary and told her not to be downcast about his coming journey to Judea. By midday, he, Lazarus, and about five other disciples set off; they walked through the night without moonlight, as the Moon was new (Jul/19/30). This mystical aspect is good for poets and dreamers. Neptune demands that the mind be clear, free from confusion. In such quietude, we may walk in realms of night unburdened by life's incessant noise.

**Sep 8: ASPECT: Sun 20° Leo square Jupiter 20° Scorpio**. The Sun shone from Jupiter's degree as Jesus and his disciples walked toward Nain. Jesus taught how to distinguish true teachers from false, saying, "Beware of false prophets, who come to you in sheep's clothing but inwardly are ravenous wolves" (Nov/12/30).

The resurrecting power of the Sun in creative tension with the Holy Spirit is like a two-edged sword, for Jupiter increases what it aspects. The question becomes: Will we *inflate*, or will we *humble* ourselves? If this is egoism, the sword wounds. If, on the other hand, it is love, the sword heals.

False prophets are masters of manipulation, yet wise Jupiter gives ample warning, informing us of the particular qualities lurking behind the masks of the wolves. When faced with the confusion of who is who, we are wise to seek the heart's counsel.

**Sep 10: ASPECT: Sun 22° Leo opposite Neptune 22° Aquarius: Death of the Blessed Virgin** (Aug/15/44). When the Sun opposes the Goddess Night, she tends to dissolve all in us that is naught but the dross of egoism. We are not to confuse this death with the death of our true "I." Indeed, when egoism rushes to the surface, expelling itself in the blush of shame, the "I" stands ever stronger.

This exact aspect occurred at the death of the Virgin Mary. The heavens thus decreed that her life had been devoted to the Goddess Night. Did not Sophia incarnate into her at the event of Pentecost? The Leo Sun asks us to resurrect from enchantment in self-interest so as to enter world-interest. This is the signature of those who hear the mighty inspirations the Goddess continuously radiates from her throne above.

**Venus enters Virgo**: "Behold worlds, O soul! **May the soul fathom worlds**, may the spirit penetrate being, work with powers of life, build upon experiences undergone, trust in blossoming worlds to come. O soul, know thou beings!" (Steiner, *Twelve Cosmic Moods*). Venus is in fall in this sign, as Virgo is opposite the place of exaltation (Pisces). Efforts are required to "fathom worlds."

**Sep 11: Mercury enters Virgo**: "Behold worlds, O soul! May the soul fathom worlds, **may the spirit penetrate being**, work with powers of life, build upon experiences undergone, trust in blossoming worlds to come. O soul, know thou beings!" (Steiner, *Twelve Cosmic Moods*). Mercury rules in this sign.

**Sep 12: ASPECT: Mars 21° Leo square Jupiter 21° Scorpio**. Mars remembers an evening in the synagogue when the Pharisees were greatly angered at Jesus's teaching, which warned against taking life too lightly—as had been done at the time of Noah or Lot. The Pharisees accused Jesus of speaking as if he were the Messiah himself, and—amid uproar—they put out the lights (Sep/4/29).

Pharisees (rigid wisdom) and anger (Mars) are fine representations of the lower nature of this aspect, and the Archangel Michael guards against uprisings from these sordid realms. Mars in Scorpio warns us to be patient, and to manage the quick and fiery temperament of this warrior force. In so doing we may gain the insights wisdom longs to bestow upon us, thus finding the strength and enthusiasm to bear all provocation in mildness of soul.

This aspect (also in fixed signs) occurred at the conception of the Nathan Jesus. There is no better example of a being whose soul was so pure that it was free of all disturbances born of aggression. In such a soul, the Holy Spirit is the creative force behind every action.

We can pray that moderation governs those who rule nations, for any increase in daring action could result in dangerous recklessness.

**Sep 13: ASPECT: Mercury conjunct Venus 4° Virgo**. Venus recalls the conception of John the Baptist (Sep/9/3 BC). Head and heart are aligned under the influence of this aspect. We can imagine the mind of John in seamless integration with his heart, even while he was held captive by Herod's black magicians.

**Sep 14: ASPECT: Full Moon 26° Aquarius opposite Sun 26° Leo.** The Moon remembers the Healing of the Nobleman's Son (Aug/3/30).

The New Moon that began this lunar cycle reminded us of the closed circle of the serpent's world and the Sabbath door through which we enter eternity. During the first quarter Moon, we remembered the "secret" places wherein we find discourse with our spiritual brothers and sisters. Did we leap, and thereby find that the net appeared as we defied the ruse of the serpent? If we indeed leapt, we may find transformational powers assisting us as we heal lingering forces that bind us to the serpent's endless circle through the forces of heredity.

Moon in Aquarius increases our relationship with the realm of consciousness that borders the day-waking consciousness to which we are often bound. From the Angel-Human, waters pour forth in flows of imaginative splendor; and from these waters the soul finds the "waters of eternal life." The brain-bound mind, however, may encounter an intellectual shock when leaping from the security of the sense-world, for the mysteries deconstruct what the senses hold dear.

We can imagine the angel holding two urns, one red and one blue, suggesting the integration of duality wherein the cooperation of peace finds its contentment. This integration is what forms the Sabbath door—it represents the neutral ground of soul silence—that leads us out of the serpent's endless circle.

Although Lucifer has torn time asunder, the angel holds the unblemished continuity of memory in the sacred archetype she holds for us: *our divine image*. Furthermore, the divine image of each and every human being is an aspect of the immaculate soul of the Angel Jesus. In him is the totality of purity we lost as we fell from Paradise. And, as the last quarter Moon reminds us of Jesus Christ commissioning his disciples to heal what has fallen, this Full Moon serves as preparation for the culminating grace this lunar cycle may bestow. We leap, we tend the night, and now we are to heal at least a small portion of the ghosts who have bound us to things of the past. The "image" held by angels, however, has in no way suffered any decrease despite the fact that our "likeness" has participated in the Fall.

The guardian Angel *cherishes* the endeavor, quest, and aspiration of the soul engaged on this way [of the soul from life to life]. This means to say that he fills in the breaks in the psychic functional organism due to the disfigurement of the likeness, and makes up for its failings—given the soul's good will toward it. For *support* never signifies substitution of the Angel's will for that of the human being. The will remains free, always and everywhere. The guardian Angel never touches on humankind's free will, and resigns himself to await the decision or choice made in the inviolable sanctuary of free will—to lend his assistance immediately if it is just, or to remain a passive observer reduced alone to prayer if it is not.[1]

The inviolable region of free will exists for human beings as well as for angels. Demons serve the purpose of assuring spiritual progress—for, without them, free will would have no venue to prove the merits of freedom. The angel stands by, offering all we could possibly need, if only we were aware of this. The angel guards, cherishes, and protects; it also visits and defends all who gather in the holy waters they continuously pour upon us.

Contemplating angelic "defense" brings us to the sorrowful fact that they must follow us wherever we choose to go, and this is how human beings contribute to the fall of angels.

In our hereditary bodies, all aspects of ourselves that have become satellites of things born of the serpent's ruse, will obstruct us from receiving our angel's healing ministrations. As we are now living in the 40th day, the day angels came to minister to Jesus Christ, it has become mandatory that we again turn to spiritual guidance. Such guidance is the mission and purpose of our angel.

The Angel depends on humankind in his creative activity. If the human being does not ask for it, if he turns away from him, the Angel has no motive for creative activity. He can then fall into a state of consciousness where all his creative geniality remains in potential and does not

---

1 Ibid., p. 376.

manifest. It is a state of vegetation or "twilight existence," comparable to sleep from the human point of view. An Angel who has nothing to exist for is a tragedy in the spiritual world.[2]

Here we touch into the fifth sacrifice of Christ, whereby he is bringing the moral ether to all humankind *through the sacrifice of the Angel Jesus*—who has sacrificed his *manas* consciousness to Christ, and thus lives in the "twilight existence" described above. When we receive the blessing of the fifth sacrifice, we awake to angels and to the Angel Jesus who resurrects *in* us. This is how we receive access to higher realms of consciousness. It is world destiny that we regain the clairvoyant capacities of old, but now this clairvoyance is not atavistic—instead, it is *manas* consciousness, i.e., filled with the power of our "I." This moral consciousness frees us from all negative aspects of heredity, allowing us to draw closer to angels. And, as we gaze up at the Aquarian Moon, we remember the Angel-Human.

Mars opposite Neptune accompanies this Full Moon, lending vigor to our strivings.

**ASPECT: Mars 22° Leo opposite Neptune 22° Aquarius.** This aspect was in the natal charts of both Francis Bacon and Jacques Lusseyran (the heroic, blind Resistance leader during World War Two). What a representation of the aspect's lower and higher possibilities! It rendered Bacon susceptible to the deceit of materialistic thinking and "natural" science, while Lusseyran spent his life exposing and fighting against the deceptions that had crept into mass consciousness—even though his sight was taken from him as a boy.

The Archangel Michael is the solar guardian of all angels, and his special charge is the Angel Jesus, in whom the purity of Paradise has been preserved. When standing across the heavens from the Goddess Night, a quickening may result. What is the nature of this quickening? We can imagine the Aquarian Angel-Human swaddling our "image" in a divine world-womb. Furthermore, we can imagine the Lion of Judah holding our "likeness" in the interior of our hearts. Thus may the difference between the two be revealed. Will we resurrect from some measure of error—and indeed *rejoice* as we glimpse a portion of our higher self?

This aspect was present (also in fixed signs) at the visitation. The Jesus child (in the womb of Mary) caused a quickening of the John child (in the womb of Elizabeth). The Old Adam (John) was touched by the New Adam (Jesus), and thus was he moved. In like manner this aspect asks us to be quickened by the resounding inspirations Neptune bestows upon our soul body (astral body), calling us to remember that we are born from the divine, and to the divine we strive.

Now inversely, the negative traits of this aspect present the possibility of deception, of drained energies, and of disappointment. *Yet, if we have not appointed ourselves to be great, we can not be disappointed when the fervor of egoism is silenced and we humbly gaze upon the self we would die to become.*

**Sep 18: Sun enters Virgo:** "Behold worlds, O soul! May the soul fathom worlds, may the spirit penetrate being, work with powers of life, build upon experiences undergone, trust in blossoming worlds to come. O soul, know thou beings!" (Steiner, *Twelve Cosmic Moods*).

The late William Bento illumines this mantra:

> The more engaged we are with the phenomena of Natura, the accompanying rhythms of social life, and the planetary and starry celestial dances above us, the more awe and wonder arise in our soul. This beholding is more than a seeing; it is an immersion into a *conscious participation mystique*. The mystery of worlds is precisely what the longing of the soul seeks to know; and so this beholding is indeed not a static event, but the movement of the soul into worlds both known and unknown.

The first decan is ruled by the Sun, and is associated with the constellation of the Cup (Crater); here we can think of the Grail chalice held by the Queen of Peace, represented by the Virgin. The virtue of Virgo is here invoked: *Courtesy becomes Tactfulness of Heart.* The inner work of descent (Persephone) brings the awareness of self-knowledge. Hydra ("the Serpent") stretches its undulating life force throughout the entire region beneath

---

[2] Ibid., pp. 378-379.

Virgo. To become self-aware, we must confront the serpent!

**Sep 19: Saturn stations direct 19° Sagittarius.** This degree of the Zodiac recalls the Sun's position as Jesus Christ commissioned the twelve to go forth and baptize. The Blessed Virgin would, of course, ask the same of us, for she swaddles us in merciful grace and she intends us to share this with all others. Moreover, as Saturn is in Sagittarius, past traditions may be resurrected through the power of truth, which necessitates that we open to apocalyptic streams of revelation.

**Sep 21: ASPECT: Jupiter 22° Scorpio square Neptune 22° Aquarius.** The Sun stood at Jupiter's degree on the day that Jesus raised from the dead the youth of Nain. Jesus and the disciples had encountered the funeral procession for the boy; Jesus commanded the coffin bearers to put down the coffin and he said the words recorded in Matthew 11:28–30: "Come to me, all who labor and are heavy laden, and I will give you rest. Take my yoke upon you, and learn from me; for I am gentle and lowly in heart, and you will find rest for your souls. For my yoke is easy, and my burden is light" (Nov/13/30).

This is the third time that this square is exact. It has been an overlighting influence this entire year. The first exact square was on January 12, the second on June 16. Today we experience the last exact square between these two heavenly bodies. This will not again occur until until 2025.

The Christ memory revealed at the time of the January square was our capacity to heal from afar in relation to sacred magic. In June the memory was the casting out of demons and the theology of their different levels of manifestation. Today we remember the raising of the youth of Nain, who later became Mani in the 3rd century, and then Parsifal in the 9th century. Regarding Mani, Rudolf Steiner had the following to say. "[Mani] will act from the power of the Grail Mysteries, and he will instruct humankind so that they may decide even about good and evil."[1]

---
1 Steiner, *From the History and Contents of the First Section of the Esoteric School*, p. 227.

A few weeks after Jesus raised the youth of Nain, he exorcised demons in Gergeza. Raising the dead and exorcising demons are practices that rest very much in the Manichaean stream of *loving evil good*. Furthermore, it was Kyot, King Charlemagne's chief Paladin, who brought his nephew Parsifal through his formation, i.e., helping him develop his wisdom-filled thinking in preparation for re-entering the Grail Castle. Both Mani and Parsifal guide us to understand the working of evil as well as respect its necessity.

This transit can bring up thoughts that can shatter our illusion of soul wellness. Suspicions, deceptions, and even paranoia may arise. Such are the accoutrements of the Woman of Babylon (lower Neptune influences). Inversely, the Goddess Night (higher Neptune influences) bestows a wealth of inspiring insights, parting the veil that has long obscured Sophianic realms of wonder.

Anne Catherine Emmerich witnessed the moment when the youth of Nain was raised from the dead, and she beheld a murky, black, cloud-like figure issuing from his body as a dark creature fled from him. Given that we live in a world woven through with dark energies, it is inevitable that energy contagions will enter us. Becoming afflicted by these murky beings is not the real problem. Not applying the healing arts of sacred magic, however, *is* a problem.

It is possible that Mani has incarnated in our time, and he indeed will be working in the light of the Grail mysteries. This light is streaming into our world through the sacrifice of the Angel Jesus, who has bequeathed to Christ his *manas* consciousness. True it is that we are now being instructed on the etheric technologies that defend against the powers of evil. Mani is inspiring many morally-focused healers to develop these new practices. As we cleanse our fields of negative energies, we are surrounded by spiritually clean air into which angels may approach us. They cannot reach us if murky pestilence engulfs us, for in so doing they would faint. And without spiritual air, angels cannot breathe. Without spiritual air, human beings—analogously—

succumb to deceptions.

This entire year has been a test of faith for humankind. Will we enter the fifth light of the Grail, or will we content ourselves with chimeras of Neptunian delusions?

**Last Quarter Moon 4° Gemini.** This Moon is conjunct both *Polaris*, the North Star, and *Betelgeuse*, the star marking the right shoulder of Orion. According to the research of Robert Powell, Betelgeuse corresponds to the earthly location of the Temple of Solomon. The Moon holds the memory of Jesus ten days before the crucifixion, when he explained his mission to his disciples. Jesus said that he would soon withdraw from humanity and from the flesh, and that whoever—with him, through him, and in him—separated himself from his own fallen nature, would at the same time commend himself to the Father (Mar/24/33).

In conjunction with the last square between Jupiter and Neptune, we enter the concluding phase of this lunar cycle. Hopefully we have tended the Sabbath door that leads us into the night—as well as into communion with angels by day. Thus have we perhaps freed ourselves from at least some aspects of binding hereditary influences. Now we enter the period of integration and interiorization. True it is that Christ is no longer physically with us; yet, for those who strive to commune with him, his etheric presence is undeniable. *Through the power of Christ, all demons can be exorcised, for he is never separate from his Bride, Sophia, who carries the force that doth penetrate all material substance—cleansing auras so as to make way for angels.*

**Sep 22: ASPECT: Mercury 19° Virgo square Saturn 19° Sagittarius.** Mercury recalls its position precisely one solar year after the baptism. After having taught at the synagogue, Jesus, at the request of a pagan priestess whose child had just died, went to the pagan quarter of the town and raised the child from the dead. He then healed many other pagan children, who were suffering because of their parents' worship of Moloch. Jesus exorcised the priestess and revealed to the assembly the nature of their idolatry; in consequence, they were determined to turn to the God of Israel (Sep/23/30). Healing Mercury has discipline when in aspect with Saturn. Our culture harbors many Molochs to whom we offer our "first born," i.e., our children. Perhaps we may learn to protect them before it is too late.

**Sept 23: Autumn Equinox, 3:50 AM, EDT: Sun 5° Virgo.** The little seed we carried from the manger in the Holy Nights of 2018/2019 has ripened as a soul force within us, bearing its fruit. That which was then only a spiritual potential can now become an achievement—if it is taken hold of and directed by our courageous will. As the Mother's breath contracts in her seasonal inhalation, we enter her inner worlds—and in these inner realms we find dragons waiting, which rest in confidence that we will not trouble ourselves with their presence. Given that we are increasingly distracting ourselves to death, this may be true for many. Yet, for the knightly, it is time to pick up Michael's sword and slay that in us which obstructs our spiritual progress. Through such efforts, a space will be newly created into which autumn's fruit will form a new seed—a seed that will be borne into winter's night for yet another beginning in the spiral of the seasons.

**Sep 25: ASPECT: Venus 19° Virgo square Saturn 19° Sagittarius.** Venus recalls Jesus taking hold of the hands of Eliud, whose wife had been unfaithful. He spoke to him lovingly about the washing of the feet. Jesus revealed to him that his children were not his own, but that his wife wanted to make amends and that he should forgive her. Jesus stood in silent prayer through Eliud's anguish, then comforted him and washed his feet. Eliud called his wife, who entered the room wearing a veil. Jesus blessed them and their children, and thereafter they remained true to one another (Aug/20/32).

The principle of mercy reigns from heavenly spheres today as the cross of Venus stands in creative tension with the Blessed Virgin. How could this not be true when Venus is love and the Virgin is holiness? This aspect is the benediction of spiritual promises pouring into the heart of the cross—where the vertical and horizontal beams meet. With Venus in Virgo, our soul may be raised above the trivialities of distraction to hear what the angel of the other wants us to speak. The artistry of knowing just how much to say is a matter of tactfulness of heart, as well as courtesy.

Inversely, if we want nothing to do with our cross, such artistry will evade us. *The restraining arms of the Virgin will instead feel like a prison of melancholy, as an unwanted weight of responsibility falls upon us*—which of course would be accompanied by negative feelings and even fears of criticism. The origin of such fears, however, lies in our own souls, for all criticism we have launched upon others may now come home to roost. Therefore, it is grand indeed that we experience what we ourselves have created—for this enables us to restore the principle of mercy, and to reintegrate our brokenness.

This aspect (although in different constellations) was present at Pentecost, when the Holy Spirit descended, through Mary, upon the disciples of Jesus Christ. Truth and tactfulness thus join forces under the influences of Sagittarius and Virgo, calling all disciples of goodness to pick up their cross and walk, leaving footprints of mercy in our wake.

**Sep 26: Mars enters Virgo:** "Behold worlds, O soul! May the soul fathom worlds, may the spirit penetrate being, **work with powers of life**, build upon experiences undergone, trust in blossoming worlds to come. O soul, know thou beings!" (Steiner, *Twelve Cosmic Moods*). **ASPECT: Mercury 25° Virgo square Pluto 25° Sagittarius.** Mercury remembers the Feast of Atonement, for which Jesus taught regarding penance. He spoke against those who practiced only bodily purification and did not restrain those desires of the soul that were evil (Sep/26/30). Virgo protects what would otherwise be left vulnerable to unholy forces. If our bodies are fit, but our souls are hardened, we only make it more difficult to find spirit; this renders our minds bereft—lost in agitated restlessness as we pursue more of what we don't need.

**Sep 28: ASPECT: New Moon 10° Virgo.** The Moon reached this degree just one hour before the Miracle of Walking on the Water (Jan/30/31).

In the fourth and fifth miracles of Jesus Christ, both the macrocosmic initiations (bread) and the microcosmic initiations (fish) were exemplified through the feeding of the five thousand and the walking on water. Herein lay the prophecy of Christ's future descent into Hell (the trial of the fish initiation) and his resurrection (the victory of the bread initiation). To walk on water, by analogy, is to have a pure and chaste etheric body. All remnants of the Fall create vortices in the etheric body that become infused with a magnetic charge able to pull one down, i.e., suck one in. From one perspective, we can view the walking on water as a seamless reflection of oneness with the radiant qualities of the life body. A whale swallowed Jonah. He spent three days inside this fish, just as Christ spent three days in Hell. Jonah's fish initiation can be regarded as the Earth Trial—wherein we descend into our inner nature to encounter all obstacles we have created, and which affect our ability to heal our life body.

Miracles, magic, and purity of heart are evoked with this New Moon. What is the source of this profundity? It is the primal revelation, streaming from the presence of God. It is the prodigious conviction of hope and faith, which vibrates both in the whole world and within each individual. The Virgin protects the sacred space that surrounds us. She asks that we listen to the womb of silence she provides for our protection. She is the voice resounding throughout the natural world, as well as the voice that sings to us within the beating of our heart.

The sea of glass surrounding the throne of God is to be reflected below in the sea of glass we create as a mantle embracing our physical being. *When we find resonance with the Virgin's purity, we gain connection with the force she generates as the primal vibration of our soul's origin.*

> Insofar as my heart beats, that I breathe, that my blood circulates—in so far, in other words, that faith and hope work in me—in so far do I take part, thereby, in the great cosmic ritual in which all beings participate, all the hierarchies from the Seraphim down to butterflies...namely, in natural religion's "sacrament of baptism," which is immersion in the waters of the "sea of glass," and natural religion's "sacrament of confirmation," which takes place day and night through the chorus of choirs of animated Nature: "Holy, holy, holy..." All beings are baptized and confirmed in natural religion. Because, in so far as they live, they have faith and hope. But the baptism and confirmation with "fire and Spirit,"

the sacraments of love, surpass those of natural religion. They bear forgiveness and healing to fallen nature.[1]

We can imagine inviting the Virgin to still the waters of our unconscious, calming us in times of angst or fear. Through her we remember Natura and our oneness in the womb of the Mother, praying to participate in the baptism and confirmation of her sacraments of love. Turning to our Mother, and remembering the great cosmic biography of the Earth, we awake a "memory" of truth regarding how we are to approach her kingdoms. Without her mantle interpenetrating our earthly mantle, we are in danger of forgetting her cosmic biography. This would result in our being swept away on the fanatical and agitated currents of the serpent's river of misery:

> Fallen Nature also has its unconscious mystery, i.e., its collective instinctivity of perception (its "waters") and its collective instinctivity of reaction (its "creatures"). Again, it is the Apocalypse of St. John that reveals this. The following is the origin of the "sea" of fallen Nature according to the Apocalypse:
>
> > The serpent poured water like a river out of his mouth after the woman, to sweep her away with the flood. But the earth came to the help of the woman, and the earth opened its mouth and swallowed the river that the dragon had poured from his mouth. (Rev. 12:15–16)
>
> The difference between the waters of the "sea of glass" before the throne and the waters poured forth by the serpent is that the former are the calm, peace and stability of contemplation, or pure perception—they are "as glass," "like crystal"—whilst the latter are in movement, "poured forth," "like a river," in the pursuit of an aim, namely that of sweeping away the woman.[2]

The waters of the serpent are tremulous, emitting a force of suction that seeks to drag us under and sweep us away from the holy woman. To walk on water means we fear not the presence of our error; rather do we accept our soul's fallen nature as we strive to name the forces which would otherwise destroy our peace. *In not fearing, we find the reciprocal light that holds us up as we enter the process of redemption.*

Our enemies surround us, yet our hearts seek to become like that of a child. For the child accepts all things as they are, ever seeking the unceasing wonder of the world. Thus does the Holy Virgin draw near to us, enfolding us in her mantle of love. When the heart speaks, courtesy flows from one heart to the other, healing discord through inspirations born of contemplative calm.

**First quarter Moon, 16° Sagittarius: Jesus reveals that Herod put John to death.**

**Full Moon, 25° Pisces: Triumphant entry into Jerusalem.**

**Last quarter Moon, 3° Cancer: Birth of John the Baptist.**

Lunar teachings of this cycle begin with the walking on water, pointing to how this can be approached at this time of the Second Coming. As the first quarter dawns, we are to act. What sacred magic can we learn to counter the current of black magic now so prevalent? As the transformational phase of the Full Moon dawns, we are reminded that there is a future awaiting us, into which all who have remained loyal to the "name" of Christ may find him. And in the closing phase of the last quarter, we are to integrate these teachings as we remember John—who represents the future stream of time and its apocalyptic realities.

This New Moon falls on Michaelmas Eve, lending strength to our contemplations.

**Sep 29. Mercury enters Libra:** "Worlds sustain worlds; in being, experience being; **in existing, embrace existence.** And being effects being to pour forth deeds unfolding, in world-enjoyment reposing. O worlds, uphold worlds!" (Steiner, *Twelve Cosmic Moods*).

**Michaelmas.** The air is alive with iron. Our blood is fortified for the battle at hand. Some are called to take up all space with goodness, whereas others are called to actually confront evil. Whatever our task may be, we can pray that it is consciously chosen. Thus may the powers of creation intercede through

---

[1] Anon., *Meditations of the Tarot*, p. 271.
[2] Ibid.

our willingness to unmask the evil that seeks to obliterate all goodness.

Like Lazarus rising from the dead, so too does human consciousness rise into wakefulness as nature falls into winter's rest. The Resurrection we celebrated last spring is now to be realized. This is not a time for sleep! Mother Earth is awaking from her summer sojourn into the vast reaches of the cosmos. She returns filled with creative and new spiritual resolves, and we are to unite our consciousness with hers. The tomb of the inner Earth is to be penetrated by the light we now carry into its darkness. We gathered this light all summer; now it illumines our way into realms of unconsciousness, so that we may cleanse the temple of our soul in preparation for the Christmas season to come.

**Sep 30: ASPECT: Venus 25° Virgo square Pluto 25° Sagittarius.** Venus was at her degree in Virgo when Jesus and the disciples arrived in Dion, where Jesus healed the sick throughout the day. Great jubilation ensued: "Blessed is he who considers the poor!" Jesus and those with him then went to the synagogue and thanked God (Sep/25/30).

The lower nature of this aspect may cause simmering tensions to rise. The higher aspect, however, creates dynamic tension between our sensory nature and suprasensory realities. Pluto/Phanes directs us to new truths that must revivify old paradigms—while, at the same time, the soul may experience fear in letting go. Our soul must move *into* the tension, embracing inner forces seeking release into the light. Long has the revelation stream been dammed from below, meeting resistance from humanity's peculiar fear of change. Yet the mystery wisdom will rise; and as we enter its river, we will find that we can swim together in seas of change, unhindered by trepidations that once held us captive. Taking up the cross of love will sustain us as we move into willingness to meet the future. Something very new is occurring, and lonely will be those who are left on the shores of the old as their friends follow the current river of truth.

This aspect may help us become conscious of our hidden fears and our need to control. What is happening is utterly uncontrollable.

# OCTOBER 2019

## Stargazing Preview

The Moon finds Jupiter on the 3rd; at sunset, look for Jupiter high in the southwest, below and slightly to the right of the Moon. On the 4th, Venus enters Libra, and she'll set less than forty minutes after the Sun. The next day brings a Moon–Saturn conjunction. They will be overhead, due south, as the Sun sets, with the Last Quarter Moon slightly to the left of Saturn. They both disappear below the western horizon at about midnight.

October's Pisces Full Moon falls on the 13th. The Moon passes Mars on the 26th, and on the following morning, watch for Mars, then the Moon, in the east as they rise about ninety minutes before the Sun. Quite late on the 27th there will be a Libra New Moon; two days later, the waxing crescent will set just after Venus, an hour before sunset. By the time the Sun sets on the following day, Venus will have moved into Scorpio.

After the final sunset of the month, look to the southwest, and you'll see the waxing Moon close to Jupiter, on its left. They set ninety minutes after Venus and Mercury, still very close to each other after their conjunction the previous day. Orion will rise at 2000.

## October Commentaries

**Oct 3: Pluto stations direct 25° Sagittarius.** The Sun was at Pluto's degree as Jesus taught in the synagogue at Shiloh concerning reverence for the old and love of one's parents (Dec/15/29).

Traditions are ground to dust under the feet of the irreverent. "The human organism is filled with all sorts of substances, biological forces, and egoistic tendencies; in the areas of commerce, politics, and abstract intellectuality, human civilization is absorbed in profit, power, and pleasure."[1] Under such influences, respect for tradition has crumbled. Yet the young are not to blame if their elders have failed to uphold the dignity and virtue that sustain the continuity of tradition.

---
1  Valentin Tomberg, *Christ and Sophia*, p. 343.

**Oct 4: Sun 16° Virgo: Birth of the Solomon Mary (9/7/21 BC).** During the profound conversation before the Baptism, the Nathan Mary united with the Solomon Mary; thus was the Pentecost event prepared. The greater Pentecost event—for humanity as a whole—will occur as souls again experience the power of the living word. Then will conversation with the spiritual world become a conversation with actual entities of both human and hierarchal realms. This is not an ideal fabricated by lunatics; instead, it depicts the awaking of the Christ Sun in our heart. "When such conversation takes place in a light that makes the 'appearances' of spiritual beings visible and their individual 'voices' audible, then it becomes a real conversation with actual individuals."[2]

The remembrance of this conversation, in light of the mantra for Venus in Libra, invites us into the dance of synchronicity—wherein two worlds cooperate in the forming of reality.

**Venus enters Libra:** "Worlds sustain worlds; **in being, experience being**; in existing, embrace existence. And being effects being to pour forth deeds unfolding, in world-enjoyment reposing. O worlds, uphold worlds!" (Steiner, *Twelve Cosmic Moods*). Venus rules in this sign.

**Oct 5: First Quarter Moon 16° Sagittarius.** Jesus and his mother, accompanied by Peter, John, and others, went into the room where John the Baptist (who had been killed five days earlier) had been born. As they knelt together on a large rug, the Holy Virgin recounted events from the Baptist's life. Then Jesus told them that Herod had put John to death. They were stricken with grief (Jan/9/31). The New Moon revealed the trial of walking on water as the test of overcoming fear. Now we encounter the stream of black magic used by Herod's people in their treatment of John. Sacred magic is the antidote to these dark powers—for, by employing such tactics we are turned away from the torrid waters in our subconscious depths. In so turning, we may find the stream of peaceful mercy, which forgives all trespasses. Indeed, mercy is an antidote to the black magical currents that have created a "network" around us.

What is mercy? *It is the marriage of compassionate righteousness with love.* Guilt is offered the hand of mercy when we seek to make good our wrongs. For then we may ask: What is missing? This question accompanies the therapeutic gaze, which beholds what the other is striving to become. Herod's priests inverted the quality of mercy; and instead of expressing awe for what would become of John's new mission, they murdered him.

At the time of John's beheading, powerful stellar influences were at work. Herod's priests intended to use these benevolent forces in their inversion to capture and possess the powerful thought-life John would bring into etheric worlds upon his death. John was to become the shepherd of the circle of twelve disciples, increasing their understanding of the divine mission they were serving.

Had the black magicians succeeded, John's mighty spiritualized future would also have been slaughtered by the murderous evil ones, after which this future would then be served to the disciples *in inversion*. Doubt would then have triumphed over faith, and this would have destroyed the circle of twelve. John remained faithful through the intercession of Christ, who knew the powerful stellar configurations that were then forming. Christ was thereby able to bring the boundless force of white magic to bear against the forces of black magic—thus averting what would have been a terrible tragedy.

We remember that white magic multiplies in the spiritual world like the mustard seed, while black magic's multiplication is limited to the periphery of the sense world—which reflects the subearthly realms wherein the souls of proclaimed atheists are held captive after their deaths. Sacred magic prevented the *spiritual* beheading of John, and thus were the magicians of Herod defeated.

**Oct 7: ASPECT: Sun 19° Virgo square Saturn 19° Sagittarius.** The Sun was at Saturn's degree at the Commissioning of the Disciples. Jesus and the twelve disciples climbed a mountain north of Capernaum while a large crowd remained below. Jesus had compassion for those in the crowd, as they were harassed and helpless—like sheep without a shepherd. He then said to the disciples: "The harvest is plentiful, but the laborers are few; pray

---

2 Ibid., p. 345.

SIDEREAL GEOCENTRIC LONGITUDES : OCTOBER 2019 Gregorian at 0 hours UT

| DAY | ☉ | ☽ | ☊ | ☿ | ♀ | ♂ | ♃ | ♄ | ♅ | ♆ | ♇ |
|---|---|---|---|---|---|---|---|---|---|---|---|
| 1 TU | 12 ♍ 31 | 13 ♎ 46 | 18 ♊ 29R | 1 ♎ 36 | 25 ♍ 24 | 2 ♍ 56 | 23 ♏ 10 | 19 ♐ 2 | 10 ♈ 39R | 21 ♒ 45R | 25 ♐ 37R |
| 2 WE | 13 30 | 28 9 | 18 21 | 3 4 | 26 38 | 3 35 | 23 18 | 19 3 | 10 37 | 21 43 | 25 37 |
| 3 TH | 14 29 | 12 ♏ 1 | 18 16 | 4 30 | 27 53 | 4 13 | 23 27 | 19 4 | 10 35 | 21 42 | 25 37 |
| 4 FR | 15 28 | 25 24 | 18 13 | 5 55 | 29 8 | 4 52 | 23 35 | 19 6 | 10 33 | 21 40 | 25 37D |
| 5 SA | 16 27 | 8 ♐ 20 | 18 12 | 7 19 | 0 ♎ 22 | 5 31 | 23 44 | 19 7 | 10 31 | 21 39 | 25 37 |
| 6 SU | 17 26 | 20 53 | 18 12 | 8 42 | 1 37 | 6 9 | 23 53 | 19 9 | 10 29 | 21 37 | 25 37 |
| 7 MO | 18 25 | 3 ♑ 8 | 18 11 | 10 5 | 2 51 | 6 48 | 24 2 | 19 11 | 10 26 | 21 36 | 25 37 |
| 8 TU | 19 24 | 15 9 | 18 9 | 11 26 | 4 6 | 7 27 | 24 11 | 19 13 | 10 24 | 21 35 | 25 37 |
| 9 WE | 20 24 | 27 3 | 18 5 | 12 46 | 5 21 | 8 5 | 24 20 | 19 15 | 10 22 | 21 33 | 25 37 |
| 10 TH | 21 23 | 8 ♒ 54 | 17 58 | 14 4 | 6 35 | 8 44 | 24 29 | 19 17 | 10 20 | 21 32 | 25 38 |
| 11 FR | 22 22 | 20 44 | 17 49 | 15 22 | 7 50 | 9 23 | 24 39 | 19 19 | 10 17 | 21 30 | 25 38 |
| 12 SA | 23 21 | 2 ♓ 37 | 17 36 | 16 38 | 9 4 | 10 1 | 24 48 | 19 21 | 10 15 | 21 29 | 25 38 |
| 13 SU | 24 21 | 14 36 | 17 23 | 17 53 | 10 19 | 10 40 | 24 58 | 19 23 | 10 13 | 21 28 | 25 38 |
| 14 MO | 25 20 | 26 40 | 17 8 | 19 6 | 11 33 | 11 19 | 25 8 | 19 26 | 10 10 | 21 26 | 25 39 |
| 15 TU | 26 19 | 8 ♈ 52 | 16 55 | 20 17 | 12 48 | 11 58 | 25 18 | 19 28 | 10 8 | 21 25 | 25 39 |
| 16 WE | 27 19 | 21 12 | 16 43 | 21 27 | 14 3 | 12 36 | 25 27 | 19 31 | 10 6 | 21 24 | 25 39 |
| 17 TH | 28 18 | 3 ♉ 41 | 16 34 | 22 35 | 15 17 | 13 15 | 25 38 | 19 34 | 10 3 | 21 23 | 25 40 |
| 18 FR | 29 18 | 16 20 | 16 27 | 23 41 | 16 32 | 13 54 | 25 48 | 19 37 | 10 1 | 21 21 | 25 40 |
| 19 SA | 0 ♎ 17 | 29 11 | 16 24 | 24 44 | 17 46 | 14 33 | 25 58 | 19 39 | 9 58 | 21 20 | 25 41 |
| 20 SU | 1 17 | 12 ♊ 16 | 16 23 | 25 45 | 19 1 | 15 12 | 26 8 | 19 42 | 9 56 | 21 19 | 25 41 |
| 21 MO | 2 17 | 25 38 | 16 24D | 26 44 | 20 15 | 15 51 | 26 19 | 19 45 | 9 54 | 21 18 | 25 42 |
| 22 TU | 3 16 | 9 ♋ 19 | 16 24R | 27 39 | 21 30 | 16 30 | 26 29 | 19 49 | 9 51 | 21 17 | 25 42 |
| 23 WE | 4 16 | 23 21 | 16 22 | 28 31 | 22 45 | 17 9 | 26 40 | 19 52 | 9 49 | 21 16 | 25 43 |
| 24 TH | 5 16 | 7 ♌ 43 | 16 19 | 29 19 | 23 59 | 17 47 | 26 51 | 19 55 | 9 46 | 21 14 | 25 43 |
| 25 FR | 6 15 | 22 23 | 16 12 | 0 ♏ 3 | 25 14 | 18 26 | 27 2 | 19 59 | 9 44 | 21 13 | 25 44 |
| 26 SA | 7 15 | 7 ♍ 17 | 16 4 | 0 43 | 26 28 | 19 5 | 27 13 | 20 2 | 9 41 | 21 12 | 25 44 |
| 27 SU | 8 15 | 22 15 | 15 54 | 1 18 | 27 43 | 19 44 | 27 24 | 20 6 | 9 39 | 21 11 | 25 45 |
| 28 MO | 9 15 | 7 ♎ 10 | 15 43 | 1 47 | 28 57 | 20 23 | 27 35 | 20 9 | 9 36 | 21 10 | 25 46 |
| 29 TU | 10 15 | 21 51 | 15 34 | 2 10 | 0 ♏ 12 | 21 2 | 27 46 | 20 13 | 9 34 | 21 9 | 25 47 |
| 30 WE | 11 15 | 6 ♏ 11 | 15 26 | 2 26 | 1 27 | 21 41 | 27 57 | 20 17 | 9 31 | 21 8 | 25 47 |
| 31 TH | 12 15 | 20 6 | 15 21 | 2 36 | 2 41 | 22 21 | 28 9 | 20 21 | 9 29 | 21 8 | 25 48 |

| INGRESSES : | | |
|---|---|---|
| 2 ☽ → ♏ 3: 9 | 23 ☽ → ♌ 11:10 | |
| 4 ☽ → ♐ 8:26 | 24 ☿ → ♏ 22: 8 | |
| ♀ → ♎ 16:51 | 25 ☽ → ♍ 12:17 | |
| 6 ☽ → ♑ 17:49 | 27 ☽ → ♎ 12:26 | |
| 9 ☽ → ♒ 5:57 | 28 ♀ → ♏ 20: 9 | |
| 11 ☽ → ♓ 18:42 | 29 ☽ → ♏ 13:33 | |
| 14 ☽ → ♈ 6:34 | 31 ☽ → ♐ 17:35 | |
| 16 ☽ → ♉ 16:56 | | |
| 18 ☉ → ♎ 17: 0 | | |
| 19 ☽ → ♊ 1:30 | | |
| 21 ☽ → ♋ 7:43 | | |

| ASPECTS & ECLIPSES : | | | | |
|---|---|---|---|---|
| 1 ♀ □ ♇ 4:13 | 12 ☽ ☍ ♂ 15:42 | 21 ☽ ☍ ♇ 0: 5 | 29 ☽ ☌ ♀ 15:12 | |
| 3 ☽ ☌ ♃ 20:39 | ♀ ☍ ♅ 22: 4 | ☉ □ ☽ 12:38 | ☽ ☌ ☿ 17:33 | |
| 5 ☉ □ ☽ 16:46 | 13 ☽ □S ☊ 5:26 | ♂ □ ☊ 20:19 | 30 ☿ ☌ ♀ 22: 4 | |
| ☽ ☌ ☋ 18:48 | ☉ ☍ ☽ 21: 6 | 24 ☽ ☍ ♆ 22: 6 | 31 ☽ ☌ ♃ 14:28 | |
| ☽ ☌ ♄ 20:38 | 14 ☉ □ ♇ 7:32 | 26 ☽ ☌ P 10:43 | | |
| 6 ☽ ☌ ♇ 9:13 | 15 ☽ ☌ ♅ 2:27 | ☽ N□ ☊ 13:55 | | |
| ☉ □ ☊ 18:25 | ☽ ☍ ♀ 8:32 | ☽ ☌ ♂ 19:46 | | |
| 7 ☿ ☍ ♅ 6:14 | 16 ☽ ☍ ☿ 0:31 | 27 ♂ □ ♄ 14:29 | | |
| ☉ □ ♄ 19: 6 | 18 ☽ ☍ ♃ 17:56 | 28 ☉ ☌ ☽ 3:37 | | |
| 10 ☽ ☌ A 18:26 | 20 ☽ ☌ ☊ 7:27 | ☽ ☍ ♅ 3:56 | | |
| 11 ☽ ☌ ♆ 1:33 | ☽ ☍ ♄ 13:28 | ☉ ☍ ♅ 8:12 | | |

SIDEREAL HELIOCENTRIC LONGITUDES : OCTOBER 2019 Gregorian at 0 hours UT

| DAY | Sid. Time | ☿ | ♀ | ⊕ | ♂ | ♃ | ♄ | ♅ | ♆ | ♇ | Vernal Point |
|---|---|---|---|---|---|---|---|---|---|---|---|
| 1 TU | 0:37:46 | 16 ♏ 21 | 13 ♎ 25 | 12 ♓ 31 | 27 ♌ 11 | 3 ♐ 31 | 24 ♐ 43 | 9 ♈ 17 | 22 ♒ 26 | 27 ♐ 16 | 4 ♓ 59' 4" |
| 2 WE | 0:41:43 | 19 6 | 15 1 | 13 30 | 27 38 | 3 36 | 24 45 | 9 18 | 22 26 | 27 16 | 4 ♓ 59' 4" |
| 3 TH | 0:45:39 | 21 50 | 16 37 | 14 29 | 28 4 | 3 41 | 24 47 | 9 19 | 22 26 | 27 17 | 4 ♓ 59' 4" |
| 4 FR | 0:49:36 | 24 35 | 18 13 | 15 28 | 28 30 | 3 46 | 24 48 | 9 19 | 22 27 | 27 17 | 4 ♓ 59' 4" |
| 5 SA | 0:53:32 | 27 20 | 19 49 | 16 28 | 28 57 | 3 51 | 24 50 | 9 20 | 22 27 | 27 17 | 4 ♓ 59' 3" |
| 6 SU | 0:57:29 | 0 ♐ 5 | 21 25 | 17 27 | 29 23 | 3 56 | 24 52 | 9 21 | 22 27 | 27 18 | 4 ♓ 59' 3" |
| 7 MO | 1: 1:25 | 2 52 | 23 1 | 18 26 | 29 50 | 4 0 | 24 54 | 9 21 | 22 28 | 27 18 | 4 ♓ 59' 3" |
| 8 TU | 1: 5:22 | 5 38 | 24 37 | 19 25 | 0 ♍ 16 | 4 5 | 24 56 | 9 22 | 22 28 | 27 18 | 4 ♓ 59' 3" |
| 9 WE | 1: 9:19 | 8 26 | 26 13 | 20 24 | 0 43 | 4 10 | 24 57 | 9 23 | 22 28 | 27 19 | 4 ♓ 59' 3" |
| 10 TH | 1:13:15 | 11 16 | 27 48 | 21 23 | 1 9 | 4 15 | 24 59 | 9 23 | 22 29 | 27 19 | 4 ♓ 59' 3" |
| 11 FR | 1:17:12 | 14 7 | 29 24 | 22 23 | 1 36 | 4 20 | 25 1 | 9 24 | 22 29 | 27 19 | 4 ♓ 59' 3" |
| 12 SA | 1:21: 8 | 16 59 | 1 ♏ 0 | 23 22 | 2 2 | 4 25 | 25 3 | 9 25 | 22 30 | 27 19 | 4 ♓ 59' 3" |
| 13 SU | 1:25: 5 | 19 54 | 2 36 | 24 21 | 2 29 | 4 30 | 25 5 | 9 25 | 22 30 | 27 20 | 4 ♓ 59' 2" |
| 14 MO | 1:29: 1 | 22 50 | 4 11 | 25 21 | 2 55 | 4 35 | 25 6 | 9 26 | 22 30 | 27 20 | 4 ♓ 59' 2" |
| 15 TU | 1:32:58 | 25 49 | 5 47 | 26 20 | 3 22 | 4 39 | 25 8 | 9 27 | 22 31 | 27 20 | 4 ♓ 59' 2" |
| 16 WE | 1:36:54 | 28 51 | 7 22 | 27 19 | 3 48 | 4 44 | 25 10 | 9 27 | 22 31 | 27 21 | 4 ♓ 59' 2" |
| 17 TH | 1:40:51 | 1 ♑ 56 | 8 58 | 28 19 | 4 15 | 4 49 | 25 12 | 9 28 | 22 31 | 27 21 | 4 ♓ 59' 2" |
| 18 FR | 1:44:48 | 5 4 | 10 33 | 29 18 | 4 42 | 4 54 | 25 14 | 9 29 | 22 32 | 27 21 | 4 ♓ 59' 2" |
| 19 SA | 1:48:44 | 8 15 | 12 9 | 0 ♈ 18 | 5 8 | 4 59 | 25 16 | 9 29 | 22 32 | 27 22 | 4 ♓ 59' 2" |
| 20 SU | 1:52:41 | 11 30 | 13 44 | 1 18 | 5 35 | 5 4 | 25 17 | 9 30 | 22 32 | 27 22 | 4 ♓ 59' 1" |
| 21 MO | 1:56:37 | 14 50 | 15 20 | 2 17 | 6 2 | 5 9 | 25 19 | 9 31 | 22 33 | 27 22 | 4 ♓ 59' 1" |
| 22 TU | 2: 0:34 | 18 14 | 16 55 | 3 17 | 6 28 | 5 14 | 25 21 | 9 31 | 22 33 | 27 22 | 4 ♓ 59' 1" |
| 23 WE | 2: 4:30 | 21 42 | 18 30 | 4 17 | 6 55 | 5 19 | 25 23 | 9 32 | 22 34 | 27 23 | 4 ♓ 59' 1" |
| 24 TH | 2: 8:27 | 25 16 | 20 6 | 5 16 | 7 22 | 5 23 | 25 25 | 9 33 | 22 34 | 27 23 | 4 ♓ 59' 1" |
| 25 FR | 2:12:23 | 28 55 | 21 41 | 6 16 | 7 48 | 5 28 | 25 26 | 9 33 | 22 34 | 27 23 | 4 ♓ 59' 1" |
| 26 SA | 2:16:20 | 2 ♒ 39 | 23 16 | 7 16 | 8 15 | 5 33 | 25 28 | 9 34 | 22 35 | 27 24 | 4 ♓ 59' 1" |
| 27 SU | 2:20:17 | 6 30 | 24 51 | 8 16 | 8 42 | 5 38 | 25 30 | 9 35 | 22 35 | 27 24 | 4 ♓ 59' 0" |
| 28 MO | 2:24:13 | 10 28 | 26 26 | 9 16 | 9 9 | 5 43 | 25 32 | 9 35 | 22 35 | 27 24 | 4 ♓ 59' 0" |
| 29 TU | 2:28:10 | 14 32 | 28 1 | 10 16 | 9 36 | 5 48 | 25 34 | 9 36 | 22 36 | 27 25 | 4 ♓ 59' 0" |
| 30 WE | 2:32: 6 | 18 44 | 29 37 | 11 15 | 10 2 | 5 53 | 25 35 | 9 37 | 22 36 | 27 25 | 4 ♓ 59' 0" |
| 31 TH | 2:36: 3 | 23 3 | 1 ♐ 12 | 12 15 | 10 29 | 5 58 | 25 37 | 9 37 | 22 36 | 27 25 | 4 ♓ 59' 0" |

| INGRESSES : | |
|---|---|
| 5 ☿ → ♐ 23:12 | |
| 7 ♂ → ♍ 9:17 | |
| 11 ♀ → ♏ 8:57 | |
| 16 ☿ → ♑ 8:59 | |
| 18 ⊕ → ♈ 16:44 | |
| 25 ☿ → ♒ 7: 2 | |
| 30 ♀ → ♐ 5:54 | |

| ASPECTS (HELIOCENTRIC +MOON(TYCHONIC)) : | | | | | |
|---|---|---|---|---|---|
| 3 ☿ □ ♆ 5:14 | 8 ☽ □ ♀ 22: 1 | ☿ ☌ ♇ 12: 5 | ☽ ☍ ☿ 20:17 | ⊕ ☌ ♅ 7:56 | |
| ☿ ☌ A 7:56 | 11 ☽ ☌ ♆ 3:32 | 16 ⊕ □ ♇ 0:28 | 23 ☿ □S ☊ 12:32 | 30 ☿ ☌ ♆ 21:33 | |
| ☽ □ ♆ 18:36 | ☽ ☍ ♂ 22:46 | 17 ☽ ☍ ♀ 11:30 | 24 ☽ □ ♀ 22:42 | 31 ☽ □ ♆ 4:25 | |
| ☽ ☌ ☿ 22: 6 | 12 ☽ □ ♃ 3:37 | 18 ☽ □ ♆ 11:37 | 25 ☽ ☍ ♆ 0:17 | ☽ □ ☿ 7:43 | |
| 4 ☽ □ ♂ 5:52 | 13 ☽ □ ☿ 13:56 | ♂ □ ♃ 13:41 | ♀ ☌ ☋ 2:27 | ☽ ☌ ♀ 22:25 | |
| ☽ ☌ ♃ 15:31 | ⊕ □ ♄ 18: 5 | 19 ☿ □ ♅ 9:11 | ♀ □ ♆ 13:31 | | |
| 5 ☿ □ ♂ 16:43 | ☽ □ ♄ 20:53 | ☽ ☍ ♃ 10:45 | ☽ □ ♃ 21:12 | | |
| 6 ☽ ☌ ♄ 7:46 | 14 ☽ □ ♇ 1:18 | ☽ □ ♂ 11:21 | 26 ☽ ☌ ♂ 1:36 | | |
| ☽ ☌ ♇ 12:30 | ☿ ☌ ♄ 18:28 | 20 ☽ ☍ ♄ 23:26 | 27 ☽ □ ♄ 5:12 | | |
| 7 ☿ ☌ ♃ 10:13 | 15 ☽ ☌ ♅ 1: 7 | 21 ☽ ☍ ♇ 3: 4 | ☽ □ ♇ 8:15 | | |
| ☽ □ ♅ 12:24 | ☿ □ ⊕ 6: 4 | 22 ☽ □ ♅ 0:21 | 28 ☽ ☍ ♅ 3:55 | | |

therefore the Lord of the harvest to send out laborers into his harvest" (Dec/10/30).

The resurrecting power of the Sun, in dynamic tension with the Holy Virgin, offers a test of our character. Despite the fact that we face overwhelming opposition, we are not to see ourselves as "sheep without a shepherd." Though the laborers may be few, the power inherent in the "word" must become an inner experience: "Because the great mass of antichristian and unchristian forces fills our entire life sphere, we must allow the power of thought, the life of the heart, and the feeling for truth to live in the word and to oppose the hostile world with the other world that can be experienced in the word."[1] The apparently "little strength" in the word is, in reality, far more powerful than the colossal forces set against it.

This aspect asks us to lovingly accept the restraints of the Virgin, transforming our perception of constriction, wherein we see the benevolence of the Virgin's mantle as our protection against becoming "lost sheep." Then do our burdens become light and our yokes easy.

**ASPECT 2: Mercury 10° Libra opposite Uranus 10° Aries.** Mercury at this degree remembers Jesus teaching in Shiloh from the stone teacher's chair. He spoke of God's mercy toward the people of Israel, the destruction of the temple, and the present time of grace, whereby he made it quite clear that it was he himself who was to bring salvation (Oct/5/30). *Can we receive the scintillating light of revelation wherein are borne cosmic imaginations that illumine a new way forward?*

**Oct 12: ASPECT: Venus 10° Libra opposite Uranus 10° Aries.** Venus recalls Jesus as he healed the blind youth of Manahem, who had the gift for prophecy. That evening, he spoke in the synagogue about Noah, the ark, and the rainbow as the sign of God's mercy (Oct/6/30).

Manahem had been born physically blind and yet he retained his capacity to spiritually see through his clairvoyant visionary capacities. The gift of spiritual sight was ordinary to human beings dwelling in Paradise, wherein we saw all things as a revelation of God. But with the Fall a transformation of human seeing took place, whereby the eyes of human beings were opened, and henceforth they saw the "bare facts" of the world without the illumination of God. They no longer saw the world as an expression of God, which is spiritual seeing, but for its *own* sake, estranged from God, which is ordinary seeing.[2]

*The eye that sees beauty, sees God.* The cross of Venus in Libra stimulates an elevation of conscience, and in opposition to Uranus in Aries, we stand with the world before the power of change. Will we open our spiritual eye, or will we continue to set our focus on all that has estranged itself from God? This has become the trial of all humanity. To receive cosmic imaginations (Uranus) we must pose the question: What do we love, God or Mammon?

Uranus sends messages on the wings of the Holy Spirit directly from the heart of our galaxy. When standing across the heavens from Venus, these messages are to find their resurrection in human hearts. The godless world we have created is not the problem; rather is the problem the fact that, instead of leaping into change, we are falling into ever greater soul pathologies. The Paradisiacal vision we once had is now to rise as a new kind of seeing, wherein we are again able to behold the work of the gods in all things. To receive the mandate of change now upon us, we must discipline our consciousness, lifting it above the fray of ordinary love so as to rise again into the *extra*ordinary. If we are to reorient ourselves to a "tomorrow" already upon us, we must participate in the apocalyptic nature of the stream of time moving toward us from the future. This will necessitate overcoming the hardening of our heart and the intellect's obstinate denial of the suprasensory world. Then, and only then, are we prepared to behold the unimaginable.

**Oct 13: ASPECT: Full Moon 25° Pisces (square Pluto) opposite Sun 25° Virgo: Triumphant Entry into Jerusalem** (Mar/19/33). The Moon reached this degree as the Sun was rising on this day, about six hours before the solar eclipse that marked the event.

---

1 Ibid., p. 344.

2 *CHA*, The Sun Chronicle in the Life of the Messiah.

The eclipse on the hill of Golgotha is an analogy for the eclipse of spirit vision, which subsequently has led to the vanquishing of almost every remnant of Christ in our sciences, politics, arts, and even in our religions—for compromise has shrouded and truncated the mysteries whence religions first emerged. Furthermore, the eclipse negates the promise of a New Jerusalem into which we could otherwise triumphantly begin to enter. What is this New Jerusalem? It is a city on a hill, i.e., a place where the creative force of the Word still resounds. And the "little strength" of the word will be remembered in the Aquarian age to come, for we will then come to understand how the living word represents truth.

Although the Aquarian age is still in our future, we are not to be led astray by believing the word to be weak or insignificant. For words are not merely words when the soul speaking them has faith at first hand of how, in the beginning, all things were created *through the word*. The word is magical and remains the only power that can stand against the colossal forces we face in the world of facts, i.e., the serpent's world of ruse and illusion.

Confronting the eclipse places us before the *fire trial*, wherein we encounter the darkness of the abstract intellectuality that has delivered us into the loneliness of separateness. This trial tests us to birth greater consciousness of our higher "I." Furthermore, as we live in the culminating few centuries of the age of Pisces—and as it is likely that our next incarnation will be in the age of Aquarius—chances are that this is our last incarnation under this influence. If we are to find our place in the Aquarian cultural epoch, wherein we will be in the umbra of its glory, seeds must now be planted. The entire mission of the Aquarian age is to awake our spiritual-eye and join together with all of our brothers and sisters who will be collaboratively forming a city on a hill—a community of people whose eye has opened to the eternal power of the creative word—where we keep holy the word and we do not deny Christ's name.

Imagine forming our words in consciousness of the fact that each word creates a vessel for one kind of energy or another! Would not the world grow silent? So many words are void of life; expunging these would indeed increase the world's silence. If we are to plant seeds for our future, we must understand that what is to be accomplished in one cultural age must be experienced and realized in the occultism of the preceding age. *This foreordains that there are now people gathering in communities to realize—behind the scenes of ordinary life—the occultism already carrying us into the next age.* These are the communities of Eternal Israel, comprising those who are tending the garden of evolution in conscious devotion to the power of the word and the future that is already being created.

The Pisces glyph depicts two half circles united with a horizontal line, a bridge. In this picture we can imagine that we must travel over this bridge to leave the past so as to enter the future. One world is dying, the other newly forming. Not all will make the crossing.

> This is the position between a world that seems to be able to live only *in the word* and exercise influence *through the word*, and a world whose rapacious power is eager to show that it can stifle and swallow up all free spiritual life. This position between two worlds (in fidelity to the world that initially seems to have no power or influence other than the word spoken by the human voice) is referred to in the Apocalypse as "keeping the word of my patience." This is exactly the path that the soul must follow to make the transition from the consciousness soul to the spirit self. It involves an immense strengthening of awareness in the consciousness soul and, at the same time, a specific orientation toward the spirit self.[1]

We gain the strength to speak the living word by resisting the world of facts and all the menacing powers that cunningly weave in this fabricated manifestation of godlessness. In developing the "little strength" of the word, we will birth life forces that will allow us to see through the lies and deceptions—thus freeing us from the colossal powers that have nothing but their sheer magnitude, through which they make themselves believed and

---

1 Tomberg, *Christ and Sophia*, p. 344.

even feared. This we are to do without wavering, for the life-bestowing forces are greater by far than the death-engendering forces of godlessness.

Travelers crossing the bridge between the two worlds, as represented in the Pisces glyph, are working selflessly for the future world reality that all who are devoted to truth will eventually enter triumphantly.

The inaugurating New Moon of this cycle remembered the walking on water; it also pointed to how this miracle can be approached at this time of the Second Coming. The first quarter Moon asked us to act, making the change from being merely silent victims of the world's collapsing morality to becoming learned collaborators in the art of sacred magic. Through deepening into the power of our words, we are now entering into a small measure of transformation. The upcoming culmination phase of the last quarter will invoke the revelatory future of John's apocalypse, reminding us that we will be able to unveil the new mysteries by *interiorizing love*.

**Oct 14: ASPECT: Sun 26° Virgo square Pluto 26° Sagittarius.** The Sun at this degree recalls Jesus speaking concerning Isaac's sacrifice, which was associated with the two-day New Year festival. Jesus and the disciples then proceeded to Abila, where a pillar was erected in memory of Elijah. He taught there, in the open (Sep/18/30).

The resurrecting powers of the Sun, in dynamic tension with the Father God (Phanes/Pluto), test us to rid ourselves of egoism. This nails us to the cross of Mammon. When carrying this cross, we cannot die into Christ. Realizing that we are not in control, however, grants us the possibility to awake into the eternal power wielded by the Lord of Karma—Christ—who holds command over *all* things. If we are to free ourselves from the escalating darkness that threatens to devour all aspects of spiritual life, we can now face our deeply rooted fears.

The "I" has three citadels within us: it lives in the organization of the blood; it comes to consciousness in our nerve-sense system; and it is enthroned in our heart, our inner Sun. From this holy sanctuary of the heart, we can offer it up in sacrifice for something higher than ourselves, for the "I" alone *is* our very own. When we sacrifice our "I" to the Father God, we become servants of prophecy. This is represented in the sacrifice made by Elijah—for thus could the gods speak through him.

Abraham was willing to sacrifice his son Isaac in obedience to his God. What are we willing to sacrifice? With the god of the underworld (Pluto/Hades) in Sagittarius, we are faced with the choice of awaking to truth, or falling still deeper into the delusions of Ahriman's theater.

Virgo asks us to protect what has been divinely given to us—our "I."

**Oct 18: Sun enters Libra:** "Worlds sustain worlds; in being experience being; in existing, embrace existence. And being effects being to pour forth deeds unfolding, in world-enjoyment reposing. O worlds, uphold worlds!" (Steiner, *Twelve Cosmic Moods*).

The late William Bento illumines this mantra:

Everything is connected to everything, and so it is with any attempt to grasp how the Cosmos has given birth to worlds that sustain worlds. Nothing can be truly understood when it is taken out of the context of relatedness. Modern scientific thinking has unfortunately lost this understanding and continues to attempt to explain the complexity of nature, man, and the heavens by abstracting it from its natural habitat. The result is a kind of lifelessness. *The antidote to this edifice of abstractions is to apply the principles of a spiritual scientific thinking, which is based on the premise that "worlds sustain worlds."*

The first decan is ruled by the Moon and is associated with the constellation of Bootes the Ploughman. The deeper meaning of Bootes has to do with the Hebrew *Bo*, which means "coming"; hence Bootes is "The Coming One." How appropriate that the baptism of the Coming One, the Messiah, took place when the Sun entered this decan! Libra calls for balanced thought, which becomes balanced action, as well as a certain standard of uprightness that requires an alignment with higher consciousness. *In Libra, contentment becomes equanimity—whereby we enter the connectivity of all creation.*

**Oct 21: Last Quarter Moon 3° Cancer: Birth of John the Baptist** (Jun/4/2 BC). John, who had been Elijah (and, subsequently, became Raphael and then Novalis), is united with the "waiting and searching church" of the Second Coming. Three pillars are depicted in the fourth seal of the Apocalypse, the blue pillar representing the tree of life. When humanity lost the tree of life, we also lost the grace of being born from the divine. Instead, we had to be born out of heredity lines. This is the tragedy of losing the tree of life. Very often we find that the bodies we must inhabit are not suitable vehicles for our soul/spirit. Nonetheless, we must carry this bag of bones and flesh along with us, ever striving to rise above its restriction.

In Paradise, the Cherubim continue to guard the tree of life, hiding both the secrets of evil and the secrets of good. Uniting with the apocalyptic stream of John will open us to these revelations that have long been hidden from us. Unmasking evil was a task given to both Elijah and John. Now this is *our* task. Yet we must also remember that we live during the time of the historic unfolding of the 40th day, and we must therefore be witnesses to a new light that is manifesting. We are equally tasked with bearing witness to evil as well as to a new revelation of the Good. This light of the new revelation is indeed far more powerful than anything the darkness can conjure.

As this lunar cycle enters into its concluding phase, we interiorize and integrate. Have we recognized the suction force of error that seeks to pull us into subconscious realms of instinct—instead of supporting us from realms of supraconsciousness? Have we practiced deeds of sacred magic against the black magical powers that surround us? Are we willing to cross the bridge into the future, employing the power of the "little strength" indwelling the word? All efforts directed toward these goals can now become new forces of life if we are willing to awake into the waiting arms of the church that longs to embrace us. This is the church of John, wherein we meet cathartic (Cancer) forces of redemption.

John's church works *with* Peter's church. Yet as we draw nearer to the Aquarian Age, the cleansing waters in-streaming from the future will restore and heal all that has become ill in the mystery traditions of the past. Thus can Peter's church find rejuvenation, radiating its original splendor. Moreover, this restoration will most likely birth a renewal of *true interest* in the Petrine tradition.

**Oct 24: Mercury enters Scorpio:** "Existence consumes being; yet, in being, existence endures. **In activity growth disappears**; in growth, activity persists. In chastising world-activation, in punishing self-formation, being sustains beings" (Steiner, *Twelve Cosmic Moods*).

**Oct 27: ASPECT: New Moon 9° Libra.** This Moon recalls the Scourging of Jesus Christ (Apr/3/33). In his last words, spoken from the cross, Christ said: "My God, my God, how you have glorified me!" These precious words are connected to the Jupiter chakra, which is located between the brows and is most commonly referred to as the *third-eye*. During his Scourging, Christ yielded neither to Ahriman nor to Lucifer, who both attacked him from left and right. Instead, he maintained vertical alignment with his Father in Heaven. The inner strength he exemplified can help us to understand "chastity." For it is chasteness that prevents us from falling prey to the second temptation. This was the temptation of both Lucifer and Ahriman: approaching Christ, and tempting him to plunge from the pinnacle of the temple—while assuring him that angels would catch him. The angels they referred to, however, were not the good angels. Plunging from the pinnacle is, by analogy, plunging from consciousness into the murky waters of the subconscious, where *fallen* angels are dwelling. Christ was bringing the *true* kingdom to humanity, the kingdom unknown since the Fall from Paradise.

> The stage of Scourging is one of bearing suffering without struggling against it. To bear suffering was Eve's curse. It is the task that falls most of all upon the woman, also constitutionally. Woman suffers.[1]

Before Christ was Scourged, he had washed the feet of his disciples. In so doing, he established

---
1 Valentin Tomberg, *Lord's Prayer Course*, p. 40.

an indelible stream of spiritual force, uniting the heights with the depths. The destruction of this stream was the aim of both Lucifer and Ahriman, who approached him not only at the beginning of the ministry, but also at its end, for they were Christ's tormentors at the Scourging: Lucifer with his pride and egoism, and Ahriman with his cold cynicism. This was the cosmic aspect of the Scourging.

From the *human* aspect, [however], it is necessary that the human being learns to stand without wavering. The decision underlying the will to create the [vertical] stream [of the foot washing] must prove itself in the trial of Scourging. *One has to learn to stand without wavering.* What are the forces that one must call upon in order that one can really remain standing?

Lucifer works with pride, haughtiness, and egotism, which are overcome through *humility:* to have the consciousness that one has earned the blows, and thus to accept them.

One has protection against Ahriman when one never lets out of one's consciousness the worth of the cause that one serves. *Always have present in one's consciousness the worth and the holiness of the cause that one serves.* This it the protection against Ahriman.

<u>Exercise</u>: One imagines oneself to be in the following situation:

One wants to accomplish something Great and Holy as a karmic mission [task]. Then two people come who want to convince one that it is debasing and stupid.

The one appeals to pride and egotism. The other puts forward terribly realistic arguments (to the point of cynicism) based on ["realistic"] experience, [and appealing to] fear and indifference. However, after this dialogue one makes clear to oneself the necessity of the mission [task] that one has, that one is unworthy, that one accepts it as [a karmic] debt, as [a karmic] cross that one has <u>earned</u>, with the decision to bear it, i.e., to strive honestly to become more worthy [to accomplish it].[2]

Every task that has true merit is one in which we will inevitably find ourselves unworthy. Lofty spiritual beings do not waste our time by giving us work that will be easy to accomplish; instead, the tasks they assign have everything to do with *increasing* us. Thus, we will find that we need the *strength of humility* to achieve our destined mission. Having this strength ensures that we hold the vertical of spiritual conviction, leaning neither to left nor to right. Having this humility ensures that we bear the weight of our decision while understanding that the outcome is unknown, for we will be tempted to compromise if things become too difficult.

In such situations the stakes are indeed high, for compromise would entail the destruction of the vertical stream—the scales (Libra) would tip to one devil or the other; we would either justify through egoism, or else cynically denigrate the worth of the task. In either case, we would lose the center point of balance, whereby our conscience is diminished.

Nowadays it is common that the woman in birth can also avoid the suffering of the Scourging. We have many medical interventions that come to her rescue. When this occurs, the infant struggles alone as it enters the world, and the mother loses something in this as well. Yet "the suffering woman" does not only refer to women, for the woman is in the man too, although residing in the etheric nature. Therefore, men must also take responsibility for birth. They must birth the authority of "father"; they must hold to a moral path despite being offered an easier path through compromise; and they must birth ideas that remain true to the vertical spiritual current under which they strive to realize their humanity.

This New Moon asks us if we have a *spiritual vertical* that we would defend regardless of the two devils who seek to destroy this. Imagine how the world could change if more of us successfully passed through the trial of the Scourging!

**First quarter Moon, 17° Capricorn: First temptation.**

**Full Moon, 25° Aries: Healing of the woman possessed.**

**Last quarter Moon, 2° Leo: Jesus speaks of how his enemies have hated him since the raising of Lazarus.**

---

2  Ibid., pp. 144-145.

Lunar teaching of this cycle begins with the memory of the Scourging of Jesus. We were asked if we have a spiritual vertical that we would die to defend. As the first quarter Moon dawns, we face the temptation by Lucifer, who asked Christ to bow to him and to the world he was creating. The Full Moon places us in the transformational time of healing. What unknown evil possesses us, dragging us through the world as it tears us apart? This cycle culminates with the memory of Jesus speaking of his many enemies and their outrage after he raised Lazarus from the dead. Indeed, all the dead that we raise to the light will attract the enemies of Christ, for such raisings draw us closer to him. Moreover, as we increase, our morality is tested, whereby the spiritual world determines if we can be entrusted with that which has been given.

**ASPECT: Mars 20° Virgo square Saturn 20° Sagittarius.** Mars remembers the death of Thomas (Dec/18/72).

The Archangel Michael in dynamic tension with the Holy Virgin offers the trial of surrender. What are we to surrender? *We are to relinquish our frustration before the necessities of our destiny tasks.* Thomas was the disciple representing Libra (today's New Moon), who had to overcome his doubt. In so doing he became a great proclaimer of the Incarnation, life, and promised future of Jesus Christ. The New Moon today reminds us of the Scourging of Jesus, and this aspect further reminds us of the walking on water—the miracle connected to the chakra located in the region of the larynx (the Mars chakra).

When Jesus approached the boat carrying his disciples (the destiny community then forming), Peter jumped from the boat to meet him, only to sink as he then cried out for Jesus to save him. Peter's doubt exemplifies the future promise of all doubt—the redeemer will reach out his hand to save us. Faith is the opposite of doubt, and this must be *born from within* if we are to overcome the malignant forces that seek to pull us under. The moral compass of our absolute vertical is founded in the third-eye, and it is tested through scourging.

Doubt, hate, and fear are the enemies of faith, for just as faith descends as certainty from above, doubt, hate, and fear ascend as byproducts of faithlessness. This was what Thomas overcame as he touched into the wounds of the Risen One.

The mantle of the Holy Virgin restrains us to lead us along the path that has been preordained. Struggling against this will inevitably result in heaviness, loneliness, and even cowardliness. Overcoming doubt, however, delivers us into acceptance of the trials we ourselves have set before us, and this acceptance converts frustration into the power of discipline. Thus do our burdens become light as we courageously persevere—even when frustration would otherwise have us shriveling in the face of our difficulties.

**Oct 28: ASPECT: Sun 10° Libra opposite Uranus 10° Aries.** Uranus reached its current degree in March of 1936, when Hitler's German Army remilitarized the Rhineland (the region west of the Rhine that had been "demilitarized"—i.e., established as a buffer from German aggression—through the 1919 Treaty of Versailles).

The resurrecting power of the Sun, standing across from Uranus, is the harbinger of sudden and unexpected change. The specific nature of the change, however, depends on the source of light. There is the light of the Holy Spirit, which streams as unmediated revelation directly from the heart of the galaxy. Inverse to this is the luciferic light, which streams from the "Belt of Lies" he has set up, which surrounds the entire globe. It is not an easy task to discern between the two. One certain indicator, however, is the light's effect. The true light increases humility, while the false light increases egoism, even to the point of "inflation."

This aspect arouses a need for freedom. Freedom grants us the ability to choose which tasks we will take up in service to the future; and in so doing, we expand our horizons beyond the limits of the sense world. Egoistic freedom, on the other hand, seeks the pursuit of pleasure, although void of the burden of responsibility—which increases our bondage to it as it narrows our horizons. What egoism confines us?

The light of the Holy Spirit was not manifesting when, in the 1930s, Hitler was amassing his armies of vengeance against an unsuspecting world; instead, it was the will-to-power that was developing. This would lead to a murderous future. Yet despite the all-engulfing fear that had paralyzed the German people, a small group of German youths initiated the White Rose movement in opposition to the evil of Hitler. This would later result in the hanging of several of these brave souls who so fearlessly took up tasks in service to the holy light.

Will history tell of a courageous few who stood against evil in our time?

**Venus enters Scorpio:** "Existence consumes being; **yet, in being, existence endures.** In activity, growth disappears; in growth, activity persists. In chastising world-activation, in punishing self-formation, being sustains beings" (Steiner, *Twelve Cosmic Moods*).

**Oct 30: ASPECT: Mercury conjunct Venus 2° Scorpio.** Venus stands in memory of Jesus healing the sick and possessed at a town well. Later he visited the leper-house to cure the lepers. That afternoon, Bartholomew and Simon introduced Jesus to Judas Iscariot; Jesus was friendly but was filled with indescribable sorrow. Judas said, "Master, I pray thee allow me to join your teaching" (Oct/24/30). Heart and mind, in harmony, have powers of perception far greater than ordinary sensing. Jesus saw into the heart of Judas, and thus he was filled with sorrow. As this conjunction occurs in Scorpio, we are afforded the task of revealing what is hidden beneath the surface of things.

# NOVEMBER 2019

## Stargazing Preview

On the 9th of this month, Jupiter, having just entered Sagittarius, will set about two hours after the Sun. Two days later, Mars, which rises at 0600, moves into Libra. The bright star very near Mars is Spica.

We'll all be able to enjoy the Full Aries Moon on the 12th. The evening of the 17th provides the best chance to see the Leonid meteor showers. As the name suggests, these appear to earthly eyes to radiate from the Lion (though they can make an appearance anywhere in the night sky). Though the large waning Moon (rising around 2200) will make viewing more difficult, try looking NW, below the pan of Ursa Major; the radiant will be below the horizon.

Venus progresses into Sagittarius on the 21st; she now sets about ninety minutes after the Sun. When the Moon rises moments before Mars on the morning of the 24th, they'll be just shy of a conjunction. Also on this day, you'll see the year's second conjunction of Venus and Jupiter, this time at 3° Sagittarius. It's a truly beautiful sight to see them together, but you won't have much time to do so, as they set around 1800. The Moon conjuncts the Sun (for a New Moon) on the 26th, Jupiter and Venus on the 28th, and Saturn on the following day. On the 29th, then, the planetary setting order (staring ninety minutes after sunset) is: Jupiter, Venus, Saturn, and Moon. They will all be in Sagittarius, along with Pluto. More heat!

Orion, now almost opposite the Sun, will be visible throughout the night.

## November Commentaries

**Nov 4: First Quarter Moon 17° Capricorn: First Temptation in the Wilderness** (Nov/27/29). According to the research of Robert Powell, this temptation occurred at four in the afternoon. The Moon, conjunct Venus, passed in front of this degree of the Goat around noon that day. At this hour the planets were arranged in a tall cross, with the vertical axis situated between the Sun and Pluto at the top of the chart, straddling the Midheaven, and Saturn directly below. The vertical beam was crossed by the horizontal beam that was formed by the square aspect between the Moon and Venus on the eastern side and Mars on the west.

The New Moon remembered the Scourging of Jesus Christ and how this works in our time as the "fire trial." Did we strengthen our unwavering *spiritual vertical*? Today we are to put into action what has been gained. Two worlds confront us: the kingdom of luciferic/ahrimanic delusions and—in juxtaposition to it—the enchristed kingdom that is rising with the Dharma Sun.[1] Without an unwavering verticality, we will not be able to withstand the hateful blows directed against the "I" in us. Instead, we will be swept away along with the godless masses.

In response to the first temptation, Jesus spoke: "My kingdom is not of this world." Eventually all of humanity will understand the meaning in his words. For now, *lest we petrify our spirit in the crystallized tomb of the intellect*, we muster the courage to choose fluidic imaginations that will lead us to his kingdom.

**Nov 5: ASPECT: Mars 26° Virgo square Pluto 26° Sagittarius.** This same aspect occurred at the second healing of the daughter of Jairus (Dec/1/30). Informed that she was again close to death, Jesus agreed to go to her. On the way, he was told that she had died, but still they went on. When he reached her, he repeated the raising of Salome (the daughter) from the dead.

How many times have our souls been resurrected from death? Mars, in dynamic tension with Pluto/Hades, tends to lure aggressiveness to the surface—and thereby causes confrontation. Thus are we able to see the work we have yet to do. In contrast, when Pluto–Phanes governs over our soul's lower forces, we may find that our words have strength. The gift of the Holy Word then renders our speech not only harmless, but also chaste; i.e., words become *inseparate* from the power of original creation.

The serpent has taken broken fragments to piece together a world of his own making. Streaming from the future age of Aquarius, however, comes the mantra to awake to the "little strength" of the word—which stands alone as a force that dismantles the world assembled through the *stolen word*—i.e., the word issuing from the mouth of the serpent.

Words are powerful, and this aspect allows us to discern the god who speaks with us, whether that be Phanes or Hades.

**Nov 6: Mercury enters Libra:** "Worlds sustain worlds; in being, experience being; **in existing, embrace existence**. And being effects being to pour forth deeds unfolding, in world enjoyment reposing. O worlds, uphold worlds! In existing embrace existence" (Steiner, *Twelve Cosmic Moods*). May our minds grasp the true reality of our existence, so that we may participate in sustaining the world-goodness that is ever-present.

**Nov 9: Jupiter enters Sagittarius:** "Growth attains power of existence; in existence, growth's power dies. Attainment concludes joyful striving in life's active force of will. **World-activity matures in dying;** forms vanish in re-forming. May existence feel existence!" (Steiner, *Twelve Cosmic Moods*). Jupiter rules Sagittarius, and this benevolent planet will spend approximately one year under the auspices of the constellation of truth (Sagittarius). Therefore, the next twelve months promise that attainments will be gained if we joyfully await the spirit that arises from all that is dying.

**Nov 11: ASPECT: Inferior conjunction of Sun and Mercury 24° Libra.** This conjunction recalls the position of the Sun at the onset of the present Age of Michael (Nov/10/1879).

The superior conjunction that preceded this inferior conjunction occurred at 16° Leo, recalling a time when Jesus taught to a crowd prior to his Baptism. At this event were gathered some of his future disciples. All the cosmic forces of will that have streamed into us since then are now rising to imaginative levels of spirit beholding. Would not such imaginations reveal great world truths, granting us renewed courage in the work of not only unmasking evil, *but also of bearing witness to the incredible work of angels*? Mind and heart align to sustain *world goodness* through the light engendered by embracing *world truth*.

**Mars enters Libra:** "Worlds sustain worlds; in being, experience being; in existing, embrace existence. **And being effects being** to pour forth deeds unfolding, in world enjoyment reposing. O worlds, uphold worlds!" (Steiner, *Twelve Cosmic Moods*). Mars is in its detriment when in Libra, as it stands opposite its rulership in Aries. It will take extra effort to rescue the forces of will from entanglement with all that disdains the world's destined promise.

---

[1] See "The Rising of the Dharma Sun" in this volume of *Star Wisdom*.

| SIDEREAL GEOCENTRIC LONGITUDES : | NOVEMBER 2019 Gregorian at 0 hours UT | | | | | | | | | | |
|---|---|---|---|---|---|---|---|---|---|---|---|
| DAY | ☉ | ☽ | ☊ | ☿ | ♀ | ♂ | ♃ | ♄ | ♅ | ♆ | ♇ |
| 1 FR | 13 ♎ 15 | 3 ♐ 33 | 15 ♊ 18R | 2 ♏ 37R | 3 ♏ 56 | 23 ♍ 0 | 28 ♏ 20 | 20 ♐ 25 | 9 ♈ 26R | 21 ♒ 7R | 25 ♐ 49 |
| 2 SA | 14 15 | 16 33 | 15 17 | 2 29 | 5 10 | 23 39 | 28 32 | 20 29 | 9 24 | 21 6 | 25 50 |
| 3 SU | 15 15 | 29 9 | 15 18D | 2 13 | 6 25 | 24 18 | 28 43 | 20 33 | 9 22 | 21 5 | 25 51 |
| 4 MO | 16 15 | 11 ♑ 27 | 15 18 | 1 47 | 7 39 | 24 57 | 28 55 | 20 37 | 9 19 | 21 4 | 25 52 |
| 5 TU | 17 15 | 23 30 | 15 18R | 1 12 | 8 54 | 25 36 | 29 7 | 20 42 | 9 17 | 21 3 | 25 53 |
| 6 WE | 18 15 | 5 ♒ 25 | 15 17 | 0 27 | 10 8 | 26 15 | 29 19 | 20 46 | 9 14 | 21 3 | 25 54 |
| 7 TH | 19 15 | 17 16 | 15 13 | 29 ♎ 33 | 11 23 | 26 55 | 29 31 | 20 51 | 9 12 | 21 2 | 25 55 |
| 8 FR | 20 16 | 29 8 | 15 6 | 28 30 | 12 37 | 27 34 | 29 43 | 20 55 | 9 9 | 21 1 | 25 56 |
| 9 SA | 21 16 | 11 ♓ 4 | 14 58 | 27 20 | 13 52 | 28 13 | 29 55 | 21 0 | 9 7 | 21 1 | 25 57 |
| 10 SU | 22 16 | 23 8 | 14 49 | 26 5 | 15 6 | 28 52 | 0 ♐ 7 | 21 4 | 9 5 | 21 0 | 25 58 |
| 11 MO | 23 16 | 5 ♈ 21 | 14 38 | 24 46 | 16 21 | 29 31 | 0 19 | 21 9 | 9 2 | 21 0 | 25 59 |
| 12 TU | 24 17 | 17 45 | 14 29 | 23 26 | 17 35 | 0 ♎ 11 | 0 31 | 21 14 | 9 0 | 20 59 | 26 0 |
| 13 WE | 25 17 | 0 ♉ 21 | 14 20 | 22 8 | 18 50 | 0 50 | 0 44 | 21 19 | 8 58 | 20 59 | 26 1 |
| 14 TH | 26 17 | 13 8 | 14 14 | 20 53 | 20 4 | 1 29 | 0 56 | 21 24 | 8 55 | 20 58 | 26 2 |
| 15 FR | 27 18 | 26 6 | 14 10 | 19 46 | 21 19 | 2 9 | 1 9 | 21 29 | 8 53 | 20 58 | 26 3 |
| 16 SA | 28 18 | 9 ♊ 16 | 14 8 | 18 46 | 22 33 | 2 48 | 1 21 | 21 34 | 8 51 | 20 57 | 26 5 |
| 17 SU | 29 18 | 22 37 | 14 8D | 17 57 | 23 48 | 3 28 | 1 34 | 21 39 | 8 48 | 20 57 | 26 6 |
| 18 MO | 0 ♏ 19 | 6 ♋ 9 | 14 9 | 17 19 | 25 2 | 4 7 | 1 46 | 21 44 | 8 46 | 20 56 | 26 7 |
| 19 TU | 1 19 | 19 55 | 14 11 | 16 53 | 26 17 | 4 46 | 1 59 | 21 50 | 8 44 | 20 56 | 26 8 |
| 20 WE | 2 20 | 3 ♌ 52 | 14 11R | 16 38 | 27 31 | 5 26 | 2 12 | 21 55 | 8 42 | 20 56 | 26 10 |
| 21 TH | 3 21 | 18 3 | 14 10 | 16 34D | 28 45 | 6 5 | 2 25 | 22 1 | 8 39 | 20 56 | 26 11 |
| 22 FR | 4 21 | 2 ♍ 23 | 14 7 | 16 42 | 0 ♐ 0 | 6 45 | 2 37 | 22 6 | 8 37 | 20 55 | 26 13 |
| 23 SA | 5 22 | 16 52 | 14 3 | 17 0 | 1 14 | 7 24 | 2 50 | 22 12 | 8 35 | 20 55 | 26 14 |
| 24 SU | 6 22 | 1 ♎ 23 | 13 57 | 17 27 | 2 29 | 8 4 | 3 3 | 22 17 | 8 33 | 20 55 | 26 15 |
| 25 MO | 7 23 | 15 51 | 13 51 | 18 2 | 3 43 | 8 43 | 3 16 | 22 23 | 8 31 | 20 55 | 26 17 |
| 26 TU | 8 24 | 0 ♏ 10 | 13 46 | 18 45 | 4 58 | 9 23 | 3 29 | 22 29 | 8 29 | 20 55 | 26 18 |
| 27 WE | 9 25 | 14 14 | 13 41 | 19 35 | 6 12 | 10 3 | 3 43 | 22 34 | 8 27 | 20 55 | 26 20 |
| 28 TH | 10 25 | 27 58 | 13 39 | 20 30 | 7 26 | 10 42 | 3 56 | 22 40 | 8 25 | 20 55D | 26 21 |
| 29 FR | 11 26 | 11 ♐ 20 | 13 38 | 21 31 | 8 41 | 11 22 | 4 9 | 22 46 | 8 23 | 20 55 | 26 23 |
| 30 SA | 12 27 | 24 19 | 13 38D | 22 36 | 9 55 | 12 2 | 4 22 | 22 52 | 8 21 | 20 55 | 26 24 |

INGRESSES :

| | |
|---|---|
| 3 ☽ → ♑ 1:37 | 19 ☽ → ♌ 17:22 |
| 5 ☽ → ♒ 13: 3 | 21 ☽ → ♍ 20: 1 |
| 6 ☿ → ♎ 12:31 | 22 ♀ → ♐ 0: 2 |
| 8 ☽ → ♓ 1:45 | 23 ☽ → ♎ 21:42 |
| 9 ♃ → ♐ 10:24 | 25 ☽ → ♏ 23:43 |
| 10 ☽ → ♈ 13:31 | 28 ☽ → ♐ 3:37 |
| 11 ♂ → ♎ 17:25 | 30 ☽ → ♑ 10:42 |
| 12 ☽ → ♉ 23:20 | |
| 15 ☽ → ♊ 7: 8 | |
| 17 ☽ → ♋ 13: 8 | |
| ☉ → ♏ 16:28 | |

ASPECTS & ECLIPSES :

| | | | |
|---|---|---|---|
| 1 ☽ ☌ ☋ 21:38 | 12 ☽ ☍ ☿ 9:50 | 23 ☽ ☌ P 7:45 | 30 ☽ ☌ ♇ 3:55 |
| 2 ☽ ☌ ♄ 7:27 | ☉ ☍ ☽ 13:33 | 24 ☽ ☌ ♂ 11:35 | |
| ☽ ☌ ♇ 17:37 | 14 ☽ ☍ ♀ 14:14 | ☽ ☍ ♅ 11:50 | |
| 4 ☉ □ ☽ 10:22 | ♀ □ ♆ 17:12 | ♀ ☌ ♃ 13:32 | |
| 5 ♂ □ ♇ 10:19 | 15 ☽ ☍ ♃ 9:23 | ♂ ☍ ♅ 16:47 | |
| 7 ☽ ☌ ♆ 7:37 | 16 ☽ ☌ ☊ 8:47 | 25 ☽ ☌ ☿ 3:48 | |
| ☽ ☌ A 8:43 | ☽ ☍ ♄ 22:16 | 26 ☉ ☌ ☽ 15: 4 | |
| 9 ☽ □S ☊ 7:41 | 17 ☽ ☍ ♇ 6:13 | 28 ☽ ☌ ♃ 10:48 | |
| 10 ☽ ☍ ♂ 11:57 | 19 ☉ □ ☽ 21: 9 | ☽ ☌ ♀ 18:41 | |
| 11 ☽ ☌ ♅ 7: 8 | 21 ☽ ☍ ♆ 4:50 | 29 ☽ ☌ ☋ 4:12 | |
| ☉ i☌ ☿ 15:20 | 22 ☽ N□ ☊ 19:21 | ☽ ☌ ♄ 21:15 | |

| SIDEREAL HELIOCENTRIC LONGITUDES : | NOVEMBER 2019 Gregorian at 0 hours UT | | | | | | | | | | |
|---|---|---|---|---|---|---|---|---|---|---|---|
| DAY | Sid. Time | ☿ | ♀ | ⊕ | ♂ | ♃ | ♄ | ♅ | ♆ | ♇ | Vernal Point |
| 1 FR | 2:39:59 | 27 ♒ 31 | 2 ♐ 47 | 13 ♈ 15 | 10 ♍ 56 | 6 ♐ 3 | 25 ♐ 39 | 9 ♈ 38 | 22 ♒ 37 | 27 ♐ 25 | 4 ♓ 59' 0" |
| 2 SA | 2:43:56 | 2 ♓ 6 | 4 22 | 14 15 | 11 23 | 6 7 | 25 41 | 9 39 | 22 37 | 27 26 | 4 ♓ 59' 0" |
| 3 SU | 2:47:52 | 6 50 | 5 57 | 15 16 | 11 50 | 6 12 | 25 43 | 9 39 | 22 38 | 27 26 | 4 ♓ 58'59" |
| 4 MO | 2:51:49 | 11 44 | 7 32 | 16 16 | 12 17 | 6 17 | 25 45 | 9 40 | 22 38 | 27 26 | 4 ♓ 58'59" |
| 5 TU | 2:55:46 | 16 46 | 9 7 | 17 16 | 12 44 | 6 22 | 25 46 | 9 41 | 22 38 | 27 27 | 4 ♓ 58'59" |
| 6 WE | 2:59:42 | 21 57 | 10 42 | 18 16 | 13 11 | 6 27 | 25 48 | 9 41 | 22 39 | 27 27 | 4 ♓ 58'59" |
| 7 TH | 3: 3:39 | 27 17 | 12 17 | 19 16 | 13 38 | 6 32 | 25 50 | 9 42 | 22 39 | 27 27 | 4 ♓ 58'59" |
| 8 FR | 3: 7:35 | 2 ♈ 47 | 13 52 | 20 16 | 14 5 | 6 37 | 25 52 | 9 42 | 22 39 | 27 28 | 4 ♓ 58'59" |
| 9 SA | 3:11:32 | 8 25 | 15 27 | 21 16 | 14 32 | 6 42 | 25 54 | 9 43 | 22 40 | 27 28 | 4 ♓ 58'59" |
| 10 SU | 3:15:28 | 14 11 | 17 1 | 22 17 | 14 59 | 6 47 | 25 55 | 9 44 | 22 40 | 27 28 | 4 ♓ 58'59" |
| 11 MO | 3:19:25 | 20 5 | 18 36 | 23 17 | 15 26 | 6 51 | 25 57 | 9 44 | 22 40 | 27 28 | 4 ♓ 58'58" |
| 12 TU | 3:23:21 | 26 6 | 20 11 | 24 17 | 15 53 | 6 56 | 25 59 | 9 45 | 22 41 | 27 29 | 4 ♓ 58'58" |
| 13 WE | 3:27:18 | 2 ♉ 14 | 21 46 | 25 18 | 16 20 | 7 1 | 26 1 | 9 46 | 22 41 | 27 29 | 4 ♓ 58'58" |
| 14 TH | 3:31:15 | 8 26 | 23 21 | 26 18 | 16 48 | 7 6 | 26 3 | 9 46 | 22 42 | 27 29 | 4 ♓ 58'58" |
| 15 FR | 3:35:11 | 14 40 | 24 56 | 27 18 | 17 15 | 7 11 | 26 4 | 9 47 | 22 42 | 27 30 | 4 ♓ 58'58" |
| 16 SA | 3:39: 8 | 21 1 | 26 31 | 28 19 | 17 42 | 7 16 | 20 6 | 9 48 | 22 42 | 27 30 | 4 ♓ 58'58" |
| 17 SU | 3:43: 4 | 27 20 | 28 6 | 29 19 | 18 9 | 7 21 | 26 8 | 9 48 | 22 43 | 27 30 | 4 ♓ 58'58" |
| 18 MO | 3:47: 1 | 3 ♊ 39 | 29 41 | 0 ♉ 20 | 18 37 | 7 26 | 26 10 | 9 49 | 22 43 | 27 31 | 4 ♓ 58'57" |
| 19 TU | 3:50:57 | 9 55 | 1 ♑ 15 | 1 20 | 19 4 | 7 31 | 26 12 | 9 50 | 22 43 | 27 31 | 4 ♓ 58'57" |
| 20 WE | 3:54:54 | 16 8 | 2 50 | 2 21 | 19 31 | 7 36 | 26 14 | 9 50 | 22 44 | 27 31 | 4 ♓ 58'57" |
| 21 TH | 3:58:50 | 22 16 | 4 25 | 3 21 | 19 59 | 7 40 | 26 15 | 9 51 | 22 44 | 27 31 | 4 ♓ 58'57" |
| 22 FR | 4: 2:47 | 28 18 | 6 0 | 4 22 | 20 26 | 7 45 | 26 17 | 9 52 | 22 44 | 27 32 | 4 ♓ 58'57" |
| 23 SA | 4: 6:44 | 4 ♋ 13 | 7 35 | 5 22 | 20 53 | 7 50 | 26 19 | 9 52 | 22 45 | 27 32 | 4 ♓ 58'57" |
| 24 SU | 4:10:40 | 9 59 | 9 10 | 6 23 | 21 21 | 7 55 | 26 21 | 9 53 | 22 45 | 27 32 | 4 ♓ 58'57" |
| 25 MO | 4:14:37 | 15 37 | 10 45 | 7 24 | 21 48 | 8 0 | 26 23 | 9 54 | 22 46 | 27 33 | 4 ♓ 58'56" |
| 26 TU | 4:18:33 | 21 6 | 12 19 | 8 24 | 22 16 | 8 5 | 26 24 | 9 54 | 22 46 | 27 33 | 4 ♓ 58'56" |
| 27 WE | 4:22:30 | 26 25 | 13 54 | 9 25 | 22 43 | 8 10 | 26 26 | 9 55 | 22 46 | 27 33 | 4 ♓ 58'56" |
| 28 TH | 4:26:26 | 1 ♌ 34 | 15 29 | 10 26 | 23 11 | 8 15 | 26 28 | 9 56 | 22 47 | 27 34 | 4 ♓ 58'56" |
| 29 FR | 4:30:23 | 6 34 | 17 4 | 11 27 | 23 38 | 8 20 | 26 30 | 9 56 | 22 47 | 27 34 | 4 ♓ 58'56" |
| 30 SA | 4:34:19 | 11 24 | 18 39 | 12 27 | 24 6 | 8 25 | 26 32 | 9 57 | 22 47 | 27 34 | 4 ♓ 58'56" |

INGRESSES :

| |
|---|
| 1 ☿ → ♓ 13: 6 |
| 7 ☿ → ♈ 11:56 |
| 12 ☿ → ♉ 15:17 |
| 17 ☿ → ♊ 10: 8 |
| ⊕ → ♉ 16:13 |
| 18 ♀ → ♑ 4:55 |
| 22 ☿ → ♋ 6:50 |
| 27 ☿ → ♌ 16:36 |

ASPECTS (HELIOCENTRIC +MOON(TYCHONIC)) :

| | | | | | |
|---|---|---|---|---|---|
| 1 ☽ ☌ ♃ 4:34 | ☽ ☌ ♆ 10:54 | 13 ☽ ☌ ☿ 6:54 | 18 ☽ □ ♅ 6:25 | ☿ □ ♅ 23:33 | ☽ ☌ ♇ 6: 6 |
| ☽ □ ♂ 14: 2 | 8 ♀ □ ♂ 4:41 | 14 ☽ □ ♆ 17:43 | ☿ ☍ ♃ 14:38 | 24 ♀ □ ♅ 11: 1 | ☿ □ ⊕ 6:46 |
| 2 ☿ □ ♀ 17:18 | ☽ □ ♃ 15:10 | 15 ♀ ☌ ♄ 17:40 | 20 ☿ □ ♂ 14:15 | ☽ ☍ ♅ 14: 5 | |
| ☽ ☌ ♄ 17:21 | 9 ☿ ☌ ♅ 5:29 | ☽ ☍ ♃ 20:21 | 21 ☽ ☍ ♆ 7:52 | ☽ □ ♀ 14:27 | |
| ☽ ☌ ♇ 20:40 | ☽ ☍ ♂ 7:11 | 16 ☿ □ ♆ 6:26 | ☿ ☍ ♄ 15:53 | ☽ □ ☿ 23:21 | |
| ☿ □ ♃ 20:46 | ☽ □ ♀ 10: 3 | ☿ ☌ P 6:36 | ☿ ☍ ♇ 20:54 | 26 ☿ N□ ☊ 10:58 | |
| 3 ♀ ☌ ♃ 4: 7 | 10 ☽ □ ♄ 5:31 | ♀ ☌ ♇ 15: 0 | 22 ☽ □ ♃ 8:57 | 27 ☽ □ ♆ 14:51 | |
| ☽ □ ♅ 20:28 | ☽ □ ♇ 8:33 | ☽ □ ♂ 15:44 | 23 ☽ ☌ ♂ 6:52 | 28 ☽ ☌ ♃ 18:31 | |
| 4 ☿ ☍ ♂ 2:57 | 11 ☽ ☌ ♅ 8:32 | 17 ☽ ☍ ♄ 6:17 | ☽ □ ♄ 15:39 | ♀ ☌ A 20:17 | |
| 6 ☿ □ ♄ 17:29 | ☿ ☌ ☊ 13:51 | ☽ ☍ ♇ 8:42 | ☽ □ ♇ 17:38 | 29 ☽ □ ♂ 23:34 | |
| 7 ☿ □ ♇ 0:44 | ☿ ☌ ⊕ 15:20 | ☽ ☍ ♀ 11: 3 | ☿ ☍ ♀ 19:12 | 30 ☽ ☌ ♄ 4: 9 | |

May our deeds courageously serve the "being" who sustains worlds.

**Nov 12: ASPECT: Full Moon 25° Aries opposite Sun 25° Libra.** The Moon recalls the day of the healing of Mara, the adulteress. Around midday, Jesus went to the place of baptism, where he taught and prepared those waiting. Afterward, he went to the house of Mara the Suphanite, to exorcise her (she was possessed) and to forgive her sins. Following a festive meal, Mara and her three children presented Jesus with costly spices (Sep/4/30).

The New Moon that began this cycle reminded us of the Scourging of Christ and the absolute necessity to maintain our vertical spiritual alignment. Moreover, the two-petalled lotus was our particular focus. The first quarter Moon reminded us of the first temptation in the wilderness. As we enter the transformational phase of the Full Moon, we contemplate possession—and what may be in us, yet not of us. This is both the plague and the blessing of our time, for becoming aware of our investments in Mammon's world blesses us with the invitation to invest instead in what truly sustains us.

At his Baptism, Jesus was possessed by Christ:

> At the Baptism in the Jordan one can see the wings of the dove as the working of the spirit, not only horizontally, but also vertically. The clouds [represent] a picture of the force of Love streaming in from the right and from the left, winning space from Ahriman and Lucifer—i.e., not only in a line descending from above, as in the case of the prophets, but taking possession of the whole human being; Ahriman and Lucifer—who are otherwise right and left in the human being—are thereby driven out. This complete taking possession [of the human being] is the [meaning of] "for theirs is the kingdom of heaven" (after having become empty and "poor in spirit").[1]

The dove descended into Jesus and spread its wings. Thus was the Cross of Love borne into the world. This cross bears the promise that each of us will eventually overcome the tempters who assault us through our desires and fears; and in casting out the tempters, we become possessed instead by the kingdom of heaven. Possession by "things"—to which we cling—reveals our confinement in the prison of want and need. Those whose attention is ruled by much desire will tend also to bear much fear. Indeed, desire and fear *lure evil to us*, for these soul states emit a kind of substance upon which evil feasts.

In the last three days of Christ's 39 days of continual temptation, he met the archetypal temptations we know as the will-to-power, plunging from the pinnacle of consciousness, and turning stones to bread. These temptations are, respectively: an encounter with conceiving oneself to be at the center of things (i.e., egoism); intoxications born of superstitions and dedication to the subconscious; and the intrusion of the outer world into the inner world—i.e., becoming as stones in the cold cynical ahrimanic creation.

There is also the *4th temptation*. If not met with spiritual forces, it will often result in a dangerous possession, marking a further stage along the path of decline. This temptation has its roots in the fire earth (the 6th subearthly sphere), which causes a sucking effect that feeds on warmth. Furthermore, as forces from the fire earth suck up all soul warmth, the densified soul easily falls into discipleship with Ahriman. This is a predominate threatening possession of our time.

Imagine gazing upon the world from the third eye in either a cynical way (Ahriman) or through idealistic lies (Lucifer). Through the eye of Ahriman we behold the world in a godless manner; and through the eye of Lucifer we behold the world through a veil of deception.

The mission of humankind in the age of Pisces is to recognize the kingdom of heaven—and in so doing, set its compass to the shores of angelic worlds. Our individual angels long to help us as they protect the star of our eternal self. The false power of Ahriman withers before their light—and before all the "Christ stars" they protect. *Above each one of us shines our eternal star, and our goal is to surrender to its radiance.*

Transformational experiences are born when we actively seek to raise our spiritual gaze into realms

---

1 Tomberg, *The Lord's Prayer Course*, p. 79.

of light. The formula for compromise, however, brings the two-petalled lotus to its ruin. We are to overcome the world of cold "facts," and the world of hot "desire." Then will we be raised into the vertical spiritual, while bearing the cross of light that is the promise of our future destiny. We are not gods, and yet we claim rights and prerogatives as if we were.

Waywardly listing to either left or right, in alignment with one of the two tempters, is symptomatic of beginning an initiation into black magic. The solution to the antidotal path of white magic, however, is offered by Tomberg:

> One experiences *the force of longing* as the initiative underlying all true thinking. All thought initiative is for this purpose: to experience the outer world as the revelation of God; and the inner world, the spiritual world within, as [offering the possibility of] drawing near to God. Thus one finds God again. If one really finds God, as before the Fall, the human being would recognize everything from the outer world in the *inner* world, and he would not need to think at all.[2]

The beings working from the constellation of Aries test the resoluteness of our thinking. Can we tame the wild nature of our thinking? Concentration births the discipline of discipleship. In such a state of command over thought, we may participate in the greatness of world-thoughts that are constantly alive in our surroundings.

As the last quarter Moon dawns, we will be reminded of how eager the enemies of Christ are to eliminate his presence from our thinking, feeling, and willing.

**Nov 14: ASPECT: Venus 21° Scorpio square Neptune 21° Aquarius: First Conversion of Mary Magdalene** (Venus). Jesus invited those who were weary and laden with guilt to come to him, do penance, and share the kingdom with him. As Jesus then offered some words of consolation—actually meant for Mary Magdalene—she was converted. During the evening meal, she anointed Jesus' head with costly ointment (Nov/8/30).

This is the third and last square between Venus and Neptune this year—whereby the holy cross and the Goddess Night again find the creative tension whence springs healing. It is of utmost importance that we raise our consciousness when dealing with Venus—i.e., away from the miasma of *personal soul angst* and toward the devotion of *transpersonal soul light*.

Lovely Venus has been the undoing of many, for as Cupid's arrow wounds, the blood of lust is released. This marks the soul's undoing; it tears and breaks as it is dragged through the world's vanities.

The beings indwelling the Venus sphere guard a future period of Earth's unfolding evolution: the time of inspirational consciousness, i.e., inner spiritual hearing. At present, we are far too focused on ourselves, which renders us deaf to the inspirations that could otherwise find us. Enveloped in trivialities, our soul's virtue is diminished.

The foundational core of all matter is love, and this virginal force is what the true alchemists sought to discover. Thinking has to be turned inside out if we are to reach into these primal realms of Venus energy, and to touch into this we will have to develop heart-thinking. This is what frees us from our isolation in the loneliness of *maya*. *Our willingness to love our brokenness is the key to achieve this elevation to heart thinking.*

Venus sets a trap before us, testing our spiritual weight; many fail the test, instead falling in love with themselves, with outer beauty, with fortune, and with desire for prosperity. Magdalene stands as our perfect exemplar of rising above the petty so as to engage in the profound—to die into Christ's heart and lovingly carry his cross. To discover the great purpose of evolution, guarded by the Venus beings, we must awake the sleeping beauty in our soul. Whereas sleeping beauty represents one coffin, there are six others, and together they represent the wisdom of the seven planetary genii. Through the efforts of our moral will, we are to fill these empty coffins by rediscovering our communion with the star beings. In so doing, we fill the empty coffins with life, thereby awaking the sleeping forces within us.

Every trauma we have experienced has created gaps in our soul's perfect mandala. Our mandala holds our song, constantly resounding the love

---

2 Ibid., p. 355.

that we are. Trauma introduces a foreign sound—one that agitates, causing us to contract—and in so doing we lose our cross. Instead of hearing our perfection, we hear the noise of soul intruders who have entered us through the gaps of our brokenness. The noise of trauma tears our mandala, thereby making us vulnerable to diseases of body, soul, or spirit. Yet, no matter how loud the foreign noise may become, the Goddess Night (Neptune) continuously resounds our true song, ever guarding the perfection of our wholeness.

Venus forms a pentagram as she travels through the Zodiac. We are to follow the pentagram, representing the star of our higher self. This will heal our brokenness as we soar above entrapment in the paltry nonsense usually ascribed to poor Venus, such as jealousy, rivalry, and similar unworthy attitudes of soul. In so doing we will take up our cross and ever so gradually hear our soul's song. This is represented in the transformation undergone by Magdalene in her conversions.

In square to the Goddess Night (Neptune), Venus creates a dynamic tension between the vanity of our "smaller" self and the self we are striving to become. This aspect bestows benevolence when we are able to love our brokenness and befriend the angst of trauma as the "not us" in us. For love alone is the power that can restore to wholeness, all that has been wounded in the stream of time.

**Nov 17: Sun enters Scorpio: "Existence consumes being**; yet, in being, existence endures. In activity, growth disappears; in growth, activity persists. In chastising world-activation, in punishing self-formation, being sustains beings" (Steiner, *Twelve Cosmic Moods*). Consciousness is a force that consumes being; at the same time, it is the force of evolution's endurance.

**Nov 19: Last Quarter Moon 2° Leo.** The Moon was at this degree during Jesus Christ's last Saturday before the Passion (Mar/28/33). In the temple, Jesus spoke of his departure, saying that since the raising of Lazarus his enemies had wanted to kill him. He spoke also of Eve, and remarked plainly that he was the Savior who would free human beings from the power of sin.

The New Moon that inaugurated this cycle reminded us of the Scourging, and how we must establish an unwavering relationship to spirit. As the first quarter Moon dawned, we remembered the first temptation. Hopefully we have acted by awaking to the seductive powers of Lucifer and Ahriman, who endlessly seek to pull us from spiritual alignment. The Full Moon recalled possession as the trial of our times. Now we integrate and interiorize what has been given.

At the raising of Lazarus, the Sun was 3° Leo, and the Moon was 4° Leo. This last quarter Moon indeed is a time to interiorize the meaning of becoming a Christ initiate as was Lazarus—following in his footsteps. Furthermore, we must find our willingness to raise our dead, despite the presence of countless enemies who will stop at nothing in their attempts to deter us.

The letter to the Angel of Sardis (Piscean age) asks us to hallow the Name of all others. In so doing, we will receive the cloak of our Name—i.e., the star of our higher "I" shall envelop us in white raiment. This raiment protects us from all enemies, for it leads us to the open door that no one can shut. This is the door to the future promise that opens as we find the "little strength" of the "word" to overcome the colossal illusion evil has spun around us; and when we refrain from "denying Christ's name." Once the Name has drawn near—proclaiming a deeper acceptance of Christ—we will encounter even greater enemies. Compassion is key, for what we cannot love in others is merely an indication of our *compression in darkness*. This compression marks the boneyard where dwell the corpses we have not yet raised.

**Nov 21: Venus enters Sagittarius:** "Growth attains power of existence; **in existence, growth's power dies.** Attainment concludes joyful striving in life's active force of will. World-activity matures in dying; forms vanish in re-forming. May existence feel existence!" (Steiner, *Twelve Cosmic Moods*). Indeed, as we age, the power of growth must elevate itself to mingle with the etheric archetypes that overlight all manifestations of material form.

**Nov 24: ASPECT: Venus conjunct Jupiter 3° Sagittarius.** Venus remembers the first raising of Jairus' daughter from the dead (Nov/18/30). Jairus was the chief of the synagogue in Capernaum, and he pleaded with Jesus to heal his daughter, Salome, who was near death. Jesus agreed; but on their way, they were met with news of her death. Jesus, in his mercy then performed the miracle of bringing her back to life. The negative attitude of her parents toward Jesus is what led to her illness.

The lovely cross of Venus, in communion with the Holy Spirit (Jupiter), brings wisdom and love together. The boneyard of corpses that we carry along with us are naught but the tombs wherein lie lost aspects of our own soul. In each shadow, no matter how dark, a light eternally burns; this is our *sleeping light*. This conjunction grants us the fortitude to plunge into what appears to be darkness to resurrect our light. Furthermore, as this conjunction occurs in Sagittarius, we are to carefully govern our speech, sublimating all that is negative and harmful. This self-mastery births discernment for truth.

Godless speech is being spilt throughout the world, cluttering the air with a heaviness that creates weariness. These fallen words are an actual contagion, one we are to avoid. With Jupiter and Venus standing very near where the Sun was at the healing of the man born blind, we are reminded of a sphere of truth-filled grace that now radiates toward us from just beyond the realms of the sense-world—wherein divisiveness masquerades as reality. This reality is collapsing, and will become ever more dangerous for those who choose to remain susceptible to its delusion.

This aspect awakes an ability to wisely use the power of love to call our dead from the tomb of deceit, which then resurrects our *sleeping light*.

**ASPECT 2: Mars 8° Libra opposite Uranus 8° Aries.** Mars remembers its heliocentric position at the birth of the Nathan Jesus (Dec/6/2 BC). Under this aspect, we must beware of impulsive actions. Relationships will be tested (Libra). Uranus flows from subearthly electrical currents as well as from supra-earthly founts of divine light. The quality of the light determines the recklessness or carefulness of resultant actions. The eternal source of light is the Angel Jesus, who ministers to all who keep their lower forces in check. Moreover, by meeting our lower forces, we are afforded the possibility of understanding what has yet been sublimated, i.e., brought under the governance of our "I."

We can pray that world events are governed by the Jesus light rather than the subearthly light. The Archangel Michael asks that we have the courage to grasp hold of thoughts hitherto unimaginable. The "not yet imagined" is rising with the Sun of Satya Yuga. To realize these new thoughts, we must form new concepts. Our ability to do so determines whether civilization will move into the future of brotherhood and sisterhood, or instead be dragged into further mechanization. Evil seeks to slaughter the future and then serve it to a people who, while sensing its inherent element of truth, miss the cunning manipulation that has actually destroyed it. Thus can even the elect be deceived.

Words are vessels into which one or another energy will be conjured. *Chastity marks the virtue of words when they are filled with the life force of creation.* When this is not the case, however, we thirst and know it not. We are each tasked to carry a burden in service to the future, and we will find such tasks if we awake to what Uranus sends to Earth from the heights of heaven.

Will we accept what the new light reveals, and then take up our tasks in service to the world's becoming? Did not Jesus do just this?

**Nov 26: ASPECT: New Moon 9° Scorpio: Death of Moses** (Sep/28/1250 BC). Commemorating the death of Moses, this New Moon recalls the life of Rudolf Steiner. Just as Moses, in Genesis, gave us the seven days of creation in a form that was proper for the people of his time, so too did Steiner give us the seven stages of the unfolding of the *cosmic biography* of the Earth: Saturn, Sun, Moon, Earth, future Jupiter, future Venus, and future Vulcan. In remembering Moses, we remember the manna offered to his people, which they gathered every morning during their long sojourn through the desert. Is this not exactly what we need, as we travel through the barren desert of our material world? How do we turn from the "golden calf" of idol worship to gain the manna of *our* time?

Moses had a perfectly developed two-petalled lotus flower, and this was the means through which the commandments of his God Jehovah were written on the stony tablets of his nerve–sense system (i.e., on his consciousness). When Moses beheld Christ in the Burning Bush, proclaiming: "I am the I am," he met the fire of divinity that does not consume, but instead *awakes*.

We live in the later stage of the age of Pisces, wherein revelation is most assuredly streaming into time; and in the light of this revelation, evil is unmasked. *The danger of our time is that of over-focusing on the theater of Ahriman. This causes fear as well as desire, for if one spends a great deal of time tracking evil, one desires to find it. Fear and desire draw the devil closer.*

Over the past centuries, consciousness has been taken over by succumbing to logic, facts, and "hurry." In the meantime, evil has worked ever so secretly to obtain great worldly power. Over the past few decades, people have increasingly been tasked with naming the damaging threat we face from the evil and merciless powers lurking behind the lords of money and power. Yes, it is important to be aware of this activity—but not to the extent that we miss the major event of our times: *the emerging of powerful fields of light.*

The world of facts, logic, and coercion is falling apart. The collapse of the old paradigm is clearly evident in the escalation of grievous social pathologies. The human being is collapsing, falling apart. We have allowed ourselves to become victims to "world rulers"; now it is time that we realize, together, that we live at the dawn of evil's irrelevance. Forces supporting the awaking of consciousness are here with us. *Manas* consciousness was extraordinary in the time of Moses; now, as the Piscean age draws toward its end, it must become ordinary.

The first stage of *manas* consciousness is union with the Holy Spirit. This is followed by the second stage, wherein we become aware of our fidelity to nature and our task to heal her kingdoms. Lastly, we come to the third stage of *manas* consciousness, wherein we transform the darkest evil into the highest good—i.e., we see the activity of the Father God in all creation as we concurrently see the darkest of all beings who stand against the him.

*Manas* consciousness was exemplified in Moses, and now we are to achieve the three levels of this consciousness out of our own inner efforts. Three inhibiting forces work against us: our luciferic double, our karmic double, and the ahrimanic double. The luciferic double is freed through honesty and selflessness, making way for the descent of the Holy Spirit. The karmic double is freed when we become aware of its presence and become master over it. The ahrimanic double is freed when we cast it out, for the human being cannot redeem it.

Moses reminds us of the Ten Commandments, which tell us what we must do to avoid the threat of evil. Christ gave us the Lord's Prayer, which directs us to freedom—through which we will learn how to open our third-eye. What we do, and what we focus upon, determines whether we are chained or free.

This New Moon shines from the constellation of Scorpio, asking us to reveal both the mysteries of evil and the mysteries of good. If we are to transform the Scorpion into the Johannine Eagle, we must strengthen our spirit-eye (the third-eye)—so that, like Moses, we too may read the revelatory inscriptions the Holy Spirit authors.

**First quarter Moon, 17° Aquarius: the third temptation in the wilderness.**
**Full Moon, 25° Taurus: death of Moses.**
**Last quarter Moon, 2° Virgo: beginning of 40 days.**

Lunar teachings of this cycle begin with Moses and the power of the Holy Spirit that awakes us to *manas* consciousness. As the first quarter Moon dawns, and as we remember the temptation to stones into bread, we will encounter the first challenge to deepening our spirit-eye. *This is now occurring in reverse, as it is the bread of life that is being turned to stone through the duplicity the anti-Holy Spirit is cunningly etching into our astral bodies.*

The transformative period of the Full Moon finds us again with Moses, recalling his death. Moses died before he reached the Promised Land—which, by analogy, is the age of Aquarius now before us. Our "little self" grows smaller, dying to the light, as we approach the shores of this future of brotherhood and sisterhood. All seeds now planted will protect us as we later emerge into this coming age.

As the culminating phase of the last quarter dawns, we must accept our confrontation with temptations. Not only are we confronted with the three, we are also confronted with the 4th temptation—which comprises the three, together, and asks us: "In whose name do you come?" Indeed, we must make our way through the wilderness of our time while bearing witness to the light that will increasingly illumine the world. And those who bear witness to this light will grow in number.

# DECEMBER 2019

## Stargazing Preview

Venus catches up to Saturn on the 11th; you can see them set, Saturn first, two hours past sundown. You'll be able to admire December's Full Moon on the following day, shining high above Orion's belt. The Geminid meteor showers peak on the night of the 13th. You'll want to look northeast for the best chance of seeing them. The large waning Moon will make viewing more difficult, as it's in the sky from 1700 until 0800 the next morning.

On the 16th, Venus, still visible low in the west for two hours after sunset, enters Capricorn. Early on the morning of the 22nd you'll be able to see the Moon rise just ahead of Mars. The New Moon on the 26th creates an Annular Solar Eclipse over Australia, Asia, and India, and the Sun is positioned as it was at the third temptation in the wilderness. The Moon passes Saturn on the 27th; look for Saturn setting right before the Moon about an hour after sunset. On the 28th, the Moon and Venus will set together, in nearly perfect conjunction, two to three hours after the Sun moves below the western horizon for its nightly rest.

By the 31st of the month, Orion will be seen rising a little over an hour before the setting of the Sun. Have a glorious New Year!

## December Commentaries

**Dec 1:** Today is the first Sunday of Advent. We prepare for the celebration of the birth of the Nathan Jesus. The Jesus being has renounced his higher rank to unite directly with humankind.

Since the Lemurian Epoch, the Jesus *being*,[1] who was partly embodied in the Nathan Jesus, has exercised a harmonizing influence on the human organism. He was an archangelic being who descended to the angelic hierarchy to be associated directly with humankind. Rudolf Steiner describes the effect of the threefold permeation of the Jesus being by Christ (during the Lemurian epoch, the first third of the Atlantean epoch, and the final third of the Atlantean epoch) as harmonizing, respectively, the senses, the life processes, and the soul forces.[2]

Tomberg goes on to describe how the human being is held together as a *complete* being by the force of love. Extraordinary! The fourth deed of Christ Jesus harmonized the "I," and this was possible only because of the working together of Buddha, Elijah, and Jesus. We now live in the time of the fifth deed, the birth of *manas* consciousness, which is the theme of this lunar cycle.

Rudolf Steiner brings the following perspective:

> Hidden knowledge was now flowing, although imperceptible to begin with, into people's ways of thinking. It is self-evident that intellectual forces have continued to reject this knowledge right into the present. But what must happen *will* happen, in spite of any temporary rejection. Symbolically, this hidden knowledge, which is taking hold of humanity from the other side and will do so increasingly in the future, can be called "the knowledge of the Grail." If we learn to understand the deeper meaning of this symbol as it is presented in stories and legends, we will discover a significant image of what has been described above as the new initiation knowledge with the Christ mystery at its center. Therefore, modern initiates can also be known as "Grail initiates."[3]

---
1 This refers to the supra-personality aspect.
2 Tomberg, *Christ and Sophia*, p. 73.
3 Steiner, *An Outline of Esoteric Science*, p. 388.

SIDEREAL GEOCENTRIC LONGITUDES : DECEMBER 2019 Gregorian at 0 hours UT

| DAY | ☉ | ☽ | ☊ | ☿ | ♀ | ♂ | ♃ | ♄ | ♅ | ♆ | ♇ |
|---|---|---|---|---|---|---|---|---|---|---|---|
| 1 SU | 13 ♏ 28 | 6 ♑ 58 | 13 ♊ 39 | 23 ♎ 45 | 11 ♐ 9 | 12 ♎ 41 | 4 ♐ 35 | 22 ♐ 58 | 8 ♈ 19R | 20 ♒ 55 | 26 ♐ 26 |
| 2 MO | 14 28 | 19 18 | 13 41 | 24 57 | 12 24 | 13 21 | 4 49 | 23 4 | 8 17 | 20 55 | 26 27 |
| 3 TU | 15 29 | 1 ♒ 24 | 13 43 | 26 12 | 13 38 | 14 1 | 5 2 | 23 10 | 8 15 | 20 55 | 26 29 |
| 4 WE | 16 30 | 13 21 | 13 44 | 27 30 | 14 52 | 14 40 | 5 15 | 23 16 | 8 14 | 20 56 | 26 31 |
| 5 TH | 17 31 | 25 13 | 13 43R | 28 50 | 16 7 | 15 20 | 5 29 | 23 22 | 8 12 | 20 56 | 26 32 |
| 6 FR | 18 32 | 7 ♓ 6 | 13 42 | 0 ♏ 11 | 17 21 | 16 0 | 5 42 | 23 29 | 8 10 | 20 56 | 26 34 |
| 7 SA | 19 33 | 19 4 | 13 40 | 1 34 | 18 35 | 16 40 | 5 56 | 23 35 | 8 8 | 20 56 | 26 36 |
| 8 SU | 20 34 | 1 ♈ 10 | 13 36 | 2 59 | 19 49 | 17 20 | 6 9 | 23 41 | 8 7 | 20 57 | 26 37 |
| 9 MO | 21 35 | 13 29 | 13 33 | 4 24 | 21 4 | 17 59 | 6 23 | 23 47 | 8 5 | 20 57 | 26 39 |
| 10 TU | 22 36 | 26 3 | 13 29 | 5 51 | 22 18 | 18 39 | 6 36 | 23 54 | 8 4 | 20 58 | 26 41 |
| 11 WE | 23 37 | 8 ♉ 53 | 13 26 | 7 18 | 23 32 | 19 19 | 6 50 | 24 0 | 8 2 | 20 58 | 26 42 |
| 12 TH | 24 37 | 21 59 | 13 24 | 8 46 | 24 46 | 19 59 | 7 4 | 24 7 | 8 1 | 20 58 | 26 44 |
| 13 FR | 25 38 | 5 ♊ 20 | 13 23 | 10 15 | 26 0 | 20 39 | 7 17 | 24 13 | 7 59 | 20 59 | 26 46 |
| 14 SA | 26 39 | 18 56 | 13 23D | 11 44 | 27 14 | 21 19 | 7 31 | 24 20 | 7 58 | 21 0 | 26 48 |
| 15 SU | 27 40 | 2 ♋ 43 | 13 23 | 13 13 | 28 28 | 21 59 | 7 45 | 24 26 | 7 56 | 21 0 | 26 50 |
| 16 MO | 28 41 | 16 40 | 13 24 | 14 43 | 29 42 | 22 39 | 7 58 | 24 33 | 7 55 | 21 1 | 26 51 |
| 17 TU | 29 43 | 0 ♌ 43 | 13 25 | 16 14 | 0 ♑ 56 | 23 19 | 8 12 | 24 40 | 7 54 | 21 1 | 26 53 |
| 18 WE | 0 ♐ 44 | 14 51 | 13 26 | 17 45 | 2 10 | 23 59 | 8 26 | 24 46 | 7 53 | 21 2 | 26 55 |
| 19 TH | 1 45 | 29 2 | 13 27 | 19 16 | 3 24 | 24 39 | 8 40 | 24 53 | 7 51 | 21 3 | 26 57 |
| 20 FR | 2 46 | 13 ♍ 13 | 13 26R | 20 47 | 4 38 | 25 19 | 8 53 | 25 0 | 7 50 | 21 4 | 26 59 |
| 21 SA | 3 47 | 27 23 | 13 26 | 22 18 | 5 52 | 25 59 | 9 7 | 25 7 | 7 49 | 21 4 | 27 1 |
| 22 SU | 4 48 | 11 ♎ 28 | 13 25 | 23 50 | 7 6 | 26 39 | 9 21 | 25 13 | 7 48 | 21 5 | 27 2 |
| 23 MO | 5 49 | 25 26 | 13 24 | 25 22 | 8 20 | 27 20 | 9 35 | 25 20 | 7 47 | 21 6 | 27 4 |
| 24 TU | 6 50 | 9 ♏ 15 | 13 23 | 26 55 | 9 34 | 28 0 | 9 48 | 25 27 | 7 46 | 21 7 | 27 6 |
| 25 WE | 7 51 | 22 52 | 13 22 | 28 27 | 10 48 | 28 40 | 10 2 | 25 34 | 7 45 | 21 8 | 27 8 |
| 26 TH | 8 52 | 6 ♐ 14 | 13 22 | 0 ♐ 0 | 12 1 | 29 20 | 10 16 | 25 41 | 7 44 | 21 9 | 27 10 |
| 27 FR | 9 54 | 19 20 | 13 22D | 1 33 | 13 15 | 0 ♏ 0 | 10 30 | 25 48 | 7 44 | 21 10 | 27 12 |
| 28 SA | 10 55 | 2 ♑ 10 | 13 22 | 3 6 | 14 29 | 0 41 | 10 44 | 25 55 | 7 43 | 21 11 | 27 14 |
| 29 SU | 11 56 | 14 44 | 13 22 | 4 40 | 15 43 | 1 21 | 10 58 | 26 2 | 7 42 | 21 12 | 27 16 |
| 30 MO | 12 57 | 27 3 | 13 22 | 6 14 | 16 56 | 2 1 | 11 11 | 26 9 | 7 42 | 21 13 | 27 18 |
| 31 TU | 13 58 | 9 ♒ 10 | 13 22R | 7 48 | 18 10 | 2 42 | 11 25 | 26 16 | 7 41 | 21 14 | 27 20 |

INGRESSES :

| | | |
|---|---|---|
| 2 ☽ → ♒ 21:11 | 21 ☽ → ♎ 4:27 | |
| 5 ☽ → ♓ 9:39 | 23 ☽ → ♏ 7:53 | |
| ☿ → ♏ 20:43 | 25 ☽ → ♐ 12:45 | |
| 7 ☽ → ♈ 21:41 | 26 ☿ → ♐ 0: 0 | |
| 10 ☽ → ♉ 7:26 | ♂ → ♏ 23:42 | |
| 12 ☽ → ♊ 14:27 | 27 ☽ → ♑ 19:54 | |
| 14 ☽ → ♋ 19:17 | 30 ☽ → ♒ 5:48 | |
| 16 ♀ → ♑ 5:43 | | |
| ☽ → ♌ 22:46 | | |
| 17 ☉ → ♐ 6:52 | | |
| 19 ☽ → ♍ 1:37 | | |

ASPECTS & ECLIPSES :

| | | | | |
|---|---|---|---|---|
| 3 ♀ ☍ ☊ 1:34 | 12 ☉ ☍ ☽ 5:11 | ☿ □ ♆ 4:24 | ☽ ☌ ♇ 14:40 | |
| 4 ☉ □ ☽ 6:57 | 13 ☽ ☍ ♃ 3:31 | ☉ □ Π 23:43 | ☉ ☌ ♃ 18:24 | |
| ☽ ☌ ♆ 15:18 | ☽ ☌ ☊ 14:14 | 21 ☽ ☍ ♅ 17:45 | 28 ☉ □ Π 19: 5 | |
| 5 ☽ ☌ A 4:13 | ♀ ☌ ♇ 15:11 | 22 ♀ □ ♅ 13:28 | 29 ☽ ☌ ♀ 2: 5 | |
| 6 ☽ □S ☊ 13:13 | 14 ☽ ☍ ♄ 9:31 | 23 ☽ ☌ ♂ 3:26 | 30 ☉ ☍ ☊ 9:55 | |
| 8 ☉ □ ♆ 9: 7 | ☽ ☍ ♇ 13:45 | 25 ☽ ☌ ☿ 11:17 | | |
| ☽ ☌ ♅ 13:33 | ☽ ☍ ♀ 15:55 | 26 ☉ ☌ ☽ 5:12 | | |
| ☉ □ Π 15:11 | 18 ☽ ☍ ♆ 10:28 | ☉ ● A 5:17 | | |
| 9 ☽ ☍ ♂ 9: 8 | ☽ ☌ P 20:49 | ☽ ☌ ♃ 7:28 | | |
| 10 ☽ ☍ ☿ 20:42 | 19 ☉ □ ☽ 4:56 | ☽ ☌ ☋ 13: 0 | | |
| 11 ♀ ☌ ♄ 10: 3 | 20 ☽ □N ☊ 0:22 | 27 ☽ ☌ ♄ 12: 7 | | |

SIDEREAL HELIOCENTRIC LONGITUDES : DECEMBER 2019 Gregorian at 0 hours UT

| DAY | Sid. Time | ☿ | ♀ | ⊕ | ♂ | ♃ | ♄ | ♅ | ♆ | ♇ | Vernal Point |
|---|---|---|---|---|---|---|---|---|---|---|---|
| 1 SU | 4:38:16 | 16 ♌ 5 | 20 ♑ 14 | 13 ♉ 28 | 24 ♍ 34 | 8 ♐ 30 | 26 ♐ 33 | 9 ♈ 58 | 22 ♒ 48 | 27 ♐ 34 | 4 ♓ 58'56" |
| 2 MO | 4:42:13 | 20 37 | 21 49 | 14 29 | 25 1 | 8 34 | 26 35 | 9 58 | 22 48 | 27 35 | 4 ♓ 58'56" |
| 3 TU | 4:46: 9 | 25 0 | 23 24 | 15 30 | 25 29 | 8 39 | 26 37 | 9 59 | 22 48 | 27 35 | 4 ♓ 58'55" |
| 4 WE | 4:50: 6 | 29 15 | 24 59 | 16 31 | 25 57 | 8 44 | 26 39 | 10 0 | 22 49 | 27 35 | 4 ♓ 58'55" |
| 5 TH | 4:54: 2 | 3 ♍ 22 | 26 34 | 17 32 | 26 24 | 8 49 | 26 41 | 10 0 | 22 49 | 27 36 | 4 ♓ 58'55" |
| 6 FR | 4:57:59 | 7 22 | 28 9 | 18 33 | 26 52 | 8 54 | 26 43 | 10 1 | 22 49 | 27 36 | 4 ♓ 58'55" |
| 7 SA | 5: 1:55 | 11 14 | 29 44 | 19 33 | 27 20 | 8 59 | 26 44 | 10 2 | 22 50 | 27 36 | 4 ♓ 58'55" |
| 8 SU | 5: 5:52 | 15 0 | 1 ♒ 19 | 20 34 | 27 48 | 9 4 | 26 46 | 10 2 | 22 50 | 27 37 | 4 ♓ 58'55" |
| 9 MO | 5: 9:48 | 18 40 | 2 54 | 21 35 | 28 16 | 9 9 | 26 48 | 10 3 | 22 51 | 27 37 | 4 ♓ 58'55" |
| 10 TU | 5:13:45 | 22 14 | 4 29 | 22 36 | 28 44 | 9 14 | 26 50 | 10 4 | 22 51 | 27 37 | 4 ♓ 58'54" |
| 11 WE | 5:17:42 | 25 42 | 6 4 | 23 37 | 29 12 | 9 19 | 26 52 | 10 4 | 22 51 | 27 37 | 4 ♓ 58'54" |
| 12 TH | 5:21:38 | 29 6 | 7 39 | 24 38 | 29 40 | 9 24 | 26 53 | 10 5 | 22 52 | 27 38 | 4 ♓ 58'54" |
| 13 FR | 5:25:35 | 2 ♎ 25 | 9 14 | 25 39 | 0 ♎ 8 | 9 28 | 26 55 | 10 6 | 22 52 | 27 38 | 4 ♓ 58'54" |
| 14 SA | 5:29:31 | 5 40 | 10 49 | 26 40 | 0 36 | 9 33 | 26 57 | 10 6 | 22 52 | 27 38 | 4 ♓ 58'54" |
| 15 SU | 5:33:28 | 8 50 | 12 24 | 27 41 | 1 4 | 9 38 | 26 59 | 10 7 | 22 53 | 27 39 | 4 ♓ 58'54" |
| 16 MO | 5:37:24 | 11 58 | 13 59 | 28 42 | 1 32 | 9 43 | 27 1 | 10 7 | 22 53 | 27 39 | 4 ♓ 58'54" |
| 17 TU | 5:41:21 | 15 2 | 15 35 | 29 43 | 2 0 | 9 48 | 27 2 | 10 8 | 22 53 | 27 39 | 4 ♓ 58'53" |
| 18 WE | 5:45:17 | 18 3 | 17 10 | 0 ♊ 44 | 2 28 | 9 53 | 27 4 | 10 9 | 22 54 | 27 40 | 4 ♓ 58'53" |
| 19 TH | 5:49:14 | 21 1 | 18 45 | 1 45 | 2 57 | 9 58 | 27 6 | 10 9 | 22 54 | 27 40 | 4 ♓ 58'53" |
| 20 FR | 5:53:11 | 23 57 | 20 20 | 2 46 | 3 25 | 10 3 | 27 8 | 10 10 | 22 55 | 27 40 | 4 ♓ 58'53" |
| 21 SA | 5:57: 7 | 26 50 | 21 55 | 3 47 | 3 53 | 10 8 | 27 10 | 10 11 | 22 55 | 27 40 | 4 ♓ 58'53" |
| 22 SU | 6: 1: 4 | 29 42 | 23 31 | 4 49 | 4 21 | 10 13 | 27 12 | 10 11 | 22 55 | 27 41 | 4 ♓ 58'53" |
| 23 MO | 6: 5: 0 | 2 ♏ 32 | 25 6 | 5 50 | 4 50 | 10 18 | 27 13 | 10 12 | 22 56 | 27 41 | 4 ♓ 58'53" |
| 24 TU | 6: 8:57 | 5 21 | 26 41 | 6 51 | 5 18 | 10 23 | 27 15 | 10 13 | 22 56 | 27 41 | 4 ♓ 58'52" |
| 25 WE | 6:12:53 | 8 9 | 28 17 | 7 52 | 5 47 | 10 28 | 27 17 | 10 13 | 22 56 | 27 42 | 4 ♓ 58'52" |
| 26 TH | 6:16:50 | 10 55 | 29 52 | 8 53 | 6 15 | 10 32 | 27 19 | 10 14 | 22 57 | 27 42 | 4 ♓ 58'52" |
| 27 FR | 6:20:46 | 13 41 | 1 ♓ 27 | 9 54 | 6 44 | 10 37 | 27 21 | 10 15 | 22 57 | 27 42 | 4 ♓ 58'52" |
| 28 SA | 6:24:43 | 16 26 | 3 3 | 10 55 | 7 12 | 10 42 | 27 22 | 10 15 | 22 57 | 27 43 | 4 ♓ 58'52" |
| 29 SU | 6:28:40 | 19 11 | 4 38 | 11 57 | 7 41 | 10 47 | 27 24 | 10 16 | 22 58 | 27 43 | 4 ♓ 58'52" |
| 30 MO | 6:32:36 | 21 55 | 6 13 | 12 58 | 8 10 | 10 52 | 27 26 | 10 17 | 22 58 | 27 43 | 4 ♓ 58'52" |
| 31 TU | 6:36:33 | 24 40 | 7 49 | 13 59 | 8 38 | 10 57 | 27 28 | 10 17 | 22 59 | 27 43 | 4 ♓ 58'52" |

INGRESSES :

| | |
|---|---|
| 4 ☿ → ♍ 4:17 | |
| 7 ♀ → ♒ 4: 6 | |
| 12 ☿ → ♎ 6:28 | |
| ♂ → ♎ 17:25 | |
| 17 ⊕ → ♊ 6:37 | |
| 22 ☿ → ♏ 2:29 | |
| 26 ♀ → ♓ 2: 2 | |

ASPECTS (HELIOCENTRIC +MOON(TYCHONIC)) :

| | | | | | |
|---|---|---|---|---|---|
| 1 ☽ □ ♅ 5:47 | ☽ ☍ ♂ 17: 5 | ☽ □ ♂ 21: 2 | ☽ ☌ ♂ 11:27 | ☽ □ ♅ 15:24 | |
| 2 ☽ ☌ ♀ 5:41 | 8 ☽ ☌ ♅ 17:20 | 15 ☿ ☍ ♅ 9:46 | ♀ ☌ ♆ 15: 3 | 30 ☿ ☌ A 7:13 | |
| ☿ ☍ ♆ 11:51 | 10 ⊕ □ ♆ 5:50 | ☽ □ ♅ 12:46 | ☽ ☍ ♅ 21:49 | ☿ □ ♆ 9:10 | |
| 4 ☽ ☌ ♆ 19: 7 | ☽ □ ♀ 18: 2 | ☽ □ ☿ 13:38 | 23 ☽ ☌ ☿ 15:27 | | |
| 5 ♂ □ ♄ 15: 2 | 11 ☿ □ ♄ 8:10 | 18 ☽ ☍ ♀ 4:23 | 25 ☽ □ ♆ 0: 8 | | |
| 6 ☽ ☍ ☿ 0:47 | ☿ □ ♇ 13:31 | ☽ ☍ ♆ 13:37 | ☽ □ ♀ 10:58 | | |
| ☽ □ ♃ 3:38 | 12 ☽ □ ♆ 1:36 | 19 ☽ □ ♃ 18:35 | 26 ☽ ☌ ♃ 7:53 | | |
| ☿ □ ♃ 9:38 | ☿ ☌ ♂ 4:41 | ☿ ☌ ☋ 20:44 | 27 ☽ ☌ ♄ 14:56 | | |
| 7 ♂ □ ♇ 14: 7 | 13 ☽ ☍ ♃ 7:23 | 20 ♀ □S ☊ 22:45 | ☽ ☌ ♇ 15:35 | | |
| ☽ □ ♄ 15:17 | 14 ☽ ☍ ♄ 14: 2 | ☽ □ ♄ 23:38 | ⊕ ☍ ♃ 18:24 | | |
| ☽ □ ♇ 16:58 | ☽ ☍ ♇ 15:12 | 21 ☽ □ ♇ 0:30 | 28 ☽ □ ♂ 9:56 | | |

These are mighty thoughts to contemplate as we enter Advent.

**Dec 4: First Quarter Moon 17° Aquarius.** This Moon remembers its position shortly after sundown on the day Jesus Christ faced the last temptation in the wilderness (Nov/29/29). In this season of Advent, we remember the overcoming of evil through the words uttered by Jesus Christ: "Humankind does not live by bread alone, but by every word issued from the mouth of God."

The New Moon remembered Moses and the opening of the third-eye. In this phase, we make use of practices that strengthen our spirit-vision—i.e., *we sacrifice what we think we know*. In such emptiness, we may find that higher knowing approaches us; and through this union, not only do we know, *we become "known,"* i.e., we become visible in worlds above.

The beings indwelling the constellation of Aquarius ask us to unite with our angel. Although the practice of angel-awareness may not at first bear seeds, it will inevitably do so as our practice matures. Angels long to help us. Taking our angel everywhere we go—striving to see what she is seeing in our every deed, thought, and feeling—would be an example of change. Especially will we hear her response to words we speak.

In light of this practice during our daily activities, our evening review of the day (*Ruckschau*) will be greatly enhanced.

**Dec 5: Mercury enters Scorpio:** "Existence consumes being; yet, in being existence endures. **In activity, growth disappears;** in growth, activity persists. In chastising world-activation, in punishing self-formation, being sustains beings" (Steiner, *Twelve Cosmic Moods*).

**Dec 8: ASPECT: Sun 21° Scorpio square Neptune 21° Aquarius.** The Sun was at Neptune's degree as three secret disciples came to Bethany from Jerusalem to see Jesus, reporting that the high priests and Pharisees wanted to send out spies so that they could capture him as soon as he came back to Jerusalem (Feb/8/33).

Indeed, "spies" have been sent out. Nonetheless, we have the choice to walk upon the path whereon spies cannot travel—the narrow path illumined by angels (Aquarius), inspired by wisdom (Neptune), and protected by the love we offer even to our enemies.

**Dec 11: ASPECT: Venus conjunct Saturn 24° Sagittarius.** Venus stands in memory of Jesus as he spoke of the fourth beatitude: *Blessed are those who hunger and thirst for righteousness, for they shall be satisfied*. Afterward, he went with the twelve disciples to the east shore of the lake, where he gave them authority to cast out unclean spirits (Dec/4/30).

The Venus cross stands with the Holy Virgin (Saturn). Where must we suffer our brokenness? The "I" of Christ broke into as many fragments as there are individuals in his Father's creation; yet, despite this fact, he was never separated from his wholeness. His crucifixion (Venus) bestowed the power of redemption upon each of us. This is proof of his enduring mercy. *The redemptive power of mercy is a balm for our brokenness*; it is an actual substance, for imperfections are *wounds* seeking the light. This realization gives us courage to accept ourselves exactly as we are. In so doing, our angel reveals where we have lost our patient faithfulness when confronted by the trials of our destiny.

The healing arms of the Virgin (Saturn) protect our karmic destiny, ever leading us to rise from all that is immoral and ugly. Venus longs for beauty, elegance, and all that is refined. When Saturn restrains her, she is granted introspective power. And when such isolation is freely accepted, we are granted glimpses into the deeper meaning of our life—we gain depth. When we fight against this, on the other hand, isolation becomes a constraining prison that can result in despair and depression.

Venus and Saturn were conjunct during the time when Nathan Mary visited her cousin Elizabeth. Both were pregnant: Mary with Jesus; Elizabeth with John. The karmic bond between the two boys (the old Adam, John, in the womb of Elizabeth; and the new Adam, Jesus, in the womb of Mary), made possible the deepest mystery of Earth evolution: the Mystery of Golgotha. Karma preserves truth, guiding us toward the restoration of cosmic order—an order we know in the depths of our heart. Indeed, the underlying principle within this order serves to birth conscience. When we take up our cross, our heart opens. Inversely, when we do not, our heart contracts into the loneliness of sorrowful privation.

As this aspect occurs in Sagittarius, we are asked to mind our speech. *Ugly thoughts spill darkness. Beautiful thoughts open portals to the light.* This conjunction affords an opportunity to commune with interiorized love, strengthening our ability to love others. The power of love casts out demons.

**Dec 12: ASPECT: Full Moon 25° Taurus opposite Sun 25° Scorpio.** The Moon remembers Jesus as he arrived at his mother's house in Capernaum. She and the other holy women who gathered there were veiled because of the day of fasting that commemorated the death of Moses (Feb/28/30).

The New Moon recalled Moses and the power of spiritual sight. As the first quarter dawned, the third temptation was our focus, reminding us how easily the duplicitous anti-Holy Spirit can masquerade as the true Holy Spirit. Now we arrive at the transformational time of the Full Moon in Taurus, again remembering Moses.

Moses died before he reached the Promised Land, which by analogy is the age of Aquarius now before us. Our "little self" must grow smaller as we die into the light that streams from the shores of this bright future. The seeds of brotherhood and sisterhood—now planted—will protect us as we later re-emerge in this coming age.

The point of crossing into a promised land, resides between the continual activity of ordinary consciousness and the domain of memory. What is this land? It is the resurrection zone into which our dead rise, seeking to be known. For in discerning the dead we drag along with us, we free aspects of consciousness that were previously relegated to remain in the darkness of memory.

Psychic memory of the individual is but a fragment of what has been written in the great book of the World Memory, i.e., the akashic chronicle. While the former is transient, the latter is eternal—it is moral memory:

> Moral memory presents a tableau of the past where the context indicates facts and sequences of facts not in so far as they took place or in so far as they played a relevant logical role, but above all in so far as they reveal *moral value and meaning*. In old age, moral memory more and more replaces logical memory; and the force of memory then depends on moral force—on the intensity of the moral and spiritual life of the person in question. And as there is nothing in the world which is so insignificant that it is beneath moral and spiritual values—and as there is nothing so lofty that it is above them—the moral memory in old age of a person with an awakeed heart can, in principle, replace without fault all the functions of automatic memory and logical memory.[1]

In bringing moral memory to bear, we recall all in us that has transgressed against our heart. In a sense, we must swallow the book of our biography—while noting that although it is sweet on our tongue, it is bitter in our stomach. The *sweetness* represents our divine potential; the *bitterness* represents all damage we have rendered upon this potential.

The Ten Commandments are teachings that protect us from error. In the case of Moses, these commandments prepared an entire race to receive the incarnation of Jesus Christ. Jesus gave his disciples one commandment: *Love one another*. To this end, we strive to avoid all that kills trust, faith, hope, or love—for all that kills is a sin. Evil, on the other hand, results from calling sin a good thing. For example, fracking is evil, for it harms the Mother; yet evil tells us it is good, for it gathers the energy we need. Another example is that of GMO seeds, which kill spiritual archetypes. Evil justifies this by claiming that such practices will increase food supplies. Yet another example is that of people who beat their own children, claiming this is for their own good.

If we are to open our third-eye to the world wisdom, we will need to discern the difference between sin and evil. The former can be transformed; the latter must be seen for what it is.

We began this lunar cycle with consideration regarding Moses and the power of the Holy Spirit. At the first quarter Moon, when we met

---

[1] Anon., *Meditations on the Tarot*, p. 563.

the third temptation in the wilderness, we were asked to beware of the intoxicating wine of the false Holy Spirit. Now we again remember Moses and the preparation that is underway for birthing the impending Aquarian age. As the last quarter Moon dawns, we will interiorize our knowledge of the 40 days in full conscious of the spiritual wilderness through which we walk. Moreover, we may awake to a fourth temptation, that of coming in one's own name.

**Dec 13: ASPECT: Venus conjunct Pluto 26° Sagittarius.** Venus recalls the healing of the two possessed youths from Gergesa whose demons Jesus drove out into a herd of swine, which then plunged down into the lake (Dec/6/30).

The Venus cross in communion with Pluto/Phanes increases depth. Venus marks the sphere wherein dwell the archai, who govern over long epochs of time. Under this influence we can imagine karmic communities penetrating more deeply into their collective mission.

Every great wave of time brings groups of people to Earth who carry a common purpose. The mission of our time is to name evil and bring forth the good. *This necessitates that we enter the secrets of "electrical fire" and the intoxication born of counter-intuition.* Such fiery intoxications are to be feared when they arise in community as human-engendered demons, i.e., as *egregores*.

> The Canaan Moloch who demanded the bloody sacrifice of the first born, mentioned so often in the Bible, is not a hierarchical entity—either of good or of evil—but rather an evil *egregore*, i.e., a demon created artificially and collectively by human communities infatuated with the thrill of fear. The Mexican Quetzalcoatl is a similar instance of this. There, also, it was a matter of a demon created and worshipped collectively.[2]

With Venus conjunct Pluto, communities are given fair warning, for none are immune to the infiltration of these subtle organisms of ill will. The specter of communism that haunted Europe is another example of an *egregore*. It stole the future promise of the Aquarian age and thus beguiled the Slavic people into accepting, prematurely, a distorted Marxist caricature of the sisterhood and brotherhood yet to come. Indeed, this *egregore* made way for the terror of Stalin.

The West has its ideological superstructures as well, formed from human will and imagination to support a goal that benefits only a few. Nonetheless, such ghoulish ideologies become the obsession of the masses through the cunning manipulations of powerful organisms, with propaganda being their greatest weapon.

> The Word and idols, revealed truth and "ideological superstructures" of the human will, operate simultaneously in the history of the human race. Has there been a single century when the servants of the Word have not had to confront the worshippers of idols, *egregores*?[3]

No, not a single century. The idol of the West is money. How many people successfully avoid captivity by this demon? The tragedy of the *egregore* is that, once created, it enslaves the creator; thus locking the system into endless cycles of increasing greed. How do we stop creating these demons? First we must become aware of them.

> And having this knowledge, is it not time that we said to ourselves: let us be silent. Let us make our arbitrary will and imagination silent; let us impose on them the discipline of silence. Is this not one of the four traditional rules of Hermeticism: to dare, to will, to know, *to be silent!* To be silent is more than to keep things secret; it is more even than to guard oneself from profaning the holy things to which a respectful silence is owed. To be silent is, above all, *the great magical commandment of not engendering demons* through our arbitrary will and imagination; it is the task of silencing arbitrary will and imagination.[4]

The teaching offered by the Venus/Pluto conjunction is that we must employ silence in our *personal* will if we are to become free of the demons of *mass* will. This means: we must cease "wanting." What if we had enough? What if we slowed down? What if we spent more time with friends

---

2 Ibid., 405.

3 Ibid., p. 409.

4 Ibid., p. 409.

and family? Would not our riches grow? We have tasks appointed by very high beings. We are not here simply to amuse ourselves; we are here, instead, to serve the evolution of the Earth and humanity. *We cannot just be spiritual, and not also religious.* How can we say we are spiritual if we refuse to exert the effort necessary to understand what spirit is? Theology, and in particular *Christology*, is essential to the science of spirit.

Christ could walk on water because nothing pulled him under—no gravity held command over his being. Instead, he was aligned with all the stars in the heavens. Thus was he united with celestial gravitation. Demons create "sucking pockets" that pull us from the light, whereas light drives out darkness. Therefore, vigilance is needed if we are to protect our communities from the intoxication of mass-thought. A demon recognized is already rendered impotent!

Today's aspect offers penetrating depths into the mission, progress, and purity of community.

**Dec 17: Sun enters Sagittarius: "Growth attains power of existence"** (Steiner, *Twelve Cosmic Moods*). The late William Bento illumines this mantra:

> When existence is regarded not merely as a noun, but also as a verb, we enter the realm of becoming. It is being—in dynamic movement. Such movement is purposeful, for being seeks a state in which it can be a power of "presence," a reality of the here and now. *This achievement "to be" is the drama of human potential.* Each human being seeks "to be" what he or she has resolved to become. The arrival of that becoming is both a joyful and an empowering experience, where there is nothing to do but *be*.

Control of Speech becomes Feeling for Truth. Blessed are the self-disciplined, for they shall awake a feeling for truth.

**Venus enters Capricorn:** "May the future rest upon the past. **May the past feel the future** to be strong in the present. In face of life's inner resistance, may world-being's vigilance grow in power, and may the might of life's activity flower. May the past bear the future!" (Steiner, *Twelve Cosmic Moods*).

**Dec 18: Last Quarter Moon 2° Virgo.** The Moon, aligned with *Alkaid*, was at this degree shortly before midnight on the day that began Jesus Christ's forty days in the wilderness (Oct/21/29). *Alkaid* is the outer star of the handle of the Big Dipper; it bears a correspondence to Saturn.

As we enter the concluding phase of this lunar cycle, we are reminded of the wilderness of materialism that entraps all who know not of its prison. Last year we entered into the 40th day, the day angels came to minister to Christ Jesus. To receive the new light now radiating, we must first have the courage to name the evil that has engulfed us. In naming it, we rise above its clawing magnetism; we are then also able to stand witness to the fact that spiritual ministers now watch over those who have turned their mind's eye to a new dawn.

**Dec 21: Winter Solstice.** As the Holy Nights open three days from now, we are afforded a journey into magical realms of wonder. The seed of our future spiritual potential, which we carried through this past cycle of the seasons, has spent itself—and in doing so, it has birthed a new seed. This we carry into the days and nights to come.

In the Holy Nights, we are born into the womb of the Mother. Pagans, in pre-Christian Europe, called this time the Night of the Mothers. We descend, as soul seeds, into the earthly depths to gather the spiritual forces we will need if we are to meet the trials that await us in the coming year. In these blessed nights we are reminded that much of the world's suffering is brought about by our false beliefs.

As we consciously celebrate this time of pause in the yearly rhythm of the seasons, our hearts are granted new forces. This engenders the courage we will need to face our trials with equanimity of soul and stalwartness of spirit. By living into the Shambhala mysteries now being unveiled, we are strengthened to serve peace in the world.

**Dec 22: ASPECT: Venus 8° Capricorn square Uranus 8° Aries.** Venus recalls Jesus speaking in the synagogue of the second beatitude: *Blessed are they that mourn, for they shall be comforted* (Dec/15/30).

The cross of Venus, in dynamic tension with the Holy Spirit (Uranus), asks us to willingly suffer truth into time. The old almost always oppose the new. When we suffer, our heart breaks—opening for something new to fall through the cracks. If we are unwilling to suffer, we will remain slaves in old paradigms that aggress against notions that threaten the status quo. Indeed, contentment is often a prison with golden bars!

**Dec 23: Sun 7° Sagittarius:** The first temptation in the wilderness (Nov/27/29).

The first temptation was the temptation to bow to the prince of this world. Satan hung a globe from his hand in which all the marvels of the world were contained. Jesus would not look into the globe, but instead spoke the words: "My kingdom is not of this world." Thus, the will-to-power was overcome. This globe of Satan seems very much like the "globe" of virtual and augmented realities.

*If we cannot imagine spiritual reality, we are sentenced to life in unspiritual time: days running endlessly until we take our last breath.* Communion and the sacraments wither in the absence of persevering faith.

*When the inner spiritual light fades, we hold neither karmic concerns nor the necessity for righteousness of action.* Thus do we become vulnerable to the possibility of possession. We forget the Father, and are left with inner dullness.

The Rosicrucian mantra *Ex Deo nascimur* (from God we are born) aligns us with the truth that we have been born from the Divine. We must not sleep while confronted by the necessities of developing moral consciousness. We are to live into the eternal vastness that holds the beings of Time themselves—the mighty archai who reveal to us our place in the great evolutionary wave to which we belong. Thus does the past become the foundation stone for the revelation of Time's future.

In answer to the first temptation, Christ replied: *My kingdom is not of this world.* At this time of the fifth sacrifice of Christ, a new kingdom is forming, one that is born of the moral ether.

As we gather with friends and family to celebrate the miracle that tomorrow evening, in winter's darkest night, is to be born anew, may we find the holiness of Christ's etheric embrace.

**Dec 24: Christmas Eve and the beginning of the Holy Nights.** This is the time when Christ and his chorus of archangels gather together around the Earth, bestowing the blessing of peace to all who are of good will. The archangels, whose wings hold the memory of creation are drawing near—encircling the Earth. Indeed, we can imagine them so near that their wings touch!

At the Ascension, Christ rose through all the spiritual hierarchies, bestowing new teachings into each of these higher spheres. Emanations from the Cosmic Christ now reach us via the Angel Jesus and the archangels, who radiate love to groups and nations, as well as to the entirety of the global human family.

For the next twelve days and nights, we enter extraordinary time, wherein the splendor of miracles abound:

In the archangels' wings are contained the records and histories of the peoples for whom they have stewardship.... And their wings are emanations of what is in their hearts. I beheld Christ bearing the entire history of all peoples within his own being.

He was the ultimate archangelic being when he entered into their realm. He became one of them; and indeed in every realm that he entered during the Ascension, he became the ultimate ideal of whatever beings he encountered. When in the human realm, he was the ultimate Human. When he rose into the angelic realm, he became the ultimate angel. Thus he showed the angels the way of their own evolution, what they were to ultimately achieve. He bore in his being the experience of being an angel in its totality, to its greatest fulfillment; and all angels witnessed this great Being who would bend to meet them at their present level of being and then uplift them to the next higher level. He did this by becoming one with them—just as he had become one with humanity by meeting humanity at its level. He descended below all things and then ascended to the angelic realm, and then to the archangelic realm, and continued onward from there.

In the Ascension, he brought to the archangels full account of his deeds on the Earth—what he had done for humankind. And symbolically he laid this great gift at the feet of the archangels who were spiraling around him.[1]

As the door to the Holy days and nights opens, we are called to contemplate the nearness of holy beings and the eternal oneness that weaves among all peoples of the Earth. The portal now opening reaches not only into the heavenly heights, but also into the the earthly depths. In these depths we find the inner Earth mysteries, Shambhala mysteries. Paradise rests at the Earth's center, wherein lies the holy manger. In mysterious ways, we journey during these sacred nights to this manger and light the fire of hope that will sustain us in the unfolding year to come.

**Sun 7°53' Sagittarius: The second temptation in the wilderness** (Nov/28/29). Throughout the period of temptations, Christ was the representative of human freedom. In times of temptation we must make our decisions not from the spiritual world, but from within ourselves. After finding our pure, divine conviction—born of freedom and human discretion—the spiritual world will again open before us, and the angels will come to minister to us.

Now is a time when true human freedom hangs in the balance. And, as we pass through this bleak period of global temptation, we must all make decisions out of our sovereign freedom.

The second temptation asked Jesus Christ to plunge from the pinnacle of the temple. Instead, he rejected the onslaught of the adversaries and spoke the words: "Thou shalt not tempt the Lord thy God." When this temptation succeeds, the abyss into which we thus plunge is made up of the instinctive urges that are hidden from consciousness. *This creates a desire for miracles without any conscious effort.* We then surrender, often quite unwittingly, to something unknown and unseen from the lower worlds.

Moreover, the temptation to plunge from the pinnacle of our highest consciousness is increasing in our time, as witnessed for example by the wildly rampant increase in the use of mind altering drugs—whether medically prescribed or illicit. Many other forms of addiction are also becoming prevalent nowadays throughout the world. Indeed, when we fall into the instinctual forces of the unconscious, the angels who will catch us are *not* the good ones!

The Rosicrucian mantra *In Christo morimur* (In Christ, death becomes new life) strengthens us to stay awake in each moment, to feel the presence of the Etheric Christ in the encircling round, and to await his touch in moments of silent devotion.

**Dec 25: Christian celebration of Christmas.** Insanity approaches the mind when our experience of time loses its connection to the great rhythms of the cosmic year. The seasons, celebrations, and festival life all contribute to our feeling of belonging to something greater than ourselves. Every year we visit the "manger": the heart of the Mother in the center of the earthly depths. This manger holds the memory of the entirety of human history, and each of our true Names is etched into this cradle of love. Initiates follow their star to find the manger, where upon they kneel before the Midnight Sun—the eternal Christ child who lives in each heart. As these holy days and nights begin, we too will go to the manger—some of us in wakeful consciousness, and many of us merely in our dreams. This is the sacred journey of renewal that resounds, as if for the first time, year after year.

The annual repetition of the nativity of Christ is a real event on the spiritual plane—like those of his miracles, his passion, his resurrection and ascension—which means to say that just as the external Sun eternally repeats springtime, summer, autumn and winter, so does the spiritual Sun reveal his *eternal* springtime aspect—his infancy—at Christmas; his *eternal* summer aspect—his miracles; his *eternal* autumnal aspect—his passion and resurrection; and his *eternal* winter aspect—his ascension. This means to say, again, that the ages are eternal—that infancy, youth, middle age, and old age are eternal. The Christ is eternally Child, Master, Crucified, and Resurrected. Man bears in himself at one and the same time the child, the young man, the mature man, and the old man. Nothing of the past is lost or destroyed; the past simply passes from the stage [of life] into the wings—from the framework of the

---

1 Isaacson (unpublished manuscript).

conscious to the domain of the unconscious, from where it operates in a no-less active way. It is the same with past epochs and civilizations of human history; they have not disappeared, but are present and active in the instinctivity of our epoch and civilization. It is to the great merit of C. G. Jung that he discovered the presence of the remote past in contemporary psychic life and established the existence of "archaeological layers" in human psychic life—just as archaeology did for the material objects of past civilizations and as paleontology did for material fossils of the biological past. Thanks to the work of Jung, "psychological excavations" can be added to archaeological and paleontological excavations, and can come to their aid. The difference between the vestiges of the past with which archaeology and paleontology work and the "psychic layers" of the past established by Jung is that the latter are *living*—although outside of the framework of consciousness dominated and determined by intelligence—whilst the materials of archaeology and paleontology are *dead*: they are only skeletons of the past.[2]

May this most precious time of the year be a celebration of the miracle that continually bestows its grace upon us from the radiance of the spiritual Sun.

**Sun 9° Sagittarius:** The third temptation in the wilderness (Nov/29/29).

The end of the historic period of the third temptation (1988-2018) has come to an end. We are now in the 40th day, the day when angels came to minister to Christ. May we notice their ministering presence as they draw near to us as well.

The third temptation was not overcome, for Ahriman held something back that Jesus Christ could not encounter. Only later, when Jesus sweated blood in the Garden of Gethsemane, would Ahriman approach again to thrust his last blows against the incarnated Son of God. The temptation to turn stones into bread is an ominous and continual threat that is currently working through money and through seed manipulation—and indeed also through a perpetual need to be continuously "hooked up" in the ever more intricate and expanding grid of technological realities.

Religious life is dying, and in its place the quantitative aspects of life have triumphed over the qualitative aspects. Materialism causes humankind to see a world mournfully void of spiritual guidance, a world devoid of direction. Behind this lurks a fear of karma and—ultimately—a fear of judgment. Without deference to karmic consequences, we are freed from feelings of responsibility; we can instead rest in self-justified, albeit illusory, contentment. Yet, this can cause us to fall into the hallucination that life can be mechanized—i.e., abstracted from its living reality. Lower beings can thus find their way into our consciousness, feigning importance and giving false direction. Finally, the bread of life and the stones of Ahriman become equal—and then the latter ominously begin to supersede the former.

The Rosicrucian mantra *Per spiritum sanctum reviviscimus* (In the world thoughts of the spirit, the soul awakes) is the antidote to this temptation.

When we receive the impulses streaming from the future, we serve what is in the process of becoming. Space becomes an open field of possibilities—of weaving light, bestowing revelation. In the kingdom forming through Christ's etheric presence, Grail nourishment can be found; and it *will* be found as we develop new capacities now in their infancy. This kingdom is part of the new miracle that accompanies Christ's fifth sacrifice: *the forming of the moral ether.*

As we gather to celebrate the sacred birth of Jesus, we can imagine that the foods we share are not only filled with the blessings of the Mother, but that they also bear the living word of God. When time reaches its end, we will come to know the eternal truth—that we live not by bread alone, but by every word that is issued from the mouth of God.

**Mercury enters Sagittarius:** "Attainment concludes joyful striving" (Steiner, *Twelve Cosmic Moods*).

**Dec 26: ASPECT: New Moon 9° Sagittarius and Annular Solar Eclipse over much of Asia and Australia.** The Moon remembers Jesus as he went to the house of a rich herd owner who had died suddenly in one of his fields. His wife and children were very sad and had sent for Jesus, begging him to come to the funeral. Jesus agreed, and later spoke to the

---

2 *MOT*, p. 532.

wife of the dead man, whose name was Nazor. He said that if she and her children would believe in his teaching and follow him, and if they would keep silence on the matter, Nazor would be raised to life again. For, he said, Nazor's soul had not yet passed on to be judged but was still present over the place in the field where he had died. Jesus called Nazor back to his body, and they later found him sitting upright in his coffin. Nazor climbed out of his coffin and cast himself down at Jesus' feet (Sep/1/32).

The year approaches its end as the Lady of the Night unites with the Sun—this represents the immaculate conception of something newly dawning. A new Saturn–Pluto cycle will commence in January of 2020, in the constellation of Sagittarius. As we conclude the current cycle, which began in Libra, we prepare to receive the truth that rewards all who have mustered the courage to name evil. In so doing, one is able to rise above the contention of controversy. Anne Catherine Emmerich bore witness to the globe of Satan's trick-show; now we, too, must *all* bear such witness. If we cannot, we will not be able to meet the rising of the Dharma Sun that now illumines a truth that soars above the despair of falsehood. This is the truth that will meet all pilgrims of a new world order, whose noble loyalty to love will shine a light into the darkness, thus withering the illusions that have long held us captive.

In the words of Emmerich, who saw Satan's temptation of Jesus:

> Then he showed him a piece of apparatus that hung on his hand; it was like a globe, or—perhaps still more—like a birdcage. Jesus would not look at the tempter, much less into the globe as Satan desired; Jesus then left the grotto, turning his back on Satan. I saw that a look into Satan's trick-show disclosed the most magnificent scenes from nature. There were lovely pleasure gardens, full of shady groves, as well as cool fountains, richly laden fruit trees, and luscious grapes—among other such delights. All of this seemed to be within one's reach, and all was constantly dissolving into ever more beautiful, more enticing scenes. Jesus, however, simply turned his back on Satan, and vanished!

This was another temptation to interrupt the fast of Jesus, who now began to thirst and to experience the pangs of hunger. Satan did not yet know what to think of him. He was aware, it is true, of the prophecies relating to him, and he felt that he exercised power over himself; but he did not yet know that Jesus was God. He did not know even that Jesus was indeed the Messiah, whose advent he so dreaded—since he had beheld him fasting, hungering, and enduring temptation; since he saw him so poor, suffering in so many ways; in a word, since he saw him in all things so like an ordinary man. In this, Satan was as blind as the Pharisees. He looked upon Jesus merely as a holy man whom temptation might lead to a fall.[1]

Enraptured within Satan's trick show, we all believe in the splendorous, magnificent world of the fifth kingdom. Within this world we compromise, we mechanize, we abstract to death all life through depersonalization. Thus can we justify evil as good, knowing not that we have been captured.

Like Jesus, we are to avoid this "bird cage"—*for it is naught but the glamour of dangerous illusion.* The Pharisees refused to see that the Messiah had indeed been born to them. If we refuse to see the rising Sun of a new age, we will enter Satan's world and cling to that which brings only death—all while living in a time of resurrecting life. How tragic!

Nazor's healing is today remembered. He was healed from afar as Jesus manifested the art of sacred magic. Positive etheric technology is an art we all must learn if we are to maintain fields of light into which angels may minister to us. In our heart's emptiness we enter a void; and in such a void, miracles become ordinary.

When gnosis reveals the reality of new truths, we may find an eagerness to rise above all discord—the origin of which always consists of the noxious vapors emanating from the "birdcage." As we then arise out of the limitations of the past and advance into realms of possibility hitherto unattained, may we, too, put on the armor of God!

**Mars enters Scorpio:** "Existence consumes being; yet, in being, existence endures. In activity, growth

---

1 *The Visions of Anne Catherine Emmerich, Book I*, p. 369.

disappears; **in growth, activity persists**. In chastising world-activation, in punishing self-formation, being sustains beings" (Steiner, *Twelve Cosmic Moods*).

**Dec 27: ASPECT: Sun conjunct Jupiter 11° Sagittarius.** The Sun stood here as Jesus preached concerning the third beatitude: *Blessed are the meek, for they shall inherit the earth*. During the event, men tried to bring a paralytic on a bed to where Jesus stood, but were unable to make their way through the crowd. The men then lowered him through the roof; and when Jesus saw their faith, he said to the paralytic, "Man, your sins are forgiven you!" (Dec/1/30).

The resurrecting power of the Sun, united with the Holy Spirit, is exactly the force that can reveal new mysteries. In fields of light, angels are able to draw near to us, leading our broken hearts into realms of wonder. May joy embrace us as we turn to the dawning of 2020.

# GLOSSARY

This glossary of entries relating to Esoteric Christianity lists only some of the specialized terms used in the articles and commentaries of *Star Wisdom*. Owing to limited space, the entries are very brief, and the reader is encouraged to study the foundational works of Rudolf Steiner for a more complete understanding of these terms.

**Ahriman**: An adversarial being identified by the great prophet Zarathustra during the ancient Persian cultural epoch (5067–2907 BC) as an opponent to the Sun God *Ahura Mazda* (obs.; "Aura of the Sun"). Also called Satan, Ahriman represents one aspect of the Dragon. Ahriman's influence leads to materialistic thinking devoid of feeling, empathy, and moral conscience. Ahriman helps inspire science and technology, and works through forces of sub-nature such as gravity, electricity, magnetism, radioactivity—forces that are antithetical to life. The influence of Ahriman's activity upon the human being limits human cognition to what is derived from sense perception, hardens thinking (materialistic thoughts), attacks the etheric body by way of modern technology (electromagnetic radiation, etc.), and hardens hearts (cold and calculating).

**ahrimanic beings**: Spiritual beings who have become agents of Ahriman's influences.

**Angel Jesus**: A pure immaculate Angelic being who sacrifices himself so that the Christ may work through him. This Angelic being is actually of the status of an Archangel, who has descended to work on the Angelic level to be closer to human beings and to assist them on the path of confrontation with evil.

**Ascension**: An unfathomable process at the start of which, on May 14, AD 33, Christ united with the etheric realm that surrounds and permeates the Earth with Cosmic Life. Thus began his cosmic ascent to the realm of the heavenly Father, with the goal of elevating the Earth spiritually and opening pathways between the Earth and the spiritual world for the future.

**astral body**: Part of the human being that is the bearer of consciousness, passion, and desires, as well as idealism and the longing for perfection.

**Asuras**: Fallen Archai (Time Spirits) from the time of Old Saturn, whose opposition to human evolution comes to expression through promoting debauched sexuality and senseless violence among human beings. So low is the regard that the Asuras have for the sacredness of human life, that as well as promoting extreme violence and debauchery (for example, through the film industry), they do not hold back from the destruction of the physical body of human beings. In particular, the activity of the Asuras retards the development of the consciousness soul.

**bodhisattva**: On the human level a bodhisattva is a human being far advanced on the spiritual path, a human being belonging to the circle of twelve great teachers surrounding the Cosmic Christ. One who incarnates periodically to further the evolution of the Earth and humanity, working on the level of an angelic, archangelic, or higher being in relation to the rest of humanity. Every 5,000 years, one of these great teachers from the circle of bodhisattvas takes on a special mission, incarnating repeatedly to awake a new human faculty and capacity. Once that capacity has been imparted through its human bearer, this bodhisattva then incarnates upon the Earth for the last time, ascending to the level of a Buddha to serve humankind from spirit realms. See also Maitreya Bodhisattva.

**Central Sun**: Heart of the Milky Way, also called the Galactic Center. Our Sun orbits this Central Sun over a period of approximately 225 million years.

**chakra**: One of seven astral organs of perception through which human beings develop higher levels of cognition such as clairvoyance, telepathy, and so on.

**Christ**: The eternal being who is the second member of the Trinity. Also called the "Divine 'I AM,'" the Son of God, the Cosmic Christ, and the Logos/Word. Christ began to fully unite with the human vessel (Jesus) at the Baptism in the Jordan, and for 3½ years penetrated as the *Divine I AM* successively into the astral body, etheric body, and physical body of Jesus, spiritualizing each member. Through the Mystery of Golgotha Christ united with the Earth, kindling the spark of Christ consciousness (*Not I, but Christ in me*) in all human beings.

**consciousness soul**: The portion of the human soul in which "I" consciousness is awaking not only to its own sense of individuality and to the individualities of others, but also to its higher self—spirit self (Sanskrit: *manas*). Within the consciousness soul, the "I" perceives truth, beauty, and goodness; within the spirit self, the "I" becomes truth, beauty, and goodness.

**crossing the threshold**: a term applicable to our time, as human beings are increasingly encountering the spiritual world—in so doing, crossing the threshold between the sense-perceptible realm and non-physical realms of existence. To the extent that spiritual capacities have not been cultivated, this encounter with non-physical realms beyond the sense world signifies a descent into the subconscious (for example, through drugs) rather than an ascent to knowledge of higher worlds through the awaking of higher levels of consciousness.

**Decan**: The zodiac of 360° is divided into twelve signs, each of 30°. A decan is 10°, thus one third of one sign or 1/36 of the zodiac.

**Devil**: Another name for Lucifer.

**Dragon**: As used in the Apocalypse of John, there are different appearances of the dragon, each one representing an adversarial being opposed to Michael, Christ, and Sophia. For example, the great red dragon of chapter 12 opposes Sophia, the woman clothed with the Sun (Sophia is the pure Divine-Cosmic Feminine Soul of the World). The imagery from chapter 12 of Revelations depicts the woman clothed with the Sun as pregnant and that the great red dragon attempts to devour her child as soon as it is born. The child coming to birth from the woman clothed with the Sun represents the Divine-Cosmic "I AM" born through the assistance of the pure Divine Feminine Soul of the World. The dragon is cast down from the heavenly realm by the mighty Archangel Michael. Cast down to the Earth, the dragon continues with attempts to devour the cosmic child (the Divine-Cosmic "I AM") coming to birth among humankind.

**ego**: The soul sheath through which the "I" begins to incarnate and to experience life on Earth (to be distinguished from the term *ego* used in Freudian and Jungian psychology—hence written capitalized "Ego" to make this distinction). The terms *ego*, "I," and *soul* are often used interchangeably in Spiritual Science. The ego maintains threads of integrity and continuity through memory, while experiencing new sensations and perceptions through observation and thinking, feeling, and willing. The ego is capable of moral discernment and also experiences temptation. Thus, it is often stated that the "I" comprises both a higher nature ("Ego") and a lower nature ("ego").

**Emmerich, Anne Catherine** (also "Sister Emmerich"): A Catholic stigmatist (1774–1824) whose visions depicted the daily life of Jesus, beginning some weeks before the event of the descent of Christ into the body of Jesus at the Baptism in the River Jordan and extending for a period of several weeks after the Crucifixion.

**Ephesus**: The area in Asia Minor (now Turkey) to which the Apostle John (also called John Zebedee, the brother of James the Greater) accompanied the Virgin Mary approximately three years after the death of Jesus Christ. Ephesus was a very significant ancient mystery center where cosmic mysteries of the East found their way into the West. Initiates at Ephesus were devoted to the goddess Artemis, known as "Artemis of Ephesus," whose qualities are more those of a Mother goddess than is the case with the Greek goddess Artemis, although there is a certain degree of overlap between Artemis and Artemis of Ephesus with regard to many of their respective characteristics. A magnificent Ionic mystery temple was built in honor of Artemis of Ephesus at a location close to the Aegean Sea. Mary's house, built by John, was located high up above, on the nearby hill known as Mount

Nightingale, about six miles from the temple of Artemis at Ephesus.

**etheric body:** The body of life forces permeating and animating the physical body. The etheric body was formed during Ancient Sun evolution. The etheric body's activity is expressed in the seven life processes permeating the seven vital organs. The etheric body is related to the movements of the seven visible planets.

**Fall, The:** A fall from oneness with spiritual worlds. The Fall, which took place during the Lemurian period of Earth evolution, was a time of dramatic transition in human evolution when the soul descended from "Paradise" into earthly existence. Through the Fall the human soul began to incarnate into a physical body upon the Earth and experience the world from "within" the body, perceiving through the senses.

**Fifth Gospel:** The writings and lectures of Rudolf Steiner based on new spiritual perceptions and insights into the mysteries of Christ's life on Earth, including the Second Coming of Christ—his appearance in the etheric realm in our time, beginning in the twentieth century.

**Golgotha, Mystery of:** Rudolf Steiner's designation for the entire mystery of the coming of Christ to the Earth. Sometimes this term is used more specifically to refer to the events surrounding the Crucifixion and Resurrection. In particular, the Crucifixion—the sacrifice on the cross—marked the birth of Christ's union with the Earth. Also referred to as the "Turning Point of Time," whereby at the Crucifixion Christ descended from the sphere of the Sun and became the "Spirit of the Earth."

**Grail:** An etheric chalice into which Christ can work to transform earthly substance into spiritual substance. The term *Grail* has many deep levels of meaning and refers on the one hand to a spiritual stream in service of Christ, and on the other hand to the means by which the human "I" penetrates and transforms evil into good. The power of transubstantiation expresses something of this process of transformation of evil into good.

**Grail Knights:** Those trained to confront evil and transform it into something good, in service of Christ. Members of a spiritual stream that existed in the past and continues to exist—albeit in metamorphosed form—in the present. Every human being striving for the good can potentially become a Grail Knight.

**I AM:** One's true individuality, that—with few exceptions—never fully incarnates but works into the developing "I" and its lower bodies (astral, etheric, and physical). The **Cosmic I AM** is the "I AM" of Christ, through which—on account of the Mystery of Golgotha—we are all graced with the possibility of receiving a divine spark therefrom.

**Jesus** (see Nathan Jesus and Solomon Jesus): The pure human being who received the Christ at the Baptism in the River Jordan.

**Jesus Christ:** The Divine-Human being; the God-Man; the union of the Divine with the Human. The presence of the Cosmic Christ in the physical body of the human being called the Nathan Jesus during the 3½ years of the ministry.

**Jesus of Nazareth:** The name of the human being whose birth is celebrated in the Gospel of Luke, also referred to as the Nathan Jesus. When Jesus of Nazareth reached the age of twelve, the spirit of the Solomon Jesus (Gospel of Matthew) united with the body and sheaths of the pure Nathan Jesus. This union lasted for about 18 years, until the Baptism in the River Jordan. During these eighteen years, Jesus of Nazareth was a composite being comprising the Nathan Jesus and the spirit ("I") of the Solomon Jesus. Just before the Baptism, the spirit of the Solomon Jesus withdrew, and at the Baptism Jesus became known as "Jesus Christ" through the union of Christ with the sheaths of Jesus.

**Jezebel:** Wife of King Ahab, approximately 900 BC, who worked through the powers of black magic against the prophet Elijah.

**Kali Yuga:** Yugas are ages of influence referred to in Hindu cosmography, each yuga lasting a certain numbers of years in length (always a multiple of 2,500). The Kali Yuga is also known as the Dark Age, which began with the death of Krishna in 3102 BC (-3101). Kali Yuga lasted 5,000 years and ended in AD 1899.

**Kingly Stream:** Biblically, the line of heredity from King David into which the Solomon Jesus (Gospel of Matthew) was born. The kings (the three magi) were initiates who sought to bring the cosmic will of the heavenly Father to expression on the Earth through spiritual forces working from spiritual beings dwelling in the stars. The minds of the wise kings were enlightened by the coming of Jesus Christ.

**Krishna:** A cosmic-human being, the sister soul of Adam that overlighted Arjuna as described in the Bhagavad Gita. The overlighting by Krishna of Arjuna could be described as an incorporation of Krishna into Arjuna. An incorporation is a partial incarnation. The cosmic-human being known as Krishna later fully incarnated as Jesus of Nazareth (Nathan Jesus—Gospel of Luke).

**Lazarus:** The elder brother of Mary Magdalene, Martha, and Silent Mary. At his raising from the dead, Lazarus became the first human being to be fully initiated by Christ (see Lazarus–John).

**Lazarus–John:** At the raising of Lazarus from the dead by Christ, the spiritual being of John the Baptist united with Lazarus. The higher spiritual members of John (spirit body, life spirit, spirit self) entered into the members of Lazarus, which were developed to the level of the consciousness soul.

**Lucifer:** The name of a fallen spiritual being, also called the Light-Bearer, who acts as a retarding force within the human astral body and also in the sentient soul. Lucifer inflames egoism and pride within the human being, often inspiring genius and supreme artistry. Arrogance and self-importance are stimulated, without humility or sacrificial love. Lucifer stirs up forces of rebellion, but cannot deliver true freedom—just its illusion.

**luciferic beings:** Spiritual beings who have become agents of Lucifer's influences.

**magi:** Initiates in the mystery school of Zarathustra, the Bodhisattva who incarnated as Zoroaster (Zaratas, Nazaratos) in the sixth century BC and who, after he came to Babylon, became a teacher of the Chaldean priesthood. At the time of Jesus, the magi were still continuing the stargazing tradition of the school of Zoroaster. The task of the magi was to recognize when their master would reincarnate. With their visit to the newborn Jesus child in Bethlehem (Gospel of Matthew), to this child who was the reincarnated Zarathustra/Zoroaster, they fulfilled their mission. The three magi are the "priest kings from the East" referred to in the Gospel of Matthew.

**Maitreya Bodhisattva:** The bodhisattva individuality that is preparing to become the successor of Gautama Buddha and will be known as the Bringer of the Good. This bodhisattva was incarnated in the second century BC as Jeshu ben Pandira, the teacher of the Essenes, who died about 100 BC. Rudolf Steiner indicated that Jeshu ben Pandira reincarnated at the beginning of the twentieth century as a great bodhisattva individuality to fulfill the lofty mission of proclaiming Christ's coming in the etheric realm, beginning around 1933: "He will be the actual herald of Christ in his etheric form" (lecture about Jeshu ben Pandira held in Leipzig on November 4, 1911). There are differing points of view as to who this individuality actually was in his twentieth century incarnation.

**manas:** Also called the spirit self; the purified astral body, lifted into full communion with truth and goodness by becoming the true and the good within the essence of the higher self of the human being. Manas is the spiritual source of the "I," and as it is the eternal part of the human being that goes from life to life, manas bears the human being's true "eternal name" through its union with the Holy Spirit. The "eternal name" expresses the human being's true mission from life to life.

**Mani:** The name of a lofty initiate who lived in Babylon in the third century AD. The founder of the Manichean stream, whose mission is the transformation of evil into goodness through compassion and love. Mani reincarnated as Parzival in the ninth century AD. Mani/Parzival is one of the leading initiates of our present age—the age of the consciousness soul (AD 1414–3574). One of the highest beings ever to incarnate upon the Earth, he will become the future Manu beginning in the astrological age of Sagittarius. This future Manu will oversee the spiritual evolution of a sequence of seven ages, comprising the seven cultural epochs of the Sixth Great Age of Earth evolution from the Age of Sagittarius to the Age of Gemini—lasting a total of 7 x 2,160 years (15,120 years), since each zodiacal age lasts 2,160 years.

**Manu:** Like the word Buddha, the word Manu is a title. A Manu has the task of spiritually overseeing one Great Age of Earth evolution, comprising seven astrological ages (seven cultural epochs)—lasting a total of 7 x 2,160 years (15,120 years), since each zodiacal age lasts 2,160 years. The present Age of Pisces (AD 215–2375)—with its corresponding cultural epoch (AD 1414–3574)—is the fifth epoch during the Fifth Great Age of Earth evolution. (Lemuria was the Third Great Age, Atlantis the Fourth Great Age, and since the great flood that destroyed Atlantis, we are now in the Fifth Great Age.) The present Manu is the exalted Sun-initiate who guided humanity out of Atlantis during the ancient flooding that destroyed the continent of Atlantis formerly in the region of the Atlantic Ocean—the Flood referred to in the Bible in connection with Noah. He is the overseer of the seven cultural epochs corresponding to the seven astrological ages from the Age of Cancer to the Age of Capricorn, following the sequence: Cancer, Gemini, Taurus, Aries, Pisces, Aquarius, Capricorn. The present Manu was the teacher of the Seven Holy Rishis who were the founders of the ancient Indian cultural epoch (7227–5067 BC) during the Age of Cancer. He is known in the Bible as Noah, and in the Flood story belonging to the Gilgamesh epic he is called Utnapishtim. Subsequently this Manu appeared to Abraham as Melchizedek and offered Abraham an agape ("love feast") of bread and wine. Jesus "was designated by God to be high priest in the order of Melchizedek" (Heb. 5:10).

**Mary:** Rudolf Steiner distinguishes between the Nathan Mary and the Solomon Mary (see corresponding entries). The expression "Virgin Mary" refers to the Solomon Mary, the mother of the child Jesus whose birth is described in the Gospel of Matthew.

**Mary Magdalene:** Sister of Lazarus, whose soul was transformed and purified as Christ cast out seven demons who had taken possession of her. Christ thus initiated Mary Magdalene. Later, she anointed Jesus Christ. And she was the first to behold the Risen Christ in the Garden of the Holy Sepulcher on the morning of his resurrection.

**megastar:** Stars with a luminosity greater than 10,000 times that of our Sun.

**Nain, Youth of:** Referred to in the Gospel of Luke as the son of the widow of Nain. The Youth of Nain—at the time he was twelve years old—was raised from the dead by Jesus. The Youth of Nain later reincarnated as the Prophet Mani (third century AD) and subsequently as the Grail King Parzival (ninth century AD).

**Nathan Jesus:** From the priestly line of David, as described in the Gospel of Luke. An immaculate and pure soul whose one and only physical incarnation was as Jesus of Nazareth (Nathan Jesus).

**Nathan Mary:** A pure being who was the mother of the Nathan Jesus. The Nathan Mary died in AD 12, but her spirit united with the Solomon Mary at the time of the Baptism of Jesus in the River Jordan. From this time on, the Solomon Mary—spiritually united with the Nathan Mary—was known as the Virgin Mary.

**New Jerusalem:** A spiritual condition denoting humanity's future existence that will come into being as human beings free themselves from the *maya* of the material world and work together to bring about a spiritualized Earth.

**Osiris:** *Osiris* and *Isis* are names given by the Egyptians to the preincarnatory forms of the spiritual beings who are now known as Christ and Sophia.

**Parzival:** Son of Gahmuret and Herzeloyde in the epic *Parzival* by Wolfram von Eschenbach. Although written in the thirteenth century, this work refers to actual people and events in the ninth century AD, one of whom (the central figure) bore the name Parzival. After living a life of dullness and doubt, Parzival's mission was to seek the Castle of the Grail and to ask the question "What ails thee?" of the Grail King, Anfortas—moreover, to ask the question without being bidden to do so. Parzival eventually became the new Grail King, the successor of Anfortas. Parzival was the reincarnated prophet Mani. In the incarnation preceding that of Mani, he was incarnated as the Youth of Nain (Luke 7:11–15). Parzival is a great initiate responsible for guiding humanity during the Age of Pisces, which has given birth to the cultural epoch of the development of the consciousness soul (AD 1414–3574).

**Pentecost:** Descent of the Holy Spirit fifty days after Easter, whereby the cosmic "I AM" was birthed among the disciples and those individuals close to Christ. They received the capacity to develop manas, or spirit self, within the community of striving human individuals, whereby the birth of the spirit self is facilitated through the soul of the Virgin Mary. See also World Pentecost.

**phantom body:** The pure spiritual form of the human physical body, unhindered by matter. The far-distant future state of the human physical body when it has become purified and spiritualized into a body of transformed divine will.

**Presbyter John:** Refers to Lazarus–John who moved to Ephesus about twenty years after the Virgin Mary had died there. In Ephesus he became a bishop. He is the author of the Book of Revelations, the Gospel of St. John, and the Letters of John.

**Risen One:** The initial appearance of Christ in his phantom body (resurrection body), beginning with his appearance to Mary Magdalene on Easter Sunday morning. Christ frequently appeared to the disciples in his phantom body during the forty days leading from Easter to Ascension.

**Satan:** The traditional Christian name for Ahriman.

**Serpent:** Another name for Lucifer, but sometimes naming a combination of Lucifer and Ahriman: "The great dragon was hurled down—that ancient serpent called the devil, or Satan, who leads the whole world astray" (Rev. 12:9).

**Shepherd Stream:** Biblically, the genealogical line from David the shepherd through his son Nathan. It was into this line that the Nathan Jesus was born, whose birth is described in the Gospel of Luke. Rudolf Steiner describes the shepherds, who—according to Luke—came to pay homage to the newborn child, as those servants of pure heart who perceive the goodwill streaming up from Mother Earth. The hearts of the shepherds were kindled with the fire of Divine Love by the coming of the Christ. The shepherds can be regarded as precursors of the heart stream of humanity that now intuits the being of Christ as the spirit of the Earth.

**Solomon Jesus:** Descended from the genealogical line from David through his son Solomon. This line of descent is described in the Gospel of Matthew. The Solomon Jesus was a reincarnation of Zoroaster (sixth century BC). In turn, Zoroaster was a reincarnation of Zarathustra (6000 BC), the great prophet and founder of the ancient Persian religion of Zoroastrianism. He was a bodhisattva, who as the founder of this new religion that was focused upon the Sun Spirit Ahura Mazda, helped prepare humanity for the subsequent descent into incarnation of Ahura Mazda, the cosmic Sun Spirit, as Christ.

**Solomon Mary:** The wise mother of the Solomon Jesus, who adopted the Nathan Jesus after the death of the Nathan Mary. At the time of the Baptism of Jesus in the River Jordan, the spirit of the Nathan Mary united with the Solomon Mary. Usually referred to as the Virgin Mary or Mother Mary, the Solomon Mary bore witness at the foot of the cross to the Mystery of Golgotha. She died in Ephesus eleven years after Christ's Ascension.

**Sophia:** Part of the Divine Feminine Trinity comprising the Mother (counterpart of the Father), the Daughter (counterpart of the Son), and the Holy Soul (counterpart of the Holy Spirit). Sophia, also known as the Bride of the Lamb, is the Daughter aspect of the threefold Divine Feminine Trinity. To the Egyptians Sophia was known as Isis, who was seen to belong to the starry realm surrounding the Earth. In the Book of Proverbs, attributed to King Solomon, Sophia's temple has seven pillars (Proverbs 9:1). The seven pillars in Sophia's temple represent the seven great stages of Earth evolution (from Ancient Saturn to Future Vulcan).

**Sorath:** The great enemy of Christ who works against the "I" in the human being. Sorath is identified with the two-horned beast that rises up from the depths of Earth, as described in the Apocalypse of St. John. Sorath is the Sun Demon, and is identified by Rudolf Steiner as the Antichrist. According to the Book of Revelations his number is 666.

**Sun Demon:** Another name for Sorath.

**Transfiguration:** The event on Mt. Tabor where Jesus Christ was illumined with Divine Light raying forth from the purified etheric body of Jesus, which the Divine "I AM" of Christ had penetrated. The Gospels of Matthew and Luke describe the Transfiguration. The sunlike radiance that shone forth from Jesus Christ on Mt. Tabor was an expression of the purified etheric body that had its origin during the Old Sun period of Earth evolution.

**Transubstantiation:** Sacramental transformation of physical substance—for example, the transubstantiation of bread and wine during the Mass to become the body and blood of Christ. During the Holy Eucharist the bread and wine are transformed in such a way that the substances of bread and wine are infused with the life force (body) and light (blood) of Christ. Thereby the bread and wine are reunited with their divine archetypes and are no longer "merely" physical substances, but are bearers on the physical level of a spiritual reality.

**Turning Point of Time:** Transition between involution and evolution, as marked by the Mystery of Golgotha. The descending stream of involution culminated with the Mystery of Golgotha. With the descent of the Cosmic Christ into earthly evolution, through his sacrifice on Golgotha an ascending stream of evolution began. This sacrifice of Christ was followed by the events of his Resurrection and Ascension, which were followed in turn by Whitsun (Pentecost)—all expressing the ascending stream of evolution. This path of ascent was also opened up to all human beings by way of the power of the divine "I AM" bestowed—at least, potentially—on all humanity by Christ through his sacrifice on the cross.

**Union in the Temple:** The event of the union of the spirit of the Solomon Jesus with the twelve-year-old Nathan Jesus. This union of the two Jesus children signified the uniting of the priestly (Nathan) line and the kingly (Solomon) line—both lines descended from King David.

**Whitsun:** "White Sunday"; Pentecost.

**World Pentecost** is the gradual event of cosmic revelation becoming human revelation as a signature of the end of the Dark Age (Kali Yuga). Anthroposophy (Spiritual Science) is a language of spiritual truth that could awake a community of striving human beings to the presence of the Holy Spirit and the founding of the New Jerusalem.

**Zarathustra:** The great teacher of the ancient Persians in the sixth millennium BC (around 6000 BC). In the sixth century BC, Zarathustra reincarnated as Zoroaster. He then reincarnated as the Solomon Jesus (6 BC–AD 12), whose birth is described in the Gospel of Matthew.

**Zoroaster:** An incarnation of Zarathustra. Zarathustra–Zoroaster was a Bodhisattva. Zoroaster lived in the sixth century BC. He was a master of wisdom. Among his communications as a teacher of wisdom was his specification as to how the zodiac of living beings in the heavens comes to expression in relation to the stars comprising the twelve zodiacal constellations. Zoroaster subsequently incarnated as the Solomon Jesus, whose birth is described in the Gospel of Matthew, to whom the three magi came from the East bearing gifts of gold, frankincense, and myrrh.

---

"The stars are the expression of love in the cosmic ether.... To see a star means to feel a caress that has been prompted by love.... To gaze at the stars is to become aware of the love proceeding from divine spiritual beings.... The stars are signs and tokens of the presence of gods in the universe." (*Karmic Relationships,* vol. 7, June 8, 1924)

"We must see in the shining stars the outer signs of colonies of spirits in the cosmos. Wherever a star is seen in the heavens, there—in that direction—is a colony of spirits." (*Karmic Relationships,* vol. 6, June 1, 1924)

"They looked up above all to what is represented by the zodiac. And they regarded what the human being bears within as the spirit in connection with the constellations, the glory of the fixed stars, the spiritual powers whom they knew to be there in the stars." (*Karmic Relationships,* vol. 4, Sept. 12, 1924)

# BIBLIOGRAPHY AND REFERENCES

*See "Literature" on page 10 for an annotated list of books on Astrosophy.*

Andreev, Daniel. *The Rose of the World*. Gr. Barrington, MA: Lindisfarne Books, 1997.

Anonymous. *Meditations on the Tarot: A Journey into Christian Hermeticism*. New York: Tarcher/Putman, 2002.

Courtois, Stéphane, et al. *The Black Book of Communism: Crimes, Terror, Repression*. Cambridge, MA: Harvard University, 1997.

Crowe, Michael J. *The Extraterrestrial Life Debate, 1750–1900*. New York: Dover, 1986.

Dorsan, Jacques. *The Clockwise House System: A True Foundation for Sidereal and Tropical Astrology*. Gr. Barrington, MA: Lindisfarne Books, 2011.

Emmerich, Anne Catherine. *Visions of the Life of Christ* (3 vols.). Kettering, OH: Angelico Press, 2015.

Fagan, Cyril. *Astrological Origins*. St. Paul, MN: Llewellyn, 1971.

———. *Zodiacs Old and New: A Probe into Antiquity and What Was Found*. London: Anscombe, 1951.

Freeland, Elena. *Chemtrails, HAARP, and the Full Spectrum Dominance of Planet Earth*. Port Townsend, WA: Feral House, 2014.

Geyer, Martin H., and Janohannes Paulmann (eds.). *The Mechanics of Internationalism: Culture, Society, and Politics from the 1840s to the First World War*. Oxford, UK: Oxford University, 2001.

Greub, Werner. *How the Grail Sites Were Found*. Amsterdam: Willehalm Institute, 2013.

Hale, George Ellery. *The Study of Stellar Evolution: An Account of Some Recent Methods of Astrophysical Research*. Chicago: University of Chicago, 1908.

Isaacson, Estelle. *The Grail Bearer: Tellings from the Ever Primal Story: Through the Eyes of Repanse de Schoye*. Peterborough, NH: LogoSophia, 2016.

———. *Through the Eyes of Mary Magdalene*, 3 vols. Taos, NM: LogoSophia, 2012–2015.

———. *The Younger Kyot: Tellings of Mages and Maidens: Shimmerings through the Grail Land of Grace*. Peterborough, NH; LogoSophia 2017.

Kirschenbaum, Lisa A. *Small Comrades: Revolutionizing Childhood in Soviet Russia, 1917–1932*. New York: Routledge, 2001.

Krisciunas, Kevin, and Bill Yenne. *The Pictorial Atlas of the Universe*. New York: BDD, 1989.

Longerich, Peter. *Heinrich Himmler: A Life*. New York: Oxford University, 2012.

Lusseyran, Jacques. *And There Was Light: The Extraordinary Memoir of a Blind Hero of the French Resistance in World War II*. Novato, CA: New World Library, 1963.

McLaren Lainson, Claudia. *The Circle of Twelve and the Legacy of Valentin Tomberg*. Boulder: Windrose Academy, 2015.

Mayer, W. August. *Uncle Joe, FDR and the Deep State*. San Francisco: PipeLineMedia, 2017.

Powell, Robert. *The Christ Mystery*. Fair Oaks, CA: Rudolf Steiner College, 1999.

———. *Christian Hermetic Astrology: The Star of the Magi and the Life of Christ*. Gr. Barrington, MA: Lindisfarne Books, 2009.

———. *Chronicle of the Living Christ: The Life and Ministry of Jesus Christ: Foundations of Cosmic Christianity*. Hudson, NY: Anthroposophic Press, 1996.

———. *Cultivating Inner Radiance and the Body of Immortality: Awakening the Soul through Modern Etheric Movement*. Gr. Barrington, MA: Lindisfarne Books, 2012.

———. *Elijah Come Again: A Prophet for Our Time: A Scientific Approach to Reincarnation*. Gr. Barrington, MA: Lindisfarne Books, 2009.

———. *Hermetic Astrology*, vols. 1 and 2. San Rafael, CA: Sophia Foundation Press, 2006.

———. *History of the Zodiac*. San Rafael, CA: Sophia Academic Press, 2007.

———. *The Most Holy Trinosophia: The New Revelation of the Divine Feminine*. Gr. Barrington, MA: SteinerBooks, 2000.

———. *The Mystery, Biography, and Destiny of Mary Magdalene: Sister of Lazarus–John & Spiritual Sister of Jesus*. Gr. Barrington, MA: Lindisfarne Books, 2008.

———. *Prophecy-Phenomena-Hope: The Real Meaning of the year 2012*. Gr. Barrington, MA: SteinerBooks, 2011.

———. *The Sign of the Son of Man in Heaven*. San Rafael, CA: Sophia Foundation, 2007.

———. *The Sophia Teachings: The Emergence of the Divine Feminine in Our Time*. Gr. Barrington, MA: Lindisfarne Books, 2007.

Powell, Robert, and David Bowden. *Astrogeographia: Correspondences between the Stars and Earthly Locations: Earth Chakras and the Bible of Astrology*. Gr. Barrington, MA: SteinerBooks, 2012.

Powell, Robert, and Kevin Dann. *The Astrological Revolution: Unveiling the Science of the Stars as a Science of Reincarnation and Karma*. Gr. Barrington, MA: SteinerBooks, 2010.

———. *Christ and the Maya Calendar: 2012 and the Coming of the Antichrist*. Gr. Barrington, MA: SteinerBooks, 2009.

Powell, Robert, and Estelle Isaacson. *Gautama Buddha's Successor: A Force for Good in our Time*. Gr. Barrington, MA: SteinerBooks, 2013.

———. *The Mystery of Sophia: Bearer of the New Culture: The Rose of the World*. Gr. Barrington, MA: SteinerBooks, 2014.

Powell, Robert, and Lacquanna Paul. *Cosmic Dances of the Planets*. San Rafael, CA: Sophia Foundation Press, 2006.

Powell, Robert, and Peter Treadgold. *The Sidereal Zodiac*. Tempe, AZ: AFA, 1985.

Solzhenitsyn, Aleksandr, *The Gulag Archipelago, 1918–1956, Volume 1: An Experiment in Literary Investigation*. New York: Harper, 2007.

Stein, Walter Johannes. *The Ninth Century and the Holy Grail*. Forest Row, UK: Temple Lodge, 2009.

Steiner, Rudolf. *Approaching the Mystery of Golgotha*. Gr. Barrington, MA: Anthroposophic Press, 2006.

———. *Artistic Sensitivity as a Spiritual Approach to Knowing Life and the World*. Gr. Barrington, MA: Anthroposophic Press, 2018.

———. *Astronomy and Astrology: Finding a Relationship to the Cosmos*. Forest Row, UK: Rudolf Steiner Press, 2009.

———. *The Book of Revelation: And the Work of the Priest*. Forest Row, UK: Rudolf Steiner Press, 2008.

———. *Calendar 1912–1913: Facsimile Edition of the Original Book Containing the Calendar Created by Rudolf Steiner for the Year 1912–1913*. Gr. Barrington, MA: SteinerBooks, 2004.

———. *Christ and the Spiritual World and the Search for the Holy Grail*. Forest Row, UK: Rudolf Steiner Press, 1963.

———. *Death as Metamorphosis of Life: Including "What Does the Angel Do in Our Astral Body?" and "How Do I Find Christ?"* Gr. Barrington, MA: SteinerBooks, 2008.

———. *The Electronic Doppelgänger: The Mystery of the Double in the Age of the Internet*. Forest Row, UK: Rudolf Steiner Press, 2016.

———. *An Esoteric Cosmology: Evolution, Christ, and Modern Spirituality*. Gr. Barrington, MA: SteinerBooks, 2008.

———. *The Fall of the Spirits of Darkness*. Forest Row, UK: Rudolf Steiner Press, 1993.

———. *The Foundations of Human Experience*. Hudson, NY: Anthroposophic Press, 1996.

———. *Founding a Science of the Spirit* (previous title, *At the Gates of Spiritual Science*). Forest Row, UK: Rudolf Steiner Press, 1999.

———. "The Four Sacrifices of Christ." in *Approaching the Mystery of Golgotha*. Gr. Barrington, MA: SteinerBooks, 2006.

———. *The Four Seasons and the Archangels*. Forest Row, UK: Rudolf Steiner Press, 1968.

———. *From the History and Contents of the First Section of the Esoteric School: Letters, Documents, and Lectures: 1904–1914*. Gr. Barrington, MA: SteinerBooks, 2010.

———. *Guidance in Esoteric Training: From the Esoteric School*. Forest Row, UK: Rudolf Steiner Press, 1998.

———. *How to Know Higher Worlds: A Modern Path of Initiation*. Hudson, NY: Anthroposophic Press, 1994.

———. *The Karma of Untruthfulness: Secret Societies, the Media, and Preparations for the Great War* (2 vols.). Forest Row, UK: Rudolf Steiner Press, 2005.

———. *Karmic Relationships: Esoteric Studies*, vol. 4. Forest Row, UK: Rudolf Steiner Press, 2017.

———. *Life between Death and Rebirth*. Hudson, NY: Anthroposophic Press, 1975.

———. *Occult History*. London: Rudolf Steiner Press, 1983.

———. *An Outline of Esoteric Science*. Hudson, NY: Anthroposophic Press, 1997.

———. *The Reappearance of Christ in the Etheric: The Second Coming of Christ*. Gr. Barrington, MA: SteinerBooks, 2003.

———. *The Spiritual Foundation of Morality: Francis of Assisi and the Christ Impulse*. Hudson, NY: Anthroposophic Press, 1995.

———. *Spiritual Guidance of the Individual and Humanity: Some Results of Spiritual-Scientific Research into Human History and Development*. Hudson, NY: Anthroposophic Press, 1992.

———. *The Spiritual Hierarchies and the Physical World: Zodiac, Planets, and Cosmos*. Gr. Barrington, MA: SteinerBooks, 2008.

———. *Towards Social Renewal: Rethinking the Basis of Society*. Forest Row, UK: Rudolf Steiner Press, 2000.

———. *True and False Paths in Spiritual Investigation*. London: Rudolf Steiner Press, 1969.

———. *Understanding Society through Spiritual-Scientific Knowledge: Social Threefolding, Christ, Lucifer, and Ahriman*. Forest Row, UK: Rudolf Steiner Press, 2017.

Steiner, Rudolf, and Marie Steiner-von Sivers. *Correspondence and Documents 1901–1925*. Hudson, NY: Anthroposophic Press, 1988.

Sucher, Willi. *The Drama of the Universe*. Larkfield, UK: Landvidi Research Centre, 1958.

———. *Isis Sophia I: Introducing Astrosophy*. Meadow Vista, CA: Astrosophy Research Center, 1999.

———. *Isis Sophia II: An Outline of a New Star Wisdom*. Meadow Vista, CA: Astrosophy Research Center, 1985.

Tomberg, Valentin. *Christ and Sophia: Anthroposophic Meditations on the Old Testament, New Testament, and Apocalypse*. Gr. Barrington, MA: SteinerBooks, 2006.

———. *Studies on the Foundation Stone Meditation*. San Rafael, CA: LogoSophia, 2010.

von Halle, Judith. *And if He Had not Been Raised...: The Stations of Christ's Path to Spirit Man*. Forest Row, UK: Temple Lodge Press, 2007.

———. *Descent into the Depths of the Earth on the Anthroposophic Path of Schooling*. Forest Row, UK: Temple Lodge Press, 2011.

———. *Illness and Healing: And the Mystery Language of the Gospels*. Forest Row, UK: Temple Lodge, 2009.

———. *Secrets of the Stations of the Cross and the Grail Blood: The Mystery of Transformation*. Forest Row, UK: Temple Lodge Press, 2007.

von Eschenbach, Wolfram. *Parzival*. London; David Nutt, 1894.

———. *Parzival*. London; Penguin Classics, 1980.

Vreede, Elisabeth. *Astronomy and Spiritual Science: The Astronomical Letters of Elisabeth Vreede*. Gr. Barrington, MA: SteinerBooks, 2007.

Winchester, Simon. *Krakatoa: The Day the World Exploded: August 27, 1883*. HarperCollins, 2003.

---

## EVENING MEDITATION

In the evening meditate on the Earth as a great radiant green star shining out into the cosmos, and allow the heart to speak:

*May this prayer from my warm heart unite*

*With the Earth's Light which reveres the Christ-Sun,*

*That I may find Spirit in the Light of the Spirit,*

*Breath of the Soul in the World's Breath,*

*Human Strength in the Life of the Earth.*

Given by Rudolf Steiner, March 9, 1924, to Maud B. Monges of Spring Valley, NY (translated by RP)

# ABOUT THE CONTRIBUTORS

 **DANIEL ANDREEV** (1906–1959) was born in Berlin. His father was the well-known Russian writer Leonid Andreev. His mother, Alexandra Veligorsky, died during childbirth. Daniel's father, overcome with grief, gave up Andreev to Alexandra's sister Elizabeth Dobrov, who lived in Moscow. It was a critical event in Daniel Andreev's life, for in contrast to many of the Russian intelligentsia at the time, the family maintained its Russian Orthodox faith. Daniel's childhood included contact with persons such as his godfather Maxim Gorky. Daniel was conscripted as a noncombatant in the Soviet Army in 1942, and after the war he returned to writing fiction and poetry. He was arrested in 1947, along with his wife and many of his relatives and friends, and sentenced to twenty-five years in prison, while his wife received twenty-five years of labor camp. All of his previous writings were destroyed. With the rise of Khrushchev, Andreev's case was reviewed and his sentence reduced to ten years. He was released to his wife in 1957, his health ruined following a heart attack in prison. While in prison, he had written the first drafts of *The Rose of the World* and *Russian Gods* (a collection of poetry), as well as *The Iron Mystery*, a play in verse. Andreev spent the last two years of his life finishing these works. Andreev's wife Alla, realizing the negative reception the books would get from the Soviet authorities, hid them until the mid-1970s and did not publish them until Gorbachev and glasnost. The first edition of *The Rose of the World* (100,000 copies) quickly sold out, and since then several editions have been equally popular in Russia.

 **KEVIN DANN**, PhD, has taught history at SUNY Plattsburgh, the University of Vermont, and Rutgers University. His books include *Bright Colors Falsely Seen* (1998); *Across the Great Border Fault* (2000); *Lewis Creek Lost and Found* (2001); *A Short Story of American Destiny, 1909–2009* (2008); and (with Robert Powell) *Christ & the Maya Calendar: 2012 & the Coming of the Antichrist* (2009) and *The Astrological Revolution: Unveiling the Science of the Stars as a Science of Reincarnation and Karma* (2010).

 **ESTELLE ISAACSON** is a contemporary mystic and seer whose first books were published by LogoSophia in 2012: *Through the Eyes of Mary Magdalene: Early Years and Soul Awakening*. In volume 1 in her trilogy on the life of Mary Magdalene, Estelle Isaacson presents her visions of the life of Christ as seen through Magdalene's own eyes. Volume 2, *Through the Eyes of Mary Magdalene: From Initiation to the Passion*, enters the profound mysteries of Christ's Passion, culminating in the Resurrection. Estelle is coauthor with Robert Powell of *Gautama Buddha's Successor: A Force for Good in Our Time* (2013) and *The Mystery of Sophia: Bearer of the New Culture: The Rose of the World* (2014).

 **JULIE HUMPHREYS** is a graduate of Stanford and a former pediatric nurse and Waldorf mom. An early interest in astrology lay dormant for more than three decades until she was introduced to the sidereal system, the works of Robert Powell, and the visions of Anne Catherine Emmerich. She has taken great joy in researching astrological phenomena for the *Journal for Star Wisdom*. Julie lives in Carmel, California, where shooting stars and the Milky Way are often visible.

 **CLAUDIA MCLAREN LAINSON** is a teacher and Therapeutic Educator. She has been working in the field of Anthroposophy since 1982, when she founded her first Waldorf program in Boulder, Colorado. She lectures nationally on various topics related to Spiritual Science, human development, the evolution of consciousness and the emerging Christ and Sophia mysteries of the twenty-first century. Claudia is the founder of Windrose Farm and Academy near Boulder. Windrose is a biodynamic

## About the Contributors

farm and academy for collaborative work in anthroposophic courses, therapeutic education, cosmic and sacred dance, and nature-based educational programs. Claudia most recently founded the School for the Sophia Mysteries at Windrose. She is the author of *The Circle of Twelve and the Legacy of Valentin Tomberg* (windroseacademypress.com).

**JOEL PARK** is a coworker at Plowshare Farm (a Camphill Affiliate) in Greenfield, NH. He has been house-holding with his wife and children there since 2011, primarily identifying as a farmer. He is working toward a certification in social therapy through the Camphill Academy. Joel's path to Astrosophy began at Pentecost 2008, when he became a student of Rudolf Steiner. Later, during Christmastime 2008, he became a student of Valentin Tomberg. He first encountered the work of Robert Powell in 2009, and since then he has grown increasingly familiar with it, culminating in April 2015, when he joined the Grail Knighthood, founded by Robert. Subsequent to meeting Robert at the Knight's Blessing, a good rapport began to unfold between them, ultimately resulting in Joel lending a hand to Robert's Astrosophical karma research. This collaboration is a work in progress, hopefully soon to bear fruit. This is Joel's first contribution to *Journal for Star Wisdom*. A selection of some of his other, more informal pieces can be found at www.treehouse.live.

**ROBERT POWELL**, PhD, is an internationally known lecturer, author, eurythmist, and movement therapist. He is founder of the Choreocosmos School of Cosmic and Sacred Dance, and cofounder of the Sophia Foundation of North America. He received his doctorate for his thesis *The History of the Zodiac*, available as a book from Sophia Academic Press. His published works include *The Sophia Teachings*, a six-tape series (Sounds True Recordings), as well as *Elijah Come Again: A Prophet for Our Time*; *The Mystery, Biography, and Destiny of Mary Magdalene*; *Divine Sophia—Holy Wisdom*; *The Most Holy Trinosophia and the New Revelation of the Divine Feminine*; *Chronicle of the Living Christ*; *Christian Hermetic Astrology*; *The Christ Mystery*; *The Sign of the Son of Man in the Heavens*; *Cultivating Inner Radiance and the Body of Immortality*; and the yearly *Journal for Star Wisdom* (previously *Christian Star Calendar*). He translated the spiritual classic *Meditations on the Tarot* and co-translated Valentin Tomberg's *Lazarus, Come Forth!* Robert is coauthor with David Bowden of *Astrogeographia: Correspondences between the Stars and Earthly Locations* and coauthor with Estelle Isaacson of *Gautama Buddha's Successor* and *The Mystery of Sophia*. Robert is also coauthor with Kevin Dann of *The Astrological Revolution: Unveiling the Science of the Stars as a Science of Reincarnation and Karma* and *Christ and the Maya Calendar: 2012 & the Coming of the Antichrist*; and coauthor with Lacquanna Paul of *Cosmic Dances of the Zodiac* and *Cosmic Dances of the Planets*. He teaches a gentle form of healing movement: the sacred dance of eurythmy, as well as the Cosmic Dances of the Planets and signs of the zodiac. Through the Sophia Grail Circle, Robert facilitates sacred celebrations dedicated to the Divine Feminine. He offers workshops in Europe and Australia, and with Karen Rivers, cofounder of the Sophia Foundation, leads pilgrimages to the world's sacred sites: Turkey, 1996; the Holy Land, 1997; France, 1998; Britain, 2000; Italy, 2002; Greece, 2004; Egypt, 2006; India, 2008; Turkey, 2009; the Grand Canyon, 2010; South Africa, 2012; Peru, 2014; the Holy Land, 2016; and Bali, 2018. Visit www.sophiafoundation.org and www.astrogeographia.org.

# A Note from Lindisfarne / SteinerBooks

SteinerBooks is a 501 (c) 3 not-for-profit organization, incorporated in New York State since 1928 to promote the progress and welfare of humanity and to increase public awareness of Rudolf Steiner (1861–1925), the Austrian-born polymath writer, lecturer, spiritual scientist, philosopher, cosmologist, educator, psychologist, alchemist, ecologist, Christian mystic, comparative religionist, and evolutionary theorist, who was the creator of Anthroposophy ("human wisdom") as a path uniting the spiritual in the human being with the spiritual in the universe; and to this end publish and distribute books for adults and children, utilize the electronic media, hold conferences, and engage in similar activities making available his works and exploring themes arising from, and related to, them and the movement that he founded.

- We commission translations of books by Rudolf Steiner unpublished in English, as well as new translations for updated editions.
- Our aim is to make works on Anthroposophy available to all by publishing and distributing both introductory and advanced works on spiritual research.
- New books are publish for both print and digital editions to reach the widest possible readership.
- Recent technology also makes it efficient for us to make our previously out-of-print works available for the next generation.

SteinerBooks depends on our readers' financial support, which is greatly needed, appreciated, and tax-deductible. Please consider a donation by check or other means to SteinerBooks, 610 Main St., Great Barrington, MA 01230. We also accept donations via PayPal on our website. For more information about supporting our work, send email to friends@steinerbooks.org or call 413-528-8233.